Draft
THE ^ STANDARD

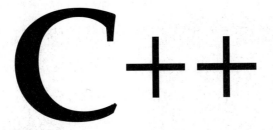

C++

LIBRARY

P.J. Plauger

Prentice Hall PTR
Upper Saddle River, NJ 07458

Library of Congress Cataloging-in-Publication Data

Plauger, P. J., 1944-
    The draft Standard C++ library / P.J. Plauger.
      p.   cm.
    Includes bibliographical refernces and index.
      1. C++ (Computer program language)   I. Title
  QA76.73.C153P47 1994
  005. 13'3--dc20   94-36379
                                                    CIP

Editorial/production supervision: *Mary Rottino*
Manufacturing buyer: *Alexis Heydt*
Cover design: *Aren Graphics*

Published by Prentice Hall PTR
Prentice-Hall, Inc.
A Simon & Schuster Company
Upper Saddle River, New Jersey 07458

The author and publisher have used their best efforts in preparing this book. These efforts include the development, research, and testing of the programs to determine their effectiveness. The author and publisher make no warranty of any kind, expressed or implied, with regard to these programs or the documentation contained in this book. The author and publisher shall not be liable in any event for incidental or consequential damages in connection with, or arising out of, the furnishing, performance, or use of these programs.

For additional licensing of the code, see page xv. The code version shown here is 2.1.

Printed in the United States of America
10 9 8 7 6 5 4 3 2

ISBN 0-13-117003-1

Prentice-Hall International (UK) Limited, *London*
Prentice-Hall of Australia Pty. Limited, *Sydney*
Prentice-Hall of Canada Inc., *Toronto*
Prentice-Hall Hispanoamericana, S.A., *Mexico*
Prentice-Hall of India Private Limited, *New Dehli*
Prentice-Hall of Japan, Inc., *Tokyo*
Simon & Schuster Asia Pte. Ltd., *Singapore*
Editora Prentice-Hall do Brasil, Ltda., *Rio de Janerio*

for Geoff

PERMISSIONS

TRADEMARKS

TYPOGRAPHY

Contents

Preface

This book shows you how to use the library classes and functions mandated by the draft ANSI/ISO Standard for the programming language C++. I have chosen to focus on the library exclusively, since many other books describe the language proper. In fact, remarkably little has been written about the basic library that accompanies nearly every C++ translator to date. The library portion of the draft C++ Standard describes what *will* accompany all implementations of C++ in the near future. On that topic, practically *nothing at all* has been written, outside of occasional magazine articles. That's because the draft has only recently coalesced to the point where its basic intent is clear and precise enough to describe.

Informal Review Draft The watershed event was the publication, in February 1994, of the draft C++ Standard for informal public review. (See **Koe94** in Appendix D: References.) I refer to it here as the Informal Review Draft. This draft marks the first time that the entire language and library have been described completely and in one place. It also marks the first time that the draft C++ Standard has been made available to the public in any sort of official manner. Until now, much of the material has not been spelled out, or has been available only as working papers within ANSI committee X3J16 or ISO committee WG21, the groups charged with developing the C++ Standard. Hence, the Informal Review Draft serves as the basis for this book.

You will find here a *complete and verbatim* presentation of the library portion of the Informal Review Draft. As the editor of that portion, I brought together in a more uniform style all the separate proposals approved for inclusion in the Standard C++ library. The presentation here differs from the Informal Review Draft only in matters of typesetting.

Naturally, the draft C++ Standard continues to evolve. But the major changes adopted since the Informal Review Draft add features not traditionally part of most C++ implementations. These new features rely heavily on template technology and extensions that are just beginning to get good commercial support. I believe that this book captures well the *existing practice* represented in the Standard C++ library. It is the part that is stable enough to describe and to start using. Even those parts still likely to change in outward appearance illustrate *functionality* that is not likely to disappear. I include in each chapter a section on **Future Directions**, to describe changes already made or under serious consideration.

The book also shows you how to *implement* the Standard C++ library. I present about 9,000 lines of tested, working code that is designed to be portable across the most popular current implementations of C++. To a large extent, the code presented here works atop any ANSI/ISO Standard C library. It is designed to work particularly well, however, with an enhanced version of the portable implementation I provide in my earlier book, *The Standard C Library* (**Pla92**). That work was also published by Prentice-Hall, in 1992. (Similarities between this Preface and the one in that book are neither accidental nor a matter of casual copying.)

One way or another, you can use the code presented here to gain valuable early experience using the library that is destined to become the Standard for the C++ world. Equally important, I believe that seeing a realistic implementation of the Standard C++ library can help you better understand how to use it.

And that introduces yet another goal. Besides presenting the Informal Review Draft for the library, and working code to implement it, this book also serves as a tutorial on how to use the library. You will find here useful background information on how the library came to take its present form, how it was *meant* to be used, and how it *should* be used. You don't have to read and understand all the code presented here to achieve that basic goal. Even a cursory study is beneficial. You certainly don't have to be a sophisticated user to profit from this book, but the programmer who is just an occasional sophisticate will find the information presented here invaluable.

Teaching you how to write C++ is *not* a goal of this book. I assume you know enough about C++ to read straightforward code. Where the code presented is not so straightforward, I explain the trickery involved.

the Standard C++ library The Standard C++ library is fairly ambitious. It provides considerable power in many different environments, through an assortment of utilitarian classes and templates. It promises well-defined name spaces for both user and implementor. It imposes fairly strict requirements on the robustness and precision of its numerical conversions and other mathematical operations. And it pioneers in supporting the use of new C++ features such as templates, exceptions, and *namespace* declarations.

To benefit from these ambitions, a user should be aware of numerous subtleties. To satisfy these ambitions, an implementor must provide for them. These subtleties are not always addressed in the draft C++ Standard proper. It is not the primary purpose of a standard to educate implementors. Nor are many of these subtleties well explained in the piecemeal descriptions published to date on the C++ library. This book endeavors to highlight the subtle and make it more obvious.

The pioneering features I mentioned above are not found in traditional implementations of C++ libraries. An implementation now uses templates where once "clever" macros had to suffice. The library throws exceptions where once it returned error codes that were often ignored. And the library is now wrapped with *namespace* declarations where once it provided an untidy soup of names. Little or no prior art exists for these new features. Hence, even the most experienced C++ programmers need guidance in understanding library templates, exceptions, and *namespace* declarations. Particular attention is given here to these topics.

designing   Still another purpose of this book is to teach programmers how to design
libraries and implement class libraries in general. By its very nature, the library provided with a programming language is a mixed bag. An implementor needs a broad spectrum of skills to deal with the varied contents of the bag. It is not enough to be a competent class designer or numerical analyst, or to be skilled in manipulating character strings efficiently, or to be knowledgeable in the ways of operating system interfacing. Writing a library demands all these skills and more.

Good books have been written on how to write mathematical functions. Other books present specialized class libraries for a variety of purposes. They show you how to use the library presented. Some may even justify many of the design choices for the particular library in question. Few, if any, endeavor to teach the skills required for library building in general. Those that do tend to have a narrower focus of applicability than this book.

reusability   A number of books present general principles for designing and implementing software. The disciplines they present have names such as structured analysis, structured design, object-oriented design, and object-oriented programming. Most examples in these books consider only programs written for a custom application. Nevertheless, the principles and disciplines apply equally well to the writing of reusable libraries.

The goal of reusability simply raises the stakes. If a library class is not highly cohesive, in the structured-design sense, then it is less likely to find new uses. If it does not have low coupling to other classes, in the same sense, it is harder to use. Similarly, a collection of classes must hide implementation details and provide complete functionality. Otherwise, it fails at implementing reusable data abstractions, in the best sense of object-oriented design and programming.

So the final purpose of this book is to address the design and implementation issues peculiar to C++ library building. The design of the Standard C++ library is still amazingly fluid. Nevertheless, the standardized existing practice shown here is a good design in many ways and worthy of discussion. Implementations of the Standard C++ library can vary even while conforming to the draft C++ Standard. Any number of choices are strongly dictated by general principles, such as correctness and maintainability. Other choices are dictated by priorities peculiar to a project, such as the need for very high performance, portability, or small size. These choices and principles are also worthy of discussion.

structure   The book is structured much like the Standard C++ library itself. Thirty-
of this eight headers declare or define all the names in the library. Eighteen of those
book are inherited from the Standard C library and Amendment 1 to the C Standard. A single chapter discusses how the Standard C library changes

to meet the needs of C++. For the rest, a separate chapter covers each header. I discuss them in their order of presentation within the Informal Review Draft.

Most of the headers have reasonably cohesive contents. That makes for reasonably cohesive discussions. One or two, however, are catchalls. Their corresponding chapters are perforce wider ranging. And many headers cooperate to implement the extensive "iostreams" facility. Their descriptions are necessarily intertwined.

I include in each chapter excerpts from relevant portions of the Informal Review Draft. The excerpts supplement the narrative description of how each portion of the library is customarily used. They also help make this book a more complete reference (that is nevertheless more readable than the Informal Review Draft alone). I warn of any future changes to that portion of the draft, either already adopted, imminent, or at least very likely to occur. I also show all C++ code needed to implement that portion and to test the implementation.

Each chapter ends with a set of exercises. In a university course based on this book, the exercises can serve as homework problems. Many of them are simple exercises in using the library, or in code rewriting. They drive home a point or illustrate reasonable variations in implementation. The more ambitious exercises are labeled as such. They can serve as a basis for more extended projects. The independent reader can use the exercises as stimulus for further thought.

The Code

The code presented in this book has been tested with C++ compilers from Borland, Microsoft, Sun Microsystems, Metrowerks, and the Edison Design Group. It has passed the widely used Plum Hall Validation Suite tests. While I have taken pains to minimize errors, I cannot guarantee that none remain. Please note the disclaimer on the copyright page.

Please note also that the code in this book is protected by copyright. It has *not* been placed in the public domain. Nor is it shareware. It is not protected by a "copyleft" agreement, like code distributed by the Free Software Foundation (Project GNU). I retain all rights.

fair use   You are welcome to transcribe the code to machine-readable form for your personal use. You can purchase the code in machine-readable from Plum Hall Inc. in Kamuela, Hawaii. In either case, what you do with the code is limited by the "fair use" provisions of copyright law. Fair use does *not* permit you to distribute copies of the code, either hard copy or machine-readable, either free or for a fee.

Having said that, I do permit one important usage that goes well beyond fair use. You can compile portions of the library and link the resultant binary object modules with your own code to form an executable file. I hereby permit you to distribute unlimited copies of such an executable file. I ask no royalty on any such copies. I do, however, require that you document the presence of the library, whatever amount you use, either modified or unmodified. Please include somewhere in the executable file the following sequence of characters: **Portions of this work are derived from The Standard C++ Library, copyright (c) 1995 by P.J. Plauger, published by Prentice-Hall, and are used with permission.** The same message should appear prominently, and in an appropriate place, on any documentation that you distribute with the executable image. If you omit either message, you infringe the copyright. (These are the same terms on which I have offered the Standard C library for several years now.)

licensing   You can also obtain permission to do more. You can distribute the entire library in the form of binary object modules. You can make the source code available on a network to a group of co-workers. You can even distribute copies of the source files from this book, either modified or unmodified. You can, in short, incorporate the library into a product that lets people use it to make executable programs. To do so, however, requires a license. You pay a fee for the license. Contact Plum Hall Inc. for licensing terms and for on-going support of the library.

Despite the mercenary tone of these paragraphs, my goal is not simply to flog a commercial product. I believe this is a reasonable basis for the Standard C++ library. While I have contributed little to the technical content, I have worked hard to help refine its expression and specification. I want to raise public awareness of this, the first really universal library for writing C++ programs. I wrote this implementation, and this book, to help achieve that important goal.

Acknowledgments

The Library Working Group within both X3J16 and WG21 has worked for years to bring the draft Standard C++ library to its present useful state. I happily acknowledge the contributions of the many people who have served in the Library Working Group, and to two people in particular. Mike Vilot has chaired that group from the outset. Jerry Schwarz has borne the brunt of the effort needed to turn the specification for his popular iostreams package into an international standard. More than anything, this book is intended as a tribute to the extensive efforts of the Library Working Group.

Paul Becker, my Publisher at Prentice-Hall, has provided his usual patient support. He has maintained his enthusiasm for this project even as it has grown from one year to nearly three. I appreciate his professional focus, and I'm grateful that he favors quiet encouragement over nagging.

Tom Plum has provided extraordinary support in the development, testing, and packaging of the code in this book. He has devoted many hours to porting the code to popular platforms, to automating builds and tests, and to coordinating the efforts of beta testers. He has also contrived solutions to any number of nasty design problems, along the way. Michael Marcotty of Metrowerks has also been most helpful in reporting both bugs and fixes for them.

Tim Prince kindly provided the coefficients needed for the revised Standard C math library, in all three floating-point precisions. His contribution is not directly visible in this book, but it serves as a vital underpinning to the complex arithmetic classes. Also invisible, but most helpful, have been the excellent math tests from Cody and Waite (**C&W80**). They were instrumental in proving in the math functions.

I have benefited from several discussions with Dan Saks and Chuck Allison. Their greater experience with C++ has often shown me graceful solutions to seemingly intractable problems. I have enjoyed the illuminating perspectives of Beman Dawes and Pete Becker, also active participants in the Library Working Group, and of Tony Hansen, Andy Koenig, and Bjarne Stroustrup. Knowingly or not, all these folks have influenced the presentation in this book, I think to advantage. (But I respect their right to disagree, or to disclaim any intentional influence.)

Much of the material presented here first appeared in monthly installments in *The C Users Journal*. I thank Robert Ward, as publisher, for enabling me to blend so easily dual careers as magazine writer/editor and author of textbooks. I am likewise grateful to John Levine, editor and publisher of *The Journal of C Language Translation*. Some of my quarterly contributions to that publication have also found their way into this book.

Those who reviewed this manuscript for gaffes, typos, and infelicities include Chuck Allison and Tom Plum. For making this a more readable book, they deserve your thanks at least as much as mine.

Finally, I acknowledge the wonderfully supportive environment provided by my family. My son, Geoffrey, assisted with the layout and typographic design of this book. My wife, Tana, was ever ready to off-load any tiresome administrative chores. And far more important, both provided ample reason and reward for doing the bits that weren't always fun.

P.J. Plauger
Concord, Massachusetts

Chapter 0: Introduction

Background

A *library* is a collection of program components that can be reused in many programs. Most programming languages include some form of library. The programming language C++ is no exception. It inherits a great number of useful *functions* from the Standard C library, right from the start. These functions help you classify characters, manipulate character strings, read input, and write output — to name just a few categories of services.

overloading
and operators To these can be added even more functions that profit from the special notation of C++. You can *overload* a function name, for example:

```
float_complex pow(float_complex, float_complex);
float_complex pow(float_complex, float);
float_complex pow(float_complex, int);
float_complex pow(float, float_complex);
```

Different versions of a function get called depending on the types and number of arguments in a particular function call. For the object `X` of type `float_complex`, `pow(X, X)` and `pow(X, 3.0F)` call different functions.

You can overload *operators* as well, as in:

```
float_complex operator+(float_complex, float_complex);
float_complex operator+(float_complex, complex);
float_complex operator+(float, float_complex);
```

Different versions of an operator function get called depending on the types of operands for that operator in a particular expression. So `X + X` and `X + 3.0F` also call different functions.

classes
and
templates You can also define *classes*. A class encapsulates all the data needed to model a particular instance of some abstract entity, along with all the functions you need to manipulate that data. Properly designed, a class is likely to be a more reusable program component than a function. Finally, you can declare *template functions* and *template classes*. A template has one or more parameters, usually including type parameters. You can, for example, instantiate different versions of a template that perform essentially the same services for operands of different types.

The C++ library described in this book adds an assortment of capabilities to those it inherits from Standard C. These capabilities include:

- an *iostreams* package that overloads the operators `<<` and `>>` for convenient and type-safe input and output

- a *string* package that overloads several operators for convenient manipulation of text strings

- a *complex* package that overloads most of the arithmetic operators for complex arithmetic, based on a variety of floating-point data types

As you might expect, these packages and their brethren make use of function and operator overloading, class definitions, and templates.

What you might not expect, however, is the particular choice of capabilities described here. C++ is rightly praised as a boon to writing reusable code. A well crafted library of classes can model a given application domain to advantage for a broad range of related programs. Classes provide uniformity, centralization of concepts, and enforced semantics across project boundaries. But this book is not about designing such classes, at least not exactly.

The question addressed here is somewhat different — what functions and classes are sufficiently useful that they should be available to *all* C++ programs? That constitutes library design in the same spirit as programming-language design. In that spirit, this book is a sequel to my earlier opus, *The Standard C Library* (**Pla92**). There, I described the library mandated by ISO/IEC 9899:1990, the international standard for the programming language C (**ANS89** and **ISO90**). By the inheritance I mentioned earlier, that means I have already described a large chunk of the Standard C++ library. The purpose of this book is to describe *everything else* needed to make the Standard C++ library, at least as of a given point in time. (Amendment 1 to the C Standard, now in the final stages of ISO balloting, adds a bunch of C functions for manipulating very large character sets (**ISO94**). I describe them here only in passing.)

What follows is a number of definitions that pertain to the business of describing, using, and implementing a library in C++. Much of this chapter is cribbed heavily, and unapologetically, from the corresponding introduction to *The Standard C Library*. C++ is built atop C in many senses. Both languages are best described in terms of a common vocabulary.

a few You must *declare* a typical function before you use it in a program. The
definitions only safe way to do so is to incorporate into the program a *header* that declares all the library functions and classes in a given category. A header can also define any associated *type definitions* and *macros*. A header is as much a part of the library as the functions themselves. Most often, a header is a *text file* just like the file you write to make a program.

You use the **#include** directive in a C++ source file to make a header part of the *translation unit*. For example, the header **<stdio.h>** declares the Standard C functions that perform input and output. A program that prints a simple message with the function **printf** looks much like the corresponding C program. It consists of the single C++ source file:

```
// a simple C-ish test program
#include <stdio.h>

int main(void)
    {                                                    // say hello
    printf("Hello\n");
    return (0);
    }
```

Even better, you can use the header `<iostream>` to make use of the iostreams package in an equally simple C++ source file:

```
// a simple C++-ish test program
#include <iostream>

int main(void)
    {                                                    // say hello
    cout << "Hello" << endl;
    return (0);
    }
```

A *translator* converts each translation unit to an *object module*, a form suitable for use with a given *computer architecture* (or *machine*). A *linker* combines all the object modules that make up a program. It incorporates any object modules you use from the Standard C++ library as well. The most popular form of translator is a *compiler*. It produces an *executable file*. Ideally at least, an executable file contains only those object modules from the library that contain functions actually used by the program. That way, the program suffers no size penalty as the Standard C++ library grows more extensive. (Another form of translator is an *interpreter*. It may include the entire Standard C++ library, directly or indirectly, as part of the program that interprets your program.)

making a You can construct your own libraries. A typical C++ compiler has a
library *librarian*, a program that assembles a library from the object modules you specify. The linker knows to select from *any* library only the object modules used by the program. The C++ library is seldom a special case.

You can write part or all of a library in C++. The translation unit you write to make a library object module is not that unusual:

- A library object module should contain no definition of the function **main** with external linkage. A programmer is unlikely to reuse code that insists on taking control at program startup.

- The object module should contain only functions that are easy to declare and use. Provide a header that declares the functions and defines any associated classes and macros.

- Most important, a library object module should be usable in a variety of contexts. Writing code that is highly reusable is a skill you develop only with practice and by studying successful libraries.

After you have read this book, you should be comfortable designing, writing, and constructing specialized libraries in C++.

the C++   The C++ library itself is typically written in C or C++. That is often *not*
library   the case with other programming languages. Earlier languages (other than
in C++   C) had libraries written in *assembly language*. Different computer architectures have different assembly languages. To move the library to another
computer architecture, you had to rewrite it completely. C++ lets you write
powerful and efficient code that is also highly *portable*. You can move
portable code simply by translating it with a different C++ translator.

Here, for example, is the Standard C library function **strlen**, declared
in **<string.h>**. The function returns the length of a null-terminated string.
Its pointer argument points to the first element of the string:

```
// strlen function
#include <string.h>

size_t (strlen)(const char *s)
    {                                          // find length of s[]
    const char *sc;
    for (sc = s; *sc != '\0'; ++sc)
        ;
    return (sc - s);
    }
```

strlen is a small function, one fairly easy to write. It is also fairly easy to
write incorrectly in many small ways. **strlen** is widely used. You might
want to provide a special version tuned to a given computer architecture.
But you don't have to. This version is correct, portable, and reasonably
efficient.

Other contemporary languages cannot be used to write significant portions of their own libraries. You cannot, for example, write the Pascal library
function **writeln** in portable Pascal. By contrast, you *can* write the equivalent C or C++ library function **printf** in portable C++. The comparison is
a bit unfair because C++ type checking is weaker in this case, at least for
varying length argument lists. (That's partly why the Standard C++ library
adds iostreams.) Nevertheless, the underlying point is significant — the
C++ library has been expressible from its earliest beginnings almost completely in C++.

nonportable   Sometimes the code for a library function cannot be written in *portable*
code   C++. The code you write in C++ may work for a large class of computer
architectures, but not all. In such a case, the important thing is to document
clearly the nonportable portions that may have to change. You should also
isolate nonportable code as much as possible. Even nonportable C++ code
is easier to write, debug, and maintain than assembly language. You write
assembly language only where it is unavoidable. Those places are few and
far between in the Standard C++ library.

Of particular help is the existence of the Standard C library. Most places
where nonportable code is required are already encapsulated by functions
from the older library. Thus, the added code presented here for the Standard
C++ library can usually avoid portability problems simply by calling
functions from the Standard C library as necessary.

This book shows you how to use the Standard C++ library presented here. Along the way, it also shows you how to write this library in C++. That can help you understand how the library works. And it illustrates many aspects of designing and writing a nontrivial library in C++.

What the Draft C++ Standard Says

Bjarne Stroustrup developed "C with classes" at AT&T Bell Laboratories in the early 1980s, which evolved over time into C++. It was built atop the highly successful programming language C, and has maintained a considerable amount of upward compatibility with the older language. As ever larger projects have felt the limitations of C, more programmers have looked to C++ for its class machinery and stronger type checking. By late 1989, sentiment became strong to commence standardizing C++.

ANSI X3J16 The American National Standards Institute, or ANSI, standardizes com-
ISO WG21 puter programming languages in the United States. X3J16 is the name of the ANSI-authorized committee that began developing the Standard for C++, starting in 1989. The International Organization for Standardization, or ISO [sic], has a similar responsibility in the international arena. ISO formed the technical committee JTC1/SC22/WG21 in 1991 to work with X3J16 in forming a simultaneous ANSI/ISO Standard for C++. The *Committee* is thus shorthand for both X3J16 and WG21, which meet together three times per year, each time for a week of intense effort, and will do so for years to come.

The words I quote in this book are the library portion of the first complete draft produced by the Committee (**Koe94**). That draft, which I call here the *Informal Review Draft*, is also the first document released for informal public review. Thus, it serves as a double milestone in the development of the C++ Standard. The draft continues to change, sometimes markedly in outward appearance, but the "codification of existing practice" shown here is much more stable. Until a version survives the public review process, and can be widely implemented, the Informal Review Draft is a good stationary target.

You will find the draft C++ Standard hard to read from time to time. Remember that it is cast intentionally in a kind of legalese. A standard must be precise and accurate first. Readability comes a distant second. The document is not intended to be tutorial.

I include in each chapter a direct quote from the relevant portion of the Informal Review Draft. This first quote introduces the Library section of the draft C++ Standard. It provides a few definitions and lays down several important ground rules that affect the library as a whole. Note how I have marked distinctly each quote from the Informal Review Draft. The type face differs from the running text of the book. A bold rule runs down the left side. (The notes to the left of the rule are mine.)

I typeset the quotes from the Informal Review Draft from the same machine-readable text used to produce the draft C++ Standard itself. Line and page breaks differ, of course. Be warned, however, that the draft is still subject to repeated change and has not been officially approved. The final authority on C++ will be the printed C++ Standard you eventually obtain from ISO, ANSI, or another participating national standards body.

17 Library

17.1 Introduction

A C++ implementation provides a *Standard C++ library* that defines various entities: types, macros, objects, and functions. Each of these entities is declared or defined (as appropriate) in a *header,* whose contents are made available to a translation unit when it contains the appropriate **#include** preprocessing directive.[48] Objects and functions defined in the library and required by a C++ program are included in the program prior to program startup.

17.1.1 Standard C library

This International Standard includes by reference clause 7 of the C Standard and clause 4 of Amendment 1 to the C Standard (1.2). The combined library described in those clauses is hereinafter called the *Standard C library*. With the qualifications noted in this subclause 17.1 and in subclause 17.2, the Standard C library is a subset of the Standard C++ library.

17.1.2 Headers

The Standard C++ library provides 39 *primary headers*, each with a corresponding *secondary header*, as shown in Table 13:

Table 13 — Library headers

PRIMARY	SECONDARY	PRIMARY	SECONDARY
`<all.ns>`	`<all>`	`<bits.ns>`	`<bits>`
`<cassert.ns>`	`<assert.h>`	`<bitstring.ns>`	`<bitstring>`
`<cctype.ns>`	`<ctype.h>`	`<defines.ns>`	`<defines>`
`<cerrno.ns>`	`<errno.h>`	`<dynarray.ns>`	`<dynarray>`
`<cfloat.ns>`	`<float.h>`	`<exception.ns>`	`<exception>`
`<ciso646.ns>`	`<iso646.h>`	`<fstream.ns>`	`<fstream>`
`<climits.ns>`	`<limits.h>`	`<iomanip.ns>`	`<iomanip>`
`<clocale.ns>`	`<locale.h>`	`<ios.ns>`	`<ios>`
`<cmath.ns>`	`<math.h>`	`<iostream.ns>`	`<iostream>`
`<complex.ns>`	`<complex>`	`<istream.ns>`	`<istream>`
`<csetjmp.ns>`	`<setjmp.h>`	`<new.ns>`	`<new>`
`<csignal.ns>`	`<signal.h>`	`<ostream.ns>`	`<ostream>`
`<cstdarg.ns>`	`<stdarg.h>`	`<ptrdynarray.ns>`	`<ptrdynarray>`
`<cstddef.ns>`	`<stddef.h>`	`<sstream.ns>`	`<sstream>`
`<cstdio.ns>`	`<stdio.h>`	`<streambuf.ns>`	`<streambuf>`
`<cstdlib.ns>`	`<stdlib.h>`	`<string.ns>`	`<string>`
`<cstring.ns>`	`<string.h>`	`<strstream.ns>`	`<strstream>`
`<ctime.ns>`	`<time.h>`	`<typeinfo.ns>`	`<typeinfo>`
`<cwchar.ns>`	`<wchar.h>`	`<wstring.ns>`	`<wstring>`
`<cwctype.ns>`	`<wctype.h>`		

If the name (enclosed in angle brackets) of a secondary header ends in **.h**, that header and its corresponding primary header are associated with the Standard C library and are called *C headers*. All other headers are called *C++ headers*.

If a header is implemented as a source file, the derivation of the file name from the header name is implementation-defined. If a file has a name equivalent to the derived file name for one of the above headers, is not provided as part of the implementation, and is placed in any of the standard places for a source file to be included, the behavior is undefined.

The header **<all.ns>** includes all other primary headers. The header **<all>** includes all other secondary headers.

A translation unit may include these headers in any order. Each may be included more than once, with no effect different from being included exactly once, except that the effect of including either **<cassert.ns>** or **<assert.h>** depends each time on the lexically current definition of **NDEBUG**. A translation unit shall include a header only outside of any external declaration or definition, and shall include the header lexically before the first reference to any of the entities it declares or first defines in that translation unit.

Certain types, macros, and namespace aliases are defined in more than one header. For such an entity, a second or subsequent header that also defines it may be included after the header that provides its initial definition.

None of the C headers includes any of the other headers, except that each secondary C header includes its corresponding primary C header. Except for the headers **<all.ns>** and **<all>**, none of the C++ headers includes any of the C headers. However, any of the C++ headers can include any of the other C++ headers, and must include a C++ header that contains any needed definition.[49]

17.1.3 Namespaces

Except for the header **<all.ns>**, each C++ header whose name has the form **name.ns** declares or defines all entities within the namespace **iso_standard_library::name**.[50]

Except for the header **<all>**, each C++ header whose name has the form **name** includes its corresponding primary header **name.ns**, followed by the declaration:

```
using namespace iso_standard_library::name
```

In addition, the header **<new>** contains the declarations:[51]

```
using iso_standard_library::new::operator delete
using iso_standard_library::new::operator new
```

Each C header whose name has the form **cname.ns** declares or defines all entities within the namespace **iso_standard_library::c::name**.

Each C header whose name has the form **name.h** includes its corresponding primary header **cname.ns**, followed by the declaration

```
using namespace iso_standard_library::c::name
```

In addition, for each function or object **X** declared with external linkage in its corresponding primary header **cname.ns**, the header **name.h** contains the declaration[52]

```
using iso_standard_library::c::name::X
```

Descriptions of header contents in this clause name the secondary headers instead of the primary headers. A statement such as "**X** is defined or declared in **<ios>**" is equivalent to "**X** is defined or declared by including **<ios>**, which includes **<ios.ns>** to obtain the actual declaration or definition."

17.1.4 Reserved names

A translation unit that includes a header shall not contain any macros that define names declared or defined in that header. Nor shall such a translation unit define macros for names lexically identical to keywords.

Each header defines the namespace **iso_standard_library** and its alias **std**. Each header declares or defines all names listed in its associated subclause. Each header also optionally declares or defines names which are always reserved to the implementation for any use and names reserved to the implementation for use at file scope.

Each name defined as a macro in a header is reserved to the implementation for any use if the translation unit includes the header.[53]

Certain sets of names and function signatures are reserved whether or not a translation unit includes a header:

- Each name that begins with an underscore and either an uppercase letter or another underscore is reserved to the implementation for any use.
- Each name that begins with an underscore is reserved to the implementation for use as a name with file scope or within the namespace **iso_standard_library** in the ordinary name space.
- Each name declared as an object with external linkage in a header is reserved to the implementation to designate that library object with external linkage.[54]
- Each global function signature declared with external linkage in a header is reserved to the implementation to designate that function signature with external linkage.[55]
- Each name having two consecutive underscores is reserved to the implementation for use as a name with both **extern "C"** and **extern "C++"** linkage.
- Each name declared with external linkage in a C header is reserved to the implementation for use as a name with **extern "C"** linkage.
- Each function signature declared with external linkage in a C header is reserved to the implementation for use as a function signature with both **extern "C"** and **extern "C++"** linkage.[56]

It is unspecified whether a name declared with external linkage in a C header has either **extern "C"** or **extern "C++"** linkage.[57]

If the program declares or defines a name in a context where it is reserved, other than as explicitly allowed by this clause, the behavior is undefined.

No other names or global function signatures are reserved to the implementation.[58]

17.1.5 Restrictions and conventions

17.1.5.1 Restrictions on macro definitions

restrictions
on macro
definitions

All object-like macros defined by the Standard C++ library and described in this clause as expanding to integral constant expressions are also suitable for use in **#if** preprocessing directives, unless explicitly stated otherwise.

17.1.5.2 Restrictions on arguments

restrictions
on arguments

Each of the following statements applies to all arguments to functions defined in the Standard C++ library, unless explicitly stated otherwise in this clause.

- If an argument to a function has an invalid value (such as a value outside the domain of the function, or a pointer invalid for its intended use), the behavior is undefined.
- If a function argument is described as being an array, the pointer actually passed to the function shall have a value such that all address computations and accesses to objects (that would be valid if the pointer did point to the first element of such an array) are in fact valid.

17.1.5.3 Restrictions on exception handling

restrictions
on exception
handling

Any of the functions defined in the Standard C++ library can report a failure to allocate storage by calling **ex.raise()** for an object **ex** of type **xalloc**. Otherwise, none of the functions defined in the Standard C++ library throw an exception that must be caught outside the function, unless explicitly stated otherwise.

None of the functions defined in the Standard C++ library catch any exceptions, unless explicitly stated otherwise.[59)]

17.1.5.4 Alternate definitions for functions

alternate definitions for functions

This clause describes the behavior of numerous functions defined by the Standard C++ library. Under some circumstances, however, certain of these function descriptions also apply to functions defined in the program:

- Four function signatures defined in the Standard C++ library may be displaced by definitions in the program. Such displacement occurs prior to program startup.[60)]
- Certain handler functions are determined by the values stored in pointer objects within the Standard C++ library. Initially, these pointer objects store null pointers or designate functions defined in the Standard C++ library. Other functions, however, when executed at run time, permit the program to alter these stored values to point at functions defined in the program.
- Virtual member function signatures defined for a base class in the Standard C++ library may be overridden in a derived class by definitions in the program.

In all such cases, this clause distinguishes two behaviors for the functions in question:

- *Required behavior* describes both the behavior provided by the implementation and the behavior that shall be provided by any function definition in the program.
- *Default behavior* describes any specific behavior provided by the implementation, within the scope of the required behavior.

Where no distinction is explicitly made in the description, the behavior described is the required behavior.

If a function defined in the program fails to meet the required behavior when it executes, the behavior is undefined.

17.1.5.5 Objects within classes

objects within classes

Objects of certain classes are sometimes required by the external specifications of their classes to store data, apparently in member objects. For the sake of exposition, this clause provides representative declarations, and semantic requirements, for private member objects of classes that meet the external specifications of the classes. The declarations for such member objects and the definitions of related member types in this clause are enclosed in a comment that ends with **exposition only**, as in:

```
// streambuf* sb;                          exposition only
```

Any alternate implementation that provides equivalent external behavior is equally acceptable.

17.1.5.6 Optional members

optional members

The definitions of some member types and the declarations of some member functions in this clause are enclosed in a comment that ends with **optional**, as in:

```
// void clear(io_state state_arg = 0);                  optional
```

Whether such definitions and declarations are actually present is implementation-defined.

17.1.5.7 Functions within classes

For the sake of exposition, this clause repeats in a derived class declarations for all the virtual member functions inherited from a base class. All such declarations are enclosed in a comment that ends with *inherited*, as in:

```
// virtual void do_raise();                              inherited
```

If a virtual member function in the base class meets the semantic requirements of the derived class, it is unspecified whether the derived class provides an overriding definition for the function signature.

An implementation can declare additional non-virtual member function signatures within a class:

- by adding arguments with default values to a member function signature described in this clause;[61]
- by replacing a member function signature with default values by two or more member function signatures with equivalent behavior;
- by adding a member function signature for a member function name described in this clause.

A call to a member function signature described in this clause behaves the same as if the implementation declares no additional member function signatures.[62]

For the sake of exposition, this clause describes no copy constructors, assignment operators, or (non-virtual) destructors with the same apparent semantics as those that can be generated by default. It is unspecified whether the implementation provides explicit definitions for such member function signatures, or for virtual destructors that can be generated by default.

17.1.5.8 Global functions

A call to a global function signature described in this clause behaves the same as if the implementation declares no additional global function signatures.[63]

17.1.5.9 Unreserved names

Certain types defined in C headers are sometimes needed to express declarations in other headers, where the required type names are neither defined nor reserved. In such cases, the implementation provides a synonym for the required type, using a name reserved to the implementation. Such cases are explicitly stated in this clause, and indicated by writing the required type name in *constant-width italic* characters.

Certain names are sometimes convenient to supply for the sake of exposition, in the descriptions in this clause, even though the names are neither defined nor reserved. In such cases, the implementation either omits the name, where that is permitted, or provides a name reserved to the implementation. Such cases are also indicated in this clause by writing the convenient name in *constant-width italic* characters.

For example:

The class **filebuf**, defined in **<fstream>**, is described as containing the private member object:

```
FILE* file;
```

This notation indicates that the member *file* is a pointer to the type **FILE**, defined in **<stdio.h>**, but the names **file** and **FILE** are neither defined nor reserved in **<fstream>**. An implementation need not implement class **filebuf** with an explicit member of type **FILE***. If it does so, it can choose 1) to replace the name *file* with a name reserved to the implementation, and 2) to replace *FILE* with an incomplete type whose name is reserved, such as in:

```
struct _Filet* _Fname;
```

If the program needs to have type **FILE** defined, it must also include **<stdio.h>**, which completes the definition of **_Filet**.

17.1.5.10 Implementation types

Certain types defined in this clause are based on other types, but with added constraints.

17.1.5.10.1 Enumerated types

enumerated types

Several types defined in this clause are *enumerated types*. Each enumerated type can be implemented as an enumeration or as a synonym for an enumeration. The enumerated type **enumerated** can be written:

```
enum secret {
    V0, V1, V2, V3, .....};
typedef secret enumerated;
static const enumerated C0(V0);
static const enumerated C1(V1);
static const enumerated C2(V2);
static const enumerated C3(V3);
    .....
```

Here, the names **C0**, **C1**, etc. represent *enumerated elements* for this particular enumerated type. All such elements have distinct values.

17.1.5.10.2 Bitmask types

bitmask types

Several types defined in this clause are *bitmask types*. Each bitmask type can be implemented as an enumerated type that overloads certain operators. The bitmask type **bitmask** can be written:

```
enum secret {
    V0 = 1 << 0, V1 = 1 << 1, V2 = 1 << 2, V3 = 1 << 3, .....};
typedef secret bitmask;
static const bitmask C0(V0);
static const bitmask C1(V1);
static const bitmask C2(V2);
static const bitmask C3(V3);

    .....
bitmask& operator&=(bitmask& X, bitmask Y)
    {X = (bitmask)(X & Y); return (X); }
bitmask& operator|=(bitmask& X, bitmask Y)
    {X = (bitmask)(X | Y); return (X); }
bitmask& operator^=(bitmask& X, bitmask Y)
    {X = (bitmask)(X ^ Y); return (X); }
bitmask operator&(bitmask X, bitmask Y)
    {return ((bitmask)(X & Y)); }
bitmask operator|(bitmask X, bitmask Y)
    {return ((bitmask)(X | Y)); }
bitmask operator^(bitmask X, bitmask Y)
    {return ((bitmask)(X ^ Y)); }
bitmask operator~(bitmask X)
    {return ((bitmask)~X); }
```

Here, the names **C0**, **C1**, etc. represent *bitmask elements* for this particular bitmask type. All such elements have distinct values such that, for any pair **Ci** and **Cj**, **Ci & Ci** is nonzero and **Ci & Cj** is zero.

The following terms apply to objects and values of bitmask types:

- To *set* a value **Y** in an object **X** is to evaluate the expression **X |= Y**.
- To *clear* a value **Y** in an object **X** is to evaluate the expression **X &= ~Y**.
- The value **Y** *is set* in the object **X** if the expression **X & Y** is nonzero.

17.1.5.10.3 Derived classes

derived classes

Certain classes defined in this clause are derived from other classes in the Standard C++ library:

- It is unspecified whether a class described in this clause as a base class is itself derived from other base classes (with names reserved to the implementation).
- It is unspecified whether a class described in this clause as derived from another class is derived from that class directly, or through other classes (with names reserved to the implementation) that are derived from the specified base class.

In any case:

- A base class described as virtual in this clause is always virtual;
- A base class described as non-virtual in this clause is never virtual;
- Unless explicitly stated otherwise, types with distinct names in this clause are distinct types.[64]

17.1.5.11 Protection within classes

protection within classes

It is unspecified whether a member described in this clause as private is private, protected, or public. It is unspecified whether a member described as protected is protected or public. A member described as public is always public.

It is unspecified whether a function signature or class described in this clause is a friend of another class described in this clause.

17.1.5.12 Definitions

definitions

The Standard C++ library makes widespread use of characters and character sequences that follow a few uniform conventions:

- A *letter* is any of the 26 lowercase or 26 uppercase letters in the basic execution character set.
- The *decimal-point character* is the (single-byte) character used by functions that convert between a (single-byte) character sequence and a value of one of the floating-point types. It is used in the character sequence to denote the beginning of a fractional part. It is represented in this clause by a period, `'.'`, which is also its value in the `"C"` locale, but may change during program execution by a call to `setlocale(int, const char*)`, declared in `<locale.h>`.
- A *character sequence* is an array object **A** that can be declared as **T A[N]**, where **T** is any of the types **char**, **unsigned char**, or **signed char**, optionally qualified by any combination of **const** or **volatile**. The initial elements of the array have defined contents up to and including an element determined by some predicate. A character sequence can be designated by a pointer value **s** that points to its first element.
- A *null-terminated byte string,* or *NTBS,* is a character sequence whose highest-addressed element with defined content has the value zero (the *terminating null* character).[65]
- The *length of an NTBS* is the number of elements that precede the terminating null character. An *empty NTBS* has a length of zero.
- The *value of an NTBS* is the sequence of values of the elements up to and including the terminating null character.
- A *static NTBS* is an NTBS with static storage duration.[66]
- A *null-terminated multibyte string,* or *NTMBS,* is an NTBS that constitutes a sequence of valid multibyte characters, beginning and ending in the initial shift state.[67]
- A *static NTMBS* is an NTMBS with static storage duration.

- A *wide-character sequence* is an array object **A** that can be declared as *T* **A[N]**, where *T* is type **wchar_t**, optionally qualified by any combination of **const** or **volatile**. The initial elements of the array have defined contents up to and including an element determined by some predicate. A character sequence can be designated by a pointer value **s** that designates its first element.
- A *null-terminated wide-character string,* or *NTWCS*, is a wide-character sequence whose highest-addressed element with defined content has the value zero.[68]
- The *length of an NTWCS* is the number of elements that precede the terminating null wide character. An *empty NTWCS* has a length of zero.
- The *value of an NTWCS* is the sequence of values of the elements up to and including the terminating null character.
- A *static NTWCS* is an NTWCS with static storage duration.[69]

Footnotes:

48) A header is not necessarily a source file, nor are the sequences delimited by < and > in header names necessarily valid source file names.
49) Including any one of the C++ headers can introduce all of the C++ headers into a translation unit, or just the one that is named in the **#include** preprocessing directive.
50) Macro definitions nevertheless occupy a disjoint name space.
51) Including the header **<new>** permits references of the form **::operator new**.
52) Including the C secondary header permits references of the form **::X**.
53) It is not permissible to remove a library macro definition by using the **#undef** directive.
54) The list of such reserved names includes **errno**, declared or defined in **<errno.h>**.
55) The list of such reserved function signatures with external linkage includes **setjmp(jmp_buf)**, declared or defined in **<setjmp.h>**, and **va_end(va_list)**, declared or defined in **<stdarg.h>**.
56) The function signatures declared in **<wchar.h>** and **<wctype.h>** are always reserved, notwithstanding the restrictions imposed in subclause 4.5.1 of Amendment 1 to the C Standard for their corresponding secondary headers.
57) The only reliable way to declare an object or function signature from the Standard C library is by including the header that declares it, notwithstanding the latitude granted in subclause 7.1.7 of the C Standard.
58) A global function cannot be declared by the implementation as taking additional default arguments. Also, the use of "masking macros" for function signatures declared in C headers is disallowed, notwithstanding the latitude granted in subclause 7.1.7 of the C Standard. The use of a masking macro can often be replaced by defining the function signature as *inline.*
59) A function can catch an exception not documented in this clause provided it rethrows the exception.
60) The function signatures, all declared in **<new>**, are **operator delete(void*)**, **operator delete[](void*)**, **operator new(size_t)**, and **operator new[](size_t)**.
61) Hence, taking the address of a member function has an unspecified type. The same latitude does *not* extend to the implementation of virtual or global functions, however.

62) A valid C++ program always calls the expected library member function, or one with equivalent behavior. An implementation may also define additional member functions that would otherwise not be called by a valid C++ program.

63) A valid C++ program always calls the expected library global function. An implementation may also define additional global functions that would otherwise not be called by a valid C++ program.

64) An implicit exception to this rule are types described as synonyms for basic integral types, such as **size_t** and **streamoff**.

65) Many of the objects manipulated by function signatures declared in **<string.h>** are character sequences or NTBSs. The size of some of these character sequences is limited by a length value, maintained separately from the character sequence.

66) A string literal, such as **"abc"**, is a static NTBS.

67) An NTBS that contains characters only from the basic execution character set is also an NTMBS. Each multibyte character then consists of a single byte.

68) Many of the objects manipulated by function signatures declared in **<wchar.h>** are wide-character sequences or NTWCSs.

69) A wide string literal, such as **L"abc"**, is a static NTWCS.

Future Directions

This "front matter" to clause 17 lays down ground rules that cover the entire library portion of the draft C++ Standard. While there is continuing restatement or rearrangement of this material, many of the ground rules now appear to be widely accepted. A few areas, however, are still somewhat volatile. Some have, in fact, already changed.

headers   To begin with, the header **<all>** has been deleted. Also, you need no longer worry about the distinction between "primary" and "secondary" headers (17.1.2). The Committee has already scrubbed all those files whose names end in **.ns**. The nearest thing to a replacement is a set of new C++ headers with names like **<cassert>** (corresponding to **<assert.h>**), **<cctype>** (corresponding to **<ctype.h>**), and so on for all 18 C headers. You might not recognize three of these C headers, by the way. Amendment 1 to the C Standard introduces **<iso646.h>**, **<wchar.h>**, and **<wctype.h>** (**ISO94**).

The relationship is much as before. The header **<cctype>**, for example, declares all its functions inside a *namespace* declaration (17.1.3). A *namespace* declaration encloses a sequence of declarations much like a class does, but without all the other semantics implied by a class declaration. The library *namespace* declaration nesting has also been radically simplified. Now, each C++ header simply contributes to the single library *namespace* declaration **std**, as in this skeleton for **<cctype>**:

```
// possible skeleton for <cctype>
namespace std {
    int isalnum(int);
    int isalpha(int);
    .....                                    // and so on
};
```

If you include `<cctype>` in a translation unit, you can refer to the functions by their qualified names, such as `std::isalnum`, `std::isalpha`, and so on. With this approach, you don't have to worry about library names colliding with any names your program defines, other than macro names. Or you can "hoist" names into file scope by writing (at file scope):

```
#include <cctype>
using std::isdigit;
```

From that point on, the name `isdigit` behaves as in the past. You can use it either qualified or unqualified. And, of course, it can also collide with names your program defines.

The corresponding C header does this hoisting for you. The skeleton for `<ctype.h>` now looks like:

```
// possible skeleton for <ctype.h>
#include <cctype>
using std::isalnum;
using std::isalpha;
    .....                                     // and so on
```

The primary change here is the omission of the *using* declaration for hoisting all names from the (now nonexistent) nested *namespace* declaration peculiar to the header.

whither   Old hands at C++ will note the absence of traditional headers such as
`<iostream.h>`   `<iostream.h>` and `<new.h>`. (See, for example, **Tea93**.) They have so far been intentionally omitted from the draft C++ Standard. If they reappear, I suspect they will behave much like the C headers, to ease migration of existing code. If they do not, you can be sure that vendors of C++ translators will supply them anyway.

It is not clear to me at this writing whether a header such as `<iostream>` will hoist its names. I doubt that even the most ardent proponents of *namespace* declarations will happily write `std::cout` repeatedly throughout a program. But a header that hoists may well be added with a different name (such as the venerable `<iostream.h>`, in this particular case).

The code in this book assumes, as the Informal Review Draft states, that such hoisting does indeed occur. It may have been more prudent to protect the code from changes in header conventions. Certainly, they have been a volatile and inventive area for some time now. But I chose not to add such protection. In fact, I provide only the C++ headers with no file extension, such as `<iostream>`. And these contain no *namespace* or *using* declarations. (I currently have access to no translators, commercial or otherwise, that even implement *namespace* declarations.) As a result, the code may need widespread changes when the C++ headers eventually settle down.

user-defined   Some sentiment has also been expressed for reducing the bite taken out
macros   of the library namespace by user-defined macros (17.1.4). Various schemes have been proposed for inhibiting or prohibiting user-defined macro expansion within library headers. One benefit of such a change would be that implementors could more easily add member functions to library classes. Old hands at C++ will inevitably note, and mourn, the absence of certain

features intentionally omitted during standardization. (**ios::fd()** is one example, for those of you in the know.) Vendors dare not add them back if their names can be masked by user-defined macros. The headers will simply translate improperly.

exceptions   The exception-handling machinery has been overhauled repeatedly, and bids fair to be modified still further. The class name **xalloc** (17.1.5.3), for example, is now **bad_alloc**. And the convention of throwing all library exceptions by calling the member function **raise()** for the exception object is under review. I discuss this matter at greater length in Chapter 3: **<exception>**, particularly under **Future Directions**.

optional   For backward compatibility with existing practice, the Informal Review
members Draft permits several member functions within library classes to be over-loaded with "old-fashioned" versions of three enumerated types. These older types are **ios::io_state** (replaced by **ios::iostate**), **ios:: open_mode** (replaced by **ios::openmode**), and **ios::seek_dir** (replaced by **ios::seekdir**). Member functions that use the older types are branded "optional members" here (17.1.5.6). You will see more of these beginning with Chapter 6: **<ios>**.

The Committee has already decided, however, to describe such additions in a non-normative annex as "deprecated features." I suspect that the practical effect of this change of emphasis will be minimal. Wise vendors will continue to supply the "old-fashioned" member functions because the draft C++ Standard permits the practice. More important, they will do so because users will demand the backward compatibility.

Using the Library

The draft C++ Standard has a lot to say about how the library looks to the user. Two important issues are how to use library headers and how to create names in a program

using   The Standard C++ library provides 38 standard headers that should
headers meet your daily needs. These include 18 *C headers,* inherited along with the Standard C library:

C headers

`<assert.h>`	`<limits.h>`	`<stdarg.h>`	`<string.h>`
`<ctype.h>`	`<locale.h>`	`<stddef.h>`	`<time.h>`
`<errno.h>`	`<math.h>`	`<stdio.h>`	`<wchar.h>`
`<float.h>`	`<setjmp.h>`	`<stdlib.h>`	`<wctype.h>`
`<iso646.h>`	`<signal.h>`		

Among these are the three relatively exotic standard headers introduced by Amendment 1 to the C Standard. The remaining are 20 *C++ headers,* added to describe facilities specific to C++:

C++ headers

`<bits>`	`<exception>`	`<istream>`	`<streambuf>`
`<bitstring>`	`<fstream>`	`<new>`	`<string>`
`<complex>`	`<iomanip>`	`<ostream>`	`<strstream>`
`<defines>`	`<ios>`	`<ptrdynarray>`	`<typeinfo>`
`<dynarray>`	`<iostream>`	`<sstream>`	`<wstring>`

file extensions   Note the absence of a *file extension*, such as `.h`. C++ implementations have followed an assortment of conventions for identifying C++ headers by file extension, including `.hpp` and the traditional `.h`. The Committee felt it wisest to standardize none of these. Instead, they chose header names with *no* file extension. An implementation is free to map these header names to file names with extensions, or to use them unchanged as file names.

The code in this book assumes the latter course — the file `defines`, for example, implements the header `<defines>`. As a sop to several popular operating systems with restricted file names, however, I chop the names of header files to eight letters. Thus, for example, `ptrdynar` implements the header `<ptrdynarray>`.

Of course, you may well have lots of C++ code with different ideas. Header names such as `<iomanip.h>`, `<iostream.h>`, and `<new.h>` occur widely. In most cases, you can simply make files with these names that include their standardized equivalents. Or, if duplicating source code doesn't give you the willies, you can copy the file `iostream` to `iostream.h`, and so on. That may speed the translation process slightly, but at the risk of violating the One Definition Rule, described below.

header properties   Any predefined name not defined in the language proper is declared or defined in one or more of these standard headers. The headers have several properties:

- They are *idempotent.* You can include the same standard header more than once. The effect is as if you included it exactly once.

- They are *mutually independent.* No standard header requires that the program first include another standard header to work properly. Instead, a C++ header itself includes any other C++ headers it needs. No header includes another C header.

- They are equivalent to *file-level declarations.* You must include a standard header before you refer to anything it defines or declares. You must not include a standard header within a declaration. And you must not mask any keywords, or names declared or defined by the standard header, with macro definitions before you include the standard header.

C++ headers must include each other because of the *One Definition Rule.* This principle (not yet well stated in the draft C++ Standard) requires that each entity be defined exactly once among all the headers and source files that make up a program. Officially, you can't get by with synonyms or duplicated chunks of source text, as you can in Standard C, even if you can apparently outsmart the translator in doing so. Less officially, you should at least make duplicated definitions as identical as possible. Thus, all you know when you include one or more C++ headers in a translation unit is that you have made visible *at least* what those headers declare and define. You can, in principle, include any one C++ header and get them all — but you can't depend on it.

<all>   An easy out is simply to include the header **<all>**. It includes all the C++ headers listed above. You can thus make a habit of including **<all>** atop each C++ translation unit you write. I can't bring myself to be so casual, however. I include at least the minimum set of C++ headers needed to ensure that all relevant headers get dragged in. And I avoid including any headers demonstrably not needed by a translation unit.

header   The universal convention among C++ programmers is to include all
placement headers near the beginning of a C++ source file. Only an identifying comment precedes the **#include** directives. You can write the headers in any order — I prefer to list all C headers first, then all C++ headers. Within each group, I sort the headers alphabetically by name. Include the headers for *every* Standard C library function that you use. Never mind what the C Standard says about declaring functions other ways. The draft C++ Standard is more demanding in this regard.

Your program may require its own header files. Don't use any of the standard header names as the names of your header files. You might get away with it on one system and come to grief on another. A widespread convention, if not universal, is to choose portable C or C++ source file names and header file names that take the following form:

- Begin the name with a lowercase letter.
- Follow with one to seven lowercase letters and digits.
- End with an extension of **.c** for a C or C++ source file, **.h** for a header file.

Examples are **i80486.h**, **matrix.c**, and **plot.h**. Names of this form are portable to a wide variety of C/C++ translators. You can achieve even wider portability by using at most *five* additional lowercase letters and digits. That's what the C Standard suggests. I find these longer names quite portable (and cryptic) enough, however.

extern "C"   An alternate extension for C++ source files is **.cpp**. As the pragmatic distinction between C and C++ fades over time, however, I find the uniform naming more sensible and convenient. I also find it more sensible to translate C programs as C++ code. That avoids the need to declare C functions in some "alien" form within C++ headers, as with the **extern "C"** storage-class qualifier. I use such warts only to access a C library that cannot be recompiled as C++.

A header file you write may require declarations or definitions from a standard header. If so, it is a wise practice to include the standard header near the top of your header file. That eliminates the need for you to include headers in a specific order within your C or C++ source files. Don't worry if you end up including the same standard header more than once within a translation unit. That's what idempotence is all about.

It is a good practice to use a different form of the **#include** directive for your own header files. Delimit the name with double quotes instead of angle brackets. Use the angle brackets only with the standard headers. For example, you might write at the top of a C++ source file:

```
#include <iostream>
#include "plot.h"
```

My practice is to list the standard headers first. If you follow the advice I gave above, however, that practice is not mandatory. I follow it simply to minimize the arbitrary.

name The Standard C++ library has fairly clean *name spaces*. The library defines **spaces** a couple hundred external names, and hundreds more nested within various classes. (See Apendix B: Names.) Beyond that, it reserves certain sets of names for use by the implementors. All other names belong to the users of the language. Figure 0.1 shows the name spaces that exist in a C++ program. It is adapted from Plauger and Brodie, *Standard C* (**P&B92**). The figure shows that you can define an open-ended set of name spaces:

- A new *ordinary* name space is created for each block (enclosed in braces within a function) or *namespace* declaration. It contains all names declared as type definitions, functions, objects, enumeration constants, enumeration tags, class tags, structure tags, and union tags.

- A new name space is created for each class, structure, or union you define. It contains the names of all the members.

- A new name space is created for each function prototype you declare. It contains the names of all the parameters.

- A new name space is created for each function you define. It contains the names of all the *goto* labels.

Figure 0.1:
C++ Name
Spaces

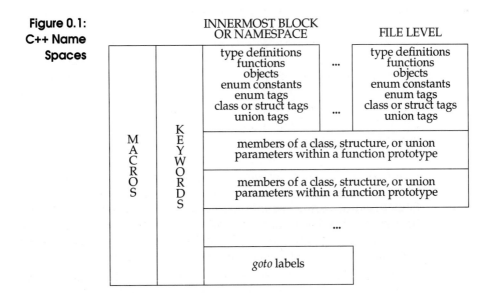

You can use a name only one way within a given name space. If the translator recognizes a name as belonging to a given name space, it may fail to see another use of the name in a different name space. In the figure, a name space box masks any name space box to its right. Thus, a macro can mask a keyword. And either of these can mask any other use of a name. (That makes it impossible for you to define an object whose name is **while**, for example.)

reserved
names
In practice, you should treat *all* keywords and library names as reserved in *all* name spaces, as much as possible. Use function overloading only to provide similar functionality for different parameter types. That minimizes confusion both for you and future readers of your code. Rely on the separate name spaces, or inadvertent overloading, to save you only when you forget about a rarely used name in the library. If you must do something rash, like defining a macro that masks a keyword, do it carefully and document the practice clearly. You must also avoid using certain sets of names when you write programs. They are reserved for use by the implementors. Don't use:

- names of functions and objects with external linkage that begin with an underscore, such as **_abc** or **_DEF**

- names of macros that begin with an underscore followed by a second underscore or an uppercase letter, such as **__abc** or **_DEF**.

Remember that a macro name can mask a name in any other name space. The second class of names is effectively reserved in *all* name spaces.

implementation
latitude
The draft C++ Standard permits some flexibility in implementation. A member function declared with a default argument, such as:

```
string& assign(char ch, size_t n = 1);
```

can be replaced by two declarations, as in:

```
string& assign(char ch,);
string& assign(char ch, size_t n);
```

The draft C++ Standard even allows an implementation to *add* default arguments not specified in the member function declaration. What this latitude costs the programmer is a bit of uncertainty. Taking the address of a library member function is now potentially ambiguous. (If you must do so, write a wrapper function that calls the one you want, then take the address of the wrapper.)

This latitude is limited, however. An implementation must *not* overload member functions to avoid other kinds of conversions. That could lead to ambiguities in a program that would be otherwise unambiguous. So the latitude granted implementors is specifically limited to playing games with default arguments. That still helps the draft C++ Standard offer a "thicker" interface without specifying so many different member functions. And it lets implementors decide how best to offer the required services.

By the way, the same latitude does *not* extend to external functions in the library. There are relatively few of these, and many of them are serious candidates for having their addresses taken on a regular basis.

Implementing the Library

The code that follows in this book makes several assumptions. If you want to use any of the code with a given C++ implementation, you must verify that the assumptions are valid for that implementation.

assumptions ■ *You can replace a standard header with a C++ source file of the same name, such as* **iostream**. An implementation is permitted to treat the names of the standard headers as reserved. Including a standard header can simply turn on a set of definitions built into the translator. An implementation that does so will cause problems when you try to replace headers.

■ *You can replace the standard headers piecemeal.* You may wish to experiment only with portions of the code presented here. Even if you eventually want to try it all, you don't want to have to make it all work at once.

■ *You can replace a predefined function with a C++ source file containing a conventional definition for the function.* An implementation is permitted to treat the external names of library functions as reserved (with just a few notable exceptions). Calling a library function can simply expand to inline code. An implementation that does so will cause problems.

■ *You can replace the predefined functions piecemeal.* An implementation is permitted to combine multiple library functions into a single module. The same arguments also apply as for replacing standard headers.

■ *File names for C++ source can have at least eight lowercase letters, followed by a dot and a single lowercase letter.* This is the form I described on page 18.

■ *External names may or may not map all letters to a single case.* The code presented here works correctly either way.

It is unlikely that your implementation violates any of these assumptions. If it does, the implementation can probably be made to cooperate by some ruse. Most C++ vendors write their libraries in C and C++, and use their own translators. They need this behavior too.

coding style The code in this book obeys a number of style rules. Most of the rules make sense for any project. A few are peculiar.

■ Each *visible* function in the library is either defined inline in the header that declares it or can be found in some C++ source file. The file name consists of at most eight characters, followed by **.c**. I group functions in a single file only when the likelihood is high that all will be used together. That makes for some rather small files in a few cases. Appendix B: Names shows each visible name defined in the library, giving the file name and initial page number where you can find the file that defines the name at least once.

■ Each *secret* name begins with an underscore followed by an uppercase letter, as in **_Getint**. Appendix B: Names also lists each secret name that is declared in a standard header.

■ Code layout is reasonably uniform. I usually declare objects within functions at the innermost possible nesting level. I indent religiously to show the nesting of control structures. I also follow each left brace (**{**) inside a function with a one-line comment. Inline functions are written more compactly than function definitions in C++ source files. (Even with this additional sacrifice in readability, some of the header files are still quite large.)

- The code contains no **register** declarations. They are hard to place wisely and they clutter the code. Besides, modern compilers should allocate registers much better than a programmer can.

- This book displays each C++ source file as a figure with a box around it. The figure caption gives the name of the file. Larger files appear on two or more pages — the figure caption on each page warns you that the code on that page represents only part of a C source file. I present two-page files on facing pages, but several files extend to three or more pages. I resisted the temptation to break these up along artificial boundaries, merely for the sake of presentation in this book.

- Each figure displays C++ source code with horizontal tab stops set every four columns. Displayed code differs from the actual C++ source file in two ways — comments to the right of code are right justified on the line, and a box character (□) marks the end of the last line of code in each C++ source file.

The resulting code is quite dense at times. For a typical coding project, I would add white space to make it at least 20 per cent larger. I would expand the inline functions in headers even more. I compressed the code aggressively to keep this book from getting even thicker.

The code also contains a number of files that could easily be merged. Placing all visible functions in separate files sometimes results in ridiculously small object modules, as I indicated above. The extra modules may sometimes be unappealing from the standpoint of good design, but they help both readability and portability in the real world.

all   For openers, here is a particularly simple example of a C++ file. Figure 0.2 shows the file **all**, which implements the header **<all>**. It consists only of a sequence of **#include** directives, for the remaining headers.

implementing   A number of the source files in this implementation are the standard **headers** headers. I listed several properties of standard headers earlier — idempotence, mutual independence, and declaration equivalence. Each of the properties has an impact on how you implement the standard headers.

Idempotence is easy to manage. You use a *macro guard* for most of the standard headers. For example, you can protect **<iostream>** by conditionally including its contents at most one time:

idempotence
```
#ifndef _IOSTREAM_
#define _IOSTREAM_
    .....                                        // body of <iostream>
#endif
```

The funny macro name **_IOSTREAM_** is, of course, in the class of names reserved to the implementor.

Figure 0.2:
all

```
// all standard header
#ifndef _ALL_
#define _ALL_
#include <assert.h>
#include <ctype.h>
#include <errno.h>
#include <float.h>
#include <iso646.h>
#include <limits.h>
#include <locale.h>
#include <math.h>
#include <setjmp.h>
#include <signal.h>
#include <stdarg.h>
#include <stddef.h>
#include <stdio.h>
#include <stdlib.h>
#include <string.h>
#include <time.h>
#include <wchar.h>
#include <wctype.h>
#include <bits>
#include <bitstring>
#include <complex>
#include <defines>
#include <dynarray>
#include <exception>
#include <fstream>
#include <iomanip>
#include <ios>
#include <iostream>
#include <istream>
#include <new>
#include <ostream>
#include <ptrdynarray>
#include <sstream>
#include <streambuf>
#include <string>
#include <strstream>
#include <typeinfo>
#include <wstring>
#endif
```

      You can't use this mechanism for the C header **<assert.h>**, by the way. Its behavior is controlled by the macro name **NDEBUG** that *the programmer* can choose to define. Each time the program includes this header, the header turns the **assert** macro off or on, depending upon whether or not **NDEBUG** has a macro definition at that point in the translation unit.

mutual
independence

      Maintaining mutual independence among the C++ headers is easier than in C because the C++ headers can include each other as they see fit. "Mutual independence" merely requires that the C++ headers do all the necessary including, rather than leave the job to the programmer. Problems occur only when a C++ header would dearly love to include a C header. The draft C++ Standard mitigates this problem by introducing the standard header **<defines>**. (See Chapter 2: **<defines>**.) Among other things, it defines several types also defined widely throughout C headers, the most popular being **size_t**. It is the type that results from applying the **sizeof** operator, and it occurs frequently as a function parameter type or return value type.

But this service causes a potential clash between **<defines>** and various C headers. A program must be able to include two different headers that define the same name without causing an error. The type definition **size_t** is a classic example. In Standard C, the canonical way to protect against multiple definitions of this type is with another macro guard:

```
#ifndef _SIZET
#define _SIZET
typedef unsigned int size_t;
#endif
```

This technique extends easily to C++ headers as well (but see the further discussion on page 47.)

benign   The macro **EOF** is another example. Both the C header **<stdio.h>** and
redefinition the C++ header **<streambuf>** define it. **EOF** signals end-of-file when extracting characters from a stream, or an invalid return value. One way to define this macro is:

```
#define EOF (-1)
```

It does no harm to include multiple instances of this macro definition in a translation unit. Both Standard C and the draft C++ Standard permit *benign redefinition* of a macro. Two definitions for the same macro name must have the same sequence of *tokens*. They can differ only in the *white space* (in this case, spaces and horizontal tabs) between tokens. You need not protect against including two definitions that match in this sense.

You do have to provide the same definition for several entities in multiple places, however. That is an annoying maintenance problem. Two solutions are:

- Write the same definition in multiple places. Be prepared to hunt down all occurrences if the definition changes.

- Place the definition in a separate header file. Give the file a name that should not collide with file names created by the programmer. Include the file in each header that requires it.

<yxvals.h> I chose the second solution (most of the time) because it simplifies adapting the library to different implementations of C++. The header **<yxvals.h>**, peculiar to the implementation of the Standard C++ library in this book, is a catchall. It holds configuration-specific macros and type definitions, as well as definitions that must be shared with C headers. (The analogous header in my implementation of the Standard C library is **<yvals.h>**). Appendix A: Interfaces summarizes the various contributions to this "internal" header.

A related issue arises with the classes **stdiobuf**, **istdiostream**, and **ostdiostream**, described in Chapter 13: **<fstream>**. All have constructors that take a parameter of type *pointer to* **FILE**. But that type is not defined in this particular header. It is defined only in the C header **<stdio.h>**. How can this be?

synonyms   The answer is simple, if a bit subtle. The header **<fstream>** must contain a *synonym* for the type **FILE**. The synonym has a name from the set reserved for macros. That's all that's needed within the standard header to declare each of the three constructors. (Of course, the implementor faces the same problems replicating either visible definitions or synonyms in multiple headers.)

It's rather difficult for you as a programmer to *use* any of these functions without a definition for **FILE**. (It can be done, but it's probably not good style.) That means you probably want to include the header **<stdio.h>** any time you make use of any of these functions. Still, it's the programmer's problem. The implementation need not (and must not) drag in **<stdio.h>** every time the program includes **<streambuf>**.

headers at   The final property of standard headers is primarily for the benefit of
file level   implementors. The programmer must include a standard header only where a file-level declaration is permitted. That means the **#include** directive must not occur anywhere inside another declaration. Most standard headers must contain one or more *external declarations*. These are permissible only in certain contexts. Without the caveat, many standard headers would be impossible to write as ordinary C++ source files.

Testing the Library

Testing can be a never-ending proposition. Only the most trivial functions can be tested exhaustively. Even these can never be tested for all possible interactions with nontrivial programs that use them. You would have to test all possible input values, or at least exercise all possible paths through the code. If your goal is to prove conclusively that a function contains no bugs, you will often fall far short of your goal.

validating   A less ambitious goal is *validation*. Here, your goal is to demonstrate how
specifications   well the code meets its specification. You pointedly ignore any implementation details. Thus, it is often called "black-box testing." A vendor may know implementation details that are not easily visible to the customer. It is in the vendor's best interest to test the internal structure of the code as well as its external characteristics. A customer, however, should be concerned primarily with validating that a product meets its specification, particularly when comparing two or more competing products.

testing   Another form of testing is to write tests that exercise every statement in
all paths   the executable code. That is a far cry from testing every possible path through the code. It is good enough, however, to build a high level of

confidence that the code is essentially correct. To write such tests, you must know:

- what the code is supposed to do (the specification)
- how it does it (the code itself)

You must then contrive tests that test each detail of the specification. (I intentionally leave vague what a "detail" might be.) In principle, those tests should visit every cranny of the code. Every piece of code should help implement some part of the specification. In practice, you must always add tests you don't anticipate when you first analyze the specification.

The result is a complex piece of code closely tied to the code you intend to test. It was commonly called "white-box testing," although "glass-box testing" is now more often used, and more apropos. The test program can be as complex as the program to be tested, or more so. That can double the quantity of code you must maintain in future. A change to either piece often necessitates a change to the other. You use each piece of code to debug the other. Only when the two play in harmony can you say that testing is complete — at least for the time being. The payoff for all this extra investment is a significant improvement in code reliability.

performance   Still another form of testing is for *performance*. To many people perform-
testing ance means speed, pure and simple. But other factors can matter as much or more — such as memory and disk requirements, both temporary and permanent, or predictable worst-case timings.

Good performance tests:

- measure parameters that are relevant to the way the code is likely to be used
- can be carried out by independent agents
- have reproducible results
- have reasonable criteria for "good enough"
- have believable criteria for "better than average" and "excellent"

An amazing number of so-called performance tests violate most or all of these principles. Many test what is easy to test for, not what is worth testing.

The wise code developer invests in as many of these forms of testing as possible, given the inevitable limits on time and money. You design a test plan alongside the code to be tested. You develop comprehensive tests as part of the project. Ideally, you have different programmers write the code and tests. You obtain vendor-independent validation suites from outside sources. You institutionalize retesting after any changes. You provide for maintenance of test machinery as well as the delivered code itself.

I heartily endorse such professionalism in developing code. Having paid lip service to that ideal, however, I intend to stop somewhat short of it. The code presented here has been validated a number of different ways, by several different parties. But I have not yet produced test programs to exercise every part of the executable code. This book is already overstuffed with code. To add a full set of proper tests would make it truly unwieldy.

simple testing

Instead, I present a number of simple test programs. Each tests part or all of the facilities provided by one of the standard headers in the Standard C++ library. You will find that these test programs focus primarily on external behavior. That means, essentially, that they comprise a simple validation suite. Occasionally, however, they stray into the realm of testing internal structure. Some implementation errors are so common, and so pernicious, that I can't resist testing for them. Rarely do the programs stray into the realm of performance testing.

Most of all, you will find these tests to be remarkably superficial and simplistic, given what I just said about proper testing. Nevertheless, even simple tests serve a useful purpose. You can verify that a function satisfies its basic design goals with just a few lines of code. That reassures you that your implementation is sane. When you make changes (as you inevitably will), repeating the tests renews that assurance. Simple tests are well worth writing, and keeping around.

I found that the best simple confidence tests have a number of common properties:

- Print a standard reassuring message and exit with successful status to report correct execution.

- Identify any other unavoidable output to minimize confusion on the part of the reader.

- Provide interesting implementation-dependent information that you may find otherwise difficult to obtain.

- Say nothing else.

I have adopted the convention of preceding each header name with a **t** (then chopping, as necessary, to eight letters before the **.c** file extension) to construct test file names. Thus, **tdefines.c** tests the header **<defines>**. It verifies that the header defines what it is supposed to. It prints the sizes of several flexible object types. And it ends by displaying the reassuring message:

```
SUCCESS testing <defines>
```

then takes a normal exit. That way, you can run this and other tests from a command script and simply test the exit status, if you choose.

Note that each of these files defines its own **main**. You link each with the Standard C++ library to produce a separate test program. Do *not* add any of these files to your Standard C++ object-module library. I chose **t** as the leading character to follow the same convention as for my implementation of the Standard C library. File naming is more arbitrary in this implementation of the Standard C++ library than in the earlier work, so there is no fear of name conflicts.

Exercises

Exercise 0.1 Which of the following are *good* reasons for including a class in a library?

- The class is widely used.
- Performance of the member functions in the class can be improved dramatically by special optimizations.
- The class is easy to write and can be written several different ways.
- The class is hard to write correctly.
- Writing the class poses several interesting challenges.
- The class proved very useful in a past application.
- The class performs a number of services that are loosely related.

Exercise 0.2 Write a (correct) program that contains the line:

```
x: x::x.x = x(5);
```

Describe the five distinct uses of **x**. Can you make a case for using any two of these meanings at once in a sensible program?

Exercise 0.3 A library class **x** declares a member function **y**. What happens if the program defines a macro named **y** before it includes the header that defines the class **x**?

Exercise 0.4 What happens if the program includes the header that defines **x**, as above, then defines a macro named **y** *after* it includes the header?

Exercise 0.5 If any standard header can include any other, what style must you adopt to avoid problems?

Exercise 0.6 [**Harder**] If a standard header can define arbitrary names, what must a programmer do to ensure that a large program runs correctly when moved from another implementation?

Exercise 0.7 [**Very hard**] Describe an implementation that tolerates arbitrary names, even keywords, being masked by macros when you include standard headers.

Exercise 0.8 [**Very hard**] Describe an implementation that tolerates standard headers being included inside class declarations, function definitions, or at any arbitrary place within a source file.

Chapter 1: Standard C Library

Background

An important reason for the success of C++ is that it's built atop C. That confers several immediate advantages:

- C++ inherits C's well thought out technology for basic types, expression evaluation, and flow of control.
- C++ profits from C's popularity and portability.
- C++ programs can make use of the extensive Standard C library.

And herein lies an interesting irony. For it is the *limitations* of C that inspired many of the features of C++. Just as C made C++ possible, it also made it arguably *necessary* to many people.

class libraries One of the major advantages of C++ over C is the ability to write class libraries instead of function libraries. A class encapsulates much more than just a type definition and a handful of related functions. It can enforce information hiding and proper protocols for using member functions. A well designed class, or template class, or set of classes, is bound to be more reusable than the equivalent collection of functions.

Nevertheless, the Standard C library endures as an important adjunct to C++. It has not been displaced by a superior set of classes. (The iostreams package does replace much of what's in `<stdio.h>`, but not all.) If anything, I believe that the presence of such a rich function library has inhibited, or at least delayed, the growth of the kind of class library that many C++ programmers would prefer. As is so often the case, that which is *good enough* wins out over that which is arguably the best.

What the Draft C++ Standard Says

For a variety of reasons, some of which I indicated above, the C++ library includes the Standard C library as a subset. From a purely descriptive standpoint, the draft C++ Standard avoids repetition as much as possible. Rather than copy great gobs of wording from the C Standard, the draft C++ Standard includes the library portion of the C Standard "by reference" (**ISO90**). The focus is thus on what must change to make the Standard C library work properly as part of the Standard C++ library.

17.2 Standard C library

This subclause summarizes the explicit changes in definitions, declarations, or behavior within the Standard C library when it is part of the Standard C++ library. (Subclause 17.1 imposes some *implicit* changes in the behavior of the Standard C library.)

17.2.1 Modifications to headers

modifications to headers | Each C header whose name has the form **cname.ns** declares or defines those entities declared or defined in the corresponding header **name.h** in the C Standard.[70]

17.2.2 Modifications to definitions

17.2.2.1 Type wchar_t

wchar_t | **wchar_t** is a keyword in this International Standard. It does not appear as a type name defined in any of **<stddef.h>**, **<stdlib.h>**, or **<wchar.h>**.

17.2.2.2 Macro NULL

NULL | The macro **NULL**, defined in any of **<locale.h>**, **<stddef.h>**, **<stdio.h>**, **<stdlib.h>**, **<string.h>**, **<time.h>**, or **<wchar.h>**, is an implementation-defined C++ null-pointer constant in this International Standard.[71]

17.2.2.3 Header <iso646.h>

<iso646.h> | The tokens **and**, **and_eq**, **bitand**, **bitor**, **compl**, **not_eq**, **not**, **or**, **or_eq**, **xor**, and **xor_eq** are keywords in this International Standard. They do not appear as macro names defined in **<iso646.h>**.

17.2.3 Modifications to declarations

17.2.3.1 memchr(const void*, int, size_t)

memchr | The function signature **memchr(const void*, int, size_t)**, declared in **<string.h>** in the C Standard, does not have the declaration

```
    void* memchr(const void* s, int c, size_t n);
```

in this International Standard. Its declaration in **<string.h>** is replaced by the two declarations:

```
    const void* memchr(const void* s, int c, size_t n);
          void* memchr(      void* s, int c, size_t n);
```

both of which have the same behavior as the original declaration.

17.2.3.2 strchr(const char*, int)

strchr | The function signature **strchr(const char*, int)**, declared in **<string.h>** in the C Standard, does not have the declaration:

```
    char* strchr(const char* s, int c);
```

in this International Standard. Its declaration in **<string.h>** is replaced by the two declarations:

```
    const char* strchr(const char* s, int c);
          char* strchr(      char* s, int c);
```

both of which have the same behavior as the original declaration.

17.2.3.3 strpbrk(const char*, const char*)

strpbrk | The function signature **strpbrk(const char*, const char*)**, declared in **<string.h>** in the C Standard, does not have the declaration:

```
    char* strpbrk(const char* s1, const char* s2);
```

in this International Standard. Its declaration in **<string.h>** is replaced by the two declarations:

```
    const char* strpbrk(const char* s1, const char* s2);
          char* strpbrk(      char* s1, const char* s2);
```

both of which have the same behavior as the original function signature.

17.2.3.4 strrchr(const char*, int)

strrchr

The function signature **strrchr(const char*, int)**, declared in **<string.h>** in the C Standard, does not have the declaration:
```
char* strrchr(const char* s, int c);
```
in this International Standard. Its declaration in **<string.h>** is replaced by the two declarations:
```
const char* strrchr(const char* s, int c);
      char* strrchr(      char* s, int c);
```
both of which have the same behavior as the original declaration.

17.2.3.5 strstr(const char*, const char*)

strstr

The function signature **strstr(const char*, const char*)**, declared in **<string.h>** in the C Standard, does not have the declaration:
```
char* strstr(const char* s1, const char* s2);
```
in this International Standard. Its declaration in **<string.h>** is replaced by the two declarations:
```
const char* strstr(const char* s1, const char* s2);
      char* strstr(      char* s1, const char* s2);
```
both of which have the same behavior as the original declaration.

17.2.4 Modifications to behavior

17.2.4.1 Macro offsetof

offsetof

The macro **offsetof(type, member-designator)**, defined in **<stddef.h>**, accepts a restricted set of **type** arguments in this International Standard. **type** shall be a POD structure or a POD union.

17.2.4.2 longjmp(jmp_buf, int)

longjmp

The function signature **longjmp(jmp_buf jbuf, int val)**, declared in **<setjmp.h>**, has more restricted behavior in this International Standard. If any automatic objects would be destroyed by a thrown exception transferring control to another (destination) point in the program, then a call to **longjmp(jbuf, val)** at the throw point that transfers control to the same (destination) point has undefined behavior.

17.2.4.3 Storage allocation functions

storage
allocation
functions

The function signatures **calloc(size_t)**, **malloc(size_t)**, and **realloc(void*, size_t)**, declared in **<stdlib.h>**, do not attempt to allocate storage by calling **operator new(size_t)**, declared in **<new>**.

17.2.4.4 exit(int)

exit

The function signature **exit(int status)**, declared in **<stdlib.h>**, has additional behavior in this International Standard:

- First, all functions **f** registered by calling **atexit(f)**, are called, in the reverse order of their registration.[72] The function signature **atexit(void (*)())**, is declared in **<stdlib.h>**.
- Next, all static objects are destroyed in the reverse order of their construction. (Automatic objects are not destroyed as a result of calling **exit(int)**.)[73]
- Next, all open C streams (as mediated by the function signatures declared in **<stdio.h>**) with unwritten buffered data are flushed, all open C streams are closed, and all files created by calling **tmpfile()** are removed.[74] The function signature **tmpfile()** is declared in **<stdio.h>**.

- Finally, control is returned to the host environment. If **status** is zero or **EXIT_SUCCESS**, an implementation-defined form of the status *successful termination* is returned. If **status** is **EXIT_FAILURE**, an implementation-defined form of the status *unsuccessful termination* is returned. Otherwise the status returned is implementation-defined. The macros **EXIT_FAILURE** and **EXIT_SUCCESS** are defined in **<stdlib.h>**.

The function signature **exit(int)** never returns to its caller.

Footnotes:

Footnotes

70) The header **<stdlib.h>**, for example, makes all declarations and definitions available in the global name space, much as in the C Standard. The header **<cstdlib.ns>** provides the same declarations and definitions within the namespace **iso_standard_library::c::stdlib**.
71) Possible definitions include **0** and **0L**, but not **(void*)0**.
72) A function is called for every time it is registered.
73) Automatic objects are all destroyed in a program whose function **main** contains no automatic objects and executes the call to **exit**. Control can be transferred directly to such a **main** by throwing an exception that is caught in **main**.
74) Any C streams associated with **cin**, **cout**, etc. are flushed and closed when static objects are destroyed in the previous phase.

Future Directions

I believe most of the tough decisions have been made in the area of compatibility between the Standard C and Standard C++ libraries. The toughest decision was not to try to "fix" the Standard C library. Maintaining backward compatibility with widespread C practice has an obvious payoff. Outlawing irregular or inconvenient features may make for a prettier library, but raises the cost of migrating from C to C++. So the Committee has mandated changes in the Standard C library only when it felt a pressing need. I can think of only a few open issues:

locales   The Committee has voted in extensive additions to the machinery associated with C locales. These additions encapsulate locales within "locale objects," permit different input and output streams to operate in different locales, and extend the set of locale-specific operations. Superficially, nothing need change in the C header **<locale.h>**, but in practice, C locales may in future be implemented atop C++ locale objects. Or both may be implemented atop a common foundation.

math functions   The C Standard supplies a number of common math functions, with names like **exp**, **sin**, and **sqrt**, that operate on *double* operands and produce *double* results. It also reserves names for a parallel set of *float* functions (such as **expf**, **sinf**, and **sqrtf**), and for a similar set of *long double* functions (such as **expl**, **sinl**, and **sqrtl**). But these latter two groups are not required by the Standard C library.

The draft C++ Standard defines complex arithmetic classes in all three precisions. (See Chapter 21: **<complex>**.) They require these additional math functions implicitly, whether or not their presence is explicitly called out. Thus, it might be a kindness to programmers to spell out such a requirement. That way, the functions will assuredly be present with standard names, and hence more widely available.

<stdarg.h>   The macros defined in **<stdarg.h>** barely work, in most implementations of Standard C. To ask them to deal with reference parameters, and references to objects of type **va_list**, is probably pushing things a bit too far. The Informal Review Draft doesn't address this subject, but there has been some discussion within the Committee about limiting what the programmer can expect of these macros. And a typical implementation of C++ will almost certainly fail if the macros are pushed too hard. I'm sure the draft C++ Standard will eventually restrict what's expected of **<stdarg.h>**.

Using the Standard C Library

I can't begin to describe the entire Standard C library here. To do it justice would literally double the size of this book. (See **ISO90**, **ISO94**, **Pla92**, **P&B92**, and **Plu89** for other books on this subject.) I confine my attention in this book to what is *different* about the Standard C library when it forms a part of the Standard C++ library. Here are some of the qualifications you need to keep in mind:

First and foremost, *always* include the relevant C headers for any facilities you use from the Standard C library. (I explain why on page 37.) Eliminate any inline declarations of Standard C functions or objects. Sooner or later, they'll clash with some change mandated by a valid implementation of the Standard C++ library.

wchar_t   In C, the type **wchar_t** is defined in the headers **<stddef.h>** and **<stdlib.h>**. It serves as a synonym for one of the other integer types (used by the translator to represent wide characters). In C++, **wchar_t** is now a keyword that names a distinct type. That lets you overload functions and reliably distinguish between arguments of types *char* and **wchar_t**. But it also means that **wchar_t** is in a program name space whether or not you include any of the traditional C headers that define this type.

NULL   In C, the macro **NULL** can be defined as any of **0**, **0L**, or **(void *)0**. In C++, the third option is no longer permissible (and the second one is of little benefit). One use for **NULL** in a C program is to emphasize that you're talking about a null pointer, and not just any old zero. A more important use, however, was in the early days of C, when pointers tended to be all the same size and function prototypes were nonexistent. By writing **NULL** as a null pointer argument, you were sure to get a zero of the proper size. It is important to point out, however, that the C Standard doesn't require **NULL** for the first use and doesn't guarantee that it's always suitable for the second. So for a variety of reasons, mostly stylistic, you should probably not use **NULL** in C++ programs anyway.

offsetof   In C, structures are pretty simple creatures. They consist only of the member objects you declare, in the order you declare those members. At worst, the translator throws in a few holes to get storage boundaries right. In C++, a structure may inherit member objects from one or more base classes. Some of those member objects may be private. And the structure may contain one or more pointers to virtual tables. Thus, it is a little harder to say what is meant by "the offset of" a member object in an arbitrary C++ structure (class). It makes no sense at all to talk about the offset of a member class (nested class), a member template, or a member function.

For all these reasons, the macro **offsetof** is defined only for the "plain old data structures" of C. These are essentially the kind of structures or unions you can declare in a C program, with a few minor additions. Don't try to apply this macro to anything more sophisticated.

<stdarg.h>   Much the same sort of thing can be said about most of the machinery that lets you walk varying length argument lists. As I mentioned earlier, the macros defined in **<stdarg.h>** probably won't work properly with constructs peculiar to C++. Avoid:

- a scalar argument in a varying length list that changes representation when subject to default argument promotion (integer types smaller than *int*, or the type *float*)

- an aggregate argument in a varying length list other than a "plain old data structure"

- references to objects of type **va_list**

- a reference "**parmN**" parameter (the parameter argument to **va_start**)

The first constraint also applies to Standard C programs, but programmers occasionally forget it, to their detriment when they have to chase subtle bugs. The second constraint also rules out array types as arguments to **va_arg**, even for Standard C programs. (The translator converts an array argument expression to a pointer expression.)

longjmp   Some people would like to ban **setjmp** and **longjmp** entirely from C++
setjmp   programs. Indeed, these functions will eventually be no longer strictly necessary. Exception handling has been added to the draft C++ Standard to perform the same operations, but in a safer and more structured fashion.

The major problem is skipped destructors. Calling **longjmp** peels back the stack an arbitrary number of levels to get back to the context where **setjmp** was called for the **jmp_buf** argument. Any automatic storage constructed on the way down just gets abandoned on the way back out. A thrown exception, by contrast, makes a point of calling all the destructors in the proper order on the way from the *throw* expression to the *catch* clause that handles the exception. (See Chapter 3: **<exception>**.)

It is an obvious fact of life, however, that the world is full of C code that calls **setjmp** and **longjmp**. Certainly, the C++ community is eager to pave the migration of C code to C++. Thus, the draft C++ Standard attempts to avoid any gratuitous changes that require existing C code to be rewritten. This is the well known principle of keeping C++ "as close as possible to C, but no closer" (**K&S89**).

So the compromise is to permit a C++ program to contain calls to **setjmp** and **longjmp**. The only problem arises when a call to **longjmp** skips over destructor calls. That's not likely to happen in code you first migrate to C++, since no C code calls any destructors. The draft C++ Standard simply decrees that this behavior is undefined. Just be careful not to insert code that calls destructors before you've eliminated any **longjmp** calls that might bypass it.

exit   Some people would also like to ban **exit** from C++ programs. The traditional behavior is for **exit** to call the destructors for all static data, but *not* for any automatic data still alive at the time of the **exit** call. This is not considered quite so bad as **longjmp** skipping destructors — at least the program is terminating. But it's still not nice. Some classes depend on destructors to perform cleanup that is important even in the throes of program termination.

There has been some discussion in support of having **exit** call those skipped destructors. Effectively, a call to **exit** would throw an exception that is caught by the agent that calls **main**. But such a change could add significant overheads to all C++ programs and is controversial for other reasons as well. Right now, its behavior is simply documented in its traditional form. I expect it to remain that way.

You should hunt down and eliminate any calls to **exit** in C code that you migrate to C++. (Throw an exception and catch it in **main**, for example, if you really have to terminate from deep within the function-call hierarchy.) Sooner or later, you will regret a destructor call that gets missed.

storage   Another minor conflict lies in the set of functions declared in
allocation **<stdlib.h>** that allocate and free storage. C++ provides **operator new(size_t)**, **operator delete(void *)**, and their array counterparts to do the same thing in a somewhat more structured fashion. (Constructors and destructors get called at the proper times, for one thing.)

But once again, lots of migrated code calls **malloc, free,** and their buddies. Even a few pure C++ programs have occasion to call these functions directly. (For some justifiable uses of these functions in C++, see Chapter 15: **<string>**, Chapter 16: **<wstring>**, and Chapter 18: **<bitstring>**.)

So the question arises, what is the relationship between **operator new** and **malloc**? The answer comes in two parts:

- There is no guarantee that the two mechanisms are compatible. What you allocate with **operator new** you'd better free with the corresponding **operator delete**. What you allocate with **malloc** (or its buddies) you'd better free with **free**.

- If you replace an **operator new** with your own version, it's okay to have it call **malloc** to buy storage. Put another way, **malloc** is guaranteed *not* to call **operator new(size_t)** to do its thing. No fear of an infinite loop here.

string　A handful of functions declared in **<string.h>** have a form that is
functions　inconvenient to many a C++ program. Consider:

```
void *memchr(const void *s, int c, size_t n);
char *strchr(const char *s, int c);
char *strpbrk(const char *s1, const char *s2);
char *strrchr(const char *s, int c);
char *strstr(const char *s1, const char *s2);
```

Each of these takes a pointer to a constant argument that designates a
sequence of characters, and returns a pointer to somewhere inside that
sequence (or a null pointer). But the return type is *not* declared as a pointer
to a constant type. C++ is rather more finicky than C about mixing pointers
to constant and non-constant things. As a result, you find yourself writing
type casts practically all the time when you use these functions from C++.

The solution is to replace **strrchr**, for example, with:

```
const char *strrchr(const char *s, int c);
      char *strrchr(      char *s, int c);
```

The idea is to eliminate the need for most type casts. The declarations tend
to be more honest in the bargain. (I personally favor dropping the second
form, however, as being even more honest. That's the way the analogous
wide-character functions are now declared in Amendment 1 to the C
Standard, described below.)

Amendment 1　One other document is included by reference in the draft C++ Standard.
Amendment 1 to the ISO C Standard provides numerous additions to the
Standard C library — to support reading, writing, and manipulation of
large character sets (**ISO94**). The Committee has agreed to include it as part
of the Standard C++ library, even before it is formally approved.

So far, only one qualification is spelled out for Amendment 1 contributions. Part of that Amendment is the addition of a new header, **<iso646.h>**,
which defines a number of macros as aliases for certain operators. These
are mostly the operators that are hard to write in national variants of ISO
646, which often replace the conventional graphics for C operators such as
|=. Thus, for example, the macro **or_eq** expands to |=.

But this presents a problem in C++ similar to **wchar_t**. It seems the draft
C++ Standard has already made keywords of all the macros defined in
<iso646.h>. Thus, you need never include the header. I can imagine only
the rarest of circumstances under which you might wish to include this
header anyway.

Implementing the Standard C Library

C++ is not exactly the same language as C. It is no surprise, therefore, to
find that the Standard C library cannot survive completely unchanged in a
C++ environment. The draft C++ Standard includes a number of qualifications to the behavior of the Standard C library. You cannot, for example,
declare a library function inline, as in:

```
extern double sqrt(double);
```

In a C++ program, you must include the header `<math.h>` to be sure the function is declared properly. And that header almost certainly must be modified to some extent. Here are a couple of reasons why:

- The Standard C library can be implemented as "alien" C code, decorated with lots of `extern "C"` qualifiers. Equally, it can be implemented as C++ code. Thus, all the external names from that library are reserved in the space of `extern "C"` names, but the function names are still not guaranteed to be of that flavor. That effectively rules out writing declarations for any of these functions, as permitted by the C Standard, instead of including its header. Include the appropriate header, or perish.

- C++ cares about *function signatures*, not just names. A program can overload `sqrt`, for example, even if it includes `<math.h>`. Thus, only the external function signatures explicitly defined by the Standard C++ library are reserved. That effectively rules out the use of any masking macros in the Standard C headers, despite what the C Standard normally promises.

C++ ready   To make an existing Standard C library "C++ ready" generally requires attention to many small details. List a C header from a combined C/C++ implementation and you will see what I mean. Likely enough, you will find liberal use of conditional preprocessing, with lines that read something like:

```
#ifdef __cplusplus
    .....                                                       // C++ code
#else
    .....                                                       // C code
#endif
```

The builtin macro `__cplusplus` is defined by all C++ translators, and should not be defined by any C translators. This approach handles differences such as whether type `wchar_t` is predefined or needs to be defined in a C header.

Converting a Standard C library to work with C++ does not necessarily require a major rewrite, unless the library is *very* old. If the library is written in the style encouraged by the C Standard, it will be close to what is required by the draft C++ Standard. I've completed this exercise for my implementation from *The Standard C Library* (**Pla92**). The two biggest enhancements were almost pure additions:

- adding code to implement Amendment 1 of the C Standard, and modifying the facilities provided by `<stdio.h>` to work with "wide streams"

- adding all the optional *float* and *long double* math functions, to provide proper support for the complex classes

The rest was dusting and cleaning, by comparison.

needed   There is another side to the coin. To a surprising extent, the Standard
extensions C++ library sits neatly atop the Standard C library. The code in this book, with few exceptions, can run unchanged atop any implementation of Standard C. The exceptions lie in two areas:

- Sometimes the Standard C++ library code must be privy to implementation-dependent information. In the previous chapter (page 24), I mentioned the added header **<yxvals.h>**. It is one convenient vehicle for conveying such information — such as how the Standard C library protects itself from defining **size_t** twice in the same translation unit.

- A few operations cannot be performed well, if at all, purely within Standard C. In these cases, I have enhanced my implementation of the Standard C library to provide proper support for C++. Some of these enhancements involve low-level operations that are not easily described in a book of this nature. Nevertheless, I endeavor to clarify here the functional requirements of each enhancement. I also show compromise approaches, in more portable C++, that are adequate for many needs.

Testing the Standard C Library

Testing Standard C implementations is a serious business. Several companies offer commercial C validation suites, and several nations around the world use these suites to provide official validation of C translators. (One of the major players in the C/C++ validation game is Plum Hall Inc. of Kamuela HI, the same folks who license this implementation of the Standard C++ library.) I couldn't begin to replicate here the technology brought to bear in this important arena.

validation suites   I can say that a commercial Standard C validation suite should have no problems with a library that has been made C++ ready. None of the changes required by the draft C++ Standard should make a Standard C library any less conformant to the C Standard. You may have a problem proving this, however. Some C validation suites may not themselves operate in the environment needed to test a modified Standard C library. In particular, if all the C code is translated as C++ code, the suite may also have to be translated as C++ code to make the necessary tests.

The other problem area is the need for additions to the typical Standard C library, as I outlined above. An implementation without the features described in Amendment 1 to the C Standard does not, strictly speaking, conform to the draft C++ Standard. But this requirement is sufficiently new — and specialized for the international marketplace — that many programmers will not complain about a failure to satisfy it. Similarly, only a fraction of all programmers really care about complex arithmetic that is both efficient and precise. Many others will be content with complex classes all built on the conventional *double* functions.

I provide coarse tests for conformance in *The Standard C Library*. The tests at the end of each chapter verify that the basic functionality is present, and that a library at least performs its most obvious duties. I have augmented that set of tests with similar tests for Amendment 1 functionality, *float* math, and *long double* math. Running these tests is often sufficient to determine whether a given library can serve as an adequate starting point.

Exercises

Exercise 1.1 C headers traditionally generate inline code for a library function by masking its declaration with a macro, as in:

```
#define isdigit(c) (_Ctype[(int)(c)] & _DI)
```

Write a valid C++ code sequence that fails to translate properly in the presence of such a macro definition.

Exercise 1.2 How can you alter a C header so that it still generates inline code for a library function in the absence of a masking macro?

Exercise 1.3 Write a valid (portable) C++ code sequence that can detect whether the header **<string.h>** has the modified function declarations required by the draft C++ Standard.

Exercise 1.4 A C++ version of the header **<math.h>** could, in principle, overload existing function names, as in:

```
double sin(double);
float sin(float);
long double sin(long double);
```

rather than use the distinct names reserved by the C Standard (such as **sinf** and **sinl**). Is there any reason why this might not be a good idea? (Hint: Does any Standard C program change meaning when translated as C++ with such a revised header?)

Exercise 1.5 [**Harder**] Revise a C++ implementation of the C header **<stdarg.h>** to work properly with:

- a scalar argument in a varying length list that changes representation when subject to default argument promotion (integer types smaller than *int*, or the type *float*)

- an aggregate argument in a varying length list other than a "plain old data structure"

- references to objects of type **va_list**

- a reference **parmN** parameter (the parameter argument to **va_start**)

Exercise 1.6 [**Very hard**] Write the specification for a true *null pointer constant* in C++. Describe the properties it should have:

- when assigned to a pointer object

- when assigned to an arithmetic object

- when type cast to all other scalar types

- when used as the actual argument on a call to an overloaded function

- when used as the actual argument in a varying length argument list

Chapter 2: `<defines>`

Background

The header `<defines>` is an invention of the Committee. It was added to serve as a repository for several definitions needed throughout the Standard C++ library. Writing, and describing, several C++ headers proved to be a nuisance without these definitions. On the other hand, no existing header seemed appropriate as a parking place for any one of the items defined here. Thus, the header `<defines>` has a history and *raison d'être* similar to the C header `<stddef.h>`.

What the Draft C++ Standard Says

This section of the draft C++ Standard is called "language support" because it, more than any other part of the C++ library, is on rather intimate terms with the language proper. The header `<defines>` communicates implementation-dependent type information from the translator to the program. Later headers define classes used implicitly by translated code. In some cases, a translator will generate code that implicitly calls functions declared here. You will also find quite a few fellow travelers, not directly connected to language support. But the tie is there, nevertheless.

17.3 Language support

This subclause describes the function signatures that are called implicitly, and the types of objects generated implicitly, during the execution of some C++ programs. It also describes the headers that declare these function signatures and define any related types.

17.3.1 Header `<defines>`

`<defines>`   The header `<defines>` defines a constant and several types used widely throughout the Standard C++ library. Some are also defined in C headers.
The constant is:
```
const size_t NPOS = (size_t)(-1);
```
which is the largest representable value of type `size_t`.

17.3.1.1 Type `fvoid_t`

`fvoid_t`
```
typedef void fvoid_t();
```

The type **fvoid_t** is a function type used to simplify the writing of several declarations in this clause.

17.3.1.2 Type ptrdiff_t

ptrdiff_t

```
typedef T ptrdiff_t;
```

The type **ptrdiff_t** is a synonym for **T**, the implementation-defined signed integral type of the result of subtracting two pointers.

17.3.1.3 Type size_t

size_t

```
typedef T size_t;
```

The type **size_t** is a synonym for **T**, the implementation-defined unsigned integral type of the result of the **sizeof** operator.

17.3.1.4 Type wint_t

wint_t

```
typedef T wint_t;
```

The type **wint_t** is a synonym for **T**, the implementation-defined integral type, unchanged by integral promotions, that can hold any value of type **wchar_t** as well as at least one value that does not correspond to the code for any member of the extended character set.[75]

17.3.1.5 Type capacity

capacity

```
typedef T capacity;
static const capacity default_size;
static const capacity reserve;
```

The type **capacity** is an enumerated type (indicated here as **T**), with the elements:

default_size
- **default_size**, as an argument value indicates that no reserve capacity argument is present in the argument list;

reserve
- **reserve**, as an argument value indicates that the preceding argument specifies a reserve capacity.

Footnotes:

Footnotes

75) The extra value is denoted by the macro **WEOF**, defined in **<wchar.h>**. It is permissible for **WEOF** to be in the range of values representable by **wchar_t**.

Future Directions

<stddef>   This header has already been renamed **<stddef>**.

The header **<defines>** is a catchall for definitions needed throughout the Standard C++ library. Hence, it is likely to accrete more material as time goes on. The type definitions inherited from Standard C are least likely to change, but the others are all invented to serve the needs of C++. They are being refined over time.

fvoid_t   Some people have objected to the type **fvoid_t**, for example, as being too generalized and too primitive. Earlier editions of the draft C++ Standard used specialized versions of this type for each of its applications (such as **set_terminate** and **set_new_handler**). The Committee has already restored these specializations, and eliminated **fvoid_t** as a communal type in the bargain.

ptrdiff_t The type **ptrdiff_t** is not actually used in any of the C++ headers. In fact, it's not actually used for much of anything. It may well be removed from this header.

capacity The enumeration **capacity** is used to disambiguate certain constructors, as described below. The classes that use this trick are all serious candidates for major changes, as I describe later in this book. (See, for example, Chapter 18: **<bitstring>**.) Also, the language weakness that leads to these ambiguities may very well be patched in the near future. If either or both of these events occurs, the need for **capacity** will disappear.

Using <defines>

Chances are good that, if you include *any* C++ header in a translation unit, **<defines>** will be included as well. You include it explicitly only if you need one or more of the definitions it provides and you can't count on another C++ header to drag it in. But chances are also good that you *will* need one or more of the entities defined in this header. If you get a translator diagnostic that, say, **size_t** is undefined, remember that you can satisfy the need cheaply by including this header.

Here's a brief run-down of the definitions in **<defines>**:

fvoid_t Several functions in the Standard C++ library register *handlers* — functions that get called when certain events occur. Typically, a handler is called with no arguments and is expected to return no value. It might even be required *not* to return at all. In all such cases, the classic way to declare such a handler **hand** is:

```
void hand(void);
```

The type **fvoid_t** declares a pointer to such a function, which is typically the type of a parameter that conveys the address of a handler.

ptrdiff_t When you subtract two pointers in a C++ expression, the result has type **ptrdiff_t**. It is an integer type that can represent negative values. Almost certainly it is either *int* or *long*. It is often the signed type that has the same number of bits as the unsigned type chosen for **size_t**, described below.

For reasons that I won't go into here, the type **ptrdiff_t** often proves to be inadequate for its intended purpose. (See **Pla92**, Chapter 11: **<stddef.h>** for more details.) If you can't think of a reason to use it, don't worry.

size_t When you apply the **sizeof** operator in a C++ expression, the result has type **size_t**. It is an unsigned integer type that can represent the size of the largest object you can declare. Almost certainly it is either *unsigned int* or *unsigned long*. It is typically the unsigned type that has the same number of bits as the signed type chosen for **ptrdiff_t**, described above.

Unlike **ptrdiff_t**, however, **size_t** is *very* useful. It is the most portable type to represent any integer object you use as an array subscript. You don't have to worry if a small array evolves to a very large one as the program changes. Subscript arithmetic will never overflow when performed in type `size_t`. You don't have to worry if the program moves to a machine with peculiar properties, such as 32-bit bytes and 1-byte *longs*. Type `size_t` offers the greatest chance that your code won't be unduly surprised. The only sensible type to use for computing the sizes of objects is `size_t`.

The Standard C++ library makes extensive use of the type `size_t`. You will find that many function arguments and return values are declared to have this type. You too should make a point of using type `size_t` *anywhere* your program performs array subscripting or address arithmetic. Be warned, however, that unsigned-integer arithmetic has more pitfalls than signed. You cannot run an unsigned counter down until it goes negative — it never will. If the translator doesn't warn you of a silly test expression, the program may loop forever. You may find, in fact, that counting down to zero sometimes leads to clumsy tests. You will occasionally miss the convenience of using negative values (such as `EOF`, defined in `<streambuf>` to signal end-of-file) and testing for them easily. Nevertheless, the improvement in robustness is well worth the learning investment.

The code in this book uses type `size_t` wherever it is appropriate. You may see an occasional place where *int* objects hold subscripts. In all such cases, however, the size of related array objects should be naturally limited to a safe range of sizes. I indulge in such practices only when I have an overriding need to mix negative values with proper subscript values.

`wint_t`   To understand the need for `wint_t`, you must first understand the importance of the closely related type `wchar_t`. You write a *wide character constant* as, for example, `L'x'`. It has type `wchar_t`. You write a *wide character string literal* as, for example, `L"hello"`. It has type *constant array of* `wchar_t`. `wchar_t` is an integer type that can represent all the code values for all wide-character encodings supported by the implementation. You use `wchar_t` to represent *all* objects that must hold wide characters. (See, for example, Chapter 16: `<wstring>`.)

For an implementation with only minimal support for wide characters, `wchar_t` may be as small as *char*. For a very ambitious implementation, it may be as large as *unsigned long*. More likely, `wchar_t` is a synonym for an integer type that has at least a 16-bit representation, such as *short* or *unsigned short*. It is considered sufficiently important that the draft C++ Standard has made `wchar_t` a keyword, and the type it represents a distinct integer type. Thus, you can safely overload a function name by distinguishing the parameter types *char* and `wchar_t` — they are always distinct types even if they happen to have the same representation.

Amendment 1 to the C Standard (**ISO94**) introduces type `wint_t` as a companion to `wchar_t`. They bear the same relation as the types *char* and *int* when performing character-at-a-time input with the functions declared in `<stdio.h>`. Several of these functions signal end-of-file by returning the *int* value `EOF` instead of a character code. `EOF` is guaranteed to be distinguishable from any value that can be represented as type *unsigned char*.

Similarly, the wide-character input functions declared in **<wchar.h>** signal end-of-file by returning the **wint_t** value **WEOF** instead of a character code. **WEOF** is guaranteed to be distinguishable from any *valid* wide-character code that can be representable as type **wchar_t**. (The emphasis on "valid" is critical — the types **wchar_t** and **wint_t** are permitted to have the same representation. Hence, **WEOF** may be representable as type **wchar_t**, so long as it doesn't pun with a valid wide-character code.)

As it turns out, type **wint_t** isn't used in any of the C++ headers described in the Informal Review Draft. Wide-character input disappeared from an earlier draft and reappeared later in the form of iostream templates. (See page 119.) That mechanism will probably cause this definition to disappear from the header **<defines>**. For now, you would use it only in conjunction with the wide-character input/output defined in **<wchar.h>**, which also defines **wint_t**. Thus, this definition has marginal utility.

capacity   The enumeration **capacity** is something of a kludge. C++ has the unfortunate habit of treating all single-argument constructors as conversion functions. For example, the class definitions:

```
class W;
class X {
public:
    X(W);
    X(int);
    .....
};
```

introduce implicit conversions to class **x**, in many contexts, from objects of class **w** and from all sorts of arithmetic expressions. The latter include values as diverse as **0**, **'x'**, and even **3.2**. It is much too easy to turn a typographical error into a valid expression, under such circumstances. It is also very easy to introduce surprising conversion ambiguities, when two or more related classes permit conversions from (almost) the same scalar types.

One way to avoid the problem is to turn single-parameter constructors into two-parameter constructors. In many cases within the Standard C++ library, that second parameter has type **capacity**. (See Chapter 15: **<string>**, Chapter 16: **<wstring>**, Chapter 19: **<dynarray>**, and Chapter 20: **<ptrdynarray>**.) The value of the enumeration constant further serves to specify how to interpret the first argument:

default_size ▪ **default_size** — treat the first argument as the initial size of the newly constructed object, initializing its elements to zero (for a scalar object), or a default constructor (for a class object).

reserve ▪ **reserve** — treat the first argument as the optimum reserve capacity to set aside for the newly constructed object, but give it an actual initial size of zero.

I characterize this approach (perhaps unfairly) as something of a kludge because it solves the underlying problem of unwanted conversions rather indirectly. For now, however, it's one of the few palatable options available.

Figure 2.1:
defines

```
// defines standard header
#ifndef _DEFINES_
#define _DEFINES_
#ifndef _YXVALS_
 #include <yxvals.h>
#endif
            // type definitions
typedef void fvoid_t();
#ifndef _PTRDIFFT
 #define _PTRDIFFT
 typedef _Ptrdifft ptrdiff_t;
#endif
#ifndef _SIZET
 #define _SIZET
 typedef _Sizet size_t;
#endif
#ifndef _WCHART
 #define _WCHART
 typedef _Wchart wchar_t;
#endif
#ifndef _WINTT
 #define _WINTT
 typedef _Wintt wint_t;
#endif
enum capacity {default_size, reserve};
            // constants
const size_t NPOS = (size_t)(-1);
            // functions
void _Nomemory();
#endif                                          □
```

NPOS   **NPOS** is the constant value **(size_t)(-1)**, the largest value representable as type **size_t**. Hence, it serves as an effective code either for:

- This size is too huge to be valid.

- This argument value isn't a size — do something else to determine it.

Several library classes describe objects that can hold a varying number of elements. They all use **NPOS** with one or both of these special meanings. (See Chapter 15: **<string>**, Chapter 16: **<wstring>**, Chapter 18: **<bitstring>**, Chapter 19: **<dynarray>**, and Chapter 20: **<ptrdynarray>**.)

Yes, it is indeed possible to declare a repetition count of **NPOS** in some declarations. This convention rules out those largest-possible repetition counts, in the interest of providing a handy code that can be copied about as just another value of type **size_t**. The Committee felt it was a small sacrifice to lower the upper limit for a repetition count to **NPOS - 1**, for a handful of library classes at least. I'm inclined to agree.

Most of the time, you'll find that **NPOS** is the default value for an argument. You'll probably have few occasions to actually write this symbol in your code. But you should be comfortable with *both* potential meanings for **NPOS**, and learn to recognize which applies in each case.

Implementing **<defines>**

The specification for the header **<defines>** is deceptively simple. It suggests that the header could be as simple as:

```
#ifndef _DEFINES_
#define _DEFINES_
typedef void fvoid_t();
typedef int ptrdiff_t;
typedef unsigned int size_t;
typedef unsigned short wint_t;
enum capacity {default_size, reserve};
const size_t NPOS = (size_t)(-1);
#endif
```

But this simple approach fails to deal with several issues:

- Including various C headers also provides definitions for some of these types. Some shared mechanism is needed to avoid duplicate definitions.

- Several of the type definitions vary among implementations. Some mechanism is needed to convey the implementation-dependent implementation to code that is itself common to all implementations.

- **wchar_t** is not yet a distinct type, much less a keyword, in all current implementations of C++. Where the type is not predefined, **<defines>** is the natural place to define it.

- An implementation typically needs to define an occasional entity (with secret names) that are also widely available. Once again, **<defines>** is the obvious vehicle for such definitions.

<yxvals.h> To handle the first three issues, I introduce the header **<yxvals.h>**, which is peculiar to this implementation. Here is the place to put those magic, and ugly, bits of code to deal with the harsher realities. Appendix A: Interfaces discusses this header at length. Throughout this book, I discuss bits and pieces of it as they are relevant to the problem at hand. Where appropriate, I also show examples of how to write those bits to work with my implementation of the Standard C library and with others.

macro For example, here's the way I chose to avoid introducing the same type
guard definition for **size_t** twice into a translation unit. You protect each **typedef** declaration with a macro guard, much the way you protect the entire contents of a header:

```
#ifndef _SIZET
 #define _SIZET
 typedef _Sizet size_t;
#endif
```

In my implementation of the Standard C library, a header defines the macro **_SIZET** whenever it provides a definition for **size_t**. (The draft C++ Standard now permits benign redefinition of type synonyms with **typedef**, but I've kept the older machinery to aid compatibility with Standard C.)

This code sequence also conveys the implementation-dependent type of the result of the **sizeof** operator. The header **<yxvals.h>** defines **_Sizet** appropriately for each implementation.

defines   Figure 2.1 shows the file **defines**. You can see this technique at work in defining all the types shared with C headers. Note that the type **wchar_t** looks like all the others. For a C++ implementation that predefines this type, the header **<yxvals.h>** simply defines the macro **_WCHART**, and the translator skips the type definition in **<defines>**.

_Nomemory   You can also see one of the secret names I mentioned earlier. Any number of classes within the Standard C++ library attempt to allocate storage from time to time. When such an attempt fails, a member function may have to report the failure itself. In all such cases, a call to the function **_Nomemory()** does the actual reporting by throwing an exception. (See Chapter 3: **<exception>**.)

Testing <defines>

tdefines.c   Figure 2.2 shows the file **tdefines.c**. It is fairly simple, since the header is rather small and has little to test in the bargain. Mostly, it checks for the overt presence of all the definitions. It then prints the sizes of the flexible types with which it is preoccupied. If all goes well, the program prints something like:

```
sizeof (ptrdiff_t) = 4;
sizeof (size_t) = 4;
sizeof (wchar_t) = 2;
sizeof (wint_t) = 4;
SUCCESS testing <defines>
```

and takes a normal exit.

Exercises

Exercise 2.1 Rewrite the declarations:

```
fvoid_t* set_new_handler(fvoid_t* new_nh);
fvoid_t* set_terminate(fvoid_t* new_th);
fvoid_t* set_unexpected(fvoid_t* new_uh);
```

so that the address of, say, a *new* handler cannot be registered as a *terminate* handler.

Exercise 2.2 What would be the advantage in making **size_t** a keyword and a distinct type?

Exercise 2.3 What would be the advantage in making **wint_t** a keyword and a distinct type?

Exercise 2.4 Define at least one additional use for type **capacity**, besides specifying **default_size** or **reserve**.

Exercise 2.5 [Harder] Devise a method that eliminates the need to reserve the value **(size_t)(-1)** for **NPOS**. Revise the declarations in class **string** to use this method. (See Chapter 15: **<string>**.)

Exercise 2.6 [Very hard] Devise a method for distinguishing conversions from pure constructors in a class declaration.

Figure 2.2:
tdefines.c

```
// test <defines>
#include <assert.h>
#include <limits.h>
#include <defines>
#include <iostream>

        // static data
static capacity cap[] = {default_size, reserve};
static char *pc = 0;
static fvoid_t *fv = 0;

int main()
    {                   // test basic workings of defines definitions
    ptrdiff_t pdiff = &pc[INT_MAX] - &pc[0];
    wchar_t wc = _L('Z');
    wint_t wi = _L('Z');

    assert(sizeof (size_t) == sizeof (sizeof (char)));
    assert(pdiff == &pc[INT_MAX] - &pc[0]);
    assert(wc == _L('Z'));
    assert(wi == _L('Z'));
    assert(cap[0] != cap[1]);
    assert(NPOS == (size_t)(-1));
    cout << "sizeof (ptrdiff_t) = " << sizeof (ptrdiff_t)
        << endl;
    cout << "sizeof (size_t) = " << sizeof (size_t) << endl;
    cout << "sizeof (wchar_t) = " << sizeof (wchar_t) << endl;
    cout << "sizeof (wint_t) = " << sizeof (wint_t) << endl;
    cout << "SUCCESS testing <defines>" << endl;
    return (0);
    }                                                       □
```

Chapter 3: `<exception>`

Background

Exceptions represent a significant departure in C++ from past programming practice in C. Much of what you write in C++ translates one for one to very similar C code. The rest may get longer winded in C, and a bit harder to read, but it's still conventional C. Exception handling, however, changes the underlying model of how functions get called, automatic storage gets allocated and freed, and control gets passed back to the calling functions.

A compiler *can* generate reasonably portable C code to handle exceptions, but that code can have serious performance problems — even for programs that don't use exceptions. The very *possibility* that an exception can occur in a called function changes how you generate code for the caller. Alternatively, a compiler can generate code directly that can't quite be expressed in C — and face a different set of problems. It may be hard to mix such C++ code with that generated from C or another programming language. Perhaps you can see now why C++ vendors have generally been slow to add this important new feature to the language.

`longjmp` `setjmp` What makes exception handling important is that it stylizes a common operation expressible in C only in a rather dirty fashion. You can think of exception handling, in fact, as a disciplined use of the notorious functions `setjmp` and `longjmp`, declared in `<setjmp.h>`. (Strictly speaking, `setjmp` is a macro, but I won't not pursue that distraction for now.)

In a C program, you call `setjmp` at a point to which you expect to "roll back." The function memorizes enough context to re-establish the roll-back point, then returns the value zero. A later call to `longjmp` can occur anywhere within the same function or a function called from that function, however deep in the call stack. By unspecified magic, the call stack gets rolled back and control returns once again from `setjmp`. The only difference is, this time you can tell from the nonzero return value that a `longjmp` call initiated the return.

That all adds up to a clever bit of machinery, used to pull off all sorts of error-recovery logic over the past couple of decades. The only trouble is, it's too clever by half. Many implementations have trouble determining how to roll back all the automatic storage properly. The C Standard is obligingly vague on the subject, making life easier on the implementors at the expense of being harder on those wishing to write portable and robust code. Nobody pretends that **<setjmp.h>** is an elegant piece of design.

constructors   In C++, matters are much more critical. That language prides itself on
destructors cradle-to-grave control of objects, particularly nontrivial ones. You are assured that every object gets constructed exactly once, before anybody can peek at its stored values. And you are promised with equal fervor that every object gets destroyed exactly once. Thus, you can allocate and free auxiliary storage for an object with a discipline that ensures no files are left open, or no memory gets lost, in the hurly burly of execution.

longjmp sabotages the best efforts of C++ compilers to maintain this discipline. In rolling back the call stack, the older C function cheerfully bypasses all those implicit calls to destructors strewn about by the C++ compiler. Promises get broken, files remain open, storage on the heap gets lost. The draft C++ Standard leaves **<setjmp.h>** in the library for upward compatibility. But it discourages the use of these heavy-handed functions in the neighborhood of "real" C++ code with nontrivial destructors.

throw   Enter exceptions. In modern C++, you don't report a nasty error by
catch calling **longjmp** to roll back to a point established by **setjmp**. Instead, you evaluate a *throw* expression to roll back to a *catch* clause. The *throw* expression names an object whose type matches that expected by the *catch* clause. You can even examine the object to get a hint about what caused the exception. It's kind of like calling a function with a single argument, only you're not always sure where the function actually resides. And the function may be further *up* the call stack instead of one level further down.

Most important of all, none of those destructors get skipped in the process of rolling back the call stack. If that sounds like a nightmare in bookkeeping to you, you're absolutely right. Somehow, the executing code must at all times have a clear notion of what destructors are pending before control can pass out of a given block or a given function. It must also deal with exceptions thrown in constructors and destructors, and exceptions thrown while processing earlier exceptions. Kids, don't try this at home.

So this fancier machinery is now in the draft C++ Standard. All that remains is to decide what to do with it. You can get a few hints from other programming languages. Ada, to name just one, has had exceptions for over a decade. Their very presence changes how you design certain interfaces and how you structure programs that must respond to nasty errors. The one certainty is that you must develop a *style* for using exceptions that fits the language as a whole, then use it consistently.

library   That has serious implications for the Standard C++ library. Traditionally,
exceptions of course, the library has thrown or caught no exceptions. (There weren't any such critters to throw!) But it's a poor advertisement for this new feature if the library itself makes no use of exceptions. Put more strongly, the Standard C++ library has a moral obligation to set a good example. Many programmers will use only the exceptions defined in the library.

Others will model their own on what they see used by the library. Thus, the library is duty bound to set a good example for the children.

Early on, the Committee committed to using exceptions as part of the error-reporting machinery of the Standard C++ library. Not everyone is happy with this decision. Some people object to it because they don't want to incur the inevitable overheads of exception handling in every program that touches the Standard C++ library — and that's essentially every program you write in C++. Others object because of the putative difficulties of validating a program that throws exceptions. Some projects require that the software vendors assert that exceptions can never be thrown. So the decision to use exceptions in the library was not lightly made.

Only recently has the Committee begun to converge on an overall structure. It still suffers regular name changes and other tweaks. More changes are doubtless in the works. Still the general approach is likely to survive reasonably unchanged.

`<exception>`   All the relevant declarations and class definitions for exception handling

xmsg can be had by including the new header `<exception>`. Within this header you can find the definition for the base class **xmsg**, the mother of all exceptions thrown by the library. (Yes, that name has already changed too.) Each exception object based on class **xmsg** is accompanied by a message describing the reason for throwing the exception.

The next important notion is that an exception should have a private copy (on the heap, presumably) of its message string. A typical exception constructor allocates storage on the heap, copies the string, and sets an internal flag to note that it has done so. That way, the destructor knows to free the storage once the exception has been processed.

But then, why the flag? Well, one important exception derived from this base class is **xalloc** (also renamed). It is thrown by **operator new** when it fails to allocate storage. (See Chapter 4: `<new>`.) The last thing you want to do is try to copy a string onto the heap when you have to report that there's no more room on the heap! Thus, a special protected constructor lets you avoid such copying of strings. Of course, anyone using this constructor had better provide a string with a sufficiently long lifetime, or trouble ensues. That's why this form is discouraged, except where absolutely necessary.

raise   You'd think then that to throw an exception you write something like:

```
throw xmsg("bad input record");
```

You can certainly do so, but that is not the preferred method. Instead, for any exception object **ex** based on class **xmsg**, you're encouraged to call **ex.raise()**. That member function does three things:

- First it calls **(*ex.handler)(*this)** to call the *raise* handler. The default behavior is to do nothing, but you can hijack any thrown exception by providing your own *raise* handler with a call to **xmsg::set_raise_handler**.

- Then it calls the virtual member function **do_raise**. That lets you hijack thrown exceptions only for some particular class derived from **xmsg**.
- Finally it evaluates the expression **throw *this**.

The first escape hatch is for embedded systems and those projects I indicated above that abhor all exceptions. The program can reboot, or **longjmp** to some recovery point (and to heck with the skipped destructors). The second is for classes derived from **xmsg** that may require special handling. You can intercept just these exceptions, without interfering with any others. (But see page 64.)

The third thing is to do what exception classes were invented to do in the first place. By having *all* library exceptions be thrown through this machinery, however, the class meets the needs of several constituencies.

There's still more to library exceptions. A whole hierarchy of classes is derived from **xmsg**:

exception
hierarchy
```
xmsg
  xlogic
    xdomain
      badcast
      badtypeid (typeinfo)
    invalidargument (bits/bitstring/dynarray)
    lengtherror (bits/bitstring/dynarray/string/wstring)
    outofrange (bits/bitstring/dynarray/string/wstring)
  xruntime
    xrange
    overflow (bits)
    xalloc (new)
    ios::failure (ios)
```

I list in parentheses after each exception class the other library classes that use it. Some of these exception classes are defined in other headers, but most are to be found in **<exception>**. There are two basic groups:

xlogic ■ *logic errors*, derived from class **xlogic**, which report errors that you can, in principle, detect and avoid when writing the program

xruntime ■ *runtime errors*, derived from class **xruntime**, which report errors that you can, most likely, detect only when you run the program

xdomain   The former category is for those "can't happen" events that are often too
xrange hard to prevent, at least until after some thorough debugging. For example, **xdomain** is derived from **xlogic** for reporting a *domain error* (invalid argument value). The latter is for surprises that happen during program execution, such as running out of heap or encountering bad input from a file. **xrange** is derived from **xruntime** for reporting a *range error* (unrepresentable result). No library functions throw objects of these classes directly, however.

Exception processing code can also call two additional functions:

terminate ■ **terminate**, when exception handling must be abandoned for any of several reasons, shown below

unexpected ■ **unexpected**, when a function throws an exception that is not listed in its *exception specification*

exception specifications An exception specification is an optional qualifier such as `throw(badcast, xalloc)` that you append to a function declaration. It promises that the function, when executed, will never propagate any exception not in the specified list. The use and usefulness of exception specifications is still being debated within the Committee.

A terminate condition occurs when the exception handling mechanism:

- cannot find a handler for a thrown exception
- finds the execution stack corrupted
- executes a destructor that tries to transfer control to a calling function by throwing another exception

handlers The default behavior of `terminate` is to call the function `abort`, declared in `<stdlib.h>`. The default behavior of `unexpected` is to call `terminate`. As usual in C++, however, you can provide your own flavors of these functions. A call to `set_terminate` lets you specify a pointer to a *terminate* handler. The new function you specify must still somehow terminate the program. A call to `set_unexpected` lets you specify a pointer to an *unexpected* handler. The new function you specify can itself throw (or rethrow) an exception or terminate program execution.

As you can see, the facilities provided by `<exception>` give you considerable latitude in reporting and handling exceptions. The C++ library uses this machinery exclusively, so you can control what the library does with exceptions. You can even prevent the library from actually evaluating any *throw* expressions. Given our limited experience to date with using expressions in C++, I'm fairly confident that this is basically a good design. It is still being refined by the Committee, however.

What the Draft C++ Standard Says

This section of the draft C++ Standard is another aspect of "Language Support." A translator will generate code that uses some of the classes declared in this section, or that implicitly calls functions defined here.

For example:

- a *dynamic-cast expression* throws an exception of class `badcast` if it cannot properly initialize a reference
- a thrown exception calls `unexpected` if control leaves a function in violation of an exception specification
- a thrown exception calls `terminate` if no *catch* clause can handle the exception

There are also quite a few exception classes that are not directly connected to language support, but all such classes are interrelated.

17.3.2 Header `<exception>`

The header `<exception>` defines several types and functions related to the handling of exceptions in a C++ program.

17.3.2.1 Class `xmsg`

```
class xmsg {
public:
    typedef void (*raise_handler)(xmsg&);
    static raise_handler set_raise_handler(raise_handler
handler_arg);
    xmsg(const char* what_arg = 0, const char* where_arg = 0,
        const char* why_arg = 0);
    virtual ~xmsg();
    void raise();
    const char* what() const;
    const char* where() const;
    const char* why() const;
protected:
    virtual void do_raise();
    xmsg(const char* what_arg, const char* where_arg,
        const char* why_arg, int copyfl);
private:
//    static raise_handler handler;          exposition only
//    const char* what;                      exposition only
//    const char* where;                     exposition only
//    const char* why;                       exposition only
//    int alloced;                           exposition only
};
```

The class `xmsg` defines the base class for the types of objects thrown as exceptions by Standard C++ library functions, and certain expressions, to report errors detected during program execution. Every exception `ex` thrown by a function defined within the Standard C++ library is thrown by evaluating an expression of the form `ex.raise()`. The class defines a member type `raise_handler` and maintains several kinds of data. For the sake of exposition, the stored data is presented here as:

- **`static raise_handler handler`**, points to the function called by the member function **`raise`**. Its initial value is a null pointer;
- **`const char* what`**, stores a null pointer or points to an NTMBS intended to briefly describe the general nature of the exception thrown;
- **`const char* where`**, stores a null pointer or points to an NTMBS intended to briefly describe the point at which the exception is thrown;
- **`const char* why`**, stores a null pointer or points to an NTMBS intended to briefly describe any special circumstances behind the exception;
- **`int alloced`**, stores a nonzero value if storage for the three NTMBSs has been allocated by the object of class `xmsg`.

17.3.2.1.1 Type `xmsg::raise_handler`

```
typedef void (*raise_handler)(xmsg&);
```

The type **`raise_handler`** describes a pointer to a function called by the member function **`raise`** to perform operations common to all objects of class `xmsg`.

17.3.2.1.2 xmsg::set_raise_handler(raise_handler)

```
static raise_handler set_raise_handler(
    raise_handler handler_arg);
```

Assigns *handler_arg* to *handler* and then returns the previous value stored in *handler*.

17.3.2.1.3 xmsg::xmsg(const char*, const char*, const char*)

constructor

```
xmsg(const char* what_arg = 0, const char* where_arg = 0,
    const char* why_arg = 0);
```

Behaves the same as xmsg(*what_arg*, *where_arg*, *why_arg*, 1).

17.3.2.1.4 xmsg::~xmsg()

destructor

```
virtual ~xmsg();
```

Destroys an object of class **xmsg**. If **alloced** is nonzero, the function frees storage pointed to by **what**, **where**, and **why**.

17.3.2.1.5 xmsg::raise()

raise

```
void raise();
```

If *handler* is nonzero, calls (***handler**)(***this**). The function then calls **do_raise()**, then evaluates the expression **throw *this**.

17.3.2.1.6 xmsg::what()

what

```
const char* what() const;
```

If *what* is not a null pointer, returns *what*. Otherwise, the function returns a pointer to an empty NTBS.[76]

17.3.2.1.7 xmsg::where()

where

```
const char* where() const;
```

If *where* is not a null pointer, return *where*. Otherwise, the function returns a pointer to an empty NTBS.

17.3.2.1.8 xmsg::why()

why

```
const char* why() const;
```

If *why* is not a null pointer, returns *why*. Otherwise, the function returns a pointer to an empty NTBS.

17.3.2.1.9 xmsg::do_raise()

do_raise

```
virtual void do_raise();
```

Called by the member function **raise** to perform operations common to all objects of a class derived from **xmsg**. The default behavior is to return.

17.3.2.1.10 xmsg::xmsg(const char*, const char*, const char*, int)

constructor

```
xmsg(const char* what_arg, const char* where_arg,
    const char* why_arg, int copyfl);
```

Constructs an object of class **xmsg** and initializes *what* to *what_arg*, *where* to *where_arg*, *why* to *why_arg*, and *alloced* to *copyfl*.

If **alloced** is nonzero, for each of the three stored pointers to NTMBSs that is not a null pointer the function allocates storage for the NTMBS, copies the NTMBS to the allocated storage, and replaces the stored pointer with a pointer to the allocated storage. Otherwise, the three pointers shall either be null pointers or point to NTMBSs that have static lifetimes or lifetimes that exceed that of the constructed object.

17.3.2.2 Class xlogic

Class
xlogic

```
class xlogic : public xmsg {
public:
    xlogic(const char* what_arg = 0, const char* where_arg = 0,
        const char* why_arg = 0);
    virtual ~xlogic();
protected:
//  virtual void do_raise();                                    inherited
};
```

The class **xlogic** defines the type of objects thrown as exceptions by the implementation to report errors presumably detectable before the program executes, such as violations of logical preconditions.

17.3.2.2.1 xlogic::xlogic(const char*, const char*, const char*)

constructor

```
xlogic(const char* what_arg = 0, const char* where_arg = 0,
    const char* why_arg = 0);
```

Constructs an object of class **xlogic**, initializing the base class with **xmsg(**what_arg, where_arg, why_arg**)**.

17.3.2.2.2 xlogic::~xlogic()

destructor

```
virtual ~xlogic();
```

Destroys an object of class **xlogic**.

17.3.2.2.3 xlogic::do_raise()

do_raise

```
//  virtual void do_raise();                                    inherited
```

Behaves the same as **xmsg::do_raise()**.

17.3.2.3 Class xruntime

Class
xruntime

```
class xruntime : public xmsg {
public:
    xruntime(const char* what_arg = 0, const char* where_arg = 0,
        const char* why_arg = 0);
    virtual ~xruntime();
protected:
//  virtual void do_raise();                                    inherited
    xruntime(const char* what_arg,
        const char* where_arg,
        const char* why_arg, int copyfl);
};
```

The class **xruntime** defines the type of objects thrown as exceptions by the implementation to report errors presumably detectable only when the program executes.

17.3.2.3.1 xruntime::xruntime(const char*, const char*, const char*)

constructor

```
xruntime(const char* what_arg = 0, const char* where_arg = 0,
    const char* why_arg = 0);
```

Constructs an object of class **xruntime**, initializing the base class with **xmsg(**what_arg, where_arg, why_arg**)**.

17.3.2.3.2 xruntime::~xruntime()

destructor

```
virtual ~xruntime();
```

Destroys an object of class **xruntime**.

17.3.2.3.3 xruntime::do_raise()

do_raise

```
// virtual void do_raise();                          inherited
```
Behaves the same as **xmsg::do_raise()**.

17.3.2.3.4 xruntime::xruntime(const char*, const char*, const char*, int)

constructor
```
xruntime(const char* what_arg = 0, const char* where_arg = 0,
    const char* why_arg = 0, int copyfl);
```
Constructs an object of class **xruntime**, initializing the base class with **xmsg(what_arg, where_arg, why_arg, copyfl)**.

17.3.2.4 Class badcast

Class
badcast
```
class badcast : public xlogic {
public:
    badcast();
    virtual ~badcast();
protected:
// virtual void do_raise();                          inherited
};
```
The class **badcast** defines the type of objects thrown as exceptions by the implementation to report the execution of an invalid *dynamic-cast* expression.

17.3.2.4.1 badcast::badcast()

constructor
```
badcast();
```
Constructs an object of class **badcast**, initializing the base class **xlogic** with an unspecified constructor.

17.3.2.4.2 badcast::~badcast()

destructor
```
virtual ~badcast();
```
Destroys an object of class **badcast**.

17.3.2.4.3 badcast::do_raise()

do_raise
```
// virtual void do_raise();                          inherited
```
Behaves the same as **xmsg::do_raise()**.

17.3.2.5 Class invalidargument

Class
invalid-
argument
```
class invalidargument : public xlogic {
public:
    invalidargument(const char* where_arg, const char* why_arg);
    virtual ~invalidargument();
protected:
// virtual void do_raise();                          inherited
};
```
The class **invalidargument** defines the base class for the types of all objects thrown as exceptions, by functions in the Standard C++ library, to report an invalid argument.

17.3.2.5.1 invalidargument::invalidargument(const char*, const char*)

constructor
```
invalidargument(const char* where_arg = 0,
    const char* why_arg = 0);
```
Constructs an object of class **invalidargument**, initializing the base class with **xlogic(what_arg, where_arg, why_arg)**, where the NTMBS pointed to by **what_arg** is unspecified.

destructor

17.3.2.5.2 invalidargument::~invalidargument()

```
virtual ~invalidargument();
```

Destroys an object of class **invalidargument**.

17.3.2.5.3 invalidargument::do_raise()

do_raise

```
// virtual void do_raise();                              inherited
```

Behaves the same as **xmsg::do_raise()**.

17.3.2.6 Class lengtherror

Class lengtherror

```
class lengtherror : public xlogic {
public:
    lengtherror(const char* where_arg, const char* why_arg);
    virtual ~lengtherror();
protected:
// virtual void do_raise();                              inherited
};
```

The class **lengtherror** defines the base class for the types of all objects thrown as exceptions, by functions in the Standard C++ library, to report an attempt to produce an object whose length equals or exceeds **NPOS**.

17.3.2.6.1 lengtherror::lengtherror(const char*, const char*)

constructor

```
lengtherror(const char* where_arg = 0,
    const char* why_arg = 0);
```

Constructs an object of class **lengtherror**, initializing the base class with **xlogic(**_what_arg_, _where_arg_, _why_arg_**)**, where the NTMBS pointed to by _what_arg_ is unspecified.

17.3.2.6.2 lengtherror::~lengtherror()

destructor

```
virtual ~lengtherror();
```

Destroys an object of class **lengtherror**.

17.3.2.6.3 lengtherror::do_raise()

do_raise

```
// virtual void do_raise(); inherited
```

Behaves the same as **xmsg::do_raise()**.

17.3.2.7 Class outofrange

Class outofrange

```
class outofrange : public xlogic {
public:
    outofrange(const char* where_arg, const char* why_arg);
    virtual ~outofrange();
protected:
// virtual void do_raise();                              inherited
};
```

The class **outofrange** defines the base class for the types of all objects thrown as exceptions, by functions in the Standard C++ library, to report an out-of-range argument.

17.3.2.7.1 outofrange::outofrange(const char*, const char*)

constructor

```
outofrange(const char* where_arg = 0, const char* why_arg = 0);
```

Constructs an object of class **outofrange**, initializing the base class with **xlogic(**_what_arg_, _where_arg_, _why_arg_**)**, where the NTMBS pointed to by _what_arg_ is unspecified.

17.3.2.7.2 outofrange::~outofrange()

destructor

```
virtual ~outofrange();
```

Destroys an object of class **outofrange**.

17.3.2.7.3 outofrange::do_raise()

do_raise

```
//  virtual void do_raise();                              inherited
```

Behaves the same as **xmsg::do_raise()**.

17.3.2.8 Class overflow

**Class
overflow**

```
class overflow : public xruntime {
public:
    overflow(const char* where_arg, const char* why_arg);
    virtual ~overflow();
protected:
//  virtual void do_raise();                              inherited
};
```

The class **overflow** defines the base class for the types of all objects thrown as exceptions, by functions in the Standard C++ library, to report an arithmetic overflow.

17.3.2.8.1 overflow::overflow(const char*, const char*)

constructor

```
overflow(const char* where_arg = 0, const char* why_arg = 0);
```

Constructs an object of class **overflow**, initializing the base class with **xruntime(***what_arg, where_arg, why_arg***)**, where the NTMBS pointed to by *what_arg* is unspecified.

17.3.2.8.2 overflow::~overflow()

destructor

```
virtual ~overflow();
```

Destroys an object of class **overflow**.

17.3.2.8.3 overflow::do_raise()

do_raise

```
//  virtual void do_raise(); inherited
```

Behaves the same as **xmsg::do_raise()**.

17.3.2.9 Class xdomain

**Class
xdomain**

```
class xdomain : public xlogic {
public:
    xdomain(const char* what_arg = 0,
        const char* where_arg = 0,
        const char* why_arg = 0);
    virtual ~xdomain();
protected:
//  virtual void do_raise();                              inherited
};
```

The class **xdomain** defines the type of objects thrown as exceptions by the implementation to report violations of a precondition.

17.3.2.9.1 xdomain::xdomain(const char*, const char*, const char*)

constructor

```
xdomain(const char* what_arg = 0, const char* where_arg = 0,
    const char* why_arg = 0);
```

Constructs an object of class **xdomain**, initializing the base class with **xlogic(***what_arg, where_arg, why_arg***)**.

destructor

17.3.2.9.2 `xdomain::~xdomain()`

```
virtual ~xdomain();
```

Destroys an object of class **xdomain**.

17.3.2.9.3 `xdomain::do_raise()`

do_raise

```
//  virtual void do_raise();                              inherited
```

Behaves the same as **xmsg::do_raise()**.

**Class
xrange**

17.3.2.10 Class **xrange**

```
class xrange : public xruntime {
public:
    xrange(const char* what_arg = 0, const char* where_arg = 0,
        const char* why_arg = 0);
    virtual ~xrange();
protected:
//  virtual void do_raise();                              inherited
};
```

The class **xrange** defines the type of objects thrown as exceptions by the implementation to report violations of a postcondition.

17.3.2.10.1 `xrange::xrange(const char*, const char*, const char*)`

constructor

```
xrange(const char* what_arg = 0, const char* where_arg = 0,
    const char* why_arg = 0);
```

Constructs an object of class **xrange**, initializing the base class with **xruntime(**what_arg**,** where_arg**,** why_arg**)**.

17.3.2.10.2 `xrange::~xrange()`

destructor

```
virtual ~xrange();
```

Destroys an object of class **xrange**.

17.3.2.10.3 `xrange::do_raise()`

do_raise

```
//  virtual void do_raise();                              inherited
```

Behaves the same as **xmsg::do_raise()**.

17.3.2.11 `set_terminate(fvoid_t*)`

```
fvoid_t* set_terminate(fvoid_t* new_p);
```

**set_
terminate**

Establishes a new handler for terminating exception processing. The function stores **new_p** in a static object that, for the sake of exposition, can be declared as:

```
fvoid_t* terminate_handler = &abort;
```

where the function signature **abort()** is defined in **<stdlib.h>**. **new_p** shall not be a null pointer.

The function returns the previous contents of **terminate_handler**.

17.3.2.12 `set_unexpected(fvoid_t*)`

```
fvoid_t* set_unexpected(fvoid_t* new_p);
```

**set_
unexpected**

Establishes a new handler for an unexpected exception thrown by a function with an *exception-specification*. The function stores **new_p** in a static object that, for the sake of exposition, can be declared as:

```
fvoid_t* unexpected_handler = &terminate;
```

new_p shall not be a null pointer.

The function returns the previous contents of **unexpected_handler**.

17.3.2.13 terminate()

terminate

```
void terminate();
```

Called by the implementation when exception handling must be abandoned for any of several reasons, such as:

- when a thrown exception has no corresponding handler;
- when a thrown exception determines that the the execution stack is corrupted;
- when a thrown exception calls a destructor that tries to transfer control to a calling function by throwing another exception.

Using the notation of subclause 17.3.2.11, the function evaluates the expression:

```
(*terminate_handler)()
```

The required behavior of any function called by this expression is to terminate execution of the program without returning to the caller. The default behavior is to call **abort()**, declared in **<stdlib.h>**.

17.3.2.14 unexpected()

unexpected

```
void unexpected();
```

Called by the implementation when a function with an *exception-specification* throws an exception that is not listed in the *exception-specification*. Using the notation of subclause 17.3.2.12, the function evaluates the expression:

```
(*unexpected_handler)()
```

The required behavior of any function called by this expression is to throw an exception or terminate execution of the program without returning to the caller. The called function may perform any of the following operations:

- rethrow the exception;
- throw another exception;
- call **terminate()**;
- call either **abort()** or **exit(int)**, declared in **<stdlib.h>**.

The default behavior is to call **terminate()**.

Footnotes:

Footnotes

76) An empty NTBS is also an empty NTMBS.

Future Directions

Practically every name has changed at least once in the exception hierarchy since the Informal Review Draft quoted here. And the hierarchy itself has been repeatedly rearranged. Here are the current names, and arrangement. If the name has changed, I show the old name in parentheses:

revised
hierarchy

```
exception (xmsg)
   logic_error (xlogic)
      domain_error (xdomain)
      invalid_argument (invalidargument)
      length_error (lengtherror)
      out_of_range (outofrange)
      bad_cast (badcast)
      bad_typeid (badtypeid)
   runtime_error (xruntime)
      range_error (xrange)
      overflow_error (overflow)
      bad_alloc (xalloc)
   ios::failure
```

<stdexcept> Moreover, some of the exceptions have been moved to a new header called **<stdexcept>**. The Committee is still tinkering with naming conventions to make the Standard C++ library more uniform.

what A more fundamental change is in the representation of message text. Gone are the **where** and **why** components. The **what** component is now an object of class **string**. (See Chapter 15: **<string>**.) In fact, the member function **exception::what()** is now virtual. A protected constructor lets certain derived classes (**runtime** and **alloc**) avoid allocating storage for the message. In this case, **what()** yields an implementation-defined result.

raise The Committee has eliminated the **raise()** machinery. Not everyone appreciates the need for a standard way to control the handling of library-generated exceptions. Others begrudge the amount of complexity involved in solving the problem. The mechanism described here must thus be reworked using secret names, or eliminated altogether.

It didn't help that the current machinery is underspecified. The whole idea of an exception hierarchy is to provide nested levels of control. Catching an exception of class **xalloc** should ignore all others, even if they're derived from a common base. Catching an exception of class **xlogic** should also catch any type derived from that class, but no exceptions derived from **xruntime**. And catching an exception of class **xmsg** should catch the whole family. But it takes a bit of work to pull all that off.

A class derived from **xmsg** must override the default definition for the virtual member function **do_raise()**. For example:

```
void overflow::do_raise()
    {     // throw an overflow
    throw *this;
    }
```

Otherwise, the actual throw occurs in **xmsg::raise()**. All exceptions thrown this way are of class **xmsg** — any information about derived classes gets lost.

An implementation that chooses to retain the **raise()** machinery has to live with this annoyance, or find some way to fix it.

exception A related issue still under debate is the use of exception specifications. **specifications** The Committee voted separately on a number of proposals which now constitute the library portion of the draft C++ Standard. Some of these proposals described library classes with exception specifications. Many did not. All exception specifications were omitted from the Informal Review Draft, however, until the Committee could agree on a uniform style for using them. That style has yet to be spelled out.

Opinions vary on whether the Standard C++ library should use exception specifications at all. Some Committee members even favor removing this feature from the language altogether. Whatever the outcome, however, there is likely to be little resulting change in the functionality, or implementation, of the affected library classes.

bool   Finally, the Committee has introduced a first-class Boolean type called **bool**. It replaces any parameter or return value within the Standard C library that is tested only for having a nonzero value. The practical effect of this change should be minimal.

Using **<exception>**

The header **<exception>** has two distinct uses:

- It defines much of the hierarchy of exception classes thrown by the Standard C++ library. You include this header to use the defined classes directly, and not just in conjunction with other library classes.

- It declares the functions **set_terminate** and **set_unexpected**. You include this header to register handlers that can be called when *any* exceptions are later thrown.

exception   I strongly encourage you to follow the lead of (this version of) the
classes   Standard C++ library in the use of exceptions:

- Throw only objects of one or more classes derived from **xmsg** (or more recently **exception**).

- Use the most appropriate exception class defined in the Standard C++ library, wherever possible.

- If you must introduce a new exception class, derive it from the most appropriate library exception class.

- If you introduce a new exception class, override **do_raise** to evaluate the expression **throw *this**, as I showed above.

- *Always* throw an exception object **ex** by evaluating the expression **ex.raise()**. Even better, supply a function to throw each exception.

- Throw exceptions only to report conditions that require truly distinct processing — where possible, favor "in-channel" status reporting, such as returning special error values. (**EOF** and **NPOS** are two examples.)

Exceptions are not universally implemented. And the draft C++ Standard is particularly volatile in this area. So for the near to medium term, I have to add another piece of advice. *Encapsulate* exception handling, to localize and minimize change as implementations evolve.

_Nomemory   I follow my own advice throughout this implementation. In the previous chapter (page 48), I introduced the function **_Nomemory()**, declared in **<defines>**. It reports an out-of-memory condition by throwing an object of class **xalloc** (or more recently **bad_alloc**). Later in this book, you will see secret member functions added to throw other exceptions peculiar to a class. (See Chapter 15: **<string>**, Chapter 16: **<wstring>**, Chapter 17: **<bits>**, Chapter 18: **<bitstring>**, and Chapter 19: **<dynarray>**.) I am also careful to use only the **what** message component, since its two companions have already been eliminated from the draft C++ Standard. I persist, however, in calling the member function **raise**, for a variety of reasons.

Encapsulation of exception handling has one additional advantage. You may have to write code intended to run on a variety of implementations. If some have implemented exceptions and others have not, the tendency is strong to avoid using exceptions altogether. But that approach costs you the use of a powerful language feature, one that often helps you better structure a program. Better to start thinking now about how best to incorporate exception handling, even if you have to disable much of the machinery, than to put off learning an important discipline.

set_ **raise_handler** One transitional approach, using library exception classes as defined here, is to intercept all thrown exceptions before they actually evaluate a *throw* expression. You can write something like:

```
#include <stdlib.h>
#include <iostream>

void my_raise(xmsg& ex)
    {                                           // abort on any throw
    cerr < "exception: " < ex.what() < endl;
    abort();
    }
.....
    xmsg::set_raise_handler(&my_raise);
```

A *raise* handler can also call **longjmp**, declared in **<setjmp.h>**, to roll back to a safe recovery point. To do so, however, you typically need some way to reinitialize static objects and recover allocated storage. This is the sort of thing you can, and often must, do only in an embedded application. The draft C++ Standard specifies no portable way to perform such a "reboot" in a hosted application.

You can ignore the library exception classes and still have occasion to include **<exception>**. You sometimes want to take control of two other aspects of exception handling: calls to **terminate()** and to **unexpected()**.

terminate Throwing an exception results in a call to **terminate**:

- if the exception has no corresponding handler
- if the execution stack appears to be corrupted
- if a destructor throws another exception along the way

The default behavior of **terminate** is to call **abort()**, declared in **<stdlib.h>**. Any *terminate* handler you provide must not return to its caller. And it probably should not do too much before it terminates execution. But you can probably get away with a more orderly shutdown, as in:

set_ **terminate**
```
#include <stdlib.h>
#include <iostream>

void my_terminate()
    {                                           // exit on any throw
    cerr < "exception: " < ex.what() < endl;
    exit(EXIT_FAILURE);
    }
.....
    set_terminate(&my_terminate);
```

unexpected Throwing an exception results in a call to **unexpected** if a function declaration has an exception specification, if control passes out of the function, and if the type of the thrown exception is not listed in the exception specification. The default behavior of **unexpected** is to call **terminate()**. Any *unexpected* handler you provide must not return to its caller. The draft C++ Standard lists four general ways to transfer control from an *unexpected* handler:

- rethrow the exception (by evaluating the expression **throw**)

- throw another exception

- call **terminate()**

- call either **abort()** or **exit(int)**, declared in **<stdlib.h>**

set_ You call **set_unexpected** much the same way as you call **set_termi-**
unexpected **nate**. I won't bother to give another example. I note instead that a function definition **void f() throw(badcast, xalloc)** is merely shorthand for:

```
void f()
    {                          // throw only badcast or xalloc
    try
        .....                  // body of function
    catch (badcast)
        throw;
    catch (xalloc)
        throw;
    catch (...)
        unexpected();
    }
```

If you follow this form, you can replace the call to **unexpected()** with code tailored to each function. Given the uncertain future of exception specifications, you may be better off cultivating this style from the outset.

Implementing `<exception>`

exceptio Figure 3.1 shows the file **exceptio**, which implements the header **<exception>**. It consists mostly of declarations for the various exception classes, beginning with the base class **xmsg**. Declarations for the various exception handling functions bring up the rear.

copying and The draft C++ Standard doesn't declare any copy constructors or assign-
assignment ment operators whose *overt* behavior is what the translator supplies by default. Similarly, I don't bother to provide any such creatures whose *actual* behavior can be supplied by default. Here is a case, however, where actually copying the member objects from one object of class **xmsg** to another is inadequate. The result can be message strings that get freed more than once — a debugging nightmare. So I declare **xmsg** as having an explicit copy constructor and assignment operator, and provide definitions for them.

_Bool I have changed to type **_Bool** those declarations that have been changed to type **bool** in the draft C++ Standard. The header **<yxvals.h>** defines **_Bool** as type *int*, if the new keyword is not yet defined.

```
// exception standard header
#ifndef _EXCEPTION_
#define _EXCEPTION_
#include <defines>
            // class xmsg
class xmsg {
public:
    typedef void(*raise_handler)(xmsg&);
    static raise_handler set_raise_handler(raise_handler);
    xmsg(const char * = 0, const char * = 0, const char * = 0);
    xmsg(const xmsg&);
    xmsg& operator=(const xmsg&);
    virtual ~xmsg();
    void raise();
    const char *what() const;
    const char *where() const;
    const char *why() const;
    static void _Throw(xmsg *);
protected:
    virtual void do_raise();
    xmsg(const char *, const char *, const char *, _Bool);
private:
    void _Tidy();
    static raise_handler _Handler;
    const char *_What, *_Where, *_Why;
    _Bool _Alloced;
    };
            // class xlogic
class xlogic : public xmsg {
public:
    xlogic(const char * = 0, const char * = 0, const char * = 0);
    virtual ~xlogic();
protected:
    virtual void do_raise();
    };
            // class xruntime
class xruntime : public xmsg {
public:
    xruntime(const char * = 0, const char * = 0,
        const char * = 0);
    virtual ~xruntime();
protected:
    xruntime(const char *, const char *, const char *, _Bool);
    virtual void do_raise();
    };
            // class badcast
class badcast : public xlogic {
public:
    badcast(const char * = 0, const char * = 0, const char * = 0);
    virtual ~badcast();
protected:
    virtual void do_raise();
    };
            // class invalidargument
class invalidargument : public xlogic {
```

```
public:
    invalidargument(const char * = 0, const char * = 0,
        const char * = 0);
    virtual ~invalidargument();
protected:
    virtual void do_raise();
    };
        // class lengtherror
class lengtherror : public xlogic {
public:
    lengtherror(const char * = 0, const char * = 0,
        const char * = 0);
    virtual ~lengtherror();
protected:
    virtual void do_raise();
    };
        // class outofrange
class outofrange : public xlogic {
public:
    outofrange(const char * = 0, const char * = 0,
        const char * = 0);
    virtual ~outofrange();
protected:
    virtual void do_raise();
    };
        // class overflow
class overflow : public xruntime {
public:
    overflow(const char * = 0, const char * = 0,
        const char * = 0);
    virtual ~overflow();
protected:
    virtual void do_raise();
    };
        // class xdomain
class xdomain : public xlogic {
public:
    xdomain(const char * = 0, const char * = 0, const char * = 0);
    virtual ~xdomain();
protected:
    virtual void do_raise();
    };
        // class xrange
class xrange : public xruntime {
public:
    xrange(const char * = 0, const char * = 0, const char * = 0);
    virtual ~xrange();
protected:
    virtual void do_raise();
    };
        // function declarations
fvoid_t *set_terminate(fvoid_t *);
fvoid_t *set_unexpected(fvoid_t *);
void terminate(), unexpected();
#endif
```

```
// exception -- exception members
#include <signal.h>
#include <stdlib.h>
#include <string.h>
#include <iostream>

xmsg::raise_handler xmsg::_Handler = 0;

static const char *hs(const char *s)
    {                                           // copy string to heap
    const char *d;
    return (s == 0
        || (d = (const char *)malloc(strlen(s) + 1)) == 0
        ? 0 : (const char *)strcpy((char *)d, s));
    }

xmsg::raise_handler xmsg::set_raise_handler(raise_handler pnew)
    {                                           // set new raise handler
    const raise_handler pold = _Handler;
    _Handler = pnew;
    return (pold);
    }

xmsg::xmsg(const char *what, const char *where,
    const char *why)
    : _What(hs(what)), _Where(hs(where)), _Why(hs(why)),
        _Alloced(1)
    {                                           // construct an xmsg
    }

xmsg::xmsg(const xmsg& rhs)
    : _What(hs(rhs.what())), _Where(hs(rhs.where())),
        _Why(hs(rhs.why())), _Alloced(1)
    {                                           // copy an xmsg
    }

xmsg& xmsg::operator=(const xmsg& rhs)
    {                                           // assign an xmsg
    if (this != &rhs)
        {                                       // not the same, copy
        _Tidy();
        _What = hs(rhs.what());
        _Where = hs(rhs.where());
        _Why = hs(rhs.why());
        _Alloced = 1;
        }
    return (*this);
    }

xmsg::~xmsg()
    {                                           // destruct an xmsg
    _Tidy();
    }
```

```
void xmsg::raise()
    {                                           // raise an xmsg
    if (_Handler)
        (*_Handler)(*this);
    do_raise();
    _RAISE(*this);
    }

const char *xmsg::what() const
    {                               // return non-null What pointer
    return (_What != 0 ? _What : "");
    }

const char *xmsg::where() const
    {                               // return non-null Where pointer
    return (_Where != 0 ? _Where : "");
    }

const char *xmsg::why() const
    {                               // return non-null Why pointer
    return (_Why != 0 ? _Why : "");
    }

void xmsg::do_raise()
    {                       // do no special raise handling by default
    }

xmsg::xmsg(const char *what, const char *where,
    const char *why, _Bool copyfl)
    : _What(copyfl ? hs(what) : what),
        _Where(copyfl ? hs(where) : where),
        _Why(copyfl ? hs(why) : why),
        _Alloced(copyfl)
    {                               // construct an xmsg, optional copy
    }

void xmsg::_Throw(xmsg *pex)
    {                               // handle an unthrowable xmsg
    cerr << "exception: " << (pex ? pex->what() : "??") << endl;
    ::raise(SIGABRT);
    }

void xmsg::_Tidy()
    {                               // free storage for an xmsg
    if (_Alloced)
        {                           // free any allocated strings
        free((void *)_What);
        free((void *)_Where);
        free((void *)_Why);
        _Alloced = 0;
        }
    }
```

_Throw   Exception handling is still sufficiently problematic that I avoid writing explicit *throw* expressions or *catch* clauses in the code. An implementation that doesn't support exceptions instead calls the secret static member function **xmsg::_Throw** to terminate execution. (See Figure 3.2.)

_Tidy   Class **xmsg** also adds the protected member function **xmsg::_Tidy()**. The destructor and the assignment operator both call this function to free any storage previously allocated for messages. Several classes in this implementation use a function of this name for much the same purpose.

exceptio.c   Figure 3.2 shows the file **exceptio.c**. It defines all the objects and functions likely to be required by any object of class **xmsg**. (You could argue that **what()** and **why()** are seldom used, but they are also an unfortunate size — not worth making inline and not worth placing in separate translation units.) The static function **hs(const char *)** is used only within this translation unit. It performs the tedious little chore of allocating a private copy of any non-null strings. You can see how it simplifies the writing of several constructors and the assignment operator. **hs** calls **malloc** instead of using a *new* expression to avoid throwing yet another exception.

_RAISE   The function **xmsg::raise()** replaces the expression **throw *this** with the macro invocation **_RAISE(*this)**. As usual, the header **<yxvals.h>** supplies an appropriate definition. If the macro cannot expand to a *throw* expression, because the implementation doesn't support exceptions, it expands to **xmsg::_Throw()**.

xlogic.c   The rest of the exception classes are minor variations on the same theme.
xruntime.c   Figure 3.3 shows the file **xlogic.c**, which implements the class **xlogic**. Figure 3.4 shows the file **xruntime.c**, which implements the class **xruntime**. Note the slight asymmetry. The latter class has an extra protected constructor, as I described earlier, which is supposed to be used only by **xalloc**. (See Chapter 4: **<new>**.)

Figure 3.3:
xlogic.c

```
// xlogic -- xlogic members
#include <exception>

xlogic::xlogic(const char *what, const char *where,
    const char *why)
    : xmsg(what, where, why)
    {                                           // construct an xlogic
    }

xlogic::~xlogic()
    {                                           // destruct an xlogic
    }

void xlogic::do_raise()
    {                                           // throw an xlogic
    _RAISE(*this);
    }                                                              □
```

Figure 3.4:
xruntime.c

```
// xruntime -- xruntime members
#include <exception>

xruntime::xruntime(const char *what, const char *where,
    const char *why)
    : xmsg(what, where, why)
    {                                         // construct an xruntime
    }

xruntime::~xruntime()
    {                                         // destruct an xruntime
    }

xruntime::xruntime(const char *what, const char *where,
    const char *why, _Bool copyfl)
    : xmsg(what, where, why, copyfl)
    {                            // construct an xruntime, optional copy
    }

void xruntime::do_raise()
    {                                         // throw an xruntime
    _RAISE(*this);
    }                                                              □
```

Figure 3.5:
xdomain.c

```
// xdomain -- xdomain members
#include <exception>

xdomain::xdomain(const char *what, const char *where,
    const char *why)
    : xlogic(what, where, why)
    {                                         // construct an xdomain
    }

xdomain::~xdomain()
    {                                         // destruct an xdomain
    }

void xdomain::do_raise()
    {                                         // throw an xdomain
    _RAISE(*this);
    }                                                              □
```

xdomain.c   Two more classes are derived from these to report mathematical errors.
xrange.c   Figure 3.5 shows the file xdomain.c, which implements the class xdomain.
Figure 3.6 shows the file xrange.c, which implements the class xrange.

badcast.c   Figure 3.7 shows the file badcast.c, which implements the class bad-
cast. Objects of class badcast are thrown implicitly by expressions generated by the translator. The only other exception class on such intimate terms with the language is badtypeid. (See Chapter 5: <typeid>.)

Figure 3.6:
xrange.c

```
// xrange -- xrange members
#include <exception>

xrange::xrange(const char *what, const char *where,
    const char *why)
    : xruntime(what, where, why)
    {                                          // construct an xrange
    }

xrange::~xrange()
    {                                          // destruct an xrange
    }

void xrange::do_raise()
    {                                          // throw an xrange
    _RAISE(*this);
    }                                                                □
```

Figure 3.7:
badcast.c

```
// badcast -- badcast members
#include <exception>

badcast::badcast(const char *what, const char *where,
    const char *why)
    : xlogic(what, where, why)
    {                                          // construct a badcast
    }

badcast::~badcast()
    {                                          // destruct a badcast
    }

void badcast::do_raise()
    {                                          // throw a badcast
    _RAISE(*this);
    }                                                                □
```

Figure 3.8:
invalida.c

```
// invalidargument -- invalidargument members
#include <exception>

invalidargument::invalidargument(const char *what,
    const char *where, const char *why)
    : xlogic(what, where, why)
    {                                    // construct an invalidargument
    }

invalidargument::~invalidargument()
    {                                    // destruct an invalidargument
    }

void invalidargument::do_raise()
    {                                    // throw an invalidargument
    _RAISE(*this);
    }                                                                □
```

Figure 3.9:
lengther.c

```
// lengtherror -- lengtherror member functions
#include <exception>

lengtherror::lengtherror(const char *what, const char *where,
    const char *why)
    : xlogic(what, where, why)
    {                                          // construct a lengtherror
    }

lengtherror::~lengtherror()
    {                                          // destruct a lengtherror
    }

void lengtherror::do_raise()
    {                                          // throw a lengtherror
    _RAISE(*this);
    }                                                                    □
```

Figure 3.10:
outofran.c

```
// outofrange -- outofrange members
#include <exception>

outofrange::outofrange(const char *what, const char *where,
    const char *why)
    : xlogic(what, where, why)
    {                                          // construct an outofrange
    }

outofrange::~outofrange()
    {                                          // destruct an outofrange
    }

void outofrange::do_raise()
    {                                          // throw an outofrange
    _RAISE(*this);
    }                                                                    □
```

Figure 3.11:
overflow.c

```
// overflow -- overflow members
#include <exception>

overflow::overflow(const char *what, const char *where,
    const char *why)
    : xruntime(what, where, why)
    {                                          // construct an overflow
    }

overflow::~overflow()
    {                                          // destruct an overflow
    }

void overflow::do_raise()
    {                                          // throw an overflow
    _RAISE(*this);
    }                                                                    □
```

Figure 3.12:
terminat.c

```
// terminate -- terminate support functions
#include <stdlib.h>
#include <exception>

static fvoid_t *terminate_handler = &abort;

fvoid_t *set_terminate(fvoid_t *pnew)
    {                      // store terminate handler pointer, return old
    fvoid_t *pold = terminate_handler;
    terminate_handler = pnew;
    return (pold);
    }

void terminate()
    {                               // call terminate handler or abort
    if (terminate_handler != 0)
        (*terminate_handler)();
    abort();
    }                                                                     □
```

Figure 3.13:
unexpect.c

```
// unexpected -- unexpected support functions
#include <exception>

static fvoid_t *unexpected_handler = &terminate;

fvoid_t *set_unexpected(fvoid_t *pnew)
    {                    // store unexpected handler pointer, return old
    fvoid_t *pold = unexpected_handler;
    unexpected_handler = pnew;
    return (pold);
    }

void unexpected()
    {                               // call unexpected handler or terminate
    if (unexpected_handler != 0)
        (*unexpected_handler)();
    terminate();
    }                                                                     □
```

invalida.c   The remaining four files in this group are much the same. They imple-
lengther.c ment the exception classes thrown by other classes in the Standard C++
outofran.c library. Figure 3.8 shows the file **invalida.c**, which implements the class
overflow.c **invalidargument**. Figure 3.9 shows the file **lengther.c**, which implements the class **lengtherror**. Figure 3.10 shows the file **outofran.c**, which
implements the class **outofrange**. And Figure 3.11 shows the file **over-
flow.c**, which implements the class **overflow**.

terminat.c   Finally, Figure 3.12 shows the file **terminat.c**, which defines the func-
unexpect.c tions **terminate** and **set_terminate**. And Figure 3.13 shows the file
unexpect.c, which defines the functions **unexpected** and **set_unex-
pected**. Both are straightforward.

Testing **<exception>**

texcepti.c   Figure 3.14 shows the file **texcepti.c**. It faces the difficult task of testing as much of **<exception>** as possible even when exceptions are not implemented. And because it deals with various extraordinary transfers of control, the logic is rather twisty. Ironically, the tests depend heavily on **setjmp** and **longjmp** — two functions designed to be obsoleted by exception handling.

The program tests four ways that control can be transferred:

- to a **do_raise()** member function of a derived exception class
- to a *raise* handler registered with **set_raise_handler**
- to a *terminate* handler registered with **set_terminate**
- to an *unexpected* handler registered with **set_unexpected**

All four tests report a failure to transfer control properly with the idiom:

```
assert("message" == 0);
```

Since a string literal never converts to a null pointer, the assertion always fails. That prints the message, along with source file and line number identification, then exits abnormally.

_RAISE   As a grand finale, the program attempts to throw an exception and catch it. To do so, it uses the **_RAISE** macro I described on page 72 to throw the exception, if possible. It also uses yet another set of related macros, defined in **<yxvals.h>**, designed to catch an arbitrary exception:

_TRY_BEGIN	**_TRY_BEGIN**	
_CATCH_ALL	.....	// **try block**
_CATCH_END	**_CATCH_ALL**	
	.....	// **catch block**
	_CATCH_END	

If exceptions are implemented, these macros expand to:

```
try {
    .....                       // try block
} catch (...) {
    .....                       // catch block
}
```

Otherwise, the expansion is:

```
{ {
    .....                       // try block
} if (0) {
    .....               // catch block (never executed)
} }
```

The remaining bulk of the program is mostly declarations. Don't worry that the program makes no further use of many of the declared objects. The idea is to "touch" various definitions to make sure they're there and behave more or less as expected. You will find that sort of thing in all the tests that follow in this book. If all goes well, the program prints:

```
SUCCESS testing <exception>
```

and takes a normal exit.

```
// test <exception>
#include <assert.h>
#include <setjmp.h>
#include <signal.h>
#include <stdlib.h>
#include <exception>
#include <iostream>

    // static data
static jmp_buf jbuf;

    // derived exception
class myex : public xmsg {
public:
    myex(const char *what = 0)
        : xmsg(what) {}
protected:
    virtual void do_raise();
    };

void myex::do_raise()
    {                                  // capture raised exception
    longjmp(jbuf, 1);
    }

void abort_hand(int)
    {                               // field abort when throwing exception
    cout << "Exceptions are not implemented" << endl;
    cout << "SUCCESS testing <exception>" << endl;
    exit(0);
    }

void jmpback()
    {                                  // longjmp back to caller
    longjmp(jbuf, 1);
    }

void raiseback(xmsg&)
    {                                  // jump back from raise handler
    longjmp(jbuf, 1);
    }

void try_myex_hand()
    {                                     // test do_raise machinery
    if (setjmp(jbuf) == 0)
        {                       // see if handler returns control
        myex("testing myex::do_raise").raise();
        assert("myex::raise() returned" == 0);
        }
    }
```

```
void try_raise_hand()
    {                                   // test set_raise_handler machinery
    xmsg::raise_handler save_hand =
        xmsg::set_raise_handler(&raiseback);
    if (setjmp(jbuf) == 0)
        {                               // see if handler returns control
        xmsg("testing raise handler").raise();
        assert("xmsg::raise() returned" == 0);
        }
    assert(xmsg::set_raise_handler(save_hand) == &raiseback);
    }

void try_terminate()
    {                                   // test terminate machinery
    fvoid_t *save_hand = set_terminate(&jmpback);
    if (setjmp(jbuf) == 0)
        terminate(), assert("terminate() returned" == 0);
    assert(set_terminate(save_hand) == &jmpback);
    }

void try_unexpected()
    {                                   // test unexpected machinery
    fvoid_t *save_hand = set_unexpected(&jmpback);
    if (setjmp(jbuf) == 0)
        unexpected(), assert("terminate() returned" == 0);
    assert(set_unexpected(save_hand) == &jmpback);
    }

int main()
    {               // test basic workings of exception definitions
    xmsg x1("xmsg what", "where", "why");
    xlogic x2("xlogic what", "where", "why");
    xruntime x3("xruntime what", "where", "why");
    badcast x4("badcast what", "where", "why");
    invalidargument x5("invalidargument what", "where", "why");
    lengtherror x6("lengtherror what", "where", "why");
    outofrange x7("outofrange what", "where", "why");
    overflow x8("overflow what", "where", "why");
    xdomain x9("xdomain what", "where", "why");
    xrange x10("xrange what", "where", "why");
    try_myex_hand();
    try_raise_hand();
    try_terminate();
    try_unexpected();
    cout << "About to throw an exception" << endl;
    signal(SIGABRT, &abort_hand);
    _TRY_BEGIN
        _RAISE(x1), assert("throw returned" == 0);
    _CATCH_ALL
        cout << "Exceptions are implemented" << endl;
    _CATCH_END
    cout << "SUCCESS testing <exception>" << endl;
    return (0);
    }                                                               □
```

Exercises

Exercise 3.1 An argument value on a function call is determined by a nontrivial expression evaluation. If the value is invalid for the function specification, does that constitute a logic error or a runtime error?

Exercise 3.2 If a constructor throws an exception, should its corresponding destructor be called?

Exercise 3.3 If a constructor allocates storage and it can possibly throw an exception (other than for a storage-allocation failure), how can you avoid "memory leaks," where storage is repeatedly allocated and never gets freed?

Exercise 3.4 You need to construct an object that can throw two or more different exceptions during construction. Describe a discipline that avoids memory leaks in all cases.

Exercise 3.5 Rewrite the macro **assert**, defined in **<assert.h>**, to throw an exception when the assertion fails. The message stored with the exception object should convey at least as much information as the existing **assert** macro displays (source file name, source line number, and the source code of the offending predicate).

Exercise 3.6 [Harder] Can you implement **setjmp** and **longjmp** purely in terms of exceptions? If so, do so. If not, explain why not.

Exercise 3.7 [Harder] Can you implement exceptions purely in terms of **setjmp** and **longjmp**? If so, do so. If not, explain why not.

Exercise 3.8 [Very hard] Write a version of **setjmp** and **longjmp** that calls all necessary destructors, and properly restores all objects with dynamic storage duration, on a **longjmp** call. Why would you want such a capability?

Chapter 4: <new>

Background

Exceptions can be thought of as a way to structure the use of **setjmp** and **longjmp**, as I discussed in the previous chapter. Similarly, the addition of **new** and **delete** to C++ essentially structures the use of **malloc** and **free**. By writing the declaration:

```
Thing *p = new Thing;
```

you are assured that the program constructs the object of type **Thing** after it is successfully allocated and before it can be accessed through **p**. Similarly, the expression statement:

```
delete p;
```

ensures that the program destroys the object before it deallocates its storage.

You don't have to include any headers before writing expressions like these — **new** and **delete** are indeed built right into the language. But you can also play a variety of games with storage allocation if you choose. To do so, you begin by including the header **<new>**. Then you can supply a handler function that gets control when an allocation request can't be honored. Or you can even *replace* one or more of the Standard C++ library functions that manage storage with a function definition in the program.

treaties   As an aside, the draft C++ Standard is a bit harder to write than the C Standard. In C, the implementation provides all Standard C library functions and you the programmer cannot replace them. The C Standard has to describe only a single interface between implementation and program. In C++, however, the program can replace functions otherwise supplied by the Standard C++ library. The draft C++ Standard must spell out the environment promised to such a displacing function. And it must spell out what is expected of the displacing function so the program doesn't get surprised.

Here is another example from the previous chapter. A *terminate* handler (called by the function **terminate()**) is not supposed to return to its caller. If you provide one that prints a message and returns, you can cause the Standard C++ library severe problems. The draft C++ Standard says so. That gives the library permission to misbehave if you don't hold up your end of the bargain. So when you read the descriptions that follow in this chapter, remember that the "treaty" between programmer and implementor can be multifaceted. The extra complexity of the draft C++ Standard is one of the prices you pay for extra flexibility in this area.

set_
new_handler   The simplest game you can play with the storage-allocation functions is to gain control when an allocation request can't be honored. The function **set_new_handler** lets you register a *new* handler for this condition. In principle, the draft C++ standard says you can "make more storage available for allocation and then return," but the method you use will be implementation dependent. Calling **free** to liberate storage may help, but there is no requirement that storage be actually allocated by calling **malloc**. Deleting one or more allocated objects may also help, but even that is not guaranteed. More likely, you will want to throw an exception or terminate execution at this point.

exceptions   The default *new* handler does, in fact, throw an exception, of class **xalloc** (or, more recently, **bad_alloc**). As I described in the previous chapter, all library exceptions derive from the base class **xmsg** (or, more recently, **exception**). Special provision is made for constructing an **xalloc** object without allocating storage on the heap. Moreover, the Standard C++ library (currently) throws all exceptions by calling **ex.raise()**, for some object **ex** of class **xmsg**. Unless you seize control of the process in one of the ways I described earlier, the eventual outcome is that a failed allocation will throw an exception, which will in turn terminate execution of the program.

null
pointers   This is a significant change from universal past practice, which has been to quietly yield a null pointer as a result of the *new* expression. The Committee anguished quite a bit before making this change. But eventually, the predominant wisdom was that the Standard C++ library had bloody well better use the full language in this case, not just the bits that were available when **new** and **delete** were first added to C++.

A persuasive argument is that very few programs truly check all *new* expressions for null pointers. Those that don't may well stumble about when the heap is exhausted — they're almost certainly better off dying a clean death. Those that do check all such expressions often simply abort — the path to abnormal termination is now just slightly different. It is only those few sophisticated programs that try to do something nontrivial when the heap is exhausted that need a bit of rewriting. Most of the Committee felt this was a necessary price to pay to introduce exceptions at this critical juncture.

Even so, some sympathy remains for being able to revert to the old behavior. For a variety of reasons, the Committee has not spelled out a portable way to do so. But it has identified what it thinks should be a common extension. Calling **set_new_handler** with a null pointer argument is otherwise undefined behavior. It seems natural to use this nonportable call as a way for an implementation to know that it should revert to the older behavior.

operator
new   If you want more certain control over the business of allocating storage, your best bet is to provide your own versions of **operator new(size_t)**

and/or **operator delete(void *)**. These functions have a peculiar dispensation — the Standard C++ library provides a version of each, but you can replace (or "knock out") those versions by defining your own. (Only the array versions of these two operators, described below, also enjoy this special status within the Standard C++ library.)

But first note an important distinction. When you write:

```
Thing *p = new Thing;
```

the subexpression **new Thing** is called a *new* expression. It calls **operator new(size_t)** to allocate storage, but it also does other things, such as constructing the newly allocated object. All that **operator new(size_t)** has to worry about is providing the number of requested "raw" bytes, suitably aligned, or dealing with inadequate heap storage. Similarly:

```
delete p;
```

is an expression statement containing a *delete* expression. It calls **operator delete(void *)** to free storage, but it first calls the destructor for the object (only if the pointer is not null, of course). All that **operator delete(void *)** has to worry about is freeing storage for the object.

So one thing you might do is replace **operator delete(void *)** with a function that doesn't really free the storage. That could be handy while you're debugging a program, provided of course that you have enough heap to run your test cases. Or you might replace both **operator new(size_t)** and **operator delete(void *)** with versions that are simpler, or faster, or more sophisticated than the library versions. It is important to replace both, because the latter function in the library only knows how to free storage for objects allocated by the former.

In either case, you probably don't have to bother with **set_new_handler**. You are at liberty to do whatever you want when you run out of heap. No need to call the *new* handler, which you can't do portably anyway.

Yet another latitude granted by Standard C++ is to provide an arbitrary set of additional arguments in a *new* expression, as in:

```
Thing *get_special(T1 stuff, T2 more_stuff)
    {                           // special allocator for Thing
    return (new (stuff, more_stuff) Thing);
    }
```

This form implicitly calls the function:

```
void *operator new(size_t, T1, T2);
```

which you are obliged to supply as part of your program. I leave it to your imagination what extra parameters might be useful when you're allocating some of your more sophisticated objects.

It doesn't take too much imagination, however, to see a very common need. Sometimes you know exactly where you want a C++ object to be constructed — you have reason to believe that the storage area **x** is large enough and suitably aligned to hold an object of type **Thing**. Moreover, you're confident that no object has been constructed there already for which a nontrivial destructor will later be called. (Whew!)

To deal with this twilight zone between C and C++ programming, you can write:

```
Thing *p = new ((void *)&X) Thing;
```

This, naturally enough, calls the function:

```
void *operator new(size_t, void *);
```

which can simply return its second argument, as in:

```
void *operator new(size_t, void *p)
    {                               // return placement address
    return (p);
    }
```

The Standard C++ library provides this one version of a "placement **operator new**." (Don't forget to include the header **<new>** to be sure it is properly declared.) Any fancier placement variants are up to you to provide.

member new Yet another way exists for controlling how objects get allocated. For any class, you can overload all the variants of **operator new** and/or **operator delete** that I've mentioned so far. Perhaps you want to write your own definitions of:

```
void Thing::operator delete(void *);
void *Thing::operator new(size_t);
```

that do a really fast job of allocating and freeing objects of class **Thing**. (You declare them as static member functions in the class definition.) They can, for example, maintain a list of previously freed objects and hand them back quickly for future allocation requests. Unless you get really tricky, you can even ignore the **size_t** first argument to all variants of **operator new**, since you know how big a **Thing** is likely to be. (How do you get tricky? Well, you can declare an **operator new** in a base class and fail to override it in a derived class. An object of the derived class may well require more storage than for the base object. But thinking about things like that gives me a headache.)

allocating arrays So you see that you can exercise pretty fine control over how all objects, or even individual objects, get allocated. But that leads to one last residual problem, regarding the allocation and freeing of arrays. You can, for example, write:

```
Thing *p = new Thing[N];
```

to allocate an array of **N** elements each of type **Thing**. The program constructs each of the elements in order, starting with the first (element zero). In this case, you *must* write the expression statement:

```
delete[] p;
```

to delete the array, not just a simple:

```
delete p;
```

as before. Why? Because the "array *new* expression" above has to somehow memorize how many elements **N** it has allocated. It needs to know how to locate this memorized information and use it to destroy the appropriate number of elements and free the appropriate amount of storage. Yes, some existing implementations of C++ let you be cavalier about deleting arrays the wrong way, but don't count on that license in a portable program.

This requirement presents another problem. What happens if you've provided a member **operator new(size_t)** for class **Thing**, as above? It cannot, in general, know whether it's being asked to allocate storage for a single element or a whole array. (Remember the potential trickery I mentioned above.) So what C++ has done in the past is to ignore any such member functions and call the external **operator new(size_t)** for all array allocations. This has been a less than satisfactory solution.

delete[] The Committee has plugged this control gap by permitting you to define
new[] the member functions **operator new[](size_t)** and **operator delete[](void *)**. Defining these functions gives you control over the allocation and freeing of arrays as well as the class objects themselves.

You can't necessarily tell how many array elements are being allocated, by the way. An array *new* expression can ask for extra storage for its own bookkeeping, so you'd better honor the **size_t** argument blindly. But at least you can maintain private storage pools now for array objects.

For completeness, the draft C++ Standard also includes the external versions of these array operators:

```
void operator delete[](void *);
void *operator new[](size_t);
void *operator new[](size_t, void *);
```

The Standard C++ library versions of these functions effectively just turn around and call the non-array library versions. And you can indeed replace the first two of these functions with your own definitions, but I'm not sure why you'd bother. I'm sure *someone* can find a reason to do so, however.

What the Draft C++ Standard Says

The description of header **<new>** consists mostly of a recitation of the functions it declares. The tricky part to specify is the interaction between a *new* handler and **operator new(size_t)**.

17.3.3 Header <new>

<new> The header **<new>** defines a type and several functions that manage the allocation of storage in a program, as described in subclauses 5.3 and 12.

17.3.3.1 Class xalloc

Class
xalloc
```
class xalloc : public xruntime {
public:
    xalloc(const char* where_arg = 0,
           const char* why_arg = 0);
    virtual ~xalloc();
protected:
//  virtual void do_raise(); inherited
};
```

The class **xalloc** defines the type of objects thrown as exceptions by the implementation to report a failure to allocate storage.

17.3.3.1.1 xalloc::xalloc(const char*, const char*)

constructor

```
xalloc(const char* where_arg = 0, const char* why_arg = 0);
```

Constructs an object of class **xalloc**, initializing the base class with **xruntime(what_arg, where_arg, why_arg, 0)**, where the NTMBS pointed to by **what_arg** is unspecified.[77]

17.3.3.1.2 xalloc::~xalloc()

destructor

```
virtual ~xalloc();
```

Destroys an object of class **xalloc**.

17.3.3.1.3 xalloc::do_raise()

do_raise

```
//  virtual void do_raise(); inherited
```

Behaves the same as **xmsg::do_raise()**.

17.3.3.2 set_new_handler(fvoid_t*)

set_new_handler

```
fvoid_t* set_new_handler(fvoid_t* new_p);
```

Establishes a new handler to be called by the default versions of **operator new(size_t)** and **operator new[](size_t)** when they cannot satisfy a request for additional storage. The function stores **new_p** in a static object that, for the sake of exposition, can be called **new_handler** and can be declared as:

```
fvoid_t* new_handler = &new_hand;
```

where, in turn, **new_hand** can be defined as:

```
static void new_hand()
{   // raise xalloc exception
    static const xalloc ex("operator new");
    ex.raise();
}
```

The function returns the previous contents of **new_handler**.

17.3.3.3 operator delete(void*)

delete

```
void operator delete(void* ptr);
```

Called by a **delete** expression to render the value of **ptr** invalid. The program can define a function with this function signature that displaces the default version defined by the Standard C++ library. The required behavior is to accept a value of **ptr** that is null or that was returned by an earlier call to **operator new(size_t)**.

The default behavior for a null value of **ptr** is to do nothing. Any other value of **ptr** shall be a value returned earlier by a call to the default **operator new(size_t)**.[78] The default behavior for such a non-null value of **ptr** is to reclaim storage allocated by the earlier call to the default **operator new(size_t)**. It is unspecified under what conditions part or all of such reclaimed storage is allocated by a subsequent call to **operator new(size_t)** or any of **calloc(size_t)**, **malloc(size_t)**, or **realloc(void*, size_t)**, declared in **<stdlib.h>**.

17.3.3.4 operator delete[](void*)

delete[]

```
void operator delete[](void* ptr);
```

Called by a **delete[]** expression to render the value of **ptr** invalid. The program can define a function with this function signature that displaces the default version defined by the Standard C++ library.

The required behavior is to accept a value of **ptr** that is null or that was returned by an earlier call to **operator new[](size_t)**.

The default behavior for a null value of **ptr** is to do nothing. Any other value of **ptr** shall be a value returned earlier by a call to the default **operator new[](size_t)**.[79] The default behavior for such a non-null value of **ptr** is to reclaim storage allocated by the earlier call to the default **operator new[](size_t)**. It is unspecified under what conditions part or all of such reclaimed storage is allocated by a subsequent call to **operator new(size_t)** or any of **calloc(size_t)**, **malloc(size_t)**, or **realloc(void*, size_t)**, declared in **<stdlib.h>**.

17.3.3.5 operator new(size_t)

new

```
void* operator new(size_t size);
```

Called by a **new** expression to allocate **size** bytes of storage suitably aligned to represent any object of that size. The program can define a function with this function signature that displaces the default version defined by the Standard C++ library.

The required behavior is to return a non-null pointer only if storage can be allocated as requested. Each such allocation shall yield a pointer to storage disjoint from any other allocated storage. The order and contiguity of storage allocated by successive calls to **operator new(size_t)** is unspecified. The initial stored value is unspecified. The returned pointer points to the start (lowest byte address) of the allocated storage. If **size** is zero, the value returned shall not compare equal to any other value returned by **operator new(size_t)**.[80]

The default behavior is to execute a loop. Within the loop, the function first attempts to allocate the requested storage. Whether the attempt involves a call to the Standard C library function **malloc** is unspecified. If the attempt is successful, the function returns a pointer to the allocated storage. Otherwise (using the notation of subclause 17.3.3.2), if **new_handler** is a null pointer, the result is implementation-defined.[81] Otherwise, the function evaluates the expression **(*new_handler)()**. If the called function returns, the loop repeats. The loop terminates when an attempt to allocate the requested storage is successful or when a called function does not return.

The required behavior of a function called by **(*new_handler)()** is to perform one of the following operations:

- make more storage available for allocation and then return;
- execute an expression of the form **ex.raise()**, where **ex** is an object of type **xalloc**, declared in **<exception>**;
- call either **abort()** or **exit(int)**, declared in **<stdlib.h>**.

The default behavior of a function called by **(*new_handler)()** is described by the function **new_hand**, as shown in subclause 17.3.3.2.

The order and contiguity of storage allocated by successive calls to **operator new(size_t)** is unspecified, as are the initial values stored there.

17.3.3.6 operator new[](size_t)

new[]

```
void* operator new[](size_t size);
```

Called by a **new[]** expression to allocate **size** bytes of storage suitably aligned to represent any array object of that size or smaller.[82] The program can define a function with this function signature that displaces the default version defined by the Standard C++ library.

The required behavior is the same as for **operator new(size_t)**.

The default behavior is to return **operator new(size)**.

new

17.3.3.7 `operator new(size_t, void*)`

```
void* operator new(size_t size, void* ptr);
```
Returns *ptr*.

17.3.3.8 `operator new[](size_t, void*)`

new[]
```
void* operator new[](size_t size, void* ptr);
```
Returns *ptr*.

___

Footnotes:

Footnotes

77) Note that *where_arg* and *why_arg* must either be null pointers or point to NTMBSs whose lifetime exceeds that of the constructed object.

78) The value must not have been invalidated by an intervening call to **operator delete(size_t)**, or it would be an invalid argument for a Standard C++ library function call.

79) The value must not have been invalidated by an intervening call to **operator delete[](size_t)**, or it would be an invalid argument for a Standard C++ library function call.

80) The value cannot legitimately compare equal to one that has been invalidated by a call to **operator delete(size_t)**, since any such comparison is an invalid operation.

81) A common extension when *new_handler* is a null pointer is for **operator new(size_t)** to return a null pointer, in accordance with many earlier implementations of C++.

82) It is not the direct responsibility of **operator new[](size_t)** or **operator delete[](void*)** to note the repetition count or element size of the array. Those operations are performed elsewhere in the array **new** and **delete** expressions. The array **new** expression, may, however, increase the *size* argument to **operator new[](size_t)** to obtain space to store supplemental information.

Future Directions

As I mentioned in the previous chapter, the exception class **xalloc** has been renamed **bad_alloc**, with rather different properties inherited from its base class. Its definition has twice been moved, but is currently back in the header **<exception>**.

Otherwise, this header has been reasonably stable of late.

Using <new>

You include **<new>** only if you want to take extraordinary control of the storage-allocation process. Left to its own devices, the Standard C++ library allocates all storage off a common heap. If it can't honor an allocation request, it throws an exception. And if exception handling is left to its own devices, the thrown exception causes the program to terminate abnormally. For many programs, that's acceptable behavior.

You may do some storage allocation of your own. If so, a polite way for your specialized allocator to return failure is to mimic what the Standard C++ library does. In principle, that means you should include **<new>**, declare an object **ex** of class **xalloc**, and call **ex.raise()**. In practice, I encourage you *not* to be so direct. The exception machinery of the Standard C++ library is still volatile. Better you should call some common function to do this job for you.

_Nomemory   This implementation includes the function **_Nomemory**, declared in **<defines>**. (See page 48.) It encapsulates the business of reporting a storage-allocation failure. If you can't or won't use this function, I encourage you to write a similar one and use it religiously.

set_   The traditional method for gaining control when storage allocation fails
new_handler is to register a *new* handler by calling **set_new_handler**. But as I discussed earlier (on page 82), this facility offers only limited control. You may have code that does something useful with an existing implementation of C++, but don't expect it to be portable to another.

A more likely reason to call **set_new_handler** might be to revert to another traditional behavior. You may have code that expects a *new* expression to yield a null pointer when storage allocation fails. The call:

```
set_new_handler(0);
```

while not defined by the draft C++ Standard, is suggested as the way to roll back the clock. For any new code you write, however, I strongly urge you *not* to consider such antics.

replacing   You may have occasion to knock out some or all of the storage-allocation
functions functions. If you do, keep such functions simple, lest they call a function that allocates storage. And note that only certain combinations make sense:

- You can choose to replace only **operator delete(void *)** and/or **operator delete[](void *)**, provided you make no attempt to actually free the storage.

- If you replace **operator new(size_T)**, you *must* also replace **operator delete(void *)**.

- If you replace **operator new[](size_T)**, you *must* also replace **operator delete[](void *)**.

I suspect, however, that you have little occasion to replace the array versions.

Implementing <new>

new   Figure 4.1 shows the file **new**. It (currently) declares the exception class **xalloc**. Otherwise, its principal business is to declare the various functions associated with storage allocation.

HAS   The array versions of these functions are a fairly recent invention. An
ARRAY_NEW implementation that doesn't recognize the new forms must be protected, lest it diagnose syntax errors in the header. Thus, the header **<yxvals.h>** supplies yet another implementation-dependent indicator. It defines the macro **_HAS_ARRAY_NEW** only if the implementation recognizes the new array versions.

Figure 4.1:
new

```
// new standard header
#ifndef _NEW_
#define _NEW_
#include <exception>
        // class xalloc
class xalloc : public xruntime {
public:
    xalloc(const char * = 0, const char * = 0,
        const char * = 0);
    virtual ~xalloc();
protected:
    virtual void do_raise();
    };
        // function and object declarations
fvoid_t *set_new_handler(fvoid_t *);
void operator delete(void *);
void *operator new(size_t);
inline void *operator new(size_t, void *_P)
    {return (_P); }
#if _HAS_ARRAY_NEW
void operator delete[](void *);
void *operator new[](size_t);
inline void *operator new[](size_t, void *_P)
    {return (_P); }
#endif
extern fvoid_t (*_New_hand);
#endif                                                              □
```

new.c   Figure 4.2 shows the file **new.c**. It supplies all the machinery you need to call or register *new* handlers. Note that this includes the various support functions for the exception class **xalloc**. Here is also where the implementation-specific function **_Nomemory** resides.

newop.c   Four functions must each reside in separate modules, so they can be
delop.c replaced. Figure 4.3 shows the file **newop.c**, which implements the function **operator new(size_t)**. This implementation calls **malloc**, declared in **<stdlib.h>** to do the actual allocation. It loops until storage allocation succeeds or the *new* handler fails to return. Figure 4.4 shows the file **delop.c**, which implements the companion function **operator delete(void *)**. It naturally enough calls **free**, also declared in **<stdlib.h>**, the companion to **malloc**.

newaop.c   Figure 4.5 shows the file **newaop.c**. It implements the function **operator**
delaop.c **new[](size_t)**, which lets **operator new(size_t)** do all the work. Note the use of macro **_HAS_ARRAY_NEW** to guard the new function syntax. For an older implementation, this source file yields a translation unit with no definitions. Figure 4.6 shows the file **delaop.c**. As you might expect, it relies on **operator delete(void *)** and it too is guarded by the same macro.

Figure 4.2:
new.c

```
// new -- operator new support functions
#include <new>

static xalloc nomem("no memory");

static void new_handler()
    {                               // default new handler -- raise xalloc
    nomem.raise();
    }

xalloc::xalloc(const char *what, const char *where,
    const char *why)
    : xruntime(what, where, why, 0)
    {                                           // construct an xalloc
    }

xalloc::~xalloc()
    {                                           // destruct an xalloc
    }

void xalloc::do_raise()
    {                                           // throw an xalloc
    _RAISE(*this);
    }

fvoid_t *_New_hand = &new_handler;

fvoid_t *set_new_handler(fvoid_t *pnew)
    {                                           // point at new handler
    fvoid_t *pold = _New_hand;
    _New_hand = pnew;
    return (pold);
    }

void _Nomemory()
    {                                           // report out of memory
    nomem.raise();
    }                                                                   □
```

Figure 4.3:
newop.c

```
// newop operator new(size_t) REPLACEABLE
#include <stdlib.h>
#include <new>

void *operator new(size_t size)
    {                                           // try to allocate size bytes
    void *p;
    while ((p = malloc(size)) == 0 && _New_hand != 0)
        (*_New_hand)();
    return (p);
    }                                                                   □
```

Figure 4.4:
delop.c

```
// delop -- operator delete(void *) REPLACEABLE
#include <stdlib.h>
#include <new>

void operator delete(void *p)
        {                                               // free an allocated object
        free(p);
        }                                                                           □
```

Figure 4.5:
newaop.c

```
// newaop -- operator new[](size_t) REPLACEABLE
#include <new>

#if _HAS_ARRAY_NEW
void *operator new[](size_t size)
        {                               // try to allocate size bytes for an array
        return (operator new(size));
        }
#endif                                                                              □
```

Figure 4.6:
delaop.c

```
// delaop -- operator delete[](void *) REPLACEABLE
#include <new>

#if _HAS_ARRAY_NEW
void operator delete[](void *p)
        {                                               // free an allocated object
        operator delete(p);
        }
#endif                                                                              □
```

Testing <new>

tnew.c   Figure 4.7 shows the file **tnew.c**. It tests the basic functionality of the storage-allocation functions supplied by the Standard C++ library. The only function it attempts to knock out is **operator delete[](void *)**. Naturally enough, it makes that test only if **_HAS_ARRAY_NEW** says it's wise to even try. In this regard, **tnew.c** is *not* a portable test for an arbitrary implementation of the Standard C++ library. To do a proper job of that would require a suite of additional programs, which I chose not to provide in this book.

One useful service comes with this compromise in portability. The program reports whether or not an implementation supports the array operators. If all goes well, the program prints either:

```
Array new/delete are replaceable
SUCCESS testing <new>
```

or

```
Array new/delete are not replaceable
SUCCESS testing <new>
```

and takes a normal exit.

Figure 4.7:
tnew.c

```
// test <new>
#include <assert.h>
#include <string.h>
#include <new>
#include <iostream>

        // class abc
class abc {
public:
    abc(const char *s)
        {strcpy(buf, s); }
    char *ptr()
        {return (buf); }
private:
    char buf[10];
    };

        // static data
static int del_called = 0;

static void nop()
    {                                           // dummy new handler
    }

#if _HAS_ARRAY_NEW
void operator delete[](void *p)
    {                                           // free an allocated object
    del_called = 1;
    operator delete(p);
    }
#endif

int main()
    {                           // test basic workings of new definitions
    xalloc x1("xalloc what", "xalloc where", "xalloc why");
        // test set_new_handler
    fvoid_t *save_hand = set_new_handler(&nop);
    assert(set_new_handler(save_hand) == &nop);
        // test new, placement new, and delete
    abc *p = new abc("first");
    assert(strcmp(p->ptr(), "first") == 0);
    assert(new (p) abc("second") == (void *)p);
    assert(strcmp(p->ptr(), "second") == 0);
    delete p;
        // test array new, array delete
    char *s = new char[10];
    delete[] s;
    cout << "Array new/delete are"
        << (del_called ? " " : " not ")
        << "replaceable" << endl;
    cout << "SUCCESS testing <new>" << endl;
    return (0);
    }                                                              □
```

Exercises

Exercise 4.1 Can you use a placement **new** expression to "reconstruct" an arbitrary object? If not, can you list the constraints that must be satisfied for this operation to be safe?

Exercise 4.2 Where does the program store size information when a *new* expression allocates an array object? If you can't determine how a given implementation does the job, suggest one or more mechanisms that might work.

Exercise 4.3 Some people have suggested the need for a "renew" operator, which reallocates storage for an object that changes size. (It is inspired in part by the function **realloc**, declared in **<stdlib.h>**.) Specify a syntax for such an operator, and sensible semantics to go with it. What do you do about calling constructors and destructors?

Exercise 4.4 Write replacement versions of **operator new(size_t)** and **operator delete(void *)** that report "storage leaks" (a failure to free all allocated storage between two matching checkpoints. Why would you want such a capability?

Exercise 4.5 Many programs allocate and free numerous objects of just a few different sizes. Write replacement versions of **operator new(size_t)** and **operator delete(void *)** that perform faster (on average) under these circumstances. Measure performance for a nontrivial program, with and without your replacement functions, to demonstrate any improvement.

Exercise 4.6 Write replacement versions of **operator new(size_t)** and **operator delete(void *)** that detect most or all invalid attempts to free storage.

Exercise 4.7 [Harder] Alter the specification for *new* handlers, **operator new(size_t)**, and **operator delete(void *)** so that a *new* handler can portably supply additional storage. Why would you want such a capability?

Exercise 4.8 [Very hard] Write portable versions of **operator new(size_t)** and **operator delete(void *)** that do not allocate storage by calling **malloc**. Do you have to add any features to the language or to the Standard C++ library to support this code?

Chapter 5: `<typeinfo>`

Background

A relatively recent significant addition to the draft C++ Standard is "runtime type identification" (or RTTI, for short). Basically, it adds the operator **typeid** for obtaining various bits of information on the type of an object (or expression). The expression **typeid x** yields an object of class **typeinfo**, defined in the header `<typeinfo>`.

RTTI was added to Standard C++ to help solve a few nagging problems. Fundamental to the design of C++ is the notion of *static typing*. The translator knows enough about the type of every operand and subexpression to make safe, and reasonably efficient, decisions about how to translate each subexpression into executable code. It can do so even in the presence of derived classes with virtual member functions. You can pretend that an object of a derived class *is* an object of the base class, so long as you confine yourself to operations valid for the base class alone. You can even tailor behavior defined for the base class a bit by overriding virtual member functions in the derived class.

But you can't do everything. Sometimes, you have a pointer to an object of some base class and you really want to know the actual derived type of the object. With multiple inheritance (more than one base class) and derivation to arbitrary depth, this can be a nontrivial question to answer. A traditional way to determine an actual derived type is to provide a "tag" member object in the base class. Each time you construct a derived object, you make a point of initializing the tag to describe the actual derived type. Such a practice is an error-prone duplication of the work of the type system, however. Alternatively, you can define a virtual member function that reports the type of the object. You provide an overriding definition in each derived class. This beats having to get all those constructors right, but it is still repetitious.

dynamic casts Still another method has been recently introduced into the Standard C++ language. A *dynamic-cast* expression can be used to safely "down cast" a pointer to an object of a base class so that it points at the containing object of some derived class. The result is a null pointer if the pointer does not truly designate an object of the proper derived type. This solves many type-identification problems, but it still leads to some tedious code.

Enter RTTI. You can apply the operator **typeid** to an arbitrary expression. For many expressions, the type can be determined statically at translation time. For a pointer to an object of some base-class type, however, the program may have to do some work at runtime. In either event, the result is an object of class **typeinfo**.

badtypeid   The exception **badtypeid** is reported in some cases where the type cannot be determined statically at translation time. If, in the process of chasing down the actual object, the program encounters a null pointer, you can guess what happens.

name   What can you do with an object of class **typeinfo**? Well, you can obtain some sort of name for the type, for one thing. **typeinfo::name()** yields a null-terminated multibyte string (NTMBS) that presumably says something meaningful about the type. There are no standard names defined, so far, not even for the builtin types.

operator==   You can also compare two objects of class **typeinfo** for equality or
operator!=   inequality. Within any given program, you can expect two such objects to compare equal only if they derive from two expressions of the same type. Don't expect to be able to remember these critters in files, however, and check for type equality across programs. Even running the same program twice doesn't promise to yield the same representation of a **typeinfo** object for the same type each time.

before   Finally, you can impose an ordering on all the types within a program. **typeinfo::before(const typeinfo&)** returns nonzero for an object that represents a type earlier in the pecking order than the argument object. Once again, however, no promises are made about the rules for determining this order, or whether they're even the same each time you run the program.

Far more can be said about the uses of RTTI, but this is not the place to say it. I know of little practical experience with the standardized form of this new feature. For now, I can report only on what facilities the Standard C++ library provides in support of RTTI.

What the Draft C++ Standard Says

The discussion of the header **<typeinfo>** is remarkably brief. Mostly that's because the library machinery is fairly simple in this area.

17.3.4 Header **<typeinfo>**

<typeinfo>   The header **<typeinfo>** defines two types associated with type information generated by the implementation.

17.3.4.1 Class **badtypeid**

Class
badtypeid
```
class badtypeid : public xlogic {
public:
    badtypeid();
    virtual ~badtypeid();
```

```
protected:
//  virtual void do_raise(); inherited
};
```

The class **badtypeid** defines the type of objects thrown as exceptions by the implementation to report a null pointer *p* in an expression of the form **typeid (*p)**.

17.3.4.1.1 badtypeid::badtypeid()

constructor

```
badtypeid();
```

Constructs an object of class **badtypeid**, initializing the base class **xlogic** with an unspecified constructor.

17.3.4.1.2 badtypeid::~badtypeid()

destructor

```
virtual ~badtypeid();
```

Destroys an object of class **badtypeid**.

17.3.4.1.3 badtypeid::do_raise()

do_raise

```
//  virtual void do_raise(); inherited
```

Behaves the same as **xmsg::do_raise()**.

17.3.4.2 Class typeinfo

Class typeinfo

```
class typeinfo {
public:
    virtual ~typeinfo();
    int operator==(const typeinfo& rhs) const;
    int operator!=(const typeinfo& rhs) const;
    int before(const typeinfo& rhs);
    const char* name() const;
private:
//  const char* name;          exposition only
//  T desc;                    exposition only
    typeinfo(const typeinfo& rhs);
    typeinfo& operator=(const typeinfo& rhs);
};
```

The class **typeinfo** describes type information generated within the program by the implementation. Objects of this class effectively store a pointer to a name for the type, and an encoded value suitable for comparing two types for equality or collating order. The names, encoding rule, and collating sequence for types are all unspecified and may differ between programs.

For the sake of exposition, the stored objects are presented here as:

- **const char* *name***, points at a static NTMBS;
- ***T desc***, an object of a type *T* that has distinct values for all the distinct types in the program, stores the value corresponding to ***name***.

17.3.4.2.1 typeinfo::~typeinfo()

destructor

```
virtual ~typeinfo();
```

Destroys an object of type **typeinfo**.

17.3.4.2.2 typeinfo::operator==(const typeinfo&)

operator==

```
int operator==(const typeinfo& rhs) const;
```

Compares the value stored in ***desc*** with ***rhs.desc***. Returns a nonzero value if the two values represent the same type.

17.3.4.2.3 typeinfo::operator!=(const typeinfo&)

operator!=

```
int operator!=(const typeinfo& rhs) const;
```

Returns a nonzero value if `!(*this == rhs)`.

17.3.4.2.4 typeinfo::before(const typeinfo&)

before

```
int before(const typeinfo& rhs) const;
```

Compares the value stored in *desc* with *rhs.desc*. Returns a nonzero value if `*this` precedes *rhs* in the collation order.

17.3.4.2.5 typeinfo::name()

name

```
const char* name() const;
```

Returns *name*.

17.3.4.2.6 typeinfo::typeinfo(const typeinfo&)

constructor

```
typeinfo(const typeinfo& rhs);
```

Constructs an object of class `typeinfo` and initializes *name* to *rhs.name* and *desc* to *rhs.desc*.[83]

17.3.4.2.7 typeinfo::operator=(const typeinfo&)

operator=

```
typeinfo& operator=(const typeinfo& rhs);
```

Assigns *rhs.name* to *name* and *rhs.desc* to *desc*. The function returns `*this`.

Future Directions

bad_typeid
The exception class has been renamed. The class **badtypeid** is currently **bad_typeid**, derived from the class **logic**. This is part of a general renaming of exceptions. (See Chapter 3: **<exception>**.)

constructor
Class **typeinfo** currently declares the copy constructor and assignment operator private to the class. Both should probably be protected instead, but this issue has yet to be addressed by the Committee.

standard names
There is ongoing debate about whether there should be standard names for the scalar types (the predefined types mostly inherited from Standard C). Some even argue that there should be rules for determining the spelling of an arbitrary type name. Type names could then be preserved and interchanged with different program executions.

name mangling
But this requirement skirts dangerously close to the business of "name mangling," where type information is appended to external names to implement type checking through traditional linker technology. The Committee has resisted the temptation to standardize how names get mangled, in part because such tricks are *not* an essential part of all Standard C++ implementations. A weaker requirement may be that the names of all scalar types and types defined in the Standard C++ library are standardized.

My bet is that modifications to this subclause will appear only after the user community gains more experience with this particular method of specifying RTTI.

Using <typeinfo>

You include **<typeinfo>** only if you use the operator **typeid**. An expression of the form **typeid x** is the *only* way to construct a (temporary) **typeinfo** object. The class has only a private copy constructor. Since the assignment operator is also private, you cannot copy or assign objects of class **typeinfo** either. You give a name, and a longer lifetime, to a **typeinfo** object by initializing a reference to it, as in:

```
typeinfo& tix = typeid x;
```

The simplest use of RTTI is to test whether two expressions denote objects of the same derived class, irrespective of their static types. Write:

```
if (typeid x == typeid y)
    .....                          // dynamic types are the same
```

to invoke the comparison **typeinfo::operator==(const typeinfo&)**.

badtypeid   You should also be prepared to handle exceptions if you use RTTI. Remember that operator **typeid** can throw an object of class **badtypeid** under some circumstances. You must either avoid those circumstances, be willing to have the program abort, or catch the thrown exception. Remember also that exception handling is a volatile area of the draft C++ Standard. Try to localize any dependence on the name of the exception class, or any of its other properties.

before   You may have a number of types to distinguish using RTTI. In that case, pairwise equality comparisons start to get tedious, inefficient, and error prone. Beyond a certain point, you should consider building an ordered data structure — such as a list, tree, or hash table. In any event, you can perform all necessary ordering comparisons using the equality and inequality operators and the member function **typeinfo::before(const typeinfo&)**. Remember, however, that you cannot construct, copy, or assign objects of class **typeinfo**. Plan your data structures around pointers to **typeinfo** references, as shown above, not the objects themselves.

name   Finally, you may have occasion to display the names associated with objects of class **typeinfo**. The member function **typeinfo::name()** delivers up an NTMBS for your reading enjoyment. The name can be handy during debugging, for example. But remember that these names are not standardized. What may be readable and informative in one implementation may prove useless in another.

Implementing <typeinfo>

typeinfo   Figure 5.1 shows the file **typeinfo**. It declares the exception class **badtypeid** and the RTTI class **typeinfo**. Both are fairly simple.

_Typedesc   Once again, I invoke the implementation-specific header **<yxvals.h>**. In this case, it provides a definition of the type **_Typedesc**, the type chosen by the implementation to encode type identification. Absent any guidance from an implementation that supports RTTI, I have currently chosen to define this as type *int*.

Figure 5.1:
typeinfo

```
// typeinfo standard header
#ifndef _TYPEINFO_
#define _TYPEINFO_
#include <exception>
            // class badtypeid
class badtypeid : public xlogic {
public:
    badtypeid(const char * = 0, const char * = 0,
        const char * = 0);
    virtual ~badtypeid();
protected:
    virtual void do_raise();
    };
            // class typeinfo
class typeinfo {
public:
    virtual ~typeinfo();
    _Bool operator==(const typeinfo&) const;
    _Bool operator!=(const typeinfo& _Rop) const
        {return (!(*this == _Rop)); }
    _Bool before(const typeinfo&) const;
    const char *name() const
        {return (_Name); }
private:
    const char *_Name;
    _Typedesc _Desc;
    typeinfo(const typeinfo&);
    typeinfo& operator=(const typeinfo&);
    };
#endif                                                     □
```

typeinfo.c   Figure 5.2 shows the file **typeinfo.c**. It defines all the support functions
needed to manipulate objects of class **typeinfo**. Note the assumptions
made here about objects of type **_Typedesc**:

- You can assign such objects with the conventional assignment operator.

- You can compare such objects for equality with **operator==**.

- You can determine whether an object precedes another with **operator<**.

A non-scalar implementation of **_Typedesc** must supply these definitions.

badtypei.c   Finally, Figure 5.3 shows the file **badtypei.c**. It defines the usual member functions for an exception class.

Testing <typeinfo>

ttypeinf.c   Figure 5.4 shows the file **ttypeinf.c**. It tests just the most basic properties of the library support for RTTI. For one thing, there is little to test so
far. For another, I have access to no system that actually implements RTTI.

HAS   As is my practice, I provide yet another parameter to guard implemen-
TYPEINFO   tations that lack a recent language addition. The header **<yxvals.h>** defines the macro **_HAS_TYPEINFO** only for implementations that support the

Figure 5.2:
typeinfo.c

```
// typeinfo -- typeinfo members
#include <typeinfo>

typeinfo::~typeinfo()
    {                                              // destruct a typeinfo
    }

_Bool typeinfo::operator==(const typeinfo& rhs) const
    {                                  // compare two typeinfos for equality
    return (_Desc == rhs._Desc);
    }

_Bool typeinfo::before(const typeinfo& rhs) const
    {                                  // compare two typeinfos for order
    return (_Desc < rhs._Desc);
    }

typeinfo::typeinfo(const typeinfo& rhs)
    : _Name(rhs._Name), _Desc(rhs._Desc)
    {                                  // construct a typeinfo from copy
    }

typeinfo& typeinfo::operator=(const typeinfo& rhs)
    {                                          // assign a typeinfo
    _Name = rhs._Name, _Desc = rhs._Desc;
    return (*this);
    }                                                          □
```

Figure 5.3:
badtypei.c

```
// badtypeid -- badtypeid members
#include <typeinfo>

badtypeid::badtypeid(const char *what, const char *where,
    const char *why)
    : xlogic(what, where, why)
    {                                          // construct a badtypeid
    }

badtypeid::~badtypeid()
    {                                          // destruct a badtypeid
    }

void badtypeid::do_raise()
    {                                          // throw a badtypeid
    _RAISE(*this);
    }                                                          □
```

operator **typeid**. Thus, **ttypeinf.c** is no more portable than **texcepti.c** (see page 78), but it is equally robust during this transitional period in the adoption of Standard C++ features.

The program reports whether or not an implementation supports RTTI. If all goes well, the program prints either:

```
RTTI is implemented.
SUCCESS testing <typeinfo>
```

or:

```
RTTI is not implemented
SUCCESS testing <typeinfo>
```

and takes a normal exit.

Exercises

Exercise 5.1 A *catch* clause catches only thrown objects of a suitable type. Can you use exception handling to determine the actual derived type of an object?

Exercise 5.2 What should the standard RTTI names be for the scalar types?

Exercise 5.3 [Harder] Devise a rule based on these names that predicts the name of an arbitrary type.

Exercise 5.4 [Very hard] Add the constructor **typeinfo(const char *tname)** to class **typeinfo**. For a valid RTTI name (from the previous exercise) it should construct an object **tinfo** that yields the same name on the call **tinfo.name()** and compares equal to other such objects with the same name. Write this constructor. Why would you want such a capability?

Figure 5.4:
ttypeinf.c

```
// test <typeinfo>
#include <assert.h>
#include <string.h>
#include <typeinfo>
#include <iostream>

int main()
        {                    // test basic workings of typeinfo definitions
        badtypeid x1("badtypeid what", "where", "why");
        typeinfo *p1 = 0;
        typeinfo *p2 = 0;
#if _HAS_TYPEINFO
        p1 = typeid (x1);
        p2 = typeid (int);
#endif
        cout << "RTTI is" << (p1 != 0 ? " " : " not ")
                << "implemented" << endl;
        if (p1 != 0)
                {                          // test typeinfo member functions
                assert(p2 != 0);
                assert(!(*p1 == *p2));
                assert(*p1 != *p2);
                assert(p1->before(*p2) || p2->before(*p1));
                assert(strcmp(p1->name(), p2->name()) != 0);
                }
        cout << "SUCCESS testing <typeinfo>" << endl;
        return (0);
        }
```

Chapter 6: `<ios>`

Background

The largest single component of the Standard C++ library is the package called "iostreams." It consists of a whole slew of classes that work together to make input and output look simple. The commonest application is probably the classic:

```
#include <iostream>
.....
    cout << "Hello, world." << endl;
```

which writes the message **Hello, world.** followed by a newline character to the standard output stream (the same stream as controlled by **stdout**).

This simple expression is the tip of a rather large iceberg. Look a bit below the surface. As you might guess, the header **<iostream>** declares all the necessary classes and objects. The class of interest for this example is **ostream**, each of whose objects controls a stream into which you can *insert* characters. That stream can be an output file, a text string that grows dynamically in memory, or lots of other things.

cout   In this particular case, **cout** is a static object of class **ostream** whose name has external linkage. It conspires rather intimately with **stdout**, the familiar Standard C library object of type pointer to **FILE**, to help you write formatted text to the standard output stream. You can freely intermix expressions such as the one above with more traditional calls such as to **putchar** or **printf** and get the result you'd expect. (Translation: you don't have to worry about two different buffering mechanisms saving up characters and writing reordered blocks of characters to the standard output stream. Again, existing implementations don't always make this promise, at least not unless you perform some magic incantation at runtime. And then you can often expect a degradation of performance. The draft C++ Standard hopes to encourage better synchronization of C and C++ I/O, if only to the standard streams.)

The header **<iostream>** declares two similar objects of class **ostream**:

cerr ▪ **cerr**, which controls writes of unbuffered text to the standard error stream, in cooperation with **stderr**, and

clog ▪ **clog**, which also cooperates with **stderr** but which won't necessarily force text to be written out at the end of each insertion operation.

Now take a closer look at the first part of the example expression:

```
cout << "Hello, world." .....
```

inserters The class **ostream** overloads the left-shift operator repeatedly with member functions to provide a rich set of *inserters*. These each encode a right-hand operand by various rules (akin to the conversion specifications for **printf**), then insert the encoded text in the stream controlled by the **ostream** object. In this particular case, the inserter called is:

```
ostream& ostream::operator<<(const char* s);
```

This function knows to write the null-terminated string pointed to by **s** to the output stream controlled by **cout**. Put another way, the function inserts each of the characters from the string into the controlled stream up to but not including the terminating null.

More complicated inserters turn binary integer and floating-point values into sequences of characters that human beings can read. For example, the inserter:

```
ostream& ostream::operator<<(int n);
```

lets you write expressions like:

```
cout << i;
```

that inserts, say, the sequence **-123** in the controlled stream to represent the value –123 stored in the integer object **i**.

C programmers have been doing the same sort of thing for decades by writing:

```
printf("%s %d\n", s, i);
```

So what's the big deal? Well, the inserter approach offers several advantages:

- The translator picks the appropriate inserter to match the right-hand operand type. No need to make sure that conversion specifications in a format string line up with the proper arguments. There is that much less chance that the value will be interpreted incorrectly.

- The notation is often convenient. You can string inserters out left to right, as in the original example above, to perform a series of insertions one after the other.

- The notation can be augmented in various clever ways, as with the **endl** in the original example.

manipulators I won't elaborate much on that last point until later. (See pages 124 and 244.) All you need to know for now is that inserting **endl** in an output stream has the effect of inserting a newline character (**'\n'**) then flushing output to the controlled stream. It is but one of many interesting *manipulators* you can use with the inserter notation.

Other manipulators make up for one of the shortcomings of the inserter notation. Remember that with **printf** you can write some pretty fancy conversion specifications, such as:

```
printf("%+10d\n", i);
```

to force a plus sign on positive output and pad the generated text to (at least) ten characters. But **operator<<** takes only two operands. There is no place to smuggle in that extra formatting information.

The solution is to squirrel away the extra information in the **cout** object before performing the insertion. You can do this by calling member functions, as in the sequence of expression statements:

```
cout.setf(showpos), cout.width(10);
cout < i;
```

Or you can use still more magic manipulators to achieve the same effect, as in the single expression statement:

```
cout << showpos << setw(10) << i;
```

As you can see, it's possible to have manipulators that take arguments. But that involves even more chicanery — a topic for much later. (See Chapter 10: **<iomanip>**.)

In case you're wondering, the effect of **showpos** endures for subsequent inserter calls, in either of the above forms. I'll show how to turn it off later. But the field width evaporates after the first inserter that makes use of it.

cin   You can probably guess what's coming next. The header **<iostream>** also supports reading and decoding text from various streams, including input files. It declares the object **cin**, which helps you *extract* characters from the standard input stream, in cooperation with **stdin**. As you might further guess, this object is of class **istream**, the obvious companion to **ostream**.

extractors   Thus, you can write code involving *extractors*, such as:

```
int n;
cin >> n;
```

to read a sequence of characters and decode them by the usual rules for encoded integer input. The "usual" rules are much as for the function **scanf**:

- Skip any leading white space.

- Gobble one or more characters that look like a valid encoded integer and convert them to *int* representation.

- If no such characters are found, or if the result can't be properly represented as type *int*, report a failure.

One small difference exists between inserters and extractors. You can insert the *value* of an expression into a stream. (This is traditionally called an "rvalue" by C programmers.) But you extract from a stream into an *object*. (Those same C programmers would call this an "lvalue," but the times and the terms they are a changing.) A corresponding difference appears in C — you call **printf** with arbitrary expressions for value arguments and you call **scanf** with pointer arguments to designate the objects to store into.

In C++, you declare extractors with *reference* parameters, as in:

```
istream& istream::operator>>(int& n);
```

That ampersand lets you write a bald **n**, but still ensures that a real live lvalue gets bound to the corresponding parameter within the function. No worry about null pointers or other pointer type mismatches.

You can also play tricks with extractors, by the way, much like that **endl** shorthand I showed earlier. If all you want to do, for example, is consume any pending white space from the standard input stream, you can write:

```
cin >> ws;
```

and the job is done. Similarly, you can communicate various bits of formatting information through other manipulators. much as with output streams. Once again, I won't begin to explain the magic behind that bald **ws** manipulator until later. (See page 214.) Just note for now that such tricks are possible.

history   Iostreams has several clear advantages over the formatted I/O functions of the Standard C library. Little wonder that every implementation of C++ has for years offered some version of iostreams, however much the implementation may vary in its support for other common library classes. Jerry Schwarz, now at Lucid Technology, gets credit for fleshing out an early version of iostreams, for helping it become widespread, and for seeing the package through more than one major revision. He is also responsible for drafting the specification of iostreams in the draft Standard C++ library.

Unfortunately, little has been written on the detailed architecture of iostreams. About the only commercially available guide is a book by Steve Teale (**Tea93**), which deals with a slightly dated version of the package. Since the draft C++ Standard progresses even beyond the current field version, Teale's book offers only limited guidance. Still, it's better than what you typically get from the vendor of a C++ translator.

extensibility   For many class libraries this lack of information would not be a problem. But iostreams is designed to be extensible in several important ways:

- You can overload **operator<<** to define additional inserters, or **operator>>** to define additional extractors, for classes you define.

- You can define a host of manipulators that work with objects of class **istream**, class **ostream**, or both.

- You can derive new classes from class **streambuf**, then override several of its virtual member functions, to control sources and sinks of characters of your own devising.

Such power is not without its complexity. And complexity can be mastered safely only with careful guidance. To date, programmers have relied on access to bits and pieces of library source code to get that guidance. Where such code is not available, or where it varies among implementations, adequate guidance has been lacking. Standardizing iostreams is thus a major step toward helping the package realize its full potential.

ios   I begin with some basic architecture. Classes **istream** and **ostream** have several requirements in common:

- Both must control a stream through the agency of some object of class **streambuf**.

- Both must maintain some notion of the state of the controlled stream, including a history of any errors that have occurred and how to report future errors.

- Both must memorize a host of formatting options, as I described earlier.

- Both must define a number of common types for describing the member functions and objects needed to effectuate the above requirements.

<ios>   To provide all these services, both classes derive from the virtual public base class **ios**. And that is the topic of this chapter. This base class is sufficiently large, and comes with enough related functions, that the draft C++ Standard assigns it a header of its very own, called **<ios>**.

Note that class **ios** is a *virtual* base for both **istream** and **ostream**. That is more a matter of compatibility with past practice than of necessity. Existing implementations control a stream that can be both read and written by declaring an object of class **iostream**, defined something like:

iostream
```
class iostream
    : public istream, ostream {
    ..... };
```

Were the base **ios** not virtual, this class would end up with *two* such subobjects, not just one. That would lead to all sorts of confusion in trying to control the bidirectional stream. Making the base virtual adds a bit of complexity here and there, particularly with initialization, but it permits the traditional definition of class **iostream** for those who want to use it.

This class is *not* a part of the draft C++ Standard, however, because it is no longer necessary. The preferred way to control a bidirectional stream is with two separate objects, one of class **istream** and one of class **ostream**. Both point to the same **streambuf** object, which is the only agent that really has to know that the stream can be both read and written. (That is part of the reason why an object of class **ios** contains a pointer to a separate **streambuf** object, instead of the object itself. See page 122.)

coming
attractions Class **ios** lies at the heart of the iostreams machinery, so I deal with it first. You have to understand it in detail to make sense of its more visible descendants, the classes **istream** and **ostream**. But it is far from the whole story. That tale spreads out over the next *eight* chapters as well. Here is a brief overview of what you can expect.

streambuf Class **streambuf** is equally fundamental to iostreams. (See Chapter 7: **<streambuf>**.) You can get quite a lot of use out of iostreams without ever declaring a **streambuf** object directly. But if you want to know how the whole works hangs together, or if you want to extend iostreams in nontrivial ways, you *must* know how this class behaves in detail.

manipulators Manipulators are yet another topic. Many are simple and easy to explain
istream once you know the basics of classes **ios**, **istream** (Chapter 8: **<istream>**),
ostream and **ostream** (Chapter 9: **<ostream>**). But all those manipulators with

arguments derive from one of several "interesting" template classes. (See Chapter 10: **<iomanip>**.) Of course, in many existing implementations, they are built atop even more interesting macros.

strstreambuf   Two library classes show some of the power of class **streambuf**. Class
stringbuf   **strstreambuf** provides capabilities akin to the Standard C library function **sprintf**. (See Chapter 11: **<strstream>**.) You can use inserters and extractors to manipulate in-memory text strings. Class **stringbuf** is similar, except that it eases conversion between such in-memory strings and objects of the standard library class **string**. (See Chapter 12: **<sstream>**.) I discuss class **string** after I've presented the last of iostreams. (See Chapter 15: **<string>**.)

filebuf   Finally, I return to the objects that manipulate external files. Class **file-**
cin   **buf** lets you open files by name, much as with **fopen**, then manipulate them
cout   as iostreams. (See Chapter 13: **<fstream>**.) And the objects **cin**, **cout**, **cerr**,
cerr   and **clog** have their own tale as well. (See Chapter 14: **<iostream>**.) It turns
clog   out that initializing these creatures, as required by the draft C++ Standard, is no mean feat.

class   As a quick overview, here are the two hierarchies that subsume most of
hierarchy   the classes that make up iostreams. One is based on class **ios**, the topic of this chapter. The other is based on class **streambuf**, which I cover in the next chapter:

```
ios
    istream                        streambuf
        istrstream                     strstreambuf
        istringstream                  stringbuf
        ifstream                       filebuf
        istdiostream                   stdiobuf
    ostream
        ostrstream
        ostringstream
        ofstream
        ostdiostream
```

The description of the iostreams facilities occupies about half the library portion of the Informat Review Draft. It's going to take quite some time to cover it in adequate detail.

What the Draft C++ Standard Says

Class **ios** takes a lot of declaring, as you can well imagine from this brief introduction. For all that, it is neither a big nor a very complex class. Mostly, it involves a lot of small details that come into focus in ensuing chapters. Still, all that declaring demands a comparable amount of explaining. And class **ios** does lie at the heart of the entire iostreams class hierarchy. So you will find a lot of standardese here. And a deal of description to follow.

If you are familiar with some existing implementation of iostreams, be particularly alert. Many small differences in past practice have been ironed out here. Some are bound to surprise practically everybody.

17.4 Input/output

This subclause describes a number of headers that together support input, output, and internal data conversions.

17.4.1 Header `<ios>`

The Header `<ios>` defines a type and several function signatures for controlling how to interpret text input from a sequence of characters and how to generate text output to a sequence of characters.

17.4.1.1 Class `ios`

```
class ios {
public:
    class failure : public xmsg {
    public:
        failure(const char* where_val = 0,
            const char* why_val = 0);
        virtual ~failure();
    protected:
//      virtual void do_raise();                              inherited
    };
    typedef T1 fmtflags;
    static const fmtflags dec;
    static const fmtflags fixed;
    static const fmtflags hex;
    static const fmtflags internal;
    static const fmtflags left;
    static const fmtflags oct;
    static const fmtflags right;
    static const fmtflags scientific;
    static const fmtflags showbase;
    static const fmtflags showpoint;
    static const fmtflags showpos;
    static const fmtflags skipws;
    static const fmtflags unitbuf;
    static const fmtflags uppercase;
    static const fmtflags adjustfield;
    static const fmtflags basefield;
    static const fmtflags floatfield;
    typedef T2 iostate;
    static const iostate badbit;
    static const iostate eofbit;
    static const iostate failbit;
    static const iostate goodbit;
    typedef T3 openmode;
    static const openmode app;
    static const openmode ate;
    static const openmode binary;
    static const openmode in;
    static const openmode out;
    static const openmode trunc;
    typedef T4 seekdir;
    static const seekdir beg;
    static const seekdir cur;
    static const seekdir end;
```

```
//  typedef T5 io_state;                                    optional
//  typedef T6 open_mode;                                   optional
//  typedef T7 seek_dir;                                    optional
    class Init {
    public:
        Init();
        ~Init();
    private:
//      static int init_cnt;                                exposition only
    };
    ios(streambuf* sb_arg);
    virtual ~ios();
    operator void*() const
    int operator!() const
    ios& copyfmt(const ios& rhs);
    ostream* tie() const;
    ostream* tie(ostream* tiestr_arg);
    streambuf* rdbuf() const;
    streambuf* rdbuf(streambuf* sb_arg);
    iostate rdstate() const;
    void clear(iostate state_arg = goodbit);
//  void clear(io_state state_arg);                         optional
    void setstate(iostate state_arg);
//  void setstate(io_state state_arg);                      optional
    int good() const;
    int eof() const;
    int fail() const;
    int bad() const;
    iostate exceptions() const;
    void exceptions(iostate except_arg);
//  void exceptions(io_state except_arg);                   optional
    fmtflags flags() const;
    fmtflags flags(fmtflags fmtfl_arg);
    fmtflags setf(fmtflags fmtfl_arg);
    fmtflags setf(fmtflags fmtfl_arg, fmtflags mask);
    void unsetf(fmtflags mask);
    int fill() const;
    int fill(int ch);
    int precision() const;
    int precision(int prec_arg);
    int width() const;
    int width(int wide_arg);
    static int xalloc();
    long& iword(int index_arg);
    void*& pword(int index_arg);
protected:
    ios();
    void init(streambuf* sb_arg);
private:
//  streambuf* sb;                                          exposition only
//  ostream* tiestr;                                        exposition only
//  iostate state;                                          exposition only
//  iostate except;                                         exposition only
//  fmtflags fmtfl;                                         exposition only
//  int prec;                                               exposition only
```

```
//  int wide;                                          exposition only
//  char fillch;                                       exposition only
//  static int index;                                  exposition only
//  int* iarray;                                       exposition only
//  void** parray;                                     exposition only
};
```

The class **ios** serves as a base class for the classes **istream** and **ostream**. It defines several member types:

- a class **failure** derived from **xmsg**;
- a class **Init**;
- three bitmask types, **fmtflags**, **iostate**, and **openmode**;
- an enumerated type, **seekdir**.

It maintains several kinds of data:

- a pointer to a *stream buffer,* an object of class **streambuf**, that controls sources (input) and sinks (output) of character sequences;
- state information that reflects the integrity of the stream buffer;
- control information that influences how to interpret (format) input sequences and how to generate (format) output sequences;
- additional information that is stored by the program for its private use.

For the sake of exposition, the maintained data is presented here as:

- **streambuf* sb**, points to the stream buffer;
- **ostream* tiestr**, points to an output sequence that is *tied* to (synchronized with) an input sequence controlled by the stream buffer;
- **iostate state**, holds the control state of the stream buffer;
- **iostate except**, holds a mask that determines what elements set in **state** cause exceptions to be thrown;
- **fmtflags fmtfl**, holds format control information for both input and output;
- **int wide**, specifies the field width (number of characters) to generate on certain output conversions;
- **int prec**, specifies the precision (number of digits after the decimal point) to generate on certain output conversions;
- **char fillch**, specifies the character to use to pad (fill) an output conversion to the specified field width;
- **static int index**, specifies the next available unique index for the integer or pointer arrays maintained for the private use of the program, initialized to an unspecified value;
- **int* iarray**, points to the first element of an arbitrary-length integer array maintained for the private use of the program;
- **void** parray**, points to the first element of an arbitrary-length pointer array maintained for the private use of the program.

17.4.1.1.1 Class ios::failure

failure
```
class failure : public xmsg {
public:
    failure(const char* where_arg = 0, const char* why_arg = 0);
    virtual ~failure();
protected:
//  virtual void do_raise();                              inherited
};
```

The class **failure** defines the base class for the types of all objects thrown as exceptions, by functions in the Standard C++ library, to report errors detected during stream buffer operations.

17.4.1.1.1.1 ios::failure::failure(const char*, const char*)

constructor

```
failure(const char* where_arg = 0, const char* why_arg = 0);
```

Constructs an object of class **failure**, initializing the base class with **xmsg(**_what_arg_**,** _where_arg_**,** _why_arg_**)**, where the NTMBS pointed to by _what_arg_ is unspecified.

17.4.1.1.1.2 ios::failure::~failure()

destructor

```
virtual ~failure();
```

Destroys an object of class **failure**.

17.4.1.1.1.3 ios::failure::do_raise()

do_raise

```
// virtual void do_raise(); inherited
```

Behaves the same as **xmsg::do_raise()**.

17.4.1.1.2 Type ios::fmtflags

fmtflags

```
typedef T1 fmtflags;
```

The type **fmtflags** is a bitmask type (indicated here as _T1_) with the elements:

- **dec**, set to convert integer input or to generate integer output in decimal base;
- **fixed**, set to generate floating-point output in fixed-point notation;
- **hex**, set to convert integer input or to generate integer output in hexadecimal base;
- **internal**, set to add fill characters at a designated internal point in certain generated output;
- **left**, set to add fill characters on the right (final positions) of certain generated output;
- **oct**, set to convert integer input or to generate integer output in octal base;
- **right**, set to add fill characters on the left (initial positions) of certain generated output;
- **scientific**, set to generate floating-point output in scientific notation;
- **showbase**, set to generate a prefix indicating the numeric base of generated integer output;
- **showpoint**, set to generate a decimal-point character unconditionally in generated floating-point output;
- **showpos**, set to generate a + sign in non-negative generated numeric output;
- **skipws**, set to skip leading white space before certain input operations;
- **unitbuf**, set to flush output after each output operation;
- **uppercase**, set to replace certain lowercase letters with their uppercase equivalents in generated output.

Type **fmtflags** also defines the constants:

- **adjustfield**, the value **left | right | internal**;
- **basefield**, the value **dec | oct | hex**;
- **floatfield**, the value **scientific | fixed**.

17.4.1.1.3 Type ios::iostate

iostate

```
typedef T2 iostate;
```

The type **iostate** is a bitmask type (indicated here as _T2_) with the elements:

- **badbit**, set to indicate a loss of integrity in an input or output sequence (such as an irrecoverable read error from a file);

- **eofbit**, set to indicate that an input operation reached the end of an input sequence;
- **failbit**, set to indicate that an input operation failed to read the expected characters, or that an output operation failed to generate the desired characters.

Type **iostate** also defines the constant:

- **goodbit**, the value zero.

17.4.1.1.4 Type ios::openmode

openmode

```
typedef T3 openmode;
```

The type **openmode** is a bitmask type (indicated here as **T3**) with the elements:

- **app**, set to seek to end-of-file before each write to the file;
- **ate**, set to open a file and seek to end-of-file immediately after opening the file;
- **binary**, set to perform input and output in binary mode (as opposed to text mode);
- **in**, set to open a file for input;
- **out**, set to open a file for output;
- **trunc**, set to truncate an existing file when opening it.

17.4.1.1.5 Type ios::seekdir

seekdir

```
typedef T4 seekdir;
```

The type **seekdir** is an enumerated type (indicated here as **T4**) with the elements:

- **beg**, to request a seek (positioning for subsequent input or output within a sequence) relative to the beginning of the stream;
- **cur**, to request a seek relative to the current position within the sequence;
- **end**, to request a seek relative to the current end of the sequence.

17.4.1.1.6 Type ios::io_state

io_state

```
// typedef T5 io_state;                                    optional
```

The type **io_state** is a synonym for an integer type (indicated here as **T5**) that permits certain member functions to overload others on parameters of type **iostate** and provide the same behavior.

17.4.1.1.7 Type ios::open_mode

open_mode

```
// typedef T6 open_mode;                                   optional
```

The type **open_mode** is a synonym for an integer type (indicated here as **T6**) that permits certain member functions to overload others on parameters of type **openmode** and provide the same behavior.

17.4.1.1.8 Type ios::seek_dir

seek_dir

```
// typedef T7 seek_dir;                                    optional
```

The type **seek_dir** is a synonym for an integer type (indicated here as **T7**) that permits certain member functions to overload others on parameters of type **iostate** and provide the same behavior.

17.4.1.1.9 Class ios::Init

Class
ios::Init

```
class Init {
public:
    Init();
    ~Init();
private:
```

```
//  static int init_cnt;                              exposition only
};
```

The class **Init** describes an object whose construction ensures the construction of the four objects declared in **<iostream>** that associate file stream buffers with the standard C streams provided for by the functions declared in **<stdio.h>**. For the sake of exposition, the maintained data is presented here as:

• **static int** *init_cnt*, counts the number of constructor and destructor calls for class **Init**, initialized to zero.

17.4.1.1.9.1 ios::Init::Init()

constructor

```
Init();
```

Constructs an object of class **Init**. If *init_cnt* is zero, the function stores the value one in *init_cnt*, then constructs and initializes the four objects **cin** (17.4.9.1), **cout** (17.4.9.2), **cerr** (17.4.9.3), and **clog** (17.4.9.4). In any case, the function then adds one to the value stored in *init_cnt*.

17.4.1.1.9.2 ios::Init::~Init()

destructor

```
~Init();
```

Destroys an object of class **Init**. The function subtracts one from the value stored in *init_cnt* and, if the resulting stored value is one, calls **cout.flush()**, **cerr.flush()**, and **clog.flush()**.

17.4.1.1.10 ios::ios(streambuf*)

constructor

```
ios(streambuf* sb_arg);
```

Constructs an object of class **ios**, assigning initial values to its member objects by calling **init(sb_arg)**.

17.4.1.1.11 ios::~ios()

destructor

```
virtual ~ios();
```

Destroys an object of class **ios**.

17.4.1.1.12 ios::operator void*()

operator void*

```
operator void*() const
```

Returns a non-null pointer (whose value is otherwise unspecified) if **failbit | badbit** is set in *state*.

17.4.1.1.13 ios::operator!()

operator!

```
int operator!() const
```

Returns a nonzero value if **failbit | badbit** is set in *state*.

17.4.1.1.14 ios::copyfmt(const ios&)

copyfmt

```
ios& copyfmt(const ios& rhs);
```

Assigns to the member objects of ***this** the corresponding member objects of *rhs*, except that:

• *sb* and *state* are left unchanged;

• *except* is altered last by calling **exception(rhs.except)**.

If any newly stored pointer values in ***this** point at objects stored outside the object *rhs*, and those objects are destroyed when *rhs* is destroyed, the newly stored pointer values are altered to point at newly constructed copies of the objects.

The function returns ***this**.

17.4.1.1.15 ios::tie()

tie

```
ostream* tie() const;
```

Returns *tiestr*.

17.4.1.1.16 ios::tie(ostream*)

tie

```
ostream* tie(ostream* tiestr_arg);
```

Assigns *tiestr_arg* to *tiestr* and then returns the previous value stored in *tiestr*.

17.4.1.1.17 ios::rdbuf()

rdbuf

```
streambuf* rdbuf() const;
```

Returns *sb*.

17.4.1.1.18 ios::rdbuf(streambuf*)

rdbuf

```
streambuf* rdbuf(streambuf* sb_arg);
```

Assigns *sb_arg* to *sb*, then calls **clear()**. The function returns the previous value stored in *sb*.

17.4.1.1.19 ios::rdstate()

rdstate

```
iostate rdstate() const;
```

Returns *state*.

17.4.1.1.20 ios::clear(iostate)

clear

```
void clear(iostate state_arg = goodbit);
```

Assigns *state_arg* to *state*. If *sb* is a null pointer, the function then sets **badbit** in *state*. If *state & except* is zero, the function returns. Otherwise, the function calls *fail.raise()* for an object *fail* of class *failure*, constructed with argument values that are implementation-defined.

17.4.1.1.21 ios::clear(io_state)

clear

```
//  void clear(io_state state_arg);                              optional
```

Calls **clear((iostate)**_state_arg_**)**.

17.4.1.1.22 ios::setstate(iostate)

setstate

```
void setstate(iostate state_arg);
```

Calls **clear(**_state_ **|** _state_arg_**)**.

17.4.1.1.23 ios::setstate(io_state)

setstate

```
//  void setstate(io_state state_arg);                           optional
```

Calls **clear((iostate)(**_state_ **|** _state_arg_**))**.

17.4.1.1.24 ios::good()

good

```
int good() const;
```

Returns a nonzero value if *state* is zero.

17.4.1.1.25 ios::eof()

eof

```
int eof() const;
```

Returns a nonzero value if **eofbit** is set in *state*.

17.4.1.1.26 ios::fail()

fail

```
int fail() const;
```

Returns a nonzero value if **badbit** or **failbit** is set in *state*.

17.4.1.1.27 ios::bad()

bad

```
int bad() const;
```

Returns a nonzero value if **badbit** is set in *state*.

17.4.1.1.28 ios::exceptions()

exceptions

```
 iostate exceptions() const;
```

Returns *except*.

17.4.1.1.29 ios::exceptions(iostate)

exceptions

```
 void exceptions(iostate except_arg);
```

Assigns *except_arg* to *except*, then calls **clear(*state*)**.

17.4.1.1.30 ios::exceptions(io_state)

exceptions

```
 // void exceptions(io_state except_arg);                          optional
```

Calls **exceptions((iostate)*except_arg*)**.

17.4.1.1.31 ios::flags()

flags

```
 fmtflags flags() const;
```

Returns *fmtfl*.

17.4.1.1.32 ios::flags(fmtflags)

flags

```
 fmtflags flags(fmtflags fmtfl_arg);
```

Assigns *fmtfl_arg* to *fmtfl* and then returns the previous value stored in *fmtfl*.

17.4.1.1.33 ios::setf(fmtflags)

setf

```
 fmtflags setf(fmtflags fmtfl_arg);
```

Sets *fmtfl_arg* in *fmtfl* and then returns the previous value stored in *fmtfl*.

17.4.1.1.34 ios::setf(fmtflags, fmtflags)

setf

```
 fmtflags setf(fmtflags fmtfl_arg, fmtflags mask);
```

Clears *mask* in *fmtfl*, sets *fmtfl_arg* & *mask* in *fmtfl*, and then returns the previous value stored in *fmtfl*.

17.4.1.1.35 ios::unsetf(fmtflags)

unsetf

```
 void unsetf(fmtflags mask);
```

Clears *mask* in *fmtfl*.

17.4.1.1.36 ios::fill()

fill

```
 int fill() const;
```

Returns *fill*.

17.4.1.1.37 ios::fill(int)

fill

```
 int fill(int fillch_arg);
```

Assigns *fillch_arg* to *fillch* and then returns the previous value stored in *fillch*.

17.4.1.1.38 ios::precision()

precision

```
 int precision() const;
```

Returns *prec*.

17.4.1.1.39 ios::precision(int)

precision

```
 int precision(int prec_arg);
```

Assigns *prec_arg* to *prec* and then returns the previous value stored in *prec*.

17.4.1.1.40 ios::width()

width

```
 int width() const;
```

Returns *wide*.

17.4.1.1.41 ios::width(int)

width
   `int width(int wide_arg);`

Assigns *wide_arg* to *wide* and then returns the previous value stored in *wide*.

17.4.1.1.42 ios::xalloc()

xalloc
   `static int xalloc();`

Returns *index++*.

17.4.1.1.43 ios::iword(int)

iword
   `long& iword(int idx);`

If *iarray* is a null pointer, allocates an array of **int** of unspecified size and stores a pointer to its first element in *iarray*. The function then extends the array pointed at by *iarray* as necessary to include the element *iarray[idx]*. Each newly allocated element of the array is initialized to zero. The function returns *iarray[idx]*. After a subsequent call to **iword(int)** for the same object, the earlier return value may no longer be valid.[84]

17.4.1.1.44 ios::pword(int)

pword
   `void* & pword(int idx);`

If *parray* is a null pointer, allocates an array of pointers to *void* of unspecified size and stores a pointer to its first element in *parray*. The function then extends the array pointed at by *parray* as necessary to include the element *parray[idx]*. Each newly allocated element of the array is initialized to a null pointer. The function returns *parray[idx]*. After a subsequent call to **pword(int)** for the same object, the earlier return value may no longer be valid.

17.4.1.1.45 ios::ios()

constructor
   `ios();`

Constructs an object of class **ios**, assigning initial values to its member objects by calling **init(0)**.

17.4.1.1.46 ios::init(streambuf*)

init
   `void init(streambuf* sb_arg);`

Assigns:
- *sb_arg* to *sb*;
- a null pointer to *tiestr*;
- **goodbit** to *state* if *sb_arg* is not a null pointer, otherwise **badbit** to *state*;
- **goodbit** to *except*;
- **skipws | dec** to *fmtfl*;
- zero to *wide*;
- 6 to *prec*;
- the space character to *fillch*;
- a null pointer to *iarray*;
- a null pointer to *parray*.

17.4.1.2 dec(ios&)

dec
   `ios& dec(ios& str);`

Calls *str*.setf(ios::dec, ios::basefield) and then returns *str*.[85]

17.4.1.3 fixed(ios&)

fixed
   `ios& fixed(ios& str);`

Calls *str*.setf(ios::fixed, ios::floatfield) and then returns *str*.

17.4.1.4 `hex(ios&)`

hex

   `ios& hex(ios& `*`str`*`);`

Calls *`str`*`.setf(ios::hex, ios::basefield)` and then returns *`str`*.

17.4.1.5 `internal(ios&)`

internal

   `ios& internal(ios& `*`str`*`);`

Calls *`str`*`.setf(ios::internal, ios::adjustfield)` and then returns *`str`*.

17.4.1.6 `left(ios&)`

left

   `ios& left(ios& `*`str`*`);`

Calls *`str`*`.setf(ios::left, ios::adjustfield)` and then returns *`str`*.

17.4.1.7 `noshowbase(ios&)`

noshowbase

   `ios& noshowbase(ios& `*`str`*`);`

Calls *`str`*`.unsetf(ios::showbase)` and then returns *`str`*.

17.4.1.8 `noshowpoint(ios&)`

noshowpoint

   `ios& noshowpoint(ios& `*`str`*`);`

Calls *`str`*`.unsetf(ios::showpoint)` and then returns *`str`*.

17.4.1.9 `noshowpos(ios&)`

noshowpos

   `ios& noshowpos(ios& `*`str`*`);`

Calls *`str`*`.unsetf(ios::showpos)` and then returns *`str`*.

17.4.1.10 `noskipws(ios&)`

noskipws

   `ios& noskipws(ios& `*`str`*`);`

Calls *`str`*`.unsetf(ios::skipws)` and then returns *`str`*.

17.4.1.11 `nouppercase(ios&)`

nouppercase

   `ios& nouppercase(ios& `*`str`*`);`

Calls *`str`*`.unsetf(ios::uppercase)` and then returns *`str`*.

17.4.1.12 `oct(ios&)`

oct

   `ios& oct(ios& `*`str`*`);`

Calls *`str`*`.setf(ios::oct, ios::basefield)` and then returns *`str`*.

17.4.1.13 `right(ios&)`

right

   `ios& right(ios& `*`str`*`);`

Calls *`str`*`.setf(ios::right, ios::adjustfield)` and then returns *`str`*.

17.4.1.14 `scientific(ios&)`

scientific

   `ios& scientific(ios& `*`str`*`);`

Calls *`str`*`.setf(ios::scientific, ios::floatfield)` and then returns *`str`*.

17.4.1.15 `showbase(ios&)`

showbase

   `ios& showbase(ios& `*`str`*`);`

Calls *`str`*`.setf(ios::showbase)` and then returns *`str`*.

17.4.1.16 `showpoint(ios&)`

showpoint

   `ios& showpoint(ios& `*`str`*`);`

Calls *`str`*`.setf(ios::showpoint)` and then returns *`str`*.

17.4.1.17 `showpos(ios&)`

showpos

   `ios& showpos(ios& `*`str`*`);`

Calls **str.setf(ios::showpos)** and then returns **str**.

17.4.1.18 skipws(ios&)

skipws

```
ios& skipws(ios& str);
```

Calls **str.setf(ios::skipws)** and then returns **str**.

17.4.1.19 uppercase(ios&)

uppercase

```
ios& uppercase(ios& str);
```

Calls **str.setf(ios::uppercase)** and then returns **str**.

Footnotes:

Footnotes

84) An implementation is free to implement both the integer array pointed at by **iarray** and the pointer array pointed at by **parray** as sparse data structures, possibly with a one-element cache for each.

85) The function signature **dec(ios&)** can be called by the function signature **ostream& stream::operator<<(ostream& (*)(ostream&))** to permit expressions of the form **cout << dec** to change the format flags stored in **cout**.

Future Directions

optional members
As I mentioned earlier, the Committee has changed the status of the "optional members" that use the older types **ios::io_state, ios:: open_mode**, and **ios::seek_dir**. (See page 16.) These are now "deprecated features." There's no harm, and much good, in continuing to provide them as part of a Standard C++ library, however.

locale objects
As I also mentioned earlier, the Committee has added locale objects as well. (See page 32.) You can now *imbue* a stream with a *locale object*, which encapsulates some locale. Inserters and extractors operating on that stream follow the conventions specified by the imbued locale. The visible effect on class **ios** is the addition of member functions for imbuing a locale object and later accessing it to determine locale-specific behaviors.

wide-character streams
Far more ambitious is a change that replaces all of the iostreams machinery with templates. The idea is to ease the introduction of "wide-character streams." These are streams that traffic in wide characters (elements of type **wchar_t**), rather than the traditional single-byte characters (elements of type *char*). Cultures that use very large character sets — such as in Japan and China — are a growing force in both commercial programming and international programming-language standards. The people who serve these rapidly growing markets naturally want the same power that has been available to cultures with smaller character sets. In this case, the drive is toward providing *all* of iostreams in parallel versions, for both single-byte and wide characters (and for possibly other "characters" as well).

Redefining iostreams in terms of templates has certain advantages. The draft C++ Standard can describe the common properties of all flavors of iostreams just once. (By contrast, see Chapter 15: **<string>** and Chapter 16: **<wstring>**.) The relatively few differences are then easier to summarize and highlight. Moreover, templates are open ended. The Standard C++

library may be obliged to provide instantiations only for single-byte and wide characters, but programmers are free to instantiate more. That can prove to be a boon should unforeseen uses arise.

template On the other hand, templates pose certain problems as well. The current **limitations** state of the art does not encourage ambitious use of templates. Existing implementations favor different organizations of source files (still within the scope of the draft C++ Standard). It can be a challenge to write a nontrivial template that works unchanged with multiple C++ translators. Some of those implementations also suffer surprising capacity limitations when processing templates. Experienced C++ programmers know to keep templates small and simple, for now, if they hope to move them about freely.

Naturally, all such limitations should disappear over time. The draft C++ Standard has added several new features to the language, including exceptions, templates, runtime type identification (RTTI), and *namespace* declarations. The Standard C++ library cannot ignore these language additions simply because current support is weak. It is a delicate balancing act to specify a Standard C++ library that can be implemented adequately in the short term, but that uses the full language in the long term.

functional Please note, however, that the basic *functionality* of traditional (single-**compatibility** byte) iostreams does not change with the introduction of templates. A program written to match the Informal Review Draft should remain essentially unchanged. Only a (very new) program that uses, say, wide-character streams will notice the lack of iostreams templates. So even with all the machinery of iostreams officially replaced by templates, the lessons of this and subsequent chapters still prove useful. So, in fact, is the code presented here. Think of it as an efficient specialization of iostreams for type *char*.

Using `<ios>`

You have little or no occasion to include the header `<ios>` directly. It is, in fact, one of a handful of headers invented by the Committee simply to split the iostreams declarations into more manageable pieces. But the chances are very good that you'll use the *contents* of `<ios>` in a program. Class `ios` is the base class for both `istream` and `ostream`, which mediate practically all input and output in the iostreams package. The base class summarizes what is *common* to both input and output. And the functions defined in this header, which operate on objects of class `ios`, are sometimes useful both for input and output.

member Class `ios` defines several member types. Some are used directly within **types** the class, others are not. But all are involved in the operation of iostreams. Packing this assortment of types within class `ios` is an attempt, from the earliest days of iostreams, to reduce the clutter of names.

Here is the first use made of two flavors of types introduced in the "front matter" of the library portion of the draft C++ Standard (see page 11):

enumerated types ■ An *enumerated type* (17.1.5.10.1) is an "honest" enumeration. It defines one or more *enumerated elements,* which are all distinct values. You assign such elements only to an object of the proper enumerated type, and you compare such stored values only for equality with these elements.

bitmask types ■ A *bitmask type* (17.1.5.10.2) is an enumerated type with the bitwise operations (such as AND, OR, and EXCLUSIVE OR) defined for it. It defines one or more *bitmask elements,* whose values typically each have just one distinct bit set. It may also define *bitmask constants,* whose values are the union of zero or more bitmask elements. You perform bitwise operations only between values of the same bitmask type.

The draft C++ Standard introduces these definitions for several reasons. One is to give implementors some latitude in how they specify such types. Nobody wants to have to slavishly duplicate all those **static const** declarations. (See, for example, page 109.) An **enum** is much tidier. On the other hand, **enum** doesn't tell the whole story. So the draft C++ Standard defines a term that has additional constraints.

enumeration overloading The Committee has added the ability to overload on enumerations. Now you can, and must, write a passel of functions to define the bitwise operations, as the draft C++ Standard shows. Otherwise, you'll find yourself writing lots of **(int)** type casts, to combine bitmask values, and even more type casts to bless the *int* results before storing them in bitmask objects.

All of this machinery is designed to improve the type safety of programs that fiddle bits. Too often, innocent programmers confuse two flavors of bitmask elements and mix them inappropriately in an expression. The resulting mishmash goes undiagnosed if all the operands have type *int*. Subsequent debugging is a pain.

optional types Nevertheless, the draft C++ Standard permits an implementation to retain support for several of the older types as well. I list them below, for completeness, but I suggest you avoid using them. I also suggest you exercise caution in using the new enumerated and bitmask types. Not all implementations support overloading on enumerations yet. The type safety promised by the draft C++ Standard can't always be delivered. But get in the habit of pretending that the stronger type checking is there. Otherwise, you'll have lots of code to rewrite later.

The member types in class **ios** are:

failure ■ **ios::failure** — an exception class that describes all objects thrown as exceptions by the Standard C++ library to report iostreams problems

fmtflags ■ **ios::fmtflags** — a bitmask type that specifies combinations of formatting attributes for input and/or output

iostate ■ **ios::iostate** — a bitmask type that specifies combinations of status indications for an associated **streambuf** object

openmode ■ **ios::openmode** — a bitmask type that specifies combinations of qualifiers when opening a file

seekdir ■ **ios::seekdir** — an enumerated type that specifies what kind of positioning operation to perform on a **streambuf** object

io_state ■ **ios::io_state** — the precursor to **iostate**, retained for backward compatibility

open_mode ■ **ios::open_mode** — the precursor to **openmode**, retained for backward compatibility

seek_dir ■ **ios::seek_dir** — the precursor to **seekdir**, retained for backward compatibility

I write all these nested types with the **ios::** access qualifier as a reminder. Typically, you must write the fully qualified name for any use you make of these types in a program. It doesn't hurt to make a habit of doing so.

stream buffers Perhaps the single most important role for an object of class **ios** is to keep tabs on an associated object of class **streambuf**, also known as a *stream buffer*. All the actual inserting and extracting of character sequences occurs under control of a stream buffer. An **ios** object merely takes notes. It remembers formatting preferences for objects (typically of the derived classes **istream** or **ostream**) that convert between these character sequences and values of various types within a program. And it remembers the status of earlier operations on the stream buffer. I deal with the latter first.

rdbuf The member function **rdbuf()** returns the stored pointer to an object of class **streambuf**. The pointer can be null. Often, the pointer value is stored when the **ios** object is first constructed and never changes afterward. But you can also store a different pointer in an **ios** object **x** by calling **x.rdbuf(sb)**, or even **x.rdbuf(0)**. Yes, the name is a misnomer, since the **rd** suggests that you can only "read" the stored pointer.

One reason to call **rdbuf** is to set up a bidirectional stream. (See page 107.) You might write something like:

```
#include <fstream>
    .....
    ifstream istr("abc", ios::in | ios::out);
    ostream ostr(istr.rdbuf());
```

This sequence constructs two objects. **istr** has a type derived from class **istream** (and hence from **ios**). This particular constructor opens the file **"abc"**, places it under control of a stream buffer, and then points at that stream buffer (if the open was successful). The stream buffer is a member object within **istr**. **ostr** is a generic **ostream** object (also derived from **ios**). Here, it is constructed with a specific pointer to **streambuf** argument. The expression **istr.rdbuf()** supplies the pointer to the stream buffer to be shared between the two objects.

Equally, you might write something like:

```
#include <fstream>
    .....
    ifstream istr("abc", ios::in | ios::out);
    ostream ostr;
    ostr.rdbuf(istr.rdbuf());
```

to achieve the same effect with somewhat less grace.

The only other time you have occasion to use **rdbuf** is to access **streambuf** member functions directly. (See Chapter 7: **<streambuf>**.) You can do quite a lot with iostreams, however, without descending to this level.

An operation on a stream buffer that fails sets one or more status bits within an **ios** object. These status bits inhabit a member object of type **iostate**. Call:

clear ■ **x.clear()** to clear all status bits

clear ■ **x.clear(new_stat)** to reset the status bits to the value **new_stat** (yes, it's another misnomer)

setstate ■ **setstate(mask)** to set the status bits in **mask** without clearing other status bits

rdstate   Other member functions let you read and test the status bits in various ways. The simplest call is **x.rdstate()**, which returns all the status bits. The remaining member functions of this ilk are more specific:

good ■ **good()** (same as **rdstate() == (iostate)0**) indicates *no* errors

bad ■ **bad()** (same as **rdstate() & ios::badbit**) indicates a null stream-buffer pointer, a read/write error, or some other loss of integrity of the associated stream buffer

eof ■ **eof()** (same as **rdstate() & ios::eofbit**) indicates that an earlier extraction operation has encountered the end of the input stream

fail ■ **fail()** (same as **rdstate() & (ios::badbit | ios::failbit)**) indicates that an earlier extraction operation has failed to match the required pattern of input text

ipfx   Any functions you write to manipulate an **istream** or **ostream** object
opfx should be careful to test the status bits before trying anything rash. You don't want to reach for a stream buffer that isn't there, for example. Typically this service is provided for you by the functions **istream::ipfx** (page 196) or **ostream::opfx** (page 238). If you get more deeply involved in manipulating objects based on class **ios**, however, you may have occasion to call the above member functions directly.

exception   What if you don't want your program simply to keep stumbling on in the presence of iostream failures? Or what if you don't want to test the result of every operation that calls in turn on iostreams functions? That's where the newly added *exception mask* comes in. An **ios** object contains a second member object of type **iostate**, in addition to the status bits. You can obtain its stored value by calling **x.exception()**, or set it by calling **x.exception(iostate)**. Any change of status, or of the exception mask, that results in **x.rdstate() & x.exceptions()** becoming nonzero throws an exception of class **ios::failure**. (As usual, the "throw" of the exception object **ex** is actually the call **ex.raise()**.)

Initially, the exception mask is zero for any object of class **ios**. If you don't believe in exceptions, or don't want to be bothered by them here, you can simply ignore this machinery.

operator!   Class **ios** has one other bit of cuteness with regard to testing its status
void * flags. It overloads the unary **operator!()** and the unary type cast **opera-**
tor void *() as a quick way of testing whether either of the status bits
ios::failbit or **ios::badbit** is nonzero. Thus, you can write:

```
if (!(cin >> obj))
    cerr << "can't read obj" << endl;
```

because the type of **cin** is derived from class **ios**. Be warned, however, that
the traditional effect of some tests like this is not always the same as for the
draft C++ Standard. Check your old code carefully when upgrading it to
conform.

formatting   The second most important role for class **ios**, after keeping tabs on a
information stream buffer, is remembering formatting information. The member functions that do so are mostly trivial. Quite a few, in fact, merely store a new
value in one of the private member objects, then return the previously
stored value. Many others just return the stored value. It is up to the derived
classes **istream**, **ostream**, and their kin to actually *do* something with all
this information.

manipulators   You alter or access formatting information directly by calling member
functions for objects of class **ios**. A more indirect approach is to invoke
manipulators. These exploit clever member functions in classes derived from
ios. Class **istream**, for example, defines the extractor member function:

```
istream& operator>>(ios& (*_F)(ios&))
    {(*_F)(*(ios *)this); return (*this); }
```

which interacts neatly with a declaration such as:

```
ios& dec(ios&);
```

The net effect is that, for an **istream** object such as **cin**, you can write:

```
cin >> dec;
```

and obtain the same effect as the call:

```
dec(cin);
```

It takes a bit of study to see why this is true, but the time is well repaid.

Naturally, class **ostream** defines a similar inserter member function to
support the same clever notation. Some manipulators work only with
extractors, some only with inserters, and some with both. The ones that
work with both are declared in **<ios>** if they require no additional arguments. Otherwise, they are declared in **<iomanip>**.

Here is a summary of the stored values used as formatting information.
I describe each in terms of the member function that returns the value. Far
more often, you call a member function of the same name, but with a
different function signature, to store a new value. But that is not necessarily
the best way to do so. The manipulators described later in this chapter, and
in Chapter 10: **<iomanip>**, are often more convenient.

fill ■ **fill()** — returns the *fill* character that some inserters use to pad to a
setfill specified field width. **fill(int)** stores a new value, but the inserter
setfill(int) (17.4.5.4.4) is often handier.

precision ■ **precision()** — returns the *precision* value that floating-point inserters
setprecision   use to determine the number of digits to insert. **precision(int)** stores
                a new value, but the inserter **setprecision(int)** (17.4.5.4.5) is often
                handier.

width ■ **width()** — returns the *width* value that the extractor **istream& opera-**
setw   **tor>>(char*)** uses to determine the maximum number of characters to
        extract, and that many inserters use to determine the minimum number
        of characters to insert. An extractor or inserter that makes use of the
        width invariably sets it to zero — this is the one piece of formatting
        information that is transient. **width(int)** stores a new value, but the
        inserter **setw(int)** (17.4.5.4.6) is often handier.

xalloc ■ **xalloc()** — returns an index, suitable for use with **iword** or **pword**
        below, that is unique among *all* **ios** objects during a given program
        execution. This machinery lets you store in an **ios** object some integer
        or object pointer values used only by inserters or extractors you supply.
        This extensibility is handy when simply recycling the fill character,
        precision, and/or width doesn't do the job. Typically, you call **xalloc**
        once for each unique index you need, and store the index in a static
        object. The functions that need to access the values stored with the **ios**
        object then use this index to select the appropriate elements. (If you don't
        understand why you might need this capability, you're probably not
        ready to indulge in such antics.)

iword ■ **iword(int n)** — returns a reference to element **n**, of type *long*, of an
        extensible sequence peculiar to each **ios** object. Each element is initial-
        ized to zero. The reference remains valid, even for storing a new value,
        until the next call to either **iword** or **pword** for the **ios** object. The
        last-stored values of all elements are retained for the lifetime of the **ios**
        object and are copied as part of its value.

pword ■ **pword(int n)** — returns a reference to element **n**, of type *pointer to void*,
        of an extensible sequence peculiar to each **ios** object. Otherwise, its
        behavior is the same as for **iword**, above.

tie ■ **tie()** — returns a pointer to an **ostream** object that is *tied* to the **ios**
      object and is "flushed" (synchronized with any external files) before any
      insertion or extraction controlled by the **ios** object. **tie(ostream *)**
      stores a new value. You are likely to use this machinery only on those
      rare occasions when you set up your own interactive files. (See Chapter
      14: **<iostream>** for the commonest use of tieing.)

flags ■ **flags()** — returns the *format flags* that many extractors and inserters
        use to qualify their behavior.

        Format flags make a significant topic in its own right. Most flags (which
        are bitmask elements) act independently, but some belong to one of three
        groups that are always considered together. The flag **skipws** affects only
        extractors. Nearly all other flags affect only inserters, but one group (**base-
        field**) affects both. And essentially all flags are defined precisely in terms
        of *conversion specifications* for the Standard C library functions **fprintf** or

fscanf, declared in **<stdio.h>**. (See **P&B92** for a readable summary of the conversion specifications.) The flags, and their groupings, are:

adjustfield ■ **adjustfield** is the union of the flags **internal**, **left**, and **right**. The
internal width value can call for an inserter to generate additional fill characters,
left besides the minimum character sequence required to represent the
right inserted value. This group determines whether fill characters are inserted at some specified internal point in the character sequence (**internal**), before the character sequence (**right**), or after the character sequence (any other flag settings, but preferably **left** for clarity).

basefield ■ **basefield** is the union of the flags **dec**, **hex**, and **oct**. Inserters and
dec extractors can convert integer values with a variety of assumed numeric
hex bases. This group determines whether the base is 16 (**hex**), 8 (**oct**), or
oct decimal (any other flag settings, but preferably **dec** for clarity). More precisely, an integer *extractor* takes a zero value for these three flags as special license to determine the base from the form of the input field, the same as the **i** conversion specifier does for **fscanf**.

floatfield ■ **floatfield** is the union of the flags **fixed** and **scientific**. Inserters
fixed can convert floating-point values in several formats, which are best
scientific characterized by the analogous conversion specifiers for **fprintf**. This group determines whether the behavior is the same as for a conversion specifier of **f** (**fixed**), **e** (**scientific**), or **g** (any other flag settings).

showbase ■ **showbase** determines whether an integer inserter generates the prefix **0x** or **0X** for base 16 conversion, or **0** for base 8 conversion (the same as the **#** conversion qualifier for **fprintf**).

showpoint ■ **showpoint** determines whether a floating-point inserter generates a trailing decimal point that would otherwise be suppressed (the same as the **#** conversion qualifier for **fprintf**). The Standard C library function **localeconv**, declared in **<locale.h>**, defines what constitutes the decimal point for the current locale.

showpos ■ **showpos** determines whether an integer or floating-point inserter generates a **+** before a non-negative value (the same as the **+** conversion qualifier for **fprintf**).

skipws ■ **skipws** determines whether most extractors first extract and discard all white-space characters before extracting the characters to convert. The Standard C library function **isspace**, declared in **<ctype.h>**, defines what constitutes white space for the current locale.

unitbuf ■ **unitbuf** determines whether an inserter flushes the **ostream** object upon completion. You set this flag for a stream whose associated output file should be kept in close synchronization with the program, such as an interactive device or a debugging trace file. Otherwise, you should leave this flag reset and favor the often dramatic improvement in performance that comes with more aggressive buffering of output streams.

uppercase ■ **uppercase** determines whether an integer or floating-point inserter generates any letters as uppercase instead of lowercase (the same as an uppercase conversion specifier for **fprintf**).

flags   Class **ios** provides a variety of member functions to manipulate format
setf   flags. You can replace all flags with **flags(fmtflags)**, set selected flags
unsetf   with **setf(fmtflags)**, clear selected flags with **unsetf(fmtflags)**, and
set selected flags under a mask with **setf(fmtflags, fmtflags)**. The last
member function is useful for setting one flag in a group and clearing the
rest in that group, as in **setf(dec, basefield)**.

resetiosflags   Once again, you may find a manipulator handier for fiddling with
setbase   format flags. You can set selected flags with **setiosflags(ios::fmt-**
setiosflags   **flags)** or clear selected flags with **resetiosflags(ios::fmtflags)**. To
set one of the common bases (8, 10, or 16), use **setbase(int)**. Any other
value for base clears all flags in this group, resulting in adaptive extraction
or decimal (base 10) insertion. All these manipulators are declared in
<iomanip>. (See Chapter 10: **<iomanip>**.)

more   The header **<ios>** also declares a gazillion manipulators that set and
manipulators   clear format flags, singly and in groups:

```
internal          left              right
dec               hex               oct
fixed             scientific
noshowbase        showbase
noshowpoint       showpoint
noshowpos         showpos
noskipws          skipws
nouppercase       uppercase
```

While the set isn't complete, it does meet the commonest needs.

A good style for manipulating formatting information is to leave the
most-used values, and all flags, in their default state most of the time:
format flags are **skipws | dec**, width is zero, precision is 6, and fill
character is space. The width reverts to zero as soon as it's used. The others
you should revert before you forget.

copyfmt   One handy addition made by the Committee eases saving and restoring
all the formatting information at once. The member function **copy-**
fmt(const ios&) copies everything but the pointer to stream buffer and
the status bits from one **ios** object to another. Thus, you might write:

```
const static ios default_ios;
ios save;
save.copyfmt(stdout);                        // save old info
stdout.copyfmt(default_ios);          // revert to defaults
stdout << setbase(16) << showbase << uppercase;
.....                                  // muck with stdout freely
stdout.copyfmt(save);                       // restore old info
```

Here is probably the only occasion you will have to declare objects of class
ios not in captivity.

A small warning, however. The expression **x.copyfmt(y)** also copies
the exception mask to **x**. Its last act before returning is to test whether
x.rdstate() & x.exceptions() is nonzero. If so, the function throws an
ios::failure exception. Even if you plan for such exceptions, the timing
here can be surprising.

init   As a final note, class **ios** is more public than most about how it handles
Init initializations. The protected member function **init** initializes an **ios**
subobject in a base class. Constructing an object of class **ios::Init** ensures
that the standard streams (**cin**, etc.) are properly initialized. Chances are
slim that you will have need to call on either of these mechanisms explicitly.
I suggest you resist the temptation to play with them. (I show how the
Stndard C++ library uses them on your behalf in this and subsequent
chapters.)

Implementing <ios>

ios   Figure 6.1 shows the file **ios**, which implements the standard header
<ios>. Much of it follows directly from the requirements of the draft C++
Standard. But it also includes a number of mysteries required by this
particular implementation.

_CATCH_IO_   The draft C++ Standard dictates how inserters and extractors should
EXCEPTIONS handle exceptions. (See Chapter 8: **<istream>** and Chapter 9: **<ostream>**.)
I anticipate, however, that not everybody will want the added overhead of
exception handling, particularly in every inserter and extractor. Thus, the
internal header **<yxvals.h>** must define the macro **_CATCH_IO_EXCEP-**
TIONS to turn on exception handling within iostreams.

_TRY_IO_BEGIN   Even if you want to conform exactly to the draft C++ Standard, not all
_CATCH_IO_END C++ implementations support exception handling. I define the set of
_CATCH_IO_(x) macros **_TRY_IO_BEGIN**, **_CATCH_IO_END**, and **_CATCH_IO_(x)** to encapsu-
late the code changes needed to deal with diverse environments. Within a
member function of a class derived from **ios**, you can write:

```
_TRY_IO_BEGIN
.....      // perform streambuf operations
_CATCH_IO_END
```

This expands to code that catches all exceptions thrown between the two
macros. The *catch* clause sets the status bit **ios::failbit** and propagates
the exception. Within any other function that operates on an object **x**
derived from **ios**, you replace the second macro with **_CATCH_IO_(x)**.

_RERAISE   The above macros are mostly based, in turn, on macros introduced for
the header **<exception>**. (See pages 72 and 77.) The only new creature is
the macro **_RERAISE**. The internal header **<yxvals.h>** defines this macro
as the expression **throw**, to propagate a pending exception, if exceptions
are implemented, or as **xmsg::_Throw(0)** if not. (See page 72.)

enumeration   Still another implementation artifact is the handling of enumeration
overloading overloading. As I mentioned on page 121, the Committee has added
enumeration overloading to C++, but not all implementations have caught
up with this change. That poses several problems in the writing of this and
later standard headers. The draft C++ Standard specifies that several
bitmask types be defined as enumerations with bitwise operators overloaded. But older implementations balk at such antics. So an implementation provides these overloaded operator definitions for a bitmask type only

Figure 6.1:
ios
Part 1 of 3

```
// ios standard header
#ifndef _IOS_
#define _IOS_
#include <exception>
            // I/O exception macros
#if _CATCH_IO_EXCEPTIONS
 #define _TRY_IO_BEGIN    _TRY_BEGIN
 #define _CATCH_IO_END    _CATCH_ALL \
     setstate(badbit); _RERAISE; _CATCH_END
 #define _CATCH_IO_(x)    _CATCH_ALL \
     (x).setstate(ios::badbit); _RERAISE; _CATCH_END
#else
 #define _TRY_IO_BEGIN    {
 #define _CATCH_IO_END    }
 #define _CATCH_IO_(x)    }
#endif
class ostream; class streambuf;
            // class ios
class ios {
public:
                // class failure
    class failure : public xmsg {
    public:
        failure(const char *_X = 0, const char *_Y = 0,
            const char *_Z = 0)
            : xmsg(_X, _Y, _Z) {};
        virtual ~failure();
    protected:
        virtual void do_raise();
    };
    enum _Fmtflags {skipws = 0x0001, unitbuf = 0x0002,
        uppercase = 0x0004, showbase = 0x0008,
        showpoint = 0x0010, showpos = 0x0020,
        left = 0x0040, right = 0x0080, internal = 0x0100,
        dec = 0x0200, oct = 0x0400, hex = 0x0800,
        scientific = 0x1000, fixed = 0x2000,
        adjustfield = 0x01c0, basefield = 0x0e00,
        floatfield = 0x3000, _Fmtmask = 0x3fff, _Fmtzero = 0};
    enum _Iostate {goodbit = 0x0, eofbit = 0x1,
        failbit = 0x2, badbit = 0x4, _Statmask = 0x7};
    enum _Openmode {in = 0x01, out = 0x02, ate = 0x04,
        app = 0x08, trunc = 0x10, binary = 0x20};
    enum seekdir {beg = 0, cur = 1, end = 2};
    _BITMASK(_Fmtflags, fmtflags);
    _BITMASK(_Iostate, iostate);
    _BITMASK(_Openmode, openmode);
    typedef short io_state, open_mode, seek_dir;
    enum _Uninitialized {_Noinit};
                // class Init
    class Init {
    public:
        Init();
        ~Init();
    private:
        static int _Init_cnt;
```

```
        };
                // class _Iosarray
class _Iosarray {
public:
    _Iosarray(int _Idx, _Iosarray *_Link = 0)
        : _Next(_Link), _Index(_Idx), _Lo(0), _Vp(0) {}
    _Iosarray *_Next;
    int _Index;
    long _Lo;
    void *_Vp;
    };
ios(streambuf *_S)
    {init(_S); }
ios(const ios& _R)
    {init(0), *this = _R; }
ios& operator=(const ios&);
virtual ~ios();
operator void *() const
    {return (void *)(!*this ? 0 : this); }
_Bool operator!() const
    {return ((_State & (failbit|badbit)) != 0); }
ios& copyfmt(const ios&);
ostream *tie() const
    {return (_Tiestr); }
ostream *tie(ostream *);
streambuf *rdbuf() const
    {return (_Sb); }
streambuf *rdbuf(streambuf *);
iostate rdstate() const
    {return (_State); }
void clear(iostate = goodbit);
void clear(io_state _St)
    {clear((iostate)_St); }
void setstate(iostate _St)
    {clear(_State | _St); }
void setstate(io_state _St)
    {setstate((iostate)_St); }
_Bool good() const
    {return (_State == goodbit); }
_Bool eof() const
    {return (_State & eofbit); }
_Bool fail() const
    {return (_State & (badbit | failbit)); }
_Bool bad() const
    {return (_State & badbit); }
iostate exceptions() const
    {return (_Except); }
void exceptions(iostate);
void exceptions(io_state _St)
    {exceptions((iostate)_St); }
fmtflags flags() const
    {return (_Fmtfl); }
fmtflags flags(fmtflags);
fmtflags setf(fmtflags);
fmtflags setf(fmtflags, fmtflags);
```

```
        void unsetf(fmtflags);
        int fill() const
            {return (_Fillch); }
        int fill(int);
        int precision() const
            {return (_Prec); }
        int precision(int);
        int width() const
            {return (_Wide); }
        int width(int);
        static int xalloc()
            {return (_Index++); }
        long& iword(int _Idx)
            {return (_Findarr(_Idx)._Lo); }
        void *& pword(int _Idx)
            {return (_Findarr(_Idx)._Vp); }
protected:
        ios()
            {init(0); }
        ios(_Uninitialized)
            {}
        void init(streambuf *);
private:
        streambuf *_Sb;
        ostream *_Tiestr;
        iostate _State, _Except;
        fmtflags _Fmtfl;
        int _Prec, _Wide;
        char _Fillch;
        static int _Index;
        _Iosarray *_Arr;
        _Iosarray& _Findarr(int);
        void _Tidy();
        };
            // manipulators
ios& dec(ios&);
ios& fixed(ios&);
ios& hex(ios&);
ios& internal(ios&);
ios& left(ios&);
ios& noshowbase(ios&);
ios& noshowpoint(ios&);
ios& noshowpos(ios&);
ios& noskipws(ios&);
ios& nouppercase(ios&);
ios& oct(ios&);
ios& right(ios&);
ios& scientific(ios&);
ios& showbase(ios&);
ios& showpoint(ios&);
ios& showpos(ios&);
ios& skipws(ios&);
ios& uppercase(ios&);
#endif
```

if it supports enumeration overloading. Otherwise, an implementation defines each of the bitmask types as a synonym for *int*.

But the draft C++ Standard also specifies several "optional" types for backward compatibility. These are all traditionally synonyms for type *int*. A number of member functions are overloaded on the newer bitmask type and the older type. To avoid ambiguous function signatures, this implementation defines the optional types as synonyms for type *short*.

_Fmtflags
_Iostate
_Openmode
Perhaps now you can see why the bitmask types are defined in two stages. The first stage declares an enumeration with a secret name — **_Fmtflags**, **_Iostate**, or **_Openmode**. The second stage ties the secret name to the public name — **fmtflags**, **iostate**, or **openmode**, respectively. It also supplies the overloaded function definitions, if the implementation supports enumeration overloading. Otherwise, the public name is defined as a synonym for *int*.

_BITMASK
The macro **_BITMASK** encapsulates this tedious process. The internal header **<yxvals.h>** contains either the macro definition:

```
#define _BITMASK(E, T) \
E& operator&=(E& _X, E _Y) \
    {_X = (E)(_X & _Y); return (_X); } \
E& operator|=(E& _X, E _Y) \
    {_X = (E)(_X | _Y); return (_X); } \
E& operator^=(E& _X, E _Y) \
    {_X = (E)(_X ^ _Y); return (_X); } \
E& operator&(E _X, E _Y) \
    {return ((E)(_X & _Y)); } \
E& operator|(E _X, E _Y) \
    {return ((E)(_X | _Y)); } \
E& operator^(E _X, E _Y) \
    {return ((E)(_X ^ _Y)); } \
E& operator~(E _X) \
    {return ((E)~_X); } \
typedef E T
```

if enumerations are overloadable. or:

```
#define _BITMASK(E, T) typedef int T
```

(Yes, much of the first definition can be replaced by a template, but not all of it. And templates aren't available in some current implementations.)

_Uninitialized
Another piece of implementation-specific magic is the secret enumeration **_Uninitialized**. I use it as an explicit warning that something unusual is happening. The draft C++ Standard requires that the standard streams be usable even within static constructors. No reliable way currently exists for ordering initialization among static constructors in separate translation units. Hence, the objects that implement the standard streams cannot rely on the normal workings of static constructors to get the streams ready in time.

double construction
The solution is to *double construct* certain critical objects in the iostreams portion of the Standard C++ library. (While the theology of this practice is still questionable, every implementation of C++ that I know of makes it work right, of necessity.) To ensure that the actual object initialization occurs only when expected, the static constructors for these critical objects

must assuredly do nothing. (So too must certain destructors, but that's another part of the story.) I discuss these matters at greater length in Chapter 14: **<iostream>**.

_Noinit   Thus, certain iostream constructors have a single parameter of type **_Uninitialized**. (See, for example, Chapter 7: **<streambuf>**, Chapter 8: **<istream>**, Chapter 9: **<ostream>**, and Chapter 13: **<fstream>**.) The only legitimate value of this type is **_Noinit**. A constructor such as **streambuf(ios::_Noinit)** clearly advertizes that it performs *no* initialization of its object members.

_Iosarray   One more implementation artifact is worthy of remark. The member functions **iword** and **pword** demand some internal representation for extensible arrays. I chose to represent both, for simplicity, in one singly linked list. Class **_Iosarray** describes a list element. An object of this class stores:

- a value of type *long*
- a value of type *pointer to void*
- the index value for the element
- a link to the next element in the list

The list is not kept in any particular order.

_Findarr   The private member function **_Findarr** maintains a linked list of these elements for each **ios** object. As you can see, both **iword** and **pword** are implemented in terms of a single call to **_Findarr**.

ios.c   Figure 6.2 shows the file **ios.c**. It defines all the member functions likely to be required by any object of class **ios**. That includes overrides for virtual member functions in the exception class **ios::failure**.

clear   Three of the member functions are workhorses. **clear(iostate)** is the
init one place that checks whether to throw an **ios::failure** exception. You
_Tidy will find that all other functions with this responsibility pass it off to this member function. **init(streambuf *)** likewise performs all initializations of **ios** objects. And **_Tidy** performs all cleanups. Its primary responsibility is to free any list elements allocated by **_Findarr**.

destructor   The destructor for class **ios** is bizarre. For an arbitrary **ios** object, it is obliged to call **_Tidy**. But for the objects that control the four standard streams, it is obliged *not* to do so. Just as these four objects must survive double construction, so too must they endure double destruction. Otherwise, you could not safely use the standard streams from static destructors, which the draft C++ Standard explicitly allows. I chose this overt kludge, over more subtle methods, to handle this unusual requirement.

iosassig.c   Figure 6.3 shows the file **iosassig.c**, which defines the assignment operator for class **ios**. The default versions of this function and the copy constructor are unacceptable because of the need to copy an allocated list. It is also conceivable that the act of copying will trip across the need to throw an exception. Neither member function is large, but both have their fragile aspects.

Figure 6.2:
ios.c

```
// ios -- ios basic members
#include <iostream>

int ios::_Index = 0;

ios::failure::~failure()
    {                                          // destruct a failure
    }

void ios::failure::do_raise()
    {                                          // throw an ios::failure
    _RAISE(*this);
    }

ios::~ios()
    {                        // destruct an ios -- DO (ALMOST) NOTHING
    if (this != (ios *)&cin && this != (ios *)&cout
        && this != (ios *)&cerr && this != (ios *)&clog)
        _Tidy();
    }

void ios::clear(iostate ns)
    {                              // clear all but selected state bits
    _State = ns & _Statmask;
    if (_Sb == 0)
        _State |= badbit;
    if (_State & _Except)
        failure(_State & badbit ? "ios::badbit set"
            : _State & failbit ? "ios::failbit set"
            : "ios::eofbit set").raise();
    }

void ios::init(streambuf *sb)
    {                                          // initialize a new ios
    _Sb = sb;
    _Tiestr = 0;
    _Except = goodbit;
    _Fmtfl = skipws | dec;
    _Prec = 6;
    _Wide = 0;
    _Fillch = ' ';
    _Arr = 0;
    clear(goodbit);
    }

void ios::_Tidy()
    {                                      // discard storage for an ios
    _Iosarray *q1, *q2;
    for (q1 = _Arr; q1 != 0; q1 = q2)
        q2 = q1->_Next, delete q1;
    _Arr = 0;
    }
```

Figure 6.3:
iosassig.c

```
// iosassign -- ios::operator=(const ios&)
#include <ios>

ios& ios::operator=(const ios& rhs)
    {                                           // assign to an ios
    if (this != &rhs)
        {                                       // safe to copy
        _Sb = rhs._Sb;
        _State = rhs._State;
        copyfmt(rhs);                           // cause any throw at end
        }
    return (*this);
    }                                                               □
```

Figure 6.4:
ioscopyf.c

```
// ioscopyfmt -- ios::copyfmt(const ios&)
#include <ios>

ios& ios::copyfmt(const ios& rhs)
    {                               // copy format info from another ios
    if (this != &rhs)
        {                                   // copy all but _Sb and _State
        _Tidy();
        _Tiestr = rhs._Tiestr;
        _Fmtfl = rhs._Fmtfl;
        _Prec = rhs._Prec;
        _Wide = rhs._Wide;
        _Fillch = rhs._Fillch;
        _Iosarray *p = rhs._Arr;
        for (_Arr = 0; p != 0; p = p->_Next)
            if (p->_Lo != 0 || p->_Vp != 0)
                {                       // copy over nonzero array values
                iword(p->_Index) = p->_Lo;
                pword(p->_Index) = p->_Vp;
                }
        exceptions(rhs._Except);            // cause any throw at end
        }
    return (*this);
    }                                                               □
```

Figure 6.5:
iosexcep.c

```
// iosexceptions -- ios::exceptions(iostate)
#include <ios>

void ios::exceptions(iostate ne)
    {                                       // set selected exception bits
    _Except = ne & _Statmask;
    clear(_State);
    }                                                               □
```

ioscopyf.c   Figure 6.4 shows the file **ioscopyf.c**, which defines the member func-
iosexcep.c   tion copyfmt(const ios&). Note that it, too, is careful to complete its work
              before risking an operation that can throw an exception. Figure 6.5 shows
              the file **ioexcep.c**, which defines the member function **excep-**

Figure 6.6:
iosfill.c

```
// iosfill -- ios::fill(int)
#include <ios>

int ios::fill(int nf)
    {                                       //   set fill character
    char of = _Fillch;
    _Fillch = nf;
    return (of);
    }                                                              □
```

Figure 6.7:
iosflags.c

```
// iosflags -- ios::flags(fmtflags)
#include <ios>

ios::fmtflags ios::flags(fmtflags nf)
    {                                       // replace format bits
    fmtflags of = _Fmtfl;
    _Fmtfl = nf & _Fmtmask;
    return (of);
    }                                                              □
```

Figure 6.8:
iospreci.c

```
// iosprecision -- ios::precision(int)
#include <ios>

int ios::precision(int np)
    {                                       // set precision
    int op = _Prec;
    _Prec = np;
    return (op);
    }                                                              □
```

Figure 6.9:
iosrdbuf.c

```
// iosrdbuf -- ios::rdbuf(streambuf *)
#include <ios>

streambuf *ios::rdbuf(streambuf *nb)
    {                                       // set new streambuf
    streambuf *ob = _Sb;
    _Sb = nb;
    clear(goodbit);
    return (ob);
    }                                                              □
```

Figure 6.10:
iossetf1.c

```
// iossetf1 -- ios::setf(fmtflags)
#include <ios>

ios::fmtflags ios::setf(fmtflags nf)
    {                                       // set format bits
    ios::fmtflags of = _Fmtfl;
    _Fmtfl |= nf & _Fmtmask;
    return (of);
    }                                                              □
```

Figure 6.11:
`iossetf2.c`

```
// iossetf2 -- ios::setf(fmtflags, fmtflags)
#include <ios>

ios::fmtflags ios::setf(fmtflags nf, fmtflags mask)
    {                               // set format bits under mask
    ios::fmtflags of = _Fmtfl;
    _Fmtfl = (_Fmtfl & ~mask) | (nf & mask & _Fmtmask);
    return (of);
    }                                                          □
```

Figure 6.12:
`iostie.c`

```
// iostie -- ios::tie(ostream *)
#include <ios>

ostream *ios::tie(ostream *nt)
    {                                              // set new tie
    ostream *ot = _Tiestr;
    _Tiestr = nt;
    return (ot);
    }                                                          □
```

Figure 6.13:
`ioswidth.c`

```
// ioswidth -- ios::width(int)
#include <ios>

int ios::width(int nw)
    {                                                // set width
    int ow = _Wide;
    _Wide = nw;
    return (ow);
    }                                                          □
```

`tions(iostate)`. It in turn relies on `clear(iostate)`, as I described above, to throw an exception as needed.

A whole slew of functions simply store a new value in one of the private member objects within an object of class `ios`. They also return the previously stored value:

`iosfill.c` ■ Figure 6.6 shows the file `iosfill.c`, which defines the member function `fill(int)`.

`iosflags.c` ■ Figure 6.7 shows the file `iosflags.c`, which defines the member function `flags(fmtflags)`.

`iospreci.c` ■ Figure 6.8 shows the file `iospreci.c`, which defines the member function `precision(int)`.

`iosrdbuf.c` ■ Figure 6.9 shows the file `iosrdbuf.c`, which defines the member function `rdbuf(streambuf *)`.

`iossetf1.c` ■ Figure 6.10 shows the file `iossetf1.c`, which defines the member function `setf(fmtflags)`.

`iossetf2.c` ■ Figure 6.11 shows the file `iossetf2.c`, which defines the member function `setf(fmtflags, fmtflags)`. The second operand serves as a

Figure 6.14:
iosunset.c

```
// iosunsetf -- ios::unsetf(fmtflags)
#include <ios>

void ios::unsetf(fmtflags mask)
    {                                          // reset format bits under mask
    _Fmtfl &= ~mask;
    }                                                                          □
```

Figure 6.15:
iosarray.c

```
// iosarray -- ios::_Findarr(int)
#include <ios>

ios::_Iosarray& ios::_Findarr(int idx)
    {                         // locate or make a variable array element
    _Iosarray *p, *q;
    if (idx < 0)
        failure("invalid ios::iword/pword index").raise();
    for (p = _Arr, q = 0; p != 0; p = p->_Next)
        if (p->_Index == idx)
            return (*p);
        else if (q == 0 && p->_Lo == 0 && p->_Vp == 0)
            q = p;
    if (q != 0)
        {                                          // recycle existing element
        q->_Index = idx;
        return (*q);
        }
    if ((_Arr = new _Iosarray(idx, _Arr)) == 0)
        _Nomemory();
    return (*_Arr);
    }                                                                          □
```

mask. The function replaces format flags selected by the second operand
with corresponding flags from the first operand.

iostie.c ■ Figure 6.12 shows the file **iostie.c**, which defines the member function
tie(ostream *).

ioswidth.c ■ Figure 6.13 shows the file **ioswidth.c**, which defines the member
function **width(int)**.

iosunset.c Figure 6.14 shows the file **iosunset.c**, which defines the member
function **unsetf(fmtflags)**. Unlike its fellow flag-twiddling functions, it
makes no attempt to return the previous stored value.

iosarray.c Figure 6.15 shows the file **iosarray.c**, which defines the function
_Findarr. It locates an existing list element with the desired index, if
possible. Otherwise, it recycles a list element or allocates a new one.

The remaining source files implement manipulators for class **ios**:

dec.c ■ Figure 6.16 shows the file **dec.c**, which defines the function **dec(ios&)**.

fixed.c ■ Figure 6.17 shows the file **fixed.c**, which defines the function
fixed(ios&).

hex.c ■ Figure 6.18 shows the file **hex.c**, which defines the function **hex(ios&)**.

internal.c	■ Figure 6.19 shows the file **internal.c**, which defines the function **internal(ios&)**.
left.c	■ Figure 6.20 shows the file **left.c**, which defines the function **left(ios&)**.
noskipws.c	■ Figure 6.21 shows the file **noskipws.c**, which defines the function **noskipws(ios&)**.
noupperc.c	■ Figure 6.22 shows the file **noupperc.c**, which defines the function **nouppercase(ios&)**.
nshowbas.c	■ Figure 6.23 shows the file **nshowbas.c**, which defines the function **noshowbase(ios&)**.
nshowpoi.c	■ Figure 6.24 shows the file **nshowpoi.c**, which defines the function **noshowpoint(ios&)**.
nshowpos.c	■ Figure 6.25 shows the file **nshowpos.c**, which defines the function **noshowpos(ios&)**.
oct.c	■ Figure 6.26 shows the file **oct.c**, which defines the function **oct(ios&)**.
right.c	■ Figure 6.27 shows the file **right.c**, which defines the function **right(ios&)**.
scientif.c	■ Figure 6.28 shows the file **scientif.c**, which defines the function **scientific(ios&)**.
showbase.c	■ Figure 6.29 shows the file **showbase.c**, which defines the function **showbase(ios&)**.
showpoin.c	■ Figure 6.30 shows the file **showpoin.c**, which defines the function **showpoint(ios&)**.
showpos.c	■ Figure 6.31 shows the file **showpos.c**, which defines the function **showpos(ios&)**.
skipws.c	■ Figure 6.32 shows the file **skipws.c**, which defines the function **skipws(ios&)**.
uppercas.c	■ Figure 6.33 shows the file **uppercas.c**, which defines the function **uppercase(ios&)**.
Init	I defer discussion of the code for class **ios::Init** until much later, for reasons that will become apparent. (See Chapter 14: **<iostream>**.)

Figure 6.16:
dec.c

```
// dec -- dec(ios&)
#include <ios>

ios& dec(ios& strios)
    {                                // set decimal input/output mode
    strios.setf(ios::dec, ios::basefield);
    return (strios);
    }                                                            □
```

Figure 6.17:
fixed.c

```
// fixed -- fixed(ios&)
#include <ios>

ios& fixed(ios& strios)
    {                                             // set fixed output mode
    strios.setf(ios::fixed, ios::floatfield);
    return (strios);
    }                                                                      □
```

Figure 6.18:
hex.c

```
// hex -- hex(ios&)
#include <ios>

ios& hex(ios& strios)
    {                                      // set hexadecimal input/output mode
    strios.setf(ios::hex, ios::basefield);
    return (strios);
    }                                                                      □
```

Figure 6.19:
internal.c

```
// internal -- internal(ios&)
#include <ios>

ios& internal(ios& strios)
    {                                           // set internal output mode
    strios.setf(ios::internal, ios::adjustfield);
    return (strios);
    }                                                                      □
```

Figure 6.20:
left.c

```
// left -- left(ios&)
#include <ios>

ios& left(ios& strios)
    {                                               // set left output mode
    strios.setf(ios::left, ios::adjustfield);
    return (strios);
    }                                                                      □
```

Figure 6.21:
noskipws.c

```
// noskipws -- nosskipws(ios&)
#include <ios>

ios& noskipws(ios& strios)
    {                                           // clear skipws input mode
    strios.unsetf(ios::skipws);
    return (strios);
    }                                                                      □
```

```
// nouppercase -- nouppercase(ios&)
#include <ios>

ios& nouppercase(ios& strios)
    {                                    // clear uppercase output mode
    strios.unsetf(ios::uppercase);
    return (strios);
    }                                                              □
```

```
// nshowbase -- noshowbase(ios&)
#include <ios>

ios& noshowbase(ios& strios)
    {                                    // clear showbase output mode
    strios.unsetf(ios::showbase);
    return (strios);
    }                                                              □
```

```
// nshowpoint -- noshowpoint(ios&)
#include <ios>

ios& noshowpoint(ios& strios)
    {                                    // clear showpoint output mode
    strios.unsetf(ios::showpoint);
    return (strios);
    }                                                              □
```

```
// nshowpos -- noshowpos(ios&)
#include <ios>

ios& noshowpos(ios& strios)
    {                                    // clear showpos output mode
    strios.unsetf(ios::showpos);
    return (strios);
    }                                                              □
```

```
// oct -- oct(ios&)
#include <ios>

ios& oct(ios& strios)
    {                                    // set octal input/output mode
    strios.setf(ios::oct, ios::basefield);
    return (strios);
    }                                                              □
```

Figure 6.27:
right.c

```
// right -- right(ios&)
#include <ios>

ios& right(ios& strios)
    {                                           // set right output mode
    strios.setf(ios::right, ios::adjustfield);
    return (strios);
    }                                                                □
```

Figure 6.28:
scientif.c

```
// scientific -- scientific(ios&)
#include <ios>

ios& scientific(ios& strios)
    {                                           // set scientific output mode
    strios.setf(ios::scientific, ios::floatfield);
    return (strios);
    }                                                                □
```

Figure 6.29:
showbase.c

```
// showbase -- showbase(ios&)
#include <ios>

ios& showbase(ios& strios)
    {                                           // set showbase output mode
    strios.setf(ios::showbase);
    return (strios);
    }                                                                □
```

Figure 6.30:
showpoin.c

```
// showpoint -- showpoint(ios&)
#include <ios>

ios& showpoint(ios& strios)
    {                                           // set showpoint output mode
    strios.setf(ios::showpoint);
    return (strios);
    }                                                                □
```

Figure 6.31:
showpos.c

```
// showpos -- showpos(ios&)
#include <ios>

ios& showpos(ios& strios)
    {                                           // set showpos output mode
    strios.setf(ios::showpos);
    return (strios);
    }                                                                □
```

Figure 6.32:
skipws.c

```
// skipws -- sskipws(ios&)
#include <ios>

ios& skipws(ios& strios)
    {                                           // set skipws input mode
    strios.setf(ios::skipws);
    return (strios);
    }                                                        □
```

Figure 6.33:
uppercas.c

```
// uppercase -- uppercase(ios&)
#include <ios>

ios& uppercase(ios& strios)
    {                                           // set uppercase output mode
    strios.setf(ios::uppercase);
    return (strios);
    }                                                        □
```

Testing <ios>

tios.c   Figure 6.34 shows the file **tios.c**. It exercises the numerous member functions of class **ios**. To inspect a couple of nontrivial **ios** objects, the program obtains pointers to the base subobjects of **cin** and **cout**. Some of the tests that follow depend on the required initial values stored in these objects. (See Chapter 14: **<iostream>**.)

tios.c is hardly exhaustive, but it tries to be a bit finicky about details. I found it handy in testing the code written specially for this implementation. If you are testing an existing implementation for conformance to the draft C++ Standard, you might also appreciate this level of attention. Small variations in class **ios** among existing implementations lead to nuisancy problems in porting code, and in bringing the code into conformance.

Exercises

Exercise 6.1 Write a manipulator **ioreset** that restores all formatting information to its initial values.

Exercise 6.2 Write a manipulator **myset** that restores all formatting information to a set of values that you specify. Describe at least three sensible ways to specify such a set of values.

Exercise 6.3 What is the purpose of having the member function signature **fill(int)** instead of **fill(char)**?

Exercise 6.4 This implementation of **ios::_Findarr(int)** recycles allocated elements that contain only zeros. (See page 138.) Why do you think it does so? Write a simpler version of the member function that avoids this extra work. What caveats would you give programmers concerning the use of this simplified version?

```
// test <ios>
#include <assert.h>
#include <limits.h>
#include <ios>
#include <iostream>

        // static data
static ios::fmtflags ffl[] = {
    ios::dec, ios::fixed, ios::hex, ios::internal, ios::left,
    ios::oct, ios::right, ios::scientific, ios::showbase,
    ios::showpoint, ios::showpos, ios::skipws, ios::unitbuf,
    ios::uppercase, ios::adjustfield, ios::basefield,
    ios::floatfield};
static ios::iostate ifl[] = {
    ios::badbit, ios::eofbit, ios::failbit, ios::goodbit};
static ios::openmode ofl[] = {
    ios::app, ios::ate, ios::binary, ios::in, ios::out,
    ios::trunc};
static ios::seekdir sfl[] = {
    ios::beg, ios::cur, ios::end};

static ios::Init init_object;

int main()
    {                           // test basic workings of ios definitions
    ios *pi = &cin;
    ios *po = &cout;
    ios x(pi->rdbuf());
        // test fmtflags groups
    assert((ios::left | ios::right | ios::internal)
        == ios::adjustfield);
    assert((ios::dec | ios::oct | ios:: hex) == ios::basefield);
    assert((ios::scientific | ios::fixed) == ios::floatfield);
        // test assignment and control functions
    assert((void *)x != 0 && !x == 0);
    assert(x.tie(&cerr) == 0 && x.tie() == &cerr);
    assert(x.rdbuf(po->rdbuf()) == pi->rdbuf()
        && x.rdbuf() == po->rdbuf());
    x.clear(), assert(x.good() && x.rdstate() == ios::goodbit);
    x.clear(ios::badbit);
    assert(x.bad() && x.rdstate() == ios::badbit);
    x.setstate(ios::failbit);
    assert(x.fail() && !x.eof()), x.setstate(ios::eofbit);
    assert(x.rdstate()
        == (ios::badbit | ios::eofbit | ios::failbit));
    x.clear(ios::eofbit), pi->clear(ios::failbit);
    assert(x.copyfmt(*pi).rdstate() == ios::eofbit);
    x.exceptions(ios::badbit);
    assert(x.exceptions() == ios::badbit);
        // test format control functions
    assert(x.flags(ios::oct) == (ios::skipws | ios::dec)
        && x.flags() == ios::oct);
    assert(x.setf(ios::showbase) == ios::oct);
    assert(x.setf(ios::scientific)
        == (ios::oct | ios::showbase));
```

```
    assert(x.setf((ios::fmtflags)~0, ios::unitbuf)
        == (ios::oct | ios::scientific | ios::showbase));
    x.unsetf(ios::oct | ios::showbase);
    assert(x.flags() == (ios::scientific | ios::unitbuf));
    assert(x.precision(INT_MIN) == 6
        && x.precision() == INT_MIN);
    assert(x.width(INT_MAX) == 0 && x.width() == INT_MAX);
    assert(x.fill('y') == ' ' && x.fill() == 'y');
        // test additional storage
    int i = pi->xalloc();
    int j = pi->xalloc();
    assert(i == j - 1 && pi->iword(i) == 0 && pi->pword(j) == 0);
    pi->iword(i) = 3, pi->pword(j) = (void *)&cerr;
    x.copyfmt(*pi).iword(j) = 4;
    assert(pi->iword(i) == 3 && pi->pword(i) == 0);
    assert(pi->iword(j) == 0 && pi->pword(j) == (void *)&cerr);
    assert(x.iword(i) == 3 && x.pword(i) == 0);
    assert(x.iword(j) == 4 && x.pword(j) == (void *)&cerr);
        // test manipulators
    pi->unsetf((ios::fmtflags)~0);
    dec(fixed(internal(showbase(showpoint(*pi)))));
    assert(pi->flags() == (ios::dec | ios::fixed | ios::internal
        | ios::showbase | ios:: showpoint));
    po->unsetf((ios::fmtflags)~0);
    hex(left(scientific(showpos(skipws(*po)))));
    assert(po->flags() == (ios::hex | ios::left
        | ios::scientific | ios::showpos | ios::skipws));
    noshowbase(noshowpoint(noshowpos(noskipws(*po))));
    uppercase(oct(right(*po)));
    assert(po->flags() == (ios::oct | ios::right
        | ios:: scientific | ios::uppercase));
    scientific(nouppercase(*po));
    assert(po->flags() == (ios::oct | ios::right
        | ios::scientific));
    cout << "SUCCESS testing <ios>" << endl;
    return (0);
    }
```

Exercise 6.5 This implementation of `ios::_Findarr(int)`, on the other hand, contains few additional optimizations besides the one discussed in the previous exercise. Show how you would alter it if:

- both `ios::iword(int)` and `ios::pword(int)` are used heavily, or
- list elements are numerous, seldom altered, but often accessed

Exercise 6.6 A wide-character stream traffics in elements of type `wchar_t` instead of type *char* (a single-byte stream). What would you have to change in class `ios` to make it suitable for use with a wide stream? Can you change the class in such a way that it is suitable for use with both wide-character and single-byte streams?

Exercise 6.7 [Harder] Define the class `ins` that retains only the information required for extractions, and the class `outs` that retains only the information required for insertions. Is there sufficient benefit to define both in terms of a common base that retains overlapping information? Is there any reason *not* to do so?

Exercise 6.8 [**Very hard**] Devise a method for specifying the order of construction of static objects across translation units. You want to be able to specify that the standard streams objects are constructed first and destroyed last. You also want the programmer to be able to use the same machinery for program-specific purposes.

Chapter 7: `<streambuf>`

Background

The header `<streambuf>` has as its primary focus the class `streambuf`, which serves as the driving engine for all iostreams operations. It also defines the type `streamoff` and the class `streampos`, both of which aid in altering the next character position to insert to or extract from in a sequence controlled by an object of class `streambuf`.

`streamoff`   The type `streamoff` is a (conceptual) borrowing from the Standard C library. It is used to represent signed offsets for positioning operations within a stream controlled by a `streambuf` object. That, of course, includes C streams controlled by objects of type `FILE`. A `streamoff` object must thus be able to represent the offsets used by the functions `fseek` and `ftell`, both declared in `<stdio.h>`. Hence, the type is pretty much constrained to have the same representation as type *long*. Sadly, type `streamoff` has the same double meaning as its Standard C counterpart:

- It can be a signed offset relative to some position within a stream. All values are meaningful.

- It can be an absolute position within some stream. Negative values are nonsensical. (And a file, in particular, may be so large that it has positions not representable as values of type `streamoff`.)

It is not always clear from context which meaning is intended.

`EOF`   Yet another definition is borrowed from the Standard C library. Macro `EOF` has exactly the same definition, and meaning, as in the header `<stdio.h>`. It is an integer value distinguishable from any value representable as type *unsigned char*. And, as in the Standard C library, it is used here to signal either end-of-file when reading or some other kind of input/output failure. The Standard C I/O model also influences the iostreams machinery in more subtle ways. In particular, the remainder of header `<streambuf>` defines two classes:

- `streampos`, for describing arbitrary positions within a stream
- `streambuf`, for controlling input and output to a stream

Both strive to be abstract data types. The "streams" they control can be files in the Standard C sense, or text strings that grow and shrink dynamically in memory, or an open-ended set of user-defined sources and sinks.

Nevertheless, an important use for both these classes is to interface with their Standard C counterparts. Hence, class **streampos** is shaped internally by the needs of the Standard C functions **fgetpos** and **fsetpos**, declared in **<stdio.h>**. And class **streambuf** is obliged to work well with the streams of Standard C. Like it or not (and many C++ purists definitely *do not* like it), you will find artifacts of Standard C in both these classes.

streampos   As you might guess by now, class **streampos** is an attempt to improve upon the type **fpos_t**, defined in **<stdio.h>**. In many ways it succeeds:

- You can add a **streamoff** value to a **streampos** object, or subtract a **streamoff** value from a **streampos** object, to determine a new stream position.

- You can subtract a **streampos** object from another **streampos** object to obtain a **streamoff** difference.

- You can compare two **streampos** objects for equality or inequality.

fpos_t   By comparison, an **fpos_t** value is just a magic cookie. All you can do is obtain a current file position by calling **fgetpos**, copy the value about, and use that value to restore the same file position by calling **fsetpos** (for the same open stream, of course).

For an in-memory stream, a **streamoff** value stored inside a **streampos** object probably suffices to represent all sensible stream positions. The same is true of most disk files in a UNIX environment. All this arithmetic makes sense and is easy to perform. But for a C stream running under an arbitrary operating system, you have to rely in the end on the Standard C file-positioning functions. If they can't do what you ask, all this flexibility is for naught. Operating-system support for file positioning is sufficiently varied that you dare not be too ambitious, at least not in a program you hope to keep portable.

streambuf   I save many of the details of class **streambuf** for later chapters that describe classes *derived* from this class. For now, I focus on what you need to know to understand how this class functions as a base class for more interesting offspring. That's a hard enough tale to tell.

Conceptually, every **streambuf** object controls an input stream and an output stream. Often, one of the two streams doesn't really exist. All operations on the nonexistent stream simply fail. If there are indeed two streams, there need be no connection between them, but usually there is. Each stream can maintain a separate position indicator, but they can also be tied together and move in concert.

inserters   Class **streambuf** describes a very general engine for managing input
extractors   and output character sequences. The class offers a public interface for civilian use. Typically, the inserters associated with an **ostream** object, such as **cout**, call on member functions in this public interface to "insert characters into an output sequence." And the extractors associated with an **istream** object, such as **cin**, call on other member functions in this public interface to "extract characters from an input sequence."

buffer   An object of class **streambuf** stores six pointers. These point at the
pointers beginning, current character, and just past the end of the input and output
buffers. The member function that inserts a character need make only a
single pointer comparison to determine whether space exists in the buffer
(and perhaps a check that the buffer exists). And the member functions that
extract (or peek at) a character need make only a similar comparison to
determine whether a character exists in the buffer. An implementation
typically provides inline definitions of all these member functions, so
inserters and extractors can move characters as efficiently as possible.

But what happens when an output buffer is full (or nonexistent)? Or
what if an input buffer is empty (or nonexistent)? Then, and only then, do
the public member functions call in turn on protected virtual member
functions. Here is where the flexibility comes in. A class derived from
streambuf can override these virtuals all sorts of ways:

- For true buffered file I/O, they can endeavor to read and write hundreds
  or thousands of characters at a time using allocated buffers.

- For unbuffered file I/O, they can read or write a single character at a
  time, never setting up a buffer.

- For an in-memory stream buffer, they can allocate and free storage as
  needed to hold a character sequence that varies in length.

The possibilities are, in fact, endless. I've merely outlined the kinds of
stream buffers provided as part of the Standard C++ library. Once you see
a few variations on the **streambuf** virtual member functions, you can use
your own imagination to contrive more.

What the Draft C++ Standard Says

If you think you know iostreams well, be prepared for a few surprises
here. Class **streambuf** has been worked over considerably to make it more
portable across different operating systems and to make it more compatible
with the Standard C library. You will find more virtual member functions,
and a lot of tricky standardese at work trying to describe them accurately.

seekg   In particular, positioning functions with names like **seekg** and **tellg**
tellg have been replaced. See instead the public member functions **pubseekoff**
and **pubseekpos**, and their underlying protected virtual member functions
seekoff and **seekpos**.

pbackfail   Another important change is in the protected virtual member functions
uflow that support extractors. The existing functions **pbackfail** and **underflow**
underflow have been augmented with a third, **uflow**. With this threesome, you can
now derive stream buffers that are completely unbuffered. They can be
"pipelined" to arbitrary depth and still handle character pushback or input
positioning operations properly. The price, as always, is a bit more complexity and a somewhat more fragile interface. (If you don't understand
this, don't worry. It's a *very* advanced use of iostreams.)

17.4.2 Header `<streambuf>`

The header `<streambuf>` defines a macro and three types that control input from and output to character sequences.

The macro is:

- **EOF**, which expands to a negative integral constant expression, representable as type **int**, that is returned by several functions to indicate end-of-file (no more input from an input sequence or no more output permitted to an output sequence), or to indicate an invalid return value.[86]

17.4.2.1 Type `streamoff`

```
typedef T1 streamoff;
```

The type **streamoff** is a synonym for one of the signed basic integral type **T1** whose representation has at least as many bits as type **long**. It is used to represent:

- a signed displacement, measured in bytes, from a specified position within a sequence;
- an absolute position within a sequence, not necessarily measured in uniform units.

In the second case, the value **(streamoff)(-1)** indicates an invalid position, or a position that cannot be represented as a value of type **streamoff**.

17.4.2.2 Class `streampos`

In this subclause, the type name *fpos_t* is a synonym for the type **fpos_t** defined in **<stdio.h>**.

```
class streampos {
public:
    streampos(streamoff off = 0);
    streamoff offset() const;
    streamoff operator-(streampos& rhs) const;
    streampos& operator+=(streamoff off);
    streampos& operator-=(streamoff off);
    streampos operator+(streamoff off) const;
    streampos operator-(streamoff off) const;
    int operator==(const streampos& rhs) const;
    int operator!=(const streampos& rhs) const;
private:
//  streamoff pos;                              exposition only
//  fpos_t fp;                                  exposition only
    };
```

The class **streampos** describes an object that can store all the information necessary to restore an arbitrary sequence, controlled by the Standard C++ library, to a previous *stream position* and *conversion state*.[87] For the sake of exposition, the data it stores is presented here as:

- **streamoff pos**, specifies the absolute position within the sequence;
- **fpos_t fp**, specifies the stream position and conversion state in the implementation-dependent form required by functions declared in **<stdio.h>**.

It is unspecified how these two member objects combine to represent a stream position.

17.4.2.2.1 `streampos::streampos(streamoff)`

```
streampos(streamoff off = 0);
```

Constructs an object of class **streampos**, initializing *pos* to zero and *fp* to the stream position at the beginning of the sequence, with the conversion state at the beginning of a new multibyte sequence in the initial shift state.[88] The constructor then evaluates the expression ***this += *off***.

17.4.2.2.2 streampos::offset()

offset

```
streamoff offset() const;
```

Determines the value of type **streamoff** that represents the stream position stored in ***pos*** and ***fp***, if possible, and returns that value. Otherwise, the function returns **(streamoff)(-1)**. For a sequence requiring a conversion state, even a representable value of type **streamoff** need not supply sufficient information to restore the stored stream position.

17.4.2.2.3 streampos::operator-(streampos&)

operator-

```
streamoff operator-(streampos& rhs) const;
```

Determines the value of type **streamoff** that represents the difference in stream positions between ***this** and ***rhs***, if possible, and returns that value. (If ***this** is a stream position nearer the beginning of the sequence than ***rhs***, the difference is negative.) Otherwise, the function returns **(streamoff)(-1)**. For a sequence that does not represent stream positions in uniform units, even a representable value need not be meaningful.

17.4.2.2.4 streampos::operator+=(streamoff)

operator+=

```
streampos& operator+=(streamoff off);
```

Adds ***off*** to the stream position stored in ***pos*** and ***fp***, if possible, and replaces the stored values. Otherwise, the function stores an invalid stream position in ***pos*** and ***fp***. For a sequence that does not represent stream positions in uniform units, the resulting stream position need not be meaningful. The function returns ***this**.

17.4.2.2.5 streampos::operator-=(streamoff)

operator-=

```
streampos& operator-=(streamoff off);
```

Subtracts ***off*** from the stream position stored in ***pos*** and ***fp***, if possible, and replaces the stored value. Otherwise, the function stores an invalid stream position in ***pos*** and ***fp***. For a sequence that does not represent stream positions in uniform units, the resulting stream position need not be meaningful. The function returns ***this**.

17.4.2.2.6 streampos::operator+(streamoff)

operator+

```
streampos operator+(streamoff off) const;
```

Returns **streampos(*this) += *off***.

17.4.2.2.7 streampos::operator-(streamoff)

operator-

```
streampos operator-(streamoff off) const;
```

Returns **streampos(*this) -= *off***.

17.4.2.2.8 streampos::operator==(const streampos&)

operator==

```
int operator==(const streampos& rhs) const;
```

Compares the stream position stored in ***this** to the stream position stored in ***rhs***, and returns a nonzero value if the two correspond to the same position within a file or if both store an invalid stream position.

17.4.2.2.9 streampos::operator!=(const streampos&)

operator!=

```
int operator!=(const streampos& rhs) const;
```

Returns a nonzero value if **!(*this == *rhs*)**.

17.4.2.3 Class streambuf

```
class streambuf {
public:
    virtual ~streambuf();
    streampos pubseekoff(streamoff off,
        ios::seekdir way,
        ios::openmode which = ios::in | ios::out);
//  streampos pubseekoff(streamoff off, ios::seek_dir way,
//      ios::open_mode which = ios::in | ios::out);     optional
    streampos pubseekpos(streampos sp,
        ios::openmode which = ios::in | ios::out);
//  streampos pubseekpos(streampos sp,
//      ios::open_mode which = ios::in | ios::out);     optional
    streambuf* pubsetbuf(char* s, int n);
    int pubsync();
    int sbumpc();
    int sgetc();
    int sgetn(char* s, int n);
    int snextc();
    int sputbackc(char c);
    int sungetc();
    int sputc(int c);
    int sputn(const char* s, int n);
protected:
    streambuf();
    char* eback() const;
    char* gptr() const;
    char* egptr() const;
    void gbump(int n);
    void setg(char* gbeg_arg, char* gnext_arg, char* gend_arg);
    char* pbase() const;
    char* pptr() const;
    char* epptr() const;
    void pbump(int n);
    void setp(char* pbeg_arg, char* pend_arg);
    virtual int overflow(int c = EOF);
    virtual int pbackfail(int c = EOF);
    virtual int underflow();
    virtual int uflow();
    virtual int xsgetn(char* s, int n);
    virtual int xsputn(const char* s, int n);
    virtual streampos seekoff(streamoff off, ios::seekdir way,
        ios::openmode which = ios::in | ios::out);
    virtual streampos seekpos(streampos sp,
        ios::openmode which = ios::in | ios::out);
    virtual streambuf* setbuf(char* s, int n);
    virtual int sync();
private:
//  char* gbeg;                                         exposition only
//  char* gnext;                                        exposition only
//  char* gend;                                         exposition only
//  char* pbeg;                                         exposition only
//  char* pnext;                                        exposition only
//  char* pend;                                         exposition only
};
```

The class **streambuf** serves as an abstract base class for deriving various *stream buffers* whose objects each control two character sequences:

- a (single-byte) character input sequence;
- a (single-byte) character output sequence.

Stream buffers can impose various constraints on the sequences they control. Some constraints are:

- The controlled input sequence can be not readable.
- The controlled output sequence can be not writable.
- The controlled sequences can be associated with the contents of other representations for character sequences, such as external files.
- The controlled sequences can support operations *directly* to or from associated sequences.
- The controlled sequences can impose limitations on how the program can read characters from a sequence, write characters to a sequence, put characters back into an input sequence, or alter the stream position.

Each sequence is characterized by three pointers which, if non-null, all point into the same array object. The array object represents, at any moment, a (sub)sequence of characters from the sequence. Operations performed on a sequence alter the values stored in these pointers, perform reads and writes directly to or from associated sequences, and alter the stream position and conversion state as needed to maintain this subsequence relationship. The three pointers are:

- the *beginning pointer,* or lowest element address in the array (called *xbeg* here);
- the *next pointer,* or next element address that is a current candidate for reading or writing (called *xnext* here);
- the *end pointer,* or first element address beyond the end of the array (called *xend* here).

The following semantic constraints shall always apply for any set of three pointers for a sequence, using the pointer names given immediately above:

- If *xnext* is not a null pointer, then *xbeg* and *xend* shall also be non-null pointers into the same array, as described above.
- If *xnext* is not a null pointer and *xnext* < *xend* for an output sequence, then a *write position* is available. In this case, **xnext* shall be assignable as the next element to write (to put, or to store a character value, into the sequence).
- If *xnext* is not a null pointer and *xbeg* < *xnext* for an input sequence, then a *putback position* is available. In this case, *xnext* **[-1]** shall have a defined value and is the next (preceding) element to store a character that is put back into the input sequence.
- If *xnext* is not a null pointer and *xnext* < *xend* for an input sequence, then a *read position* is available. In this case, **xnext* shall have a defined value and is the next element to read (to get, or to obtain a character value, from the sequence).

For the sake of exposition, the maintained data is presented here as:

- **char*** *gbeg*, the beginning pointer for the input sequence;
- **char*** *gnext*, the next pointer for the input sequence;
- **char*** *gend*, the end pointer for the input sequence;
- **char*** *pbeg*, the beginning pointer for the output sequence;
- **char*** *pnext*, the next pointer for the output sequence;

• `char* pend`, the end pointer for the output sequence.

17.4.2.3.1 streambuf::~streambuf()

destructor

```
virtual ~streambuf();
```

Destroys an object of class `streambuf`.

17.4.2.3.2 streambuf::pubseekoff(streamoff, ios::seekdir, ios::openmode)

pubseekoff

```
streampos pubseekoff(streamoff off, ios::seekdir way,
    ios::openmode which = ios::in | ios::out);
```

Returns `seekoff(off, way, which)`.

17.4.2.3.3 streambuf::pubseekoff(streamoff, ios::seek_dir, ios::open_mode)

pubseekoff

```
//  streampos pubseekoff(streamoff off, ios::seek_dir way,
//          ios::open_mode which = ios::in | ios::out);    optional
```

Returns `pubseekoff(off, (ios::seekdir)way, (ios::open-mode)which)`.

17.4.2.3.4 streambuf::pubseekpos(streampos, ios::openmode)

pubseekpos

```
streampos pubseekpos(streampos sp,
    ios::openmode which = ios::in | ios::out);
```

Returns `seekpos(sp, which)`.

17.4.2.3.5 streambuf::pubseekpos(streampos, ios::open_mode)

pubseekpos

```
//  streampos pubseekpos(streampos sp,
//          ios::open_mode which = ios::in | ios::out);    optional
```

Returns `pubseekpos(sp, (ios::openmode)which)`.

17.4.2.3.6 streambuf::pubsetbuf(char*, int)

pubsetbuf

```
streambuf* pubsetbuf(char* s, int n);
```

Returns `setbuf(s, n)`.

17.4.2.3.7 streambuf::pubsync()

pubsync

```
int pubsync();
```

Returns `sync()`.

17.4.2.3.8 streambuf::sbumpc()

sbumpc

```
int sbumpc();
```

If the input sequence does not have a read position available, returns `uflow()`. Otherwise, the function returns `(unsigned char)*gnext++`.

17.4.2.3.9 streambuf::sgetc()

sgetc

```
int sgetc();
```

If the input sequence does not have a read position available, returns `underflow()`. Otherwise, the function returns `(unsigned char)*gnext`.

17.4.2.3.10 streambuf::sgetn(char*, int)

sgetn

```
int sgetn(char* s, int n);
```

Returns `xsgetn(s, n)`.

17.4.2.3.11 streambuf::snextc()

snextc

```
int snextc();
```

Calls `sbumpc()` and, if that function returns `EOF`, returns `EOF`. Otherwise, the function returns `sgetc()`.

17.4.2.3.12 streambuf::sputbackc(char)

sputbackc

```
int sputbackc(char c);
```

If the input sequence does not have a putback position available, or if **c !=** *gnext*[**-1**], returns **pbackfail(c)**. Otherwise, the function returns **(unsigned char)*--***gnext*.

17.4.2.3.13 streambuf::sungetc()

sungetc

```
int sungetc();
```

If the input sequence does not have a putback position available, returns **pbackfail()**. Otherwise, the function returns **(unsigned char)*--***gnext*.

17.4.2.3.14 streambuf::sputc(int)

sputc

```
int sputc(int c);
```

If the output sequence does not have a write position available, returns **overflow(c)**. Otherwise, the function returns **(unsigned char)(****pnext++** **=** **c)**.

17.4.2.3.15 streambuf::sputn(const char*, int)

sputn

```
int sputn(const char* s, int n);
```

Returns **xsputn(***s*, *n***)**.

17.4.2.3.16 streambuf::streambuf()

constructor

```
streambuf();
```

Constructs an object of class **streambuf()** and initializes all its pointer member objects to null pointers.[89]

17.4.2.3.17 streambuf::eback()

eback

```
char* eback() const;
```

Returns *gbeg*.

17.4.2.3.18 streambuf::gptr()

gptr

```
char* gptr() const;
```

Returns *gnext*.

17.4.2.3.19 streambuf::egptr()

egptr

```
char* egptr() const;
```

Returns *gend*.

17.4.2.3.20 streambuf::gbump(int)

gbump

```
void gbump(int n);
```

Assigns *gnext* + *n* to *gnext*.

17.4.2.3.21 streambuf::setg(char*, char*, char*)

setg

```
void setg(char* gbeg_arg, char* gnext_arg, char* gend_arg);
```

Assigns *gbeg_arg* to *gbeg*, *gnext_arg* to *gnext*, and *gend_arg* to *gend*.

17.4.2.3.22 streambuf::pbase()

pbase

```
char* pbase() const;
```

Returns *pbeg*.

17.4.2.3.23 streambuf::pptr()

pptr

```
char* pptr() const;
```

Returns *pnext*.

17.4.2.3.24 streambuf::epptr()

epptr

```
char* epptr() const;
```

Returns *pend*.

17.4.2.3.25 streambuf::pbump(int)

pbump

```
void pbump(int n);
```

Assigns *pnext* + *n* to *pnext*.

17.4.2.3.26 streambuf::setp(char*, char*)

setp

```
void setp(char* pbeg_arg, char* pend_arg);
```

Assigns *pbeg_arg* to *pbeg*, *pbeg_arg* to *pnext*, and *pend_arg* to *pend*.

17.4.2.3.27 streambuf::overflow(int)

overflow

```
virtual int overflow(int c = EOF);
```

Appends the character designated by *c* to the output sequence, if possible, in one of three ways:

- If *c* != **EOF** and if either the output sequence has a write position available or the function makes a write position available, the function assigns *c* to `*pnext++`. The function signals success by returning **(unsigned char)** *c*.
- If *c* != **EOF** and if the function can append a character directly to the associated output sequence, the function appends *c* directly to the associated output sequence. If *pbeg* < *pnext*, the *pnext* - *pbeg* characters beginning at *pbeg* shall be first appended directly to the associated output sequence, beginning with the character at *pbeg*. The function signals success by returning **(unsigned char)** *c*.
- If *c* == **EOF**, there is no character to append. The function signals success by returning a value other than **EOF**.

If the function can succeed in more than one of these ways, it is unspecified which way is chosen. The function can alter the number of write positions available as a result of any call. How (or whether) the function makes a write position available or appends a character directly to the output sequence is defined separately for each class derived from **streambuf** in this clause.

The function returns **EOF** to indicate failure.

The default behavior is to return **EOF**.

17.4.2.3.28 streambuf::pbackfail(int)

pbackfail

```
virtual int pbackfail(int c = EOF);
```

Puts back the character designated by *c* to the input sequence, if possible, in one of five ways:

- If *c* != **EOF**, if either the input sequence has a putback position available or the function makes a putback position available, and if **(unsigned char)** *c* == **(unsigned char)** *gnext*[-1], the function assigns *gnext* - 1 to *gnext*. The function signals success by returning **(unsigned char)** *c*.
- If *c* != **EOF**, if either the input sequence has a putback position available or the function makes a putback position available, and if the function is permitted to assign to the putback position, the function assigns *c* to `*--gnext`. The function signals success by returning **(unsigned char)** *c*.
- If *c* != **EOF**, if no putback position is available, and if the function can put back a character directly to the associated input sequence, the function puts back *c* directly to the associate input sequence. The function signals success by returning **(unsigned char)** *c*.
- If *c* == **EOF** and if either the input sequence has a putback position available or the function makes a putback position available, the function assigns *gnext* - 1 to *gnext*. The function signals success by returning a value other than **EOF**.

- If **c == EOF**, if no putback position is available, if the function can put back a character directly to the associated input sequence, and if the function can determine the character **x** immediately before the current position in the associated input sequence, the function puts back **x** directly to the associated input sequence. The function signals success by returning a value other than **EOF**.

If the function can succeed in more than one of these ways, it is unspecified which way is chosen. The function can alter the number of putback positions available as a result of any call. How (or whether) the function makes a putback position available, puts back a character directly to the input sequence, or determines the character immediately before the current position in the associated input sequence is defined separately for each class derived from **streambuf** in this clause.

The function returns **EOF** to indicate failure.

The default behavior is to return **EOF**.

underflow

17.4.2.3.29 streambuf::underflow()

```
virtual int underflow();
```

Reads a character from the input sequence, if possible, without moving the stream position past it, as follows:

- If the input sequence has a read position available the function signals success by returning **(unsigned char)*gnext**.
- Otherwise, if the function can determine the character **x** at the current position in the associated input sequence, it signals success by returning **(unsigned char)x**. If the function makes a read position available, it also assigns **x** to ***gnext**.

The function can alter the number of read positions available as a result of any call. How (or whether) the function makes a read position available or determines the character **x** at the current position in the associated input sequence is defined separately for each class derived from **streambuf** in this clause.

The function returns **EOF** to indicate failure.

The default behavior is to return **EOF**.

uflow

17.4.2.3.30 streambuf::uflow()

```
virtual int uflow();
```

Reads a character from the input sequence, if possible, and moves the stream position past it, as follows:

- If the input sequence has a read position available the function signals success by returning **(unsigned char)*gnext++**.
- Otherwise, if the function can read the character **x** directly from the associated input sequence, it signals success by returning **(unsigned char)x**. If the function makes a read position available, it also assigns **x** to ***gnext**.

The function can alter the number of read positions available as a result of any call. How (or whether) the function makes a read position available or reads a character directly from the input sequence is defined separately for each class derived from **streambuf** in this clause.

The function returns **EOF** to indicate failure.

The default behavior is to call **underflow()** and, if that function returns **EOF** or fails to make a read position available, return **EOF**. Otherwise, the function signals success by returning **(unsigned char)*gnext++**.[90]

xsgetn

17.4.2.3.31 streambuf::xsgetn(char*, int)

```
virtual int xsgetn(char* s, int n);
```

Assigns up to **n** characters to successive elements of the array whose first element is designated by **s**. The characters assigned are read from the input sequence as if by repeated calls to **sbumpc()**. Assigning stops when either **n** characters have been assigned or a call to **sbumpc()** would return **EOF**. The function returns the number of characters assigned.[91]

17.4.2.3.32 streambuf::xsputn(const char*, int)

xsputn

```
virtual int xsputn(const char* s, int n);
```

Writes up to **n** characters to the output sequence as if by repeated calls to **sputc(c)**. The characters written are obtained from successive elements of the array whose first element is designated by **s**. Writing stops when either **n** characters have been written or a call to **sputc(c)** would return **EOF**. The function returns the number of characters written.

17.4.2.3.33 streambuf::seekoff(streamoff, ios::seekdir, ios::openmode)

seekoff

```
virtual streampos seekoff(streamoff off, ios::seekdir way,
    ios::openmode which = ios::in | ios::out);
```

Alters the stream positions within one or more of the controlled sequences in a way that is defined separately for each class derived from **streambuf** in this clause. The default behavior is to return an object of class **streampos** that stores an invalid stream position.

17.4.2.3.34 streambuf::seekpos(streampos, ios::openmode)

seekpos

```
virtual streampos seekpos(streampos sp,
    ios::openmode which = ios::in | ios::out);
```

Alters the stream positions within one or more of the controlled sequences in a way that is defined separately for each class derived from **streambuf** in this clause. The default behavior is to return an object of class **streampos** that stores an invalid stream position.

17.4.2.3.35 streambuf::setbuf(char*, int)

setbuf

```
virtual streambuf* setbuf(char* s, int n);
```

Performs an operation that is defined separately for each class derived from **streambuf** in this clause.

The default behavior is to return **this**.

17.4.2.3.36 streambuf::sync()

sync

```
virtual int sync();
```

Synchronizes the controlled sequences with any associated external sources and sinks of characters in a way that is defined separately for each class derived from **streambuf** in this clause. The function returns **EOF** if it fails. The default behavior is to return zero.

Footnotes:

Footnotes

86) This macro is also defined, with the same value and meaning, in **<stdio.h>**.

87) The conversion state is used for sequences that translate between wide-character and generalized multibyte encoding, as described in Amendment 1 to the C Standard.

88) The next character to read or write is the first character in the sequence.

89) The default constructor is protected for class **streambuf** to assure that only objects for classes derived from this class may be constructed.

90) A class derived from `streambuf` can override the virtual member function `underflow()` with a function that returns a value other than `EOF` without making a read position available. In that event, `streambuf::uflow()` must also be overridden since the default behavior is inadequate.

91) Classes derived from `streambuf` can provide more efficient ways to implement `xsgetn` and `xsputn` by overriding these definitions in the base class.

Future Directions

Debate continues on whether the descriptions of the `streambuf` protected virtual member functions shown here are adequate. I know of no intention to change the *functionality* described in any fundamental way. Any rewrite, however, is bound to alter the interpretation of some boundary cases. I wouldn't write code that depends on too legalistic an interpretation of extreme conditions in such a notoriously delicate area of the draft C++ Standard.

showmany   Yet another `streambuf` virtual member function has already been added. The public access function for it is called `showmany` (pronounced "ess-how-many," not "show-many"). You call this function to determine how many characters you can safely extract with no fear of blocking while waiting for additional input. When an implementation can't give an honest answer, it is permitted to give an ultraconservative answer instead.

streampos   There is still ongoing discussion of ways to make the class `streampos` more open-ended. Right now, an object of this class is obliged to store sufficient information to position an in-memory stream or a C stream. A class derived from `streambuf`, however, may have additional needs. It is possible that the definition of `streampos` may be altered to allow it to be extended.

wide-character   As I mentioned in the previous chapter, on page 119, a major change
streams already made adds wide-character streams. Class `streambuf` derives from a template class parameterized by the type of the stream element. The instantiation for type *char* has essentially the same functionality as described in this chapter. Another, for type `wchar_t`, supports streams of elements from some large character set. Class `streampos` likewise derives from a template class.

Using `<streambuf>`

You have little or no occasion to include the header `<streambuf>` directly. Like `<ios>` in the previous chapter, it is another header invented by the Committee simply to split the iostreams declarations into more manageable pieces. But the chances are equally good that you'll use the *contents* of `<streambuf>` in a program. Class `streambuf` is the base class for all stream buffers, which control all input and output in the iostreams package. The base class summarizes what is *common* to all stream buffers, or the default behavior for an unused feature in a particular stream buffer.

public   You may never have occasion to use the **streambuf** interface yourself.
interface Even if you write your own inserters and extractors, you often do the
low-level work by calling on existing inserters and extractors. In fact, I'd
discourage you from making direct calls on a **streambuf** object, at least
until you've had time to study some existing inserters and extractors and
really understand the protocol. Any abstract description you read will
never compare to first-hand practical experience. For now, I'll characterize
the public interface to class **streambuf** in the briefest of terms.

When extracting from a sequence:

sbumpc ▪ Peek at the next character by calling **sgetc()**, extract (and point past) it
sgetc   by calling **sbumpc()**, or put back the last character **ch** you extracted by
sputbackc calling **sputbackc(ch)**. (Do *not* put back a different character, even
though the draft C++ Standard permits you to do so.)

sgetn ▪ Read up to **n** characters into a buffer **buf** by calling **sgetn(buf, n)**. The
return value tells you how many characters you actually read.

snextc ▪ For various reasons of performance or reliability, avoid calling **snextc()**
sungetc or **sungetc()**. Also avoid calling **sputbackc(ch)** except as I described
above.

When inserting into a sequence:

sputc ▪ Write a character **ch** by calling **sputc(ch)**.

sputn ▪ Write up to **n** characters from a buffer **buf** by calling **sputn(buf, n)**.
The return value tells you how many characters you actually wrote,
which should always be **n**.

pubseekoff   One way to position within a sequence is to use the function **pubseekoff**. The next position to access (extract from or insert to) is determined by
an offset of type **streamoff** and a value of the enumerated type **ios::
seekdir**. The latter argument can take the values:

beg ▪ **ios::beg**, to specify an absolute offset relative to the beginning of the
sequence

cur ▪ **ios::cur**, to specify an algebraic offset relative to the current position
within the sequence

end ▪ **ios::end**, to specify an algebraic offset relative to the end of the sequence

This is the same set of positioning capabilities as provided by the Standard
C library function **fseek**, declared in **<stdio.h>**. When reading and writing a C stream, both sets suffer the same potential system-dependent
limitations. (See Chapter 13: **<fstream>**.)

openmode   An argument of type **ios::openmode** (yet another misnomer) has
in **ios::in** set to affect the input sequence, and **ios::out** set to affect the
out output sequence. The effect of various combinations of arguments depends
very strongly on the actual type derived from the base **streambuf**. A C
stream, for example, maintains only one file position indicator, so this
argument is effectively ignored. For other types of stream buffers, you may
be able to position input and output streams separately or in tandem.

pubseekpos   Note, by the way, that **pubseekoff** returns an object of class **seekpos**. You need such an object to represent an arbitrary position within an arbitrary stream. A reliable way to memorize the current stream position, in fact, is to write:

```
streampos pos = x.pubseekoff(0, ios::cur)
```

for the **streambuf** object **x**. You can later return to the memorized position by writing:

```
x.pubseekpos(pos);
```

Sometimes you *know* that a simple stream offset will do the job. An object of class **strstreambuf**, for example, deals with a sequence of characters in memory. (See Chapter 11: **<strstream>**.) In such a case, you can safely traffic in stream offsets. You can memorize a position by writing:

```
streamoff off = x.pubseekoff(0, ios::cur).offset();
```

and later restore it with:

```
x.pubseekoff(off, ios::beg);
```

I encourage you to indulge in as little stream positioning as possible, however. When you must, deal with objects of class **streampos** as much as possible. Don't count on arithmetic working properly on such objects, despite the implied promises of the draft C++ Standard. And try to confine yourself to revisiting positions that you've visited earlier, using the idiom I just showed. If you're more ambitious, expect occasional surprises, and positioning failures.

pubsetbuf   Class **streambuf** has two other public member functions. You can go a long time without having occasion to call either one. **pubsetbuf** is a general hook for conveying buffering information to a stream buffer. It calls in turn the protected virtual member **setbuf**. The only defined use for this public member function in the draft C++ Standard is for class **filebuf**. (See Chapter 13: **<fstream>**.) There, it effectively lets you call the function **setvbuf**, declared in **<stdio.h>**, on behalf of the buffer controlled by **filebuf**. (Even that operation promises little or nothing in the way of actual control over file buffering.)

pubsync   The remaining public member function for class **streambuf** is **pubsync**. It provides yet another hook, this time to the protected virtual member function **sync**. The public member function is used to synchronize a stream buffer with any separate representation of the stream it controls. For an object of class **filebuf**, the effect is the same as calling **fflush**, declared in **<stdio.h>**, for a C stream. Other types of stream buffers may have little or nothing to do to ensure synchronization. In any event, such synchronization calls often occur in the course of other iostreams operations. You may have little or no occasion to add explicit calls yourself. When you do, you will find higher-level functions that call **pubsync** with a bit more checking. (See, for example, the function **ostream::flush**, on page 221.)

protected   So much for the public interface. Class **streambuf** also offers a protected
interface interface which is even more sophisticated. You care about this interface,

naturally enough, only if you derive your own class from a **streambuf** base. (That's the only way you can even *access* this interface.)

The first part of the protected interface you can, and should, pretty much ignore. It is used by the public members to conduct their business. Here again you will find a number of funny names and irregularities. But that should be of no concern to the typical user of a class derived from **streambuf**. Look at the public member functions, nearly all of which are typically defined as inline, to get a feel for what they do, if you care.

protected   You might note, in passing, that the constructors for class **streambuf** are
constructors protected. That keeps you from constructing an object of this class outside captivity. The idea is to derive from the base class and specialize it to perform useful operations.

The second part of the protected interface is where the action is. Class **streambuf** is built around a set of virtual member functions that allow you to tailor behavior over a very wide range. Here is where insertions get turned into actual writes to some physical sink for characters. Here is where extractors get turned into actual reads from some physical source of characters. Here is where positioning operations get real, or those other hooks I mentioned earlier get something hung upon them. In short, the art of specializing **streambuf** is the art of writing virtual member functions that honor the protocol of the base class.

Until the draft C++ Standard came along, there was only one way to specialize a **streambuf**. Find some code for another specialization that more or less worked, and that you could more or less understand, and crib like crazy. Having access to the source for **streambuf** proper also helped immeasurably.

Now you have a little more help. You can read the draft C++ Standard to learn the protocol that must be honored by these virtual member functions. *Then* you can go look at some specialzation that works and that you can more or less understand, and crib like crazy. I can't honestly recommend any other way to proceed.

Why is this so? Because describing the protocol for the **streambuf** virtual member functions is the hardest piece of standardese I've ever essayed. Jerry Schwarz, the original author of iostreams, is still not happy with its current description. I think it's getting reasonably accurate and precise, but I'd never accuse this part of the draft of being a decent tutorial. Learning by imitation — and by doing — is still the safest route.

Having said that, I'll give you just the briefest of hints about what the four most critical virtual member functions do:

overflow ▪ **overflow(ch)** either writes the character **ch** to the physical sink of characters, somehow, or it "makes a write position available" (creates an in-memory buffer with a space available for writing a character) and puts the character in it.

pbackfail ■ **pbackfail(ch)** either writes the character **ch** back to the physical source of characters, somehow, or it "makes a putback position available" (creates an in-memory buffer with a space available for putting back a character) and puts the character in it.

underflow ■ **underflow()** either reads a character from the physical source of characters without consuming it, somehow, or it "makes a read position available" (creates an in-memory buffer with a character available for reading) and reads the character from it without consuming it.

uflow ■ **uflow()** either reads a character from the physical source of characters and consumes it, somehow, or it "makes a read position available" (creates an in-memory buffer with a character available for reading) and reads and consumes a character from it.

The Committee added **uflow** for reasons I indicated earlier, on page 149. The public member functions call this new protected virtual member function only to read a character and point past it. To peek at a character, without pointing past it, they call the older **underflow** instead. With this discipline, the **streambuf** protected virtual member functions can avoid buffering input characters when that proves inconvenient.

If your goal is to derive a stream buffer that works properly under these specialized circumstances, make sure you understand the reasons for this protocol and how to honor it. But in general, you can be quite comfortable starting with one of the derived stream buffers presented later in this book, as I indicated earlier.

Figure 7.1:
streambu
Part 1 of 3

```
// streambuf standard header
#ifndef _STREAMBUF_
#define _STREAMBUF_
#include <ios>
            // macros
#define EOF     (-1)
            // type streamoff
typedef long streamoff;
const streamoff _BADOFF = -1;
            // class streampos
class streampos {
public:
      streampos(streamoff = 0, const _Fpost * = 0);
      streamoff offset() const;
      streamoff operator-(const streampos&) const;
      streampos& operator+=(streamoff _O)
            {_Pos += _O; return (*this); }
      streampos& operator-=(streamoff _O)
            {_Pos -= _O; return (*this); }
      streampos operator+(streamoff _O) const
            {return (streampos(*this) += _O); }
      streampos operator-(streamoff _O) const
            {return (streampos(*this) -= _O); }
```

```
        _Bool operator==(const streampos&) const;
        _Bool operator!=(const streampos& _R) const
            {return (!(*this == _R)); }
        _Fpost *_Fpos()
            {return (&_Fp); }
private:
        streamoff _Pos;
        _Fpost _Fp;
        };
                // class streambuf
class streambuf {
public:
        virtual ~streambuf();
        streampos pubseekoff(streamoff _O, ios::seekdir _W,
            ios::openmode _M = ios::in | ios::out)
            {return (seekoff(_O, _W, _M)); }
        streampos pubseekoff(streamoff _O, ios::seek_dir _W,
            ios::open_mode _M)
            {return (pubseekoff(_O, (seekdir)_W, (openmode)_M)); }
        streampos pubseekpos(streampos _P,
            ios::openmode _M = ios::in | ios::out)
            {return (seekpos(_P, _M)); }
        streampos pubseekpos(streampos _P, ios::open_mode _M)
            {return (seekpos(_P, (openmode)_M)); }
        streambuf *pubsetbuf(char *_S, int _N)
            {return (setbuf(_S, _N)); }
        int pubsync()
            {return (sync()); }
        int sbumpc()
            {return (gptr() != 0 && gptr() < egptr()
                ? *_Gn()++ : uflow()); }
        int sgetc()
            {return (gptr() != 0 && gptr() < egptr()
                ? *_Gn() : underflow()); }
        int sgetn(char *_S, int _N)
            {return (xsgetn(_S, _N)); }
        int snextc()
            {return (sbumpc() == EOF ? EOF : sgetc()); }
        int sputbackc(char _C)
            {return (gptr() != 0 && eback() < gptr()
                && _C == gptr()[-1]
                ? *--_Gn() : pbackfail((unsigned char)_C)); }
        int sungetc()
            {return (gptr() != 0 && eback() < gptr()
                ? *--_Gn() : pbackfail()); }
        int sputc(int _C)
            {return (pptr() != 0 && pptr() < epptr()
                ? (*_Pn()++ = _C) : overflow(_C)); }
        int sputn(const char *_S, int _N)
            {return (xsputn(_S, _N)); }
protected:
        streambuf()
            {_Init(); }
```

```
    streambuf(ios::_Uninitialized)
        {}
    char *eback() const
        {return (*_IGbeg); }
    char *gptr() const
        {return (*_IGnext); }
    char *egptr() const
        {return (*_IGend); }
    void gbump(int _N)
        {*_IGnext += _N; }
    void setg(char *_B, char *_N, char *_E)
        {*_IGbeg = _B, *_IGnext = _N, *_IGend = _E; }
    char *pbase() const
        {return (*_IPbeg); }
    char *pptr() const
        {return (*_IPnext); }
    char *epptr() const
        {return (*_IPend); }
    void pbump(int _N)
        {*_IPnext += _N; }
    void setp(char *_B, char *_E)
        {*_IPbeg = _B, *_IPnext = _B, *_IPend = _E; }
    void setp(char *_B, char *_N, char *_E)
        {*_IPbeg = _B, *_IPnext = _N, *_IPend = _E; }
    unsigned char *&_Gn()
        {return ((unsigned char *&)*_IGnext); }
    unsigned char *&_Pn()
        {return ((unsigned char *&)*_IPnext); }
    virtual int overflow(int = EOF);
    virtual int pbackfail(int = EOF);
    virtual int underflow();
    virtual int uflow();
    virtual int xsgetn(char *, int);
    virtual int xsputn(const char *, int);
    virtual streampos seekoff(streamoff, ios::seekdir,
        ios::openmode = ios::in | ios::out);
    virtual streampos seekpos(streampos,
        ios::openmode = ios::in | ios::out);
    virtual streambuf *setbuf(char *, int);
    virtual int sync();
    void _Init();
    void _Init(char **, char **, char **, char **, char **,
        char **);
private:
    streambuf(const streambuf&);                                // undefined
    streambuf& operator=(const streambuf&);                     // undefined
    char *_Gbeg, *_Gnext, *_Gend;
    char *_Pbeg, *_Pnext, *_Pend;
    char **_IGbeg, **_IGnext, **_IGend;
    char **_IPbeg, **_IPnext, **_IPend;
    };
#endif                                                                    □
```

Implementing `<streambuf>`

streambu   Figure 7.1 shows the file **streambu**, which implements the standard
_BADOFF   header **<streambuf>**. I have found it convenient in this implementation to
define the secret constant **_BADOFF**. As in Standard C, it is the standard way
to indicate an invalid absolute position, of type **streamoff**. Unfortunately,
it sometimes also is used to indicate an invalid relative position, as I
mentioned earlier in this chapter, on page 147. For this usage, the value –1
is a less compelling choice.

streampos   The implementation I chose for class **streampos** endeavors to succeed
at positioning requests as often as possible, even in the teeth of possible
failure. It stores within each **streampos** object two private member objects:

- **_Pos**, of type **streamoff**, to keep track of the simple offset arithmetic
  described above

- **_Fp**, of type **fpos_t**, to keep track of a C file position when working with
  actual files

The actual declared type of the latter is **_Fpost** because the name **fpos_t**
is not necessarily defined at this point. (The draft C++ Standard pays lip
service to the need for this component of class **streampos**, but is intentionally mealy mouthed about whether it is actually present.) The internal
header **<yxvals.h>** defines this type, as necessary, to match the accompa-
nying Standard C library definition.

fpos_t   This implementation declares the structure **fpos_t** (**_Fpost**) with the
_Fpost   members:

- **_Off**, for the absolute position within a stream (**_BADOFF** if undefined)

- **_Wstate**, for the state memory when parsing a wide-character stream

The state memory, in turn, has the elements:

- **_State**, for the current parse and shift state within a multibyte stream

- **_Wchar**, for the current wide-character accumulator used by the multibyte stream parser

For all but wide-character streams, both these components are always zero.

pubsetbuf   In class **streambuf**, the functions **pubsetbuf** and **pubsync** are really just
pubsync   hooks into virtual functions that are specialized for derived classes. The
default behavior for the base class is to do nothing.

setp   Finally, I've found it useful to add a three-argument version of **setp**, a
_Gn   function **_Gn** that treats the "get next" pointer as a pointer to *unsigned char*,
_Pn   and a similar function **_Pn** for the "put next" pointer.

spos.c   Figure 7.2 shows the file **spos.c**, which defines the constructor for class
streampos. I added a default second argument to provide an optional
initial value for the **fpos_t** member object **_Fp**.

sposequa.c   Figure 7.3 shows the file **sposequa.c**, which defines the equality operator for class **streampos**. Note that an invalid file position always compares
equal to another invalid file position, and never compares equal to a valid
one. The equality check for valid file positions may be too exacting.

Figure 7.2:
spos.c

```
// spos -- streampos constructor
#include <streambuf>

static const _Fpost fpzero = {0};

streampos::streampos(streamoff off, const _Fpost *fp)
    : _Pos(off), _Fp(fp != 0 ? *fp : fpzero)
    {                                              // construct a streampos
    }                                                                    □
```

Figure 7.3:
sposequa.c

```
// sposequa -- streampos::operator==(const streampos&)
#include <streambuf>

_Bool streampos::operator==(const streampos& rop) const
    {                                              // compare for equality
    if (_Fp._Off == _BADOFF || rop._Fp._Off == _BADOFF)
        return (_Fp._Off == _BADOFF && rop._Fp._Off == _BADOFF
            ? 1 : 0);
    else
        return (_Pos + _Fp._Off == rop._Pos + rop._Fp._Off
            && _Fp._Wstate._Wchar == rop._Fp._Wstate._Wchar
            && _Fp._Wstate._State == rop._Fp._Wstate._State);
    }                                                                    □
```

Figure 7.4:
sposminu.c

```
// sposminus -- streampos::operator-(const streampos&)
#include <streambuf>

streamoff streampos::operator-(const streampos& rop) const
    {                            // subtract one streampos from another
    return (_Fp._Off == _BADOFF || rop._Fp._Off == _BADOFF
        ? _BADOFF : _Pos + _Fp._Off - rop._Pos - rop._Fp._Off);
    }                                                                    □
```

Figure 7.5:
sposoffs.c

```
// sposoffset -- streampos::offset()
#include <streambuf>

streamoff streampos::offset() const
    {                                                    // get offset
    return (_Fp._Off == _BADOFF ? _BADOFF : _Pos + _Fp._Off);
    }                                                                    □
```

sposminu.c   Figure 7.4 shows the file **sposminu.c**, which defines the subtraction operator for class **streampos**. It yields **_BADOFF** if either file position is undefined. Sadly, there is no easy way to distinguish an invalid return from the very sensible difference –1.

sposoffs.c   Figure 7.5 shows the file **sposoffs.c**, which defines the member function **offset()** for class **streampos**. Note that it ignores the algebraic offset **_Pos** if the absolute position **_Fp._Off** is invalid. (Yes, the names are backwards.)

```
// streambuf -- streambuf basic members
#include <string.h>
#include <streambuf>

streambuf::~streambuf()
    {                               // destruct a streambuf -- DO NOTHING
    }

int streambuf::overflow(int)
    {                                       // dummy overflow, always fail
    return (EOF);
    }

int streambuf::pbackfail(int)
    {                                       // dummy pbackfail, always fail
    return (EOF);
    }

int streambuf::underflow()
    {                                       // dummy underflow, always fail
    return (EOF);
    }

int streambuf::uflow()
    {                                   // consume and return a character
    return (gptr() != 0 && gptr() < egptr()
        ? *_Gn()++
        : underflow() == EOF ? EOF : *_Gn()++);
    }

int streambuf::xsgetn(char *s, int n)
    {                                       // get up to n characters
    int ch, m, ns;
    for (ns = 0; 0 < n; )
        if (gptr() != 0 && 0 < (m = egptr() - gptr()))
            {                               // move as many as possible
            if (n < m)
                m = n;
            memcpy(s, gptr(), m);
            s += m, ns += m, n -= m, gbump(m);
            }
        else if ((ch = uflow()) == EOF)
            break;
        else
            *s++ = ch, ++ns, --n;
    return (ns);
    }

int streambuf::xsputn(const char *s, int n)
    {                                       // put n characters
    int m, ns;
    for (ns = 0; 0 < n; )
        if (pptr() != 0 && 0 < (m = epptr() - pptr()))
            {                               // move as many as possible
            if (n < m)
```

```
                        m = n;
                memcpy(pptr(), s, m);
                s += m, ns += m, n -= m, pbump(m);
                }
        else if (overflow(*(const unsigned char *)s) == EOF)
                break;
        else
                ++s, ++ns, --n;
    return (ns);
    }

streampos streambuf::seekoff(streamoff, ios::seekdir,
    ios::openmode)
    {                                       // dummy seekoff, always fail
    return (streampos(_BADOFF));
    }

streampos streambuf::seekpos(streampos, ios::openmode)
    {                                       // dummy seekpos, always fail
    return (streampos(_BADOFF));
    }

streambuf *streambuf::setbuf(char *, int)
    {                                       // dummy setbuf, do nothing
    return (this);
    }

int streambuf::sync()
    {                                       // dummy sync, always succeed
    return (0);
    }

void streambuf::_Init(char **gb, char **gn, char **ge,
    char **pb, char **pn, char **pe)
    {               // initialize a streambuf with indirect pointers
    _IGbeg = gb;
    _IGnext = gn;
    _IGend = ge;
    _IPbeg = pb;
    _IPnext = pn;
    _IPend = pe;
    }

void streambuf::_Init()
    {               // initialize a streambuf with default pointers
    _IGbeg = &_Gbeg;
    _IGnext = &_Gnext;
    _IGend = &_Gend;
    _IPbeg = &_Pbeg;
    _IPnext = &_Pnext;
    _IPend = &_Pend;
    setp(0, 0);
    setg(0, 0, 0);
    }                                                               □
```

streambu.c   Figure 7.6 shows the file **streambu.c**. It defines all the member functions likely to be required by any object of class **streambuf**. I've augmented the required constructor with an optional second argument, to ease interfacing with the Standard C library. Most are dummy functions that either fail or do something innocuous. The two flavors of the secret function **_Init** show two ways to implement the six pointers that control all buffer accesses.

indirect   I found it desirable to add a level of indirection. You will notice that the **pointers** class indeed has six private pointer members. It also has six private pointers to pointers to *char*. And it is these indirect pointers that the protected member functions use to access characters in any in-memory buffers.

I chose this more ornate implementation to permit a very important optimization. Remember, I said earlier that a principal use for **streambuf** objects is to work in concert with C streams controlled by objects of type **FILE**. The obvious way to do so is to derive a class whose virtual member functions call **fgetc**, **fputc**, etc. for the corresponding **FILE** object. But that is terribly inefficient. A better way, when possible, is to have both the **streambuf** and **FILE** objects control exactly the same set of pointers into exactly the same buffers.

This I have been able to do in conjunction with my implementation of the Standard C library. The cost is this extra level of indirection within class **streambuf**. The payoff is substantially improved performance for C++ iostreams when reading and writing files. I consider it a good tradeoff.

So the six indirect pointers point directly inside a **FILE** object, whenever possible, as I will show in a later chapter. (See Chapter 13: **<fstream>**.) In this case, the six character pointers are ignored. Otherwise, the six indirect pointers point at the six character pointers.

If you don't understand **streambuf** yet, don't worry. Its use will become clearer as you see some of the ways it is specialized later in the Standard C++ library.

Testing **<streambuf>**

tstreamb.c   Figure 7.7 shows the file **tstreamb.c**. It tests the basic properties of class **streampos** and class **streambuf**. For the latter, it relies on the specialization provided by class **strstreambuf**, which is mediated in turn by class **ostrstream**. (See Chapter 11: **<strstream>**.) Since class **streambuf** itself does little, there is little to test.

Most of the serious testing of class **streambuf** occurs in connection with the derived classes presented later in this book. If all goes well, the program prints:

SUCCESS testing <streambuf>

and takes a normal exit.

```
// test <streambuf>
#include <assert.h>
#include <iostream>
#include <streambuf>
#include <strstream>

int main()
    {               // test basic workings of streambuf definitions
    streamoff soff = 3;
    streampos s1, s2(10);
    assert(s1.offset() == 0 && s2.offset() == 10);
    assert(s2 - s1 == 10);
    assert(s1 + 4 == s2 - 6);
    assert(!((s1 += soff) != (s2 -= 7)));
    assert(s1.offset() == soff && s2.offset() == soff);
        // test streambuf positioning members
    char buf[10];
    ostrstream os;
    streambuf *p = os.rdbuf();
    assert(p != 0);
    s1 = p->pubseekoff(0, ios::cur, ios::out);
    s2 = p->pubseekpos(s1, ios::out);
    assert(s1 == s2);
    p->pubsetbuf(buf, sizeof (buf));
    p->pubsync();
        // test streambuf read/write members
    assert(p->sputc('a') == 'a');
    s1 = p->pubseekoff(0, ios::cur, ios::out);
    assert(s1 != s2);
    s2 = p->pubseekpos(s1, ios::out);
    assert(s1 == s2);
    assert(p->sgetc() == 'a' && p->sbumpc() == 'a');
    assert(p->sputn("xyz", 3) == 3);
    assert(p->sgetn(buf, 10) == 3 && buf[0] == 'x');
    assert(p->sputbackc('w') == 'w' && p->sungetc() == 'y');
    assert(p->snextc() == 'w');
    assert(p->pubseekpos(s1, ios::in) == s2);
    assert(p->sputc('!') == '!' && p->sgetc() == 'x');
    assert((p->pubseekoff(0, ios::end, ios::in)).offset() != -1);
    assert(p->sungetc() == '!');
    cout << "SUCCESS testing <streambuf>" << endl;
    return (0);
    }                                                               □
```

Exercises

Exercise 7.1 Derive a class from **streambuf** that serves as a "bit bucket." Any characters you insert in its output stream disappear without remark. Why would you want such a capability?

Exercise 7.2 Derive a class from **streambuf** that serves as a "**toupper** filter." Any characters you insert in its output stream are translated to uppercase, then inserted in another stream buffer. How do you specify this destination?

Exercise 7.3 Derive a class from **streambuf** that serves as a "**toupper** filter," as in the previous exercise, except that it alters its input stream, not its output stream. Why is this version more elaborate than the previous one?

Exercise 7.4 Define the class **wstreambuf** that behaves just like **streambuf**, but manages streams of wide-characters instead of single-byte characters. What do you have to change besides appearances of the type *char*?

Exercise 7.5 Define the template class **basic_streambuf** such that it can be specialized to look like either **streambuf** or the **wstreambuf** of the previous exercise. How many parameters do you need to specify?

Exercise 7.6 [Harder] Define a clase that serves as an "**mbtowc** filter." It extracts single-byte characters from another stream buffer and converts them to a stream of wide characters, as if by repeated calls to **mbrtowc**, declared in **<wchar.h>** (ISO94). Is the reverse mapping easier or harder?

Exercise 7.7 [Very hard] Alter the class **streambuf** so that it manages *both* single-byte and wide-character streams interchangeably. How can you "cross couple" the streams to minimize surprises given a mixture of single-byte and wide-character insertions or extractions?

Chapter 8: `<istream>`

Background

The principal business of the header `<istream>` is to define the class `istream`. This class is derived from the virtual public base class `ios` to help you extract characters from a stream. The best known object of this class is `cin`, which controls input from the standard input stream — the same C stream controlled by `stdin`, declared in `<stdio.h>`. You can also create `istream` objects that control files you open by name, or strings of text stored in memory, as later chapters reveal.

istream Most of the `istream` member functions fall into one of two broad categories:

- *unformatted input functions,* which extract sequences of arbitrary *char* values, such as uninterpreted text or binary data

- *formatted input functions,* which extract sequences that match certain text patterns and convert them to encoded values of the various scalar and string data types

unformatted input The former group mostly overloads the names `get` and `read`. It is analogous to the Standard C library's `fgetc` and `fread`, declared in `<stdio.h>`, but rather easier to use. For example, you can extract a "line" of text with:

```
if (cin.getline(buf, sizeof (buf)))
    <input succeeded>
```

The test is true (nonzero) only if the member function extracts a non-empty string that can fit in `buf`, from the stream controlled by the `istream` object `cin`. A line is delimited (terminated) by an optional third argument of type *char,* which defaults to `'\n'`. The function stores the resulting null-terminated string in `buf`, discarding the delimiter.

formatted input The latter group of member functions overloads `operator>>` to make the basic family of extractors. It is analogous to the Standard C library's `fscanf` and friends, but with a variety of advantages. For example, you can extract an octal integer with:

```
int n;
if (cin >> oct >> n)
    <input succeeded>
```

The test is true only if the second extractor extracts a non-empty field that matches the pattern for octal integers, and the converted value can be properly represented in an object of type *int*.

Extractors are second in popularity only to inserters (formated output functions) as a selling point for iostreams over more conventional Standard C input and output. But they are easier to explain after you gain more familiarity with the unformatted input functions. I return to extractors later in this section.

Remember that all extractions and insertions in iostreams are mediated by objects of class **streambuf**. (See the previous chapter.) An object of class **istream** finds its related **streambuf** object via a pointer in its base subobject of class **ios**. A member function of class **istream** can extract and consume the next available input character by calling **rdbuf()->sbumpc()**. It can extract and *not* consume the next available input character (peek at it) by calling **rdbuf()->sgetc()**. And it can put back a character **ch** by calling **rdbuf()->sputbackc(ch)**. (It can perform several other related functions as well, but these are the most robust.)

ipfx   There is one small problem, however. It is perfectly permissible for the
isfx pointer to **streambuf** to be null. It is also quite possible that the pointer is non-null, but the stream is in some error state that should discourage extracting. Thus, it behooves any input function to look before it leaps. The canonical way to play safe is to wrap every extractor member function with two calls to **istream** member functions:

```
if (ipfx(noskip))
    <perform any input>
isfx();
```

The "prefix" function **ipfx(int)** verifies that the stream is both ready and willing to supply input, or at least to support calls to the **streambuf** member functions described above. It also performs other initializiation operations and, if you so request, will skip any white space in the input stream. As a rule, formatted input functions skip leading white space while unformatted input functions do not.

The "suffix" function **isfx()** performs any necessary wrapup operations after each input member function does its work. Some implementations define **isfx()** as an inline empty function — it often has nothing to do. But that is not always the case for an arbitrary implementation. If you write an input function that uses the **istream** object **x** and makes direct calls to its associated **streambuf** object, always call **x.ipfx(noskip)** and **x.isfx()** as shown above.

exception   The prefix and suffix member functions have been part of iostreams for
handling many a year. You will find similar creatures as member functions of class **ostream**. (See the next chapter.) But the draft C++ Standard introduces yet another source of surprises, which calls for even more machinery. All sorts of functions can throw exceptions. The input functions have clearly defined responsibility when exceptions occur during their execution.

If the Standard C++ library had complete control over matters, it would not have to worry so much. Input functions could simply avoid calling functions that might throw exceptions. But that is not the case. Any call to **rdbuf()->sbumpc()**, for example, can result in a call to a **streambuf** virtual member function. And any object of class **streambuf** can actually represent a derived class. In fact, it usually does. A derived stream buffer is not necessarily part of the Standard C++ library. It can have programmer-supplied virtual member functions. The library can thus never know when a call on a **streambuf** member function might throw an exception.

The draft C++ Standard is clear about what happens when an exception occurs during execution of an input (or output) member function. The function must call **setstate(badbit)**, then rethrow the exception. The structure of an arbitrary input function must now look like:

```
try {
    if (ipfx(noskip))
        <perform any input>
    isfx();
    }
catch (...) {
    setstate(badbit);
    throw;
    }
```

Note that the act of setting **badbit** can also raise an exception, of class **ios::failure**. (See page 123.) Should that happen, the original exception never gets rethrown.

get Now you have enough background to understand how the unformatted input functions work. The simplest of these is the member function **get()**. It extracts a single character — probably by calling **rdbuf()->sbumpc()** inside the sandwich shown above — and delivers it as the value of the function. A failure to extract the requested character, for any reason, is reflected in a return value of **EOF**.

gcount A failure by **get()** can also be detected another way. Each of the unformatted input functions stores within the **istream** object a count of the number of characters it extracts. You can access this stored value by calling the member function **gcount()**. In the case of **get()**, a subsequent call to **gcount()** returns a count of either zero or one. Obviously, a subsequent call to another unformatted input function for the same **istream** object replaces the stored value with a newer one.

Equally obviously, the overhead in obtaining a single character via **get()** is substantially higher than for the Standard C library function **getchar()**, declared in **<stdio.h>**. The latter is almost invariably implemented as a macro that fetches a character straight from an input buffer more often than not. Thus, it behaves much like the member function **streambuf:: sbumpc()**. But **istream::get()** is almost impossible to treat similarly, given the prefix/suffix calls and exception handling required by the draft C++ Standard. You should thus favor methods that extract many more characters for each call, whenever possible, if performance is an issue.

get   You can also extract a single character by calling the member function **get(char&)**. You call it instead of **get()** to store directly into a *char*. You can also call it if you want to chain operations, as in:

```
is.get(c1).get(c2);
```

(a practice not universally admired). The variants **get(unsigned char&)** and **get(signed char&)** behave the same as **get(char)**, but store in the other character types.

get   The function **get(char *, int, char)** also has its variants for arrays
getline of *unsigned char* and *signed char*. You use it to extract a sequence of characters up to, but not including, a delimiter character. If that sounds much like **getline(char *, int, char)**, which I described earlier, you're right. In a nutshell, both deliver null-terminated strings guaranteed not to contain an instance of the delimiter. Both set **eofbit** if they encounter end-of-file while extracting characters. Both set **failbit** if the buffer ends up holding an empty string. But **get** doesn't actually consume the delimiter, while **getline** does (without storing it). And **get** doesn't get upset if it fills the buffer before it sees a delimiter, while **getline** sets **failbit** in this case. (See the summary beginning on page 190.)

current   This behavior of **getline** is not entirely consistent with current practice,
practice by the way. In at least some implementations:

- storing a null string in the buffer sets **failbit** only if no delimiter is extracted and discarded
- filling the buffer *exactly* does not set **failbit** (if the first unstored character is the delimiter, the buffer is not considered over full)
- encountering end-of-file sets *both* **eofbit** and **failbit**, not just the former

Inconsistencies like this are a topic for on-going refinement by the Committee. Unless and until such issues are resolved, you are well advised not to write code that is vulnerable to these differences.

read   If you want rather less logic, consider the member function **read(char *, int)** (or its alternate forms for arrays of *signed char* or *unsigned char*). It simply extracts characters until the count you specify is exhausted, or until no more characters can be extracted. Once again, it has slightly different rules for setting status bits, which I discuss later in this chapter. (As before, see page 190.)

writing   Lest you think that iostreams are always at a performance disadvantage
stream buffers compared to Standard C input/output, consider the member function **get(streambuf&, char)**. It extracts characters and writes them directly to a stream buffer up to, but not including, a delimiter. Thus, you can write:

```
cin.get(*cout.rdbuf(), '\n');
```

to copy the next text line from **cin** directly to **cout**. In this case, copying can be quite fast. (A related extractor can be even faster for copying to the end of the input stream, since it doesn't have to check for delimiters. I describe it later in this chapter.)

ignore   A handful of additional member functions sometimes proves handy in
sync conjunction with the unformatted input functions. The member function
ignore(int, int), for example, extracts and discards characters up to a
specified count, or until a specified delimiter is extracted and discarded.
And the member function **sync()** simply calls the public "synchronizing"
function **rdbuf()->pubsync()** (assuming the associated **streambuf** object
is present).

Typically, such an operation flushes an output stream to the associated
external file. Some systems use calls like this to discard pending characters
from an interactive input stream, but that is *not* mandated by the draft C++
Standard. Don't count on it. For a pure input stream, there is no *portable* use
you can make of this particular member function.

peek   Several member functions let you manipulate characters from the input
putback stream one at a time. The member function **peek()** lets you see the next
unget character to be extracted without actually consuming it. It is a safer interface
to **rdbuf()->sgetc()**. The member function **putback(char)** lets you "put
back" an extracted character — a safer **rdbuf()->sputbackc()**. The next
extraction will deliver up the character you just put back. And the related
member function **unget()** backs up a character position without altering
the apparent contents of the input stream. It is a safer **rdbuf()->
sungetc()**. With either of these last two functions, you shouldn't count on
backing up more than one character position between extractions. Portable
support for such antics is not guaranteed.

extractors   Now for the formatted input functions, or extractors. These member
functions overload **operator>>** for a left parameter of type **istream&**. That
lets you write code such as:

```
float fl;
cin >> fl;
```

which extracts characters from the stream controlled by **cin** (the standard
input stream). Extraction continues so long as characters continue to match
the text pattern acceptable to the Standard C library function **strtod**,
declared in **<stdlib.h>**. The entire sequence extracted by this rule must
then be successfully converted, as if by calling **strtod**, and the resulting
value must be representable as type *float*.

If all those conditions obtain, the extractor stores the converted value in
fl and succeeds. Otherwise, the function reports failure, typically by
setting **failbit** in **cin**. In any event, all the characters extracted to make
up the valid text field (or valid prefix for such a field) are irretrievably
consumed.

If all that machinery sounds rather like **fscanf**, declared in **<stdio.h>**,
it should. Extractors serve the same function for the Standard C++ library
that the **fscanf** family serves for the Standard C library. You can, in fact,
implement extractors by calls to **fscanf**. That turns out to be not always
convenient, however:

- The source of input for a stream controlled by an **istream** object is controlled in turn by a **streambuf** object. You can't always relate that source directly to the sources accessible by **fscanf** or **sscanf**.

- You can extract characters and store them in a buffer for processing by **sscanf**. But doing so requires a buffer that is arbitrarily large. Or you end up doing so much preprocessing of the text that you duplicate much of the work done by **sscanf**.

For these reasons, it is not necessarily wise to make actual calls to **fscanf** to implement extractors. Nevertheless, the *definition* of a typical extractor member function in **istream** is in terms of **fscanf** conversion specifiers (17.4.3.1). When in doubt, you can often turn to the C Standard for a more precise description of extractor behavior.

character extractors   I begin with the extractors that perform a minimum of interpretation. These extract one or more characters from the input stream and deliver them either to memory or to an output stream. The simplest of all is **operator>>(char&)**, which extracts a single character. As usual, class **istream** also defines *unsigned char* and *signed char* versions of the same extractor.

These member functions are all similar in behavior to the member function **get(char&)** and its brethren, described earlier. The principal difference internally is the argument to **ipfx**. An unformatted input function such as **get(char&)** should call **ipfx(1)** (or with some other nonzero argument), to suppress skipping of leading white space.

The extractor, however, should call **ipfx(0)**. That encourages **ipfx** to skip leading white space before extracting the actual data to be delivered, assuming the format flag **skipws** is set within the **istream** object. (It is set by default when the object is constructed.)

ws   If you want to skip white space before invoking an extractor, regardless of the setting of **skipws**, you can always use the manipulator **ws**, declared in **<istream>**. If you write:

```
cin >> ws >> fl;
```

then the manipulator always skips white space before **fl** is extracted. (It doesn't hurt to try skipping white space more than once.)

string extractors   The member function **operator>>(char *)** extracts a sequence of characters from the input stream and stores it as a null-terminated string in the character array designated by the pointer argument. Yes, there are three flavors, once again. This is one of the few extractors that uses the width value stored in the **istream** object. If **width()** is zero, the width is taken as **INT_MAX**, defined in **<limits.h>**. Input stops with the first white-space character (which is not extracted), or when the specified number of characters, counting the terminating null, are stored in the array. Note that the width field is set to zero by this extractor, as is customary for functions that make use of this field.

stream buffer The member function **operator>>(streambuf&)** also strongly resem-
extractor bles one of the unformatted input functions shown earlier. You use it to
copy the remainder of the input stream to the output stream controlled by
the **streambuf** operand, as in:

```
cin >> cout->rdbuf();
```

As I mentioned before, this extractor version should be substantially faster
because it doesn't have to check for delimiters. Thus, it can move whole
blocks of characters at a time, if properly implemented.

scalar The remaining formatted input functions extract various scalar types.
extractors For all the integer types, you can control the assumed numeric base by how
you set the **ios::basefield** group of format flags. (See page 126.) No
controls apply to the floating-point types (other than the usual **ios::**
skipws) — integer, fixed-point, and scientific formats are all acceptable at
all times. Nor do any controls apply to the extractor for pointer to *void*, an
extractor of limited utility. (See page 192.)

user-defined You can, of course, also write your own extractors. It is commonplace,
extractors when designing a new class, to provide a tailored inserter at the very least.
If reading values of the class makes sense, then it is good manners to
provide an extractor as well. You might even want to write an extractor or
two that are not associated with a specific class.

The best style for writing new extractors is to do so in terms of the
member functions of class **istream**. If you must drop below this level and
access the associated **streambuf** object directly, then by all means match
the discipline followed in the extractors presented here. If you don't, then
it's only a matter of time before you or one of your colleagues gets burned.
Such is the blessing, and the curse, of reusable software.

What the Draft C++ Standard Says

The header **<istream>** is the third of the "big four" headers that define
the iostreams package. Like **<ios>** and **<streambuf>** in the previous two
chapters, and **<ostream>** in the next chapter, it contains a lot of niggling
detail.

It also contains a number of small deviations from common past practice.
I've warned about some of these earlier in this chapter, but I can't highlight
them all. Partly that's because of small differences among current implementations. One role of a programming-language standard is to make
choices when past practice is not uniform. In such cases, it's impossible to
please everyone with an existing investment in code. That is sometimes the
case with a package as extensive as iostreams.

17.4.3 Header `<istream>`

The header `<istream>` defines a type and a function signature that control input from a stream buffer.

17.4.3.1 Class `istream`

```
class istream : virtual public ios {
public:
    istream(streambuf* sb);
    virtual ~istream();
    int ipfx(int noskipws = 0);
    void isfx();
    istream& operator>>(istream& (*pf)(istream&));
    istream& operator>>(ios& (*pf)(ios&));
    istream& operator>>(char* s);
    istream& operator>>(unsigned char* s);
    istream& operator>>(signed char* s);
    istream& operator>>(char& c);
    istream& operator>>(unsigned char& c);
    istream& operator>>(signed char& c);
    istream& operator>>(short& n);
    istream& operator>>(unsigned short& n);
    istream& operator>>(int& n);
    istream& operator>>(unsigned int& n);
    istream& operator>>(long& n);
    istream& operator>>(unsigned long& n);
    istream& operator>>(float& f);
    istream& operator>>(double& f);
    istream& operator>>(long double& f);
    istream& operator>>(void*& p);
    istream& operator>>(streambuf& sb);
    int get();
    istream& get(char* s, int n, char delim = '\n');
    istream& get(unsigned char* s, int n, char delim = '\n');
    istream& get(signed char* s, int n, char delim = '\n');
    istream& get(char& c);
    istream& get(unsigned char& c);
    istream& get(signed char& c);
    istream& get(streambuf& sb, char delim = '\n');
    istream& getline(char* s, int n, char delim = '\n');
    istream& getline(unsigned char* s, int n, char delim = '\n');
    istream& getline(signed char* s, int n, char delim = '\n');
    istream& ignore(int n = 1, int delim = EOF);
    istream& read(char* s, int n);
    istream& read(unsigned char* s, int n);
    istream& read(signed char* s, int n);
    int peek();
    istream& putback(char c);
    istream& unget();
    int gcount() const;
    int sync();
private:
//  int chcount;                                    exposition only
};
```

The class `istream` defines a number of member function signatures that assist in reading and interpreting input from sequences controlled by a stream buffer.

Two groups of member function signatures share common properties: the *formatted input functions* (or *extractors*) and the *unformatted input functions*. Both groups of input functions obtain (or *extract*) input characters by calling the function signatures **sb.sbumpc()**, **sb.sgetc()**, and **sb.sputbackc(char)**. If one of these called functions throws an exception, the input function calls **setstate(badbit)** and rethrows the exception.

- The formatted input functions are:

```
istream& operator>>(char* s);
istream& operator>>(unsigned char* s);
istream& operator>>(signed char* s);
istream& operator>>(char& c);
istream& operator>>(unsigned char& c);
istream& operator>>(signed char& c);
istream& operator>>(short& n);
istream& operator>>(unsigned short& n);
istream& operator>>(int& n);
istream& operator>>(unsigned int& n);
istream& operator>>(long& n);
istream& operator>>(unsigned long& n);
istream& operator>>(float& f);
istream& operator>>(double& f);
istream& operator>>(long double& f);
istream& operator>>(void*& p);
istream& operator>>(streambuf& sb);
```

- The unformatted input functions are:

```
int get();
istream& get(char* s, int n, char delim = '\n');
istream& get(unsigned char* s, int n, char delim = '\n');
istream& get(signed char* s, int n, char delim = '\n');
istream& get(char& c);
istream& get(unsigned char& c);
istream& get(signed char& c);
istream& get(streambuf& sb, char delim = '\n');
istream& getline(char* s, int n, char delim = '\n');
istream& getline(unsigned char* s, int n, char delim = '\n');
istream& getline(signed char* s, int n, char delim = '\n');
istream& ignore(int n = 1, int delim = EOF);
istream& read(char* s, int n);
istream& read(unsigned char* s, int n);
istream& read(signed char* s, int n);
int peek();
istream& putback(char c);
istream& unget();
```

Each formatted input function begins execution by calling **ipfx()**. If that function returns nonzero, the function endeavors to obtain the requested input. In any case, the formatted input function ends by calling **isfx()**, then returning the value specified for the formatted input function.

Some formatted input functions endeavor to obtain the requested input by parsing characters extracted from the input sequence, converting the result to a value of some scalar data type, and storing the converted value in an object of that scalar data type. The behavior of such functions is described in terms of the conversion specification for an equivalent call to the function signature **fscanf(FILE*, const char*, ...)**, declared in **<stdio.h>**, with the following alterations:

- The formatted input function extracts characters from a stream buffer, rather than reading them from an input file.[92)]
- If **flags()** & **skipws** is zero, the function does not skip any leading white space. In that case, if the next input character is white space, the scan fails.
- If the converted data value cannot be represented as a value of the specified scalar data type, a scan failure occurs.

If the scan fails for any reason, the formatted input function calls **setstate(failbit)**.

For conversion to an integral type other than a character type, the function determines the integral conversion specifier as follows:

- If **(flags() & basefield) == oct**, the conversion specifier is **o**.
- If **(flags() & basefield) == hex**, the conversion specifier is **x**.
- If **(flags() & basefield) == 0**, the conversion specifier is **i**.

Otherwise, the integral conversion specifier is **d** for conversion to a signed integral type, or **u** for conversion to an unsigned integral type.

Each unformatted input function begins execution by calling **ipfx(1)**. If that function returns nonzero, the function endeavors to extract the requested input. It also counts the number of characters extracted. In any case, the unformatted input function ends by storing the count in a member object and calling **isfx()**, then returning the value specified for the unformatted input function.

For the sake of exposition, the data maintained by an object of class **istream** is presented here as:

- **int** *chcount*, stores the number of characters extracted by the last unformatted input member function called for the object.

17.4.3.1.1 istream::istream()

constructor

```
istream(streambuf* sb);
```

Constructs an object of class **istream**, assigning initial values to the base class by calling **ios::init(sb)**, then assigning zero to *chcount*.

17.4.3.1.2 istream::~istream()

destructor

```
virtual ~istream();
```

Destroys an object of class **istream**.

17.4.3.1.3 istream::ipfx(int)

ipfx

```
int ipfx(int noskipws = 0);
```

If **good()** is nonzero, prepares for formatted or unformatted input. First, if **tie()** is not a null pointer, the function calls **tie()->flush()** to synchronize the output sequence with any associated external C stream. (The call **tie()-> flush()** does not necessarily occur if the function can determine that no synchronization is necessary.) If *noskipws* is zero and **flags() & skipws** is nonzero, the function extracts and discards each character as long as **isspace(c)** is nonzero for the next available input character *c*. The function signature **isspace(int)** is declared in **<ctype.h>**.

If, after any preparation is completed, **good()** is nonzero, the function returns a nonzero value. Otherwise, it calls **setstate(failbit)** and returns zero.[93)]

17.4.3.1.4 istream::isfx()

isfx

```
void isfx();
```

Returns.

17.4.3.1.5 istream::operator>>(istream& (*)(istream&))

operator>>

```
istream& operator>>(istream& (*pf)(istream&));
```

Returns **(*pf)(*this)**.[94)]

17.4.3.1.6 istream::operator>>(ios& (*)(ios&))

operator>>

  istream& operator>>(ios& (*pf)(ios&));

Calls **(*(ios*)pf)(*this)**, then returns ***this**.[95)]

17.4.3.1.7 istream::operator>>(char*)

operator>>

  istream& operator>>(char* s);

A formatted input function, extracts characters and stores them into successive locations of an array whose first element is designated by **s**. If **width()** is greater than zero, the maximum number of characters stored **n** is **width()**; otherwise it is **INT_MAX**, defined in **<limits.h>**.

Characters are extracted and stored until any of the following occurs:

- **n - 1** characters are stored;
- end-of-file occurs on the input sequence;
- **isspace(c)** is nonzero for the next available input character **c**.

The function signature **isspace(int)** is declared in **<ctype.h>**.

If the function stores no characters, it calls **setstate(failbit)**. In any case, it then stores a null character into the next successive location of the array and calls **width(0)**. The function returns ***this**.

17.4.3.1.8 istream::operator>>(unsigned char*)

operator>>

  istream& operator>>(unsigned char* s);

Returns **operator>>((char*)s)**.

17.4.3.1.9 istream::operator>>(signed char*)

operator>>

  istream& operator>>(signed char* s);

Returns **operator>>((char*)s)**.

17.4.3.1.10 istream::operator>>(char&)

operator>>

  istream& operator>>(char& c);

A formatted input function, extracts a character, if one is available, and stores it in **c**. Otherwise, the function calls **setstate(failbit)**. The function returns ***this**.

17.4.3.1.11 istream::operator>>(unsigned char&)

operator>>

  istream& operator>>(unsigned char& c);

Returns **operator>>((char&)c)**.

17.4.3.1.12 istream::operator>>(signed char&)

operator>>

  istream& operator>>(signed char& c);

Returns **operator>>((char&)c)**.

17.4.3.1.13 istream::operator>>(short&)

operator>>

  istream& operator>>(short& n);

A formatted input function, converts a signed short integer (with the integral conversion specifier preceded by **h**, as in **hd** for decimal input) if one is available, and stores it in **n**. The function returns ***this**.

17.4.3.1.14 istream::operator>>(unsigned short&)

operator>>

  istream& operator>>(unsigned short& n);

A formatted input function, converts an unsigned short integer (with the integral conversion specifier preceded by **h**, as in **hu** for decimal input) if one is available, and stores it in **n**. The function returns ***this**.

17.4.3.1.15 istream::operator>>(int&)

operator>>

```
istream& operator>>(int& n);
```

A formatted input function, converts a signed integer (with the integral conversion specifier unqualified, as in **d** for decimal input) if one is available, and stores it in **n**. The function returns ***this**.

17.4.3.1.16 istream::operator>>(unsigned int&)

operator>>

```
istream& operator>>(unsigned int& n);
```

A formatted input function, converts an unsigned integer (with the integral conversion specifier unqualified, as in **u** for decimal input) if one is available, and stores it in **n**. The function returns ***this**.

17.4.3.1.17 istream::operator>>(long&)

operator>>

```
istream& operator>>(long& n);
```

A formatted input function, converts a signed long integer (with the integral conversion specifier preceded by **l**, as in **ld** for decimal input) if one is available, and stores it in **n**. The function returns ***this**.

17.4.3.1.18 istream::operator>>(unsigned long&)

operator>>

```
istream& operator>>(unsigned long& n);
```

A formatted input function, converts an unsigned long integer (with the integral conversion specifier preceded by **l**, as in **lu** for decimal input) if one is available, and stores it in **n**. The function returns ***this**.

17.4.3.1.19 istream::operator>>(float&)

operator>>

```
istream& operator>>(float& f);
```

A formatted input function, converts a **float** (with the conversion specifier **f**) if one is available, and stores it in **f**. The function returns ***this**.

17.4.3.1.20 istream::operator>>(double&)

operator>>

```
istream& operator>>(double& f);
```

A formatted input function, converts a **double** (with the conversion specifier **lf**) if one is available, and stores it in **f**. The function returns ***this**.

17.4.3.1.21 istream::operator>>(long double&)

operator>>

```
istream& operator>>(long double& f);
```

A formatted input function, converts a **long double** (with the conversion specifier **Lf**) if one is available, and stores it in **f**. The function returns ***this**.

17.4.3.1.22 istream::operator>>(void*&)

operator>>

```
istream& operator>>(void*& p);
```

A formatted input function, converts a pointer to **void** (with the conversion specifier **p**) if one is available, and stores it in **p**. The function returns ***this**.

17.4.3.1.23 istream::operator>>(streambuf&)

operator>>

```
istream& operator>>(streambuf& sb);
```

A formatted input function, extracts characters from ***this** and inserts them in the output sequence controlled by **sb**. Characters are extracted and inserted until any of the following occurs:

- end-of-file occurs on the input sequence;
- inserting in the output sequence fails (in which case the character to be inserted is not extracted);
- an exception occurs (in which case the exception is caught but not rethrown).

If the function inserts no characters, it calls **setstate(failbit)**. The function returns ***this**.

17.4.3.1.24 `istream::get()`

get | `int get();`

An unformatted input function, extracts a character *c*, if one is available. The function then returns **(unsigned char)** *c*. Otherwise, the function calls **setstate(failbit)** and then returns **EOF**.

17.4.3.1.25 `istream::get(char*, int, char)`

get | `istream& get(char* s, int n, char delim = '\n');`

An unformatted input function, extracts characters and stores them into successive locations of an array whose first element is designated by *s*. Characters are extracted and stored until any of the following occurs:

- *n* - **1** characters are stored;
- end-of-file occurs on the input sequence (in which case the function calls **setstate(eofbit)**);
- *c* == *delim* for the next available input character *c* (in which case *c* is not extracted).

If the function stores no characters, it calls **setstate(failbit)**. In any case, it then stores a null character into the next successive location of the array. The function returns ***this**.

17.4.3.1.26 `istream::get(unsigned char*, int, char)`

get | `istream& get(unsigned char* s, int n, char delim = '\n');`

Returns **get((char*)*s*, *n*, *delim*)**.

17.4.3.1.27 `istream::get(signed char*, int, char)`

get | `istream& get(signed char* s, int n, char delim = '\n');`

Returns **get((char*)*s*, *n*, *delim*)**.

17.4.3.1.28 `istream::get(char&)`

get | `istream& get(char& c);`

An unformatted input function, extracts a character, if one is available, and assigns it to *c*. Otherwise, the function calls **setstate(failbit)**. The function returns ***this**.

17.4.3.1.29 `istream::get(unsigned char&)`

get | `istream& get(unsigned char& c);`

Returns **get((char&)*c*)**.

17.4.3.1.30 `istream::get(signed char&)`

get | `istream& get(signed char& c);`

Returns **istream::get((char&)*c*)**.

17.4.3.1.31 `istream::get(streambuf&, char)`

get | `istream& get(streambuf& sb, char delim = '\n');`

An unformatted input function, extracts characters and inserts them in the output sequence controlled by *sb*. Characters are extracted and inserted until any of the following occurs:

- end-of-file occurs on the input sequence;
- inserting in the output sequence fails (in which case the character to be inserted is not extracted);
- *c* == *delim* for the next available input character *c* (in which case *c* is not extracted);
- an exception occurs (in which case, the exception is caught but not rethrown).

If the function inserts no characters, it calls **setstate(failbit)**. The function returns ***this**.

17.4.3.1.32 istream::getline(char*, int, char)

getline

```
istream& getline(char* s, int n, char delim = '\n');
```

An unformatted input function, extracts characters and stores them into successive locations of an array whose first element is designated by **s**. Characters are extracted and stored until any of the following occurs:

- **n - 1** characters are stored (in which case the function calls **setstate(failbit)**);
- end-of-file occurs on the input sequence (in which case the function calls **setstate(eofbit)**);
- **c == delim** for the next available input character **c** (in which case the input character is extracted but not stored).

If the function stores no characters, it calls **setstate(failbit)**. In any case, it then stores a null character into the next successive location of the array. The function returns ***this**.

17.4.3.1.33 istream::getline(unsigned char*, int, char)

getline

```
istream& getline(unsigned char* s, int n, char delim = '\n');
```

Returns **getline((char*)s, n, delim)**.

17.4.3.1.34 istream::getline(signed char*, int, char)

getline

```
istream& getline(signed char* s, int n, char delim = '\n');
```

Returns **getline((char*)s, n, delim)**.

17.4.3.1.35 istream::ignore(int, int)

ignore

```
istream& ignore(int n = 1, int delim = EOF);
```

An unformatted input function, extracts characters and discards them. Characters are extracted until any of the following occurs:

- if **n != INT_MAX**, **n** characters are extracted
- end-of-file occurs on the input sequence (in which case the function calls **setstate(eofbit)**);
- **c == delim** for the next available input character **c** (in which case **c** is extracted).

The last condition will never occur if **delim == EOF**.

The macro **INT_MAX** is defined in **<limits.h>**.

The function returns ***this**.

17.4.3.1.36 istream::read(char*, int)

read

```
istream& read(char* s, int n);
```

An unformatted input function, extracts characters and stores them into successive locations of an array whose first element is designated by **s**. Characters are extracted and stored until either of the following occurs:

- **n** characters are stored;
- end-of-file occurs on the input sequence (in which case the function calls **setstate(failbit)**).

The function returns ***this**.

17.4.3.1.37 istream::read(unsigned char*, int)

read

```
istream& read(unsigned char* s, int n);
```

Returns **read((char*)s, n)**.

17.4.3.1.38 istream::read(signed char*, int)

read

```
istream& read(signed char* s, int n);
```

Returns **read((char*)s, n)**.

17.4.3.1.39 istream::peek()

peek

```
int peek();
```

An unformatted input function, returns the next available input character, if possible.

If **good()** is zero, the function returns **EOF**. Otherwise, it returns **rdbuf()->sgetc()**.

17.4.3.1.40 istream::putback(char)

putback

```
istream& putback(char c);
```

An unformatted input function, calls **rdbuf->sputbackc(c)**. If that function returns **EOF**, the function calls **setstate(badbit)**. The function returns ***this**.

17.4.3.1.41 istream::unget()

unget

```
istream& unget();
```

An unformatted input function, calls **rdbuf->sungetc()**. If that function returns **EOF**, the function calls **setstate(badbit)**. The function returns ***this**.

17.4.3.1.42 istream::gcount()

gcount

```
int gcount() const;
```

Returns *chcount*.

17.4.3.1.43 istream::sync()

sync

```
int sync();
```

If **rdbuf()** is a null pointer, returns **EOF**. Otherwise, the function calls **rdbuf()->pubsync()** and, if that function returns **EOF**, calls **setstate(badbit)** and returns **EOF**. Otherwise, the function returns zero.

17.4.3.2 ws(istream&)

ws

```
istream& ws(istream& is);
```

Saves a copy of *is.fmtflags*, then clears *is.skipws* in *is.fmtflags*. The function then calls *is.ipfx()* and *is.isfx()*, and restores *is.fmtflags* to its saved value. The function returns *is*.[96]

Footnotes:

Footnotes

92) The stream buffer can, of course, be associated with an input file, but it need not be.

93) The function signatures **ipfx(int)** and **isfx()** can also perform additional implementation-dependent operations.

94) See, for example, the function signature **ws(istream&)**.

95) See, for example, the function signature **dec(ios&)**.

96) The effect of **cin >> ws** is to skip any white space in the input sequence controlled by **cin**.

Future Directions

bool   With the addition of the scalar type **bool** comes another formatted input function for class **istream**. An integer 1 converts to "true," while a zero converts to "false." The Committee has so far resisted the temptation to accept any more elaborate spellings, such as **T** or **true**.

eofbit   A later change regularizes the setting of **eofbit** when an extraction fails (presumably signaling end-of-file). In the Informal Review Draft, only a handful of the **istream** member functions promise to set this status bit as needed. Hence, **eofbit** is an unreliable indicator here.

getline   The member function **getline** has been altered to better match (at least some) current practice. See page 176 for a description of the newer functionality.

locale objects   As I mentioned earlier, the Committee has added locale objects. (See page 32.) Extractors in class **istream** are expected to access the locale object imbued within the base **ios** subobject to determine how to parse input. In principle, each **istream** object can operate within a different locale. By default, however, the locale imbued by an **istream** constructor is the **"C"** locale, *not* the current locale. Be warned.

wide-character streams   I also repeat here the warning, first mentioned on page 119, that wide-character streams have been added to the Standard C++ library. Class **istream** now derives from a template class parameterized by the type of the stream element. One instantiation, for type *char*, has essentially the same functionality as described in this chapter. Another, for type **wchar_t**, supports streams of elements from some large character set.

Using <istream>

You have little or no occasion to include the header **<istream>** directly. Like **<ios>** and **<streambuf>** in the previous two chapters, it is another header invented by the Committee simply to split the iostreams declarations into more manageable pieces. But the chances are just as good that you'll use the *contents* of **<istream>** in a program. Class **istream** is the base class for all classes that support extractions from a stream buffer, the classic way to mediate all input in the iostreams package. The base class summarizes what is *common* to all such input classes.

cin   If you include the header **<iostream>**, you can use the **istream** object **cin** to read the standard input stream. (See Chapter 14: **<iostream>**.) Otherwise, you typically create an object *derived* from **istream** to mediate input from a stream buffer you create at the same time. (See Chapter 11: **<strstream>**, Chapter 12: **<sstream>**, and Chapter 13: **<fstream>**.)

constructor   The only occasion you have for declaring an **istream** object directly is to mediate input from a stream buffer created separately. You can, for example, set up a bidirectional stream various ways. I showed one way to do so on page 122. The complementary way is:

```
#include <fstream>
    .....
    ofstream ostr("abc", ios::in | ios::out);
    istream istr(ostr.rdbuf());
```

or:

```
#include <fstream>
    .....
    ofstream ostr("abc", ios::in | ios::out);
    istream istr;
    istr.rdbuf(ostr.rdbuf());
```

Given an **istream** object **x**, you can perform a whole host of operations on it. Many are inherited from the base class **ios**, which I have already described. (See Chapter 6: `<ios>`.) You can also call:

- *predefined manipulators,* such as **x >> ws**, to alter the state of the input sequence or values stored in **x**
- *character input functions,* such as **x.get()**, to extract sequences of one or more characters
- *scalar extractors,* such as **x >> n**, for an *int* reference **n**, to extract sequences of one or more characters and convert them to scalar values
- *support functions,* such as **x.peek()**, to help you write your own manipulators and extractors

I deal with these groups of operations in order.

predefined   All the manipulators defined for class **ios** also apply to objects of class
manipulators **istream**, naturally enough. The same is true for the **ios** member functions
that have the same effect as the manipulators. (See the lengthy discussion
of formatting information beginning on page 124.) Not all have meaningful
effect, however. For an **istream** object, the relevant information is:

skipws ■ the format flag **skipws**, set (by default) to extract and discard any leading
white space, which affects all formatted input functions (extractors)

basefield ■ the format flags in the **basefield** group, which affect the numeric base
for the integer extractors

width ■ the width information, which affects only string extractors

manipulators   The header `<istream>` declares two peculiar member functions:

```
istream& operator>>(istream& (*pf)(istream&));
istream& operator>>(ios& (*pf)(ios&));
```

I described the second of these on page 124. It is the magic that makes the
manipulators defined for class **ios** work as "pseudo-extractors" with
istream objects. The first supports manipulators intended to work *only*
with **istream** objects.

ws   Only one such creature is defined by the Standard C++ library, the
manipulator **ws**, declared in `<istream>`. (But see the template class **imanip**
in Chapter 10: `<iomanip>`.) You can write:

```
x >> ws;
```

to extract and discard any white-space characters, regardless of the setting
of the format flag **skipws**.

You use this manipulator:

- to skip white space regardless of the state of **skipws**, before calling an extractor
- to skip white space selectively, with **skipws** reset, before calling certain extractors
- to skip white space before calling an unformatted input function

Put simply, the manipulator **ws** gives you more direct control over the skipping of white space.

character input functions Class **istream** provides a host of member functions for extracting sequences of one or more characters and delivering them to various places. By "deliver" I mean:

- return the character as the value of the member function
- store the character in an object
- successfully insert the character in a stream buffer

If anything, you have too many choices to keep straight. Here is my attempt to characterize them all in a way that highlights their critical differences. Each of the member functions that follows:

skipws ■ extracts and discards any leading white space only if its description says "skips white space" *and* **skipws** is set

gcount ■ stores a count of extracted characters that you can access by calling the member function **gcount()** only if its description says "defines **gcount()**"

eofbit ■ stops if it encounters end-of-file when attempting to extract a character, but sets **eofbit** only if its description says "sets **eofbit** on end-of-file"

failbit ■ sets **failbit** if it delivers no characters, unless its description explicitly says otherwise

With those blanket rules in mind, here is the list of functions you might use to extract sequences of characters:

operator>> ■ **operator>>(char& ch)**, **operator>>(signed char& ch)**, **operator>>(unsigned char& ch)** — skips white space, stores one character in **ch**

operator>> ■ **operator>>(char *s)**, **operator>>(signed char *s)**, **operator>>(unsigned char *s)** — (if **width()** is nonzero, **n** is **width()**; otherwise **n** is **INT_MAX**, defined in **<limits.h>**) skips white space, stops after storing **n - 1** characters beginning at **s** or on a white-space character (which is not extracted), always stores a terminating null character

operator>> ■ **operator>>(streambuf& sb)** — skips white space, inserts remaining characters in the streambuf **sb**, stops on an insertion failure (character not extracted) or on any exception (not rethrown)

get ■ **get()** — returns one character as the value of the function, or **EOF** on end-of-file, defines **gcount()**

get ■ **get(char& ch), get(signed char& ch), get(unsigned char& ch)** — stores one character in **ch**, defines **gcount()**

get ■ **get(char *s, int n, char delim = '\n'), get(signed char *s, int n, char delim = '\n'), get(unsigned char *s, int n, char delim = '\n')** — stops after storing **n - 1** characters beginning at **s** or on a character that matches **delim** (which is not extracted), always stores a terminating null character, defines **gcount()**, sets **eofbit** on end-of-file

get ■ **get(streambuf& sb, char delim = '\n')** — inserts remaining characters in the streambuf **sb**, stops on a character that matches **delim** (which is not extracted) or on an insertion failure (character not extracted) or on any exception (not rethrown), defines **gcount()**

getline ■ **getline(char *s, int n, char delim = '\n'), getline(signed char *s, int n, char delim = '\n'), getline(unsigned char *s, int n, char delim = '\n')** — stops after storing **n - 1** characters beginning at **s** (sets **failbit**) or on a character that matches **delim** (which is extracted but not stored), always stores a terminating null character, defines **gcount()**, sets **eofbit** on end-of-file

read ■ **read(char *s, int n), read(signed char *s, int n), read(unsigned char *s, int n)** — stops after storing **n** characters beginning at **s**, defines **gcount()**, sets **failbit** *only if* other than **n** characters stored

ignore ■ **ignore(int n = 1, int delim = EOF)** — (if **n** equals **INT_MAX**, defined in **<limits.h>**, **n** effectively becomes infitine) stops after discarding **n** characters or on a character that matches **delim** (which is extracted and discarded), defines **gcount()**, sets **eofbit** on end-of-file

Note that when the **delim** argument to **ignore** equals **EOF** (the default value), it matches *no* extracted character. This is handy behavior when you want to skip a sequence of arbitrary characters, with no delimiters.

ostream Class **ostream** also defines a member function that fits in this group. (See the next chapter.) To keep all the descriptions in one place, I present it here out of sequence:

operator<< ■ **operator<<(streambuf& sb)** — extracts remaining characters from the streambuf **sb** (and inserts them in ***this**), stops on an insertion failure (character not extracted) or on any exception (exception *is* rethrown)

I can't counsel you on which of these member functions to use. That decision depends heavily on the particular need, and the style of programming you favor. I do suggest, however, that you pick a handful of these choices, learn them well, and stick with them. It's too easy to forget details when dealing with such a rich set.

scalar extractors The scalar extractors in class **istream** are important work horses. Each converts a human-readable text sequence (or *field*) to some encoded form usable within a C++ program. The form is determined by type **T** in a member declaration of the form:

```
istream& operator>>(T& x);
```

where **x** designates the object to store into.

In all cases, the following steps occur, in order:

- If any of the status bits **badbit**, **eofbit**, or **failbit** is set, the function makes no attempt to extract characters or store a result.

- If **tie()** is not a null pointer, the function flushes the specified stream.

- If the format flag **skipws** is set, the function first extracts and discards any white space.

- The function extracts the characters that constitute the input field up to, but not including, the first white-space character or the first character that does not match the pattern for a valid field.

- If no characters match the pattern, or if the pattern is incomplete (it is only a valid *prefix*), or if the converted value cannot be represented in the designated object, the function sets **failbit**.

- Otherwise, the function stores the converted result in the object.

In all cases, the function returns ***this**, so that extractors can be chained.

integer   Integer extractors exist for the types *char, signed char, unsigned char, short,*
extractors *int, unsigned int, long,* and *unsigned long.* You *cannot* extract an integer value directly into a character object. An extractor with a character reference right operand stores a character code instead, as I described earlier. You must first extract into another integer type, (possibly) check for a value out of range, then store the value so obtained into the character object.

Remember that the **basefield** format flags determine the base for both input and output conversions. For extractors only, clearing all **basefield** flags calls for adaptive input. A character sequence that begins with a prefix, such as **0xa2e0**, determines the input conversion base — the same as for integer constants in C++ source code or text converted by the **fscanf** conversion specifier **i**.

floating-point   Floating-point extractors exist for the types *float, double,* and *long double.*
extractors They match the same patterns as the **fscanf** conversion specifier **f** (or any of the other floating-point conversion specifiers, which all behave the same way). These, in turn, are defined in terms of **strtod**, declared in **<stdlib.h>**. For niggling details, see a precise description of that function (such as in **P&B92**).

pointer   You can also extract a pointer to *void,* but the result is meaningful only
extractor under very restricted circumstances:

- The field you extract must have been generated by the corresponding inserter from class **ostream** (see next chapter)

- The pointer value must have been determined during the same program execution.

- The pointer must designate an object that has not yet been destroyed.

Only rarely are you likely to have a need for this particular extractor.

support functions The remaining member functions in class **istream** I lump together as "support functions." You call them when you want to take more direct control of the associated stream buffer. Perhaps you are defining your own extractors, as I discussed briefly on page 179, or your own manipulators. Or perhaps you just feel the need to fiddle with individual characters.

In any case, I still counsel you to keep such antics to a minimum. The member functions I have described so far represent a considerable amount of engineering. They balance caution against the need for good performance. And they are written with the limitations of various stream buffers firmly in mind. You are more likely to violate some subtle semantic constraints if you strike off on your own. So wherever possible, I urge you to write new extractors and manipulators in terms of existing ones.

get If you must do your own input parsing, then keep it simple. Extract
peek characters with **get()** or **get(char&)**. Put back the last character **ch** you
putbackc extract with **putbackc**. Then be sure to extract that character before you put back another. If you're likely to put back the next character after you extract it, you might consider calling **peek()** instead. (I never do, however.)

sync Two member functions you should *not* use, as a matter of course, are
unget **sync** and **unget**, for reasons I have touched on earlier in this book. The former has no portable input semantics. (No, it doesn't assuredly discard any type ahead from an interactive input stream.) The latter can fail more often than you can imagine when reading from C streams. And all put-back machinery gets dicey if you perform any sort of positioning operations on the stream buffer. (See the discussion beginning on page 160.)

stream buffer primitives An alternative way to write your own extractors is to model them after the ones I show here. Follow the pattern I showed on page 175. Better yet, if you're using this implementation of the Standard C++ library, follow the revised pattern I show on page 198. Note the guidelines for calling the public member functions of class **streambuf**, starting on page 160. And, wherever possible, find a working extractor similar to the one you are writing and follow its structure.

locales As a final note, I remind you that the **istream** member functions exhibit some behavior that depends upon the current locale:

- "White space" is whatever the function **isspace**, declared in **<ctype.h>**, says it is in the current locale.

- A "decimal point" in a floating-point conversion is the character **localeconv()->decimal_point[0],** where **localeconv** is declared in **<locale.h>**.

- Floating-point extractors accept whatever the function **strtod**, declared in **<stdlib.h>**, accepts in the current locale.

If your program alters the current locale by calling **setlocale**, declared in **<locale.h>**, the behavior of some extractors can thus change. Moreover, future versions of iostreams may behave differently. (See page 188.)

```cpp
// istream standard header
#ifndef _ISTREAM_
#define _ISTREAM_
#include <streambuf>
        // class istream
class istream : virtual public ios {
public:
    istream(streambuf *_S)
        : _Chcount(0), ios(_S) {}
    istream(_Uninitialized)
        : ios(_Noinit) {}
    virtual ~istream();
    _Bool ipfx(int = 0);
    void isfx()
        {}
    istream& operator>>(istream& (*_F)(istream&))
        {return ((*_F)(*this)); }
    istream& operator>>(ios& (*_F)(ios&))
        {(*_F)(*(ios *)this); return (*this); }
    istream& operator>>(char *);
    istream& operator>>(unsigned char *_S)
        {return (*this >> (char *)_S); }
    istream& operator>>(char&);
    istream& operator>>(unsigned char& _C)
        {return (*this >> *(char *)&_C); }
    istream& operator>>(short&);
    istream& operator>>(unsigned short&);
    istream& operator>>(int&);
    istream& operator>>(unsigned int&);
    istream& operator>>(long&);
    istream& operator>>(unsigned long&);
    istream& operator>>(float&);
    istream& operator>>(double&);
    istream& operator>>(long double&);
    istream& operator>>(void *&);
    istream& operator>>(streambuf&);
    int get();
    istream& get(char *, int, char = '\n');
    istream& get(unsigned char *_S, int _N, char _D = '\n')
        {return(get((char *)_S, _N, _D)); }
    istream& get(char&);
    istream& get(unsigned char& _C)
        {return (get((char&)_C)); }
    istream& get(streambuf&, char = '\n');
    istream& getline(char *, int, char = '\n');
    istream& getline(unsigned char *_S, int _N, char _D = '\n')
        {return(getline((char *)_S, _N, _D)); }
    istream& ignore(int = 1, int = EOF);
    istream& read(char *, int);
    istream& read(unsigned char *_S, int _N)
        {return(read((char *)_S, _N)); }
    int peek();
    istream& putback(char);
    istream& unget();
    int gcount() const
```

Continuing
istream
Part 2 of 2

```
                        {return (_Chcount); }
            int sync();
#if _HAS_SIGNED_CHAR
        istream& operator>>(signed char *_S)
                {return (*this >> (char *)_S); }
        istream& operator>>(signed char& _C)
                {return (*this >> *(char *)&_C); }
        istream& get(signed char *_S, int _N, char _D = '\n')
                {return (get((char *)_S, _N, _D)); }
        istream& get(signed char& _C)
                {return (get((char&)_C)); }
        istream& getline(signed char *_S, int _N, char _D = '\n')
                {return (getline((char *)_S, _N, _D)); }
        istream& read(signed char *_S, int _N)
                {return (read((char *)_S, _N)); }
#endif /* _HAS_SIGNED_CHAR */
protected:
        int _Getffld(char [_MAX_EXP_DIG + _MAX_SIG_DIG + 16]);
        int _Getifld(char [_MAX_INT_DIG], _Bool = 0);
private:
        int _Chcount;
        };
                // manipulators
istream& ws(istream&);
#endif                                                                  □
```

Implementing <istream>

istream   Figure 8.1 shows the file **istream**, which implements the standard
header **<istream>**. Its principal business is defining the class **istream**, but
it also declares the manipulator **ws**. For a description of the type **_Unin-
itialized**, and the value **_Noinit**, see page 132.

_HAS_SIGNED_   Note that half a dozen of the member functions in class **istream** are
CHAR   conditionally included. It turns out that several current implementations
of C++ have a common bug — they fail to treat *char* and *signed char* as
distinct types. Declaring all the required member functions produces ambiguities, however spurious. Thus, the internal header **<yxvals.h>** defines
the macro **_HAS_SIGNED_CHAR** only when the types are properly distinct.

_Getffld   The only other surprise should be the two protected (and secret) member
_Getifld   functions **_Getffld** and **_Getifld**. These parse and gather character sequences for conversion to floating-point or integer values, respectively. I
describe them in greater detail below. For now, I focus on their rather
unusual declarations.

In both cases, the array of *char* parameter really is equivalent to pointer
to *char*. I chose this form, for both **_Getffld** and **_Getifld**, to emphasize
in each case that the size of the argument array is known and fixed. The
sizes depend on several macros defined in the internal header **<yxvals.h>**:

_MAX_EXP_DIG ■ **_MAX_EXP_DIG** — the number of decimal digits needed to represent the
largest floating-point exponent (a comfortably large value is 8)

Figure 8.2:
istream.c

```
// istream -- istream basic members
#include <ctype.h>
#include <istream>
#include <ostream>

istream::~istream()
    {                                        // destruct an istream -- DO NOTHING
    }

_Bool istream::ipfx(int noskip)
    {                                                        // setup for input
    if (good())
        {                                            // no errors, flush and skip
        if (tie() != 0)
            tie()->flush();
        if (!noskip && flags() & skipws)
            {                                               // skip white space
            int ch;
            while (isspace(ch = rdbuf()->sbumpc()))
                ;
            if (ch != EOF)
                rdbuf()->sputbackc(ch);
            }
        if (good())
            return (1);
        }
    setstate(failbit);
    return (0);
    }
```

_MAX_INT_DIG ■ _MAX_INT_DIG — the number of decimal digits needed to represent the largest integer value (a comfortably large value is 32)

_MAX_SIG_DIG ■ _MAX_SIG_DIG — the number of decimal digits needed to represent all the meaningful significance in the largest floating-point significand (a comfortably large value is 36)

These macros appear throughout the code that parses numeric input.

istream.c   Figure 8.2 shows the file istream.c. It defines the two functions you are likely to need any time you declare an object of class istream, its destructor and ipfx(int). Note the use of the call tie() to access the stored pointer to an object of class ostream. You "tie" an output stream to another stream to ensure that it gets flushed (synchronized) at appropriate times. cout, for example, is conventionally tied to cin, and possibly cerr as well. You want to flush out any prompts to the console display before you solicit input from the console keyboard.

isxchar.c   Figure 8.3 shows the file isxchar.c, which defines the member function
_TRY_IO_BEGIN   operator>>(char&). It is the simplest of all the extractors. The only
_CATCH_IO_END   peculiar business, in fact, is the two funny macros, _TRY_IO_BEGIN and _CATCH_IO_END, that bracket the actual working code. Refer back to the generic structure for extractors that I showed on page 175. You can easily see the exception-handling code that these macros replace.

Figure 8.3:
isxchar.c

```
// isxchar -- istream::operator>>(char&)
#include <istream>

istream& istream::operator>>(char& c)
    {                               // extract an arbitrary character
    int ch;
    _TRY_IO_BEGIN
    if (!ipfx() || (ch = rdbuf()->sbumpc()) == EOF)
        setstate(failbit);
    else
        c = ch;
    isfx();
    _CATCH_IO_END
    return (*this);
    }                                                            □
```

Figure 8.4:
isxstrin.c

```
// isxstring -- istream::operator>>(char *)
#include <ctype.h>
#include <limits.h>
#include <istream>

istream& istream::operator>>(char *sa)
    {                               // extract an NTBS
    char *s = sa;
    _TRY_IO_BEGIN
    if (ipfx())
        {                           // extract arbitrary characters
        int ch;
        int n = 0 < width() ? width() : INT_MAX;
        while (0 < --n && (ch = rdbuf()->sbumpc()) != EOF)
            if (isspace(ch))
                {                   // put back white space and quit
                rdbuf()->sputbackc(ch);
                break;
                }
            else
                *s++ = ch;
        }
    if (s == sa)
        setstate(failbit);
    *s = '\0';
    width(0);
    isfx();
    _CATCH_IO_END
    return (*this);
    }                                                            □
```

Not all implementations of C++ support exceptions yet. So I've chosen to implement exception handling in input and output functions with a set of macros that can expand different ways, depending on whether or not exception handling is implemented. I described these macros briefly in conjunction with the header **<ios>**, which defines them. (See page 128.)

Figure 8.5:
isxstrea.c

```
// isxstream -- istream::operator>>(streambuf&)
#include <istream>

istream& istream::operator>>(streambuf& sb)
    {                                       // extract into streambuf
    _Bool copied = 0;
    _TRY_IO_BEGIN
    if (ipfx())
        {                                   // copy characters until failure
        char buf[512];
        int n;
        for (; 0 < (n = rdbuf()->sgetn(buf, sizeof (buf)));
            copied = 1)
            _TRY_BEGIN
                if (sb.sputn(buf, n) != n)
                    break;
            _CATCH_ALL
                break;
            _CATCH_END
        }
    if (!copied)
        setstate(failbit);
    isfx();
    _CATCH_IO_END
    return (*this);
    }                                                                    □
```

In this implementation, the generic code for an extractor looks like:

```
_TRY_IO_BEGIN
if (ipfx(noskip))
    <perform any input>
isfx();
_CATCH_IO_END
```

The obvious expansion restores the exception handling code. An alternate definition of the macros effectively turns off exception handling, for implementations that can do nothing better. The choice, as usual, is determined in the internal header **<yxvals.h>**. (See Appendix A: Interfaces for details.)

isxstrin.c   Figure 8.4 shows the file **isxstrin.c**, which defines the member function **operator>>(char *)**. It establishes the basic pattern for the various character input functions that store into memory. (See the descriptions beginning on page 190.)

isxstrea.c   Figure 8.5 shows the file **isxstrea.c**, which defines the member function **operator>>(streambuf *)**. It establishes the basic pattern for the various character input functions that insert extracted characters into a stream buffer. Note the nested logic for handling exceptions. The outer loop handles exceptions that occur during extractions, while the inner loop handles exceptions that occur during insertions.

integer extractors   Converting a field to an internal integer form is rather more complicated. You certainly want existing library functions to do the hard work, such as **strtol** or **strtoul**, declared in **<stdlib.h>**. But just setting up for one of

Figure 8.6:
isxlong.c

```
// isxlong -- istream::operator>>(long&)
#include <errno.h>
#include <stdlib.h>
#include <istream>

istream& istream::operator>>(long& lo)
    {                                              // extract a long
    _TRY_IO_BEGIN
    if (!ipfx())
        setstate(failbit);
    else
        {                                 // gather characters and convert
        char ac[_MAX_INT_DIG];
        char *ep;
        errno = 0;
        const long x = strtol(ac, &ep, _Getifld(ac));
        if (ep == ac || errno != 0)
            setstate(failbit);
        else
            lo = x;
        }
    isfx();
    _CATCH_IO_END
    return (*this);
    }                                                          □
```

Figure 8.7:
isxulong.c

```
// isxulong -- istream::operator>>(unsigned long&)
#include <errno.h>
#include <stdlib.h>
#include <istream>

istream& istream::operator>>(unsigned long& ulo)
    {                                          // extract an unsigned long
    _TRY_IO_BEGIN
    if (!ipfx())
        setstate(failbit);
    else
        {                                 // gather characters and convert
        char ac[_MAX_INT_DIG];
        char *ep;
        errno = 0;
        const unsigned long x = strtoul(ac, &ep, _Getifld(ac));
        if (ep == ac || errno != 0)
            setstate(failbit);
        else
            ulo = x;
        }
    isfx();
    _CATCH_IO_END
    return (*this);
    }                                                          □
```

Figure 8.8:
isxpoint.c

```
// isxpointer -- istream::operator>>(void *&)
#include <errno.h>
#include <stdlib.h>
#include <istream>

istream& istream::operator>>(void *& pv)
    {                                        // extract a void *
    _TRY_IO_BEGIN
    if (!ipfx())
        setstate(failbit);
    else
        {                                    // gather characters and convert
        char ac[_MAX_INT_DIG], *ep;
        const int NL = 1 +
            (sizeof (void *) - 1) / sizeof (unsigned long);
        union {
            void *pv;
            unsigned long lo[NL];
            } u;
        for (int i = 0; ; )
            {                                // gather pieces of pointer
            errno = 0;
            const unsigned long x =
                strtoul(ac, &ep, _Getifld(ac, 1));
            if (ep == ac || errno != 0)
                setstate(failbit);
            else
                u.lo[i] = x;
            if (NL <= ++i)
                break;
            const int ch = rdbuf()->sbumpc();
            if (ch != ':')
                {                            // report failure to match ':'
                if (ch != EOF)
                    rdbuf()->sputbackc(ch);
                setstate(failbit);
                break;
                }
            }
        if (good())
            pv = u.pv;
        }
    isfx();
    _CATCH_IO_END
    return (*this);
    }                                                                    □
```

these functions takes a bit of effort in its own right. Remember, nothing prevents a perverse user from generating an input sequence with 5,000 leading zeros, followed by a perfectly reasonable integer. You don't want to blindly gather characters into a buffer as part of the extraction process. I deal with this problem by doing a "smart" pre-parse.

Figure 8.9:
isgetif1.c

```
// isgetif1 -- istream::_Getifld(char *)
#include <string.h>
#include <istream>

int istream::_Getifld(char ac[_MAX_INT_DIG], _Bool hexfl)
    {                                       // extract an integer field
    _Bool sd;
    char *p;
    int base, c, dlen;
    char *const pe = &ac[_MAX_INT_DIG - 1];
    const ios::fmtflags bfl = flags() & basefield;
    static const char digits[] = "0123456789abcdefABCDEF";
    p = ac, c = rdbuf()->sbumpc();
    if (c == '+' || c == '-')
        *p++ = c, c = rdbuf()->sbumpc();
    sd = 0;
    base = hexfl ? 16 : bfl == oct ? 8 : bfl == hex ? 16
        : bfl == _Fmtzero ? 0 : 10;
    if (c == '0')
        {                                   // match possible prefix and strip it
        sd = 1;
        c = rdbuf()->sbumpc();
        if ((c == 'x' || c == 'X')
            && (base == 0 || base == 16))
            base = 16, c = rdbuf()->sbumpc(), sd = 0;
        else if (base == 0)
            base = 8;
        }
    dlen = base == 0 || base == 10 ? 10 : base == 8 ? 8 : 16 + 6;
    for (; c == '0'; sd = 1)
        c = rdbuf()->sbumpc();
    if (sd)
        *p++ = '0';
    for (; c != EOF && memchr(digits, c, dlen);
        c = rdbuf()->sbumpc(), sd = 1)
        if (p < pe)
            *p++ = c;
    if (c != EOF)
        rdbuf()->sputbackc(c);
    if (!sd)
        p = ac;
    *p = '\0';
    return (base);
    }
```

isxlong.c   Figure 8.6 shows the file **isxlong.c**, which defines the member function
operator>>(long&). It extracts a *long*. It does indeed gather characters into
a buffer, but not blindly. The secret member function **_Getifld** extracts and
parses all integer fields. I revisit this workhorse function after presenting
all the other extractors that use it.

_MAX_INT_DIG   Note that the buffer used by **_Getifld** has a bounded length, in this case
the value of the macro **_MAX_INT_DIG**, described earlier. For a typical
machine that represents *long* with 32-bits, a value of 16 is plenty big enough

```
// isxint -- istream::operator>>(int&)
#include <limits.h>
#include <istream>

istream& istream::operator>>(int& i)
    {                                              // extract an int
    long lo;
    *this >> lo;
    if (!good() || lo < INT_MIN || INT_MAX < lo)
        setstate(failbit);
    else
        i = lo;
    return (*this);
    }                                                          □
```

```
// isxuint -- istream::operator>>(unsigned int&)
#include <limits.h>
#include <istream>

istream& istream::operator>>(unsigned int& ui)
    {                                      // extract an unsigned int
    unsigned long ulo;
    *this >> ulo;
    if (!good() || UINT_MAX < ulo)
        setstate(failbit);
    else
        ui = ulo;
    return (*this);
    }                                                          □
```

```
// isxshort -- istream::operator>>(short&)
#include <limits.h>
#include <istream>

istream& istream::operator>>(short& sh)
    {                                              // extract a short
    long lo;
    *this >> lo;
    if (!good() || lo < SHRT_MIN || SHRT_MAX < lo)
        setstate(failbit);
    else
        sh = lo;
    return (*this);
    }                                                          □
```

to deal with a sign, prefix, and enough significant digits to ensure overflow if the value is indeed too large. I tend to make it 32, in the off chance that the code has to handle even larger integers.

isxulong.c   Figure 8.7 shows the file isxulong.c, which defines the member function operator>>(unsigned long&). It extracts an *unsigned long*. The es-

Figure 8.13:
isxushor.c

```
// isxushort -- istream::operator>>(unsigned short&)
#include <limits.h>
#include <istream>

istream& istream::operator>>(unsigned short& ush)
    {                                    // extract an unsigned short
    unsigned long ulo;
    *this >> ulo;
    if (!good() || USHRT_MAX < ulo)
        setstate(failbit);
    else
        ush = ulo;
    return (*this);
    }                                                            □
```

sential difference between this and the previous extractor is the choice of
functions to convert the text sequence.

Extracting a pointer to *void* is a slightly different matter. It must, of
course, work in concert with its corresponding inserter for pointer to *void*.
Both should also convert an arbitrary representation for pointers, even if it
is bigger than the largest integer. You can, and probably should, tailor
pointer conversions for each implementation. What I show here is one way
to write a pointer extractor that is both portable and robust (but may not
always choose the most appropriate text representation for pointers).

isxpoint.c   Figure 8.8 shows the file **isxpoint.c**, which defines the member function **operator>>(void *&)**. It extracts a pointer to *void*. The trick it uses is
to access the pointer from a union, where it overlaps an array of *unsigned
long*. The extractor then extracts a series of integers separated by colons and
stores them in the union as integers. It calls **_Getiffl** with a nonzero
second argument to choose hexadecimal format, regardless of the format
flags in **basefield**. The resultant pointer value is accessed from the union
in the end. So long as the corresponding inserter does the reverse, you can
be sure that a pointer value you extract matches the earlier one you inserted.

For a machine that represents pointer to *void* and *unsigned long* with the
same number of bytes, this extractor defaults to more conventional behavior. It extracts a single *unsigned long* integer, with no colons, and converts it
by storage punning in the union. (This trick does *not* always yield the same
result as type casting between pointer and integer types, by the way. The
type cast has an opportunity to change representations, if it sees fit.)

isgetifl.c   Figure 8.9 shows the file **isgetifl.c**, which defines the member function **_Getifld**. It carries out the work of gathering an integer field. This
function largely replicates the logic of **fscanf**, or even **strtol**, with an
important difference or two. It compresses all leading zeros to a single digit.
And it truncates a very big number at a value large enough to ensure
overflow, as I indicated above. It then counts on the calling function to call
strtol (for the *long* extractor) or **strtoul** (for the *unsigned long* extractor)
to do the rest of the conversion.

Figure 8.14:
isxdoubl.c

```
// isxdouble -- istream::operator>>(double&)
#include <errno.h>
#include <stdlib.h>
#include <istream>

istream& istream::operator>>(double& d)
    {                                          // extract a double
    _TRY_IO_BEGIN
    if (!ipfx())
        setstate(failbit);
    else
        {                           // gather characters and convert
        char ac[_MAX_EXP_DIG + _MAX_SIG_DIG + 16];
        char *ep;
        errno = 0;
        const double x = _Stod(ac, &ep, _Getffld(ac));
        if (ep == ac || errno != 0)
            setstate(failbit);
        else
            d = x;
        }
    isfx();
    _CATCH_IO_END
    return (*this);
    }
```
□

Figure 8.15:
xstod.c

```
/* _Stod function */
#include <stdlib.h>
#include "xmath.h"

#if !__MWERKS__
 #define NLONG 2                            /* 9 * NLONG == max digits */
#endif
double _Stod(const char *s, char **endptr, long pten)
    {                        /* convert string to double, with checking */
    double x;
    long lo[NLONG + 1];
    const int nlo = _Stoflt(s, endptr, lo, 9*NLONG);

    if (nlo == 0)
        return (0);
    if (NLONG == 1)
        x = lo[1];
    else
        {
        int i, n;
```

isxint.c   All the other integer extractors make use of either the *long* or the *unsigned*
isxuint.c   *long* extractor. Figure 8.10 shows the file **isxint.c**, which defines the
isxshort.c member function **operator>>(int&)**. It extracts an *int*. Figure 8.11 shows
isxushor.c the file **isxuint.c**, which defines the member function **operator>>(un-**
signed int&). It extracts an *unsigned int*. Figure 8.12 shows the file **isx-**

Figure 8.16:
isxfloat.c

```
// isxfloat -- istream::operator>>(float&)
#include <errno.h>
#include <stdlib.h>
#include <istream>

istream& istream::operator>>(float& f)
    {                                                // extract a float
    _TRY_IO_BEGIN
    if (!ipfx())
        setstate(failbit);
    else
        {                                // gather characters and convert
        char ac[_MAX_EXP_DIG + _MAX_SIG_DIG + 16];
        char *ep;
        errno = 0;
        const float x = _Stof(ac, &ep, _Getffld(ac));
        if (ep == ac || errno != 0)
            setstate(failbit);
        else
            f = x;
        }
    isfx();
    _CATCH_IO_END
    return (*this);
    }                                                                    □
```

Figure 8.17:
xstof.c

```
/* _Stof function */
#include <stdlib.h>

#if !__MWERKS__
#include "xmath.h"

#define NLONG  1                         /* 9 * NLONG == max digits */

float _Stof(const char *s, char **endptr, long pten)
    {                        /* convert string to float, with checking */
    float x;
    long lo[NLONG + 1];
    const int nlo = _Stoflt(s, endptr, lo, 9*NLONG);
```

short.c, which defines the member function **operator>>(short&)**. It extracts a *short*. And Figure 8.13 shows the file **isxushor.c**, which defines the member function **operator>> (unsigned short&)**. It extracts an *unsigned short*. Once one of these functions extracts a *long* or an *unsigned long*, all it has to do is make a tighter range check before storing the value.

floating-point   Converting a field to an internal floating-point form is even more
extractors complicated. Just gathering the input for a floating-point conversion function takes considerably more effort than for integer conversions. Our hypothetical perverse user now has several places to pad a numeric field with gratuitous zeros that don't alter the represented value:

Figure 8.18:
isxldoub.c

```
// isxldouble -- istream::operator>>(long double&)
#include <errno.h>
#include <stdlib.h>
#include <istream>

istream& istream::operator>>(long double& ld)
    {                                         // extract a long double
    _TRY_IO_BEGIN
    if (!ipfx())
        setstate(failbit);
    else
        {                              // gather characters and convert
        char ac[_MAX_EXP_DIG + _MAX_SIG_DIG + 16];
        char *ep;
        errno = 0;
        const long double x = _Stold(ac, &ep, _Getffld(ac));
        if (ep == ac || errno != 0)
            setstate(failbit);
        else
            ld = x;
        }
    isfx();
    _CATCH_IO_END
    return (*this);
    }                                                                □
```

Figure 8.19:
xstold.c

```
/* _Stold function */
#if !__MWERKS__
 #include <stdlib.h>
 #include "xmath.h"

#if !_DLONG                              /* 9 * NLONG == max digits */
 #define NLONG       2              /* long double same as double */
```

- leading zeros before a decimal point
- trailing zeros after a fractional part
- leading zeros before an exponent

All these places require special handling, to avoid the need for a buffer of unbounded size. Moreover, you *really* want existing library functions, such as **strtod**, to do the hard work. Constructing a floating-point value from a text representation requires cautious programming.

strtof   Sadly, the C Standard does not define a **strtold**, to convert the extra
strtold precision and range required for a *long double*. Nor does it define a **strtof**, to perform the tighter range checking required for a *float*. If you want to write the Standard C++ library in terms of the Standard C library, you're somewhat at a loss in this area.

I have effectively provided both of these functions, with secret names, in my (revised) implementation of the Standard C library. I suspect that the next revision of the C Standard will make mandatory the functions **strtof**

```
// isgetff1 -- istream::_Getffld(char *)
#include <ctype.h>
#include <locale.h>
#include <string.h>
#include <istream>

int istream::_Getffld(char ac[_MAX_EXP_DIG + _MAX_SIG_DIG + 16])
    {                                        // extract a floating field
    _Bool sd;
    char *p;
    int c, ns, pten;
    p = ac, c = rdbuf()->sbumpc(), pten = 0;
    if (c == '+' || c == '-')
        *p++ = c, c = rdbuf()->sbumpc();
    for (sd = 0; c == '0'; c = rdbuf()->sbumpc(), sd = 1)
        ;                                    // strip leading zeros
    if (sd)
        *p++ = '0';                                      // put one back
    for (ns = 0; isdigit(c); c = rdbuf()->sbumpc(), sd = 1)
        if (ns < _MAX_SIG_DIG)
            *p++ = c, ++ns;
        else
            ++pten;
    if (c == localeconv()->decimal_point[0])
        *p++ = c, c = rdbuf()->sbumpc();
    if (ns == 0)
        {                                    // strip zeros after point
        for (; c == '0'; c = rdbuf()->sbumpc(), sd = 1)
            --pten;
        if (pten < 0)
            *p++ = '0', ++pten;                          // put one back
        }
    for (; isdigit(c); c = rdbuf()->sbumpc(), sd = 1)
        if (ns < _MAX_SIG_DIG)
            *p++ = c, ++ns;
    if (sd && (c == 'e' || c == 'E'))
        {                                    // parse exponent
        *p++ = c, c = rdbuf()->sbumpc();
        if (c == '+' || c == '-')
            *p++ = c, c = rdbuf()->sbumpc();
        for (sd = 0; c == '0'; c = rdbuf()->sbumpc(), sd = 1)
            ;                                // strip leading exponent zeros
        if (sd)
            *p++ = '0';                                  // put one back
        for (ns = 0; isdigit(c); c = rdbuf()->sbumpc(), sd = 1)
            if (ns < _MAX_EXP_DIG)
                *p++ = c, ++ns;
        }
    if (c != EOF)
        rdbuf()->sputbackc(c);
    if (!sd)
        p = ac;
    *p = '\0';
    return (pten);
    }                                                                  □
```

Figure 8.21:
isget.c

```
// isget -- istream::get()
#include <istream>

int istream::get()
    {                                                        // get a character
    int ch;
    _TRY_IO_BEGIN
    if (!ipfx(1) || (ch = rdbuf()->sbumpc()) == EOF)
        setstate(failbit), _Chcount = 0, ch = EOF;
    else
        _Chcount = 1;
    isfx();
    _CATCH_IO_END
    return (ch);
    }                                                                        □
```

Figure 8.22:
isgchar.c

```
// isgchar -- istream::get(char&)
#include <istream>

istream& istream::get(char& c)
    {                                                        // get a char
    int ch = get();
    if (ch != EOF)
        c = ch;
    return (*this);
    }                                                                        □
```

and **strtold**, or something like them. Meanwhile, you can cop out by using **strtod** to perform in place of these missing functions, as I show below. This function is deficient in several ways, when used with the other two floating-point precisions, but it meets many needs.

isxdoubl.c   Figure 8.14 shows the file **isxdoubl.c**, which defines the member function **operator>>(double&)**. It extracts a *double*. It also gathers characters into a buffer with a bounded length, in this case determined by the values of the macros **_MAX_SIG_DIG** and **_MAX_EXP_DIG**, described above. For a typical machine with an 80-bit *long double* representation, you're looking at 20 or so fraction digits and four exponent digits, plus the usual assortment of signs, decimal point, and exponent character. I prefer to allow for 36 fraction digits, since 112-bit floating-point significands are already not uncommon. And I allow for a generous eight exponent digits.

_Getffld   The work of gathering a floating-point field is carried out by the pro-
_Stod tected member function **_Getffld**, which I describe below. It plays many of the same tricks as its cousin, **_Getifld**, to keep the buffer length small and bounded. The extractor itself then counts on the function **_Stod** to do the rest of the conversion. **_Stod** behaves much like **strtod**, except that it takes an additional argument computed by **_Getffld** — a power-of-ten correction factor. The final converted value is what **strtod** would produce from the compressed text field, times ten raised to the factor.

Figure 8.23:
isgstrin.c

```
// isgstring -- istream::get(char *, int, char)
#include <istream>

istream& istream::get(char *s, int n, char delim)
    {                               // get up to delimiter or count
    _Chcount = 0;
    _TRY_IO_BEGIN
    if (ipfx(1) && 0 < n)
        {                               // extract arbitrary characters
        int ch;
        for (; 0 < --n; *s++ = ch, ++_Chcount)
            if ((ch = rdbuf()->sbumpc()) == EOF)
                {                               // record eof and quit
                setstate(eofbit);
                break;
                }
            else if (ch == delim)
                {                               // put back delimiter and quit
                rdbuf()->sputbackc(ch);
                break;
                }
        }
    if (_Chcount == 0)
        setstate(failbit);
    *s = '\0';
    isfx();
    _CATCH_IO_END
    return (*this);
    }
```

xstod.c Figure 8.15 shows the file **xstod.c**, which defines a rough-and-ready version of the function **_Stod**. It simply scales the result returned by **strtod**. For my enhanced implementation of the Standard C library, I've written a proper version of _Stod (and _Stof for type *float* and _Stold for type *long double*, both of which I describe below). That library also calls these functions from **fscanf**. The proper version does better error checking, works faster, preserves precision more carefully, and avoids any floating-point overflows or underflows. But the machinery that makes all this possible is too much of a distraction to show here.

isxfloat.c Figure 8.16 shows the file **isxfloat.c**, which defines the member
xstof.c function **operator>>(double&)**. It extracts a *float*. And Figure 8.17 shows the file **xstof.c**, which defines a rough-and-ready version of the function _Stof that this extractor calls. It relies on _Stod to do the actual conversion, then makes a weak attempt at detecting and reporting overflows. On some machines, the program may trap out during the conversion of an oversize value to *float*, so the checking may well be in vain.

isxldoub.c Figure 8.18 shows the file **isxldoub.c**, which defines the member
xstold.c function **operator>>(long double&)**. It extracts a *long double*. And Figure 8.19 shows the file **xstold.c**, which defines a rough-and-ready version of the function _Stold that this extractor calls. Again, _Stod does all the work,

```
// isgline -- istream::getline(char *, int, char)
#include <istream>

istream& istream::getline(char *s, int n, char delim)
    {                                   // get up through delimiter or count
    _Bool copied = 0;
    _Chcount = 0;
    _TRY_IO_BEGIN
    if (ipfx(1) && 0 < n)
        {                               // extract arbitrary characters
        int ch;
        for (; ; )
            if (--n <= 0)
                {                       // record count failure and quit
                setstate(failbit);
                break;
                }
            else if ((ch = rdbuf()->sbumpc()) == EOF)
                {                       // record eof and quit
                setstate(eofbit);
                break;
                }
            else
                {                       // count it and test for delim
                ++_Chcount;
                if (ch == delim)
                    break;
                *s++ = ch, copied = 1;
                }
        }
    if (!copied)
        setstate(failbit);
    *s = '\0';
    isfx();
    _CATCH_IO_END
    return (*this);
    }                                                                    □
```

but this time the possible failure is different. If *long double* has greater range or precision than *double* on some architecture, this function will fail to deliver it.

isgetffl.c   Figure 8.20 shows the file **isgetffl.c**, which defines the member function _Getffld. It carries out the work of gathering a floating-point field. In many ways, it is simply a messier version of **_Getifld**, shown earlier.

isget.c   Now for the unformatted input functions. Figure 8.21 shows the file
isgchar.c **isget.c**, which defines the member function **get()**. It illustrates well the difference between just extracting a character from a stream buffer (with **streambuf()->sbumpc()**) and doing so with all the checking mandated for an **istream** member function. Figure 8.22 shows the file **isgchar.c**,

Figure 8.25:
isread.c

```
// istread -- istream::read(char *, int)
#include <istream>

istream& istream::read(char *s, int n)
    {                                         // get at most n bytes
    _Chcount = 0;
    _TRY_IO_BEGIN
    if (ipfx(1))
        {                                     // extract arbitrary characters
        int m = rdbuf()->sgetn(s, n);
        _Chcount += m;
        if (m != n)
            setstate(failbit);
        }
    isfx();
    _CATCH_IO_END
    return (*this);
    }                                                              □
```

Figure 8.26:
isignor.c

```
// isignore -- istream::ignore(int, int)
#include <limits.h>
#include <istream>

istream& istream::ignore(int n, int delim)
    {                              // discard through delimiter or count
    _Chcount = 0;
    _TRY_IO_BEGIN
    if (ipfx(1) && 0 < n)
        {                          // extract and ignore arbitrary characters
        int ch;
        for (; ; )
            if (n != INT_MAX && --n < 0)
                break;
            else if ((ch = rdbuf()->sbumpc()) == EOF)
                {                              // record eof and quit
                setstate(eofbit);
                break;
                }
            else
                {                              // count it and test for delim
                ++_Chcount;
                if (ch == delim)
                    break;
                }
        }
    isfx();
    _CATCH_IO_END
    return (*this);
    }                                                              □
```

Figure 8.27:
isgstrea.c

```
// isgstream -- istream::get(streambuf&, char)
#include <istream>

istream& istream::get(streambuf &sb, char delim)
    {                               // get into streambuf until delimiter
    _Chcount = 0;
    _TRY_IO_BEGIN
    if (ipfx(1))
        {                               // copy characters until failure
        int ch;
        for (; (ch = rdbuf()->sbumpc()) != EOF; ++_Chcount)
            _TRY_BEGIN
                if (ch == delim || sb.sputc(ch) == EOF)
                    break;
            _CATCH_ALL
                break;
            _CATCH_END
        if (ch != EOF)
            rdbuf()->sputbackc(ch);
        }
    if (_Chcount == 0)
        setstate(failbit);
    isfx();
    _CATCH_IO_END
    return (*this);
    }                                                               □
```

Figure 8.28:
ispeek.c

```
// ispeek -- istream::peek()
#include <istream>

int istream::peek()
    {                               // peek at next char
    _Chcount = 0;
    int ch;
    _TRY_IO_BEGIN
    ch = ipfx(1) ? rdbuf()->sgetc() : EOF;
    isfx();
    _CATCH_IO_END
    return (ch);
    }                                                               □
```

which defines the member function **get(char&)**. It relies on **get()** to do
all the needed checking.

isgstrin.c   Figure 8.23 shows the file **isgstrin.c**, which defines the member
isgline.c   function **get(char *, int, char)**. Figure 8.24 shows the file **isgline.c**,
isread.c   which defines the member function **getline(char *, int, char)**. Fig-
isignor.c   ure 8.25 shows the file **isread.c**, which defines the member function
read(char *, int). And Figure 8.26 shows the file **isignor.c**, which
defines the member function **ignore(int, int)**. All follow the pattern
established earlier by **isxstrin.c**, with minor variations.

Figure 8.29:
isputbac.c

```
// isputback -- istream::putback(char)
#include <istream>

istream& istream::putback(char c)
    {                                       // put back a char
    _Chcount = 0;
    _TRY_IO_BEGIN
    if (ipfx(1) && rdbuf()->sputbackc(c) == EOF)
        setstate(badbit);
    isfx();
    _CATCH_IO_END
    return (*this);
    }
```

Figure 8.30:
issync.c

```
// issync -- istream::sync()
#include <istream>

int istream::sync()
    {                                       // synchronize buffer
    int ch;
    _TRY_IO_BEGIN
    if (!good())
        ch = EOF;
    else if (rdbuf()->pubsync() == EOF)
        {                                   // note sync failure
        setstate(badbit);
        ch = EOF;
        }
    else
        ch = 0;
    _CATCH_IO_END
    return (ch);
    }
```

Figure 8.31:
isunget.c

```
// isunget -- istream::unget()
#include <istream>

istream& istream::unget()
    {                                       // put back last char
    _Chcount = 0;
    _TRY_IO_BEGIN
    if (ipfx(1) && rdbuf()->sungetc() == EOF)
        setstate(badbit);
    isfx();
    _CATCH_IO_END
    return (*this);
    }
```

isgstrea.c   Similarly, Figure 8.27 shows the file isgstrea.c, which defines the member function get(streambuf&, char). It follows the pattern established earlier by isxstrea.c, again with only minor variations.

Figure 8.32:
ws.c

```
// ws -- ws(istream&)
#include <ctype.h>
#include <istream>

istream& ws(istream& is)
    {                                          // eat white space
    _TRY_IO_BEGIN
    if (is.ipfx(1))
        {                                      // safe to eat white space
        int ch;
        while (isspace(ch = is.rdbuf()->sbumpc()))
            ;
        if (ch != EOF)
            is.rdbuf()->sputbackc(ch);
        }
    is.isfx();
    _CATCH_IO_(is);
    return (is);
    }
```

ispeek.c   The last group of **istream** member functions all call on **streambuf**
isputbac.c public member functions to perform the critical operation. Figure 8.28
issync.c   shows the file **ispeek.c**, which defines the member function **peek()**.
isunget.c Figure 8.29 shows the file **isputbac.c**, which defines the member function
putback(char). Figure 8.30 shows the file **issync.c**, which defines the
member function **sync()**. And Figure 8.31 shows the file **isunget.c**, which
defines the member function **unget()**.

ws.c   Finally, Figure 8.32 shows the file **ws.c**, which defines the manipulator
ws(istream&). I chose to replicate the logic in **istream::ipfx** for skipping
white space rather than fiddling with the format flag **skipws**. Should an
exception occur while extracting characters, it's rather messy to restore the
format flags. I didn't want to introduce more ornate macros for exception
handling just to handle one or two situations like this.

_CATCH_IO_(x)   I described the macro **_CATCH_IO_(x)** on page 128. It performs the same
function as **_CATCH_IO_END** for a function that is not a member of class
istream.

Testing <istream>

tistream.c   Figure 8.33 shows the file **tistream.c**. It tests the basic properties of
class **istream**. As in the previous chapter, I make use of classes derived
from **istream** and **streambuf** to do something concrete. This time, an
object of class **istrstream** helps construct a stream buffer (of class
strstreambuf) that delivers text from a constant character string in memory. (See Chapter 12: **<sstream>**.) The code is not completely portable
because it uses the macros **_TRY_IO_BEGIN** and **_CATCH_IO_END**, peculiar
to this implementation.

The program defines the class **Boolean**, which stores an *int* value. It then defines an extractor for this class, which maps **N** into a zero value and **Y** into a nonzero value. The program tests whether this extractor, and all the member functions of class **istream**, exhibit at least some of their required behavior.

If all goes well, the program prints:

SUCCESS testing <istream>

and takes a normal exit.

Exercises

Exercise 8.1 For a call to **istream::get(char *, int, char)**, write the predicates (tests) that distinguish whether:

- the next character to extract is a delimiter
- the function encountered end-of-file
- the buffer is full

Exercise 8.2 For a call to **istream::getline(char *, int, char)**, write the predicates (tests) that distinguish whether:

- the function extracted and discarded a delimiter character
- the function encountered end-of-file
- the buffer is full

Exercise 8.3 What kind of operations do you think **istream::isfx()** might have to perform?

Exercise 8.4 Write rules for the setting and clearing of the status flag **eofbit** by **istream** member functions to make it more consistent. In particular, if **eofbit** is set, **istream::get()** should assuredly return **EOF**.

Exercise 8.5 Can you enforce the rules of the previous exercise if two or more **istream** objects point at the same stream buffer? If so, describe how. If not, discuss the structural changes required to make such enforcement possible.

Exercise 8.6 Does the **fscanf** family of functions have any capabilities not easily modeled by **istream** extractors? Show how would you add any such missing capabilities.

Exercise 8.7 Alter the function **istream::_Getffl** (page 207) so that it need not return a power-of-ten correction factor. Instead, it should produce only a null-terminated string of bounded size that adequately represents the input field.

Exercise 8.8 [Harder] Write versions of **_Stod** (page 204), **_Stof** (page 205), and **_Stold** (page 206) that deliver full accuracy, range, and exception checking for a given architecture.

Exercise 8.9 [Very hard] Alter the functions you wrote for the previous exercise to work properly on *any* architecture.

```
// test <istream>
#include <assert.h>
#include <string.h>
#include <iostream>
#include <istream>
#include <strstream>

        // class Boolean
class Boolean {
public:
    Boolean(int v)
        : val(v) {}
    int value() const
        {return (val); }
    int value(int v)
        {return (val = v); }
private:
    int val;
    };

istream& operator>>(istream& istr, Boolean& b)
    {                                       // extract a Boolean
    _TRY_IO_BEGIN
    if (!istr.ipfx())
        istr.setstate(ios::failbit);
    else
        {                               // gather characters and convert
        const int c = istr.rdbuf()->sbumpc();
        if (c == 'Y')
            b.value(1);
        else if (c == 'N')
            b.value(0);
        else
            {                           // report failure
            istr.rdbuf()->sputbackc(c);
            istr.setstate(ios::failbit);
            }
        }
    istr.isfx();
    _CATCH_IO_END
    return (istr);
    }

int main()
    {                   // test basic workings of istream definitions
    static const char input[] = "s1 s2 s3"
        "   abc"
        " 1 23 -456 +7890   0012 00034 0"
        " 12 +3.4567e+0004-8900e-2"
        " N  Y"
        "rest of stream";
    istrstream istrstr(input);
    istream ins(istrstr.rdbuf());
    assert(ins.good() && (ins.flags() & ios::showbase) == 0);
    ins >> showbase;
```

```
    assert((ins.flags() & ios::showbase) != 0);
        // test string extractors
    char s1[10];
    signed char s2[10];
    unsigned char s3[10];
    ins >> s1 >> s2 >> s3;
    assert(strcmp(s1, "s1") == 0);
    assert(strcmp((char *)s2, "s2") == 0);
    assert(strcmp((char *)s3, "s3") == 0);
        // test character extractors
    char ch;
    signed char sch;
    unsigned char uch;
    ins >> noskipws >> ws >> ch >> sch >> uch >> skipws;
    assert(ch == 'a' && sch == 'b' && uch == 'c');
        // test integer extractors
    int i;
    long lo;
    short sh;
    unsigned int ui;
    unsigned long ulo;
    unsigned short ush;
    void *p;
    ins >> sh >> hex >> ush >> oct >> i >> dec >> ui;
    assert(sh == 1 && ush == 0x23 && i == -0456 && ui == 7890);
    ins >> lo >> ulo >> p;
    assert(lo == 12 && ulo == 34 && p == 0);
        // test floating-point extractors
    double db;
    float fl;
    long double ldb;
    ins >> fl >> db >> ldb;
    assert(fl == 12. && db == 34567. && ldb == -89.);
        // test Boolean extractor
    Boolean no(0), yes(1);
    assert(no.value() == 0 && yes.value() == 1);
    ins >> yes >> no;
    assert(no.value() == 1 && yes.value() == 0);
        // test streambuf extractor and get functions
    char buf[20], sbuf[20], ubuf[20];
    ostrstream ostr;
    ins >> *ostr.rdbuf();
    assert(ins.good() && ins.get() == EOF);
    ins.rdbuf(ostr.rdbuf());
    ins.get(buf, sizeof (buf), 'o');
    assert(strcmp(buf, "rest ") == 0);
    ins.get(sbuf, sizeof (sbuf), 's');
    assert(strcmp((char *)sbuf, "of ") == 0);
    ins.get(ubuf, sizeof (ubuf));
    assert(strcmp((char *)ubuf, "stream") == 0);
    cout << "SUCCESS testing <istream>" << endl;
    return (0);
    }
```
□

Chapter 9: `<ostream>`

Background

The principal business of the header `<ostream>` is to define the class `ostream`. This class is the obvious complement to class `istream`, which I described in the previous chapter. I have intentionally modeled this chapter after its predecessor, to highlight the structural similarities.

ostream Class `ostream` is derived from the virtual public base class `ios` to help you insert characters into a stream. The best known object of this class is `cout`, which controls output to the standard output stream — the same C stream controlled by `stdout`, declared in `<stdio.h>`. You can also create `ostream` objects that control files you open by name, or strings of text stored in memory, as later chapters reveal.

Most of the `ostream` member functions fall into one of two broad categories:

- unformatted output functions, which insert sequences of arbitrary *char* values, such as uninterpreted text or binary data
- formatted output functions, which convert encoded values of the various scalar and string data types and insert the resultant sequences

unformatted output The former group uses the name `put` and overloads the name `write`. It is analogous to the Standard C library's `fputc` and `fwrite`, declared in `<stdio.h>`, but a bit easier to use. For example, you can insert an arbitrary character sequence with:

```
if (cout.write(buf, n))
    <output succeeded>
```

The test is true (nonzero) only if the member function successfully inserts all `n` characters from `buf` to the stream controlled by the `ostream` object `cout`.

formatted output The latter group of member functions overloads `operator<<` to make the basic family of inserters. It is analogous to the Standard C library's `fprintf` and friends, but with a variety of advantages. For example, you can insert an octal integer with:

```
int n;
if (cout << oct << n)
    <output succeeded>
```

The test is true only if the second inserter inserts all the characters required to represent the *int* value **n** as an octal integer in text form.

Inserters are the single most popular selling point for iostreams over more conventional Standard C input and output. (Extractors are a close second.) But they are easier to explain after you gain more familiarity with the unformatted output functions. I return to inserters later in this section.

Remember that all extractions and insertions in iostreams are mediated by objects of class **streambuf**. (See Chapter 7: **<streambuf>**.) An object of class **ostream** finds its related **streambuf** object via a pointer in its base subobject of class **ios**. A member function of class **ostream** can then insert an output character by calling **rdbuf()->sputc()**.

opfx   There is one small problem, however. It is perfectly permissible for the
osfx pointer to **streambuf** to be null. It is also quite possible that the pointer is non-null, but the stream is in some error state that should discourage inserting. Thus, it behooves any output function to look before it leaps. The canonical way to play safe is to wrap every inserter member function with two calls to **ostream** member functions:

```
if (opfx())
    <perform any output>
osfx();
```

The "prefix" function **opfx(int)** verifies that the stream is both ready and willing to accept output, or at least to support calls to the **streambuf** member functions. It also performs other initializiation operations.

unit   The "suffix" function **osfx()** performs any necessary wrapup opera-
buffering tions after each output member function does its work. In particular, if the format flag **unitbuf** is set, the function flushes the associated stream buffer. Such "unit buffering" is often a happy compromise between the better performance of full buffering and the tighter synchronization with external files of no buffering at all. If you write an output function that uses the **ostream** object **x** and makes direct calls to its associated **streambuf** object, always call **x.opfx()** and **x.osfx()** as shown above.

exception   Inserters must also handle exceptions, for much the same reasons that
handling extractors do. (See page 174.) Any call to **rdbuf()->sputc()** can result in a call to the virtual member function **streambuf::overflow**, which can be a programmer-supplied virtual member function for a derived class. So as with extractors, the library can never know when a call on a **streambuf** member function might throw an exception.

The draft C++ Standard says that when an exception occurs during execution of an output (or input) member function, the function must call **setstate(badbit)**, then rethrow the exception. The structure of an arbitrary output function must now look like:

```
try {
    if (opfx())
        <perform any output>
    osfx();
    }
```

```
catch (...) {
    setstate(badbit);
    throw;
    }
```

Note once again that the act of setting **badbit** can also raise an exception, of class **ios::failure**. (See page 123.) Should that happen, the original exception never gets rethrown.

put　　Now you have enough background to understand how the unformatted output functions work. The simplest of these is the member function **put(char)**. It inserts a single character — probably by calling the **streambuf** member function **rdbuf()->sputc(char)** inside the sandwich shown above — and delivers it as the value of the function. A failure to insert the requested character, for any reason, is reflected in a return value of **EOF**.

　　Obviously, the overhead in inserting a single character via **put(char)** is substantially higher than for the Standard C library function **putchar(int)**, declared in **<stdio.h>**. The latter is almost invariably implemented as a macro that stores a character straight into an output buffer more often than not. Thus, it behaves much like the member function **streambuf:: sputc(char)**. But **ostream::put(char)** is almost impossible to treat similarly, given the prefix/suffix calls and exception handling required by the draft C++ Standard. You should thus favor methods that insert many more characters for each call, whenever possible, if performance is an issue.

write　　If you want rather less logic per character, consider the member function **write(const char *, int)** (or its alternate forms for constant arrays of *signed char* or *unsigned char*). It simply inserts characters until a count is exhausted, or until no more characters can be inserted.

reading　　For still faster copying from another stream buffer, consider the inserter **stream buffers** **operator<<(streambuf&)**. Actually a *formatted* input function, it extracts characters from its stream buffer argument and writes them directly to the stream buffer controlled by the **ostream** object. Thus, you can write:

```
cout << *cin.rdbuf();
```

to copy the remaining characters from **cin** directly to **cout**. In this case, copying can be quite fast. Related **istream** member functions can copy up to, but not including, a delimiter you specify. (See the summary starting on page 190.)

flush　　The member function **flush()** simply calls the public "synchronizing" function **rdbuf()->pubsync()** (assuming the associated **streambuf** object is present). Typically, such an operation flushes an output stream to the associated external file. Several mechanisms exist to ensure that synchronization occurs at judicious times:

- You can create a stream buffer that is unbuffered. (See, for example, Chapter 13: **<fstream>**.)

- You can set the format flag **unitbuf**, described above, to flush output after every call to a formatted or unformatted output function.

- You can use the manipulator **endl**, described below, to both insert a newline character (**'\n'**) and flush output.

- You can *tie* the **ostream** object to another **istream** or **ostream** object, to flush output on any call to a prefix function for that other object. (See page 125.)

And, of course, the stream buffer will be flushed when it is destroyed. You need call **flush()** for an **ostream** object only if you can't be certain that timely synchronization will occur in the normal course of affairs.

inserters   Now for the rest of the formatted output functions, or inserters. These member functions overload **operator<<** for a left parameter of type **ostream&**. That lets you write code such as:

```
float fl;
cout << fl;
```

which converts the *float* value **fl** to a character sequence and inserts those characters into the stream controlled by **cout** (the standard output stream). The character sequence is essentially the same as that produced by the Standard C library function **fprintf**, declared in **<stdio.h>**. The entire sequence must be successfully inserted in the stream buffer for the function to succeed. Otherwise, the function reports failure, typically by setting **badbit** in **cout**.

Thus, inserters serve the same function for the Standard C++ library that the **fprintf** family serves for the Standard C library. You can, in fact, implement inserters by calls to **fprintf**. That turns out to be not always convenient, however:

- The destination for output from a stream controlled by an **ostream** object is controlled in turn by a **streambuf** object. You can't always relate that destination directly to the destinations writable by **fprintf** or **sprintf**.

- You can store characters into a buffer using **sprintf** then insert them into the stream buffer. But doing so requires a buffer that is arbitrarily large. Or you end up doing so much postprocessing of the text that you duplicate much of the work done by **sprintf**.

- The program can specify an arbitrary fill character for an inserter, not just the implied space character supplied by **fprintf**. Moreover, the program can specify that this arbitrary character be used for "internal" fill, in place of the implied zero (**'0'**) supplied by **fprintf**.

For these reasons, you can't count on calls to **fprintf** to do all the hard work of implementing inserters. Nevertheless, the *definition* of a typical inserter member function in **ostream** is in terms of **fprintf** conversion specifiers (17.4.4.1). When in doubt, you can often turn to the C Standard for a more precise description of inserter behavior.

character   I begin with the inserters that perform a minimum of interpretation.
inserters These insert one or more characters from the output stream and deliver them either to memory or to an output stream. The simplest is **opera-**

adjustfield
fill
width

endl
flush

ends

string
inserters

scalar
inserters

`tor<<(char&)`, which inserts a single character. As usual, class **ostream** also has *unsigned char* and *signed char* versions of the same inserter.

These three inserters share one peculiar property. Of all the formatted output functions defined in terms of **fprintf** conversions, only these ignore the field width. All other such inserters determine a minimum field width by calling **width()**. If the conversion results in fewer characters, the result is padded with the fill character, defined by **fill()**. Where the padding goes is determined by the format flags in the group **adjustfield**. (See the summary of formatting information beginning on page 124.) But the three character inserters each insert only a single character, never padding it. Equally, none of these three inserters set the field width to zero, by calling **width(0)**, as all others do.

These member functions are all identical in behavior to the member function **put(char)**, described earlier.

If you want to insert a newline character (`'\n'`) to terminate a text line, you should favor the manipulator **endl**, declared in `<ostream>`. If you write:

```
cout << fl << endl;
```

then the manipulator inserts a newline character after **fl** is inserted. It also flushes the stream buffer, as I indicated earlier. For an output stream that might be associated with an interactive device, this is probably desirable behavior. You can also flush the output stream, without inserting a character, with the manipulator **flush**.

You can insert a null character (without flushing the output stream) with the manipulator **ends**. You seldom have occasion to write a null character to a text file — null characters are displayed, printed, and transmitted haphazardly by devices that expect only human-readable text. But a common use for an **ostream** object is to mediate output to a stream buffer that constructs an in-memory character sequence. Such a sequence often wants a terminating null character. The manipulator **ends** provides highly visible evidence that the null character is indeed being supplied.

The member function **operator<<(const char *)** inserts a sequence of characters into the output stream from a null-terminated string in the character array designated by the pointer argument. Yes, there are three flavors, once again. And yes, you can pad a string on either end with fill characters.

The remaining formatted output functions insert various scalar types. For all of these inserters, you can specify a field width, a fill character, and the format flags in the group **adjustfield**. These work together to determine whether and where to insert fill characters as padding when generating the text representation of a value. The scalar inserters further subdivide into integer types, floating-point types, and pointer to *void*. You control the behavior of each of these groups with different subsets of the format flags.

user-defined   You can, of course, also write your own inserters. It is commonplace,
inserters when designing a new class, to provide a tailored inserter at the very least.
If reading values of the class makes sense, then it is good manners to
provide an extractor as well. You might even want to write an inserter or
two that are not associated with a specific class.

The best style for writing new inserters is to do so in terms of the member
functions of class **ostream**. If you must drop below this level and access the
associated **streambuf** object directly, then by all means match the discipline
followed in the inserters presented here. Extractors are more fragile than
inserters, because of the need to look ahead in the input sequence and push
back an occasional character. But inserters are delicate enough in their own
right. Don't take unnecessary chances.

What the Draft C++ Standard Says

The header **<ostream>** is the last of the "big four" headers that define
the iostreams package. Like **<ios>**, **<streambuf>**, and **<istream>** in the
previous three chapters, it contains a lot of niggling detail.

17.4.4 Header <ostream>

<ostream> The header **<ostream>** defines a type and several function signatures that
control output to a stream buffer.

17.4.4.1 Class ostream

Class
ostream

```
class ostream : virtual public ios {
public:
    ostream(streambuf* sb);
    virtual ~ostream();
    int opfx();
    void osfx();
    ostream& operator<<(ostream& (*pf)(ostream&));
    ostream& operator<<(ios& (*pf)(ios&));
    ostream& operator<<(const char* s);
    ostream& operator<<(char c);
    ostream& operator<<(unsigned char c);
    ostream& operator<<(signed char c);
    ostream& operator<<(short n);
    ostream& operator<<(unsigned short n);
    ostream& operator<<(int n);
    ostream& operator<<(unsigned int n);
    ostream& operator<<(long n);
    ostream& operator<<(unsigned long n);
    ostream& operator<<(float f);
    ostream& operator<<(double f);
    ostream& operator<<(long double f);
    ostream& operator<<(void* p);
    ostream& operator<<(streambuf& sb);
    int put(char c);
    ostream& write(const char* s, int n);
    ostream& write(const unsigned char* s, int n);
```

```
        ostream& write(const signed char* s, int n);
        ostream& flush();
};
```

The class **ostream** defines a number of member function signatures that assist in formatting and writing output to output sequences controlled by a stream buffer.

Two groups of member function signatures share common properties: the *formatted output functions* (or *inserters*) and the *unformatted output functions*. Both groups of output functions generate (or *insert*) output characters by calling the function signature **sb.sputc(int)**. If the called function throws an exception, the output function calls **setstate(badbit)** and rethrows the exception.

- The formatted output functions are:

```
        ostream& operator<<(const char* s);
        ostream& operator<<(char c);
        ostream& operator<<(unsigned char c);
        ostream& operator<<(signed char c);
        ostream& operator<<(short n);
        ostream& operator<<(unsigned short n);
        ostream& operator<<(int n);
        ostream& operator<<(unsigned int n);
        ostream& operator<<(long n);
        ostream& operator<<(unsigned long n);
        ostream& operator<<(float f);
        ostream& operator<<(double f);
        ostream& operator<<(long double f);
        ostream& operator<<(void* p);
        ostream& operator<<(streambuf* sb);
```

- The unformatted output functions are:

```
        ostream& put(char c);
        ostream& write(const char* s, int n);
        ostream& write(const unsigned char* s, int n);
        ostream& write(const signed char* s, int n);
```

Each formatted output function begins execution by calling **opfx()**. If that function returns nonzero, the function endeavors to generate the requested output. In any case, the formatted output function ends by calling **osfx()**, then returning the value specified for the formatted output function.

Some formatted output functions endeavor to generate the requested output by converting a value from some scalar or NTBS type to text form and inserting the converted text in the output sequence. The behavior of such functions is described in terms of the conversion specification for an equivalent call to the function signature **fprintf(FILE*, const char*, ...)**, declared in **<stdio.h>**, with the following alterations:

- The formatted output function inserts characters in a stream buffer, rather than writing them to an output file.[97]

- The formatted output function uses the fill character returned by **fill()** as the padding character (rather than the space character for left or right padding, or **0** for internal padding).

If the operation fails for any reason, the formatted output function calls **setstate(badbit)**.

For conversion from an integral type other than a character type, the function determines the integral conversion specifier as follows:

- If **(flags() & basefield) == oct**, the integral conversion specifier is **o**.

- If **(flags() & basefield) == hex**, the integral conversion specifier is **x**. If **flags() & uppercase** is nonzero, **x** is replaced with **X**.

Otherwise, the integral conversion specifier is **d** for conversion from a signed integral type, or **u** for conversion from an unsigned integral type.

For conversion from a floating-point type, the function determines the floating-point conversion specifier as follows:

- If **(flags() & floatfield) == fixed**, the floating-point conversion specifier is **f**.
- If **(flags() & floatfield) == scientific**, the floating-point conversion specifier is **e**. If **flags() & uppercase** is nonzero, **e** is replaced with **E**.

Otherwise, the floating-point conversion specifier is **g**. If **flags() & uppercase** is nonzero, **g** is replaced with **G**.

The conversion specifier has the following additional qualifiers prepended to make a conversion specification:

- For conversion from an integral type other than a character type, if **flags() & showpos** is nonzero, the flag **+** is prepended to the conversion specification; and if **flags() & showbase** is nonzero, the flag **#** is prepended to the conversion specification.
- For conversion from a floating-point type, if **flags() & showpos** is nonzero, the flag **+** is prepended to the conversion specification; and if **flags() & showpoint** is nonzero, the flag **#** is prepended to the conversion specification.
- For any conversion, if **width()** is nonzero, then a field width is specified in the conversion specification. The value is **width()**.
- For conversion from a floating-point type, if **flags() & fixed** is nonzero or if **precision()** is greater than zero, then a precision is specified in the conversion specification. The value is **precision()**.

Moreover, for any conversion, padding with the fill character returned by **fill()** behaves as follows:

- If **(flags() & adjustfield) == right**, no flag is prepended to the conversion specification, indicating right justification (any padding occurs before the converted text). A fill character occurs wherever **fprintf** generates a space character as padding.
- If **(flags() & adjustfield) == internal**, the flag **0** is prepended to the conversion specification, indicating internal justification (any padding occurs within the converted text). A fill character occurs wherever **fprintf** generates a **0** as padding.[98]

Otherwise, the flag **–** is prepended to the conversion specification, indicating left justification (any padding occurs after the converted text). A fill character occurs wherever **fprintf** generates a space character as padding.

Unless explicitly stated otherwise for a particular inserter, each formatted output function calls **width(0)** after determining the field width.

Each unformatted output function begins execution by calling **opfx()**. If that function returns nonzero, the function endeavors to generate the requested output. In any case, the unformatted output function ends by calling **osfx()**, then returning the value specified for the unformatted output function.

17.4.4.1.1 ostream::ostream(streambuf*)

constructor

```
ostream(streambuf* sb);
```

Constructs an object of class **ostream**, assigning initial values to the base class by calling **ios::init(sb)**.

17.4.4.1.2 ostream::~ostream()

```
virtual ~ostream();
```
Destroys an object of class **ostream**.

17.4.4.1.3 ostream::opfx()

```
int opfx();
```
If **good()** is nonzero, prepares for formatted or unformatted output. If **tie()** is not a null pointer, the function calls **tie()->flush()**. It returns **good()**.[99]

17.4.4.1.4 ostream::osfx()

```
void osfx();
```
If **flags() & unitbuf** is nonzero, calls **flush()**.

17.4.4.1.5 ostream::operator<<(ostream& (*)(ostream&))

```
ostream& operator<<(ostream& (*pf)(ostream&))
```
Returns **(*pf)(*this)**.[100]

17.4.4.1.6 ostream::operator<<(ios& (*)(ios&))

```
ostream& operator<<(ios& (*pf)(ios&))
```
Calls **(*(ios*)pf)(*this)**, then returns ***this**.[101]

17.4.4.1.7 ostream::operator<<(const char*)

```
ostream& operator<<(const char* s);
```
A formatted output function, converts the NTBS **s** with the conversion specifier **s**. The function returns ***this**.

17.4.4.1.8 ostream::operator<<(char)

```
ostream& operator<<(char c);
```
A formatted output function, converts the **char c** with the conversion specifier **c** and a field width of zero. The stored field width (**ios::wide**) is *not* set to zero. The function returns ***this**.

17.4.4.1.9 ostream::operator<<(unsigned char)

```
ostream& operator<<(unsigned char c)
```
Returns **operator<<((char)c)**.

17.4.4.1.10 ostream::operator<<(signed char)

```
ostream& operator<<(signed char c)
```
Returns **operator<<((char)c)**.

17.4.4.1.11 ostream::operator<<(short)

```
ostream& operator<<(short n);
```
A formatted output function, converts the signed short integer **n** with the integral conversion specifier preceded by **h**. The function returns ***this**.

17.4.4.1.12 ostream::operator<<(unsigned short)

```
ostream& operator<<(unsigned short n);
```
A formatted output function, converts the unsigned short integer **n** with the integral conversion specifier preceded by **h**. The function returns ***this**.

17.4.4.1.13 ostream::operator<<(int)

```
ostream& operator<<(int n);
```
A formatted output function, converts the signed integer **n** with the integral conversion specifier. The function returns ***this**.

17.4.4.1.14 ostream::operator<<(unsigned int)

`operator<<`
> `ostream& operator<<(unsigned int n);`

A formatted output function, converts the unsigned integer **n** with the integral conversion specifier. The function returns ***this**.

17.4.4.1.15 ostream::operator<<(long)

`operator<<`
> `ostream& operator<<(long n);`

A formatted output function, converts the signed long integer **n** with the integral conversion specifier preceded by **l**. The function returns ***this**.

17.4.4.1.16 ostream::operator<<(unsigned long)

`operator<<`
> `ostream& operator<<(unsigned long n);`

A formatted output function, converts the unsigned long integer **n** with the integral conversion specifier preceded by **l**. The function returns ***this**.

17.4.4.1.17 ostream::operator<<(float)

`operator<<`
> `ostream& operator<<(float f);`

A formatted output function, converts the **float f** with the floating-point conversion specifier. The function returns ***this**.

17.4.4.1.18 ostream::operator<<(double)

`operator<<`
> `ostream& operator<<(double f);`

A formatted output function, converts the **double f** with the floating-point conversion specifier. The function returns ***this**.

17.4.4.1.19 ostream::operator<<(long double)

`operator<<`
> `ostream& operator<<(long double f);`

A formatted output function, converts the **long double f** with the floating-point conversion specifier preceded by **L**. The function returns ***this**.

17.4.4.1.20 ostream::operator<<(void*)

`operator<<`
> `ostream& operator<<(void* p);`

A formatted output function, converts the pointer to **void p** with the conversion specifier **p**. The function returns ***this**.

17.4.4.1.21 ostream::operator<<(streambuf&)

`operator<<`
> `ostream& operator<<(streambuf& sb);`

A formatted output function, extracts characters from the input sequence controlled by **sb** and inserts them in ***this**. Characters are extracted and inserted until any of the following occurs:

- end-of-file occurs on the input sequence;
- inserting in the output sequence fails (in which case the character to be inserted is not extracted);
- an exception occurs (in which case, the exception is rethrown).[102]

If the function inserts no characters, it calls **setstate(failbit)**. The function returns ***this**.

17.4.4.1.22 ostream::put(char)

`put`
> `int put(char c);`

An unformatted output function, inserts the character **c**, if possible. The function then returns **(unsigned char)c**. Otherwise, the function calls **set-state(badbit)**. It then returns **EOF**.

17.4.4.1.23 ostream::write(const char*, int)

write

```
ostream& write(const char* s, int n);
```

An unformatted output function, obtains characters to insert from successive locations of an array whose first element is designated by **s**. Characters are inserted until either of the following occurs:

- **n** characters are inserted;
- inserting in the output sequence fails (in which case the function calls **setstate(badbit)**).

The function returns ***this**.

17.4.4.1.24 ostream::write(const unsigned char*, int)

write

```
ostream& write(const unsigned char* s, int n)
```

Returns **write((const char*)s, n)**.

17.4.4.1.25 ostream::write(const signed char*, int)

write

```
ostream& write(const signed char* s, int n)
```

Returns **write((const char*)s, n)**.

17.4.4.1.26 ostream::flush()

flush

```
ostream& flush();
```

If **rdbuf()** is not a null pointer, calls **rdbuf()->pubsync()**. If that function returns **EOF**, the function calls **setstate(badbit)**.

The function returns ***this**.

17.4.4.2 endl(ostream&)

endl

```
ostream& endl(ostream& os);
```

Calls **os.put('\n')**, then **os.flush()**. The function returns **os**.[103]

17.4.4.3 ends(ostream&)

ends

```
ostream& ends(ostream& os);
```

Calls **os.put('\0')**. The function returns **os**.[104]

17.4.4.4 flush(ostream&)

flush

```
ostream& flush(ostream& os);
```

Calls **os.flush()**. The function returns **os**.

Footnotes:

Footnotes

97) The stream buffer can, of course, be associated with an output file, but it need not be.

98) The conversion specification **#o** generates a leading **0** which is *not* a padding character.

99) The function signatures **opfx()** and **osfx()** can also perform additional implementation-dependent operations.

100) See, for example, the function signature **endl(ostream&)**.

101) See, for example, the function signature **::dec(ios&)**.

102) This behavior differs from that for **istream::istream& operator>>(streambuf&)**, which does *not* rethrow the exception.

103) The effect of executing **cout << endl** is to insert a newline character in the output sequence controlled by **cout**, then synchronize it with any external file with which it might be associated.

104) The effect of executing **ostr << ends** is to insert a null character in the output sequence controlled by **ostr**. If **ostr** is an object of class **strstreambuf**, the null character can terminate an NTBS constructed in an array object.

Future Directions

bool   With the addition of the scalar type **bool** comes another formatted output function for class **ostream**. A "true" value converts to an integer 1, while "false" becomes zero.

locale   Again I remind you that the Committee has added locale objects. (See
objects page 188.) Inserters in class **ostream** are expected to access the locale object imbued within the base **ios** subobject to determine how to produce output. In principle, each **ostream** object can operate within a different locale. By default, however, the locale imbued by an **ostream** constructor is the **"C"** locale, *not* the current locale.

wide-character   I also repeat here the warning, first mentioned on page 119, that wide-
streams   character streams have been added to the Standard C++ library. Class **ostream** also becomes a template class parameterized by the type of the stream element. One instantiation, for type *char*, has essentially the same functionality as described in this chapter. Another, for type **wchar_t**, supports streams of elements from some large character set.

Using <ostream>

You have little or no occasion to include the header **<ostream>** directly. Like **<ios>**, **<streambuf>**, and **<istream>** in the previous three chapters, it is another header invented by the Committee simply to split the iostreams declarations into more manageable pieces. But the chances are just as good that you'll use the *contents* of **<ostream>** in a program. Class **ostream** is the base class for all classes that support insertions into a stream buffer, the classic way to mediate all output in the iostreams package. The base class summarizes what is *common* to all such output classes.

cout   If you include the header **<iostream>**, you can use the **ostream** object
cerr   **cout** to write the standard output stream. (See Chapter 14: **<iostream>**.)
clog   Similarly, you can use the **ostream** objects **cerr** or **clog** to write the standard error stream. Otherwise, you typically create an object *derived* from **istream** to mediate output to a stream buffer you create at the same time. (See Chapter 11: **<strstream>**, Chapter 12: **<sstream>**, and Chapter 13: **<fstream>**.)

constructor   The only occasion you have for declaring an **ostream** object directly is to mediate output to a stream buffer created separately. You can, for example, set up a bidirectional stream various ways. I repeat here the way I showed on page 122:

```
#include <fstream>
    .....
    ifstream istr("abc", ios::in | ios::out);
    ostream ostr(istr.rdbuf());
```

or:

```
#include <fstream>
    .....
```

```
ifstream istr("abc", ios::in | ios::out);
ostream ostr;
ostr.rdbuf(istr.rdbuf());
```

Given an **ostream** object **x**, you can perform a whole host of operations on it. Many are inherited from the base class **ios**, which I have already described. (See Chapter 6: **<ios>**.) You can also call:

- *predefined manipulators,* such as **x << endl**, to alter the state of the output sequence or values stored in **x**

- *character output functions,* such as **x.put()**, to insert sequences of one or more characters

- *scalar inserters,* such as **x << n**, for an *int* **n**, to convert an internal representation to a sequence of characters that represents its value and insert the seeuqnce

- *support functions,* such as **x.flush()**, to help you write your own manipulators and extractors

I deal with these groups of operations in order.

predefined   All the manipulators defined for class **ios** also apply to objects of class
manipulators **ostream**, naturally enough. The same is true for the **ios** member functions that have the same effect as the manipulators. (See the lengthy discussion of formatting information beginning on page 124.) Not all have meaningful effect, however. For an **ostream** object, the relevant information depends on the scalar type being inserted. I describe the particulars later, with the inserters for each group of types. One flag affects *all* formatted and unformatted output functions:

unitbuf ■ the format flag **unitbuf**, which calls for the output stream to be flushed by a call to the suffix function **ostream::osfx()**

The following formatting information affects all the string and scalar formatted output functions, except for the three character types:

width ■ the field width, which determines the *minimum* number of characters to insert

fill ■ the fill character, which determines the character to add repeatedly to meet the minimum width requirement

adjustfield ■ the format flags in the **adjustfield** group, which determine whether fill characters are added at some internal point in the conversion (**internal**), before the conversion (**right**), or after the conversion (**left**)

The "internal" point in a numeric conversion is generally where you would add leading zeros, or those * characters on checks. For a hexadecimal conversion, it is to the right of the **0x** or **0X** prefix. For all others, it is immediately before the leading digit.

manipulators   The header **<ostream>** declares two peculiar member functions:

```
ostream& operator<<(ostream& (*pf)(ostream&));
ostream& operator<<(ios& (*pf)(ios&));
```

I described the **istream** version of the second of these on page 124. It is the magic that makes the manipulators defined for class **ios** work as "pseudo-extractors" with **ostream** objects. The first supports manipulators intended to work *only* with **ostream** objects.

Three such creatures are defined by the Standard C++ library, all declared in **<ostream>**. (But see the template class **omanip** in Chapter 10: **<iomanip>**.) You can write:

endl   **x << endl;**

to insert a newline character (**'\n'**) and flush the output stream. This inserter is both a convenient shorthand and a useful way to synchronize the output stream periodically with an interactive file, such as a terminal display.

ends   Similarly, the manipulator **ends** inserts a null character (**'\0'**) without flushing the stream. You use this manipulator primarily to insert a terminating null character after generating an in-memory character sequence. (See Chapter 11: **<strstream>**.)

flush   The manipulator **flush** flushes the output stream without inserting a character. You use this manipulator only when you can't be certain that a necessary synchronization has occurred. (See the discussion on page 221.)

character output functions   Class **ostream** provides several member functions for inserting sequences of one or more characters. Here is my attempt to characterize them all in a way that highlights their critical differences. Each of the member functions that follows:

width   ■ pads with fill characters to the specified field width, then sets the field width to zero, only if its description says "pads to field width"

badbit   ■ sets **badbit** if it fails to insert all characters

With those blanket rules in mind, here is the list of functions you might use to insert sequences of characters:

operator<<   ■ **operator<<(char ch), operator<<(signed char ch), operator<<(unsigned char ch)** — inserts **ch**

operator<<   ■ **operator<<(const char *s)** — (**n** is **strlen(s)**, where **strlen** is declared in **<string.h>**) inserts **n** characters beginning at **s**, pads to field width

operator<<   ■ **operator<<(streambuf& sb)** — extracts remaining characters from the streambuf **sb** (and inserts them in ***this**), stops on an insertion failure (character not extracted) or on any exception (exception *is* rethrown), also described on page 191

put   ■ **put(char ch)** — inserts **ch**

write   ■ **write(const char *s, int n), write(const signed char *s, int n), write(const unsigned char *s, int n)** — inserts **n** characters beginning at **s**

As with the character input functions (page 190), I can't counsel you on which of these member functions to use. That decision depends heavily on the particular need, and the style of programming you favor. I do suggest as before, however, that you pick one or two of these choices, learn them well, and stick with them. The options are nowhere near as rich as for extracting character sequences, but it's still too easy to forget details if you try to use them all.

scalar inserters   The scalar inserters in class **ostream** are important work horses. Each converts some encoded form within a C++ program to a human-readable text sequence (or *field*). The form is determined by type **T** in a member declaration of the form:

```
ostream& operator<<(T x);
```

where **x** designates the value of the argument expression.

In all cases, the following steps occur, in order:

- If any of the status bits **badbit**, **eofbit**, or **failbit** is set, the function makes no attempt to insert characters.
- If **tie()** is not a null pointer, the function flushes the specified stream.
- The function generates the minimum-length character sequence that represents the argument value, as determined by the argument type and any relevant format flags.
- If the field width is greater than the length of this character sequence, the function pads the character sequence with fill characters as determined by the format flags in the **adjustfield** group.
- If the function cannot insert all the characters in the generated field, it sets **badbit**.
- If the format flag **unitbuf** is set, the function flushes the output stream.

In all cases, the function returns ***this**, so that inserters can be chained.

integer inserters   Integer inserters exist for the types *char, signed char, unsigned char, short, int, unsigned int, long,* and *unsigned long.* You *cannot* insert an integer value directly from a an expression of a character type. An inserter for a character type inserts the character code instead, as I described earlier. You must type cast the character expression **ch** to some integer type, as with **(int)ch**.

Remember that the **basefield** format flags determine the base for both input and output conversions. For inserters only, clearing all **basefield** flags calls for decimal output.

For all the integer types, you can control:

basefield ■ the numeric base for the text representation by how you set the **ios::basefield** group of format flags (see page 126)

showpos ■ whether non-negative values have a leading **+**, by setting the format flag **showpos**

showbase ■ whether octal values have a leading **0** or hexadecimal values have a prefix **0x** or **0X**, by setting the format flag **showbase**

uppercase ■ whether hexadecimal values use uppercase letters for **x** and the digits **a** through **f**, by setting the format flag **uppercase**

adjustfield ■ whether padding occurs after any sign and/or prefix and before the digits, by setting just the format flag **internal** in the group **adjustfield**

floating-point Floating-point inserters exist for the types *float*, *double*, and *long double*.
inserters They generate the same formats as the **fprintf** conversion specifiers **e**, **f**, and **g** (or their uppercase versions). For niggling details, see a precise description of that function (such as in **P&B92**).

For all the floating-point types, you can control:

showpos ▪ whether non-negative values have a leading **+**, by setting the format flag **showpos**

showpoint ▪ whether to preserve the decimal point along with any trailing zeros, by setting the format flag **showbase**

uppercase ▪ whether to use an uppercase letter for **e**, by setting the format flag **uppercase**

adjustfield ▪ whether padding occurs after any sign and before the digits, by setting just the format flag **internal** in the group **adjustfield**

floatfield ▪ whether to include a decimal exponent, by setting just the format flag **scientific**, or to omit a decimal exponent, by setting just the format flag **fixed**, or to choose the format that best represents the value of the number, by setting any other combination of flags in the group **float-field**

Specifically, the three formats selected by the group **floatfield** follow the same rules as for the **fprintf** conversion specifiers **e** (**scientific**), **f** (**fixed**), and **g** (any other).

pointer You can use the inserter **operator<<(void *)** to convert an arbitrary
inserter object pointer. The draft C++ Standard defines this conversion in terms of the **p** conversion specifier for **fprintf**, but the C Standard has little to add on that topic. Certainly, whatever this inserter generates should be acceptable to its corresponding **istream** extractor, and should recover the same value. (See page 192.) But little is promised about how pointers appear as character sequences.

Often, an implementation displays a pointer to *void* as one or more hexadecimal integer values. And often, the conversion is affected by the same flags that qualify hexadecimal conversions. But the draft C++ Standard is mum on this topic. Don't count on much in the way of portable behavior when inserting pointers. (I use such inserters only for debugging.) And make a point of writing an explicit **(void *)** type cast before any pointer you wish to insert. A pointer to *char* will certainly get hijacked by another inserter. And you never know when someone else might decide to write an inserter that accepts some other object pointer type.

support The remaining member function in class **ostream** is the sole "support
functions function" (unlike class **istream**, which has several). You call it when you want to take more direct cnntrol of the associated stream buffer, as when defining your own inserters (see page 179) or your own manipulators.

flush You call the member function **flush()** simply to synchronize the output stream with any external file. I discussed it and related operations earlier in this chapter, on page 221.

Generating output is a much simpler task than parsing input, but I still counsel you to keep such antics to a minimum. The member functions I have described so far also represent a considerable amount of engineering in their own way, just like extractors. You are more likely to violate some subtle semantic constraints if you strike off on your own. So wherever possible, I urge you to write new inserters and manipulators in terms of existing ones.

stream   An alternative way to write your own inserters is to model them after
buffer   the ones I show here. Follow the pattern I showed on page 220. Better yet,
primitives if you're using this implementation of the Standard C++ library, follow the revised pattern I show on page 241. Note the guidelines for calling the public member functions of class **streambuf**, starting on page 160. And, wherever possible, find a working inserter similar to the one you are writing and follow its structure.

locales   As a final note, I remind you that the **ostream** member functions exhibit some behavior that depends upon the current locale:

- A "decimal point" in a floating-point conversion is the character **lo-caleconv()->decimal_point[0],** where **localeconv** is declared in **<locale.h>**.

- Floating-point inserters may generate alternate formats outside the **"C"** locale.

If your program alters the current locale by calling **setlocale**, declared in **<locale.h>**, the behavior of some inserters can thus change. Moreover, future versions of iostreams may behave differently. (See page 188.)

Implementing **<ostream>**

ostream   Figure 9.1 shows the file **ostream**, which implements the standard header **<ostream>**. Its principal business is defining the class **ostream**, but it also declares the manipulators **endl**, **ends**, and **flush**. For a description of the type **_Uninitialized**, and the value **_Noinit**, see page 132. For a description of the macro **_HAS_SIGNED_CHAR**, see page 195.

Five protected functions with secret names perform formatted output:

_Ff ▪ **_Ff** converts the **floatfield** flags into an index value (0, 4, or 8) for floating-point conversions.

_If ▪ **_If** converts the **basefield** flags into an index value (0, 4, or 8) for integer conversions.

_Pad ▪ **_Pad** inserts the characters generated by **_Print**, plus any repetitions of the fill character or zero digits (**0**).

_Pr ▪ **_Pr** determines the (bounded) precision to use for floating-point conversions.

_Print ▪ **_Print** assembles the arguments for a call to **vsprintf**, declared in **<stdio.h>**, then calls **_Pad** to insert the padded character sequence.

Figure 9.1:
ostream
Part 1 of 2

```
// ostream standard header
#ifndef _OSTREAM_
#define _OSTREAM_
#include <streambuf>
            // class ostream
class ostream : virtual public ios {
public:
    ostream(streambuf *_S)
        : ios(_S) {}
    ostream(_Uninitialized)
        : ios(_Noinit) {}
    virtual ~ostream();
    _Bool opfx();
    void osfx();
    ostream& operator<<(ostream& (*_F)(ostream&))
        {return ((*_F)(*this)); }
    ostream& operator<<(ios& (*_F)(ios&))
        {(*_F)(*(ios *)this); return (*this); }
    ostream& operator<<(const char *);
    ostream& operator<<(char _C)
        {put(_C); return (*this); }
    ostream& operator<<(unsigned char _C)
        {return (*this << (char)_C); }
    ostream& operator<<(short _X)
        {return (_Print(&"B hoB hxB hd"[_If()], _X)); }
    ostream& operator<<(unsigned short _X)
        {return (_Print(&"B hoB hxB hu"[_If()], _X)); }
    ostream& operator<<(int _X)
        {return (_Print(&"B  oB  xB  d"[_If()], _X)); }
    ostream& operator<<(unsigned int _X)
        {return (_Print(&"B  oB  xB  u"[_If()], _X)); }
    ostream& operator<<(long _X)
        {return (_Print(&"B loB lxB ld"[_If()], _X)); }
    ostream& operator<<(unsigned long _X)
        {return (_Print(&"B loB lxB lu"[_If()], _X)); }
    ostream& operator<<(float _X)
        {return (_Print(&"P. eP. fP. g"[_Ff()], _Pr(), _X)); }
    ostream& operator<<(double _X)
        {return (_Print(&"P.leP.lfP.lg"[_Ff()], _Pr(), _X)); }
    ostream& operator<<(long double _X)
        {return (_Print(&"P.LeP.LfP.Lg"[_Ff()], _Pr(), _X)); }
    ostream& operator<<(void *);
    ostream& operator<<(streambuf&);
    ostream& put(char);
    ostream& write(const char *, int);
    ostream& write(const unsigned char *_S, int _N)
        {return (write((const char *)_S, _N)); }
    ostream& flush();
#if _HAS_SIGNED_CHAR
    ostream& operator<<(signed char _C)
        {return (*this << (char)_C); }
    ostream& write(const signed char *_S, int _N)
        {return (write((const char *)_S, _N)); }
#endif /* _HAS_SIGNED_CHAR */
```

```
protected:
     int _Ff()
          {return ((flags() & floatfield) == scientific ? 0
               : (flags() & floatfield) == fixed ? 4 : 8); }
     int _If()
          {return ((flags() & basefield) == oct ? 0
               : (flags() & basefield) == hex ? 4 : 8); }
     void _Pad(const char *, char *, int);
     int _Pr();
     ostream& _Print(const char *, ...);
     };
          // manipulators
ostream& endl(ostream&);
ostream& ends(ostream&);
ostream& flush(ostream&);
#endif
```

I warned of the limitations of using the **fprintf** functions earlier, on page 222. I use **vfprintf** anyway because it does so much of the job, and portably in the bargain. To avoid the obvious problems, **_Print** constructs a format string with no field width and with a bounded precision. Thus, an arbitrary conversion can be stored in a fixed-length buffer. The function **_Pad** does all the things that **vfprintf** does poorly, or not at all.

_Print is a specialized version of **printf**. Its first argument is a pointer to the first element of an array **code** of four formatting codes:

- **code[0]** is **B** if an integer conversion should honor the format flag **showbase**, if a floating-point conversion should honor the format flag **showpoint**, or a space character otherwise.

- **code[1]** is a dot (.) if the bounded precision **_Pr()** is the precision qualifier to use.

- **code[2]** is the conversion qualifier to use, or a space character otherwise.

- **code[3]** is the conversion specifier to use, or a space character otherwise.

Now you can understand how most of the formatted output functions work. Here, for example, is the definition of the inserter for type *short:*

```
ostream& operator<<(short _X)
     {return (_Print(&"B hoB hxB hd"[_If()], _X)); }
```

The protected member function **_If** determines the address within the string literal that is passed to **_Printf**. If, say, the group **basefield** has only the format flag **hex** set, then the call **_If()** returns 4. The first argument to **_Printf** begins with the sequence **B hx**. If the format flag **showbase** is also set, the resultant format string on the call to **vfprintf** is then **%#hx**.

With a bit of study, you should be able to understand all the inline calls to **_Printf** within the header `<ostream>` now.

Figure 9.2:
ostream.c

```
// ostream -- ostream basic members
#include <ostream>

ostream::~ostream()
        {                                      // destruct an ostream -- DO NOTHING
        }

_Bool ostream::opfx()
        {                                              // setup for output
        if (good() && tie() != 0)
                tie()->flush();
        return (good());
        }

void ostream::osfx()
        {                                              // wrapup after output
        if (flags() & unitbuf)
                flush();
        }                                                                □
```

Figure 9.3:
osipoint.c

```
// osipoint -- ostream::operator<<(void *)
#include <ostream>

ostream& ostream::operator<<(void *x)
        {                                              // insert a void *
        _TRY_IO_BEGIN
        if (!opfx())
                setstate(badbit);
        else
                {                                      // put pieces of pointer
                const int NL = 1 +
                        (sizeof (void *) - 1) / sizeof (unsigned long);
                union {
                        void *pv;
                        unsigned long lo[NL];
                        } u;
                u.lo[NL - 1] = 0, u.pv = x;
                for (int i = 0; ; )
                        {                              // put ints separated by colons
                        _Print("B lx", u.lo[i]);
                        if (NL <= ++i)
                                break;
                        rdbuf()->sputc(':');
                        }
                }
        osfx();
        _CATCH_IO_END
        return (*this);
        }                                                                □
```

ostream.c   Figure 9.2 shows the file **ostream.c**. It defines the three functions you are likely to need any time you declare an object of class **ostream**, its destructor, **opfx()**, and **osfx()**. Note the use of the call **tie()** to access the

Figure 9.4:
osprint.c

```
// osprint -- ostream::_Print(const char *, ...)
#include <ctype.h>
#include <stdarg.h>
#include <stdio.h>
#include <string.h>
#include <ostream>

ostream& ostream::_Print(const char *code, ...)
    {                                       // format data for inserter
    _TRY_IO_BEGIN
    if (!opfx())
        setstate(badbit);
    else
        {                                   // build format and convert
        char buf[_MAX_EXP_DIG + _MAX_SIG_DIG + 16];
        char fmt[8];
        char *s = fmt;
        *s++ = '%';
        if (code[0] != ' ' && flags() & showpos)
            *s++ = '+';
        if (code[0] == 'B' && flags() & showbase
            || code[0] == 'P' && flags() & showpoint)
            *s++ = '#';
        if (code[1] == '.')
            *s++ = '.', *s++ = '*';
        if (code[2] != ' ')
            *s++ = code[2];
        *s = code[3];
        if (flags() & uppercase && strchr("egx", *s) != 0)
            *s = toupper(*s);
        *++s = '\0';
        va_list ap;
        va_start(ap, code);
        _Pad(code, buf, vsprintf(buf, fmt, ap));
        va_end(ap);
        }
    osfx();
    _CATCH_IO_END
    return (*this);
    }                                                              □
```

stored pointer to an object of class **ostream**, just as in **istream::
ipfx(int)**. It can be convenient to flush one output stream when inserting
in another, just as you often want to flush an output stream before extracting
from an associated input stream.

osipoint.c   Figure 9.3 shows the file **osipoint.c**, which defines the member function **operator<<(void *)**. It is the only scalar formatted output function
that I found too elaborate to define inline within the header.

_TRY_IO_BEGIN   For a description of the macros **_TRY_IO_BEGIN** and **_CATCH_IO_END**, see
_CATCH_IO_END   page 128. They expand to different styles of exception handling, including
none at all. I showed how to use them to write a generic extractor, on page

```
// ospad -- ostream padding members
#include <string.h>
#include <ostream>

static _Bool do_rep(streambuf *sb, char c, int n)
    {                                           // put repeated char
    while (0 <= --n)
        if (sb->sputc(c) == EOF)
            return (0);
    return (1);
    }

inline _Bool rep(streambuf *sb, char c, int n)
    {                                   // put repeated char, if any
    return (0 < n ? do_rep(sb, c, n) : 1);
    }

inline _Bool send(streambuf *sb, const char *s, int n)
    {                                   // put char sequence, if any
    return (n <= 0 || sb->sputn(s, n) == n ? 1 : 0);
    }

void ostream::_Pad(const char *code, char *s, int n)
    {                                   // pad with fill char as needed
    _Bool ok = 1;
    int ni, np, nz;
    const char *sf;
    const void *sv;
    if (code[1] != '.' || (nz = precision() - _Pr()) <= 0)
        nz = 0, sf = s + n;
    else if ((sv = memchr((const void *)s, 'e', n)) != 0
        || (sv = memchr((const void *)s, 'E', n)) != 0)
        sf = (const char *)sv;
    else
        sf = s + n;
    ni = sf - s;
    if (width() == 0 || (np = width() - n - nz) < 0)
        np = 0;
    if ((flags() & adjustfield) == right)
        {                                           // put leading fill
        if (!rep(rdbuf(), fill(), np)
            || !send(rdbuf(), s, ni)
            || !rep(rdbuf(), '0', nz)
            || !send(rdbuf(), sf, n - ni))
            ok = 0;
        }
    else if ((flags() & adjustfield) != internal)
        {                                           // put trailing fill
        if (!send(rdbuf(), s, ni)
            || !rep(rdbuf(), '0', nz)
            || !send(rdbuf(), sf, n - ni)
            || !rep(rdbuf(), fill(), np))
            ok = 0;
        }
    else if (code[0] == 'B' && code[3] == 'x' && 2 <= n
```

```
                        && (s[1] == 'x' || s[1] == 'X'))
                    {                       // put internal fill after 0x or 0X
                    if (!send(rdbuf(), s, 2)
                        || !rep(rdbuf(), fill(), np)
                        || !send(rdbuf(), s + 2, ni - 2))
                        ok = 0;
                    }
            else if (0 < n && (s[0] == '-' || s[0] == '+'))
                    {                       // put internal fill after + or -
                    if (!send(rdbuf(), s, 1)
                        || !rep(rdbuf(), fill(), np)
                        || !send(rdbuf(), s + 1, ni - 1)
                        || !rep(rdbuf(), '0', nz)
                        || !send(rdbuf(), sf, n - ni - 1))
                        ok = 0;
                    }
            else
                    {                       // put internal fill as leading fill
                    if (!rep(rdbuf(), fill(), np)
                        || !send(rdbuf(), s, ni)
                        || !rep(rdbuf(), '0', nz)
                        || !send(rdbuf(), sf, n - ni))
                        ok = 0;
                    }
            width(0);
            if (!ok)
                setstate(badbit);
            }

int ostream::_Pr()
        {                                       // get bounded precision
        return (precision() <= 0 && !(flags() & fixed) ? 6
            : _MAX_SIG_DIG < precision() ? _MAX_SIG_DIG
            : precision());
        }                                                                      □
```

198. In this implementation, the corresponding generic code for an inserter looks like:

```
_TRY_IO_BEGIN
if (opfx())
    <perform any output>
osfx();
_CATCH_IO_END
```

Inserting a pointer to *void* must work in concert with extracting such a pointer. (See page 203.) In this implementation, the pointer overlaps an array of *unsigned long*. The function inserts elements of the array as hexadecimal integers, separated by colons. In the common case where one element of the array suffices, however, the converted pointer contains no colons.

osprint.c   Figure 9.4 shows the file **osprint.c**, which defines the member function **_Print**. It composes the format string for a call to **vsprintf**, which does all the hard work in converting a string or scalar value. The varying length

```
// osput -- ostream::put(char)
#include <ostream>

ostream& ostream::put(char ch)
    {                                                        // put a char
    _TRY_IO_BEGIN
    if (!opfx() || rdbuf()->sputc(ch) == EOF)
        setstate(badbit);
    osfx();
    _CATCH_IO_END
    return (*this);
    }                                                              □
```

```
// osistring -- ostream::operator<<(const char *)
#include <string.h>
#include <ostream>

ostream& ostream::operator<<(const char *x)
    {                                                    // insert a string
    _TRY_IO_BEGIN
    if (!opfx())
        setstate(badbit);
    else
        _Pad("   s", (char *)x, strlen(x));
    osfx();
    _CATCH_IO_END
    return (*this);
    }                                                              □
```

argument list that **vsprintf** expects is the list assembled for the call to **_Printf**. For a description of the macros **_MAX_EXP_DIG** and **_MAX_SIG_DIG**, see page 195. These are used, much as in several **istream** member functions, to define a safe buffer size for the conversion.

ospad.c   Figure 9.5 shows the file **ospad.c**, which defines the member functions **_Pad** and **_Pr**. The latter computes the bounded precision used by a floating-point conversion, as I indicated earlier. The macro **_MAX_SIG_DIG** establishes the upper bound, which should be large enough to capture all meaningful precision on a conversion by **vfprintf**.

Function **_Pad** is called by **_Print** to finish a formatted output operation, as I also outlined above. The logic is, to put it mildly, intricate. It must:

- determine whether any zero digits were suppressed by bounding the precision earlier, then determine where to inject any such digits
- determine whether any fill characters need be added, then determine where to inject any such padding

To keep the logic more or less readable, the code treats separately each of the five(!) places where fill characters can be injected. It also inserts all characters by calling one of two inline functions local to this translation unit:

Figure 9.8:
osistrea.c

```
// osistream -- ostream::operator<<(streambuf&)
#include <ostream>

ostream& ostream::operator<<(streambuf& sb)
    {                                       // insert from streambuf
    _Bool copied = 0;
    _TRY_IO_BEGIN
    if (opfx())
        {                                   // copy characters until failure
        char buf[512];
        int n;
        for (; 0 < (n = sb.sgetn(buf, sizeof (buf)));
            copied = 1)
            _TRY_BEGIN
                if (rdbuf()->sputn(buf, n) != n)
                    break;
            _CATCH_ALL
                setstate(failbit);
                _RERAISE;
            _CATCH_END
        }
    if (!copied)
        setstate(failbit);
    osfx();
    _CATCH_IO_END
    return (*this);
    }                                                                  □
```

- **rep**, to insert a single character repeatedly
- **send**, to insert a character sequence once

The logic is nevertheless intimately dependent on the kinds of character sequences presumably generated by **vfprintf**.

osput.c　　The remaining **ostream** member functions are relatively simple, by comparison. Figure 9.6 shows the file **osput.c**, which defines the member function **put(char)**. It simply inserts the character argument into the stream buffer, with requisite checking. Note that the character inserters all end up calling **put(char)** as well.

osistrin.c　　Figure 9.7 shows the file **osistrin.c**, which defines the member function **operator<<(const char *)**. It could have been defined inline within the header, invoking the conversion specification **%s**, but that just leads to excess wheel spinning. The member function **_Pad** can perform the only difficult operation — determining how to add any padding at either end of the inserted string.

osistrea.c　　Figure 9.8 shows the file **osistrea.c**, which defines the member function **operator<<(streambuf&)**. It closely resembles two **istream** member functions, **isxstrea.c** on page 198 and **isgstrea.c** on page 212. I discussed the macro **_RERAISE** on page 128. Once again, the inner macros handle exceptions thrown during insertion, while the outer macros handle exceptions thrown during extraction.

```
// osflush -- ostream::flush()
#include <ostream>

ostream& ostream::flush()
    {                                    // drain any buffered output
    _TRY_IO_BEGIN
    if (good() && rdbuf()->pubsync() == EOF)
        setstate(badbit);
    _CATCH_IO_END
    return (*this);
    }                                                              □
```

```
// oswrite -- ostream::write(const char *, int)
#include <ostream>

ostream& ostream::write(const char *s, int n)
    {                                              // put n bytes
    _TRY_IO_BEGIN
    if (!opfx() || rdbuf()->sputn(s, n) != n)
        setstate(badbit);
    osfx();
    _CATCH_IO_END
    return (*this);
    }                                                              □
```

```
// endl -- endl(ostream&)
#include <ostream>

ostream& endl(ostream& os)
    {                                        // terminate output line
    os.put('\n');
    os.flush();
    return (os);
    }                                                              □
```

osflush.c   Figure 9.9 shows the file **osflush.c**, which defines the member function
oswrite.c **flush()**. And Figure 9.10 shows the file **oswrite.c**, which defines the
member function **write(const char *, int)**. Both simply call the appropriate **streambuf** public member function to perform the critical operation in each case.

endl.c   Now for the three manipulators that work only with **ostream** objects.
ends.c Figure 9.11 shows the file **endl.c**, which defines the function **endl**. Figure
flush.c 9.12 shows the file **ends.c**, which defines the function **ends**. And Figure
9.13 shows the file **flush.c**, which defines the function **flush**. All three are
straightforward.

Figure 9.12:
ends.c

```
// ends -- ends(ostream&)
#include <ostream>

ostream& ends(ostream& os)
    {                                           // terminate output string
    os.put('\0');
    return (os);
    }                                                                    □
```

Figure 9.13:
flush.c

```
// flush -- flush(ostream&)
#include <ostream>

ostream& flush(ostream& os)
    {                                                      // flush output
    os.flush();
    return (os);
    }                                                                    □
```

Testing `<ostream>`

tostream.c   Figure 9.14 shows the file **tostream.c**. It tests the basic properties of class **ostream**. As in the previous chapter, I make use of classes derived from **ostream** and **streambuf** to do something concrete. This time, an object of class **ostrstream** helps construct a stream buffer (of class **strstreambuf**) that accumulates a character string in memory. (See Chapter 11: **<strstream>**.) The code is not completely portable because it uses the macros **_TRY_IO_BEGIN** and **_CATCH_IO_END**, peculiar to this implementation.

The program again defines the class **Boolean**, as does **tistream.c**, which stores an *int* value. It then defines an inserter for this class, which maps a zero value into **N** and a nonzero value into **Y**. The program tests whether this inserter, and all the member functions of class **ostream**, exhibit at least some of their required behavior.

If all goes well, the program prints:

SUCCESS testing <ostream>

and takes a normal exit.

Exercises

Exercise 9.1 Write the manipulator **general** that sets the format flags in **floatfield** to specify adaptive floating-point output (as for the **g** conversion specifier to **printf**).

Exercise 9.2 List all manipulators, not currently declared in **<ios>** or **<ostream>**, that you think might set the format flags in useful ways.

Exercise 9.3 Besides flushing the output stream, what kind of operations do you think **ostream::osfx()** might have to perform?

```
// test <ostream>
#include <assert.h>
#include <string.h>
#include <ostream>
#include <iostream>
#include <strstream>


            // class Boolean
class Boolean {
public:
    Boolean(int v)
        : val(v) {}
    int value() const
        {return (val); }
    int value(int v)
        {return (val = v); }
private:
    int val;
    };


ostream& operator<<(ostream& ostr, const Boolean& b)
    {                                   // insert a Boolean
    _TRY_IO_BEGIN
    if (!ostr.opfx())
        ostr.setstate(ios::failbit);
    else
        ostr.rdbuf()->sputc(b.value() != 0 ? 'Y' : 'N');
    ostr.osfx();
    _CATCH_IO_END
    return (ostr);
    }


int main()
    {                   // test basic workings of ostream definitions
    static const char output[] = "s1s2**s3@~s4??s5 bc\n"
        " 1 23 -456 +7890 3 12 ??010 0x??3e 0XAB 0\n"
        " +12 14.0000 -?1.68E-05 1.000 2.000E+00\n"
        " N Y\n"
        "rest of stream\n"
        " s1 s2 s3";
    ostrstream ostrstr;
    ostream outs(ostrstr.rdbuf());
    assert(outs.good() && (outs.flags() & ios::showbase) == 0);
    outs << noskipws;
    assert((outs.flags() & (ios:: dec | ios::skipws))
        == ios::dec);
        // test character inserters
    outs << "s1";
    outs.fill('*'), outs.width(4), outs << "s2";
    outs.fill('@'), outs.width(3), outs << left << "s3";
    outs.fill('~'), outs.width(3), outs << right << "s4";
    outs.fill('?'), outs.width(4), outs << internal << "s5";
    outs << ' ' << (unsigned char)'b' << (signed char)'c'
        << endl << flush;
        // test integer inserters
```

```
    outs << ' ' << (short)1 << ' ' << (unsigned short)23;
    outs << ' ' << (int)-456 << ' ';
    outs << showpos << (int)7890
         << ' ' << (unsigned int)3 << noshowpos;
    outs << ' ' << oct << (long)10;
    outs.width(5), outs << ' ' << showbase << (long)8;
    outs.width(6), outs << ' ' << hex << (unsigned long)0x3e;
    outs << ' ' << uppercase << (unsigned long)0xab;
    outs << ' ' << (unsigned long)0 << endl;
        // test floating-point inserters
    outs << ' ' << showpos << (float)12 << noshowpos;
    outs << ' ' << showpoint << (double)14 << noshowpoint;
    outs.precision(3), outs.width(10);
    outs << ' ' << (long double)-168e-7;
    outs << fixed << ' ' << 1.0;
    outs << scientific << ' ' << 2.0 << endl;
        // test Boolean inserter
    const Boolean no(0), yes(1);
    assert(no.value() == 0 && yes.value() == 1);
    outs << ' ' << no << ' ' << yes << endl;
        // test streambuf inserter and puts
    istrstream istr("rest of stream\n");
    outs << *istr.rdbuf();
    outs.put(' ').write("s1", 2);
    outs.write((unsigned char *)" s2 ", 3);
    outs.write((signed char *)" s3", 3);
    outs.flush() << ends << (void *)&output;
    assert(strcmp(ostrstr.str(), output) == 0);
    cout << "SUCCESS testing <ostream>" << endl;
    return (0);
    }                                                      □
```

Exercise 9.4 The expression statement:

```
cout << width(5) << 'x';
```

does *not* add padding to the inserted character **x**. Describe two or more ways to obtain such padding. Implement at least one of them.

Exercise 9.5 Does the **fprintf** family of functions have any capabilities not easily modeled by **ostream** inserters? Show how would you add any such missing capabilities.

Exercise 9.6 [**Harder**] Define a set of "stdargs" classes, modeled after **istream** and **ostream**, that support insertion and extraction of arbitrary scalar values *without conversion*. Why would you want such a capability? (The name should supply a good hint.)

Exercise 9.7 [**Very hard**] Augment the classes you defined for the previous exercise to provide type checking within the stream. In other words, check that a value you extract is treated as the same type as the value you earlier inserted. Why would you want such a capability?

Chapter 10: `<iomanip>`

Background

The header `<iomanip>` presents several *templates* and a handful of manipulators that exploit them. I have already presented these manipulators, alongside the `ios` member functions that perform similar operations. (See the discussion of formatting information, beginning on page 124.)

This is the first of several headers that define templates. (See also Chapter 17: `<bits>`, Chapter 19: `<dynarray>`, and Chapter 20: `<ptrdynarray>`.) It is also arguably the trickiest use of templates in the Standard C++ library, at least for now. I begin, therefore, by sketching the history that led to the templates in `<iomanip>`. I also include here a general discussion of templates, current template technology, and how I implement templates in this book.

manipulators Manipulators have lots of uses. The ones I've shown so far let you alter the formatting information stored in an object based on class `ios`, extract white space, insert special characters, and flush output streams. And they let you do so in the guise of inserting or extracting a function designator with a reasonably mnemonic name. Perhaps the happiest example of all is:

```
cout << endl;
```

which inserts a newline character to end the current text line and flushes the output to any waiting interactive display.

manipulator For all their power, however, these inserters share a common limitation. **limitations** You have no way to convey any additional, variable information. The name of the function says what it does, but that's also *all* it says. The limitation is intrinsic in the operator notation:

```
ostream& operator<<(ostream& os, X x);
```

It is clear that you can pass only one additional argument to the left shift (insertion) operator, besides the necessary `ostream&` left argument. For a manipulator, that additional argument `x` of type `X` must convey the address of the function to call, as in `(*x)(os)`. (`X` is presumably some pointer to function type, defined earlier in the translation unit.) There's hardly any room to convey additional arguments.

Or is there? Remember, `x` can be an arbitrary class. You can construct a class that stores *both* a function pointer and an extra argument, as in:

```
class X {
public:
    X(ostream& (*pf_arg)(ostream&, T), T val_arg)
        : pf(pf_arg), val(val_arg) {}
    friend ostream& operator<<(ostream&, X);
private:
    ostream& (*pf)(ostrea&&, T);
    T val;
    };
```

Presumably, **T** is defined as a type earlier in the translation unit. You can then overload the insertion operator, as in:

```
ostream& operator<<(ostream& os, X x)
    {                            // assemble function call and do it
    return ((*x.pf)(os, x.val));
    }
```

This inserter accepts an object of class **x**, digs out the pieces, and makes the desired function call. (It is a friend of the class so it can see the pieces.)

To use this machinery, you have to supply a *pair* of functions:

- the visible function, taking a single argument of type **T**, that you call to obtain the right operand of an insertion operator
- the hidden function, taking two arguments, that does the actual work

The visible function assembles an object of class **x**. Inserting that object causes the hidden function to get called.

example   Here's a realistic example. Say you want to insert an occasional integer in hexadecimal format, but you don't want to have to keep fiddling the format bits. After each such insertion, you want the integer base to revert to whatever it was before the hexadecimal insertion. To do so, you can write the function:

```
ostream& insert_hex(ostream& os, int val)
    {                                    // insert a hex integer
    ios::fmtflags old = os.setf(ios::hex, ios::basefield);
    os << val;
    os.setf(old, ios::basefield);
    return (os);
    }
```

You can then write calls such as **insert_hex(cout, mask)**. But that doesn't play so nicely with the inserter notation. Better to make this the hidden function, using the machinery I showed above. The visible function might then overload the name **hex**, as in:

```
X hex(int val)
    {                            // save info to call insert_hex(val)
    return (X(&insert_hex, val));
    }
```

Now you can write something like:

```
    cout << "mask is " << hex(mask) << endl;
```

The new **hex** assembles an object of class **x** which, when inserted, calls **insert_hex** with the stored argument. The net effect is that **mask** is inserted in hexadecimal format, regardless of the current settings for the **basefield** format flags, which are left unaltered.

Neat, huh? Even neater is the fact that you can define manipulators that work just with inserters, as above, or just with extractors, or with both. In the last case, you probably want the left operand to be an object of the base class **ios**. A subobject of class **ios** captures what is common to objects of class **ostream** (the subject of inserters) and of class **istream** (the subject of extractors). You have lots of choices.

The problem is, you have too many choices. And you have too much tedious work to do for each choice you make. It's nuisancy enough to have to write a pair of functions for each manipulator, but that's the most visible, problem-specific part. Just to *prepare* for writing this pair of functions, you need to define a class and overload one or two operators on that class. And you have to define a different class for each argument type you wish to pass, and for each object you wish to operate on (**ios**, **istream**, or **ostream**).

generic macros   The traditional approach to replicating chunks of code in C is to define macros to do it for you. In fact, typical implementations of the header **<iostream.h>** (note the **.h** suffix) contained some truly impressive macro definitions. Such *generic macros* let you write the hairy code once, then expand it on demand with a given type, or types, filled in at the critical places.

template classes   The modern approach in C++ is to define *templates* instead. A *template class* defines an open-ended set of classes with one or more parameters. Typically, a parameter specifies a type, which you write as **class T**, regardless of whether or not **T** is truly a class. That's the special power of templates that removes one more excuse to write messy macros. A parameter can also supply a value, however, such as the number of bits in a set. (See Chapter 17: **<bits>**.)

The class **X** I defined earlier, for example, converts easily to a template class. All you need to do is add a prefix to the class definition:

```
template<class T> class X {
public:
    X(ostream& (*pf_arg)(ostream&, T), T val_arg)
        : pf(pf_arg), val(val_arg) {}
    friend ostream& operator<<(ostream&, X);
private:
    ostream& (*pf)(ostream&, T);
    T val;
    };
```

Now **T** has quite a different meaning. Before, you were obliged to define **T** as a type before writing the definition for class **X**. If you wanted the same shaped class for a different type **T2**, you had to replicate all the code and alter all the references to **T**. With a template class, however, **T** is a parameter name. Much like the name of a parameter to a function call, it has special meaning within, and only within, the body of the definition that follows.

instantiating templates   To make use of such a template class, you write an *instantiation*. If, for example, you want an object that stores an argument value of type *int*, you write its type as **X<int>**. Construct such an object and the translator generates on your behalf a version of the constructor that traffics in *int* second arguments. Declare another such object and the translator can probably recycle the special code for an *int* template parameter. Declare an object of type **x<double>**, however, and the translator will most likely generate a whole 'nother constructor just for a *double* template parameter.

The point is, you can instantiate as many flavors of a given template class as your heart desires. The translator supplies whatever executable code that's necessary, on demand. If it can find clever ways to recycle existing code, so much the better for space efficiency. But in any event, you benefit from the coding convenience of writing something once and using it multiple times. And unlike macros, the translator can better check the sanity of template classes, both when they're defined and when they're instantiated.

template You can also write *template functions*. Template parameters can supply
functions types for the parameters of the function, as in:

```
template<class T> ostream& insert_hex(ostream& os, T val)
    {                           // insert a hex integer of type T
    ios::fmtflags old = os.setf(ios::hex, ios::basefield);
    os << val;
    os.setf(old, ios::basefield);
    return (os);
    }
```

A call to **insert_hex<long>(cout, mask)** instantiates a version of the function with a second parameter of type *long*.

That's handy, but the machinery doesn't stop there. You can even write **insert_hex(cout, (long)mask)**, or any call whose second argument is implicitly of type *long,* and the translator will instantiate the flavor **insert_hex<long>** for you(!) No need to spell out in advance the instantiations you expect to need. Just write the function call and leave it to the translator to guess which instantiation works best.

You can even count on a limited amount of argument type conversion, and back fitting, as part of the matching process. Here, for example, is the template function that accompanies our template class:

```
template<class T> ostream& operator<<(ostream& os, X<T> x)
    {                           // assemble function call and do it
    return ((*x.pf)(os, x.val));
    }
```

Inserting an **x<int>** does indeed instantiate the *int* version of this function.

template   Such powerful notation is a two-edged sword. The translator is obliged
limitations to guess, from the argument types, what corresponding template parameters you must have intended. You are thus obliged to help the translator in some ways:

■ Every template function parameter must affect the type of one or more function parameters in some way, however else it is used in the function definition.

■ Value parameters cannot be used as template function parameters, since they seldom can influence overload resolution.

The Committee has eliminated some of these constraints, but current implementations still have them. You can also find differences of interpretation among implementations — no surprise with any fairly new technology. So the bottom line is, don't ask too much of the machinery for automatically instantiating template functions.

implementation restrictions   Templates have other limitations as well, at least for now. Current implementations have fundamental differences in how they manage template definitions. You can, in principle, write a template class like any other. You define the template class itself in a header, but keep the member function definitions in a separate source file or files. In practice, however, not all implementations deal with this approach well, if at all. And some implementations have limited capacity for dealing with complex template definitions.

Writing inline definitions for template functions of all flavors seems to work most reliably in current implementations. Of course, you run risks in doing so, at least with certain compilers. A nontrivial inline function definition may still expand to inline code, so the compiler generates an excess of code. Other compilers choose not to inline code that contains loops, such as *for* or *while* statements. (The cfront preprocessor won't even translate such code. It favors a different template style.) Whether or not that is a good decision, the compilers still see fit to complain repeatedly about such code. I have had reasonable programs fail to compile simply because the compiler decided it had emitted too many (gratuitous) diagnostics.

template style   The style I chose for this book is to write only inline definitions for all template functions. I try to keep them small, for a host of reasons. Occasionally, I offload some work to secret functions that are shared across template instantiations. But the basic risks of this approach remain, as I outlined above. Still, I find this approach best for the sake of portability and clear presentation today. You may need to alter the representation of some templates presented here, if for no other reason than to improve translation speed, execution speed, or generated code size.

What the Draft C++ Standard Says

The header `<iomanip>` defines three template classes:

- `smanip<T>`, for use with both extractors and inserters
- `imanip<T>`, for use with extractors only
- `omanip<T>`, for use with inserters only

Each template class has one or two associated template functions for performing insertions and extractions. Note that the template classes defined here *do not* restrict public access to their member objects. Provided the member object names are secret, the effect is much the same as making each template function a friend of the template class.

The header also declares half a dozen manipulators.

17.4.5 Header `<iomanip>`

The header `<iomanip>` defines three template classes and several related functions that use these template classes to provide extractors and inserters that alter information maintained by class `ios` and its derived classes. It also defines several instantiations of these template classes and functions.

17.4.5.1 Template class `smanip<T>`

**Class
`smanip<T>`**

```
template<class T> class smanip {
public:
    smanip(ios& (*pf_arg)(ios&, T), T);
//  ios& (*pf)(ios&, T);                            exposition only
//  T manarg;                                       exposition only
};
```

The template class `smanip<T>` describes an object that can store a function pointer and an object of type `T`. The designated function accepts an argument of this type `T`. For the sake of exposition, the maintained data is presented here as:

- `ios& (*pf)(ios&, T)`, the function pointer;
- `T manarg`, the object of type `T`.

17.4.5.1.1 `smanip<T>::smanip(ios& (*)(ios&, T), T)`

constructor

```
smanip(ios& (*pf_arg)(ios&, T), T manarg_arg);
```

Constructs an object of class `smanip<T>`, initializing `pf` to `pf_arg` and `manarg` to `manarg_arg`.

17.4.5.1.2 `operator>>(istream&, const smanip<T>&)`

operator>>

```
template <class T> istream& operator>>(istream& is,
    const smanip<T>& a);
```

Calls `(*a.pf)(is, a.manarg)` and catches any exception the function call throws. If the function catches an exception, it calls `is.set-state(ios::failbit)` (the exception is not rethrown). The function returns `is`.

17.4.5.1.3 `operator<<(ostream&, const smanip<T>&)`

operator<<

```
template <class T> ostream& operator<<(ostream& os,
    const smanip<T>& a);
```

Calls `(*a.pf)(os, a.manarg)` and catches any exception the function call throws. If the function catches an exception, it calls `os.set-state(ios::failbit)` (the exception is not rethrown). The function returns `os`.

17.4.5.2 Template class `imanip<T>`

**Class
`imanip<T>`**

```
template<class T> class imanip {
public:
    imanip(istream& (*pf_arg)(istream&, T), T);
//  istream& (*pf)(istream&, T);
//  T manarg;                                       exposition only
};
```

The template class `imanip<T>` describes an object that can store a function pointer and an object of type `T`. The designated function accepts an argument of this type `T`. For the sake of exposition, the maintained data is presented here as:

- `istream& (*pf)(istream&, T)`, the function pointer;
- `T manarg`, the object of type `T`.

17.4.5.2.1 imanip<T>::imanip(istream& (*)(istream&, T), T)

constructor

```
imanip<T>::imanip(istream& (*pf_arg)(istream&, T),
    T manarg_arg);
```

Constructs an object of class **imanip<T>**, initializing **pf** to *pf_arg* and **manarg** to *manarg_arg*.

17.4.5.2.2 operator>>(istream&, const imanip<T>&)

operator>>

```
template <class T> istream& operator>>(istream& is,
    const imanip<T>& a);
```

Calls **(*a.pf)(is, a.manarg)** and catches any exception the function call throws. If the function catches an exception, it calls **is.set-state(ios::failbit)** (the exception is not rethrown). The function returns **is**.

17.4.5.3 Template class omanip<T>

Class
omanip<T>

```
template<class T> class omanip {
public:
    omanip(ostream& (*pf_arg)(ostream&, T), T);
//  ostream& (*pf)(ostream&, T);
//  T manarg;                                exposition only
};
```

The template class **omanip<T>** describes an object that can store a function pointer and an object of type **T**. The designated function accepts an argument of this type **T**. For the sake of exposition, the maintained data is presented here as:

- **ostream& (*pf)(ostream&, T)**, the function pointer;
- **T manarg**, the object of type **T**.

17.4.5.3.1 omanip<T>::omanip(ostream& (*)(ostream&, T), T)

constructor

```
omanip<T>::omanip(ostream& (*pf_arg)(ostream&, T),
    T manarg_arg);
```

Constructs an object of class **omanip<T>**, initializing **pf** to *pf_arg* and **manarg** to *manarg_arg*.

17.4.5.3.2 operator<<(istream&, const omanip<T>&)

operator<<

```
template <class T> ostream& operator<<(ostream& os,
    const omanip<T>& a);
```

Calls **(*a.pf)(os, a.manarg)** and catches any exception the function call throws. If the function catches an exception, it calls **os.set-state(ios::failbit)** (the exception is not rethrown). The function returns **os**.

17.4.5.4 Instantiations of manipulators

17.4.5.4.1 resetiosflags(ios::fmtflags)

resetiosflags

```
smanip<ios::fmtflags> resetiosflags(ios::fmtflags mask);
```

Returns **smanip<ios::fmtflags>(&f, mask)**, where **f** can be defined as:[105]

```
ios& f(ios& str, ios::fmtflags mask)
{                                        // reset specified flags
    str.setf((ios::fmtflags)0, mask);
    return (str);
}
```

17.4.5.4.2 `setiosflags(ios::fmtflags)`

```
smanip<ios::fmtflags> setiosflags(ios::fmtflags mask);
```

Returns **smanip<ios::fmtflags>**(&*f*, *mask*), where *f* can be defined as:

```
ios& f(ios& str, ios::fmtflags mask)
{                                              // set specified flags
    str.setf(mask);
    return (str);
}
```

17.4.5.4.3 `setbase(int)`

```
smanip<int> setbase(int base);
```

Returns **smanip<int>**(&*f*, *base*), where *f* can be defined as:

```
ios& f(ios& str, int base)
{                                              // set basefield
    str.setf(n == 8 ? ios::oct : n == 10 ? ios::dec
        : n == 16 ? ios::hex : (ios::fmtflags)0, ios::basefield);
    return (str);
}
```

17.4.5.4.4 `setfill(int)`

```
smanip<int> setfill(int c);
```

Returns **smanip<int>**(&*f*, *c*), where *f* can be defined as:

```
ios& f(ios& str, int c)
{                                              // set fill character
    str.fill(c);
    return (str);
}
```

17.4.5.4.5 `setprecision(int)`

```
smanip<int> setprecision(int n);
```

Returns **smanip<int>**(&*f*, *n*), where *f* can be defined as:

```
ios& f(ios& str, int n)
{                                              // set precision
    str.precision(n);
    return (str);
}
```

17.4.5.4.6 `setw(int)`

```
smanip<int> setw(int n);
```

Returns **smanip<int>**(&*f*, *n*), where *f* can be defined as:

```
ios& f(ios& str, int n)
{                                              // set width
    str.width(n);
    return (str);
}
```

Footnotes:

105) The expression **cin >> resetiosflags(ios::skipws)** clears **ios::skipws** in the format flags stored in the **istream** object **cin** (the same as **cin >> noskipws**), and the expression **cout << resetiosflags(ios::showbase)** clears **ios::showbase** in the format flags stored in the **ostream** object **cout** (the same as **cout << noshowbase**).

Future Directions

wide-character The template classes defined in `<iomanip>` are also altered by the
streams addition of wide-character streams to the Standard C++ library. (See page
119.) Additional template parameters specify the kind of stream.

Using `<iomanip>`

You include the header `<iomanip>` for one of two reasons:

- to use one or more of the predefined manipulators that take an argument
- to define one or more additional manipulators that take an argument

predefined I showed how to use the predefined manipulators much earlier, in
manipulators conjunction with the `ios` member functions that access and alter formatting
information. (See page 124.) All are based on the template class `smanip<T>`,
to work with both extractors and inserters. Very briefly:

resetiosflags ▪ `resetiosflags(fmtflags)`, clears the specified format flags

setiosflags ▪ `setiosflags(fmtflags)`, sets the specified format flags

setbase ▪ `setbase(int)`, sets the `basefield` format flags to match the specified
numeric base

setfill ▪ `setfill(int)`, alters the fill character

setprecision ▪ `setprecision(int)`, alters the floating-point precision

setw ▪ `setw(int)`, alters the field width

The manipulator notation usually results in more code generated and
executed than for direct calls to the `ios` member functions. But unless you
can demonstrate, in a particular case, that the cost is important, you should
probably use manipulators wherever possible, if only for clarity.

user-defined You can define your own manipulators as well, using the templates
manipulators defined in `<iomanip>`. A few guidelines:

- Use these templates only when you have *variable* information to convey.
  Manipulators that take no arguments are much easier to write. (See, for
  example, the predefined manipulators in Chapter 6: `<ios>`, Chapter 8:
  `<istream>`, and Chapter 9: `<ostream>`.)

- Some objects don't suffer copying about. (Objects of class `streambuf` are
  an obvious example.) For these, pass a pointer instead, if the object does
  not always exist. Otherwise, pass a reference to the object.

- If you need to pass more than one value, define a class that holds all the
  needed values. Call the manipulator with a constructor for the compos-
  ite value as its single argument value.

- Use class `smanip<T>` only for a manipulator that makes sense as both an
  inserter and an extractor, and only when the `ios` subobject is all you need
  to manipulate. Otherwise, use class `imanip<T>` or class `omanip<T>`.

As always, I encourage you to find an existing manipulator that does
something similar to what you want to do, then imitate its structure.

Figure 10.1:
iomanip
Part 1 of 2

```
// iomanip standard header
#ifndef _IOMANIP_
#define _IOMANIP_
#include <istream>
#include <ostream>
        // template class smanip
template<class _T> class smanip {
public:
    smanip(ios& (*_F)(ios&, _T), _T _A)
        : _Pf(_F), _Manarg(_A) {}
    ios& (*_Pf)(ios&, _T);
    _T _Manarg;
    };
template<class _T> inline
    istream& operator>>(istream& _I, const smanip<_T>& _M)
    {                          // apply manipulator to input stream
    _TRY_BEGIN
        (*_M._Pf)(_I, _M._Manarg);
    _CATCH_ALL
        _I.setstate(ios::failbit);
    _CATCH_END
    return (_I);
    }
template<class _T> inline
    ostream& operator<<(ostream& _O, const smanip<_T>& _M)
    {                          // apply manipulator to output stream
    _TRY_BEGIN
        (*_M._Pf)(_O, _M._Manarg);
    _CATCH_ALL
        _O.setstate(ios::failbit);
    _CATCH_END
    return (_O);
    }
        // template class imanip
template<class _T> class imanip {
public:
    imanip(istream& (*_F)(istream&, _T), _T _A)
        : _Pf(_F), _Manarg(_A) {}
    istream& (*_Pf)(istream&, _T);
    _T _Manarg;
    };
template<class _T> inline
    istream& operator>>(istream& _I, const imanip<_T>& _M)
    {                          // apply input manipulator to input stream
    _TRY_BEGIN
        (*_M._Pf)(_I, _M._Manarg);
    _CATCH_ALL
        _I.setstate(ios::failbit);
    _CATCH_END
    return (_I);
    }
        // template class omanip
template<class _T> class omanip {
public:
    omanip(ostream& (*_F)(ostream&, _T), _T _A)
```

```
                  : _Pf(_F), _Manarg(_A) {}
        ostream& (*_Pf)(ostream&, _T);
        _T _Manarg;
        };
template<class _T> inline
        ostream& operator<<(ostream& _O, const omanip<_T>& _M)
        {                               // apply manipulator to output stream
        _TRY_BEGIN
            (*_M._Pf)(_O, _M._Manarg);
        _CATCH_ALL
            _O.setstate(ios::failbit);
        _CATCH_END
        return (_O);
        }
            // instantiations
smanip<ios::fmtflags> resetiosflags(ios::fmtflags);
smanip<ios::fmtflags> setiosflags(ios::fmtflags);
smanip<int> setbase(int);
smanip<int> setfill(int);
smanip<int> setprecision(int);
smanip<int> setw(int);
#endif                                                          □
```

```
// resetiosflags -- resetiosflags(ios::fmtflags)
#include <iomanip>

static ios& rsfun(ios& iostr, ios::fmtflags mask)
    {                                       // reset specified flags
    iostr.setf(ios::_Fmtzero, mask);
    return (iostr);
    }

smanip<ios::fmtflags> resetiosflags(ios::fmtflags mask)
    {               // extractor/inserter to reset specified flags
    return (smanip<ios::fmtflags>(&rsfun, mask));
    }                                                          □
```

```
// setbase -- setbase(int)
#include <iomanip>

static ios& sbfun(ios& iostr, int n)
    {                                       // set base field
    iostr.setf(n == 8 ? ios::oct : n == 10 ? ios::dec
        : n == 16 ? ios::hex : ios::_Fmtzero, ios::basefield);
    return (iostr);
    }

smanip<int> setbase(int n)
    {                               // extractor/inserter to set base field
    return (smanip<int>(&sbfun, n));
    }                                                          □
```

Figure 10.4:
setfill.c

```
// setfill -- setfill(int)
#include <iomanip>

static ios& sffun(ios& iostr, int ch)
    {                                                 // set fill character
    iostr.fill(ch);
    return (iostr);
    }

smanip<int> setfill(int ch)
    {                               // extractor/inserter to set fill character
    return (smanip<int>(&sffun, ch));
    }                                                                        □
```

Figure 10.5:
setiosfl.c

```
// setiosflags -- setiosflags(ios::fmtflags)
#include <iomanip>

static ios& sifun(ios& iostr, ios::fmtflags mask)
    {                                                 // set specified flags
    iostr.setf(ios::_Fmtmask, mask);
    return (iostr);
    }

smanip<ios::fmtflags> setiosflags(ios::fmtflags mask)
    {                         // extractor/inserter to set specified flags
    return (smanip<ios::fmtflags>(&sifun, mask));
    }                                                                        □
```

Implementing `<iomanip>`

iomanip   Figure 10.1 shows the file **iomanip**, which implements the standard header **<iomanip>**. All template functions appear within the header as inline definitions, as I discussed earlier in this chapter. (See page 253.) Note that the template classes have public (but secret) member objects, so the template functions need not be declared as friend functions.

_TRY_IO_BEGIN   For a description of the macros **_TRY_IO_BEGIN** and **_CATCH_IO_END**, see
_CATCH_IO_END page 128. As usual, they expand to the code needed to handle exceptions for inserters and extractors. The implementation of these template classes and functions is otherwise as I outlined early in this chapter.

resetios.c   The remaining code implements the predefined manipulators. All fol-
setbase.c low the same pattern, which I also outlined earlier. Figure 10.2 shows the
setfill.c file **resetios.c**, which defines the manipulator **resetiosflags**. Figure
setiosfl.c 10.3 shows the file **setbase.c**, which defines the manipulator **setbase**.
setpreci.c Figure 10.4 shows the file **setfill.c**, which defines the manipulator
setw.c **setfill**. Figure 10.5 shows the file **setiosfl.c**, which defines the ma-
nipulator **setiosflags**. Figure 10.6 shows the file **setpreci.c**, which defines the manipulator **setprecision**. And Figure 10.7 shows the file **setw.c**, which defines the manipulator **setw**. Each of these files also defines (locally) the hidden function that the manipulator calls.

Figure 10.6:
setpreci.c

```
// setprecision -- setprecision(int)
#include <iomanip>

static ios& spfun(ios& iostr, int n)
    {                                           // set precision field
    iostr.precision(n);
    return (iostr);
    }

smanip<int> setprecision(int n)
    {                       // extractor/inserter to set precision field
    return (smanip<int>(&spfun, n));
    }                                                                □
```

Figure 10.7:
setw.c

```
// setw -- setw(int)
#include <iomanip>

static ios& swfun(ios& iostr, int n)
    {                                           // set width field
    iostr.width(n);
    return (iostr);
    }

smanip<int> setw(int n)
    {                       // extractor/inserter to set width field
    return (smanip<int>(&swfun, n));
    }                                                                □
```

Testing `<iomanip>`

tiomanip.c   Figure 10.8 shows the file `tiomanip.c`. It tests the basic properties of the template classes defined in `<iomanip>` by instantiating each template class and calling the associated manipulator. The three manipulators defined here are even arguably useful. The program also tests that the predefined manipulators do more or less what they should.

If all goes well, the program prints:

`SUCCESS testing <iomanip>`

and takes a normal exit.

Exercises

Exercise 10.1 Write the header `<iomanip2>` which defines two-parameter versions of all the template classes in `<iomanip>`. The two parameters should have independent types. Why would you want such a capability?

Exercise 10.2 Write a set of macros that behave essentially the same as the template classes defined in `<iomanip>`. Are there any circumstances where you might prefer the macros over the templates?

```
// test <iomanip>
#include <assert.h>
#include <iomanip>
#include <iostream>
#include <strstream>

static istream& clrfun(istream& iostr, ios::iostate mask)
    {                               // clear specified state flags
    iostr.clear(iostr.rdstate() & ~mask);
    return (iostr);
    }

imanip<ios::iostate> clrstate(ios::iostate mask)
    {                   // extractor to skip to specified character
    return (imanip<ios::iostate>(&clrfun, mask));
    }

static ostream& fltfun(ostream& iostr, char code)
    {                   // set fixed/scientific and uppercase flags
    ios::fmtflags fl = code == 'f' ? ios::fixed
        : code == 'e' ? ios::scientific
        : code == 'E' ? ios::scientific | ios::uppercase
        : code == 'G' ? ios::uppercase
        : (ios::fmtflags)0;
    iostr.setf(fl, ios::floatfield | ios::uppercase);
    return (iostr);
    }

omanip<char> fpfmt(char code)
    {                        // inserter to set floating-point flags
    return (omanip<char>(&fltfun, code));
    }

static ios& intfun(ios& iostr, char code)
    {                        // set dec/hex/oct and uppercase flags
    ios::fmtflags fl = code == 'd' ? ios::dec
        : code == 'o' ? ios::oct
        : code == 'x' ? ios::hex
        : code == 'X' ? ios::hex | ios::uppercase
        : (ios::fmtflags)0;
    iostr.setf(fl, ios::basefield | ios::uppercase);
    return (iostr);
    }

smanip<char> intfmt(char code)
    {                   // extractor/inserter to set integer flags
    return (smanip<char>(&intfun, code));
    }

int main()
    {                   // test basic workings of iomanip definitions
    cin.flags(0);
    assert(cin.flags() == (ios::fmtflags)0);
    cin >> setiosflags(ios::left | ios::showpoint);
    assert(cin.flags() == (ios::left | ios::showpoint));
```

```
cin >> resetiosflags(ios::showpoint);
assert(cin.flags() == ios::left);
cin >> setbase(8);
assert(cin.flags() == (ios::left | ios::oct));
cin >> setbase(10);
assert(cin.flags() == (ios::left | ios::dec));
cin >> setbase(16);
assert(cin.flags() == (ios::left | ios::hex));
cin >> setbase(-23);
assert(cin.flags() == (ios::left));
assert(cout.fill() == ' ');
cout << setfill('*');
assert(cout.fill() == '*');
assert(cout.precision() == 6);
cout << setprecision(17);
assert(cout.precision() == 17);
assert(cout.width() == 0);
cout << setw(-60);
assert(cout.width() == -60);
        // test user-defined instantiations
cin.setstate(ios::failbit);
assert(cin.fail());
cin >> clrstate(ios::failbit);
assert(!cin.fail());
cout << resetiosflags((ios::fmtflags)~0) << fpfmt('E');
assert(cout.flags() == (ios::scientific | ios::uppercase));
cout << intfmt('x');
assert(cout.flags() == (ios::hex | ios::scientific));
cin >> resetiosflags((ios::fmtflags)~0) >> intfmt('X');
assert(cin.flags() == (ios::hex | ios::uppercase));
cout << "SUCCESS testing <iomanip>" << endl;
return (0);
}                                                             □
```

Exercise 10.3 Write the manipulator **outfmt(const char *)**, based on **omanip<T>**, that alters formatting information to match the **fprintf**-style conversion specification in its format string argument. Thus, **cout << outfmt("x= %o")** **<< n** should insert the string **"x= "**, then insert the octal integer value **n**.

Exercise 10.4 Write the manipulator **infmt(const char *)**, based on **imanip<T>**, that alters formatting information to match the **fscanf**-style conversion specification in its format string argument. Thus, **cin >> infmt("x= %o") >>** **n** should extract and match the string **"x="**, skip white space, then extract an octal integer into **n**.

Exercise 10.5 [Harder] Alter the manipulators you wrote for the previous two exercises so that the format string can contain multiple conversion specifications. The manipulator **next** advances to the next conversion specification, as in:

```
cout << outfmt("(%g, %5.2f)\n") << re
      << next << im << next;
```

Exercise 10.6 [Very hard] Alter the result of the previous exercise to eliminate the need for the manipulator **next**.

Chapter 11: `<strstream>`

Background

The header `<strstream>` defines three classes that cooperate to help you read and write character sequences stored in memory:

strstreambuf ■ `strstreambuf`, derived from `streambuf` to mediate access to an in-memory character sequence and grow it on demand

istrstream ■ `istrstream`, derived from `istream` to construct a `strstreambuf` object with an input stream and to assist in extracting from the stream

ostrstream ■ `ostrstream`, derived from `ostream` to construct a `strstreambuf` object with both input and output streams and to assist in inserting into the stream

An in-memory character sequence is, in many ways, the simplest kind of stream buffer. The buffer maintained by the controlling `streambuf` object is not merely a window on some separate representation, like an external file. Rather, the buffer *is* the character sequence in its entirety.

uses Nevertheless, a `strstreambuf` object can control a variety of in-memory character sequences:

■ an array of characters all of whose elements are defined from the outset

■ an array of characters whose initial elements contain a null-terminated string

■ an initially empty array of characters that can grow on demand, with storage allocated by *new* expressions and freed by *delete* expressions

■ an initially empty array of characters that can grow on demand, with storage allocated and freed by functions supplied by the program

All these choices are reflected in a plethora of constructors for the three classes defined in `<strstream>`.

Despite all the options, three simple choices stand out. You can initialize an `istrstream` object to control a constant array of characters. You can then extract from its associated input stream, but you cannot insert to the output stream. The result is effectively an `istream` object where you dictate the stream contents purely within the program. Or you can initialize an `ostrstream` object to control a non-constant array of characters. You can then insert into its associated output stream to store into the array.

Your third simple choice is to initialize an **ostrstream** object to control an initially empty *dynamic* output stream that can grow on demand. The result is effectively an **ostream** object where you capture the stream contents purely within the program. You can then capture the final stream contents before the **ostrstream** object is destroyed. Class **strstreambuf** supplies several member functions to help you capture these contents. For an object **x** of class **strstreambuf**, here's what you can do:

str ■ Call **x.str()** to obtain a pointer to the start of the controlled character sequence. The function *freezes* the character sequence to prevent further insertions. Freezing also prevents the destructor for **x** from freeing the character sequence — you assume that responsibility when you obtain the pointer.

freeze ■ Call **x.freeze()** to freeze the character sequence, or **x.freeze(0)** to unfreeze it. The latter call is particularly helpful if you've learned what you need from an earlier **x.str()** call and now want the destructor to free the character sequence for you.

pcount ■ Call **x.pcount()** to count the number of characters inserted in the sequence. The count is useful information for arbitrary character values, or if you don't insert a null character at the end of the character sequence.

ends Here is the obvious use for the manipulator **ends**, by the way. (See page 223.) It's a clear way to supply a null character at the end of an in-memory character sequence.

sscanf I end this brief introduction by mentioning the ghost at the banquet table.
sprintf The Standard C library has long supported a similar capability. You can
vsprintf obtain formatted input from an in-memory character sequence by calling **sscanf**. You can write formatted output to an in-memory character sequence by calling **sprintf** or **vsprintf**. (All three functions are declared in **<stdio.h>**.) So how are these three classes any better? The answer is easy:

■ An **istrstream** object looks like any other **istream** object controlling an input stream. And an **ostrstream** object looks like any other **ostream** object controlling an output stream. The older functions oblige you to know that you're dealing with an in-memory character sequence. And you a;ways have to know exactly where the sequence resides.

■ Unlike **sscanf**, an **istrstream** object can control a sequence of arbitrary character values. It can have embedded null characters. Equally, it doesn't need a terminating null character.

■ **sprintf** writes to an array of fixed length whose length is nevertheless not known to the function. You avoid storage overwrites only by restricting every single conversion specification. By contrast, an **ostrstream** object can control a sequence of known length. Insertions fail before storage overwrite occurs. Or the object can control a *dynamic* sequence of arbitrary length. Insertions fail only when heap storage is exhausted.

I believe these are ample reasons to cultivate a knowledge of the header **<strstream>**.

What the Draft C++ Standard Says

Class **strstreambuf** is the first of several classes derived from **stream-buf**. (See also Chapter 12: **<sstream>** and Chapter 13: **<fstream>**.) What makes each such stream buffer unique is the way it overrides the virtual member functions in the base class. The exception classes exhibit uniqueness in a small way, by overriding the virtual member function **do_raise**. (See Chapter 3: **<exception>**.) But the stream buffers indulge in specialization big time.

The convention within the draft C++ Standard is to comment out virtual member functions in the derived class. Each such comment is labeled *inherited*. The suggestion is that an implementation need not provide an overriding definition if the definition in the base class does the job.

For the classes derived from **streambuf**, however, these comments are often misleading. Several critical virtual member functions *must* have overriding definitions to satisfy the semantic requirements of the class. The descriptions of these functions are often hard to read as well. They represent standardese at its legalistic extreme. But those descriptions are also the definitive word on how a class behaves in peculiar circumstances. Turn to them when tutorials prove inadequate.

17.4.6 Header <strstream>

<strstream>

The header **<strstream>** defines three types that associate stream buffers with (single-byte) character array objects and assist reading and writing such objects.

17.4.6.1 Class strstreambuf

Class str-
streambuf

```
class strstreambuf : public streambuf {
public:
    strstreambuf(int alsize_arg = 0);
    strstreambuf(void* (*palloc_arg)(size_t), void
(*pfree_arg)(void*));
    strstreambuf(char* gnext_arg, int n, char* pbeg_arg = 0);
    strstreambuf(unsigned char* gnext_arg, int n,
        unsigned char* pbeg_arg = 0);
    strstreambuf(signed char* gnext_arg, int n, signed char*
pbeg_arg = 0);
    strstreambuf(const char* gnext_arg, int n);
    strstreambuf(const unsigned char* gnext_arg, int n);
    strstreambuf(const signed char* gnext_arg, int n);
    virtual ~strstreambuf();
    void freeze(int = 1);
    char* str();
    int pcount();
protected:
//  virtual int overflow(int c = EOF);                      inherited
//  virtual int pbackfail(int c = EOF);                     inherited
//  virtual int underflow();                                inherited
//  virtual int uflow();                                    inherited
//  virtual int xsgetn(char* s, int n);                     inherited
//  virtual int xsputn(const char* s, int n);               inherited
```

```
//   virtual streampos seekoff(streamoff off, ios::seekdir way,
//          ios::openmode which = ios::in | ios::out);       inherited
//   virtual streampos seekpos(streampos sp,
//          ios::openmode which = ios::in | ios::out);       inherited
//   virtual streambuf* setbuf(char* s, int n);              inherited
//   virtual int sync();                                     inherited
private:
//   typedef T1 strstate;                              exposition only
//   static const strstate allocated;                 exposition only
//   static const strstate constant;                  exposition only
//   static const strstate dynamic;                   exposition only
//   static const strstate frozen;                    exposition only
//   strstate strmode;                                exposition only
//   int alsize;                                      exposition only
//   void* (*palloc)(size_t);                         exposition only
//   void (*pfree)(void*);                            exposition only
};
```

The class **strstreambuf** is derived from **streambuf** to associate the input sequence and possibly the output sequence with an object of some character array type, whose elements store arbitrary values. The array object has several attributes. For the sake of exposition, these are represented as elements of a bitmask type (indicated here as **T1**) called **strstate**. The elements are:

- **allocated**, set when a dynamic array object has been allocated, and hence should be freed by the destructor for the **strstreambuf** object;
- **constant**, set when the array object has **const** elements, so the output sequence cannot be written;
- **dynamic**, set when the array object is allocated (or reallocated) as necessary to hold a character sequence that can change in length;
- **frozen**, set when the program has requested that the array object not be altered, reallocated, or freed.

For the sake of exposition, the maintained data is presented here as:

- **strstate strmode**, the attributes of the array object associated with the **strstreambuf** object;
- **int alsize**, the suggested minimum size for a dynamic array object;
- **void* (*palloc)(size_t)**, points to the function to call to allocate a dynamic array object;
- **void (*pfree)(void*)**, points to the function to call to free a dynamic array object.

Each object of class **strstreambuf** has a *seekable area,* delimited by the pointers **seeklow** and **seekhigh**. If **gnext** is a null pointer, the seekable area is undefined. Otherwise, **seeklow** equals **gbeg** and **seekhigh** is either **pend**, if **pend** is not a null pointer, or **gend**.

17.4.6.1.1 strstreambuf::strstreambuf(int)

constructor

```
strstreambuf(int alsize_arg = 0);
```

Constructs an object of class **strstreambuf**, initializing the base class with **streambuf()**, and initializing:

- **strmode** with **dynamic**;
- **alsize** with **alsize_arg**;
- **palloc** with a null pointer;
- **pfree** with a null pointer.

17.4.6.1.2 strstreambuf::strstreambuf(void* (*)(size_t), void (*)(void*))

constructor

```
strstreambuf(void* (*palloc_arg)(size_t),
    void (*pfree_arg)(void*));
```

Constructs an object of class **strstreambuf**, initializing the base class with **streambuf()**, and initializing:

- *strmode* with *dynamic*;
- *alsize* with an unspecified value;
- *palloc* with *palloc_arg*;
- *pfree* with *pfree_arg*.

17.4.6.1.3 strstreambuf::strstreambuf(char*, int, char*)

constructor

```
strstreambuf(char* gnext_arg, int n, char *pbeg_arg = 0);
```

Constructs an object of class **strstreambuf**, initializing the base class with **streambuf()**, and initializing:

- *strmode* with zero;
- *alsize* with an unspecified value;
- *palloc* with a null pointer;
- *pfree* with a null pointer.

gnext_arg shall point to the first element of an array object whose number of elements *N* is determined as follows:

- If $n > 0$, *N* is *n*.
- If $n == 0$, *N* is **strlen(*gnext_arg*)**.
- If $n < 0$, *N* is **INT_MAX**.

The function signature **strlen(const char*)** is declared in **`<string.h>`**. The macro **INT_MAX** is defined in **`<limits.h>`**.

If **pbeg_arg** is a null pointer, the function executes:

```
setg(gnext_arg, gnext_arg, gnext_arg + N);
```

Otherwise, the function executes:

```
setg(gnext_arg, gnext_arg, pbeg_arg);
setp(pbeg_arg, pbeg_arg + N);
```

17.4.6.1.4 strstreambuf::strstreambuf(unsigned char*, int, unsigned char*)

constructor

```
strstreambuf(unsigned char* gnext_arg, int n,
    unsigned char* pbeg_arg = 0);
```

Behaves the same as **strstreambuf((char*)*gnext_arg*, n, (char*) *pbeg_arg*)**.

17.4.6.1.5 strstreambuf::strstreambuf(signed char*, int, signed char*)

constructor

```
strstreambuf(signed char* gnext_arg, int n,
    signed char* pbeg_arg = 0);
```

Behaves the same as **strstreambuf((char*)*gnext_arg*, n, (char*) *pbeg_arg*)**.

17.4.6.1.6 strstreambuf::strstreambuf(const char*, int)

constructor

```
strstreambuf(const char* gnext_arg, int n);
```

Behaves the same as **strstreambuf((char*)*gnext_arg*, n)**, except that the constructor also sets *constant* in *strmode*.

17.4.6.1.7 strstreambuf::strstreambuf(const unsigned char*, int)

constructor   `strstreambuf(const unsigned char* gnext_arg, int n);`

Behaves the same as **strstreambuf((const char*)gnext_arg, n)**.

17.4.6.1.8 strstreambuf::strstreambuf(const signed char*, int)

constructor   `strstreambuf(const signed char* gnext_arg, int n);`

Behaves the same as **strstreambuf((const char*)gnext_arg, n)**.

17.4.6.1.9 strstreambuf::~strstreambuf()

destructor   `virtual ~strstreambuf();`

Destroys an object of class **strstreambuf**. The function frees the dynamically allocated array object only if **strmode & allocated** is nonzero and **strmode & frozen** is zero. (Subclause 17.4.6.1.13 describes how a dynamically allocated array object is freed.)

17.4.6.1.10 strstreambuf::freeze(int)

freeze   `void freeze(int freezefl = 1);`

If **strmode & dynamic** is nonzero, alters the freeze status of the dynamic array object as follows: If **freezefl** is nonzero, the function sets **frozen** in **strmode**. Otherwise, it clears **frozen** in **strmode**.

17.4.6.1.11 strstreambuf::str()

str   `char* str();`

Calls **freeze()**, then returns the beginning pointer for the input sequence, **gbeg**.[106]

17.4.6.1.12 strstreambuf::pcount()

pcount   `int pcount() const;`

If the next pointer for the output sequence, **pnext**, is a null pointer, returns zero. Otherwise, the function returns the current effective length of the array object as the next pointer minus the beginning pointer for the output sequence, **pnext - pbeg**.

17.4.6.1.13 strstreambuf::overflow(int)

overflow   `// virtual int overflow(int c = EOF);`   *inherited*

Appends the character designated by **c** to the output sequence, if possible, in one of two ways:

- If **c != EOF** and if either the output sequence has a write position available or the function makes a write position available (as described below), the function assigns **c** to ***pnext++**. The function signals success by returning **(unsigned char)c**.
- If **c == EOF**, there is no character to append. The function signals success by returning a value other than **EOF**.

The function can alter the number of write positions available as a result of any call.

The function returns **EOF** to indicate failure.

To make a write position available, the function reallocates (or initially allocates) an array object with a sufficient number of elements **n** to hold the current array object (if any), plus at least one additional write position. How many additional write positions are made available is otherwise unspecified.[107] If **palloc** is not a null pointer, the function calls **(*palloc)(n)** to allocate the new dynamic array object. Otherwise, it evaluates the expression **new char[n]**. In either case, if the allocation fails, the function returns **EOF**. Otherwise, it sets **allocated** in **strmode**.

To free a previously existing dynamic array object whose first element address is *p*: If *pfree* is not a null pointer, the function calls **(*pfree)(p)**. Otherwise, it evaluates the expression **delete[] p**.

If **strmode & dynamic** is zero, or if **strmode & frozen** is nonzero, the function cannot extend the array (reallocate it with greater length) to make a write position available.

17.4.6.1.14 strstreambuf::pbackfail(int)

pbackfail

```
// virtual int pbackfail(int c = EOF);                    inherited
```

Puts back the character designated by *c* to the input sequence, if possible, in one of three ways:

- If *c* != **EOF**, if the input sequence has a putback position available, and if **(unsigned char)c == unsigned char)gnext[-1]**, the function assigns *gnext* - **1** to *gnext*. The function signals success by returning **(unsigned char)c**.

- If *c* != **EOF**, if the input sequence has a putback position available, and if **strmode & constant** is zero, the function assigns *c* to ***--gnext**. The function signals success by returning **(unsigned char)c**.

- If *c* == **EOF** and if the input sequence has a putback position available, the function assigns *gnext* - **1** to *gnext*. The function signals success by returning **(unsigned char)c**.

If the function can succeed in more than one of these ways, it is unspecified which way is chosen. The function can alter the number of putback positions available as a result of any call.

The function returns **EOF** to indicate failure.

17.4.6.1.15 strstreambuf::underflow()

underflow

```
// virtual int underflow();                               inherited
```

Reads a character from the input sequence, if possible, without moving the stream position past it, as follows:

- If the input sequence has a read position available the function signals success by returning **(unsigned char)*gnext**.

- Otherwise, if the current write next pointer *pnext* is not a null pointer and is greater than the current read end pointer *gend*, the function makes a read position available by assigning to *gend* a value greater than *gnext* and no greater than *pnext*. The function signals success by returning **(unsigned char)*gnext**.

The function can alter the number of read positions available as a result of any call.

The function returns **EOF** to indicate failure.

17.4.6.1.15 strstreambuf::uflow()

uflow

```
// virtual int uflow();                                   inherited
```

Behaves the same as **streambuf::uflow(int)**.

17.4.6.1.17 strstreambuf::xsgetn(char*, int)

xsgetn

```
// virtual int xsgetn(char* s, int n);                    inherited
```

Behaves the same as **streambuf::xsgetn(char*, int)**.

17.4.6.1.18 strstreambuf::xsputn(const char*, int)

xsputn

```
// virtual int xsputn(const char* s, int n);              inherited
```

Behaves the same as **streambuf::xsputn(char*, int)**.

17.4.6.1.19 strstreambuf::seekoff(streamoff, ios::seekdir, ios::openmode)

seekoff

```
// virtual streampos seekoff(streamoff off, ios::seekdir way,
//        ios::openmode which = ios::in | ios::out);      inherited
```

Alters the stream position within one of the controlled sequences, if possible, as described below. The function returns **streampos(*newoff*)**, constructed from the resultant offset *newoff* (of type **streamoff**), that stores the resultant stream position, if possible. If the positioning operation fails, or if the constructed object cannot represent the resultant stream position, the object stores an invalid stream position.

If *which* & **ios::in** is nonzero, the function positions the input sequence. Otherwise, if *which* & **ios::out** is nonzero, the function positions the output sequence. Otherwise, if *which* & (**ios::in** | **ios::out**) equals **ios::in** | **ios::out** and if *way* equals either **ios::beg** or **ios::end**, the function positions both the input and the output sequences. Otherwise, the positioning operation fails.

For a sequence to be positioned, if its next pointer is a null pointer, the positioning operation fails. Otherwise, the function determines *newoff* in one of three ways:

- If *way* == **ios::beg**, *newoff* is zero.
- If *way* == **ios::cur**, *newoff* is the next pointer minus the beginning pointer (*xnext* - *xbeg*).
- If *way* == **ios::end**, *newoff* is *seekhigh* minus the beginning pointer (*seekhigh* - *xbeg*).

If *newoff* + *off* is less than *seeklow* - *xbeg*, or if *seekhigh* - *xbeg* is less than *newoff* + *off*, the positioning operation fails. Otherwise, the function assigns *xbeg* + *newoff* + *off* to the next pointer *xnext*.

17.4.6.1.20 strstreambuf::seekpos(streampos, ios::openmode)

seekpos

```
// virtual streampos seekpos(streampos sp,
//        ios::openmode which = ios::in | ios::out);      inherited
```

Alters the stream position within one of the controlled sequences, if possible, to correspond to the stream position stored in *sp* (as described below). The function returns **streampos(*newoff*)**, constructed from the resultant offset *newoff* (of type **streamoff**), that stores the resultant stream position, if possible. If the positioning operation fails, or if the constructed object cannot represent the resultant stream position, the object stores an invalid stream position.

If *which* & **ios::in** is nonzero, the function positions the input sequence. If *which* & **ios::out** is nonzero, the function positions the output sequence. If the function positions neither sequence, the positioning operation fails.

For a sequence to be positioned, if its next pointer is a null pointer, the positioning operation fails. Otherwise, the function determines *newoff* from *sp*.**offset()**. If *newoff* is an invalid stream position, has a negative value, or has a value greater than *seekhigh* - *seeklow*, the positioning operation fails. Otherwise, the function adds *newoff* to the beginning pointer *xbeg* and stores the result in the next pointer *xnext*.

17.4.6.1.21 strstreambuf::setbuf(char*, int)

setbuf

```
// virtual streambuf* setbuf(char* s, int n);            inherited
```

Performs an operation that is defined separately for each class derived from **strstreambuf**.

The default behavior is the same as for **streambuf::setbuf(char*, int)**.

17.4.6.1.22 `strstreambuf::sync()`

sync
```
// virtual int sync();                              inherited
```
Behaves the same as `streambuf::sync()`.

17.4.6.2 Class `istrstream`

Class istrstream
```
class istrstream : public istream {
public:
    istrstream(const char* s);
    istrstream(const char* s, int n);
    istrstream(char* s);
    istrstream(char* s, int n);
    virtual ~istrstream();
    strstreambuf* rdbuf() const;
    char *str();
private:
//  strstreambuf sb;                              exposition only
};
```

The class `istrstream` is a derivative of `istream` that assists in the reading of objects of class `strstreambuf`. It supplies a `strstreambuf` object to control the associated array object. For the sake of exposition, the maintained data is presented here as:

- *sb*, the `strstreambuf` object.

17.4.6.2.1 `istrstream::istrstream(const char*)`

constructor
```
istrstream(const char* s);
```
Constructs an object of class `istrstream`, initializing the base class with `istream(&sb)`, and initializing *sb* with `sb(s, 0)`. *s* shall designate the first element of an NTBS.

17.4.6.2.2 `istrstream::istrstream(const char*, int)`

constructor
```
istrstream(const char* s, int n);
```
Constructs an object of class `istrstream`, initializing the base class with `istream(&sb)`, and initializing *sb* with `sb(s, n)`. *s* shall designate the first element of an array whose length is *n* elements, and *n* shall be greater than zero.

17.4.6.2.3 `istrstream::istrstream(char*)`

constructor
```
istrstream(char* s);
```
Constructs an object of class `istrstream`, initializing the base class with `istream(&sb)`, and initializing *sb* with `sb((const char*)s, 0)`. *s* shall designate the first element of an NTBS.

17.4.6.2.4 `istrstream::istrstream(char*, int)`

constructor
```
istrstream(char* s, int n);
```
Constructs an object of class `istrstream`, initializing the base class with `istream(&sb)`, and initializing *sb* with `sb((const char*)s, n)`. *s* shall designate the first element of an array whose length is *n* elements, and *n* shall be greater than zero.

17.4.6.2.5 `istrstream::~istrstream()`

destructor
```
virtual ~istrstream();
```
Destroys an object of class `istrstream`.

17.4.6.2.6 `istrstream::rdbuf()`

rdbuf
```
strstreambuf* rdbuf() const;
```

Returns `(strstreambuf*)&`*sb*.

17.4.6.2.7 istrstream::str()

str

```
char* str();
```

Returns *sb*.`str()`.

17.4.6.3 Class ostrstream

Class
ostrstream

```
class ostrstream : public ostream {
public:
    ostrstream();
    ostrstream(char* s, int n, openmode mode = out);
    virtual ~ostrstream();
    strstreambuf* rdbuf() const;
    void freeze(int freezefl = 1);
    char* str();
    int pcount() const;
private:
//    strstreambuf sb;                              exposition only
};
```

The class **ostrstream** is a derivative of **ostream** that assists in the writing of objects of class **strstreambuf**. It supplies a **strstreambuf** object to control the associated array object. For the sake of exposition, the maintained data is presented here as:

- *sb*, the **strstreambuf** object.

17.4.6.3.1 ostrstream::ostrstream()

constructor

```
ostrstream();
```

Constructs an object of class **ostrstream**, initializing the base class with `ostream(&`*sb*`)`, and initializing *sb* with `sb()`.

17.4.6.3.2 ostrstream::ostrstream(char*, int, openmode)

constructor

```
ostrstream(char* s, int n, openmode mode = out);
```

Constructs an object of class **ostrstream**, initializing the base class with `ostream(&`*sb*`)`, and initializing *sb* with one of two constructors:

- If *mode* `&` **app** is zero, then *s* shall designate the first element of an array of *n* elements. The constructor is `sb(`*s*`, `*n*`, `*s*`)`.
- If *mode* `&` **app** is nonzero, then *s* shall designate the first element of an array of *n* elements that contains an NTBS whose first element is designated by *s*. The constructor is `sb(`*s*`, `*n*`, `*s* ` + ::strlen(`*s*`))`.

The function signature `strlen(const char*)` is declared in **<string.h>**.

17.4.6.3.3 ostrstream::~ostrstream()

destructor

```
virtual ~ostrstream();
```

Destroys an object of class **ostrstream**.

17.4.6.3.4 ostrstream::rdbuf()

rdbuf

```
strstreambuf* rdbuf() const;
```

Returns `(strstreambuf*)&`*sb*.

17.4.6.3.5 ostrstream::freeze(int)

freeze

```
void freeze(int freezefl = 1);
```

Calls *sb*.`freeze(`*freezefl*`)`.

17.4.6.3.6 ostrstream::str()

str

```
char* str();
```

Returns *sb*.`str()`.

17.4.6.3.7 ostrstream::pcount()

pcount

```
int pcount() const;
```

Returns *sb*.`pcount()`.

Footnotes:

Footnotes

106) The return value can be a null pointer.

107) An implementation should consider **alsize** in making this decision.

Future Directions

str   The member function name **str** has already been changed in class **string** since the Informal Review Draft. As part of a general homogenization of names across classes, it is now **data**. That cleanup has yet to extend to the classes defined in `<strstream>`, but it might.

wide-character   As I keep mentioning where relevant, a major change is the addition of
streams   wide-character streams. (See page 119.) Class **strstreambuf** becomes a template class parameterized by the type of the stream element. One instantiation, for type *char*, has essentially the same functionality as described in this chapter. Another, for type **wchar_t**, supports streams of elements from some large character set. Classes **istrstream** and **ostrstream** change along similar lines.

Using `<strstream>`

You include the header `<strstream>` to make use of any of the classes **istrstream**, **ostrstream**, or **strstreambuf**. Objects of these classes let you read and write in-memory character sequences just as if they were conventional files. You can choose among four patterns of access:

- read only
- write only
- simple read/write
- sophisticated read/write

I deal with each of these options in turn.

read only   If all you want to do is read an in-memory character sequence, construct an object of class **istrstream** to specify the character sequence and control extractions from it. For a null-terminated string **s**, you can write:

```
istrstream strin(s);
```

The character sequence begins at **s** and continues up to, but not including, the terminating null character that follows.

To control an array of **n** characters **s** with arbitrary values, you can write:

```
istrstream strin(s, n);
```

In either case, **s** can be either a pointer to *char* or a pointer to *const char*. Whichever way you construct the **istrstream** object, the resultant stream buffer (pointed at by **strin.rdbuf()**) does not support insertions. You *must* specify an initial character sequence — class **istrstream** has no default constructor. The character sequence remains unchanged for the life of the **istrstream** object. (I suggest you refrain from altering the contents of the character sequence by other means, if that is possible, while the **istrstream** object controls accesses to it.)

stream positioning Positioning within a read-only stream is fairly simple. A **streamoff** value is effectively an index into the character sequence. Thus:

```
strin.rdbuf()->pubseekoff(0, ios::beg);
```

sets the stream position at the beginning (position zero) of the character sequence. If the length of the sequence is nonzero, the next character extracted will be the first character in the sequence. Any attempt to set the stream position to a negative value, or beyond the end of the character sequence, will fail. You can also call **streambuf::pubseekpos**, as above, but that is less necessary for an in-memory character sequence. Do so for code that shouldn't need to know what flavor stream buffer it is really dealing with. (For a general discussion of stream positioning, see page 160.)

str For what it's worth, you can also call **strin.str()** for a read-only character sequence. The call does *not* freeze the character sequence, since it is not dynamically alterable. The function merely returns a pointer to the beginning of the character sequence, just as for a character sequence you construct (as described below). This is always the beginning of the character sequence you specified when constructing the object.

pcount If you do call **strin.str()** for a read-only character sequence as above, be warned. The call **strin.rdbuf()->pcount()** will *not* return the length of the sequence. Since no output stream exists, this call returns zero. You must determine the length of the sequence by some other means, such as positioning the stream at the end and inspecting the resultant stream offset.

write only If all you want to do is create an in-memory character sequence, construct an object of class **ostrstream** to control insertions into it. You can write:

```
ostrstream strout;
```

then insert into **strout** just like any other output stream. The character sequence can grow dynamically to arbitrary length. (The actual limit is usually **INT_MAX**, defined in **<limits.h>**, or when a storage allocation request fails.)

ends pcount If you want a null-terminated string, be sure to insert a null character last, as with:

```
strout << ends;
```

It will *not* be supplied for you when you call **strout.str()**. For a sequence of arbitrary characters, you can determine the number of characters you inserted by calling **strout.pcount()**. (But see the warning below.)

stream positioning   Positioning within a write-only stream is also fairly simple. You can work mostly with **streamoff** values, as for read-only streams described above. A few caveats are in order, however:

- Current practice seems to vary on where you can set the stream position. The safest bet is to move only to character positions with values already defined — either at construction or as a result of earlier insertions.

- Some confusion is also endemic about the interaction of stream positioning requests and the value returned by a call such as **strout.pcount()**.

- Even an implementation that obeys the draft C++ Standard can still surprise. Strictly speaking, **ostrstream::pcount** calls **strstreambuf::pcount**, which does *not* return a count of all insertions. Rather, it returns the difference between *the current output stream position and the initial output stream position*. The former can be left other than at the end of the character sequence by stream-positioning requests. The latter can be set beyond the beginning of the character sequence by a more sophisticated **strstreambuf** constructor, as described below.

As usual, my advice is to avoid such delicate areas in code you hope to keep portable. If you insist on pushing the limits of clearly defined behavior, expect surprises.

str   Your goal in creating a write-only character sequence is to capture the final result, as a rule. Call **strout.str()** to freeze the character sequence and return a pointer to its initial character. Remember that freezing the character sequence tells the **strstreambuf** destructor *not* to free storage for the character sequence. You must either free the storage yourself or be sure to call **strout.freeze(0)** before **strout** is destroyed.

simple read/write   If you want to create an in-memory character sequence that you can read as well as write, you need two objects to control the input and output streams. First, construct an object of class **ostrstream** to supply the **strstreambuf** object and control insertions, then construct an object of class **istream** to control extractions. You can write:

```
ostrstream strout;
istream strin(strout.rdbuf());
```

much as I have described several times earlier for setting up a bidirectional stream. (See, for example, page 188.) You can then insert into **strout** just like any other output stream. And once you have inserted characters, you can extract them from **strin** just like any other input stream.

eofbit   A few caveats are in order, however. Try to extract beyond the last character in the sequence and you will encounter end-of-file. Once you extend the sequence by inserting characters, you can successfully extract again, but not until you clear **eofbit** if it is set in the **istream** object. Once again, this status bit proves less than trustworthy.

stream positioning   You can position the input and output streams separately or jointly. As usual, positioning operations demand a modicum of caution:

- The draft C++ Standard specifies a default third argument value **which = ios::in | ios::out** for **streambuf::pubseekoff**. (It specifies the same for the default second argument to **streambuf::pubseekpos**.) Thus, unless you supply an actual **which** argument that selects only one stream — **ios::in** or **ios::out** — a call to this member function endeavors to position both streams in tandem. Seldom does that make sense. When both reading and writing an in-memory character sequence, always specify the **which** argument on such calls.

- The draft C++ Standard is even nastier at times. If the second argument to **streambuf::pubseekoff** is **ios::cur**, a tandem positioning operation will fail. For such relative positioning requests, you should *always* specify a **which** argument that selects only one stream.

Note that the second caveat applies even to read-only or write-only in-memory character sequences.

rdbuf   As an important aside, here is a warning regarding the member function **rdbuf**. Several classes in the Standard C++ library are derived from either **istream** or **ostream**. These include **istrstream** and **ostrstream**, the topics of this chapter. All such derived classes also provide a member function **rdbuf()** that *hides* the member function in the base class **ios**.

Why is this so? All such derived classes also provide a member object of a class derived from **streambuf**. In this chapter, that derived class happens to be **strstreambuf**. Consider, for example, the call **istr.rdbuf()**, for an object **istr** of class **istrstream**. It returns a pointer to the **strstreambuf** member object in **istr**. And the return type is indeed *pointer to* **strstreambuf**, not *pointer to* **streambuf** as in the base class **ios**.

A generic pointer to the base **streambuf** gets you to all the inherited member functions. It even gets you to the proper overriding definitions of virtual member functions. But to access any member functions peculiar to the derived class, you need such a specialized pointer. Again in this particular case, the member functions **freeze, pcount**, and **str** are peculiar to class **strstreambuf**, not its base class.

Potential confusion arises, however, once you make a call such as **istr.rdbuf(strout.rdbuf())**. The critical pointer in the **ios** subobject now designates a different stream buffer. *But a subsequent call to* **istr.rdbuf()** *still returns a pointer to the member object within* **istr**. To get the pointer actually used by inserters and extractors, you must make the hairy call **((ios&)istr).rdbuf()**.

Got all that? If not, don't worry too much about it. The bottom line is that you should follow a fundamental style rule. Alter the stored stream buffer pointer *only* in an object of class **istream** or **ostream**. *Never* do so in an object of a class derived from one of these. Even better, do as I did above — use a special **istream** or **ostream** object constructed from the outset to share an existing stream buffer. With either approach, there's never a second stream buffer lying around to cause confusion.

sophisticates read/write   You can get even fancier with the classes defined in `<strstream>`. What follows is an assortment of more sophisticated setups.

Say you want to use an existing character array to store a character sequence, and you want to read the character sequence once you write it. If you declare:

```
ostrstream strout(s, n);
istream strin(strout.rdbuf());
```

then **strout** controls the sequence of **n** characters beginning at **s**. Both the read position and the write position are at the beginning of the character sequence. In this case, you cannot extend the sequence by inserting at or beyond character position **n**.

Here's a variation on this scenario. Say you want to use an existing character array to store a character sequence, and the array already stores a null-terminated string. You want to begin extracting from the beginning of the character sequence, but you want to begin inserting at the *end* of the null-terminated string (first replacing the terminating null). If you declare:

```
ostrstream strout(s, n, ios::app);
istream strin(strout.rdbuf());
```

then you get the desired behavior. Insertions effectively append characters to an initial null-terminated string, but won't continue past the end of the character array. For extractions, see the caveat above about the behavior of **eofbit**.

If you want to get fancier, you have to construct a **strstreambuf** object directly. This class has *lots* of constructors with *lots* of options. I describe here just the two that I feel are genuinely useful and safe.

preallocated buffers   Say you want to construct an in-memory character sequence that you know will get very large. You'd like to suggest, when constructing the **strstreambuf** object, that the object allocate space for a large sequence right off the mark. That can save lots of execution overhead in reallocating storage as the character sequence grows. Equally, you might want to construct a number of character sequences all of which will be fairly small. You'd like to suggest that each such object allocate only a small number of characters. That can save lots of unused storage. If you declare:

```
strstreambuf sb(n);
istream strin(&sb);
ostream strout(&sb);
```

for some *int* value **n**, the constructor should take the hint. What it does with it is up to the implementation, but at least you get to make the suggestion.

user-defined allocation   Another approach to storage allocation is to do the job yourself. So your final interesting choice is to begin with two functions like:

```
#include <stdlib.h>

void *my_alloc(size_t n)
    {                                        // allocate n chars
    return (malloc(n));
    }
```

```
void my_free(void *p)
    {                                          // free allocated storage
    free(p);
    }
```

Tailor these basic functions as you see fit. Then you can declare:

```
strstreambuf sb(&my_alloc, &my_free);
istream strin(&sb);
ostream strout(&sb);
```

The two functions you supply will be called, in place of *new* and *delete* expressions, to allocate and free storage for character sequences.

Figure 11.1:
strstrea
Part 1 of 2

```
// strstream standard header
#ifndef _STRSTREAM_
#define _STRSTREAM_
#include <istream>
#include <ostream>
            // constants
const int _ALSIZE = 512;                    // default allocation size
const int _MINSIZE = 32;                    // minimum allocation size
            // class strstreambuf
class strstreambuf : public streambuf {
public:
    enum __Strstate {_Allocated = 1, _Constant = 2,
        _Dynamic = 4, _Frozen = 8, _Noread = 16,
        _Strzero = 0};
    _BITMASK(__Strstate, _Strstate);
    strstreambuf(int _N = 0)
        {_Init(_N); }
    strstreambuf(void *(*_A)(size_t), void (*_F)(void *))
        {_Init(), _Palloc = _A, _Pfree = _F; }
    strstreambuf(char *_G, int _N, char *_P = 0,
        _Strstate _S = _Strzero)
        {_Init(_N, _G, _P, _S); }
    strstreambuf(unsigned char *_G, int _N,
        unsigned char *_P = 0)
        {_Init(_N, (char *)_G, (char *)_P); }
    strstreambuf(const char *_G, int _N)
        {_Init(_N, (char *)_G, 0, _Constant); }
    strstreambuf(const unsigned char *_G, int _N)
        {_Init(_N, (char *)_G, 0, _Constant); }
    virtual ~strstreambuf();
    void freeze(_Bool = 1);
    char *str()
        {freeze(); return (gptr()); }
    int pcount() const
        {return (pptr() == 0 ? 0 : pptr() - pbase()); }
#if _HAS_SIGNED_CHAR
    strstreambuf(signed char *_G, int _N, signed char *_P = 0)
        {_Init(_N, (char *)_G, (char *)_P); }
    strstreambuf(const signed char *_G, int _N)
        {_Init(_N, (char *)_G, 0, _Constant); }
#endif /* _HAS_SIGNED_CHAR */
protected:
```

```
        virtual int overflow(int = EOF);
        virtual int pbackfail(int = EOF);
        virtual int underflow();
        virtual streampos seekoff(streamoff, ios::seekdir,
            ios::openmode = ios::in | ios::out);
        virtual streampos seekpos(streampos,
            ios::openmode = ios::in | ios::out);
        void _Init(int = 0, char * = 0, char * = 0,
            _Strstate = _Strzero);
        void _Tidy();
        _Strstate _Strmode;
private:
        char *_Pendsave, *_Seekhigh;
        int _Alsize;
        void *(*_Palloc)(size_t);
        void (*_Pfree)(void *);
        };
        // class istrstream
class istrstream : public istream {
public:
        istrstream(const char *_S)
            : ios(&_Sb), istream(&_Sb), _Sb(_S, 0) {}
        istrstream(const char *_S, int _N)
            : ios(&_Sb), istream(&_Sb), _Sb(_S, _N) {}
        istrstream(char *_S)
            : ios(&_Sb), istream(&_Sb), _Sb((const char *)_S, 0) {}
        istrstream(char *_S, int _N)
            : ios(&_Sb), istream(&_Sb), _Sb((const char *)_S, _N) {}
        virtual ~istrstream();
        strstreambuf *rdbuf() const
            {return ((strstreambuf *)&_Sb); }
        char *str()
            {return (_Sb.str()); }
private:
        strstreambuf _Sb;
        };
        // class ostrstream
class ostrstream : public ostream {
public:
        ostrstream()
            : ios(&_Sb), ostream(&_Sb), _Sb() {}
        ostrstream(char *, int, openmode = out);
        virtual ~ostrstream();
        strstreambuf *rdbuf() const
            {return ((strstreambuf *)&_Sb); }
        void freeze(int _F = 1)
            {_Sb.freeze(_F); }
        char *str()
            {return (_Sb.str()); }
        int pcount() const
            {return (_Sb.pcount()); }
private:
        strstreambuf _Sb;
        };
#endif
```

Figure 11.2:
strstrea.c
Part 1 of 2

```
// strstreambuf -- strstreambuf basic members
#include <limits.h>
#include <string.h>
#include <strstream>

strstreambuf::~strstreambuf()
    {                                       // destruct a strstreambuf
    _Tidy();
    }

void strstreambuf::_Init(int n, char *gp, char *pp,
    _Strstate mode)
    {                               // initialize with possibly static buffer
    streambuf::_Init();
    _Pendsave = 0;
    _Seekhigh = 0;
    _Palloc = 0;
    _Pfree = 0;
    _Strmode = mode;
    if (gp == 0)
        {                                           // make dynamic
        _Alsize = _MINSIZE <= n ? n : _ALSIZE;
        _Strmode |= _Dynamic;
        }
    else if (_Strmode & _Dynamic)
        {                               // initialize a stringbuf from string
        _Alsize = _ALSIZE;
        if (0 < n)
            {                                       // copy string
            char *s = new char[n];
            if (s == 0)
                _Nomemory();
            memcpy(s, gp, n);
            _Seekhigh = s + n;
            if (!(_Strmode & _Noread))
                setg(s, s, s + n);
            if (!(_Strmode & _Constant))
                {           // make output string and maybe input
                setp(s, s + n);
                if (!gptr())
                    setg(s, s, s);
                }
            _Strmode |= _Allocated;
            }
        }
    else
        {                                           // make static
        int size = n < 0 ? INT_MAX : n == 0 ? strlen(gp) : n;
        _Alsize = 0;
        _Seekhigh = gp + size;
        if (pp == 0)
            setg(gp, gp, gp + size);
        else
            {                                       // make writable too
            if (pp < gp)
```

Continuing
strstrea.c
Part 2 of 2

```
                        pp = gp;
                  else if (gp + size < pp)
                        pp = gp + size;
                  setp(pp, gp + size);
                  setg(gp, gp, pp);
                  }
            }
      }

void strstreambuf::_Tidy()
      {                                       // discard any allocated storage
      if ((_Strmode & (_Allocated | _Frozen)) != _Allocated)
            ;
      else if (_Pfree != 0)
            (*_Pfree)(eback());
      else
            delete [] eback();
      _Seekhigh = 0;
      _Strmode &= ~(_Allocated | _Frozen);
      }
```

Implementing <strstream>

strstrea   Figure 11.1 shows the file **strstrea**, which implements the standard header **<strstream>**. It defines the classes **strstreambuf**, **istrstream**, and **ostrstream**. For a description of the macro **_BITMASK**, see page 132. For a description of the macro **_HAS_SIGNED_CHAR**, see page 195.

I have added two macros to specify in one place two values that are judgement calls. Both deal with the number of characters to allocate when creating or extending a character sequence:

_ALSIZE ■ **_ALSIZE**, the initial number of bytes to allocate, absent any hints to the contrary (currently 512)

_MINSIZE ■ **_MINSIZE**, the minimum number of additional bytes to allocate when extending (currently 32)

You may well have reasons to alter either or both of these values, based on what you know about storage size and granularity on a given implementation.

_Strstate   The bitmask type **_Strstate**, defined within the class **strstreambuf**, has much the same meaning as its counterpart *strstate* in the draft C++ Standard (17.4.6.1). I have added the element **_Noread**, which is not used by the classes defined in **<strstream>**. Adding it here, however, greatly simplifies the implementation of the classes defined in **<sstream>**. (See the next chapter.) The meaning of each of the **_Strstate** elements is:

_Allocated ■ **_Allocated**, set when the character sequence has been allocated

_Constant ■ **_Constant**, set when the character sequence is not to permit insertions

_Dynamic ■ **_Dynamic**, set when the character sequence can grow on demand

_Frozen ■ **_Frozen**, set when the character sequence has been frozen

_Noread ■ **_Noread**, set when the character sequence is not to permit extractions

Figure 11.3:
strstpro.c
Part 1 of 2

```
// strstpro -- strstreambuf protected members
#include <string.h>
#include <strstream>

int strstreambuf::overflow(int ch)
    {                                          // try to extend write area
    if (pptr() != 0 && pptr() < epptr())
        return (*_Pn()++ = ch);
    else if (!(_Strmode & _Dynamic)
        || _Strmode & (_Constant | _Frozen))
        return (EOF);
    else
        {                                      // okay to extend
        int osize = gptr() == 0 ? 0 : epptr() - eback();
        int nsize = osize + _Alsize;
        char *p = _Palloc != 0 ? (char *)(*_Palloc)(nsize)
            : new char[nsize];
        if (p == 0)
            return (EOF);
        if (0 < osize)
            memcpy(p, eback(), osize);
        else if (_ALSIZE < _Alsize)
            _Alsize = _ALSIZE;
        if (!(_Strmode & _Allocated))
            ;
        else if (_Pfree != 0)
            (*_Pfree)(eback());
        else
            delete [] eback();
        _Strmode |= _Allocated;
        if (osize == 0)
            {                                  // setup new buffer
            _Seekhigh = p;
            setp(p, p + nsize);
            setg(p, p, p);
            }
        else
            {                                  // revise old pointers
            _Seekhigh = _Seekhigh - eback() + p;
            setp(pbase() - eback() + p, pptr() - eback() + p,
                p + nsize);
            if (_Strmode & _Noread)
                setg(p, p, p);
            else
                setg(p, gptr() - eback() + p, pptr() + 1);
            }
        return (ch == EOF ? 0 : (*_Pn()++ = ch));
        }
    }

int strstreambuf::pbackfail(int ch)
    {                                          // try to putback a character
    if (gptr() == 0 || gptr() <= eback()
        || ch != EOF && (unsigned char)ch != _Gn()[-1]
            && _Strmode & _Constant)
```

```
                        return (EOF);
            else
                {                                       // safe to back up
                gbump(-1);
                return (ch == EOF ? 0 : (*_Gn() = ch));
                }
            }

int strstreambuf::underflow()
            {                               // read only if read position available
            if (gptr() == 0)
                return (EOF);
            else if (gptr() < egptr())
                return (*_Gn());
            else if (_Strmode & _Noread || pptr() == 0
                || pptr() <= gptr() && _Seekhigh <= gptr())
                return (EOF);
            else
                {                   // update _Seekhigh and expand read region
                if (_Seekhigh < pptr())
                    _Seekhigh = pptr();
                setg(eback(), gptr(), _Seekhigh);
                return (*_Gn());
                }
            }                                                                   □
```

_Init   I developed the protected secret member function **strstream-**
_Tidy **buf::_Init** as a way to handle all possible constructors, including those
for class **stringbuf** in the next chapter. Similarly, the protected secret
member function **strstreambuf::_Tidy** does all the work of the destructor. It is also used to advantage in class **stringbuf**. (See the discussion of
strstrea.c, below.)

_Pendsave   The last surprise in class **strstreambuf** (and in this header) are two
_Seekhigh additional private member objects. Each solves a different problem in
managing accesses to the controlled character sequence. **_Pendsave** stores
the end pointer for the output sequence while the stream buffer is frozen.
(See the discussion of the file **strstfre.c**, below.) **_Seekhigh** stores the
highest defined offset encountered so far within the character sequence.
The code updates its stored value in several places when that value must
be made exact.

strstrea.c   Figure 11.2 shows the file **strstrea.c**. It defines three of the functions
you are likely to need any time you declare an object of class **strstreambuf**,
its destructor, **_Init**, and **_Tidy**. Two of the three functions are straightforward, but **_Init** warrants a bit of study. It selects among multiple forms of
initialization by an intricate analysis of its arguments:

- If **gp** (the "get" pointer) is a null pointer, then **n** (the size argument) is a
  suggested initial allocation size.

- Otherwise, if **mode** has the bit **_Dynamic** set, then the initial character
  sequence is copied from one controlled by a **string** object. (See next

Figure 11.4:
strstfre.c

```
// strstfreeze -- strstreambuf::freeze(_Bool)
#include <strstream>

void strstreambuf::freeze(_Bool freezeit)
    {                                               // freeze a dynamic string
    if (freezeit && !(_Strmode & _Frozen))
        {                                           // disable writing
        _Strmode |= _Frozen;
        _Pendsave = epptr();
        setp(pbase(), pptr(), eback());
        }
    else if (!freezeit && _Strmode & _Frozen)
        {                                           // re-enable writing
        _Strmode &= ~_Frozen;
        setp(pbase(), pptr(), _Pendsave);
        }
    }                                                                      □
```

Figure 11.5:
strstpos.c
Part 1 of 2

```
// strstpos -- strstreambuf positioning members
#include <strstream>

streampos strstreambuf::seekoff(streamoff off,
    ios::seekdir way, ios::openmode which)
    {                                               // seek by specified offset
    if (pptr() != 0 && _Seekhigh < pptr())
        _Seekhigh = pptr();
    if (which & ios::in && gptr() != 0)
        {                           // set input (and maybe output) pointer
        if (way == ios::end)
            off += _Seekhigh - eback();
        else if (way == ios::cur && !(which & ios::out))
            off += gptr() - eback();
        else if (way != ios::beg || off == _BADOFF)
            off = _BADOFF;
        if (0 <= off && off <= _Seekhigh - eback())
            {                               // set one or two pointers
            gbump(eback() - gptr() + off);
            if (which & ios::out && pptr() != 0)
                setp(pbase(), gptr(), epptr());
            }
        else
            off = _BADOFF;
        }
    else if (which & ios::out && pptr() != 0)
        {                                   // set only output pointer
        if (way == ios::end)
            off += _Seekhigh - eback();
        else if (way == ios::cur)
            off += pptr() - eback();
        else if (way != ios::beg || off == _BADOFF)
            off = _BADOFF;
        if (0 <= off && off <= _Seekhigh - eback())
            pbump(eback() - pptr() + off);
        else
```

```
                    off = _BADOFF;
            }
    else                                            // nothing to set
        off = _BADOFF;
    return (streampos(off));
    }

streampos strstreambuf::seekpos(streampos sp,
        ios::openmode which)
        {                                   // seek to memorized position
    streamoff off = sp.offset();
    if (pptr() != 0 && _Seekhigh < pptr())
        _Seekhigh = pptr();
    if (off == _BADOFF)
        ;
    else if (which & ios::in && gptr() != 0)
            {                       // set input (and maybe output) pointer
        if (0 <= off && off <= _Seekhigh - eback())
                {                                   // set valid offset
            gbump(eback() - gptr() + off);
            if (which & ios::out && pptr() != 0)
                setp(pbase(), gptr(), epptr());
                }
            else
                off = _BADOFF;
            }
    else if (which & ios::out && pptr() != 0)
            {                                   // set output pointer
        if (0 <= off && off <= _Seekhigh - eback())
            pbump(eback() - pptr() + off);
            else
                off = _BADOFF;
            }
    else                                            // nothing to set
        off = _BADOFF;
    return (streampos(off));
    }                                                               □
```

chapter.) The function copies **n** characters beginning at **gp**. The calling
string constructor can independently inhibit insertions (**_Constant**)
and/or extractions (**_Noread**).

- Otherwise, the character sequence resides in an existing character array
  beginning at **gp**. If **n** is less than zero, the sequence is assumed to be
  arbitrarily large (**INT_MAX** characters). If **n** is zero, the array is assumed
  to contain a null-terminated string, which defines the character sequence. If **n** is greater than zero, it is taken as the length of the character
  sequence. The function defines an output stream only if **pp** (the "put"
  pointer) is not a null pointer and lies within the character sequence.

Be warned that this code is extremely fragile. Partly, it reflects the complexi-
ties of the numerous **strstreambuf** constructors. Partly, it is made larger
by the inclusion of support for **stringbuf** constructors. But the code also

Figure 11.6:
istrstre.c

```
// istrstream -- istrstream basic members
#include <strstream>

istrstream::~istrstream()
    {                                                  // destruct an istrstream
    }                                                                          □
```

Figure 11.7:
ostrstre.c

```
// ostrstream -- ostrstream basic members
#include <string.h>
#include <strstream>

ostrstream::ostrstream(char *s, int n, openmode mode)
    : ios(&_Sb), ostream(&_Sb),
    _Sb(s, n, s == 0 || !(mode & app) ? s : s + strlen(s))
    {                          // write at terminating null (if there)
    }

ostrstream::~ostrstream()
    {                                                  // destruct an ostrstream
    }                                                                          □
```

enforces delicate **streambuf** semantics that are hard to spell out in detail. Tinker cautiously.

strstpro.c   Figure 11.3 shows the file **strstpro.c**. It defines three functions that override **streambuf** virtual member functions to insert and extract characters — **overflow**, **pbackfail**, and **underflow**. The inherited definition of **uflow** is adequate, so no override occurs here. (See the general discussion on page 162.) Once again, two of the three functions are straightforward. Only **overflow** demands closer study.

overflow   It is the business of **overflow** to "make a write position available," then insert the argument character into it. If the write position is already available, or if none can be made available, the function has an easy job of it. The hard part comes when the function must extend, or initially create, storage for the character sequence. It must then determine the size of any existing sequence (**osize**) and the desired new size (**nsize**). Then it can try to allocate the new storage, copy over any existing sequence, and free an existing sequence that was also allocated. Finally, it must determine new settings for the **streambuf** pointers, using some very finicky arithmetic.

strstfre.c   Figure 11.4 shows the file **strstfre.c**, which defines the member function **strstreambuf::freeze**. Here is where the addition of the member object **strstreambuf::_Pendsave** saves the day. A frozen buffer must not permit insertions, but that is not an easy thing to prevent. The **streambuf** public member functions won't look past the pointers themselves if they indicate that a write position is available. So the trick is to make the output stream appear empty for a frozen stream buffer by jiggering the end pointer. **_Pendsave** stores the proper value for later restoration, should the stream buffer be unfrozen.

strstpos.c Figure 11.5 shows the file **strstpos.c**. It defines the two functions that override **streambuf** virtual member functions to alter the stream position — **seekoff** and **seekpos**. The often critical value in both functions is the member object **strstrambuf::_Seekhigh**. It is updated as needed to reflect the current "end," or high-water mark, of the character sequence. That value determines offsets relative to the end (**way** equals **ios::end**), as well as an upper bound for valid stream offsets. The logic of both functions is otherwise simple but tedious.

And that concludes the source code for class **strstreambuf**.

istrstre.c Figure 11.6 shows the file **istrstre.c**. It defines the destructor for class **istrstream**, which is the only member function not defined inline within the class.

ostrstre.c Figure 11.7 shows the file **ostrstre.c**. It defines the destructor, and a moderately messy constructor, for class **ostrstream**. I put the constructor here mostly to hide the call to the function **strlen**, declared in **<string.h>**. It is not permissible to include the C header that declares it in **<strstream>** and I didn't want to make up a version of the function with a secret name. Again this is the only source code for member functions of class **ostrstream** not defined inline within the class.

Testing `<strstream>`

tstrstre.c Figure 11.8 shows the file **tstrstre.c**. It tests the basic properties of the classes defined in **<strstream>**. It does so in four groups:

- **strstreambuf** objects for dynamic character sequences (**t1()**)
- **strstreambuf** objects for read-only character sequences (**t2()**)
- **strstreambuf** objects for read-write character sequences (**t3()**)
- **istrstream** and **ostrstream** objects (**main()**)

If all goes well, the program prints:

```
SUCCESS testing <strstream>
```

and takes a normal exit.

Exercises

Exercise 11.1 Describe the effect of the following code sequence:

```
char s[50];
ostrstream(s, sizeof (s)) < "Total = " < total < ends;
```

Exercise 11.2 A UNIX-style pipeline is a data stream that one process writes and another reads. If the writer gets too far ahead of the reader, it is made to wait. If the reader catches up with the writer, it is made to wait. In what ways is a **strstreambuf** object like a pipeline? In what ways does it differ?

Exercise 11.3 Describe alternate rules for checking arguments to **strstreambuf::seekoff** and **strstreambuf::seekpos** to make them less surprising.

```
// test <strstream>
#include <assert.h>
#include <limits.h>
#include <stdlib.h>
#include <string.h>
#include <iostream>
#include <strstream>

char buf[] = "12345678";
static int allocs = 0;
static int frees = 0;

void *salloc(size_t n)
    {                                         // allocate storage for string
    ++allocs;
    return (malloc(n));
    }

void sfree(void *p)
    {                                         // free storage for string
    ++frees;
    free(p);
    }

void t1()
    {                                         // test dynamic strstreambufs
    strstreambuf sb0, sb1(1), sb2(&salloc, &sfree);
    ostream outs(&sb0);
    outs << "dynamic strstreambuf 0" << ends;
    assert(strcmp(sb0.str(), "dynamic strstreambuf 0") == 0);
    sb0.freeze();
    outs.rdbuf(&sb1);
    outs << "dynamic strstreambuf 1" << ends;
    assert(strcmp(sb1.str(), "dynamic strstreambuf 1") == 0);
    sb1.freeze(1);
    outs.rdbuf(&sb2);
    outs << "allocating strstreambuf" << ends;
    assert(strcmp(sb2.str(), "allocating strstreambuf") == 0);
    sb2.freeze(0);
    }

void t2()
    {                                         // test read-only strstreambufs
    strstreambuf sb1((const char*)buf, 5);
    strstreambuf sb2((unsigned char *)buf, 0);
    strstreambuf sb3((signed char *)buf, -1);
    strstreambuf sb4((const char *)buf, 5);
    strstreambuf sb5((const unsigned char *)buf, 0);
    strstreambuf sb6((const signed char *)buf, -1);
    assert(strcmp(sb1.str(), buf) == 0 && sb1.pcount() == 0);
    assert(sb1.pubseekoff(0, ios::end, ios::in).offset() == 5);
    assert(sb1.pubseekoff(0, ios::cur, ios::out).offset() == -1);
    assert(strcmp(sb2.str(), buf) == 0 && sb2.pcount() == 0);
    assert(sb2.pubseekoff(0, ios::end, ios::in).offset() == 8);
    assert(sb2.pubseekoff(0, ios::cur).offset() == -1);
```

```
    assert(strcmp(sb3.str(), buf) == 0 && sb3.pcount() == 0);
    assert(sb3.pubseekoff(0, ios::end, ios::in).offset()
        == INT_MAX);
    assert(strcmp(sb4.str(), buf) == 0 && sb4.pcount() == 0);
    assert(sb4.pubseekoff(0, ios::end, ios::in).offset() == 5);
    assert(strcmp(sb5.str(), buf) == 0 && sb5.pcount() == 0);
    assert(strcmp(sb6.str(), buf) == 0 && sb6.pcount() == 0);
    }

void t3()
    {                                   // test read-write strstreambufs
    strstreambuf sb1(buf, 5, buf);
    strstreambuf sb2((unsigned char *)buf, 0,
        (unsigned char *)buf + 1);
    strstreambuf sb3((signed char *)buf, -1, (signed char *)buf);
    ostream outs(&sb1);
    outs << 'A';
    assert(strcmp(sb1.str(), "A2345678") == 0
        && sb1.pcount() == 1);
    outs << 'B';
    assert(strcmp(sb1.str(), "A2345678") == 0
        && sb1.pcount() == 1);
    assert(sb1.pubseekoff(6, ios::beg, ios::out).offset() == -1);
    assert(strcmp(sb2.str(), "A2345678") == 0
        && sb2.pcount() == 0);
    outs.rdbuf(&sb2), sb2.freeze(0), outs << 'C';
    assert(strcmp(sb2.str(), "AC345678") == 0);
    assert(sb2.pubseekoff(6, ios::beg, ios::out).offset() == 6);
    assert(sb2.pcount() == 5);
    assert(strcmp(sb3.str(), "AC345678") == 0
        && sb3.pcount() == 0);
    assert(sb3.pubseekoff(50, ios::cur, ios::out).offset()
        == 50);
    assert(sb3.pcount() == 50);
    }

int main()
    {           // test basic workings of strstream definitions
    istrstream is1("s1"), is2("s2x", 2);
    istrstream is3((char *)"s3"), is4((char *)"s4", 2);
    assert(strcmp(is1.rdbuf()->str(), "s1") == 0);
    assert(strcmp(is3.str(), "s3") == 0);
    char buf[] = "d\0fgh";
    ostrstream os1, os2("12345", 4);
    ostrstream os3(buf, sizeof (buf), ios::app);
    assert(strcmp(os2.rdbuf()->str(), "12345") == 0);
    os3 << 'e';
    assert(strcmp(os3.str(), "defgh") == 0 && os3.pcount() == 1);
    os3.freeze(0), os3 << 'F';
    assert(strcmp(os3.str(), "deFgh") == 0 && os3.pcount() == 2);
    t1(), assert(0 < allocs && 0 < frees);
    t2(), t3();
    cout << "SUCCESS testing <strstream>" << endl;
    return (0);
    }
```

Exercise 11.4 One constructor for class **ostrstream** is **ostrstream(char *, int, openmode = out)**. The function assigns no meaning to the specific value **ios::out** for the third argument. Why is this still the default value?

Exercise 11.5 The constructors for **istrstream** and **ostrstream** in this implementation all provide explicit initializers for the **ios** subobject. (See, for example, the file **strstrea** on page 280.) But so do the constructors for their base classes **istream** (page 194) and **ostream** (page 236). Why is this so? Which constructor(s) actually get called?

Exercise 11.6 Describe the discipline used in this book, as revealed by the previous exercise, for ensuring that a virtual base class always gets properly initialized. Can you think of another discipline that also works?

Exercise 11.7 [Harder] Alter the **strstreambuf** functions in the file **strstpro.c** (page 284) to manage the character sequence as a linked list of segments instead of a single array. What do you do about **strstreambuf::str**? Why would you want this alternate implementation?

Exercise 11.8 [Very hard] Alter the functions from the previous exercise to support character sequences too large to fit in storage. What do you do about **strstreambuf::str**? Why would you want this alternate implementation?

Chapter 12: `<sstream>`

Background

The header `<sstream>` is a variation on the header `<strstream>`, described in the previous chapter, to work more closely with class `string`. A `string` object controls an in-memory character sequence, supporting operations on the sequence such as assignment, concatenation, comparison, and searching. (See Chapter 15: `<string>`.)

Like `<strstream>`, `<sstream>` defines three classes that cooperate to help you read and write character sequences stored in memory:

stringbuf ■ `stringbuf`, derived from `streambuf` to mediate access to an in-memory character sequence and grow it on demand (yes, the name should be `stringstreambuf` for greater uniformity)

istringstream ■ `istringstream`, derived from `istream` to construct a `stringbuf` object with input and/or output streams and to assist in extracting from the stream

ostringstream ■ `ostringstream`, derived from `ostream` to construct a `stringbuf` object with input and/or output streams and to assist in inserting into the stream

If these classes sound suspiciously like the classes described in the previous chapter, that is hardly an accident. A `stringbuf` object supports much the same control over input and output streams as does a `strstreambuf` object. There are just a few added capabilities:

■ You can initialize the character sequence controlled by a `stringbuf` from the character sequence controlled by a `string`, when the `stringbuf` is constructed or repeatedly thereafter.

■ You can initialize the character sequence controlled by a newly constructed `string` object from the character sequence controlled by a `stringbuf`.

■ You can specify independently, when a `stringbuf` is constructed, whether the input stream is readable or the output stream is writable.

Unlike a `strstreambuf` object, however, a `stringbuf` object does *not* let you muck with a character sequence that is also controlled by a `string` object. It simply facilitates copying between two representations private to each object.

The classes **istringtream** and **ostringstream** behave much like **istrstream** and **ostrstream** in the previous chapter. They construct a **stringbuf** object for you. They also provide member functions that access the special features of a **stringbuf** object. In this case, that mostly involves copying to and from **string** objects, as described above.

What the Draft C++ Standard Says

A few subtle differences exist between the description of class **stringbuf** here and class **strstreambuf** in the previous chapter. If an object of the latter class defines an output sequence, it always defines an input sequence as well. But that is not always true for an object of class **stringbuf**. Otherwise, the two kinds of stream buffers are more alike than different.

17.4.7 Header <sstream>

<sstream>

The header **<sstream>** defines three types that associate stream buffers with objects of class **string**, as described in subclause 17.5.1.

17.4.7.1 Class stringbuf

Class
stringbuf

```
class stringbuf : public streambuf {
public:
    stringbuf(ios::openmode which = ios::in | ios::out);
    stringbuf(const string& str,
        ios::openmode which = ios::in | ios::out);
    virtual ~stringbuf();
    string str() const;
    void str(const string& str_arg);
protected:
//  virtual int overflow(int c = EOF);              inherited
//  virtual int pbackfail(int c = EOF);             inherited
//  virtual int underflow(); inherited
//  virtual int uflow();       inherited
//  virtual int xsgetn(char* s, int n);             inherited
//  virtual int xsputn(const char* s, int n);       inherited
//  virtual streampos seekoff(streamoff off, ios::seekdir way,
//      ios::openmode which = ios::in | ios::out);  inherited
//  virtual streampos seekpos(streampos sp,
//      ios::openmode which = ios::in | ios::out);  inherited
//  virtual streambuf* setbuf(char* s, int n);      inherited
//  virtual int sync();                             inherited
private:
//  ios::openmode mode;                       exposition only
};
```

The class **stringbuf** is derived from **streambuf** to associate possibly the input sequence and possibly the output sequence with a sequence of arbitrary (single-byte) characters. The sequence can be initialized from, or made available as, an object of class **string**.

For the sake of exposition, the maintained data is presented here as:

- **ios::openmode** *mode*, has **ios::in** set if the input sequence can be read, and **ios::out** set if the output sequence can be written.

For the sake of exposition, the stored character sequence is described here as an array object.

17.4.7.1.1 stringbuf::stringbuf(ios::openmode)

constructor

```
stringbuf(ios::openmode which = ios::in | ios::out);
```

Constructs an object of class **stringbuf**, initializing the base class with **streambuf()**, and initializing **mode** with **which**. The function allocates no array object.

17.4.7.1.2 stringbuf::stringbuf(const string&, ios::openmode)

constructor

```
stringbuf(const string& str,
          ios::openmode which = ios::in | ios::out);
```

Constructs an object of class **stringbuf**, initializing the base class with **streambuf()**, and initializing **mode** with **which**.

If *str*.**length()** is nonzero, the function allocates an array object *x* whose length *n* is *str*.**length()** and whose elements *x[I]* are initialized to *str[I]*. If *which* & **ios::in** is nonzero, the function executes:

```
setg(x, x, x + n);
```

If *which* & **ios::out** is nonzero, the function executes:

```
setp(x, x + n);
```

17.4.7.1.3 stringbuf::~stringbuf()

destructor

```
virtual ~stringbuf();
```

Destroys an object of class **stringbuf**.

17.4.7.1.4 stringbuf::str()

str

```
string str() const;
```

If *mode* & **ios::in** is nonzero and *gnext* is not a null pointer, returns **string(*gbeg*, *gend* - *gbeg*)**. Otherwise, if *mode* & **ios::out** is nonzero and *pnext* is not a null pointer, the function returns **string(*pbeg*, *pptr* - *pbeg*)**. Otherwise, the function returns **string()**.

17.4.7.1.5 stringbuf::str(const string&)

str

```
void str(const string& str_arg);
```

If *str_arg*.**length()** is zero, executes:

```
setg(0, 0, 0);
setp(0, 0);
```

and frees storage for any associated array object. Otherwise, the function allocates an array object *x* whose length *n* is *str_arg*.**length()** and whose elements *x[I]* are initialized to *str_arg[I]*. If *which* & **ios::in** is nonzero, the function executes:

```
setg(x, x, x + n);
```

If *which* & **ios::out** is nonzero, the function executes:

```
setp(x, x + n);
```

17.4.7.1.6 stringbuf::overflow(int)

overflow

```
// virtual int overflow(int c = EOF);                          inherited
```

Appends the character designated by *c* to the output sequence, if possible, in one of two ways:

- If *c* != **EOF** and if either the output sequence has a write position available or the function makes a write position available (as described below), the function assigns *c* to ***pnext++**. The function signals success by returning **(unsigned char)*c***.

- If *c* **==** **EOF**, there is no character to append. The function signals success by returning a value other than **EOF**.

The function can alter the number of write positions available as a result of any call.

The function returns **EOF** to indicate failure.

The function can make a write position available only if *mode* **& ios::out** is nonzero. To make a write position available, the function reallocates (or initially allocates) an array object with a sufficient number of elements to hold the current array object (if any), plus one additional write position. If *mode* **& ios::in** is nonzero, the function alters the read end pointer *gend* to point just past the new write position (as does the write end pointer *pend*).

17.4.7.1.7 stringbuf::pbackfail(int)

pbackfail
```
// virtual int pbackfail(int c = EOF);                    inherited
```

Puts back the character designated by *c* to the input sequence, if possible, in one of three ways:

- If *c* **!=** **EOF**, if the input sequence has a putback position available, and if **(unsigned char)** *c* **==** **(unsigned char)** *gnext* **[-1]**, the function assigns *gnext* **- 1** to *gnext*. The function signals success by returning **(unsigned char)** *c*.

- If *c* **!=** **EOF**, if the input sequence has a putback position available, and if *mode* **& ios::out** is nonzero, the function assigns *c* to ***--** *gnext*. The function signals success by returning **(unsigned char)** *c*.

- If *c* **==** **EOF** and if the input sequence has a putback position available, the function assigns *gnext* **- 1** to *gnext*. The function signals success by returning **(unsigned char)** *c*.

If the function can succeed in more than one of these ways, it is unspecified which way is chosen.

The function returns **EOF** to indicate failure.

17.4.7.1.8 stringbuf::underflow()

underflow
```
// virtual int underflow();                              inherited
```

If the input sequence has a read position available, signals success by returning **(unsigned char)*** *gnext*. Otherwise, the function returns **EOF** to indicate failure.

17.4.7.1.9 stringbuf::uflow()

uflow
```
// virtual int uflow();                                  inherited
```

Behaves the same as **streambuf::uflow(int)**.

17.4.7.1.10 stringbuf::xsgetn(char*, int)

xsgetn
```
// virtual int xsgetn(char* s, int n);                   inherited
```

Behaves the same as **streambuf::xsgetn(char*, int)**.

17.4.7.1.11 stringbuf::xsputn(const char*, int)

xsputn
```
// virtual int xsputn(const char* s, int n);             inherited
```

Behaves the same as **streambuf::xsputn(char*, int)**.

17.4.7.1.12 stringbuf::seekoff(streamoff, ios::seekdir, ios::openmode)

seekoff
```
// virtual streampos seekoff(streamoff off, ios::seekdir way,
//        ios::openmode which = ios::in | ios::out);     inherited
```

Alters the stream position within one of the controlled sequences, if possible, as described below. The function returns **streampos(** *newoff* **)**, constructed from the resultant offset *newoff* (of type **streamoff**), that stores the resultant stream position, if possible. If the positioning operation fails, or if the constructed object cannot represent the resultant stream position, the object stores an invalid stream position.

If *which* & **ios::in** is nonzero, the function positions the input sequence. Otherwise, if *which* & **ios::out** is nonzero, the function positions the output sequence. Otherwise, if *which* & (**ios::in** | **ios::out**) equals **ios::in** | **ios::out** and if *way* equals either **ios::beg** or **ios::end**, the function positions both the input and the output sequences. Otherwise, the positioning operation fails.

For a sequence to be positioned, if its next pointer is a null pointer, the positioning operation fails. Otherwise, the function determines *newoff* in one of three ways:

• If *way* == **ios::beg**, *newoff* is zero.

• If *way* == **ios::cur**, *newoff* is the next pointer minus the beginning pointer (*xnext* - *xbeg*).

• If *way* == **ios::end**, *newoff* is the end pointer minus the beginning pointer (*xend* - *xbeg*).

If *newoff* + *off* is less than zero, or if *xend* - *xbeg* is less than *newoff* + *off*, the positioning operation fails. Otherwise, the function assigns *xbeg* + *newoff* + *off* to the next pointer *xnext*.

17.4.7.1.13 stringbuf::seekpos(streampos, ios::openmode)

seekpos

```
// virtual streampos seekpos(streampos sp,
//         ios::openmode which = ios::in | ios::out);    inherited
```

Alters the stream position within one of the controlled sequences, if possible, to correspond to the stream position stored in *sp* (as described below). The function returns **streampos(*newoff*)**, constructed from the resultant offset *newoff* (of type **streamoff**), that stores the resultant stream position, if possible. If the positioning operation fails, or if the constructed object cannot represent the resultant stream position, the object stores an invalid stream position.

If *which* & **ios::in** is nonzero, the function positions the input sequence. If *which* & **ios::out** is nonzero, the function positions the output sequence. If the function positions neither sequence, the positioning operation fails.

For a sequence to be positioned, if its next pointer is a null pointer, the positioning operation fails. Otherwise, the function determines *newoff* from *sp*.**offset()**. If *newoff* is an invalid stream position, has a negative value, or has a value greater than *xend* - *xbeg*, the positioning operation fails. Otherwise, the function adds *newoff* to the beginning pointer *xbeg* and stores the result in the next pointer *xnext*.

17.4.7.1.14 stringbuf::setbuf(char*, int)

setbuf

```
// virtual streambuf* setbuf(char* s, int n);    inherited
```

Performs an operation that is defined separately for each class derived from **stringbuf**.

The default behavior is the same as for **streambuf::setbuf(char*, int)**.

17.4.7.1.15 stringbuf::sync()

sync

```
// virtual int sync();    inherited
```

Behaves the same as **streambuf::sync()**.

17.4.7.2 Class `istringstream`

```
class istringstream : public istream {
public:
    istringstream(ios::openmode which = ios::in);
    istringstream(const string& str,
        ios::openmode which = ios::in);
    virtual ~istringstream();
    stringbuf* rdbuf() const;
    string str() const;
    void str(const string& str);
private:
//  stringbuf sb;                            exposition only
};
```

The class **istringstream** is a derivative of **istream** that assists in the reading of objects of class **stringbuf**. It supplies a **stringbuf** object to control the associated array object. For the sake of exposition, the maintained data is presented here as:

- **sb**, the **stringbuf** object.

17.4.7.2.1 `istringstream::istringstream(ios::openmode)`

```
    istringstream(ios::openmode which = ios::in);
```

Constructs an object of class **istringstream**, initializing the base class with **istream(&sb)**, and initializing **sb** with **sb(which)**.

17.4.7.2.2 `istringstream::istringstream(const string&, ios::openmode`

```
    istringstream(const string& str,
        ios::openmode which = ios::in);
```

Constructs an object of class **istringstream**, initializing the base class with **istream(&sb)**, and initializing **sb** with **sb(str, which)**.

17.4.7.2.3 `istringstream::~istringstream()`

```
    virtual ~istringstream();
```

Destroys an object of class **istringstream**.

17.4.7.2.4 `istringstream::rdbuf()`

```
    stringbuf* rdbuf() const;
```

Returns (**stringbuf***)**&sb**.

17.4.7.2.5 `istringstream::str()`

```
    string str() const;
```

Returns **sb.str()**.

17.4.7.2.6 `istringstream::str(const string&)`

```
    void str(const string& str_arg);
```

Calls **sb.str(str_arg)**.

17.4.7.3 Class `ostringstream`

```
class ostringstream : public ostream {
public:
    ostringstream(ios::openmode which = ios::out);
    ostringstream(const string& str,
        ios::openmode which = ios::out);
    virtual ~ostringstream();
    stringbuf* rdbuf() const;
```

```
        string str() const;
        void str(const string& str);
    private:
    //  stringbuf sb;                                    exposition only
    };
```

The class **ostringstream** is a derivative of **ostream** that assists in the writing of objects of class **stringbuf**. It supplies a **stringbuf** object to control the associated array object. For the sake of exposition, the maintained data is presented here as:

• *sb*, the **stringbuf** object.

17.4.7.3.1 ostringstream::ostringstream(ios::openmode)

constructor

```
    ostringstream(ios::openmode which = ios::out);
```

Constructs an object of class **ostringstream**, initializing the base class with **ostream(&sb)**, and initializing *sb* with *sb(which)*.

17.4.7.3.2 ostringstream::ostringstream(const string&, ios::openmode

constructor

```
    ostringstream(const string& str,
        ios::openmode which = ios::out);
```

Constructs an object of class **ostringstream**, initializing the base class with **ostream(&sb)**, and initializing *sb* with *sb(str, which)*.

17.4.7.3.3 ostringstream::~ostringstream()

destructor

```
    virtual ~ostringstream();
```

Destroys an object of class **ostringstream**.

17.4.7.3.4 ostringstream::rdbuf()

rdbuf

```
    stringbuf* rdbuf() const;
```

Returns **(stringbuf*)&sb**.

17.4.7.3.5 ostringstream::str()

str

```
    string str() const;
```

Returns *sb*.**str()**.

17.4.7.3.6 ostringstream::str(const string&)

str

```
    void str(const string& str_arg);
```

Calls *sb*.**str(***str_arg***)**.

Future Directions

str   As I mentioned in the previous chapter, the member function name **str** has already been changed in class **string** since the Informal Review Draft. It is now **data**. That cleanup has yet to extend to the classes defined in `<sstream>`, but it might.

wide-character   As I also keep mentioning where relevant, a major change is the addition
streams   of wide-character streams. (See page 119.) Class **stringbuf** becomes a template class parameterized by the type of the stream element. One instantiation, for type *char*, has essentially the same functionality as described in this chapter. Another, for type **wchar_t**, supports streams of elements from some large character set. Classes **istringstream** and **ostringstream** change along similar lines.

Using <sstream>

You include the header **<sstream>** to make use of any of the classes **istringstream, ostringstream,** or **stringbuf.** Objects of these classes let you read and write in-memory character sequences just as if they were conventional files, and copy character sequences. You can choose among three patterns of access:

- read only
- write only
- read/write

I deal with each of these options in turn. For a discussion of stream-positioning operations on in-memory character sequences, see the previous chapter. The issues are essentially the same.

read only   If all you want to do is read an in-memory character sequence that is initialized from a **string** object, construct an object of class **istringstream.** If you know at construction time what **string** object **s** you wish to use, you can write:

```
istringstream strin(s);
```

The resultant stream buffer (pointed at by **strin.rdbuf()**) does not support insertions. You can, however, replace the character sequence completely from another **string** object **s2** with the call:

```
strin.str(s2);
```

The stream position is reset to the beginning of the stream. (And the resultant stream buffer *still* does not support insertions.)

You can also construct an **istringstream** object with an empty character sequence, using the default constructor. Presumably, you would later supply a non-empty character sequence, as in:

```
istringstream strin;
strin.str(s);
```

write only   If all you want to do is create an in-memory character sequence to be eventually copied to a **string** object, construct an object of class **ostringstream** to control insertions into it. You can write:

```
ostringstream strout;
```

then insert into **strout** just like any other output stream. The character sequence can grow dynamically to arbitrary length. (The actual limit is usually **INT_MAX**, defined in **<limits.h>**, or when a storage allocation request fails.) The resultant stream buffer (pointed at by **strout.rdbuf()**) does not support extractions, by the way.

str   Your goal in creating a write-only character sequence is to capture the final result in a **string** object, as a rule. Write **s = strout.str()** to construct a **string** object, initialize it to control a copy of the character sequence, and assign it to the string object **s**. The two character sequences can, of course, evolve separately thereafter.

If you want a null-terminated string, there is no real need to insert a null character last. It will *not* be supplied for you when you call **s = strout. str()**, as above. On the other hand, you must then call **s.c_str()** to get a pointer to the beginning of the character sequence. That call *will* supply a terminating null character. (See Chapter 15: **<string>**.)

read/write If you want to create an in-memory character sequence that you can read as well as write, you need two objects to control the input and output streams. The classes **istringstream** and **ostringstream** are highly symmetric. Thus, you have three equally valid ways to do the job. If you don't want to supply an initial character sequence, you can write:

```
istringstream istr(ios::in | ios::out);
ostream ostr(istr.rdbuf());
```

or:

```
ostringstream ostr(ios::in | ios::out);
istream istr(ostr.rdbuf());
```

or:

```
stringbuf sb(ios::in | ios::out);
istream istr(&sb);
ostream ostr(&sb);
```

All approaches cause **istr** to control the input stream and **ostr** to control the output stream. For a discussion of end-of-file reporting in a read/write stream of this nature, see page 277.

You can also supply an initial character sequence from a **string** object **s** in each of these three cases:

```
istringstream istr(s, ios::in | ios::out);
ostream ostr(istr.rdbuf());
```

or:

```
ostringstream ostr(s, ios::in | ios::out);
istream istr(ostr.rdbuf());
```

or:

```
stringbuf sb(s, ios::in | ios::out);
istream istr(&sb);
ostream ostr(&sb);
```

Note that both the input and output stream positions are initially at the beginning of the character sequence. That may not be what you intend. Always consider whether you want to alter the output stream position before you do anything else with such a read/write stream.

Implementing **<sstream>**

sstream Figure 12.1 shows the file **sstream**, which implements the standard header **<sstream>**. It defines the classes **stringbuf**, **istringstream**, and **ostringstream**. Note that class **stringbuf** is based on class **strstreambuf**, described in the previous chapter. The draft C++ Standard says (17.4.7.1) that **stringbuf** is derived directly from **streambuf**. Such indirect derivation is permitted by the library "front matter" (17.1.5.10.3).

Figure 12.1:
sstream

```
// sstream standard header
#ifndef _SSTREAM_
#define _SSTREAM_
#include <string>
#include <strstream>
        // class stringbuf
class stringbuf : public strstreambuf {
public:
    stringbuf(ios::openmode _W = ios::in | ios::out)
        : strstreambuf(0, 0, 0, _Mode(_W)) {}
    stringbuf(const string& _S,
        ios::openmode _W = ios::in | ios::out)
        : strstreambuf((char *)_S.c_str(), _S.length(), 0,
            _Mode(_W)) {}
    virtual ~stringbuf();
    string str() const;
    void str(const string& _S);
protected:
    _Strstate _Mode(ios::openmode);
    };
        // class istrstream
class istringstream : public istream {
public:
    istringstream(openmode _W = in)
        : ios(&_Sb), istream(&_Sb), _Sb(_W) {}
    istringstream(const string& _S, openmode _W = in)
        : ios(&_Sb), istream(&_Sb), _Sb(_S, _W) {}
    virtual ~istringstream();
    stringbuf *rdbuf() const
        {return ((stringbuf *)&_Sb); }
    string str() const
        {return (_Sb.str()); }
    void str(const string& _S)
        {_Sb.str(_S); }
private:
    stringbuf _Sb;
    };
        // class ostrstream
class ostringstream : public ostream {
public:
    ostringstream(openmode _W = out)
        : ios(&_Sb), ostream(&_Sb), _Sb(_W) {}
    ostringstream(const string& _S, openmode _W = out)
        : ios(&_Sb), ostream(&_Sb), _Sb(_S, _W) {}
    virtual ~ostringstream();
    stringbuf *rdbuf() const
        {return ((stringbuf *)&_Sb); }
    string str() const
        {return (_Sb.str()); }
    void str(const string& _S)
        {_Sb.str(_S); }
private:
    stringbuf _Sb;
    };
#endif
```

Figure 12.2:
stringbu.c

```
// stringbuf -- stringbuf basic members
#include <sstream>

stringbuf::~stringbuf()
    {                                           // destruct a stringbuf
    }

strstreambuf::_Strstate stringbuf::_Mode(ios::openmode which)
    {                               // map ios::openmode to _Strstate
    _Strstate mode = _Dynamic;
    if (!(which & ios::in))
        mode |= _Noread;
    if (!(which & ios::out))
        mode |= _Constant;
    return (mode);
    }                                                            □
```

Figure 12.3:
strbstr0.c

```
// strbstr0 -- stringbuf::str()
#include <sstream>

string stringbuf::str() const
    {                               // construct string from stringbuf
    if (gptr() != 0)
        return (string(eback(),
            (pptr() == 0 || pptr() < egptr() ? egptr() : pptr())
                - eback())));
    else if (!(_Strmode & _Constant) && pptr() != 0)
        return (string(pbase(), pptr() - pbase()));
    else
        return (string(""));
    }                                                            □
```

Figure 12.4:
strbstr1.c

```
// strbstr1 -- stringbuf::str(const string&)
#include <sstream>

void stringbuf::str(const string& str)
    {                               // construct stringbuf from string
    _Tidy();
    _Init(str.length(), (char *)str.c_str(), 0, _Strmode);
    }                                                            □
```

I chose this implementation, as I hinted in the previous chapter, because
the two derived classes are so much alike. I added a bit of logic to class
strstreambuf to close the gap:

_Noread ■ I added the element **_Noread** to the type **strstreambuf::_Strmode**, to
note when a **stringbuf** object does not support extractions.

_Init ■ The member function **strstreambuf::_Init** has a default fourth argu-
ment, of type **strstreambuf::_Strmode**, to communicate extra mode
information from a **stringbuf** constructor.

Figure 12.5:
istrings.c

```
// istringstream -- istringstream basic members
#include <sstream>

istringstream::~istringstream()
    {                                      // destruct an istringstream
    }                                                                    □
```

Figure 12.6:
ostrings.c

```
// ostringstream -- ostringstream basic members
#include <sstream>

ostringstream::~ostringstream()
    {                                      // destruct an ostringstream
    }                                                                    □
```

_Tidy ■ The member function **strstreambuf::_Tidy** is a separate function, even though it is called only by the destructor for **strstreambuf**. It thus can also be called, to advantage, by **stringbuf::str(const string&)**.

_Mode   I also added to class **stringbuf** the secret protected member function **_Mode**. It maps constructor arguments of type **ios::openmode** to their corresponding **strstreambuf::_Strmode** values:

in ■ If **ios::in** is not set, the function sets **_Strmode::_Noread** in the return value.

out ■ If **ios::out** is not set, the function sets **_Strmode::_Constant** in the return value.

The effect of all this groundwork is to dramatically reduce the amount of new code required to implement the classes defined in **<sstream>**.

stringbu.c   Figure 12.2 shows the file **stringbu.c**, which defines the two functions required for practically any use of class **stringbuf**. These are the destructor and the member function **stringbuf::_Mode**. Class **stringbuf** has only two additional member functions not defined inline, the two flavors of **str**.

strbstr0.c   Figure 12.3 shows the file **strbstr0.c**, which defines the member function **stringbuf::str()**. If an input stream exists, the complexity lies in determining the current extent of the character sequence. The calculation is reminiscent of the logic for updating the **strstreambuf** member object **_Seekhigh**. (See previous chapter.)

strbstr1.c   Figure 12.4 shows the file **strbstr1.c**, which defines the member function **stringbuf::str(const string&)**. It discards any existing character sequence and reinitializes the stream buffer to control a copy of the new one. The **strstreambuf** secret member functions really pay off here.

The remaining source files implement the other two classes defined in **<sstream>**.

istrings.c   Figure 12.5 shows the file **istrings.c**, which defines the destructor for
ostrings.c   class **istringstream**. And Figure 12.6 shows the file **ostrings.c**, which defines the destructor for class **ostringstream**. The header supplies inline definitions for all other member functions in these two classes.

```
// test <sstream>
#include <assert.h>
#include <iostream>
#include <sstream>

void t1()
    {                                               // test stringbuf
    string s0("s0"), s1("s1"), s2("s2"), s3("s3");
    stringbuf sb0, sb1(ios::in), sb2(ios::out),
        sb3(ios::in | ios::out);
    stringbuf sb10(s0), sb11(s1, ios::in), sb12(s2, ios::out),
        sb13(s3, ios::in | ios::out);
    ostream outs(&sb0);
    outs << "dynamic stringbuf 0";
    s3 = sb0.str();
    assert(s3 == "dynamic stringbuf 0");
    sb0.str(s0);
    assert(sb0.str() == "s0");
    outs.rdbuf(&sb2);
    outs << "dynamic stringbuf 2";
    assert(sb2.str() == "dynamic stringbuf 2");
    outs.rdbuf(&sb10);
    outs << "x";
    assert(sb10.str() == "x0");
    outs.rdbuf(&sb11);
    outs << "x";
    assert(!outs.good() && sb11.str() == "s1");
    outs.rdbuf(&sb12);
    outs << "x";
    assert(sb12.str() == "x");
    assert(sb12.pubseekoff(2, ios::beg).offset() == 2
        && sb12.str() == "x2");
    }

void t2()
    {                                               // test istringstream
    string s0("s0"), s1("s1"), s2("s2"), s3("s3");
    istringstream is0, is1(ios::in), is2(ios::out),
        is3(ios::in | ios::out);
    istringstream is10(s0), is11(s1, ios::in),
        is12(s2, ios::out), is13(s3, ios::in | ios::out);
    assert(is10.rdbuf()->str() == "s0");
    assert(is11.str() == "s1");
    is0.str("abc");
    assert(is0.str() == "abc");
    is0 >> s0;
    assert(s0 == "abc");
    }

void t3()
    {                                               // test ostringstream
    string s0("s0"), s1("s1"), s2("s2"), s3("s3");
    ostringstream os0, os1(ios::in), os2(ios::out),
        os3(ios::in | ios::out);
    ostringstream os10(s0), os11(s1, ios::in),
```

```
            os12(s2, ios::out), os13(s3, ios::in | ios::out);
        assert(os10.rdbuf()->str() == "");
        assert(os13.str() == "s3");
        os0.str("abc");
        assert(os0.str() == "");
        assert(os0.rdbuf()->pubseekoff(2, ios::beg).offset() == 2
            && os0.str() == "ab");
        os0 << "Cde";
        assert(os0.str() == "abCde");
        }

int main()
        {            // test basic workings of stringstream definitions
        t1();
        t2();
        t3();
        cout << "SUCCESS testing <sstream>" << endl;
        return (0);
        }                                                         □
```

Testing `<sstream>`

tsstream.c   Figure 12.7 shows the file **tsstream.c**. It tests the basic properties of the classes defined in **<sstream>**. It does so in three groups:

- **stringbuf** objects (**t1()**)

- **istringstream** objects (**t2()**)

- **ostringstream** objects (**t3()**)

The function **main()** simply performs these groups of tests in the order shown. If all goes well, the program prints:

    SUCCESS testing <sstream>

and takes a normal exit.

Exercises

Exercise 12.1 Can you construct a **stringbuf** object that permits neither insertions or deletions? If so, does it ever make sense to do so?

Exercise 12.2 Alter the classes defined in **<strstream>** to subsume the functionality of the classes defined in **<sstream>**. Would you change anything else about the classes you are redefining?

Exercise 12.3 Alter the classes defined in **<sstream>** to subsume the functionality of the classes defined in **<strstream>**. Would you omit any features?

Exercise 12.4 [Harder] Implement **stringbuf** without using the code for **strstreambuf**.

Exercise 12.5 [Very hard] Design and implement a version of **stringbuf** that allows simultaneous control of a character sequence with a **string** object. Why would you want such a capability?

Chapter 13: <fstream>

Background

The header **<fstream>** defines half a dozen classes. Three of these cooperate to help you read and write files that you open by name:

filebuf ■ **filebuf**, derived from **streambuf** to mediate access to an external stream of characters read from or written to a file

ifstream ■ **ifstream**, derived from **istream** to construct a **filebuf** object and to assist in extracting from the stream

ofstream ■ **ofstream**, derived from **ostream** to construct a **filebuf** object and to assist in inserting into the stream

The other three classes defined in **<fstream>** cooperate to help you read and write files controlled by an object of type **FILE**, declared in **<stdio.h>**:

stdiobuf ■ **stdiobuf**, derived from **streambuf** to mediate access to a stream of characters read from or written to an external stream under control of a **FILE** object

istdiostream ■ **istdiostream**, derived from **istream** to construct a **stdiobuf** object and to assist in extracting from the stream

ostdiostream ■ **ostdiostream**, derived from **ostream** to construct a **stdiobuf** object and to assist in inserting into the stream

cin Reading and writing files is an important part of iostreams. For many
cout C++ programs, it is the sole means of communication between a program and the outside world. The standard stream objects, such as **cin** and **cout**, are conventionally associated with external streams. (See the next chapter.) Even in this era of window-oriented interfaces, reading and writing files remains important. Communication between two programs, between a program and a window, or between a program and a special device are all often made to look like conventional file reads and writes. The classes defined in **<fstream>** are the preferred agents for controlling such file operations.

You do not, in principle, need two sets of classes for accessing files with iostreams. The Standard C library function **fopen**, declared in **<stdio.h>**, associates a named file with a **FILE** object. The same header declares **fclose**, for removing the association. You can associate a **FILE** object with a **stdiostream** object, as described above, and you're in business. Why the extra machinery?

history   The answer is largely historical. The iostreams package evolved *alongside* the Standard C library more than atop it. Both spent their earliest days hosted on the UNIX operating system, a particularly friendly environment for reading and writing files. As they have spread to other systems, both have also profited from the influence of UNIX on more modern operating systems. Thus, iostreams and the Standard C library have a common heritage, and many common architectural features, but they nevertheless grew up separately.

As a consequence, mixing iostreams and C stream operations has often led to an uneasy alliance. A **filebuf** object often performs reads and writes directly, using low-level operating system calls and managing an in-memory buffer directly. A **stdiobuf** object, by contrast, typically calls on the higher-level functions declared in **<stdio.h>**. The overhead per character can be *much* higher and buffering can occur in two different places within the program.

C++ programmers habitually favor the former over the latter, if only for better performance. They introduce **stdiobuf** objects only when obliged to mix iostreams and C stream reads or writes to the same file. And *then* they fret over the uncertainties that inevitably arise with double buffering. Input can be consumed in greater chunks than you expect, by the two agents. Or output from the two agents can get pasted together in bigger chunks than you intend. Often, the only safe fix is to make **stdiobuf** operations completely unbuffered. And *that* often penalizes performance even more.

responses   The draft C++ Standard addresses these historical problems:

- It defines the semantics of class **filebuf** as if it performs reads and writes through a **FILE** object. The draft C++ Standard thus rides atop the detailed descriptions of file operations from the C Standard. And it gives quick answers to many questions about the effect of mixing iostreams and C stream operations.

- It defines class **filebuf** in such a way that no **FILE** object is directly visible. The draft C++ Standard thus permits an implementation of **filebuf** atop the Standard C library, without mandating it.

- It retains class **stdiobuf**, which is defined explicitly in terms of a visible **FILE** object. Operations are *unbuffered* by default, so programs have no synchronization surprises.

- It nevertheless provides member functions to control whether **stdiobuf** operations can be buffered, if performance is more important to you than tight synchronization between iostreams and C stream operations.

- It specifies that the standard objects **cin**, **cout**, **cerr**, and **clog** behave as if they designate unbuffered **stdiostream** objects, without requiring exactly that implementation. (See next chapter.)

The basic idea is to better define the relationship between iostreams and C stream operations, and to provide as a default less surprising semantics for mixed operations. Nevertheless, the draft C++ Standard does *not* require that existing implementations of iostreams be rewritten purely in terms of calls to Standard C library functions.

open One example of shared semantics is the way you open a file by name. The **filebuf** member function **open(const char *, ios::openmode)** is the agent that does the job. It effectively calls **fopen**, declared in **<stdio.h>**. To do so, it must map its second argument to the kind of mode string acceptable to **fopen**. Thus, for example, **ios::in** becomes **"r"**. The member function is obliged to accept only those combinations of **ios::open-mode** elements for which a corresponding mode string is defined.

stream Another example is the semantics of stream positioning. The Standard
positioning C library permits a **FILE** object to mediate both reads and writes, but only in a rather stylized way. At any given time, the input stream may be readable or the output stream may be writable, but not both. (Of course, it is also possible that *neither* stream is available.) Typically, you have to perform a stream-positioning operation to switch between reading and writing. Equally, only one stream position is maintained for both reading and writing. And an arbitrary stream position requires the unspecified information stored in an **fpos_t** object, not just a **streamoff** value.

Iostreams implicitly acknowledges these limitations in several ways. By inheritance, it has the same semantic limitations on switching between extracting and inserting. (Opinions differ on this point within the Committee, however.) If you attempt to position either stream in a **filebuf** object, you position both at once. And the semantics of class **streampos** reflect the realities of the restrictions on **fpos_t** objects. (See Chapter 7: **<streambuf>**.)

I don't want to paint too rosy a picture, however. Several Committee members begrudge almost any concession to the Standard C library in the area of file operations. They may accept the narrow need for defining the semantics of the two libraries when they work together. But some feel that the Standard C++ library is better off being defined *de novo* in this area. I personally don't see how to introduce new semantics for iostreams without massively complicating the description of, say, **stdiobuf**. Others, however, may find a way over time.

What the Draft C++ Standard Says

The description of **<fstream>** depends heavily on references to functions and types declared in **<stdio.h>**, for reasons I indicated above. Please note once more, however, that such language makes no promises about how classes in this header are actually implemented. The draft C++ Standard often says, for example, that function **A** calls function **B**. Generally, this means only that **A** behaves *as if* it calls **B**. If you can write a portable program that can detect whether the call occurs — such as to a virtual member function that you can override — the call may be obligatory. Otherwise, don't be surprised if an interactive debugger fails to detect an actual call.

17.4.8 Header `<fstream>`

<fstream>

The header **<fstream>** defines six types that associate stream buffers with files and assist reading and writing files.

In this subclause, the type name ***FILE*** is a synonym for the type **FILE** defined in **<stdio.h>**.

17.4.8.1 Class `filebuf`

Class filebuf

```
class filebuf : public streambuf {
public:
    filebuf();
    virtual ~filebuf();
    int is_open() const;
    filebuf* open(const char* s, ios::openmode mode);
//  filebuf* open(const char* s, ios::open_mode mode);  optional
    filebuf* close();
protected:
//  virtual int overflow(int c = EOF);                  inherited
//  virtual int pbackfail(int c = EOF);                 inherited
//  virtual int underflow(); inherited
//  virtual int uflow();     inherited
//  virtual int xsgetn(char* s, int n);                 inherited
//  virtual int xsputn(const char* s, int n);           inherited
//  virtual streampos seekoff(streamoff off, ios::seekdir way,
//      ios::openmode which = ios::in | ios::out);      inherited
//  virtual streampos seekpos(streampos sp,
//      ios::openmode which = ios::in | ios::out);      inherited
//  virtual streambuf* setbuf(char* s, int n);          inherited
//  virtual int sync();                                 inherited
private:
//  FILE* file;                                    exposition only
};
```

The class **filebuf** is derived from **streambuf** to associate both the input sequence and the output sequence with an object of type **FILE**. Type **FILE** is defined in **<stdio.h>**. For the sake of exposition, the maintained data is presented here as:

- ***FILE *file***, points to the **FILE** associated with the object of class **filebuf**.

The restrictions on reading and writing a sequence controlled by an object of class **filebuf** are the same as for reading and writing its associated file. In particular:

- If the file is not open for reading or for update, the input sequence cannot be read.
- If the file is not open for writing or for update, the output sequence cannot be written.
- A joint file position is maintained for both the input sequence and the output sequence.

17.4.8.1.1 `filebuf::filebuf()`

constructor

```
filebuf();
```

Constructs an object of class **filebuf**, initializing the base class with **streambuf()**, and initializing ***file*** to a null pointer.

17.4.8.1.2 `filebuf::~filebuf()`

destructor

```
virtual ~filebuf();
```

Destroys an object of class **filebuf**. The function calls **close()**.

17.4.8.1.3 filebuf::is_open()

is_open

```
int is_open() const;
```

Returns a nonzero value if *file* is not a null pointer.

17.4.8.1.4 filebuf::open(const char*, ios::openmode)

open

```
filebuf* open(const char* s, ios::openmode mode);
```

If *file* is not a null pointer, returns a null pointer. Otherwise, the function opens a file, if possible, whose name is the NTBS *s*, by calling **fopen(*s, modstr*)** and assigning the return value to *file*. The NTBS *modstr* is determined from *mode* **& ~ios::ate** as follows:

- **ios::in** becomes **"r"**;
- **ios::out | ios::trunc** becomes **"w"**;
- **ios::out | ios::app** becomes **"a"**;
- **ios::in | ios::binary** becomes **"rb"**;
- **ios::out | ios::trunc | ios::binary** becomes **"wb"**;
- **ios::out | ios::app | ios::binary** becomes **"ab"**;
- **ios::in | ios::out** becomes **"r+"**;
- **ios::in | ios::out | ios::trunc** becomes **"w+"**;
- **ios::in | ios::out | ios::app** becomes **"a+"**;
- **ios::in | ios::out | ios::binary** becomes **"r+b"**;
- **ios::in | ios::out | ios::trunc | ios::binary** becomes **"w+b"**;
- **ios::in | ios::out | ios::app | ios::binary** becomes **"a+b"**.

If the resulting *file* is not a null pointer and *mode* **& ios::ate** is nonzero, the function calls **fseek(*file*, 0, SEEK_END)**. If that function returns a null pointer, the function calls **close()** and returns a null pointer. Otherwise, the function returns **this**.

The macro **SEEK_END** is defined, and the function signatures **fopen(const char*, const char*)** and **fseek(FILE*, long, int)** are declared, in **<stdio.h>**.

17.4.8.1.5 filebuf::open(const char*, ios::open_mode)

open

```
// filebuf* open(const char* s, ios::open_mode mode); optional
```

Returns **open(*s*, (ios::openmode)*mode*)**.

17.4.8.1.6 filebuf::close()

close

```
filebuf* close();
```

If *file* is a null pointer, returns a null pointer. Otherwise, if the call **fclose(*file*)** returns zero, the function stores a null pointer in *file* and returns **this**. Otherwise, it returns a null pointer.

The function signature **fclose(FILE*)** is declared, in **<stdio.h>**.

17.4.8.1.7 filebuf::overflow(int)

overflow

```
// virtual int overflow(int c = EOF);           inherited
```

Appends the character designated by *c* to the output sequence, if possible, in one of three ways:

- If *c* != **EOF** and if either the output sequence has a write position available or the function makes a write position available (in an unspecified manner), the function assigns *c* to **pnext++*. The function signals success by returning **(unsigned char)*c***.

- If *c* != **EOF**, the function appends *c* directly to the associated output sequence (as described below). If **pbeg** < **pnext**, the **pnext** - **pbeg** characters beginning at **pbeg** are first appended directly to the associated output sequence, beginning with the character at **pbeg**. The function signals success by returning **(unsigned char)** *c*.
- If *c* == **EOF**, there is no character to append. The function signals success by returning a value other than **EOF**.

If the function can succeed in more than one of these ways, it is unspecified which way is chosen. The function can alter the number of write positions available as a result of any call.

The function returns **EOF** to indicate failure. If **file** is a null pointer, the function always fails.

To append a character *x* directly to the associated output sequence, the function evaluates the expression:

```
fputc(x, file) == x
```

which must be nonzero. The function signature **fputc(int, FILE*)** is declared in **<stdio.h>**.

17.4.8.1.8 filebuf::pbackfail(int)

pbackfail

```
// virtual int pbackfail(int c = EOF);                    inherited
```

Puts back the character designated by *c* to the input sequence, if possible, in one of four ways:

- If *c* != **EOF** and if either the input sequence has a putback position available or the function makes a putback position available (in an unspecified manner), the function assigns *c* to ***--gnext**. The function signals success by returning **(unsigned char)** *c*.
- If *c* != **EOF** and if no putback position is available, the function puts back *c* directly to the associate input sequence (as described below). The function signals success by returning **(unsigned cha))** *c*.
- If *c* == **EOF** and if either the input sequence has a putback position available or the function makes a putback position available, the function assigns **gnext** - **1** to **gnext**. The function signals success by returning **(unsigned char)** *c*.
- If *c* == **EOF**, if no putback position is available, and if the function can determine the character *x* immediately before the current position in the associated input sequence (in an unspecified manner), the function puts back *x* directly to the associated input sequence. The function signals success by returning a value other than **EOF**.

If the function can succeed in more than one of these ways, it is unspecified which way is chosen. The function can alter the number of putback positions available as a result of any call.

The function returns **EOF** to indicate failure. If **file** is a null pointer, the function always fails.

To put back a character *x* directly to the associated input sequence, the function evaluates the expression:

```
ungetc(x, file) == x
```

which must be nonzero. The function signature **ungetc(int, FILE*)** is declared in **<stdio.h>**.

17.4.8.1.9 filebuf::underflow()

underflow

```
// virtual int underflow();                              inherited
```

Reads a character from the input sequence, if possible, without moving the stream position past it, as follows:

- If the input sequence has a read position available the function signals success by returning **(unsigned char)*gnext**.
- Otherwise, if the function can determine the character *x* at the current position in the associated input sequence (as described below), it signals success by returning **(unsigned char)*x**. If the function makes a read position available, it also assigns *x* to ***gnext**.

The function can alter the number of read positions available as a result of any call.

The function returns **EOF** to indicate failure. If *file* is a null pointer, the function always fails.

To determine the character *x* (of type **int**) at the current position in the associated input sequence, the function evaluates the expression:

(x = ungetc(fgetc(*file*), *file*)) != EOF

which must be nonzero. The function signatures **fgetc(FILE*)** and **ungetc(int, FILE*)** are declared in **<stdio.h>**.

17.4.8.1.10 filebuf::uflow()

uflow
```
//   virtual int uflow();                                    inherited
```
Reads a character from the input sequence, if possible, and moves the stream position past it, as follows:

- If the input sequence has a read position available the function signals success by returning **(unsigned char)*gnext++**.
- Otherwise, if the function can read the character *x* directly from the associated input sequence (as described below), it signals success by returning **(unsigned char)*x**. If the function makes a read position available (in an unspecified manner), it also assigns *x* to ***gnext**.

The function can alter the number of read positions available as a result of any call.

The function returns **EOF** to indicate failure. If *file* is a null pointer, the function always fails.

To read a character into an object *x* (of type **int**) directly from the associated input sequence, the function evaluates the expression:

(x = fgetc(*file*)) != EOF

which must be nonzero. The function signature **fgetc(FILE*)** is declared in **<stdio.h>**.

17.4.8.1.11 filebuf::xsgetn(char*, int)

xsgetn
```
//   virtual int xsgetn(char* s, int n);                      inherited
```
Behaves the same as **streambuf::xsgetn(char*, int)**.

17.4.8.1.12 filebuf::xsputn(const char*, int)

xsputn
```
//   virtual int xsputn(const char* s, int n);                inherited
```
Behaves the same as **streambuf::xsputn(char*, int)**.

17.4.8.1.13 filebuf::seekoff(streamoff, ios::seekdir, ios::openmode)

seekoff
```
//   virtual streampos seekoff(streamoff off, ios::seekdir way,
//         ios::openmode which = ios::in | ios::out);         inherited
```
Alters the stream position within the controlled sequences, if possible, as described below. The function returns a newly constructed **streampos** object that stores the resultant stream position, if possible. If the positioning operation fails, or if the object cannot represent the resultant stream position, the object stores an invalid stream position.

If *file* is a null pointer, the positioning operation fails. Otherwise, the function determines one of three values for the argument *whence*, of type **int**:

- If *way* == **ios::beg**, the argument is **SEEK_SET**;
- If *way* == **ios::cur**, the argument is **SEEK_CUR**;
- If *way* == **ios::end**, the argument is **SEEK_END**.

The function then calls **fseek(*file*, *off*, *whence*)** and, if that function returns nonzero, the positioning operation fails.

The macros **SEEK_SET**, **SEEK_CUR**, and **SEEK_END** are defined, and the function signature **fseek(FILE*, long, int)** is declared, in **<stdio.h>**.

17.4.8.1.14 filebuf::seekpos(streampos, ios::openmode)

seekpos
```
// virtual streampos seekpos(streampos sp,
//        ios::openmode which = ios::in | ios::out);        inherited
```

Alters the stream position within the controlled sequences, if possible, to correspond to the stream position stored in *sp.pos* and *sp.fp*.[108] The function returns a newly constructed **streampos** object that stores the resultant stream position, if possible. If the positioning operation fails, or if the object cannot represent the resultant stream position, the object stores an invalid stream position.

If *file* is a null pointer, the positioning operation fails.

17.4.8.1.15 filebuf::setbuf(char*, int)

setbuf
```
// virtual streambuf* setbuf(char* s, int n);        inherited
```

Makes the array of *n* (single-byte) characters, whose first element is designated by *s*, available for use as a buffer area for the controlled sequences, if possible. If *file* is a null pointer, the function returns a null pointer. Otherwise, if the call **setvbuf(*file*, *s*, _IOFBF, *n*)** is nonzero, the function returns a null pointer. Otherwise, the function returns ***this**.

The macro **_IOFBF** is defined, and the function signature **setvbuf(FILE*, char*, int, size_t)** is declared, in **<stdio.h>**.

17.4.8.1.16 filebuf::sync()

sync
```
// virtual int sync();        inherited
```

Returns zero if *file* is a null pointer. Otherwise, the function returns **fflush(*file*)**.

The function signature **fflush(FILE*)** is declared in **<stdio.h>**.

17.4.8.2 Class ifstream

**Class
ifstream**
```
class ifstream : public istream {
public:
    ifstream();
    ifstream(const char* s, openmode mode = in);
    virtual ~ifstream();
    filebuf* rdbuf() const;
    int is_open();
    void open(const char* s, openmode mode = in);
//  void open(const char* s, open_mode mode);        optional
    void close();
private:
//  filebuf fb;                                      exposition only
};
```

The class **ifstream** is a derivative of **istream** that assists in the reading of named files. It supplies a **filebuf** object to control the associated sequence. For the sake of exposition, the maintained data is presented here as:

• **filebuf** *fb*, the **filebuf** object.

17.4.8.2.1 ifstream::ifstream()

constructor

```
ifstream();
```

Constructs an object of class **ifstream**, initializing the base class with **istream(&fb)**.

17.4.8.2.2 ifstream::ifstream(const char*, openmode)

constructor

```
ifstream(const char* s, openmode mode = in);
```

Constructs an object of class **ifstream**, initializing the base class with **istream(&fb)**, then calls **open(s, mode)**.

17.4.8.2.3 ifstream::~ifstream()

destructor

```
virtual ~ifstream();
```

Destroys an object of class **ifstream**.

17.4.8.2.4 ifstream::rdbuf()

rdbuf

```
filebuf* rdbuf() const;
```

Returns **(filebuf*)&fb**.

17.4.8.2.5 ifstream::is_open()

is_open

```
int is_open();
```

Returns **fb.is_open()**.

17.4.8.2.6 ifstream::open(const char*, openmode)

open

```
void open(const char* s, openmode mode = in);
```

Calls **fb.open(s, mode)**. If the call **is_open()** returns zero, calls **setstate(failbit)**.

17.4.8.2.7 ifstream::open(const char*, open_mode)

open

```
//  void open(const char* s, open_mode mode);        optional
```

Calls **open(s, (openmode)mode)**.

17.4.8.2.8 ifstream::close()

close

```
void close();
```

Calls **fb.close()** and, if that function returns zero, calls **setstate(failbit)**.

17.4.8.3 Class ofstream

Class ofstream

```
class ofstream : public ostream {
public:
    ofstream();
    ofstream(const char* s, openmode mode = out);
    virtual ~ofstream();
    filebuf* rdbuf() const;
    int is_open();
    void open(const char* s, openmode mode = out | trunc);
//  void open(const char* s,
        open_mode mode);    optional
    void close();
private:
//  filebuf fb;                             exposition only
};
```

The class **ofstream** is a derivative of **ostream** that assists in the writing of named files. It supplies a **filebuf** object to control the associated sequence. For the sake of exposition, the maintained data is presented here as:

• filebuf *fb*, the **filebuf** object.

17.4.8.3.1 ofstream::ofstream()

constructor
```
ofstream();
```
Constructs an object of class **ofstream**, initializing the base class with **os-tream(&*fb*)**.

17.4.8.3.2 ofstream::ofstream(const char*, openmode)

constructor
```
ofstream(const char* s, openmode mode = out);
```
Constructs an object of class **ofstream**, initializing the base class with **os-tream(&*fb*)**, then calls **open(*s*, *mode*)**.

17.4.8.3.3 ofstream::~ofstream()

destructor
```
virtual ~ofstream();
```
Destroys an object of class **ofstream**.

17.4.8.3.4 ofstream::rdbuf()

rdbuf
```
filebuf* rdbuf() const;
```
Returns **(filebuf*)&*fb***.

17.4.8.3.5 ofstream::is_open()

is_open
```
int is_open();
```
Returns *fb*.**is_open()**.

17.4.8.3.6 ofstream::open(const char*, openmode)

open
```
void open(const char* s, openmode mode = out);
```
Calls *fb*.**open(*s*, *mode*)**. If **is_open()** is then false, calls **set-state(failbit)**.

17.4.8.3.7 ofstream::open(const char*, open_mode)

open
```
//  void open(const char* s, open_mode mode);            optional
```
Calls **open(*s*, (openmode)*mode*)**.

17.4.8.3.8 ofstream::close()

close
```
void close();
```
Calls *fb*.**close()** and, if that function returns zero, calls **setstate(fail-bit)**.

17.4.8.4 Class stdiobuf

Class stdiobuf
```
class stdiobuf : public streambuf {
public:
    stdiobuf(FILE* file_arg);
    virtual ~stdiobuf();
    int buffered() const;
    void buffered(int buf_fl);
protected:
//  virtual int overflow(int c = EOF);                    inherited
//  virtual int pbackfail(int c = EOF);                   inherited
//  virtual int underflow(); inherited
//  virtual int uflow();     inherited
//  virtual int xsgetn(char* s, int n);                   inherited
//  virtual int xsputn(const char* s, int n);             inherited
//  virtual streampos seekoff(streamoff off, ios::seekdir way,
//        ios::openmode which = ios::in | ios::out);      inherited
//  virtual streampos seekpos(streampos sp,
//        ios::openmode which = ios::in | ios::out);      inherited
```

```
//  virtual streambuf* setbuf(char* s, int n);        inherited
//  virtual int sync();                               inherited
private:
//  FILE* file;                                 exposition only
//  int is_buffered;                            exposition only
};
```

The class **stdiobuf** is derived from **streambuf** to associate both the input sequence and the output sequence with an externally supplied object of type **FILE**. Type **FILE** is defined in **<stdio.h>**. For the sake of exposition, the maintained data is presented here as:

- *FILE *file*, points to the **FILE** associated with the stream buffer;
- int *is_buffered*, nonzero if the **stdiobuf** object is *buffered,* and hence need not be kept synchronized with the associated file (as described below).

The restrictions on reading and writing a sequence controlled by an object of class **stdiobuf** are the same as for an object of class **filebuf**.

If an **stdiobuf** object is not buffered and *file* is not a null pointer, it is kept synchronized with the associated file, as follows:

- the call **sputc(***c***)** is equivalent to the call **fputc(***c, file***)**;
- the call **sputbackc(***c***)** is equivalent to the call **ungetc(***c, file***)**;
- the call **sbumpc()** is equivalent to the call **fgetc(***file***)**.

The functions **fgetc(FILE*)**, **fputc(int, FILE*)**, and **ungetc(int, FILE*)** are declared in **<stdio.h>**.

17.4.8.4.1 stdiobuf::stdiobuf(FILE*)

constructor

```
stdiobuf(FILE* file_arg);
```

Constructs an object of class **stdiobuf**, initializing the base class with **streambuf()**, and initializing *file* to *file_arg* and *is_buffered* to zero.

17.4.8.4.2 stdiobuf::~stdiobuf()

destructor

```
virtual ~stdiobuf();
```

Destroys an object of class **stdiobuf**.

17.4.8.4.3 stdiobuf::buffered()

buffered

```
int buffered() const;
```

Returns a nonzero value if *is_buffered* is nonzero.

17.4.8.4.4 stdiobuf::buffered(int)

buffered

```
void buffered(int buf_fl);
```

Assigns *buf_fl* to *is_buffered*.

17.4.8.4.5 stdiobuf::overflow(int)

overflow

```
//  virtual int overflow(int c = EOF);                inherited
```

Behaves the same as **filebuf::overflow(int)**, subject to the buffering requirements specified by *is_buffered*.

17.4.8.4.6 stdiobuf::pbackfail(int)

pbackfail

```
//  virtual int pbackfail(int c = EOF);               inherited
```

Behaves the same as **filebuf::pbackfail(int)**, subject to the buffering requirements specified by *is_buffered*.

17.4.8.4.7 stdiobuf::underflow()

underflow

```
//  virtual int underflow(); inherited
```

Behaves the same as **filebuf::underflow()**, subject to the buffering requirements specified by *is_buffered*.

uflow

17.4.8.4.8 `stdiobuf::uflow()`

```
//  virtual int uflow();                              inherited
```

Behaves the same as `filebuf::uflow()`, subject to the buffering requirements specified by *is_buffered*.

xsgetn

17.4.8.4.9 `stdiobuf::xsgetn(char*, int)`

```
//  virtual int xsgetn(char* s, int n);               inherited
```

Behaves the same as `streambuf::xsgetn(char*, int)`.

xsputn

17.4.8.4.10 `stdiobuf::xsputn(const char*, int)`

```
//  virtual int xsputn(const char* s, int n);         inherited
```

Behaves the same as `streambuf::xsputn(char*, int)`.

seekoff

17.4.8.4.11 `stdiobuf::seekoff(streamoff, ios::seekdir,`
   `ios::openmode)`

```
//  virtual streampos seekoff(streamoff off, ios::seekdir way,
//       ios::openmode which = ios::in | ios::out);   inherited
```

Behaves the same as `filebuf::seekoff(streamoff, ios::seekdir,`
`ios::openmode)`

seekpos

17.4.8.4.12 `stdiobuf::seekpos(streampos, ios::openmode)`

```
//  virtual streampos seekpos(streampos sp,
//       ios::openmode which =  ios::in | ios::out);   inherited
```

Behaves the same as `filebuf::seekpos(streampos, ios::openmode)`

setbuf

17.4.8.4.13 `stdiobuf::setbuf(char*, int)`

```
//  virtual streambuf* setbuf(char* s, int n);        inherited
```

Behaves the same as `filebuf::setbuf(char*, int)`

sync

17.4.8.4.14 `stdiobuf::sync()`

```
//  virtual int sync();                               inherited
```

Behaves the same as `filebuf::sync()`

17.4.8.5 Class `istdiostream`

Class
istdiostream

```
class istdiostream : public istream {
public:
    istdiostream(FILE* file_arg);
    virtual ~istdiostream();
    stdiobuf* rdbuf() const;
    int buffered() const;
    void buffered(int buf_fl);
private:
//  stdiobuf fb;                              exposition only
};
```

The class `istdiostream` is a derivative of `istream` that assists in the reading
of files controlled by objects of type `FILE`. It supplies a `stdiobuf` object to
control the associated sequence. For the sake of exposition, the maintained data
is presented here as:

• `stdiobuf` *fb*, the `stdiobuf` object.

17.4.8.5.1 `istdiostream::istdiostream(FILE*)`

constructor

```
istdiostream(FILE* file_arg);
```

Constructs an object of class `istdiostream`, initializing the base class with
`istream(&fb)` and initializing *fb* with `stdiobuf(file_arg)`.

	17.4.8.5.2 `istdiostream::~istdiostream()`
destructor	`virtual ~istdiostream();`
	Destroys an object of class `istdiostream`.
	17.4.8.5.3 `istdiostream::rdbuf()`
rdbuf	`stdiobuf* rdbuf() const;`
	Returns `(stdiobuf*)&fb`.
	17.4.8.5.4 `istdiostream::buffered()`
buffered	`int buffered() const;`
	Returns a nonzero value if *is_buffered* is nonzero.
	17.4.8.5.5 `istdiostream::buffered(int)`
buffered	`void buffered(int buf_fl);`
	Assigns *buf_fl* to *is_buffered*.
	17.4.8.6 Class `ostdiostream`

Class **ostdiostream**	`class ostdiostream : public ostream {`
	 `public:`
	     `ostdiostream(FILE* file_arg);`
	     `virtual ~ostdiostream();`
	     `stdiobuf* rdbuf() const;`
	     `int buffered() const;`
	     `void buffered(int buf_fl);`
	 `private:`
	 `//  stdiobuf fb;` *exposition only*
	 `};`

The class **ostdiostream** is a derivative of **ostream** that assists in the writing of files controlled by objects of type **FILE**. It supplies a **stdiobuf** object to control the associated sequence. For the sake of exposition, the maintained data is presented here as:

- **stdiobuf** *fb*, the **stdiobuf** object.

	17.4.8.6.1 `ostdiostream::ostdiostream(FILE*)`
constructor	`ostdiostream(FILE* file_arg);`
	Constructs an object of class **ostdiostream**, initializing the base class with **ostream(&fb)** and initializing *fb* with **stdiobuf(file_arg)**.
	17.4.8.6.2 `ostdiostream::~ostdiostream()`
destructor	`virtual ~ostdiostream();`
	Destroys an object of class **ostdiostream**.
	17.4.8.6.3 `ostdiostream::rdbuf()`
rdbuf	`stdiobuf* rdbuf() const;`
	Returns `(stdiobuf*)&fb`.
	17.4.8.6.4 `ostdiostream::buffered()`
buffered	`int buffered() const;`
	Returns a nonzero value if *is_buffered* is nonzero.
	17.4.8.6.5 `ostdiostream::buffered(int)`
buffered	`void buffered(int buf_fl);`
	Assigns *buf_fl* to *is_buffered*.

Footnotes

108) The function may, for example, call `fsetpos(file, &sp.fp)` and/or `fseek(file, sp.pos, SEEK_SET)`, declared in `<stdio.h>`.

Future Directions

showmany   As I mentioned in conjunction with the header `<streambuf>` class `streambuf` has an added virtual member function. (See page 159.) The public access function for it is called **showmany**. It endeavors to tell you how many characters you can safely extract with no fear of blocking while waiting for additional input. The derived classes `filebuf` and `stdiobuf` should have nontrivial overrides for this virtual member function.

wide-character   Once again, I note that a major change is the addition of wide-character
streams   streams. (See page 119.) The classes `filebuf` and `stdiobuf` become template classes parameterized by the type of the stream element. One instantiation, for type *char*, has essentially the same functionality as described in this chapter. Another, for type `wchar_t`, supports streams of elements from some large character set. Classes `ifstream`, `ofstream`, `istdiostream`, and `ostdiostream` change along similar lines.

Using `<fstream>`

You include the header `<fstream>` to make use of any of the classes `ifstream`, `ofstream`, `filebuf`, `istdiostream`, `ostdiostream`, or `stdiobuf`. Objects of these classes let you read and write conventional files. You can open files by name and control them, or control files already opened under control of objects of type `FILE`. For each approach, you can choose among three patterns of access:

- read only
- write only
- read/write

I deal with each of these options in turn, first for files you open by name.

read only   If all you want to do is open and read an existing text file whose name you know, construct an object of class `ifstream`. If you know at construction time what null-terminated file name **s** you wish to use, you can write:

```
ifstream fin(s);
if (fin.is_open())
    <file opened successfully>
```

is_open   If the file is not opened successfully, subsequent extractions will fail. Note, however, that the conventional tests for failure, `!fin` or `fin != 0`, will *not* be false until after you essay such an extraction. That's why I encourage you to make the explicit test `fin.is_open()` immediately after the object is constructed.

close   The resultant stream buffer (pointed at by **fin.rdbuf()**) does not sup-
open port insertions. You can, however, close any currently open file, then open
the file **s2** for reading with the two calls:

```
fin.close(), fin.open(s2);
```

Naturally, you should once again test whether the open succeeded, as
above. The stream position is reset to the beginning of the newly opened
stream. (And the resultant stream buffer *still* does not support insertions.)

You can also construct an **ifstream** object with no open file, using the
default constructor. Presumably, you would later open an existing text file
for reading, as in:

```
ifstream fin;
fin.open(s);
if (fin.is_open())
    <file opened successfully>
```

Destroying an **ifstream** objectcloses any open file associated with it.

open   The code I have shown so far always opens a *text* file, for reading only.
modes A text file can be subject to a certain amount of interpretation, such as
mapping the sequence carriage return/line feed to just line feed (newline).
A *binary* file, on the other hand, delivers each byte from the file unchanged
as a *char* value. To read a binary file, to make a file writable as well, or to
invoke various other options when you open a file, you have to specify an
explicit *open-mode* argument. (Naturally enough, it has type **ios::open-
mode**.) For all member functions that take a file-name argument **s**, the
open-mode **mode** immediately follows. The first example, above, is actually
equivalent to:

```
ifstream fin(s, ios::in);
if (fin.is_open())
    <file opened successfully>
```

You have a number of options for the value of **mode**:

- **ios::in**, to open an existing text file for reading

- **ios::out | ios::trunc**, to create a text file or to open and truncate an
  existing text file for writing

- **ios::out | ios::app**, to create a text file or to open an existing text
  file for writing, where each write occurs at the end of the file

- **ios::in | ios::binary**, to open an existing binary file for reading

- **ios::out | ios::trunc | ios::binary**, to create a binary file or to
  open and truncate an existing binary file for writing

- **ios::out | ios::app | ios::binary**, to create a binary file or to open
  an existing binary file for writing, where each write occurs at the end of
  the file

- **ios::in | ios::out**, to open an existing text file for reading and
  writing

- **ios::in | ios::out | ios::trunc**, to create a text file or to open and
  truncate an existing text file for reading and writing

- **`ios::in | ios::out | ios::app`**, to create a text file or to open an existing text file for reading and writing, where each write occurs at the end of the file

- **`ios::in | ios::out | ios::binary`**, to open an existing binary file for reading and writing

- **`ios::in | ios::out | ios::trunc | ios::binary`**, to create a binary file or to open and truncate an existing binary file for reading and writing

- **`ios::in | ios::out | ios::app | ios::binary`**, to create a binary file or to open an existing binary file for reading and writing, where each write occurs at the end of the file

If you also set **`ios::ate`** in **`mode`**, the file is positioned at end-of-file immediately after it is opened.

write only   If all you want to do is create a new text file — or truncate an existing text file — then open it for writing, construct an object of class **`ofstream`** to control insertions into it. You can write:

```
ofstream fout(s);
if (fout.is_open())
    <file opened successfully>
```

then insert into **`fout`** just like any other output stream. As with class **`ifstream`**, you can follow the file name **`s`** with a **`mode`** argument. If you omit the **`mode`** argument, as above, it defaults to **`ios::out`**.

You can also construct an **`ofstream`** object with the default constructor and later create it for writing, as in:

```
ofstream fout;
fout.open(s);
if (fout.is_open())
    <file opened successfully>
```

In either case, the resultant stream buffer (pointed at by **`fout.rdbuf()`**) does not support extractions. And, of course, destroying an **`ofstream`** object closes any open file associated with it.

read/write   If you want to open a file that you can read as well as write, you need two objects to control the input and output streams. The classes **`ifstream`** and **`ofstream`** are highly symmetric, at least in this regard. Thus, you have three equally valid ways to do the job. If you don't want to open a file initially, you can write:

```
ifstream ifile;
ostream ofile(ifile.rdbuf());
```

or:

```
ofstream ofile;
istream ifile(ofile.rdbuf());
```

or:

```
filebuf fb;
istream ifile(&fb);
ostream ofile(&fb);
```

All approaches cause **ifile** to control the input stream and **ofile** to control the output stream.

You can also open a file **s** in each of these three cases. Since the default values for the **mode** argument rarely make sense here, I show the argument explicitly in each case:

```
ifstream ifile(s, mode);
ostream ofile(ifile.rdbuf());
if (ifile.is_open())
    <file opened successfully>
```

or:

```
ofstream ofile(s, mode);
istream ifile(ofile.rdbuf());
if (ofile.is_open())
    <file opened successfully>
```

or:

```
filebuf fb;
istream ifile(&fb);
ostream ofile(&fb);
if (fb.open(s, mode))
    <file opened successfully>;
```

Note that the last test for a successful open differs from the earlier ones. As usual, when the **filebuf** object is destroyed, any open file associated with it is closed.

FILE The classes **istdiostream**, **ostdiostream**, and **stdiobuf** provide additional capability within the header **<fstream>**. They let you control files already opened under control of an object of type **FILE**. For example, the function **fopen**, declared in **<stdio.h>**, returns a non-null pointer to **FILE** when it successfully opens a file. Numerous other functions, declared in the same header, support C stream reads and writes to the opened file.

The same header also declares three well known objects of type pointer to **FILE** that control the three standard streams:

stdin ■ **stdin**, controlling the standard input stream

stdout ■ **stdout**, controlling the standard output stream

stderr ■ **stderr**, controlling the standard error stream

The header **<iostream>** declares several **istream** and **ostream** objects that work in concert with these objects to support iostreams operations on the standard streams. (See next chapter.) You can nevertheless use the facilities in **<fstream>** to control, say, **stdout** with an additional object you construct.

As usual, there are three patterns of access to discuss: read only, write only, and read/write. I cover them in order.

read only If all you want to do is read a stream controlled by a **FILE** object, construct an object of class **istdiostream**. You must know at construction time the argument value **pf**, of type *pointer to* **FILE**. You can write:

```
istdiostream fin(pf);
```

If **pf** is a null pointer, or if the stream it controls cannot be read, all
subsequent extraction operations will fail. You cannot, however, test
whether **fin** is associated with an open file.

When **fin** is destroyed, the stream ***pf** is *not* closed. Nor should you
close the stream, by calling **fclose(pf)**, before **fin** is destroyed. The call
discredits **pf**, so even a subsequent attempt to *access* the pointer itself can
cause a program to terminate abnormally. Worse, subsequent attempts to
control the file may do all sorts of insane things that are *not* diagosed.

buffered You can control the degree of buffering within **fin**. Initially, **fin.buff-
ered()** returns zero, indicating that no buffering occurs. Put simply, you
can alternate the calls **fin.get()** and **fgetc(pf)** and read alternate characters from the file.

Once you call **fin.buffered(1)**, however, **fin.buffered(1)** returns a
nonzero value. Thereafter, buffering *may* occur. Put simply, the call **fin.
get()** may encourage the stream buffer associated with **fin** to gobble an
arbitrary number of characters, not just the one you requested. A subsequent call to **fgetc(pf)** will not necessarily deliver the next character
you would expect.

If you resist the temptation to access ***pf** directly, buffering causes no
problems. On the contrary, it offers the controlling stream buffer the opportunity to improve performance, sometimes considerably. A wise rule of
thumb, therefore, is *never* to enable buffering for a file accessed both via a
stream buffer and via C stream function calls. If the stream buffer is the sole
agent accessing the file, *always* enable buffering.

write only If all you want to do is write a stream controlled by a **FILE** object,
construct an object of class **ostdiostream**. You must know at construction
time the argument value **pf**, of type *pointer to* **FILE**. You can write:

        ostdiostream fout(pf);

If **pf** is a null pointer, or if the stream it controls cannot be written, all
subsequent insertion operations will fail. As with an **istiodstream** object,
you cannot test whether **fout** is associated with an open file. The same
remarks also apply about not closing the file until **fout** is destroyed.
Equally, the same considerations apply about when to buffer, or not to
buffer, a stream associated with an **ostdiostream** object.

read/write Finally, if you want to both read and write a stream controlled by a **FILE**
object, you need two objects to control the input and output streams. The
classes **istdiostream** and **ostdiostream** are highly symmetric. Thus, you
have three equally valid ways to do the job:

        istdiostream ifile(pf);
        ostream ofile(ifile.rdbuf());

or:

        ostdiostream ofile(pf);
        istream ifile(ofile.rdbuf());

or:

```
stdiobuf sb(pf);
istream ifile(&sb);
ostream ofile(&sb);
```

In the third case, you enable buffering by calling **sb.buffered(1)**.

stream   Earlier in this chapter, I discussed the limitations on positioning within
positioning files. (See page 309.) For a discussion of stream-positioning operations in
general, see page 160. Your safest bet, as always, is to memorize a file
position you want to return to, as an object of type **streampos**. Later on in
the program, while the file is still open, you can use the value stored in this
object to return to the memorized file position.

For a binary file that is not too large, you can represent a stream position
as an object of type **streamoff**. You can thus perform arithmetic, on byte
displacements from the beginning of a file, to determine new stream
positions. The UNIX operating system represents text files the same as
binary. Hence, it extends the same latitude in stream positioning to all files,
not just binary. But few other systems share this simplicity. Don't write
portable code that counts on it.

A file opened both for reading and writing requires intervening stream-
positioning requests when switching from reading to writing, or back.
Again, some systems may relax this requirement, but don't count on it in a
portable program.

setbuf   Finally, the **streambuf** virtual member functions **setbuf** and **sync** are
sync given nontrivial semantics in the derived class **filebuf**. The former, however, is defined in terms of the function **setvbuf**, declared in **<stdio.h>**,
which does not itself promise much. And the latter is generally called as
often as necessary in the normal course of business. (See page 221.) I
recommend, therefore, that you not call either **pubsetbuf** or **pubsync**, the
public member functions that call these virtual member functions on your
behalf.

Implementing **<fstream>**

fstream   Figure 13.1 shows the file **fstream**, which implements the standard
header **<fstream>**. It defines the classes **filebuf**, **ifstream**, **ofstream**,
stdiobuf, **istdiostream**, and **ostdiostream**. I begin with several notes
on class **filebuf**, which is the workhorse class for this header.

_Filet   The incomplete type declaration **struct _Filet** is an alias for the type
FILE, declared in **<stdio.h>**. The header **<fstream>** is not permitted to
include **<stdio.h>**, but it needs to declare parameters and member function return values compatible with type **FILE**. A secret synonym solves the
problem. My implementation of the Standard C library (**Pla92**) introduces
_Filet for a similar reason. For another implementation, you may have to
alter the name, or introduce extra machinery in the internal header
<yxvals.h>, to achieve the same effect. (See Appendix A: Interfaces.)

```
// fstream standard header
#ifndef _FSTREAM_
#define _FSTREAM_
#include <istream>
#include <ostream>
            // class filebuf
struct _Filet;
class filebuf : public streambuf {
public:
    filebuf(_Filet *_F = 0)
        {_Init(_F); }
    filebuf(ios::_Uninitialized)
        : streambuf(ios::_Noinit) {}
    virtual ~filebuf();
    _Bool is_open() const
        {return ((_File != 0)); }
    filebuf *open(const char *, ios::openmode);
    filebuf *open(const char *_N, ios::open_mode _M)
        {return (open(_N, (openmode)_M)); }
    filebuf *close();
protected:
    virtual int overflow(int = EOF);
    virtual int pbackfail(int = EOF);
    virtual int underflow();
    virtual int uflow();
    virtual int xsgetn(char *, int);
    virtual int xsputn(const char *, int);
    virtual streampos seekoff(streamoff, ios::seekdir,
        ios::openmode = (ios::openmode)(ios::in | ios::out));
    virtual streampos seekpos(streampos,
        ios::openmode = (ios::openmode)(ios::in | ios::out));
    virtual streambuf *setbuf(char *, int);
    virtual int sync();
    _Filet *_Init(_Filet * = 0, _Bool = 0);
private:
    _Bool _Closef;
    _Filet *_File;
    };
            // class ifstream
class ifstream : public istream {
public:
    ifstream()
        : ios(&_Fb), istream(&_Fb) {}
    ifstream(const char *_S, openmode _M = in)
        : ios(&_Fb), istream(&_Fb) {_Fb.open(_S, _M); }
    virtual ~ifstream();
    filebuf *rdbuf() const
        {return ((filebuf *)&_Fb); }
    _Bool is_open() const
        {return (_Fb.is_open()); }
    void open(const char *_S, openmode _M = in)
        {if (_Fb.open(_S, _M) == 0)
            setstate(failbit); }
    void open(const char *_S, open_mode _M)
        {open(_S, (openmode)_M); }
```

Continuing
fstream
Part 2 of 3

```
        void close()
            {if (_Fb.close() == 0)
                setstate(failbit); }
private:
    filebuf _Fb;
    };
        // class ofstream
class ofstream : public ostream {
public:
    ofstream()
        : ios(&_Fb), ostream(&_Fb) {}
    ofstream(const char *_S, openmode _M = out | trunc)
        : ios(&_Fb), ostream(&_Fb) {_Fb.open(_S, _M); }
    virtual ~ofstream();
    filebuf *rdbuf() const
        {return ((filebuf *)&_Fb); }
    _Bool is_open() const
        {return (_Fb.is_open()); }
    void open(const char *_S, openmode _M = out | trunc)
        {if (_Fb.open(_S, _M) == 0)
            setstate(failbit); }
    void open(const char *_S, open_mode _M)
        {open(_S, (openmode)_M); }
    void close()
        {if (_Fb.close() == 0)
            setstate(failbit); }
private:
    filebuf _Fb;
    };
        // class stdiobuf
class stdiobuf : public filebuf {
public:
    stdiobuf(_Filet *_F)
        : filebuf(_F), _Is_buffered(0) {}
    virtual ~stdiobuf();
    _Bool buffered() const
        {return (_Is_buffered); }
    void buffered(_Bool _F)
        {_Is_buffered = _F; }
private:
    _Bool _Is_buffered;
    };
        // class istdiostream
class istdiostream : public istream {
public:
    istdiostream(_Filet *_F)
        : ios(&_Fb), istream(&_Fb), _Fb(_F) {}
    virtual ~istdiostream();
    stdiobuf *rdbuf() const
        {return ((stdiobuf *)&_Fb); }
    _Bool buffered() const
        {return (_Fb.buffered()); }
    void buffered(_Bool _F)
        {_Fb.buffered(_F); }
private:
```

```
        stdiobuf _Fb;
        };
            // class ostdiostream
class ostdiostream : public ostream {
public:
        ostdiostream(_Filet *_F)
            : ios(&_Fb), ostream(&_Fb), _Fb(_F) {}
        virtual ~ostdiostream();
        stdiobuf *rdbuf() const
            {return ((stdiobuf *)&_Fb); }
        _Bool buffered() const
            {return (_Fb.buffered()); }
        void buffered(_Bool _F)
            {_Fb.buffered(_F); }
private:
        stdiobuf _Fb;
        };
#endif                                                      □
```

_File   I added a constructor with the signature `filebuf(_Filet *)`. (I did so
_Init   by adding a default argument to the default constructor.) This implemen-
tation performs all file operations mediated by class `filebuf` through an
associated `FILE` object. The member object **_File** points at the associated
object, or stores a null pointer if none exists. The secret member function
_Init, described below, initializes a `filebuf` object. Its arguments specify
the initial values stored in the **_File** member objects.

_Noinit   For a description of the type **_Uninitialized**, and the value **_Noinit**,
_Uninitialized see page 132.

stdiobuf   Note that class **stdiobuf** is based on class `filebuf`. The draft C++
Standard says (17.4.8.4) that **stdiobuf** is derived directly from `streambuf`.
I pulled a similar trick in the previous chapter, deriving `stringbuf` from
`strstreambuf`. As before, such indirect derivation is permitted by the
library "front matter" (17.1.5.10.3).

_Closef   A fundamental difference exists between the classes `filebuf` and
stdiobuf, however. Destroying a `filebuf` object closes any associated file.
Destroying a **stdiobuf** object does not. I added the member object **_Closef**
to `filebuf` to tell its destructor what to do. The stored value is nonzero
only if the file is to be closed when the object is destroyed. That only
happens after `filebuf::open` successfully opens a file.

filebuf.c   Figure 13.2 shows the file `filebuf.c`, which defines a number of functions required for practically any use of class `filebuf`. On the face of it, this
implementation errs strongly on the side of portability, at the cost of
performance. All of the member functions defined here will work atop *any*
Standard C library. Moreover, none of the functions buffer reads or writes,
beyond whatever buffering that may occur in the associated `FILE` object.

_Init   Before you dismiss this as a purely tutorial implementation of class
`filebuf`, take a closer look at the last function definition in the file. As I
mentioned above, the member function **_Init** initializes all `filebuf` ob-

jects when they are constructed. It also reinitializes an object after a successful call to **filebuf::open**. And it can be made to do one very important
additional thing.

_HAS_PJP_CLIB   As I indicated much earlier, I defined the base class **streambuf** from the
outset with a bit of extra flexibility. (See page 170.) The six pointers that
control in-memory buffers are all indirect pointers. You can point them at
pointers within the **streambuf** object itself, or at pointers in another object.
For the derived class **filebuf**, you can sometimes choose the latter course
to advantage. That's why the macro **_HAS_PJP_CLIB** chooses between two
different calls to **streambuf::_Init**, which initializes all those direct and
indirect pointers in the base subobject.

For an arbitrary Standard C library, the internal header **<yxvals.h>**
should contain no definition for this macro. The code works correctly, if not
as fast as many would like. But for operation atop my implementation of
the Standard C library (**Pla92**), you can do much better. Define the macro
_HAS_PJP_CLIB in **<yxvals.h>** and the indirect pointers are set differently.
They point at the pointers stored in the **FILE** object controlling access to the
file. The pointer discipline is similar enough for things to work properly.

getchar   Here's why. I designed the **FILE** structure in C so that the macros
getchar and **putchar** could expand to inline code that is reasonably small
and generally very fast. The input and output streams are each controlled
by a triple of pointers to characters. The C++ equivalent of the macro
getchar, for example, is the inline function definition:

```
inline int getchar()
    {return ((_Files[0]->_Next < _Files[0]->_Rend
        ? *_Files[0]->_Next++ : fgetc(_Files[0]))); }
```

Compare this code with the definition of the analogous **streambuf** public
member function **sgetc**:

```
int sgetc()
    {return (gptr() != 0 && gptr() < egptr()
        ? *_Gn() : underflow()); }
```

The only real difference is a small one. **getchar** can assume that its "next"
pointer **_Files[0]->_Next** is never a null pointer. It certainly doesn't hurt
for **sgetc** to make the extra test.

What typically happens when extracting from an input stream is pretty
much what you'd hope for. If the buffer is empty, **sgetc** calls **underflow**.
The overriding definition in class **filebuf** rediscovers that the buffer is
empty and calls **fgetc** to supply a single character. Fortunately, **fgetc** often
delivers up a whole buffer full of additional characters in the bargain.

The next several hundred calls to **sgetc** simply exercise inline code that
accesses the stored character value directly from the buffer and updates the
"next" pointer to note its consumption. This is the same pointer as is used
by **getchar**, either as a macro or an inline function definition. It is also, of
course, the same pointer as is used by **fgetc**. Thus, tight synchronization
is maintained across all flavors of input. Equally important, many character

```
// filebuf -- filebuf basic members
#include <stdio.h>
#include <fstream>

filebuf::~filebuf()
    {                                          // destruct a filebuf
    if (_Closef)
        close();
    }

filebuf *filebuf::close()
    {                                          // close a file
    if (_File != 0 && fclose(_File) == 0)
        {                                      // note successful close
        _Init();
        return (this);
        }
    else
        return (0);
    }

int filebuf::overflow(int ch)
    {                                          // try to write output
    return (pptr() != 0 && pptr() < epptr()
        ? (*_Pn()++ = ch)
        : _File == 0 ? EOF : ch == EOF ? 0 : fputc(ch, _File));
    }

int filebuf::pbackfail(int ch)
    {                                          // try to pushback a character
    return (gptr() != 0 && eback() < gptr() && ch == gptr()[-1]
        ? *--_Gn()
        : _File == 0 || ch == EOF ? EOF : ungetc(ch, _File));
    }

int filebuf::underflow()
    {                                          // try to peek at input
    return (gptr() != 0 && gptr() < egptr()
        ? *_Gn()
        : _File == 0 ? EOF : ungetc(fgetc(_File), _File));
    }

int filebuf::uflow()
    {                                          // try to consume input
    return (gptr() != 0 && gptr() < egptr()
        ? *_Gn()++
        : _File == 0 ? EOF : fgetc(_File));
    }

int filebuf::xsgetn(char *s, int n)
    {                                          // read n characters
    return (_File == 0 ? 0 : fread(s, 1, n, _File));
    }
```

```
int filebuf::xsputn(const char *s, int n)
    {                                         // write n characters
    return (_File == 0 ? 0 : fwrite(s, 1, n, _File));
    }

streampos filebuf::seekoff(streamoff off, ios::seekdir way,
    ios::openmode)
    {                                         // seek by specified offset
    return (streampos(_File == 0
        || fseek(_File, off, way) != 0
         ? _BADOFF : streamoff(ftell(_File)))));
    }

streampos filebuf::seekpos(streampos sp, ios::openmode)
    {                                         // seek to memorized position
    return (_File == 0 || fsetpos(_File, sp._Fpos()) != 0
        || fseek(_File, sp.offset(), SEEK_CUR) != 0
        || fgetpos(_File, sp._Fpos()) != 0
        ? streampos(_BADOFF)
        : streampos(0, sp._Fpos())));
    }

streambuf *filebuf::setbuf(char *s, int n)
    {                                         // provide a file buffer
    return (_File == 0 || setvbuf(_File, s, _IOFBF, n) != 0
        ? 0 : this);
    }

int filebuf::sync()
    {                                         // synchronize buffer with file
    return (_File == 0 ? 0 : fflush(_File));
    }

FILE *filebuf::_Init(FILE *fp, _Bool closef)
    {                                         // initialize buffer pointers
#if _HAS_PJP_CLIB
    if (fp == 0)
        streambuf::_Init();
    else
        streambuf::_Init((char **)&fp->_Buf,
            (char **)&fp->_Next,
            (char **)&fp->_Rend,
            (char **)&fp->_Buf,
            (char **)&fp->_Next,
            (char **)&fp->_Wend);
#else
    streambuf::_Init();
#endif
    _Closef = closef;
    _File = fp;
    return (_File);
    }
```

Figure 13.3:
fiopen.c

```
// fiopen -- filebuf::open(const char *, ios::openmode)
#include <stdio.h>
#include <fstream>

filebuf *filebuf::open(const char *name, ios::openmode mode)
    {                                                    // open a file
    static const char *mods[] = {
        "r", "w", "a", "rb", "wb", "ab", "r+", "w+", "a+",
            "r+b", "w+b", "a+b", 0};
    static const int valid[] = {
        ios::in, ios::out|ios::trunc, ios::out|ios::app,
        ios::in|ios::binary, ios::out|ios::trunc|ios::binary,
        ios::out|ios::app|ios::binary, ios::in|ios::out,
        ios::in|ios::out|ios::trunc, ios::in|ios::out|ios::app,
        ios::in|ios::out|ios::binary,
        ios::in|ios::out|ios::trunc|ios::binary,
        ios::in|ios::out|ios::app|ios::binary, 0};
    FILE *fp;
    int n;
    ios::openmode atefl = mode & ios::ate;
    if (_File != 0)
        return (0);
    mode &= ~ios::ate;
    for (n = 0; valid[n] != 0 && valid[n] != mode; ++n)
        ;
    if (valid[n] == 0 || (fp = fopen(name, mods[n])) == 0)
        return (0);
    if (!atefl || fseek(fp, 0, SEEK_END) == 0)
        {                             // success, initialize and return
        _Init(fp, 1);
        return (this);
        }
    fclose(fp);                                     // can't position at end
    return (0);
    }                                                                      □
```

extractions within **istream** extractors have *no* function-call overhead whatsoever. (See Chapter 8: **<istream>**.)

Of course, the same rules apply to output streams. Most characters inserted by **streambuf::sputc** get stored directly into the output buffer, with the "next" pointer suitably updated. Thus, many character insertions within **ostream** inserters also avoid function-call overhead. (See Chapter 8: **<ostream>**.) *Quod erat demonstrandum.*

Any implementation of the Standard C library that follows this discipline for **FILE** pointers can benefit from the same performance improvement. You probably have to change the pointer member names in the definition of **filebuf::_Init**. Nothing else need change, however.

fiopen.c   Figure 13.3 shows the file **fiopen.c**, which shows the member function **filebuf::open**. It maps the **mode** argument, of type **openmode**, to the equivalent mode string expected by the function **fopen**. If that function

Figure 13.4:
ifstream.c

```
// ifstream -- ifstream basic members
#include <fstream>

ifstream::~ifstream()
    {                                          // destruct an ifstream
    }                                                                □
```

Figure 13.5:
ofstream.c

```
// ofstream -- ofstream basic members
#include <fstream>

ofstream::~ofstream()
    {                                          // destruct an ofstream
    }                                                                □
```

Figure 13.6:
stdiobuf.c

```
// stdiobuf -- stdiobuf basic members
#include <fstream>

stdiobuf::~stdiobuf()
    {                                          // destruct a stdiobuf
    }                                                                □
```

Figure 13.7:
istdiost.c

```
// istdiostream -- istdiostream basic members
#include <fstream>

istdiostream::~istdiostream()
    {                                          // destruct an istdiostream
    }                                                                □
```

Figure 13.8:
ostdiost.c

```
// ostdiostream -- ostdiostream basic members
#include <fstream>

ostdiostream::~ostdiostream()
    {                                          // destruct an ostdiostream
    }                                                                □
```

succeeds in opening the file, it reinitializes the **filebuf** object to control the associated **FILE** object.

ifstream.c   All the remaining source files needed to implement the header
ofstream.c **<fstream>** are trivial. Figure 13.4 shows the file **ifstream.c**, which defines
stdiobuf.c the destructor for class **ifstream**. Figure 13.5 shows the file **ofstream.c**,
istdiost.c which defines the destructor for class **ofstream**. Figure 13.6 shows the file
ostdiost.c **stdiobuf.c**, which defines the destructor for class **stdiobuf**. Figure 13.7
shows the file **istdiost.c**, which defines the destructor for class **istdiostream**. And Figure 13.8 shows the file **ostdiost.c**, which defines the
destructor for class **ostdiostream**.

```
// test <fstream>
#include <assert.h>
#include <stdio.h>
#include <string.h>
#include <iostream>
#include <fstream>

int main()
    {                     // test basic workings of fstream definitions
    ifstream ifs;
    ofstream ofs;
    const char *tn = tmpnam(NULL);
    assert(tn != NULL);
        // test closed file closing
    assert(!ifs.is_open() && !ifs.fail());
    ifs.close();
    assert(ifs.fail() && ifs.rdbuf()->close() == 0);
    assert(!ofs.is_open() && !ofs.fail());
    ofs.close();
    assert(ofs.fail() && ofs.rdbuf()->close() == 0);
        // test output file operations
    ofs.clear(), ofs.open(tn, ios::out | ios::trunc);
    assert(ofs.is_open() && ofs.rdbuf()->is_open());
    ofs << "this is a test" << endl;
    ofs.close();
    assert(!ofs.is_open() && ofs.good());
    assert(ofs.rdbuf()->open(tn, ios::app | ios::out) != 0);
    ofs << "this is only a test" << endl;
    ofs.close();
    assert(!ofs.is_open() && ofs.good());
        // test input file operations
    char buf[50];
    ifs.clear(), ifs.open(tn, ios::in);
    assert(ifs.is_open() && ifs.rdbuf()->is_open());
    ifs.getline(buf, sizeof (buf));
    assert(strcmp(buf, "this is a test") == 0);
    streampos p1 = ifs.rdbuf()->pubseekoff(0, ios::cur);
    ifs.getline(buf, sizeof (buf));
    assert(strcmp(buf, "this is only a test") == 0);
    assert(ifs.rdbuf()->pubseekpos(p1) == p1);
    ifs.getline(buf, sizeof (buf));
    assert(strcmp(buf, "this is only a test") == 0);
    ifs.rdbuf()->pubseekoff(0, ios::beg);
    ifs.getline(buf, sizeof (buf));
    assert(strcmp(buf, "this is a test") == 0);
    ifs.close();
    assert(!ifs.is_open() && ifs.good());
        // test combined file operations
    ifstream nifs(tn, ios::in | ios::out);
    ostream nofs(nifs.rdbuf());
    assert(nifs.is_open() && nifs.good() && nofs.good());
    nifs.rdbuf()->pubseekoff(0, ios::end);
    nofs << "this is still just a test" << endl;
    nifs.rdbuf()->pubseekoff(0, ios::beg);
    nifs.getline(buf, sizeof (buf));
```

```
        assert(strcmp(buf, "this is a test") == 0);
        nifs.getline(buf, sizeof (buf));
        assert(strcmp(buf, "this is only a test") == 0);
        nifs.getline(buf, sizeof (buf));
        assert(strcmp(buf, "this is still just a test") == 0);
        nifs.close();
        ofstream nnofs(tn, ios::in | ios::out | ios::ate);
        assert(nnofs.is_open());
        nnofs << "one last test" << endl;
        nnofs.close();
            // test stdiobuf operations
        FILE *fi = fopen(tn, "r+");
        istdiostream istd(fi);
        ostdiostream ostd(fi);
        assert(fi != 0);
        assert(istd.buffered() == 0
            && istd.rdbuf()->buffered() == 0);
        istd.rdbuf()->buffered(0), istd.buffered(1);
        assert(istd.buffered() != 0
            && istd.rdbuf()->buffered() != 0);
        assert(ostd.buffered() == 0
            && ostd.rdbuf()->buffered() == 0);
        ostd.rdbuf()->buffered(0), ostd.buffered(1);
        assert(ostd.buffered() != 0
            && ostd.rdbuf()->buffered() != 0);
        istd.getline(buf, sizeof (buf));
        assert(strcmp(buf, "this is a test") == 0);
        p1 = istd.rdbuf()->pubseekoff(0, ios::end);
        ostd << "still one more last test" << endl;
        assert(ostd.rdbuf()->pubseekpos(p1) == p1);
        istd.getline(buf, sizeof (buf));
        assert(strcmp(buf, "still one more last test") == 0);
        assert(fclose(fi) == 0 && remove(tn) == 0);
        cout << "SUCCESS testing <fstream>" << endl;
        return (0);
        }
```

Testing **<fstream>**

Figure 13.9 shows the file **tfstream.c**. It tests the basic properties of the classes defined in **<fstream>**. It does so by manipulating a temporary file whose name is obtained by calling **tmpnam**, declared in **<stdio.h>**. First it tries to write the file, then read from it, then intermix reads and writes. It also performs some modest file-positioning operations along the way. Finally, it repeats a few of these operations using the classes **istdiostream** and **ostdiostream**.

If all goes well, the program prints:

SUCCESS testing <fstream>

and takes a normal exit. It also removes the temporary file it created.

Exercises

Exercise 13.1 Is there any difference between opening a file by name twice and opening it once, then associating two **istream** or **ostream** objects with the controlling stream buffer?

Exercise 13.2 What happens if you manipulate multiple **stdiobuf** objects all associated with the same **FILE** object? Can you make the behavior predictable?

Exercise 13.3 What happens if you associate an **ostdiostream** object with **stdin**?

Exercise 13.4 Why does **filebuf::close** call **filebuf::_Init**? (See the source file **filebuf.c** on page 330.)

Exercise 13.5 Measure the performance of file reads and writes using this implementation of **<fstream>** and one that comes with a C++ compiler. If you can, also measure the performance of **filebuf.c** translated with and without the macro **_HAS_PJP_CLIB** defined.

Exercise 13.6 The function **ungetc**, declared in **<stdio.h>**, sometimes pushes characters onto a stack within the **FILE** object. While this stack is not empty, the input buffer is made to look empty so that **getchar** always calls the function **fgetc**. Should an implementation of class **filebuf** that points inside a **FILE** object point into this push-back stack? If so, describe how the stack must be implemented to support proper extractions. If not, why not?

Exercise 13.7 Modify the functions defined in **filebuf.c**, as needed, to support automatic switching between reading and writing. If, for example, a read fails, the function should perform an innocuous stream-positioning operation, then try the read again. Are there any circumstances where this added functionality can also impact performance?

Exercise 13.8 [Harder] Implement the classes defined in **<fstream>** without making use of the Standard C library. How do you deal with unbuffered operation of **stdiobuf** objects? How portable is the code?

Exercise 13.9 [Very hard] Implement a portable method for positioning arbitrary files as if they were sequences of bytes, so that you can perform arithmetic freely (and successfully) on **streampos** objects.

Chapter 14: `<iostream>`

Background

The header `<iostream>` declares four objects:

cin ▪ **cin**, to control the unbuffered standard input stream (as does **stdin**)

cout ▪ **cout**, to control the unbuffered standard output stream (as does **stdout**)

cerr ▪ **cerr**, to control the unbuffered standard error stream (as does **stderr**)

clog ▪ **clog**, to control the buffered standard error stream (as does **stderr**)

These objects are constructed for you, so they offer a particularly easy way to perform input and output in a C++ program. The three objects that are unbuffered also support reads and writes that are properly synchronized with any C file operations that the program may also perform on the standard streams. (See the previous chapter for a more precise description of buffered and unbuffered operations on stream buffers.)

The header `<iostream>` is in many ways the culmination of all the iostreams machinery that has gone before in this book. Historically, in fact, the header `<iostream.h>` includes everything represented here in the headers `<ios>`, `<streambuf>`, `<istream>`, `<ostream>`, and `<iostream>`. The general assumption has been that, if you want to work with any part of iostreams, you certainly want to declare **cin** and friends as well.

The four objects declared in `<iostream>` also share a peculiar property. They are all constructed before any expression that accesses them, even if that expression is in a constructor for a static object. Equally, none of these objects is destroyed, at least until after the execution of the last expression that accesses them, even if that expression is in a destructor for a static object. That means you can read and write the standard streams before **main** is called and after **main** returns. At the very least, such latitude is very convenient for debugging.

Pulling it off takes a bit of trickery, however. Consider the problem. Unless the Standard C++ library indulges in some extra-linguistic magic, `<iostream>` must contain declarations something like:

```
extern istream cin;
extern ostream cout;
extern ostream cerr;
extern ostream clog
```

One of the object modules linked to form a program must define these objects, if any other object module refers to them. Say a constructor for the static object **x** extracts characters from **cin**. Then **cin** must be constructed before **x** is. But C++ defines no ordering among object modules for the calling of constructors for static objects. The language cannot guarantee that the two objects are constructed in the proper order.

Fortunately, the language does define the ordering of constructor calls *within* a given object module. It promises to construct objects in the order in which they appear in the translation unit that defines the object module. You can't define **cin** early in each translation unit — exactly one instance of the object must occur throughout the entire program. But you can define *something* early enough to give you a fighting chance.

Init   That something is an object of class **ios::Init**. I promised way back in Chapter 6: **<ios>** that I'd return to this nested class, and at last I have. An important part of the trick to constructing **cin** and friends is an additional declaration in **<iostream>**. It looks something like:

```
static ios::Init _Ios_init;
```

This declares an object with the secret name **_Ios_init**, local to the translation unit. Because the name doesn't have external linkage, each translation unit that includes **<iostream>** declares a separate instance of the object. Because class **ios::Init** defines a default constructor, that constructor gets called to initialize the object. And because you must include a header before you make any reference to anything it declares or defines, that default constructor gets called in each translation unit before any static constructor can execute that references **cin** and friends.

placement   So far so good. A mechanism exists to get control in time. Presumably, it **new** can ensure that **cin** and friends are properly constructed. For that, you can use a *placement* **new** expression. (See page 83.) Say, for example, you want to construct **cin** with the single-argument constructor that specifies a pointer to the stream buffer **fin**. You can then write:

```
new (&cin) istream(&fin);
```

The effect is as if you had originally defined **cin** by writing:

```
istream cin(&fin);
```

empty   But this raises another problem. The definition for **cin** is also going to **constructor** call a constructor. Either the definition will occur before the placement **new** expression executes or after it:

- Say the definition occurs first. If it does anything nontrivial — such as allocating storage and storing a pointer to it in the constructed object — the placement **new** is going to stomp all over the result. This is bad hygiene.

- Say the placement **new** expression occurs first. If the definition later stores much anything at all in the object, it will mess up the effect of the placement **new**. This is disastrous.

The only scenario that works is to have the definition call a constructor that *does nothing at all*. Then it doesn't matter whether the definition occurs before or after. So long as the placement **new** expression does any necessary initializing before the first use of the object, everything works fine. Classes **ios**, **istream**, **ostream**, and who knows what else must each have a constructor that does nothing. For much the same reason, each of these classes must also have an empty (virtual) destructor. Otherwise, a critical object might be destroyed before it is accessed from the destructor for another static object.

nifty   The final trick is to avoid constructing **cin** and friends too many times. **counter** It's bad enough to have to *double construct* so many important objects within the iostreams package. You certainly don't want to construct them all once for each translation unit in a program that includes **<iostream>**. Class **ios::Init** again comes to the rescue by defining a static member object for counting constructor calls, as in:

```
static int _Init_cnt;
```

Such a member object is shared across all objects of class **ios::Init**. Say the member object is initialized to −1, and that the constructor for **ios::Init** increments this common counter each time it is called. Then a given call to the constructor knows whether it is the first such call. The counter increments to zero only on that first call. And *that* is the call that does the actual construction of **cin** and friends (and any support objects). This trick is known as the "nifty counter" technique. With just a little more logic, the nifty counter also can tell when to flush all the output streams, in preparation for program termination.

explicit   So there's at least one way to ensure that **cin** and friends have such an **initialization** extraordinarily useful lifetime. The trick is clever enough, but you might still wonder why the draft C++ Standard spells out so much of the machinery. Why not leave it to each implementation to solve the problem in its own way, under the hood as it were?

As it turns out, situations can arise where even all this trickery fails to deliver. Say the function **f** is defined in one translation unit and is called during the construction of a static object in another translation unit. If **f** wants to extract from **cin**, it needs to be sure that **cin** has been properly constructed, as described above. But calling a function in a translation unit does *not* ensure that static constructors for that translation unit have first been called. The nifty counter supplied by the header **<iostream>** may not come through in time.

The fix is to explicitly initialize an **ios::Init** object within **f**, as in:

```
void f()
    {                               // read during static construction
    ios::Init not_otherwise_used;
    <can now reference cin, etc>
    }
```

If this mechanism were not spelled out in the draft C++ Standard, there would be no way to solve the initialization problem portably.

What the Draft C++ Standard Says

The header **<iostream>** is deceptively short. It has been chopped down to the basics of declaring the necessary objects. Remember, however, that it drags in considerably more stuff.

17.4.9 Header <iostream>

<iostream>

The header **<iostream>** declares four objects that associate objects of class **stdiobuf** with the standard C streams provided for by the functions declared in **<stdio.h>**. The four objects are constructed, and the associations are established, the first time an object of class **ios::Init** is constructed. The four objects are *not* destroyed during program execution.[109]

17.4.9.1 Object cin

cin

```
istream cin;
```

The object **cin** controls input from an unbuffered stream buffer associated with the object **stdin**, declared in **<stdio.h>**.

After the object **cin** is initialized, **cin.tie()** returns **cout**.

17.4.9.2 Object cout

cout

```
ostream cout;
```

The object **cout** controls output to an unbuffered stream buffer associated with the object **stdout**, declared in **<stdio.h>**.

17.4.9.3 Object cerr

cerr

```
ostream cerr;
```

The object **cerr** controls output to an unbuffered stream buffer associated with the object **stderr**, declared in **<stdio.h>**.

After the object **cerr** is initialized, **cerr.flags() & unitbuf** is nonzero.

17.4.9.4 Object clog

clog

```
extern ostream clog;
```

The object **clog** controls output to a stream buffer associated with the object **stderr**, declared in **<stdio.h>**.

Footnotes:

Footnotes

109) Constructors and destructors for static objects can access these objects to read input from **stdin** or write output to **stdout** or **stderr**.

Future Directions

wide-character streams

For the last time, I note that a major change is the addition of wide-character streams. (See page 119.) The apparent effect on **<iostream>** is to leave it alone. If you want to control the standard streams as wide-character streams, you must construct the appropriate objects yourself. Still, this leaves open the effect of reading or writing the standard streams as wide-character streams. Amendment 1 (**ISO94**) says that the first operation on a C stream, standard or otherwise, makes it either "narrow oriented" or "wide oriented." Operations of the other orientation subsequently fail. Nothing in the draft C++ Standard, however, yet promises to honor this protocol in the C++ definition of wide-character streams.

Using <iostream>

You include the header **<iostream>** to make use of any of the objects **cin**, **cout**, **cerr**, or **clog**. These objects let you read and write the standard streams available to any executing C++ program:

cin ■ Extract from **cin** to read from the standard input stream.

cout ■ Insert to **cout** to write to the standard output stream.

cerr ■ Insert to **cerr** to write to the standard error stream.

clog ■ Insert to **clog** to write to the standard error stream.

Insertions to **cerr** are flushed at the end of each inserter call. (The format flag **ios::unitbuf** is set.) It is the preferred destination for debugging or error messages, lest the program crash before displaying useful output. Insertions to **clog** are more likely to be buffered. It is the preferred destination for "logging" high volumes of trace information, because insertions to it are less likely to degrade overall program performance.

_Init   These objects are constructed before any constructor is called to initialize a static object. On rare occasions, as described earlier in this chapter, you may need to be sure that **cin** and friends are initialized even earlier. In that case, be sure that program execution declares an object of class **ios::Init** before the first expression that references any of these objects.

redirection   You can redirect any of these streams by suppling a replacement pointer to **streambuf**. For example, you can alter **cin** to extract from the named file **"input"** by writing:

```
#include <fstream>
#include <iostream>
    .....
    filebuf fb;
    fb.open("input", ios::in);
    cin.rdbuf(&fb);
```

Do *not* redirect **cerr** this way, however, lest diagnostics go astray.

Implementing <iostream>

iostream   Figure 14.1 shows the file **iostream**, which implements the header **<iostream>**. It is one of those rare headers that is both short and overt. Given the general description of **<iostream>** earlier in this chapter, you should not be surprised at anything you see here.

iostream.c   Figure 14.2 shows the file **iostream.c**. Its primary business is to define the four objects declared in **<iostream>**. Its primary source of complexity is the need to double construct these and other objects, as I described earlier.

_Noinit   I first described the type **_Uninitialized**, and the value **_Noinit**, on **_Uninitialized** page 132. A constructor that takes a single argument of type **_Uninitialized** is expected to perform no initialization. A declaration with the single argument value **_Noinit** calls this constructor. Along the way, I've shown several classes that have constructors of this sort — **ios**, **streambuf**, **istream**, **ostream**, and **filebuf**. Here is where they all come into play.

Figure 14.1:
iostream

```
// iostream standard header
#ifndef _IOSTREAM_
#define _IOSTREAM_
#include <fstream>
            // standard stream declarations
extern istream cin;
extern ostream cout;
extern ostream cerr;
extern ostream clog;
static ios::Init _Ios_init;
#endif                                                              □
```

cin   Seven objects require double construction in this implementation. Four
cout are the objects declared in **<iostream>**: **cin**, **cout**, **cerr**, and **clog**. Three
cerr more are objects of type **filebuf** that do not have external linkage: **fin**,
clog **fout**, and **ferr**. All seven are constructed with placement **new** expressions
fin   in the constructor for **ios::Init**. This implementation of class **filebuf**
fout accepts a constructor with a *pointer to* **FILE** parameter. That eliminates the
ferr need for yet another do-nothing constructor, for class **stdiobuf**.

The constructor for **ios::Init** never leaves the construction count
ios::Init::_Init_cnt at zero. That way, the destructor can decrement
the contruction count with no fear of future confusion. When it decrements
the construction count to zero, the destructor knows to flush all three
objects that control output streams. Bizarre patterns of constructor and
destructor calls might cause the streams to be flushed more than once, but
no reasonable pattern should ever cause the seven objects to be constructed
more than once.

copyright   The file **iostream.c** also contains a copyright notice. It follows the form
notice I requested in the Preface. Any program that includes the object module
defined by this translation unit will satisfy the requirement I stated in the
Preface for an embedded copyright notice in an executable program.

Testing <iostream>

tiostrea.c   Figure 14.3 shows the file **tiostrea.c**. It tests the basic properties of the
objects declared in **<iostream>**. These are mostly cursory tests of the overt
properties of the objects, without altering the streams they control until the
very end. The program concludes by inserting into each of the three objects
that control output streams. If all goes well, and if the standard error stream
is directed to the same display as the standard output stream, the program
prints:

```
Can write on streams:
    cout
    cerr
    clog
SUCCESS testing <iostream>
```

and takes a normal exit.

Figure 14.2:
iostream.c

```
// iostream -- ios::Init members, standard streams
#include <iostream>
#include <new>
#include <stdio.h>

            // object declarations
int ios::Init::_Init_cnt = -1;
static filebuf fin(ios::_Noinit);
static filebuf fout(ios::_Noinit);
static filebuf ferr(ios::_Noinit);
istream cin(ios::_Noinit);
ostream cout(ios::_Noinit);
ostream cerr(ios::_Noinit);
ostream clog(ios::_Noinit);

ios::Init::Init()
    {                         // initialize standard streams first time
    if (0 <= _Init_cnt)
        ++_Init_cnt;
    else
        {                                 // initialize standard streams
        new (&fin) filebuf(stdin);
        new (&cin) istream(&fin);
        cin.tie(&cout);
        new (&fout) filebuf(stdout);
        new (&cout) ostream(&fout);
        new (&ferr) filebuf(stderr);
        new (&cerr) ostream(&ferr);
        cerr.tie(&cout);
        cerr.setf(ios::unitbuf);
        new (&clog) ostream(&ferr);
        clog.tie(&cout);
        _Init_cnt = 1;
        }
    }

ios::Init::~Init()
    {                         // flush standard streams last time
    if (--_Init_cnt == 0)
        {                                 // flush standard streams
        cout.flush();
        cerr.flush();
        clog.flush();
        }
    }

const char _PJP_CPP_Copyright[] =
"Portions of this work are derived from 'The Standard C++
Library',\n\
copyright (c) 1994 by P.J. Plauger, published by Prentice-Hall,\n\
and are used with permission.";                                    □
```

Figure 14.3:
tiostrea.c

```
// test <iostream>
#include <assert.h>
#include <iostream>
#include <iostream>

int main()
    {                    // test basic workings of iostream definitions
    assert(cin.good() && cin.exceptions() == ios::goodbit
        && cin.flags() == (ios::skipws | ios::dec)
        && cin.precision() == 6 && cin.width() == 0
        && cin.fill() == ' ');
    assert(cout.good() && cout.exceptions() == ios::goodbit
        && cout.flags() == (ios::skipws | ios::dec)
        && cout.precision() == 6 && cout.width() == 0
        && cout.fill() == ' ');
    assert(cerr.good() && cerr.exceptions() == ios::goodbit
        && cerr.flags()
            == (ios::skipws | ios::dec | ios::unitbuf)
        && cerr.precision() == 6 && cerr.width() == 0
        && cerr.fill() == ' ');
    assert(clog.good() && clog.exceptions() == ios::goodbit
        && clog.flags() == (ios::skipws | ios::dec)
        && clog.precision() == 6 && clog.width() == 0
        && clog.fill() == ' ');
    cout << "Can write on streams:" << endl;
    cout << "\tcout" << endl;
    cerr << "\tcerr" << endl;
    clog << "\tclog" << endl;
    assert(cout.good());
    assert(cerr.good());
    assert(clog.good());
    cout << "SUCCESS testing <iostream>" << endl;
    return (0);
    }
```

Exercises

Exercise 14.1 A constructor that apparently does nothing might still store into the constructed object a pointer to a table of virtual function pointers (to define its "shape"). Does this cause problems with the double-construction scheme used to initialize iostreams objects?

Exercise 14.2 What would be the constraints on using **cin** and friends if they were not constructed in a special way?

Exercise 14.3 Implement the object **cargs** that delivers the command-line argument strings one after the other. How do you delimit the arguments in the stream?

Exercise 14.4 [**Harder**] Implement **cout** so that it writes text to a window on your favorite windowing operating system.

Exercise 14.5 [**Very hard**] Implement **cin** and friends using no double construction.

Chapter 15: `<string>`

Background

One of the great strengths of C, from its earliest days, has been its ability to manipulate sequences of characters. The null-terminated sequence, or string, even has a bit of language support. You can write a string literal, such as `"abc"`, and the translator will construct for you a non-modifiable array of characters containing the sequence you specify terminated by a null character.

`<string.h>` That's about all the support you can expect from the C language proper. The Standard C library adds a number of functions, all declared in `<string.h>`, for manipulating strings and other kinds of character sequences. But you have next to no help in managing storage for these sequences. C programs abound with oversize arrays to hold character sequences of worst-case length. Or they contain ornate logic to allocate and free storage, copy strings about, and get those terminating null characters where they belong.

Little wonder, then, that writing string classes is one of the more popular indoor sports among C++ programmers. Encapsulation is an ideal tool for managing storage for strings, for hiding implementation details, and for enforcing semantic restrictions. A string class is a natural addition to any C++ library. In fact, essentially every implementation of C++ offers one, in some form or another.

And therein lies a problem. Many string classes exist in prior art, but they are many *different* string classes. The Committee faced a double challenge. It recognized a widespread demand for a standard string class, but couldn't identify an existing one to standardize on. To "codify existing practice" it had to be simultaneously inventive.

`<string>` The header `<string>` is thus an invention of the Committee, but one based heavily on prior art. It endeavors to define a class `string`, and a mess of supporting functions, that programmers will find compelling enough to use widely. That suggests reasonable efficiency in execution time and storage consumption, as well as an adequately rich assortment of operations. I believe those goals are well enough met by class `string`. Whether it wins the hearts and minds of working C++ programmers remains to be seen.

What the Draft C++ Standard Says

Class **string** has lots of member functions. The header also defines lots of additional functions that have one or more **string** parameters. But many of these come in sets of three. The idea is to provide a "fat" interface. Almost anywhere you can write a **string** argument, you should be able also to write any of:

- a pointer to a character sequence, followed by a sequence length argument
- a pointer to a null-terminated character string
- a character to be repeated, followed by a repetition count
- a single character

The Committee felt that the extra complexity in specifying class **string**, and its fellow travelers, would be more than offset by the richness and conceptual simplicity of the resulting interface.

17.5 Support classes

The Standard C++ library defines several types, and their supporting macros, constants, and function signatures, that support a variety of useful data structures.

17.5.1 Header <string>

<string>

The header **<string>** defines a type and several function signatures for manipulating varying-length sequences of (single-byte) characters.

17.5.1.1 Class **string**

Class string

```
class string {
public:
    string();
    string(size_t size, capacity cap);
    string(const string& str, size_t pos = 0, size_t n = NPOS);
    string(const char* s, size_t n = NPOS);
    string(char c, size_t rep = 1);
    string(unsigned char c, size_t rep = 1);
    string(signed char c, size_t rep = 1);
    string& operator=(const string& str);
    string& operator=(const char* s);
    string& operator=(char c);
    string& operator+=(const string& rhs);
    string& operator+=(const char* s);
    string& operator+=(char c);
    string& append(const string& str, size_t pos = 0,
        size_t n = NPOS);
    string& append(const char* s, size_t n = NPOS);
    string& append(char c, size_t rep = 1);
    string& assign(const string& str, size_t pos = 0,
        size_t n = NPOS);
    string& assign(const char* s, size_t n = NPOS);
    string& assign(char c, size_t rep = 1);
    string& insert(size_t pos1, const string& str,
```

```
            size_t pos2 = 0, size_t n = NPOS);
    string& insert(size_t pos, const char* s, size_t n = NPOS);
    string& insert(size_t pos, char c, size_t rep = 1);
    string& remove(size_t pos = 0, size_t n = NPOS);
    string& replace(size_t pos1, size_t n1, const string& str,
        size_t pos2 = 0, size_t n2 = NPOS);
    string& replace(size_t pos, size_t n1, const char* s,
        size_t n2 = NPOS);
    string& replace(size_t pos, size_t n, char c,
        size_t rep = 1);
    char get_at(size_t pos) const;
    void put_at(size_t pos, char c);
    char operator[](size_t pos) const;
    char& operator[](size_t pos);
    const char* c_str() const;
    size_t length() const:
    void resize(size_t n, char c = 0);
    size_t reserve() const;
    void reserve(size_t res_arg);
    size_t copy(char* s, size_t n, size_t pos = 0);
    size_t find(const string& str, size_t pos = 0) const;
    size_t find(const char* s, size_t pos = 0, size_t n = NPOS)
        const;
    size_t find(char c, size_t pos = 0) const;
    size_t rfind(const string& str, size_t pos = NPOS) const;
    size_t rfind(const char* s, size_t pos = NPOS,
        size_t n = NPOS) const;
    size_t rfind(char c, size_t pos = NPOS) const;
    size_t find_first_of(const string& str, size_t pos = 0)
        const;
    size_t find_first_of(const char* s, size_t pos = 0,
        size_t n = NPOS) const;
    size_t find_first_of(char c, size_t pos = 0) const;
    size_t find_last_of(const string& str, size_t pos = NPOS)
        const;
    size_t find_last_of(const char* s, size_t pos = NPOS,
        size_t n = NPOS) const;
    size_t find_last_of(char c, size_t pos = NPOS) const;
    size_t find_first_not_of(const string& str, size_t pos = 0)
        const;
    size_t find_first_not_of(const char* s, size_t pos = 0,
        size_t n = NPOS) const;
    size_t find_first_not_of(char c, size_t pos = 0) const;
    size_t find_last_not_of(const string& str,
        size_t pos = NPOS) const;
    size_t find_last_not_of(const char* s, size_t pos = NPOS,
        size_t n = NPOS) const;
    size_t find_last_not_of(char c, size_t pos = NPOS) const;
    string substr(size_t pos = 0, size_t n = NPOS) const;
    int compare(const string& str, size_t pos = 0,
        size_t n = NPOS) const;
    int compare(const char* s, size_t pos = 0, size_t n = NPOS)
        const;
    int compare(char c, size_t pos = 0, size_t rep = 1) const;
private:
```

```
//  char* ptr;                              exposition only
//  size_t len, res;                        exposition only
};
```

The class **string** describes objects that can store a sequence consisting of a varying number of arbitrary (single-byte) characters. The first element of the sequence is at position zero. Such a sequence is also called a *character string* (or simply a *string* if the type of the elements is clear from context). Storage for the string is allocated and freed as necessary by the member functions of class **string**. For the sake of exposition, the maintained data is presented here as:

- **char* ptr**, points to the initial character of the string;
- **size_t len**, counts the number of characters currently in the string;
- **size_t res**, for an unallocated string, holds the recommended allocation size of the string, while for an allocated string, becomes the currently allocated size.

In all cases, **len <= res**.

The functions described in this subclause can report two kinds of errors, each associated with a distinct exception:

- a *length* error is associated with exceptions of type **lengtherror**;
- an *out-of-range* error is associated with exceptions of type **outofrange**.

To report one of these errors, the function evaluates the expression **ex.raise()**, where **ex** is an object of the associated exception type.

17.5.1.1.1 string::string()

constructor

```
string();
```

Constructs an object of class **string** initializing:

- **ptr** to an unspecified value;
- **len** to zero;
- **res** to an unspecified value.

17.5.1.1.2 string::string(size_t, capacity)

constructor

```
string(size_t size, capacity cap);
```

Constructs an object of class **string**. If **cap** is **default_size**, the function either reports a length error if **size** equals **NPOS** or initializes:

- **ptr** to point at the first element of an allocated array of **size** elements, each of which is initialized to zero;
- **len** to **size**;
- **res** to a value at least as large as **len**.

Otherwise, **cap** shall be **reserve** and the function initializes:

- **ptr** to an unspecified value;
- **len** to zero;
- **res** to **size**.

17.5.1.1.3 string::string(const string&, size_t, size_t)

constructor

```
string(const string& str, size_t pos = 0, size_t n = NPOS);
```

Reports an out-of-range error if **pos > str.len**. Otherwise, the function constructs an object of class **string** and determines the effective length **rlen** of the initial string value as the smaller of **n** and **str.len - pos**. Thus, the function initializes:

- **ptr** to point at the first element of an allocated copy of **rlen** elements of the string controlled by **str** beginning at position **pos**;
- **len** to **rlen**;

- *res* to a value at least as large as *len*.

17.5.1.1.4 string::string(const char*, size_t)

constructor
```
string(const char* s, size_t n = NPOS);
```
If *n* equals **NPOS**, stores **strlen(*s*)** in *n*. The function signature **strlen(const char*)** is declared in **<string.h>**.

In any case, the function constructs an object of class **string** and determines its initial string value from the array of **char** of length *n* whose first element is designated by *s*. *s* shall not be a null pointer. Thus, the function initializes:

- *ptr* to point at the first element of an allocated copy of the array whose first element is pointed at by *s*;
- *len* to *n*;
- *res* to a value at least as large as *len*.

17.5.1.1.5 string::string(char, size_t)

constructor
```
string(char c, size_t rep = 1);
```
Reports a length error if *rep* equals **NPOS**. Otherwise, the function constructs an object of class **string** and determines its initial string value by repeating the character *c* for all *rep* elements. Thus, the function initializes:

- *ptr* to point at the first element of an allocated array of *rep* elements, each storing the initial value *c*;
- *len* to *rep*;
- *res* to a value at least as large as *len*.

17.5.1.1.6 string::string(unsigned char, size_t)

constructor
```
string(unsigned char c, size_t rep = 1);
```
Behaves the same as **string((char)*c*, *rep*)**.

17.5.1.1.7 string::string(signed char, size_t)

constructor
```
string(signed char c, size_t rep = 1);
```
Behaves the same as **string((char)*c*, *rep*)**.

17.5.1.1.8 string::operator=(const string&)

operator=
```
string& operator=(const string& str);
```
Returns **assign(*str*)**.

17.5.1.1.9 string::operator=(const char*)

operator=
```
string& operator=(const char* s);
```
Returns ***this = string(*s*)**.

17.5.1.1.10 string::operator=(char)

operator=
```
string& operator=(char c);
```
Returns ***this = string(*c*)**.

17.5.1.1.11 string::operator+=(const string&)

operator+=
```
string& operator+=(const string& rhs);
```
Returns **append(*rhs*)**.

17.5.1.1.12 string::operator+=(const char*)

operator+=
```
string& operator+=(const char* s);
```
Returns ***this += string(*s*)**.

17.5.1.1.13 string::operator+=(char)

operator+=
```
string& operator+=(char c);
```

Returns `*this += string(c)`.

17.5.1.1.14 string::append(const string&, size_t, size_t)

append
```
string& append(const string& str, size_t pos = 0,
    size_t n = NPOS);
```

Reports an out-of-range error if **pos > str.len**. Otherwise, the function determines the effective length **rlen** of the string to append as the smaller of **n** and **str.len - pos**. The function then reports a length error if **len >= NPOS - rlen**.

Otherwise, the function replaces the string controlled by ***this** with a string of length **len + rlen** whose first **len** elements are a copy of the original string controlled by ***this** and whose remaining elements are a copy of the initial elements of the string controlled by **str** beginning at position **pos**.

The function returns ***this**.

17.5.1.1.15 string::append(const char*, size_t)

append
```
string& append(const char* s, size_t n = NPOS);
```

Returns `append(string(s, n))`.

17.5.1.1.16 string::append(char, size_t)

append
```
string& append(char c, size_t rep = 1);
```

Returns `append(string(c, rep))`.

17.5.1.1.17 string::assign(const string&, size_t, size_t)

assign
```
string& assign(const string& str, size_t pos = 0,
    size_t n = NPOS);
```

Reports an out-of-range error if **pos > str.len**. Otherwise, the function determines the effective length **rlen** of the string to assign as the smaller of **n** and **str.len - pos**.

The function then replaces the string controlled by ***this** with a string of length **rlen** whose elements are a copy of the string controlled by **str** beginning at position **pos**.

The function returns ***this**.

17.5.1.1.18 string::assign(const char*, size_t)

assign
```
string& assign(const char* s, size_t n = NPOS);
```

Returns `assign(string(s, n))`.

17.5.1.1.19 string::assign(char, size_t)

assign
```
string& assign(char c, size_t rep = 1);
```

Returns `assign(string(c, rep))`.

17.5.1.1.20 string::insert(size_t, const string&, size_t, size_t)

insert
```
string& insert(size_t pos1, const string& str, size_t pos2 = 0,
    size_t n = NPOS);
```

Reports an out-of-range error if **pos1 > len** or **pos2 > str.len**. Otherwise, the function determines the effective length **rlen** of the string to insert as the smaller of **n** and **str.len - pos2**. The function then reports a length error if **len >= NPOS - rlen**.

Otherwise, the function replaces the string controlled by ***this** with a string of length **len + rlen** whose first **pos1** elements are a copy of the initial elements of the original string controlled by ***this**, whose next **rlen** elements are a copy of the elements of the string controlled by **str** beginning at position **pos2**, and whose remaining elements are a copy of the remaining elements of the original string controlled by ***this**.

The function returns ***this**.

17.5.1.1.21 string::insert(size_t, const char*, size_t)

insert
```
string& insert(size_t pos, const char* s, size_t n = NPOS);
```
Returns **insert(*pos*, string(*s*, *n*))**.

17.5.1.1.22 string::insert(size_t, char, size_t)

insert
```
string& insert(size_t pos, char c, size_t rep = 1);
```
Returns **insert(*pos*, string(*c*, *rep*))ÏD**.

17.5.1.1.23 string::remove(size_t, size_t)

remove
```
string& remove(size_t pos = 0, size_t n = NPOS);
```
Reports an out-of-range error if **_pos_ > _len_**. Otherwise, the function determines the effective length **_xlen_** of the string to be removed as the smaller of **_n_** and **_len_ - _pos_**.

The function then replaces the string controlled by ***this** with a string of length **_len_ - _xlen_** whose first **_pos_** elements are a copy of the initial elements of the original string controlled by ***this**, and whose remaining elements are a copy of the elements of the original string controlled by ***this** beginning at position **_pos_ + _xlen_**.

The function returns ***this**.

17.5.1.1.24 string::replace(size_t, size_t, const string&, size_t, size_t)

replace
```
string& replace(size_t pos1, size_t n1, const string& str,
    size_t pos2 = 0, size_t n2 = NPOS);
```
Reports an out-of-range error if **_pos1_ > _len_** or **_pos2_ > _str.len_**. Otherwise, the function determines the effective length **_xlen_** of the string to be removed as the smaller of **_n1_** and **_len_ - _pos1_**. It also determines the effective length **_rlen_** of the string to be inserted as the smaller of **_n2_** and **_str.len_ - _pos2_**. The function then reports a length error if **_len_ - _xlen_ >= NPOS - _rlen_**.

Otherwise, the function replaces the string controlled by ***this** with a string of length **_len_ - _xlen_ + _rlen_** whose first **_pos1_** elements are a copy of the initial elements of the original string controlled by ***this**, whose next **_rlen_** elements are a copy of the initial elements of the string controlled by **_str_** beginning at position **_pos2_**, and whose remaining elements are a copy of the elements of the original string controlled by ***this** beginning at position **_pos1_ + _xlen_**.

The function returns ***this**.

17.5.1.1.25 string::replace(size_t, size_t, const char*, size_t)

replace
```
string& replace(size_t pos, size_t n1, const char* s,
    size_t n2 = NPOS);
```
Returns **replace(*pos*, *n1*, string(*s*, *n2*))**.

17.5.1.1.26 string::replace(size_t, size_t, char, size_t)

replace
```
string& replace(size_t pos, size_t n, char c, size_t rep = 1);
```
Returns **replace(*pos*, *n*, string(*c*, *rep*))**.

17.5.1.1.27 string::get_at(size_t)

get_at
```
char get_at(size_t pos) const;
```
Reports an out-of-range error if **_pos_ >= _len_**. Otherwise, the function returns **_ptr[pos]_**.

17.5.1.1.28 string::put_at(size_t, char)

put_at

```
void put_at(size_t pos, char c);
```

Reports an out-of-range error if *pos* > *len*. Otherwise, if *pos* == *len*, the function replaces the string controlled by ***this** with a string of length *len* + 1 whose first *len* elements are a copy of the original string and whose remaining element is initialized to *c*. Otherwise, the function assigns *c* to *ptr[pos]*.

17.5.1.1.29 string::operator[](size_t)

operator[]

```
char operator[](size_t pos) const;
char& operator[](size_t pos);
```

If *pos* < *len*, returns *ptr[pos]*. Otherwise, if *pos* == *len*, the **const** version returns zero. Otherwise, the behavior is undefined.

The reference returned by the non-**const** version is invalid after any subsequent call to **c_str** or any non-**const** member function for the object.

17.5.1.1.30 string::c_str()

c_str

```
const char* c_str() const;
```

Returns a pointer to the initial element of an array of length *len* + 1 whose first *len* elements equal the corresponding elements of the string controlled by ***this** and whose last element is a null character. The program shall not alter any of the values stored in the array. Nor shall the program treat the returned value as a valid pointer value after any subsequent call to a non-**const** member function of the class **string** that designates the same object as ***this**.

17.5.1.1.31 string::length()

length

```
size_t length() const:
```

Returns *len*.

17.5.1.1.32 string::resize(size_t, char)

resize

```
void resize(size_t n, char c = 0);
```

Reports a length error if *n* equals **NPOS**. Otherwise, the function alters the length of the string designated by ***this** as follows:

- If *n* <= *len*, the function replaces the string designated by ***this** with a string of length *n* whose elements are a copy of the initial elements of the original string designated by ***this**.

- If *n* > *len*, the function replaces the string designated by ***this** with a string of length *n* whose first *len* elements are a copy of the original string designated by ***this**, and whose remaining elements are all initialized to *c*.

17.5.1.1.33 string::reserve()

reserve

```
size_t reserve() const;
```

Returns *res*.

17.5.1.1.34 string::reserve(size_t)

reserve

```
void reserve(size_t res_arg);
```

If no string is allocated, the function assigns *res_arg* to *res*. Otherwise, whether or how the function alters *res* is unspecified.

17.5.1.1.35 string::copy(char*, size_t, size_t)

copy

```
size_t copy(char* s, size_t n, size_t pos = 0);
```

Reports an out-of-range error if *pos* > *len*. Otherwise, the function determines the effective length *rlen* of the string to copy as the smaller of *n* and *len* - *pos*. *s* shall designate an array of at least *rlen* elements.

The function then replaces the string designated by *s* with a string of length *rlen* whose elements are a copy of the string controlled by *this, beginning at position *pos*.[110]

The function returns *rlen*.

17.5.1.1.36 string::find(const string&, size_t)

find

```
size_t find(const string& str, size_t pos = 0) const;
```

Determines the lowest position *xpos*, if possible, such that both of the following conditions obtain:

- *pos* <= *xpos* and *xpos* + *str.len* <= *len*;
- *ptr[xpos + I]* == *str.ptr[I]* for all elements *I* of the string controlled by *str*.

If the function can determine such a value for *xpos*, it returns *xpos*. Otherwise, it returns **NPOS**.

17.5.1.1.37 string::find(const char*, size_t, size_t)

find

```
size_t find(const char* s, size_t pos = 0, size_t n = NPOS)
    const;
```

Returns **find(string(*s*, *n*), *pos*)**.

17.5.1.1.38 string::find(char, size_t)

find

```
size_t find(char c, size_t pos = 0) const;
```

Returns **find(string(*c*), *pos*)**.

17.5.1.1.39 string::rfind(const string&, size_t)

rfind

```
size_t rfind(const string& str, size_t pos = NPOS) const;
```

Determines the highest position *xpos*, if possible, such that both of the following conditions obtain:

- *xpos* <= *pos* and *xpos* + *str.len* <= *len*;
- *ptr[xpos + I]* == *str.ptr[I]* for all elements *I* of the string controlled by *str*.

If the function can determine such a value for *xpos*, it returns *xpos*. Otherwise, it returns **NPOS**.

17.5.1.1.40 string::rfind(const char*, size_t, size_t)

rfind

```
size_t rfind(const char* s, size_t pos = NPOS,
    size_t n = NPOS) const;
```

Returns **rfind(string(*s*, *n*), *pos*)**.

17.5.1.1.41 string::rfind(char, size_t)

rfind

```
size_t rfind(char c, size_t pos = NPOS) const;
```

Returns **rfind(string(*c*, *n*), *pos*)**.

17.5.1.1.42 string::find_first_of(const string&, size_t)

find_first_of

```
size_t find_first_of(const string& str, size_t pos = 0) const;
```

Determines the lowest position *xpos*, if possible, such that both of the following conditions obtain:

- *pos* <= *xpos* and *xpos* < *len*;
- *ptr[xpos]* == *str.ptr[I]* for some element *I* of the string controlled by *str*.

If the function can determine such a value for *xpos*, it returns *xpos*. Otherwise, it returns **NPOS**.

17.5.1.1.43 string::find_first_of(const char*, size_t, size_t)

find_first_of

```
size_t find_first_of(const char* s, size_t pos = 0,
    size_t n = NPOS) const;
```

Returns `find_first_of(string(s, n), pos)`.

17.5.1.1.44 string::find_first_of(char, size_t)

find_first_of

```
size_t find_first_of(char c, size_t pos = 0) const;
```

Returns `find_first_of(string(c), pos)`.

17.5.1.1.45 string::find_last_of(const string&, size_t)

find_last_of

```
size_t find_last_of(const string& str, size_t pos = NPOS)
    const;
```

Determines the highest position *xpos*, if possible, such that both of the following conditions obtain:

- *xpos* <= *pos* and *pos* < *len*;
- *ptr[xpos]* == *str.ptr[I]* for some element *I* of the string controlled by *str*.

If the function can determine such a value for *xpos*, it returns *xpos*. Otherwise, it returns **NPOS**.

17.5.1.1.46 string::find_last_of(const char*, size_t, size_t)

find_last_of

```
size_t find_last_of(const char* s, size_t pos = NPOS,
    size_t n = NPOS) const;
```

Returns `find_last_of(string(s, n), pos)`.

17.5.1.1.47 string::find_last_of(char, size_t)

find_last_of

```
size_t find_last_of(char c, size_t pos = NPOS) const;
```

Returns `find_last_of(string(c, n), pos)`.

17.5.1.1.48 string::find_first_not_of(const string&, size_t)

find_
first_not_of

```
size_t find_first_not_of(const string& str, size_t pos = 0)
    const;
```

Determines the lowest position *xpos*, if possible, such that both of the following conditions obtain:

- *pos* <= *xpos* and *xpos* < *len*;
- *ptr[xpos]* == *str.ptr[I]* for no element *I* of the string controlled by *str*.

If the function can determine such a value for *xpos*, it returns *xpos*. Otherwise, it returns **NPOS**.

17.5.1.1.49 string::find_first_not_of(const char*, size_t, size_t)

find_
first_not_of

```
size_t find_first_not_of(const char* s, size_t pos = 0,
    size_t n = NPOS) const;
```

Returns `find_first_not_of(string(s, n), pos)`.

17.5.1.1.50 string::find_first_not_of(char, size_t)

find_
first_not_of

```
size_t find_first_not_of(char c, size_t pos = 0)
    const;
```

Returns `find_first_not_of(string(c), pos)`.

17.5.1.1.51 string::find_last_not_of(const string&, size_t)

```
size_t find_last_not_of(const string& str, size_t pos = NPOS)
    const;
```

Determines the highest position **xpos**, if possible, such that both of the following conditions obtain:

- **xpos <= pos** and **pos < len**;
- **ptr[xpos] == str.ptr[I]** for no element **I** of the string controlled by **str**.

If the function can determine such a value for **xpos**, it returns **xpos**. Otherwise, it returns **NPOS**.

17.5.1.1.52 string::find_last_not_of(const char*, size_t, size_t)

```
size_t find_last_not_of(const char* s, size_t pos = NPOS,
    size_t n = NPOS) const;
```

Returns **find_last_not_of(string(s, n), pos)**.

17.5.1.1.53 string::find_last_not_of(char, size_t)

```
size_t find_last_not_of(char c, size_t pos = NPOS)
    const;
```

Returns **find_last_not_of(string(c, n), pos)**.

17.5.1.1.54 string::substr(size_t, size_t)

```
string substr(size_t pos = 0, size_t n = NPOS) const;
```

Returns **string(*this, pos, n)**.

17.5.1.1.55 string::compare(const string&, size_t, size_t)

```
int compare(const string& str, size_t pos = 0,
    size_t n = NPOS) const;
```

Reports an out-of-range error if **pos > len**. Otherwise, if **str.len < n**, the function stores **str.len** in **n**. The function then determines the effective length **rlen** of the strings to compare as the smaller of **n** and **len - pos**. The function then compares the two strings by calling **memcmp(ptr + pos, str.ptr, rlen)**. The function signature **memcmp(const void*, const void*, size_t)** is declared in **<string.h>**.[111]

If the result of that comparison is nonzero, the function returns the nonzero result. Otherwise, the function returns:

- if **len - pos < n**, a value less than zero;
- if **len - pos == n**, the value zero;
- if **len - pos > n**, a value greater than zero.

17.5.1.1.56 string::compare(const char*, size_t, size_t)

```
size_t compare(const char* s, size_t pos = 0, size_t n = NPOS)
    const;
```

Returns **compare(string(s, n), pos)**.

17.5.1.1.57 string::compare(char, size_t, size_t)

```
size_t compare(char c, size_t pos = 0, size_t rep = 1) const;
```

Returns **compare(string(c, rep), pos)**.

17.5.1.2 operator+(const string&, const string&)

```
string operator+(const string& lhs, const string& rhs);
```

Returns **string(lhs).append(rhs)**.

operator+

17.5.1.3 operator+(const char*, const string&)
`string operator+(const char* lhs, const string& rhs);`
Returns `string(lhs) + rhs`.

operator+

17.5.1.4 operator+(char, const string&)
`string operator+(char lhs, const string& rhs);`
Returns `string(lhs) + rhs`.

operator+

17.5.1.5 operator+(const string&, const char*)
`string operator+(const string& lhs, const char* rhs);`
Returns `lhs + string(rhs)`.

operator+

17.5.1.6 operator+(const string&, char)
`string operator+(const string& lhs, char rhs);`
Returns `lhs + string(rhs)`.

operator==

17.5.1.7 operator==(const string&, const string&)
`int operator==(const string& lhs, const string& rhs);`
Returns a nonzero value if `!(lhs != rhs)` is nonzero.

operator==

17.5.1.8 operator==(const char*, const string&)
`int operator==(const char* lhs, const string& rhs);`
Returns `string(lhs) == rhs`.

operator==

17.5.1.9 operator==(char, const string&)
`int operator==(char lhs, const string& rhs);`
Returns `string(lhs) == rhs`.

operator==

17.5.1.10 operator==(const string&, const char*)
`int operator==(const string& lhs, const char* rhs);`
Returns `lhs == string(rhs)`.

operator==

17.5.1.11 operator==(const string&, char)
`int operator==(const string& lhs, char rhs);`
Returns `lhs == string(rhs)`.

operator!=

17.5.1.12 operator!=(const string&, const string&)
`int operator!=(const string& lhs, const string& rhs);`
Returns a nonzero value if `lhs.compare(rhs)` is nonzero.

operator!=

17.5.1.13 operator!=(const char*, const string&)
`int operator!=(const char* lhs, const string& rhs);`
Returns `string(lhs) != rhs`.

operator!=

17.5.1.14 operator!=(char, const string&)
`int operator!=(char lhs, const string& rhs);`
Returns `string(lhs) != rhs`.

operator!=

17.5.1.15 operator!=(const string&, const char*)
`int operator!=(const string& lhs, const char* rhs);`
Returns `lhs != string(rhs)`.

operator!=

17.5.1.16 operator!=(const string&, char)
`int operator!=(const string& lhs, char rhs);`
Returns `lhs != string(rhs)`.

operator>>	**17.5.1.17 operator>>(istream&, string&)**

```
istream& operator>>(istream& is, string& str);
```

A formatted input function, extracts characters and appends them to the string controlled by **str**. The string is initially made empty by calling **str.remove()**. Each extracted character **c** is appended as if by calling **str.append(c)**. If **width()** is greater than zero, the maximum number of characters stored **n** is **width()**; otherwise it is **INT_MAX**, defined in **<limits.h>**.

Characters are extracted and appended until any of the following occurs:

- **n** characters are appended;
- **NPOS - 1** characters are appended;
- end-of-file occurs on the input sequence;
- **isspace(c)** is nonzero for the next available input character **c** (in which case the input character is not extracted).

The function signature **isspace(int)** is declared in **<ctype.h>**.

If the function appends no characters, it calls **setstate(failbit)**. In any case, it calls **width(0)**. The function returns **is**.

getline	**17.5.1.18 getline(istream&, string&, char)**

```
istream& getline(istream& is, string& str, char delim = '\n');
```

An unformatted input function, extracts characters and appends them to the string controlled by **str**. The string is initially made empty by calling **str.remove()**. Each extracted character **c** is appended as if by calling **str.append(c)**. Characters are extracted and appended until any of the following occurs:

- **NPOS - 1** characters are appended (in which case the function calls **setstate(failbit)**);
- end-of-file occurs on the input sequence (in which case the function calls **setstate(eofbit)**);
- **c == delim** for the next available input character **c** (in which case the input character is extracted but not appended).

If the function appends no characters, it calls **setstate(failbit)**. The function returns **is**.

operator<<	**17.5.1.19 operator<<(ostream&, const string&)**

```
ostream& operator<<(ostream& os, const string& str);
```

A formatted output function, behaves the same as **os.write(str.c_str(), str.length())**.

The function returns **os**.

Future Directions

c_str	The member function **string::c_str** is now **string::data**.
put_at	The member function **string::put_at** no longer appends a character when the character sequence is accessed exactly at its end.
basic_string	The Committee has replaced class **string** with a template class called **basic_string**. One instantiation, for elements of type *char*, reproduces class **string** and related functions, as described in this chapter. Another instantiation, for elements of type **wchar_t**, reproduces class **wstring** and related functions, as described in the next chapter. This approach resembles the new templates for the iostreams classes, but is independent.

functional   As with iostreams, the basic *functionality* of class **string** does not change
compatibility   with the introduction of templates. A program written to match the Informal Review Draft should remain essentially unchanged. The code pre-
sented here is effectively an efficient specialization for type *char*.

Using <string>

You include the header **<string>** to make use of the class **string**.
Objects of this class let you manipulate in-memory character sequences that
vary dynamically in length. The **string** object allocates and frees storage
as needed to accommodate changes in length of the controlled sequence.

construction   To construct a **string** object **x0** with an initially empty character sequence, you can simply write:

```
string x0;
```

length   Each object **x** reports the *length* of its character sequence with the call
reserve **x.length()**. It also reports its *reserve size* with the call **x.reserve()**. For a
newly constructed **string** object, the reserve size suggests how much
storage to initially allocate for the character sequence. You can, for example,
specify an initial reserve size of 100 characters by writing:

capacity   **string x0(100, reserve);**

For an object with a non-empty character sequence, the reserve size suggests how much storage is currently available to hold the character sequence. Thus, **x0.length() <= x0.reserve()** at all times. As a rule, you
can ignore the reserve size. The implementation will guess it for you. (But
see the discussion on page 279.)

To construct a **string** object and define its initial character sequence,
you have a number of choices. In each case below, the string literal in the
comment shows the resulting character sequence. The implied null character at the end of this string literal is *not* part of the character sequence. You
can write:

```
string x1(5, default_size);          // "\0\0\0\0\0"
string x2('a');                       //         "a"
string x3('a', 5);                    //     "aaaaa"
string x4("abcde");                   //     "abcde"
string x5("abcdefg", 5);              //     "abcde"
```

The character argument in the constructors for **x2** and **x3** can be any of the
types *char*, *signed char*, or *unsigned char*.

substrings   You can also define the initial character sequence when you construct a
string object by selecting a *substring* from another **string** object. Given
the definition of **x5** above, you can write:

```
string x6(x5);                        //     "abcde"
string x7(x5, 1);                     //      "bcde"
string x8(x5, 1, 3);                  //       "bcd"
```

A substring thus has two default arguments. In order, these are:

- the initial position **pos** in the character sequence, counting from zero
  (default is zero)

- the maximum number of characters **n** to include from the remainder of the character sequence (default is **NPOS**, a huge value)

notation   Class **string** supports numerous combinations of argument types for practically every function that constructs or manipulates such objects. For brevity, I define here a terse and uniform style for writing various argument combinations. The resultant argument is:

- a single character, with the argument **c**
- a repetition of characters, with the arguments **c, rep**
- a null-terminated array of characters, with the argument **s**
- an array of characters with a specified length, with the arguments **s, n**
- a substring, with the arguments **x**, or **x, pos**, or **x, pos, n**, as described above

With this notation, I can more quickly summarize all the ways you can perform various operations involving **string** objects. Here, for example, is a summary of most of the constructors I showed above:

```
string x2(c);
string x3(c, rep);
string x4(s);
string x5(s, n);
string x6(x);
string x7(x, pos);
string x8(x, pos, n);
```

A number of member functions alter the character sequence controlled by a **string** object **x0**.

To assign a new character sequence, in place of any existing one:

assign
```
x0.assign(c)            x0 = c
x0.assign(c, rep)
x0.assign(s)            x0 = s
x0.assign(s, n)
x0.assign(x)            x0 = x
x0.assign(x, pos)
x0.assign(x, pos, n)
```

To append to an existing character sequence:

append
```
x0.append(c)            x0 += c
x0.append(c, rep)
x0.append(s)            x0 += s
x0.append(s, n)
x0.append(x)            x0 += x
x0.append(x, pos)
x0.append(x, pos, n)
```

To insert before position **px** in an existing character sequence:

insert
```
x0.insert(px, c)
x0.insert(px, c, rep)
x0.insert(px, s)
x0.insert(px, s, n)
x0.insert(px, x)
x0.insert(px, x, pos)
x0.insert(px, x, pos, n)
```

To replace at most **m** characters beginning with position **px** in an existing character sequence:

replace
```
x0.replace(px, m, c)
x0.replace(px, m, c, rep)
x0.replace(px, m, s)
x0.replace(px, m, s, n)
x0.replace(px, m, x)
x0.replace(px, m, x, pos)
x0.replace(px, m, x, pos, n)
```

You can remove a substring from a character sequence in various ways:

remove
```
x0.remove()                          // remove all characters
x0.remove(px)                        // remove all from px to end
x0.remove(px, n)          // remove at most n beginning at px
```

You can establish a new length **len** for a character sequence. If the new length is greater than the existing length, the character sequence is padded as stated in the comment below:

resize
```
x0.resize(len)            // pad to len with null characters
x0.resize(len, c)             // pad to len by repeating c
```

As a final alteration, you can store a new value **c** in the element at position **px** two different ways:

put_at
```
x0.put_at(px, c)
x0[px] = c
```

operator[] Be warned, however, that the subscript notation is more delicate. It returns a reference that can be invalidated by all sorts of subsequent operations on **x0**. Use it only in a very localized context, as above.

Another set of functions lets you obtain part or all of the character sequence controlled by a **string** object. The compaions to the functions immediately above are:

get_at
```
x0.get_at(px)
x0[px]
```

operator[] both of which return the character value stored at position **px**.

You can get a pointer to the beginning of the entire character sequence, complete with terminating null character, by calling:

c_str
```
x0.c_str()
```

The same caveats apply as for the subscript operator, above. Use the pointer to do any direct accessing of the character sequence quickly, before you perform any subsequent operations on **x0**. The pointer may well become invalid.

You can also copy into a character array beginning at **s** at most **n** characters from the character sequence, by writing:

copy
```
x0.copy(s, n)         // copy at most n, from the beginning
x0.copy(s, n, px)         // copy at most n, beginning at px
```

Yes, the arguments are backwards from the usual way for designating a substring.

Some functions each construct a **string** object to return as the value of the function, leaving the object **x0** unaltered. You can, for example, obtain a substring as a separate object:

substr	`x0.substr()`	`// copy all`
	`x0.substr(pos)`	`// copy remainder beginning at pos`
	`x0.substr(pos, n)`	`// copy at most n beginning at pos`

You can also construct a **string** object that appends the character sequences defined by two operands:

operator+	`x + c`
	`c + x`
	`x + s`
	`s + x`
	`x + x0`

Comparing two **string** objects involves a character-by-character comparison of corresponding values in the two character sequences, for the length of the shorter sequence. If two corresponding values are unequal, the character sequence with the larger value, treated as type *unsigned char,* compares larger. Otherwise, if the two character sequences are of equal length, they compare equal. Otherwise, the longer character sequence compares larger. To compare two complete character sequences for equality (**==**) or inequality (**!=**), you can write any of:

operator==	`x == c`	`x != c`
operator!=	`c == x`	`c != x`
	`x == s`	`x != s`
	`s == x`	`s != x`
	`x == x0`	`x != x0`

You can also call the member function **compare** to compare part or all of the character sequences. The comment that follows shows the equivalent comparison in operator notation:

compare	`x0.compare(x)`	`// x0 == x`
	`x0.compare(x, px)`	`// substr(x0, px) == x`
	`x0.compare(x, px, n)`	
		`// substr(x0, px) == substr(x, 0, n)`

Yes, the last example does *not* follow the usual pattern for specifying substrings.

A number of member functions look for substrings within a character sequence. To find the first (lowest position) occurrence of the argument character sequence within a character sequence:

find	`x0.find(c)`
	`x0.find(s)`
	`x0.find(s, 0, n)`
	`x0.find(x)`

All such calls return the beginning position of a successful match, or **NPOS** to report failure. Yes, the third example does *not* follow the usual pattern for specifying substrings. That's because the second argument, when present, is always the position **px** within the character sequence where the search begins. So to find the first occurrence of the argument character sequence *beginning on or after* **px**:

```
x0.find(c, px)
x0.find(s, px)
x0.find(s, px, n)
x0.find(x)
```

Similarly, to find the last (highest position) occurrence of the argument character sequence within a character sequence:

rfind
```
x0.rfind(c)
x0.rfind(s)
x0.rfind(s, NPOS, n)
x0.rfind(x)
```

Note the use of **NPOS** to specify a very large position. To find the last occurrence of the argument character sequence *beginning on or before* **px**:

```
x0.rfind(c, px)
x0.rfind(s, px)
x0.rfind(s, px, n)
x0.rfind(x)
```

Four sets of member functions treat the argument character sequence as a *set* of characters. Each character in the set is compared against part or all of the character sequence controlled by the **string** object. For example, to find the *first* element in the character sequence that matches *any* character in the set (**find_first_of**), or that matches *no* character in the set (**find_first_not_of**):

find_
first_of

find_
first_not_of
```
x0.find_first_of(c)            x0.find_first_not_of(c)
x0.find_first_of(s)            x0.find_first_not_of(s)
x0.find_first_of(s, 0, n)      x0.find_first_not_of(s, 0, n)
x0.find_first_of(x)            x0.find_first_not_of(x)
x0.find_first_of(c, px)        x0.find_first_not_of(c, px)
x0.find_first_of(s, px)        x0.find_first_not_of(s, px)
x0.find_first_of(s, px, n)     x0.find_first_not_of(s, px, n)
x0.find_first_of(x)            x0.find_first_not_of(x)
```

And to find the *last* element in the character sequence that matches *any* character in the set (**find_last_of**), or that matches *no* character in the set (**find_last_not_of**):

find_last_of

find_last_
not_of
```
x0.find_last_of(c)             x0.find_last_not_of(c)
x0.find_last_of(s)             x0.find_last_not_of(s)
x0.find_last_of(s, 0, n)       x0.find_last_not_of(s, 0, n)
x0.find_last_of(x)             x0.find_last_not_of(x)
x0.find_last_of(c, px)         x0.find_last_not_of(c, px)
x0.find_last_of(s, px)         x0.find_last_not_of(s, px)
x0.find_last_of(s, px, n)      x0.find_last_not_of(s, px, n)
x0.find_last_of(x)             x0.find_last_not_of(x)
```

Finally, you can insert and extract objects of class **string**. For example:

extractor
```
cin >> x0
```

extracts a character sequence from the standard input stream and assigns it to **x0**. You can set the width field nonzero in **cin** to limit the number of characters extracted. Otherwise, extraction continues up to but not including the first white-space character.

To extract up to but not including a delimiter character, you can write:

getline
```
getline(cin, x0)                        // delimiter is '\n'
getline(cin, x0, c)                      // delimiter is c
```

And last of all, you can insert the character sequence into, say, the standard output stream, by writing:

inserter
```
cout << x0
```

```
// string standard header
#ifndef _STRING_
#define _STRING_
#include <istream>
#include <ostream>
            // class string
class string {
public:
    string()
        {_Tidy(); }
    string(size_t _N, capacity _C)
        {_Tidy(), _Res = _N;
        if (_C == default_size)
            assign('\0', _N); }
    string(const string& _X, size_t _P = 0, size_t _N = NPOS)
        {_Tidy(), assign(_X, _P, _N); }
    string(const char *_S, size_t _N = NPOS)
        {_Tidy(), assign(_S, _N); }
    string(char _C, size_t _N = 1)
        {_Tidy(), assign(_C, _N); }
    string(unsigned char _C, size_t _N = 1)
        {_Tidy(), assign((char)_C, _N); }
#if _HAS_SIGNED_CHAR
    string(signed char _C, size_t _N = 1)
        {_Tidy(), assign((char)_C, _N); }
#endif /* _HAS_SIGNED_CHAR */
    ~string()
        {_Tidy(1); }
    string& operator=(const string& _X)
        {return (assign(_X)); }
    string& operator=(const char *_S)
        {return (assign(_S)); }
    string& operator=(char _C)
        {return (assign(_C)); }
    string& operator+=(const string& _X)
        {return (append(_X)); }
    string& operator+=(const char *_S)
        {return (append(_S)); }
    string& operator+=(char _C)
        {return (append(_C)); }
    string& append(const string&, size_t = 0, size_t = NPOS);
    string& append(const char *, size_t = NPOS);
    string& append(char, size_t = 1);
    string& assign(const string&, size_t = 0, size_t = NPOS);
    string& assign(const char *, size_t = NPOS);
    string& assign(char, size_t = 1);
    string& insert(size_t, const string&, size_t = 0,
        size_t = NPOS);
    string& insert(size_t, const char *, size_t = NPOS);
    string& insert(size_t, char, size_t = 1);
    string& remove(size_t = 0, size_t = NPOS);
    string& replace(size_t, size_t, const string&,
        size_t = 0, size_t = NPOS);
    string& replace(size_t, size_t, const char *,
        size_t = NPOS);
```

```
string& replace(size_t, size_t, char, size_t = 1);
char get_at(size_t) const;
void put_at(size_t, char);
char operator[](size_t _N) const
    {return (_Ptr[_N]); }
char& operator[](size_t _N)
    {return (_Ptr[_N]); }
const char *c_str() const
    {return (_Ptr != 0 ? _Ptr : ""); }
size_t length() const
    {return (_Len); }
void resize(size_t _N, char _C = 0)
    {_N <= _Len ? remove(_N) : append(_C, _N - _Len); }
size_t reserve() const
    {return (_Res); }
void reserve(size_t _N)
    {if (_Ptr == 0)
        _Res = _N; }
size_t copy(char *, size_t, size_t = 0);
size_t find(const string& _X, size_t _P = 0) const
    {return (find(_X.c_str(), _P, _X.length())); }
size_t find(const char *_S, size_t _P = 0,
    size_t _N = NPOS) const;
size_t find(char _C, size_t _P = 0) const
    {return (find((const char *)&_C, _P, 1)); }
size_t rfind(const string& _X, size_t _P = NPOS) const
    {return (rfind(_X.c_str(), _P, _X.length())); }
size_t rfind(const char *, size_t = NPOS, size_t = NPOS)
    const;
size_t rfind(char _C, size_t _P = NPOS) const
    {return (rfind((const char *)&_C, _P, 1)); }
size_t find_first_of(const string& _X, size_t _P = 0) const
    {return (find_first_of(_X.c_str(), _P, _X.length())); }
size_t find_first_of(const char *, size_t = 0,
    size_t = NPOS) const;
size_t find_first_of(char _C, size_t _P = 0) const
    {return (find((const char *)&_C, _P, 1)); }
size_t find_last_of(const string& _X, size_t _P = NPOS)
    const
    {return (find_last_of(_X.c_str(), _P, _X.length())); }
size_t find_last_of(const char *, size_t = NPOS,
    size_t = NPOS) const;
size_t find_last_of(char _C, size_t _P = NPOS) const
    {return (rfind((const char *)&_C, _P, 1)); }
size_t find_first_not_of(const string& _X,
    size_t _P = 0) const
    {return (find_first_not_of(_X.c_str(), _P,
        _X.length())); }
size_t find_first_not_of(const char *, size_t = 0,
    size_t = NPOS) const;
size_t find_first_not_of(char _C, size_t _P = 0) const
    {return (find_first_not_of((const char *)&_C, _P, 1)); }
size_t find_last_not_of(const string& _X,
    size_t _P = NPOS) const
    {return (find_last_not_of(_X.c_str(), _P,
```

```
                      _X.length())); }
    size_t find_last_not_of(const char *, size_t = NPOS,
        size_t = NPOS) const;
    size_t find_last_not_of(char _C, size_t _P = NPOS) const
        {return (find_last_not_of((const char *)&_C, _P, 1)); }
    string substr(size_t _P = 0, size_t _N = NPOS) const
        {return (string(*this, _P, _N)); }
    int compare(const string&, size_t = 0, size_t = NPOS) const;
    int compare(const char *, size_t = 0, size_t = NPOS) const;
    int compare(char, size_t = 0, size_t = 1) const;
private:
    _Bool _Grow(size_t, _Bool = 0);
    void _Tidy(_Bool = 0);
    void _Xlen() const
        {lengtherror("string too long").raise(); }
    void _Xran() const
        {outofrange("invalid string position").raise(); }
    char *_Ptr;
    size_t _Len, _Res;
    };
inline string operator+(const string& _L, const string& _R)
    {return (string(_L) += _R); }
inline string operator+(const char *_L, const string& _R)
    {return (string(_L) += _R); }
inline string operator+(char _L, const string& _R)
    {return (string(_L) += _R); }
inline string operator+(const string& _L, const char *_R)
    {return (string(_L) += _R); }
inline string operator+(const string& _L, char _R)
    {return (string(_L) += _R); }
inline _Bool operator==(const string& _L, const string& _R)
    {return (_L.compare(_R) == 0); }
inline _Bool operator==(const char * _L, const string& _R)
    {return (_R.compare(_L) == 0); }
inline _Bool operator==(char _L, const string& _R)
    {return (_R.compare(_L) == 0); }
inline _Bool operator==(const string& _L, const char *_R)
    {return (_L.compare(_R) == 0); }
inline _Bool operator==(const string& _L, char _R)
    {return (_L.compare(_R) == 0); }
inline _Bool operator!=(const string& _L, const string& _R)
    {return (!(_L == _R)); }
inline _Bool operator!=(const char *_L, const string& _R)
    {return (!(_L == _R)); }
inline _Bool operator!=(char _L, const string& _R)
    {return (!(_L == _R)); }
inline _Bool operator!=(const string& _L, const char *_R)
    {return (!(_L == _R)); }
inline _Bool operator!=(const string& _L, char _R)
    {return (!(_L == _R)); }
istream& operator>>(istream&, string&);
istream& getline(istream&, string&, char = '\n');
inline ostream& operator<<(ostream& _O, const string& _X)
    {return (_O.write(_X.c_str(), _X.length())); }
#endif
```

Implementing `<string>`

string   Figure 15.1 shows the file **string**, which implements the header
`<string>`. For a discussion of the macro **_HAS_SIGNED_CHAR**, see page 195.
The class **string** defines four secret protected member functions:

_Grow ▪ **_Grow**, which alters the storage reserved for the character sequence

_Tidy ▪ **_Tidy**, which initializes (**_Tidy()**) the member objects at construction
time or discards any character sequence (**_Tidy(1)**) and reinitializes the
member objects

_Xlen ▪ **_Xlen**, which reports a length error

_Xran ▪ **_Xran**, which reports a range error

For a discussion of the exceptions associated with length and range errors,
see Chapter 3: `<exception>`.

string.c   Figure 15.2 shows the file **string.c**. It defines the member functions
_Grow and **_Tidy**, both of which are likely to be called for any object of class
string.

MIN_SIZE   The macro **MIN_SIZE** is both a minimum size for character-sequence
storage and a minimum increment for adding more. The function **_Grow**
uses this parameter to round up requests for more storage, in the hopes of
minimizing reallocations. It also uses the parameter **trim** as an indication
that shrinking storage may be a good idea. The function is otherwise
reluctant to do so.

realloc   Note that **_Grow** allocates, or reallocates, storage by calling **realloc**,
declared in `<stdlib.h>`. That function can sometimes adjust the size of
allocated storage more efficiently than the equivalent combination of *new*
and *delete* expressions. For a description of the function **_Nomemory**, see
page 48.

Many member functions for class **string** come in groups of three. For
members of such a group I chose source file names that have a common
prefix, followed by:

▪ **c**, for an argument that is a single character or a repetition of characters

▪ **s**, for an argument that is a null-terminated string or an array of characters of specified length

▪ **x**, for an argument that is a substring or the entire character sequence
controlled by a **string** object

Often, the three flavors are just different enough to profit from distinct
function definitions.

strasc.c   As the first example, here are the three source files that define the
strass.c variations of the member function **assign**. Figure 15.3 shows the file
strasx.c **strasc.c**. Figure 15.4 shows the file **strass.c**. And Figure 15.5 shows the
file **strasx.c**. You can see the common approach. First validate the arguments, then call **_Grow** to adjust storage size for the character sequence, then
determine the new character sequence. The last act is to store the new
sequence length in the member object **_Len**. As is often the case, the

Figure 15.2:
string.c

```
// string -- string basic members
#include <stdlib.h>
#include <string>

const size_t MIN_SIZE = 31;                                    // 2^N - 1

_Bool string::_Grow(size_t n, _Bool trim)
    {                                              // grow a string as needed
    size_t osize = _Ptr == 0 ? 0 : _Res;
    if (n == 0)
        {                                              // set up a null string
        if (trim && MIN_SIZE < osize)
            _Tidy(1);
        else if (_Ptr != 0)
            _Ptr[_Len = 0] = '\0';
        return (0);
        }
    else if (n == osize || n < osize && !trim)
        return (1);
    else
        {                                          // grow or alter the string
        size_t size = _Ptr == 0 && n < _Res ? _Res : n;
        if ((size |= MIN_SIZE) == NPOS)
            --size;
        char *s;
        if ((s = (char *)realloc(_Ptr, size + 1)) == 0
            && (s = (char *)realloc(_Ptr,
                (size = n) + 1)) == 0)
            _Nomemory();
        _Ptr = s;
        _Res = size;
        return (1);
        }
    }

void string::_Tidy(_Bool constructed)
    {                                 // destroy any allocated string storage
    if (constructed && _Ptr != 0)
        free(_Ptr);
    _Ptr = 0, _Len = 0, _Res = 0;
    }                                                                       □
```

substring version requires special handling because the substring may be controlled by the same object.

strapc.c   Another set of three source files define the variations of the member
straps.c function **append**. Figure 15.6 shows the file **strapc.c**. Figure 15.7 shows
strapx.c the file **straps.c**. And Figure 15.8 shows the file **strapx.c**. All follow much the same pattern as the previous trio. In this case, however, appending part or all of a substring to itself requires little additional caution.

strinc.c   Three more source files define the variations of the member function
strins.c **insert**. Figure 15.9 shows the file **strinc.c**. Figure 15.10 shows the file
strinx.c **strins.c**. And Figure 15.11 shows the file **strinx.c**. Here the special

Figure 15.3:
strasc.c

```
// strasc -- string::assign(char, size_t)
#include <string.h>
#include <string>

string& string::assign(char ch, size_t n)
    {                                   // assign a repeated char to a string
    if (n == NPOS)
        _Xlen();
    if (_Grow(n, 1))
        {                                         // copy non-empty string
        memset(_Ptr, ch, n);
        _Ptr[_Len = n] = '\0';
        }
    return (*this);
    }                                                                      □
```

Figure 15.4:
strass.c

```
// strass -- string::assign(const char *, size_t)
#include <string.h>
#include <string>

string& string::assign(const char *s, size_t n)
    {                                       // assign an NTBS to a string
    if (n == NPOS)
        n = strlen(s);
    if (_Grow(n, 1))
        {                                         // copy non-empty string
        memcpy(_Ptr, s, n);
        _Ptr[_Len = n] = '\0';
        }
    return (*this);
    }                                                                      □
```

Figure 15.5:
strasx.c

```
// strasx -- string::assign(const string&, size_t, size_t)
#include <string.h>
#include <string>

string& string::assign(const string& str, size_t pos, size_t ns)
    {                                     // assign a substring to a string
    if (str.length() < pos)
        _Xran();
    size_t n = str.length() - pos;
    if (ns < n)
        n = ns;
    if (this == &str)
        remove(pos + n), remove(0, pos);
    else if (_Grow(n, 1))
        {                                         // copy non-empty string
        memcpy(_Ptr, &str.c_str()[pos], n);
        _Ptr[_Len = n] = '\0';
        }
    return (*this);
    }                                                                      □
```

```
// strapc -- string::append(char, size_t)
#include <string.h>
#include <string>

string& string::append(char ch, size_t nr)
    {                                   // append a repeated char to a string
    if (NPOS - _Len <= nr)
        _Xlen();
    size_t n;
    if (0 < nr && _Grow(n = _Len + nr))
        {                               // append to make non-empty string
        memset(_Ptr + _Len, ch, nr);
        _Ptr[_Len = n] = '\0';
        }
    return (*this);
    }                                                               □
```

```
// straps -- string::append(const char *, size_t)
#include <string.h>
#include <string>

string& string::append(const char *s, size_t ns)
    {                                   // append an NTBS to a string
    if (ns == NPOS)
        ns = strlen(s);
    if (NPOS - _Len <= ns)
        _Xlen();
    size_t n;
    if (0 < ns && _Grow(n = _Len + ns))
        {                               // append to make non-empty string
        memcpy(_Ptr + _Len, s, ns);
        _Ptr[_Len = n] = '\0';
        }
    return (*this);
    }                                                               □
```

```
// strapx -- string::append(const string&, size_t, size_t)
#include <string.h>
#include <string>

string& string::append(const string& str, size_t pos, size_t ns)
    {                                   // append a substring to a string
    if (str.length() < pos)
        _Xran();
    size_t n = str.length() - pos;
    if (n < ns)
        ns = n;
    if (NPOS - _Len <= ns)
        _Xlen();
    if (0 < ns && _Grow(n = _Len + ns))
        {                               // append to make non-empty string
        memcpy(_Ptr + _Len, &str.c_str()[pos], ns);
        _Ptr[_Len = n] = '\0';
        }
    return (*this);
    }                                                               □
```

Figure 15.9:
strinc.c

```
// strinc -- string::insert(size_t, char, size_t)
#include <string.h>
#include <string>

string& string::insert(size_t p0, char ch, size_t nr)
    {                               // insert a repeated char into a string
    if (_Len < p0)
        _Xran();
    if (NPOS - _Len <= nr)
        _Xlen();
    size_t n;
    if (0 < nr && _Grow(n = _Len + nr))
        {                               // insert to make non-empty string
        memmove(_Ptr + p0 + nr, _Ptr + p0, _Len - p0);
        memset(_Ptr + p0, ch, nr);
        _Ptr[_Len = n] = '\0';
        }
    return (*this);
    }                                                                      □
```

Figure 15.10:
strins.c

```
// strins -- string::insert(size_t, const char *, size_t)
#include <string.h>
#include <string>

string& string::insert(size_t p0, const char *s, size_t ns)
    {                               // insert an NTBS into a string
    if (_Len < p0)
        _Xran();
    if (ns == NPOS)
        ns = strlen(s);
    if (NPOS - _Len <= ns)
        _Xlen();
    size_t n;
    if (0 < ns && _Grow(n = _Len + ns))
        {                               // insert to make non-empty string
        memmove(_Ptr + p0 + ns, _Ptr + p0, _Len - p0);
        memcpy(_Ptr + p0, s, ns);
        _Ptr[_Len = n] = '\0';
        }
    return (*this);
    }                                                                      □
```

precaution is to sometimes call **memmove** instead of **memcpy**, both of which are declared in **<string.h>**. The former works properly even when copying a character sequence to elements that overlap the original ones.

strrem.c   Figure 15.12 shows the file **strrem.c**, which implements the member function **remove**. It too calls **memmove** to close up any hole made in the character sequence.

strrec.c   Three source files define the variations of the member function **replace**.
strres.c   Figure 15.13 shows the file **strrec.c**. Figure 15.14 shows the file **strres.c**.
strrex.c   And Figure 15.15 shows the file **strrex.c**. The logic is a bit more complex

Figure 15.11:
strinx.c

```
// strinx -- string::insert(size_t, const string&, size_t, size_t)
#include <string.h>
#include <string>

string& string::insert(size_t p0, const string& str,
    size_t pos, size_t ns)
    {                               // insert a substring into a string
    if (_Len < p0 || str.length() < pos)
        _Xran();
    size_t n = str.length() - pos;
    if (n < ns)
        ns = n;
    if (NPOS - _Len <= ns)
        _Xlen();
    if (0 < ns && _Grow(n = _Len + ns))
        {                           // insert to make non-empty string
        memmove(_Ptr + p0 + ns, _Ptr + p0, _Len - p0);
        memcpy(_Ptr + p0, &str.c_str()[pos], ns);
        _Ptr[_Len = n] = '\0';
        }
    return (*this);
    }
```

Figure 15.12:
strrem.c

```
// strrem -- string::remove(size_t, size_t)
#include <string.h>
#include <string>

string& string::remove(size_t p0, size_t nr)
    {                                       // remove a substring
    if (_Len < p0)
        _Xran();
    if (_Len - p0 < nr)
        nr = _Len - p0;
    if (0 < nr)
        {                                   // remove the substring
        memmove(_Ptr + p0, _Ptr + p0 + nr, _Len - p0 - nr);
        size_t n = _Len - nr;
        if (_Grow(n))
            _Ptr[_Len = n] = '\0';
        }
    return (*this);
    }
```

than for the earlier trios, mostly because of the need to define both old and new substrings. But it is otherwise much like what has gone before.

strget.c   Figure 15.16 shows the file **strget.c**, which defines the member func-
strput.c   tion **get_at**. And Figure 15.17 shows the file **strput.c**, which defines the companion function **put_at**. Both are simple, but as I noted earlier, the latter function has already been changed in the draft C++ Standard. It no longer appends the character when **_Len == p0**.

Figure 15.13:
strrec.c

```
// strrec -- string::replace(size_t, size_t, char, size_t)
#include <string.h>
#include <string>

string& string::replace(size_t p0, size_t n0, char ch,
    size_t nr)
    {                           // replace with a repeated char in a string
    if (_Len < p0)
        _Xran();
    if (_Len - p0 < n0)
        n0 = _Len - p0;
    if (NPOS - nr <= _Len - n0)
        _Xlen();
    size_t nm = _Len - n0 - p0;
    if (nr < n0)
        memmove(_Ptr + p0 + nr, _Ptr + p0 + n0, nm);
    size_t n;
    if ((0 < nr || 0 < n0) && _Grow(n = _Len + nr - n0))
        {                       // replace to make non-empty string
        if (n0 < nr)
            memmove(_Ptr + p0 + nr, _Ptr + p0 + n0, nm);
        memset(_Ptr + p0, ch, nr);
        _Ptr[_Len = n] = '\0';
        }
    return (*this);
    }                                                                    □
```

Figure 15.14:
strres.c

```
// strres -- string::replace(size_t, size_t, const char *,
//           size_t)
#include <string.h>
#include <string>

string& string::replace(size_t p0, size_t n0, const char *s,
    size_t ns)
    {                           // replace with an NTBS into a string
    if (_Len < p0)
        _Xran();
    if (ns == NPOS)
        ns = strlen(s);
    if (NPOS - ns <= _Len - n0)
        _Xlen();
    size_t nm = _Len - n0 - p0;
    if (ns < n0)
        memmove(_Ptr + p0 + ns, _Ptr + p0 + n0, nm);
    size_t n;
    if ((0 < ns || 0 < n0) && _Grow(n = _Len + ns - n0))
        {                       // replace to make non-empty string
        if (n0 < ns)
            memmove(_Ptr + p0 + ns, _Ptr + p0 + n0, nm);
        memcpy(_Ptr + p0, s, ns);
        _Ptr[_Len = n] = '\0';
        }
    return (*this);
    }                                                                    □
```

Figure 15.15:
strrex.c

```
// strrex -- string::replace(size_t size_t, const string&,
//           size_t, size_t)
#include <string.h>
#include <string>

string& string::replace(size_t p0, size_t n0,
    const string& str, size_t pos, size_t ns)
    {                                  // replace a substring with a string
    if (_Len < p0 || str.length() < pos)
        _Xran();
    size_t n = str.length() - pos;
    if (n < ns)
        ns = n;
    if (NPOS - ns <= _Len - n0)
        _Xlen();
    size_t nm = _Len - n0 - p0;
    if (ns < n0)
        memmove(_Ptr + p0 + ns, _Ptr + p0 + n0, nm);
    if ((0 < ns || 0 < n0) && _Grow(n = _Len + ns - n0))
        {                              // replace to make non-empty string
        if (n0 < ns)
            memmove(_Ptr + p0 + ns, _Ptr + p0 + n0, nm);
        memcpy(_Ptr + p0, &str.c_str()[pos], ns);
        _Ptr[_Len = n] = '\0';
        }
    return (*this);
    }
```

Figure 15.16:
strget.c

```
// strget -- string::get_at(size_t)
#include <string>

char string::get_at(size_t p0) const
    {                                  // get element of a string
    if (_Len <= p0)
        _Xran();
    return (_Ptr[p0]);
    }
```

Figure 15.17:
strput.c

```
// strput -- string::put_at(size_t)
#include <string>

void string::put_at(size_t p0, char ch)
    {                                  // put element to a string
    if (_Len < p0)
        _Xran();
    else if (_Len == p0)
        append(ch);
    else
        _Ptr[p0] = ch;
    }
```

Figure 15.18:
strcopy.c

```
// strcopy -- string::copy(const char *, size_t, size_t)
#include <string.h>
#include <string>

size_t string::copy(char *s, size_t n, size_t p0)
    {                                    // copy a string to a char array
    if (_Len < p0)
        _Xran();
    if (_Len - p0 < n)
        n = _Len - p0;
    memcpy(s, _Ptr + p0, n);
    return (n);
    }                                                                    □
```

Figure 15.19:
strfis.c

```
// strfis -- string::find(const char *, size_t, size_t)
#include <string.h>
#include <string>

size_t string::find(const char *s, size_t p0, size_t n) const
    {                                    // find leftmost substring in a string
    if (n == 0 || n == NPOS && (n = strlen(s)) == 0)
        return (0);
    size_t nmax;
    if (p0 < _Len && n <= (nmax = _Len - p0))
        {                                // find non-null substring in string
        const char *t, *u;
        for (nmax -= n - 1, u = _Ptr + p0;
            (t = (const char *)memchr(u, *s, nmax)) != 0;
            nmax -= t - u + 1, u = t + 1)
            if (memcmp(t, s, n) == 0)
                return (t - _Ptr);
        }
    return (NPOS);
    }                                                                    □
```

Figure 15.20:
strrfis.c

```
// strrfis -- string::rfind(const char *, size_t, size_t)
#include <string.h>
#include <string>

size_t string::rfind(const char *s, size_t p0, size_t n) const
    {                                    // find rightmost substring in a string
    if (n == 0 || n == NPOS && (n = strlen(s)) == 0)
        return (0);
    if (n <= _Len)
        for (const char *t = _Ptr
            + (p0 < _Len - n ? p0 : _Len - n); ; --t)
            if (*t == *s && memcmp(t, s, n) == 0)
                return (t - _Ptr);
            else if (t == _Ptr)
                break;
    return (NPOS);
    }                                                                    □
```

Figure 15.21:
strffs.c

```
// strffs -- string::find_first_of(const char *, size_t, size_t)
#include <string.h>
#include <string>

size_t string::find_first_of(const char *s, size_t p0, size_t n)
     const
     {                               // find leftmost set member in a string
     if (n == 0 || n == NPOS && (n = strlen(s)) == 0)
          return (0);
     if (p0 < _Len)
          {                                    // find in non-null string
          const char *const u = _Ptr + _Len;
          for (const char *t = _Ptr + p0; t < u; ++t)
               if (memchr(s, *t, n) != 0)
                    return (t - _Ptr);
          }
     return (NPOS);
     }                                                              □
```

Figure 15.22:
strfls.c

```
// strfls -- string::find_last_of(const char *, size_t, size_t)
#include <string.h>
#include <string>

size_t string::find_last_of(const char *s, size_t p0, size_t n)
     const
     {                               // find rightmost set member in a string
     if (n == 0 || n == NPOS && (n = strlen(s)) == 0)
          return (0);
     if (0 < _Len)
          for (const char *t = _Ptr
               + (p0 < _Len ? p0 : _Len - 1); ; --t)
               if (memchr(s, *t, n) != 0)
                    return (t - _Ptr);
               else if (t == _Ptr)
                    break;
     return (NPOS);
     }                                                              □
```

strcopy.c   Figure 15.18 shows the file **strcopy.c**, which defines the member function **copy**. It too is simple.

For the "find" member functions (names beginning with **find**), I found it sufficient to define the "string or array" versions (source files with names ending in **s**) only. All others are inline functions that call these versions.

strfis.c   Figure 15.19 shows the file **strfis.c**, which defines the string or array
strrfis.c   version of the member function **find**. As an optimization, it first scans for the initial character of the character sequence to match. The (mildly messy) logic could otherwise be made simpler. Figure 15.20 shows the file **strrfis.c**, which defines the string or array version of the member function **rfind**. It has no handy library function to perform the equivalent reverse scan, so its logic is perforce simpler (and possibly slower).

Figure 15.23:
strffns.c

```
// strffns -- string::find_first_not_of(const char *, size_t,
//              size_t)
#include <string.h>
#include <string>

size_t string::find_first_not_of(const char *s, size_t p0,
    size_t n) const
    {                              // find leftmost set member not in a string
    if (n == 0 || n == NPOS && (n = strlen(s)) == 0)
        return (0);
    if (p0 < _Len)
        {                                        // find in non-null string
        const char *const u = _Ptr + _Len;
        for (const char *t = _Ptr + p0; t < u; ++t)
            if (memchr(s, *t, n) == 0)
                return (t - _Ptr);
        }
    return (NPOS);
    }                                                                    □
```

Figure 15.24:
strflns.c

```
// strflns -- string::find_last_not_of(const char *, size_t,
//              size_t)
#include <string.h>
#include <string>

size_t string::find_last_not_of(const char *s, size_t p0,
    size_t n) const
    {                              // find rightmost set member not in a string
    if (n == 0 || n == NPOS && (n = strlen(s)) == 0)
        return (0);
    if (0 < _Len)
        for (const char *t = _Ptr
            + (p0 < _Len ? p0 : _Len - 1); ; --t)
            if (memchr(s, *t, n) == 0)
                return (t - _Ptr);
            else if (t == _Ptr)
                break;
    return (NPOS);
    }                                                                    □
```

strffs.c   Figure 15.21 shows the file **strffs.c**, which defines the string or array
strfls.c version of the member function **find_first_of**. And Figure 15.22 shows
the file **strfls.c**, which defines the string or array version of the member
function **find_last_of**. Compare this pair with the pair that follows.

strffns.c   Figure 15.23 shows the file **strffns.c**, which defines the string or array
strflns.c version of the member function **find_first_not_of**. And Figure 15.24
shows the file **strflns.c**, which defines the string or array version of the
member function **find_last_not_of**. All four functions are very similar.

strcoc.c   The last set of three source files define the variations of the member
strcos.c function **compare**. Figure 15.25 shows the file **strcoc.c**. Figure 15.26 shows
strcox.c the file **strcos.c**. And Figure 15.27 shows the file **strcox.c**. The messiest

Figure 15.25:
strcoc.c

```
// strcoc -- string::compare(char, size_t, size_t)
#include <string>

int string::compare(char ch, size_t p0, size_t ns) const
        {                               // compare a repeated char to a string
        if (_Len < p0)
            _Xran();
        size_t n = _Len - p0;
        for (const char *s = _Ptr + p0, *t = s + (n < ns ? n : ns);
            s < t; ++s)
            if (*s != ch)
                    return (*(unsigned char *)s < (unsigned char)ch
                        ? -1 : +1);
        return (n < ns ? -1 : n == ns ? 0 : +1);
        }                                                                    □
```

Figure 15.26:
strcos.c

```
// strcos -- string::compare(const char *, size_t, size_t)
#include <string.h>
#include <string>

int string::compare(const char *s, size_t p0, size_t ns) const
        {                               // compare an NTBS to a string
        if (_Len < p0)
            _Xran();
        size_t n = _Len - p0;
        if (ns == NPOS)
            ns = strlen(s);
        size_t ans = memcmp(_Ptr + p0, s, n < ns ? n : ns);
        return (ans != 0 ? ans : n < ns ? -1 : n == ns ? 0 : +1);
        }                                                                    □
```

Figure 15.27:
strcox.c

```
// strcox -- string::compare(const string&, size_t, size_t)
#include <string.h>
#include <string>

int string::compare(const string& str, size_t p0, size_t ns)
        const
        {                               // compare a substring to a string
        if (_Len < p0)
            _Xran();
        size_t n = _Len - p0;
        if (str.length() < ns)
            ns = str.length();
        size_t ans = memcmp(_Ptr + p0, str.c_str(),
            n < ns ? n : ns);
        return (ans != 0 ? ans : n < ns ? -1 : n == ns ? 0 : +1);
        }                                                                    □
```

part of the logic occurs when the shorter of two character sequences is a prefix of the longer one, or when the character sequences are equal.

Figure 15.28:
strxstr.c

```
// strxstr -- operator>>(istream&, string&)
#include <ctype.h>
#include <limits.h>
#include <string>

istream& operator>>(istream& is, string& str)
    {                                           // extract into a string
    _Bool changed = 0;
    str.remove();
    _TRY_IO_BEGIN
    if (is.ipfx())
        {                                  // extract arbitrary characters
        int n = 0 < is.width() ? is.width() : INT_MAX;
        for (int ch; 0 < --n && str.length() < NPOS - 1
            && (ch = is.rdbuf()->sbumpc()) != EOF; )
            if (isspace(ch))
                {                      // put back white space and quit
                is.rdbuf()->sputbackc(ch);
                break;
                }
            else
                str.append((char)ch), changed = 1;
        }
    if (!changed)
        is.setstate(ios::failbit);
    is.width(0);
    is.isfx();
    _CATCH_IO_(is);
    return (is);
    }                                                                □
```

operator>>   The last two source files define the functions that extract character
   getline sequences into **string** objects. Figure 15.28 shows the file **strxstr.c**,
            which defines the **string** version of **operator>>**. And Figure 15.29 shows
            the file **strgline.c**, which defines the **string** version of **getline**. These
            differ only in small ways from the **istream** member functions that extract
            character sequences. (See Chapter 8: **<istream>**.) They call the **istream**
            member functions differently, naturally enough. And they handle excep-
            tions using the macro **_CATCH_IO_(x)** instead of **_CATCH_IO_END**. (See page
            128.) The overall logic is otherwise quite similar.

Testing **<string>**

   tstring.c   Figure 15.30 shows the file **tstring.c**. It tests the basic properties of the
            class **string** defined in **<string>**. It does so by testing the various string
            operations in related groups, at least for their minimum functionality.

            If all goes well, the program prints:

            SUCCESS testing <string>

            and takes a normal exit.

Figure 15.29:
strgline.c

```
// strgline -- getline(istream&, string&, char)
#include <string>

istream& getline(istream& is, string& str, char delim)
    {                   // get to string up through delimiter or count
    size_t n = 0;
    str.remove();
    _Bool copied = 0;
    _TRY_IO_BEGIN
    if (is.ipfx(1))
        for (int ch; ; )
            if (NPOS - 1 <= n)
                {                       // record count failure and quit
                is.setstate(ios::failbit);
                break;
                }
            else if ((ch = is.rdbuf()->sbumpc()) == EOF)
                {                               // record eof and quit
                is.setstate(ios::eofbit);
                break;
                }
            else
                {                       // count it and test for delim
                if (ch == delim)
                    break;
                str.append((char)ch), ++n, copied = 1;
                }
    if (!copied)
        is.setstate(ios::failbit);
    is.isfx();
    _CATCH_IO_(is);
    return (is);
    }
```

Exercises

Exercise 15.1 Write a function that reverses the characters in a sequence controlled by a **string** object.

Exercise 15.2 Describe all the operations performed by functions declared in **<string.h>**, and how to do the same thing using only functions declared in **string**.

Exercise 15.3 Is it permissible to define an array of **NPOS** characters?

Exercise 15.4 Why do you think the "find" functions return **NPOS** when an argument is silly, rather than throw an exception?

Exercise 15.5 [Harder] Implement class **string** in such a way that a character sequence is actually copied only when two or more **string** objects designate the same sequence and one attempts to alter it.

Exercise 15.6 [Very hard] Define and implement a **string** class that has no limit on the length of a character sequence.

```
// test <string>
#include <assert.h>
#include <string.h>
#include <string>
#include <iostream>
#include <strstream>

int main()
    {                       // test basic workings of string definitions
    string s1, s2(30, reserve), s3(4, default_size);
    string s4("s4"), s5("s5xxx", 2), s6('a', 3);
    string s7((unsigned char)'b', 5), s8((signed char)'c');
    s1.reserve(20);
    assert(s1.reserve() == 20 && s2.reserve() == 30);
    assert(strcmp(s1.c_str(), "") == 0);
    assert(strcmp(s2.c_str(), "") == 0);
    assert(memcmp(s3.c_str(), "\0\0\0\0", 5) == 0);
    assert(strcmp(s4.c_str(), "s4") == 0);
    assert(strcmp(s5.c_str(), "s5") == 0);
    assert(strcmp(s6.c_str(), "aaa") == 0);
    assert(strcmp(s7.c_str(), "bbbbb") == 0);
    assert(strcmp(s8.c_str(), "c") == 0);
            // test assignments
    s1 = "hello", assert(strcmp(s1.c_str(), "hello") == 0);
    s1 = 'x', assert(strcmp(s1.c_str(), "x") == 0);
    s1 = s4, assert(strcmp(s1.c_str(), "s4") == 0);
    s1.assign("AB"), assert(strcmp(s1.c_str(), "AB") == 0);
    s1.assign('C'), assert(strcmp(s1.c_str(), "C") == 0);
    s1.assign(s4), assert(strcmp(s1.c_str(), "s4") == 0);
            // test appends
    s1 += "abc", assert(strcmp(s1.c_str(), "s4abc") == 0);
    s1 += 'd', assert(strcmp(s1.c_str(), "s4abcd") == 0);
    s1 += s4, assert(strcmp(s1.c_str(), "s4abcds4") == 0);
    s1 = "A", s1.append("BC");
    assert(strcmp(s1.c_str(), "ABC") == 0);
    s1.append('D'), assert(strcmp(s1.c_str(), "ABCD") == 0);
    s1.append(s4), assert(strcmp(s1.c_str(), "ABCDs4") == 0);
    assert(strcmp((s4 + s5).c_str(), "s4s5") == 0);
    assert(strcmp((s4 + "s5").c_str(), "s4s5") == 0);
    assert(strcmp(("s4" + s5).c_str(), "s4s5") == 0);
    assert(strcmp((s4 + '5').c_str(), "s45") == 0);
    assert(strcmp(('4' + s5).c_str(), "4s5") == 0);
            // test inserts
    s1 = "abc";
    s1.insert(3, "Dd").insert(1, "BC", 1).insert(0, "A");
    assert(strcmp(s1.c_str(), "AaBbcDd") == 0);
    s1.insert(7, 'E', 2).insert(4, 'C');
    assert(strcmp(s1.c_str(), "AaBbCcDdEE") == 0);
    s1.insert(10, s4).insert(0, s4, 1).insert(0, s4, 0, 1);
    assert(strcmp(s1.c_str(), "s4AaBbCcDdEEs4") == 0);
            // test removes
    s1.remove(0, 2);
    assert(strcmp(s1.c_str(), "AaBbCcDdEEs4") == 0);
    s1.remove(8), assert(strcmp(s1.c_str(), "AaBbCcDd") == 0);
    s1.remove(), assert(strcmp(s1.c_str(), "") == 0);
```

```
        // test replace
s1.replace(0, 0, "123ab789"), s1.replace(3, 2, "45678", 3);
assert(strcmp(s1.c_str(), "123456789") == 0);
s1.replace(1, 3, 'x', 2).replace(0, 0, '0');
assert(strcmp(s1.c_str(), "01xx56789") == 0);
s1.replace(3, 1, s4, 1).replace(2, 1, s4);
assert(strcmp(s1.c_str(), "01s4456789") == 0);
        // test accesses
s1.put_at(2, '2');
assert(s1.get_at(1) == '1' && s1[2] == '2');
assert((s1[3] = '3') == '3'), assert(s1.length() == 10);
s1.resize(3), assert(strcmp(s1.c_str(), "012") == 0);
s1.resize(5, 'X'), assert(strcmp(s1.c_str(), "012XX") == 0);
s1.resize(6), assert(memcmp(s1.c_str(), "012XX\0", 7) == 0);
char buf[10];
assert(s1.copy(buf, sizeof (buf)) == 6
    && strcmp(buf, "012XX") == 0);
assert(s1.copy(buf, 3, 1) == 3
    && memcmp(buf, "12X", 3) == 0);
        // test finds
s1 = "s4s4";
assert(s1.find(s4) == 0 && s1.find(s4, 1) == 2
    && s1.find(s4, 3) == NPOS);
assert(s1.find("s4") == 0 && s1.find("s4", 3) == NPOS
    && s1.find("s4XX", 1, 2) == 2);
assert(s1.find('s') == 0 && s1.find('s', 1) == 2
    && s1.find('x') == NPOS);
assert(s1.rfind(s4) == 2 && s1.rfind(s4, 1) == 0
    && s1.rfind(s5, 3) == NPOS);
assert(s1.rfind("s4") == 2 && s1.rfind("s4", 3) == 2
    && s1.rfind("s4XX", 1, 3) == NPOS);
assert(s1.rfind('s') == 2 && s1.rfind('s', 2) == 2
    && s1.rfind('x') == NPOS);
assert(s1.find_first_of(s4) == 0
    && s1.find_first_of(s4, 1) == 1
    && s1.find_first_of(s4, 4) == NPOS);
assert(s1.find_first_of("s4") == 0
    && s1.find_first_of("s4", 3) == 3
    && s1.find_first_of("abs", 1, 2) == NPOS);
assert(s1.find_first_of('s') == 0
    && s1.find_first_of('s', 1) == 2
    && s1.find_first_of('x') == NPOS);
assert(s1.find_last_of(s4) == 3
    && s1.find_last_of(s4, 1) == 1
    && s1.find_last_of(s6) == NPOS);
assert(s1.find_last_of("s4") == 3
    && s1.find_last_of("s4", 2) == 2
    && s1.find_last_of("abs", 1, 2) == NPOS);
assert(s1.find_last_of('s') == 2
    && s1.find_last_of('s', 1) == 0
    && s1.find_last_of('x') == NPOS);
assert(s1.find_first_not_of(s5) == 1
    && s1.find_first_not_of(s5, 2) == 3
    && s1.find_first_not_of(s4) == NPOS);
assert(s1.find_first_not_of("s5") == 1
```

```
        && s1.find_first_not_of("s5", 2) == 3
        && s1.find_first_not_of("s4a", 1, 2) == NPOS);
    assert(s1.find_first_not_of('s') == 1
        && s1.find_first_not_of('s', 2) == 3
        && s1.find_first_not_of('s', 4) == NPOS);
    assert(s1.find_last_not_of(s5) == 3
        && s1.find_last_not_of(s5, 2) == 1
        && s1.find_last_not_of(s4) == NPOS);
    assert(s1.find_last_not_of("s5") == 3
        && s1.find_last_not_of("s5", 2) == 1
        && s1.find_last_not_of("s4a", 1, 2) == NPOS);
    assert(s1.find_last_not_of('s') == 3
        && s1.find_last_not_of('s', 2) == 1
        && s1.find_last_not_of('s', 0) == NPOS);
        // test compares
    assert(s1.compare(s1) == 0 && s1.compare(s4, 2) == 0
        && s1.compare(s4, 2, 2) == 0);
    assert(s1.compare("s4s4") == 0 && s1.compare("s4", 2) == 0
        && s1.compare("s4xx", 2, 2) == 0);
    assert(s8.compare('c') == 0 && s1.compare('4', 3) == 0
        && s6.compare('a', 0, 3) == 0);
    assert(s1.compare(s4) != 0 && s1.compare(s1, 1) != 0
        && s1.compare(s4, 0, 2) != 0);
    assert(s1.compare("s4s5") != 0 && s1.compare("s44", 3) != 0
        && s1.compare("s4xx", 0, 2) != 0);
    assert(s1.compare('c') != 0 && s1.compare('4', 2) != 0
        && s6.compare('a', 0, 2) != 0);
    assert(s1 == s1 && s1 == "s4s4" && s8 == 'c' && "s4" == s4
        && 'c' == s8);
    assert(s1 != s4 && s1 != "xx" && s1 != 's' && "s4" != s1
        && 'a' != s6);
        // test I/O
    static const char input[] = "s1 s2 s3\n    abc";
    istrstream ins(input);
    ostrstream outs;
    ins >> s1, assert(s1 == "s1");
    ins >> s1, assert(s1 == "s2");
    getline(ins, s1), assert(s1 == " s3");
    getline(ins, s1, 'c'), assert(s1 == "    ab");
    outs << s1 << ends;
    assert(strcmp(outs.str(), "    ab") == 0);
    cout << "SUCCESS testing <string>" << endl;
    return (0);
    }
```

Chapter 16: `<wstring>`

Background

wide characters   A significant addition to Standard C (**ISO90**) is support for *wide characters*. In Standard C, type `wchar_t` is defined in `<stddef.h>` (among other places) as a synonym for one of the integer types. It can represent all the distinct codes of a large character set, otherwise known as wide characters. Hence, it is the internal representation of choice for manipulating text in languages such as Chinese and Japanese. While still a specialized style of programming, such "international" capabilities are rapidly growing in importance, for obvious commercial reasons.

Support for wide characters in Standard C, as originally specified, is minimal. The header `<stdlib.h>` defines a handful of functions for converting between wide characters and *multibyte characters* — sequences of one or more bytes that represent the same character set for external transmission. Otherwise, a program that manipulates wide characters has to supply its own utility functions.

Amendment 1   Amendment 1 to the C Standard (**ISO94**) changed all that. Standard C now includes a rich assortment of wide-character functions. You'll find analogs for all the facilities of `<ctype.h>` in `<wctype.h>`, and then some. You'll find analogs for most of the facilities of `<stdio.h>`, and all those in `<string.h>`, in `<wchar.h>`. Put simply, you can convert large quantities of text-manipulation code from single-byte to wide-character by a one-for-one replacement of header names, types, and function names.

wstring   The draft C++ Standard continues that trend. The Committee has made `wchar_t` a keyword, denoting a distinct integer type. That facilitates overloading on various character and integer types as well as `wchar_t`, with no fear of ambiguity. (See the discussions on page 33 and on page 44.) The Committee has more recently added support for iostreams-style operations on wide characters, as I've indicated several times earlier in this book. And it has earlier added to the Standard C++ library the class `wstring`.

`<wstring>`   The header `<wstring>` is a direct analog to `<string>`. It defines the class `wstring` and a number of functions that manipulate objects of this class. You will find only small differences between the two classes:

- Class `string` offers some conversions for types *signed char* and *unsigned char*. Type `wchar_t` has no analogous concerns.

- Class **string** compares two characters as if both are of type *unsigned char.* Wide characters are compared as type **wchar_t**, unaltered.

- Class **string** defines extractor and inserter functions. Type **wchar_t** has, in the Informal Review Draft, no extractors or inserters to build upon.

Otherwise, once you learn how to use class **string**, you will be quite comfortable with class **wstring**.

What the Draft C++ Standard Says

The words from the draft C++ Standard that follow are an unabashed edit of the words used to describe the header **<string>**, in the previous chapter. I outlined the small differences above. Don't look for any other surprises. As far as I know, there are none.

17.5.2 Header <wstring>

<wstring>

The header **<wstring>** defines a type and several function signatures for manipulating varying-length sequences of wide characters.

17.5.2.1 Class wstring

**Class
wstring**

```
class wstring {
public:
    wstring();
    wstring(size_t size, capacity cap);
    wstring(const wstring& str, size_t pos = 0,
        size_t n = NPOS);
    wstring(const wchar_t* s, size_t n = NPOS);
    wstring(wchar_t c, size_t rep = 1);
    wstring& operator=(const wstring& str);
    wstring& operator=(const wchar_t* s);
    wstring& operator=(wchar_t c);
    wstring& operator+=(const wstring& rhs);
    wstring& operator+=(const wchar_t* s);
    wstring& operator+=(wchar_t c);
    wstring& append(const wstring& str, size_t pos = 0,
        size_t n = NPOS);
    wstring& append(const wchar_t* s, size_t n = NPOS);
    wstring& append(wchar_t c, size_t rep = 1);
    wstring& assign(const wstring& str, size_t pos = 0,
        size_t n = NPOS);
    wstring& assign(const wchar_t*  s, size_t n = NPOS);
    wstring& assign(wchar_t c, size_t rep = 1);
    wstring& insert(size_t pos1, const wstring& str,
        size_t pos2 = 0, size_t n = NPOS);
    wstring& insert(size_t pos, const wchar_t* s,
        size_t n = NPOS);
    wstring& insert(size_t pos, wchar_t c, size_t rep = 1);
    wstring& remove(size_t pos = 0, size_t n = NPOS);
    wstring& replace(size_t pos1, size_t n1, const wstring& str,
        size_t pos2 = 0, size_t n2 = NPOS);
    wstring& replace(size_t pos, size_t n1, const wchar_t* s,
        size_t n2 = NPOS);
```

```
        wstring& replace(size_t pos, size_t n, wchar_t c,
            size_t rep = 1);
        wchar_t get_at(size_t pos) const;
        void put_at(size_t pos, wchar_t c);
        wchar_t operator[](size_t pos) const;
        wchar_t& operator[](size_t pos);
        const wchar_t* c_wcs() const;
        size_t length() const:
        void resize(size_t n, wchar_t c = 0);
        size_t reserve() const;
        void reserve(size_t res_arg);
        size_t copy(wchar_t* s, size_t n, size_t pos = 0);
        size_t find(const wstring& str, size_t pos = 0) const;
        size_t find(const wchar_t* s, size_t pos = 0,
            size_t n = NPOS) const;
        size_t find(wchar_t c, size_t pos = 0) const;
        size_t rfind(const wstring& str, size_t pos = NPOS) const;
        size_t rfind(const wchar_t* s, size_t pos = NPOS,
            size_t n = NPOS) const;
        size_t rfind(wchar_t c, size_t pos = NPOS) const;
        size_t find_first_of(const wstring& str, size_t pos = 0)
            const;
        size_t find_first_of(const wchar_t* s, size_t pos = 0,
            size_t n = NPOS) const;
        size_t find_first_of(wchar_t c, size_t pos = 0) const;
        size_t find_last_of(const wstring& str, size_t pos = NPOS)
            const;
        size_t find_last_of(const wchar_t* s, size_t pos = NPOS,
            size_t n = NPOS) const;
        size_t find_last_of(wchar_t c, size_t pos = NPOS) const;
        size_t find_first_not_of(const wstring& str,
            size_t pos = 0) const;
        size_t find_first_not_of(const wchar_t* s, size_t pos = 0,
            size_t n = NPOS) const;
        size_t find_first_not_of(wchar_t c, size_t pos = 0) const;
        size_t find_last_not_of(const wstring& str,
            size_t pos = NPOS) const;
        size_t find_last_not_of(const wchar_t* s, size_t pos = NPOS,
            size_t n = NPOS) const;
        size_t find_last_not_of(wchar_t c, size_t pos = NPOS) const;
        wstring substr(size_t pos = 0, size_t n = NPOS) const;
        int compare(const wstring& str, size_t pos = 0,
            size_t n = NPOS) const;
        int compare(const wchar_t* s, size_t pos = 0,
            size_t n = NPOS) const;
        int compare(wchar_t c, size_t pos = 0, size_t rep = 1)
            const;
private:
//  wchar_t* ptr;                                   exposition only
//  size_t len, res;                                exposition only
    };
```

The class **wstring** describes objects that can store a sequence consisting of a varying number of arbitrary wide characters. The first element of the sequence is at position zero. Such a sequence is also called a *wide-character string* (or simply a *string* if the type of the elements is clear from context). Storage for the string is allocated and freed as necessary by the member functions of class **wstring**. For the sake of exposition, the maintained data is presented here as:

- **wchar_t* *ptr***, points to the initial character of the string;
- **size_t *len***, counts the number of characters currently in the string;
- **size_t *res***, for an unallocated string, holds the recommended allocation size of the string, while for an allocated string, becomes the currently allocated size.

In all cases, ***len* <= *res***.

The functions described in this subclause can report two kinds of errors, each associated with a distinct exception:

- a *length* error is associated with exceptions of type **lengtherror**;
- an *out-of-range* error is associated with exceptions of type **outofrange**.

To report one of these errors, the function evaluates the expression ***ex*.raise()**, where ***ex*** is an object of the associated exception type.

17.5.2.1.1 wstring::wstring()

constructor
```
wstring();
```
Constructs an object of class **wstring** initializing:

- ***ptr*** to an unspecified value;
- ***len*** to zero;
- ***res*** to an unspecified value.

17.5.2.1.2 wstring::wstring(size_t, capacity)

constructor
```
wstring(size_t size, capacity cap);
```
Constructs an object of class **wstring**. If ***cap*** is ***default_size***, the function either reports a length error if ***size*** equals **NPOS** or initializes:

- ***ptr*** to point at the first element of an allocated array of ***size*** elements, each of which is initialized to zero;
- ***len*** to ***size***;
- ***res*** to a value at least as large as ***len***.

Otherwise, ***cap*** shall be ***reserve*** and the function initializes:

- ***ptr*** to an unspecified value;
- ***len*** to zero;
- ***res*** to ***size***.

17.5.2.1.3 wstring::wstring(const wstring&, size_t, size_t)

constructor
```
wstring(const wstring& str, size_t pos = 0, size_t n = NPOS);
```
Reports an out-of-range error if ***pos* > *str.len***. Otherwise, the function constructs an object of class **wstring** and determines the effective length ***rlen*** of the initial wstring value as the smaller of ***n*** and ***str.len* - *pos***. Thus, the function initializes:

- ***ptr*** to point at the first element of an allocated copy of ***rlen*** elements of the wstring controlled by ***str*** beginning at position ***pos***;
- ***len*** to ***rlen***;
- ***res*** to a value at least as large as ***len***.

17.5.2.1.4 wstring::wstring(const wchar_t*, size_t)

constructor
```
wstring(const wchar_t* s, size_t n);
```
If ***n*** equals **NPOS**, stores **wcslen(*s*)** in ***n***. The function signature **wcslen(const wchar_T*)** is declared in **<wchar.h>**.

In any case, the function constructs an object of class **wstring** and determines its initial string value from the array of **wchar_t** of length *n* whose first element is designated by *s*. *s* shall not be a null pointer. Thus, the function initializes:

- *ptr* to point at the first element of an allocated copy of the array whose first element is pointed at by *s*;
- *len* to *n*;
- *res* to a value at least as large as *len*.

17.5.2.1.5 wstring::wstring(wchar_t, size_t)

constructor

```
wstring(wchar_t c, size_t rep = 1);
```

Reports a length error if *rep* equals **NPOS**. Otherwise, the function constructs an object of class **wstring** and determines its initial string value by repeating the character *c* for all *rep* elements. Thus, the function initializes:

- *ptr* to point at the first element of an allocated array of *rep* elements, each storing the initial value *c*;
- *len* to *rep*;
- *res* to a value at least as large as *len*.

17.5.2.1.6 wstring::operator=(const wchar_t*)

operator=

```
wstring& operator=(const wstring& str);
```

Returns **assign(*str*)**.

17.5.2.1.7 wstring::operator=(const wchar_t*)

operator=

```
wstring& operator=(const wchar_t* s);
```

Returns ***this = string(*s*)**.

17.5.2.1.8 wstring::operator=(wchar_t)

operator=

```
wstring& operator=(wchar_t c);
```

Returns ***this = string(*c*)**.

17.5.2.1.9 wstring::operator+=(const wstring&)

operator+=

```
wstring& operator+=(const wstring& rhs);
```

Returns **append(*rhs*)**.

17.5.2.1.10 wstring::operator+=(const wchar_t*)

operator+=

```
wstring& operator+=(const wchar_t* s);
```

Returns ***this += string(*s*)**.

17.5.2.1.11 wstring::operator+=(wchar_t)

operator+=

```
wstring& operator+=(wchar_t c);
```

Returns ***this += string(*c*)**.

17.5.2.1.12 wstring::append(const wstring&, size_t, size_t)

append

```
wstring& append(const wstring& str, size_t pos = 0,
    size_t n = NPOS);
```

Reports an out-of-range error if *pos* > *str.len*. Otherwise, the function determines the effective length *rlen* of the string to append as the smaller of *n* and *str.len* - *pos*. The function then reports a length error if *len* >= **NPOS** - *rlen*.

Otherwise, the function replaces the string controlled by ***this** with a string of length *len* + *rlen* whose first *len* elements are a copy of the original string controlled by ***this** and whose remaining elements are a copy of the initial elements of the string controlled by *str* beginning at position *pos*.

The function returns ***this**.

17.5.2.1.13 wstring::append(const wchar_t*, size_t)

append | `wstring& append(const wchar_t* s, size_t n = NPOS);`

Returns `append(wstring(s, n))`.

17.5.2.1.14 wstring::append(wchar_t, size_t)

append | `wstring& append(wchar_t c, size_t rep = 1);`

Returns `append(wstring(c, rep))`.

17.5.2.1.15 wstring::assign(const wstring&, size_t, size_t)

assign | `wstring& assign(const wstring& str, size_t pos = 0,`
`    size_t n = NPOS);`

Reports an out-of-range error if *pos* > *str.len*. Otherwise, the function determines the effective length *rlen* of the string to assign as the smaller of *n* and *str.len - pos*.

The function then replaces the string controlled by ***this** with a string of length *rlen* whose elements are a copy of the string controlled by *str* beginning at position *pos*.

The function returns ***this**.

17.5.2.1.16 wstring::assign(const wchar_t*, size_t)

assign | `wstring& assign(const wchar_t* s, size_t n = NPOS);`

Returns `assign(wstring(s, n))`.

17.5.2.1.17 wstring::assign(wchar_t, size_t)

assign | `wstring& assign(wchar_t c, size_t rep = 1);`

Returns `assign(wstring(c, rep))`.

17.5.2.1.18 wstring::insert(size_t, const wstring&, size_t, size_t)

insert | `wstring& insert(size_t pos1, const wstring& str,`
`    size_t pos2 = 0, size_t n = NPOS);`

Reports an out-of-range error if *pos1* > *len* or *pos2* > *str.len*. Otherwise, the function determines the effective length *rlen* of the string to insert as the smaller of *n* and *str.len - pos2*. The function then reports a length error if *len* >= NPOS - *rlen*.

Otherwise, the function replaces the string controlled by ***this** with a string of length *len + rlen* whose first *pos1* elements are a copy of the initial elements of the original string controlled by ***this**, whose next *rlen* elements are a copy of the elements of the string controlled by *str* beginning at position *pos2*, and whose remaining elements are a copy of the remaining elements of the original string controlled by ***this**.

The function returns ***this**.

17.5.2.1.19 wstring::insert(size_t, const wchar_t*, size_t)

insert | `wstring& insert(size_t pos, const wchar_t* s, size_t n = NPOS);`

Returns `insert(pos, wstring(s, n))`.

17.5.2.1.20 wstring::insert(size_t, wchar_t, size_t)

insert | `wstring& insert(size_t pos, wchar_t c, size_t rep = 1);`

Returns `insert(pos, wstring(c, rep))`.

17.5.2.1.21 wstring::remove(size_t, size_t)

remove | `wstring& remove(size_t pos = 0, size_t n = NPOS);`

Reports an out-of-range error if *pos* > *len*. Otherwise, the function determines the effective length *xlen* of the string to be removed as the smaller of *n* and *len* - *pos*.

The function then replaces the string controlled by *this* with a string of length *len* - *xlen* whose first *pos* elements are a copy of the initial elements of the original string controlled by *this*, and whose remaining elements are a copy of the elements of the original string controlled by *this* beginning at position *pos* + *xlen*.

The function returns *this*.

17.5.2.1.22 wstring::replace(size_t, size_t, const wstring&, size_t, size_t)

replace

```
wstring& replace(size_t pos1, size_t n1, const wstring& str,
    size_t pos2 = 0, size_t n2 = NPOS);
```

Reports an out-of-range error if *pos1* > *len* or *pos2* > *str.len*. Otherwise, the function determines the effective length *xlen* of the string to be removed as the smaller of *n1* and *len* - *pos1*. It also determines the effective length *rlen* of the string to be inserted as the smaller of *n2* and *str.len* - *pos2*. The function then reports a length error if *len* - *xlen* >= NPOS - *rlen*.

Otherwise, the function replaces the string controlled by *this* with a string of length *len* - *xlen* + *rlen* whose first *pos1* elements are a copy of the initial elements of the original string controlled by *this*, whose next *rlen* elements are a copy of the initial elements of the string controlled by *str* beginning at position *pos2*, and whose remaining elements are a copy of the elements of the original string controlled by *this* beginning at position *pos1* + *xlen*.

The function returns *this*.

17.5.2.1.23 wstring::replace(size_t, size_t, const wchar_t*, size_t)

replace

```
wstring& replace(size_t pos, size_t n1, const wchar_t* s,
    size_t n2 = NPOS);
```

Returns **replace(*pos*, *n1*, wstring(*s*, *n2*))**.

17.5.2.1.24 wstring::replace(size_t, size_t, wchar_t, size_t)

replace

```
wstring& replace(size_t pos, size_t n, wchar_t c,
    size_t rep = 1);
```

Returns **replace(*pos*, *n*, wstring(*c*, *rep*))**.

17.5.2.1.25 wstring::get_at(size_t)

get_at

```
wchar_t get_at(size_t pos) const;
```

Reports an out-of-range error if *pos* >= *len*. Otherwise, the function returns *ptr[pos]*.

17.5.2.1.26 wstring::put_at(size_t, wchar_t)

put_at

```
void put_at(size_t pos, wchar_t c);
```

Reports an out-of-range error if *pos* > *len*. Otherwise, if *pos* == *len*, the function replaces the string controlled by *this* with a string of length *len* + 1 whose first *len* elements are a copy of the original string and whose remaining element is initialized to *c*. Otherwise, the function assigns *c* to *ptr[pos]*.

17.5.2.1.27 wstring::operator[](size_t)

operator[]

```
wchar_t operator[](size_t pos) const;
wchar_t& operator[](size_t pos);
```

If *pos* < *len*, returns *ptr[pos]*. Otherwise, if *pos* == *len*, the **const** version returns zero. Otherwise, the behavior is undefined.

The reference returned by the non-**const** version is invalid after any subsequent call to **c_wcs** or any non-**const** member function for the object.

17.5.2.1.28 wstring::c_wcs()

c_wcs

```
const wchar_t* c_wcs() const;
```

Returns a pointer to the initial element of an array of length **len + 1** whose first **len** elements equal the corresponding elements of the string controlled by ***this** and whose last element is a null character. The program shall not alter any of the values stored in the array. Nor shall the program treat the returned value as a valid pointer value after any subsequent call to a non-**const** member function of the class **wstring** that designates the same object as ***this**.

17.5.2.1.29 wstring::length()

length

```
size_t length() const:
```

Returns **len**.

17.5.2.1.30 wstring::resize(size_t, wchar_t)

resize

```
void resize(size_t n, wchar_t c = 0);
```

Reports a length error if **n** equals **NPOS**. Otherwise, the function alters the length of the string designated by ***this** as follows:

- If **n <= len**, the function replaces the string designated by ***this** with a string of length **n** whose elements are a copy of the initial elements of the original string designated by ***this**.

- If **n > len**, the function replaces the string designated by ***this** with a string of length **n** whose first **len** elements are a copy of the original string designated by ***this**, and whose remaining elements are all initialized to **c**.

17.5.2.1.31 wstring::reserve()

reserve

```
size_t reserve() const;
```

Returns **res**.

17.5.2.1.32 wstring::reserve(size_t)

reserve

```
void reserve(size_t res_arg);
```

If no string is allocated, the function assigns **res_arg** to **res**. Otherwise, whether or how the function alters **res** is unspecified.

17.5.2.1.33 wstring::copy(wchar_t*, size_t, size_t)

copy

```
size_t copy(wchar_t* s, size_t n, size_t pos = 0);
```

Reports an out-of-range error if **pos > len**. Otherwise, the function determines the effective length **rlen** of the string to copy as the smaller of **n** and **len - pos**. **s** shall designate an array of at least **rlen** elements.

The function then replaces the string designated by **s** with a string of length **rlen** whose elements are a copy of the string controlled by ***this**, beginning at position **pos**.[112)]

The function returns **rlen**.

17.5.2.1.34 wstring::find(const wstring&, size_t)

find

```
size_t find(const wstring& str, size_t pos = 0) const;
```

Determines the lowest position **xpos**, if possible, such that both of the following conditions obtain:

- **pos <= xpos** and **xpos + str.len <= len**;
- **ptr[xpos + I] == str.ptr[I]** for all elements **I** of the string controlled by **str**.

If the function can determine such a value for **xpos**, it returns **xpos**. Otherwise, it returns **NPOS**.

17.5.2.1.35 `wstring::find(const wchar_t*, size_t, size_t)`

find
```
size_t find(const wchar_t* s, size_t pos = 0, size_t n = NPOS)
    const;
```
Returns `find(wstring(s, n), pos)`.

17.5.2.1.36 `wstring::find(wchar_t, size_t)`

find
```
size_t find(wchar_t c, size_t pos = 0) const;
```
Returns `find(wstring(c), pos)`.

17.5.2.1.37 `wstring::rfind(const wstring&, size_t)`

rfind
```
size_t rfind(const wstring& str, size_t pos = NPOS) const;
```
Determines the highest position *xpos*, if possible, such that both of the following conditions obtain:

- *xpos* `<=` *pos* and *xpos* `+` *str.len* `<=` *len*;
- *ptr[xpos* `+` *I]* `==` *str.ptr[I]* for all elements *I* of the string controlled by *str*.

If the function can determine such a value for *xpos*, it returns *xpos*. Otherwise, it returns **NPOS**.

17.5.2.1.38 `wstring::rfind(const wchar_t*, size_t, size_t)`

rfind
```
size_t rfind(const wchar_t* s, size_t pos = NPOS,
    size_t n = NPOS) const;
```
Returns `rfind(wstring(s, n), pos)`.

17.5.2.1.39 `wstring::rfind(wchar_t, size_t)`

rfind
```
size_t rfind(wchar_t c, size_t pos = NPOS) const;
```
Returns `rfind(wstring(c, n), pos)`.

17.5.2.1.40 `wstring::find_first_of(const wstring&, size_t)`

find_first_of
```
size_t find_first_of(const wstring& str, size_t pos = 0) const;
```
Determines the lowest position *xpos*, if possible, such that both of the following conditions obtain:

- *pos* `<=` *xpos* and *xpos* `<` *len*;
- *ptr[xpos]* `==` *str.ptr[I]* for some element *I* of the string controlled by *str*.

If the function can determine such a value for *xpos*, it returns *xpos*. Otherwise, it returns **NPOS**.

17.5.2.1.41 `wstring::find_first_of(const wchar_t*, size_t, size_t)`

find_first_of
```
size_t find_first_of(const wchar_t* s, size_t pos = 0,
    size_t n = NPOS) const;
```
Returns `find_first_of(wstring(s, n), pos)`.

17.5.2.1.42 `wstring::find_first_of(wchar_t, size_t)`

find_first_of
```
size_t find_first_of(wchar_t c, size_t pos = 0) const;
```
Returns `find_first_of(wstring(c), pos)`.

17.5.2.1.43 `wstring::find_last_of(const wstring&, size_t)`

find_last_of
```
size_t find_last_of(const wstring& str, size_t pos = NPOS)
    const;
```
Determines the highest position *xpos*, if possible, such that both of the following conditions obtain:

- *xpos* `<=` *pos* and *pos* `<` *len*;

- `ptr[xpos] == str.ptr[I]` for some element `I` of the string controlled by `str`.

If the function can determine such a value for `xpos`, it returns `xpos`. Otherwise, it returns `NPOS`.

17.5.2.1.44 wstring::find_last_of(const wchar_t*, size_t, size_t)

find_last_of

```
size_t find_last_of(const wchar_t* s, size_t pos = NPOS,
    size_t n = NPOS) const;
```

Returns `find_last_of(wstring(s, n), pos)`.

17.5.2.1.45 wstring::find_last_of(wchar_t, size_t)

find_last_of

```
size_t find_last_of(wchar_t c, size_t pos = NPOS) const;
```

Returns `find_last_of(wstring(c, n), pos)`.

17.5.2.1.46 wstring::find_first_not_of(const wstring&, size_t)

find_first_
not_of

```
size_t find_first_not_of(const wstring& str, size_t pos = 0)
    const;
```

Determines the lowest position `xpos`, if possible, such that both of the following conditions obtain:

- `pos <= xpos` and `xpos < len`;
- `ptr[xpos] == str.ptr[I]` for no element `I` of the string controlled by `str`.

If the function can determine such a value for `xpos`, it returns `xpos`. Otherwise, it returns `NPOS`.

17.5.2.1.47 wstring::find_first_not_of(const wchar_t*, size_t, size_t)

find_first_
not_of

```
size_t find_first_not_of(const wchar_t* s, size_t pos = 0,
    size_t n = NPOS) const;
```

Returns `find_first_not_of(wstring(s, n), pos)`.

17.5.2.1.48 wstring::find_first_not_of(wchar_t, size_t)

find_first_
not_of

```
size_t find_first_not_of(wchar_t c, size_t pos = 0)
    const;
```

Returns `find_first_not_of(wstring(c), pos)`.

17.5.2.1.49 wstring::find_last_not_of(const wstring&, size_t)

find_last_
not_of

```
size_t find_last_not_of(const wstring& str, size_t pos = NPOS)
    const;
```

Determines the highest position `xpos`, if possible, such that both of the following conditions obtain:

- `xpos <= pos` and `pos < len`;
- `ptr[xpos] == str.ptr[I]` for no element `I` of the string controlled by `str`.

If the function can determine such a value for `xpos`, it returns `xpos`. Otherwise, it returns `NPOS`.

17.5.2.1.50 wstring::find_last_not_of(const wchar_t*, size_t, size_t)

find_last_
not_of

```
size_t find_last_not_of(const wchar_t* s, size_t pos = NPOS,
    size_t n = NPOS) const;
```

Returns `find_last_not_of(wstring(s, n), pos)`.

find_last_ not_of

17.5.2.1.51 `wstring::find_last_not_of(wchar_t, size_t)`

```
size_t find_last_not_of(wchar_t c, size_t pos = NPOS)
    const;
```

Returns `find_last_not_of(wstring(c, n), pos)`.

substr

17.5.2.1.52 `wstring::substr(size_t, size_t)`

```
wstring substr(size_t pos = 0, size_t n = NPOS) const;
```

Returns `wstring(*this, pos, n)`.

compare

17.5.2.1.53 `wstring::compare(const wstring&, size_t, size_t)`

```
int compare(const wstring& str, size_t pos, size_t n = NPOS)
    const;
```

Reports an out-of-range error if *pos* > *len*. Otherwise, if *str.len* < *n*, the function stores *str.len* in *n*. The function then determines the effective length *rlen* of the strings to compare as the smaller of *n* and *len* - *pos*. The function then compares the two strings by calling `wcscmp(ptr + pos, str.ptr, rlen)`. The function signature `wmemcmp(const wchar_t*, const wchar_t*, size_t)` is declared in `<wchar.h>`.

If the result of that comparison is nonzero, the function returns the nonzero result. Otherwise, the function returns:

- if *len* < *rlen*, a value less than zero;
- if *len* == *rlen*, the value zero;
- if *len* > *rlen*, a value greater than zero.

compare

17.5.2.1.54 `wstring::compare(const wchar_t*, size_t)`

```
size_t compare(const wchar_t* s, size_t n = NPOS) const;
```

Returns `compare(wstring(s, n), pos)`.

compare

17.5.2.1.55 `wstring::compare(wchar_t, size_t)`

```
size_t compare(wchar_t c, size_t rep = 1) const;
```

Returns `compare(wstring(c, rep), pos)`.

operator+

17.5.2.2 `operator+(const wstring&, const wstring&)`

```
wstring operator+(const wstring& lhs, const wstring& rhs);
```

Returns `wstring(lhs).append(rhs)`.

operator+

17.5.2.3 `operator+(const wchar_t*, const wstring&)`

```
wstring operator+(const wchar_t* lhs, const wstring& rhs);
```

Returns `wstring(lhs) + rhs`.

operator+

17.5.2.4 `operator+(wchar_t, const wstring&)`

```
wstring operator+(wchar_t lhs, const wstring& rhs);
```

Returns `wstring(lhs) + rhs`.

operator+

17.5.2.5 `operator+(const wstring&, const wchar_t*)`

```
wstring operator+(const wstring& lhs, const wchar_t* rhs);
```

Returns `lhs + wstring(rhs)`.

operator+

17.5.2.6 `operator+(const wstring&, wchar_t)`

```
wstring operator+(const wstring& lhs, wchar_t rhs);
```

Returns `lhs + wstring(rhs)`.

operator==

17.5.2.7 `operator==(const wstring&, const wstring&)`

```
int operator==(const wstring& lhs, const wstring& rhs);
```

Returns a nonzero value if *lhs.*`compare(rhs)` is zero.

operator==	**17.5.2.8** operator==(const wchar_t*, const wstring&) `int operator==(const wchar_t* lhs, const wstring& rhs);` Returns **wstring(lhs) == rhs**.
operator==	**17.5.2.9** operator==(wchar_t, const wstring&) `int operator==(wchar_t lhs, const wstring& rhs);` Returns **wstring(lhs) == rhs**.
operator==	**17.5.2.10** operator==(const wstring&, const wchar_t*) `int operator==(const wstring& lhs, const wchar_t* rhs);` Returns **lhs == wstring(rhs)**.
operator==	**17.5.2.11** operator==(const wstring&, wchar_t) `int operator==(const wstring& lhs, wchar_t rhs);` Returns **lhs == wstring(rhs)**.
operator!=	**17.5.2.12** operator!=(const wstring&, const wstring&) `int operator!=(const wstring& lhs, const wstring& rhs);` Returns a nonzero value if **!(lhs == rhs)** is nonzero.
operator!=	**17.5.2.13** operator!=(const wchar_t*, const wstring&) `int operator!=(const wchar_t* lhs, const wstring& rhs);` Returns **wstring(lhs) != rhs**.
operator!=	**17.5.2.14** operator!=(wchar_t, const wstring&) `int operator!=(wchar_t lhs, const wstring& rhs);` Returns **wstring(lhs) != rhs**.

operator!=	**17.5.2.15** operator!=(const wstring&, const wchar_t*)
	`int operator!=(const wstring& lhs,`
	`    const wchar_t* rhs);`
	Returns **lhs != wstring(rhs)**.

operator!=	**17.5.2.16** operator!=(const wstring&, wchar_t) `int operator!=(const wstring& lhs, wchar_t rhs);` Returns **lhs != wstring(rhs)**.

Footnotes:

Footnotes 112) The function does not append a null wide character to the string.

Future Directions

c_wcs   The member function **wstring::c_wcs** is now **wstring::data**.

put_at ▪ The member function **wstring::put_at** no longer appends a wide character when the sequence is accessed exactly at its end.

basic_string   As I mentioned in the previous chapter, the Committee has replaced class **wstring** with a template class called **basic_string**. One instantiation, for elements of type *char*, reproduces class **string** and related functions, as described in the previous chapter. Another instantiation, for elements of type **wchar_t**, reproduces class **wstring** and related functions, as described in this chapter. (See the discussion on page 357.) As before, the code presented here is effectively an efficient specialization for type **wchar_t**.

Using `<wstring>`

The description that follows closely resembles the one for the header `<wstring>` in the previous chapter. I present it here to keep the discussion of class `wstring` localized. Also, there are just enough differences to remember that interpolating from the description of class `string` can mislead.

You include the header `<wstring>` to make use of the class `wstring`. Objects of this class let you manipulate in-memory wide-character sequences that vary dynamically in length. The `wstring` object allocates and frees storage as needed to accommodate changes in length of the controlled sequence.

construction To construct a `wstring` object `x0` with an initially empty wide-character sequence, you can simply write:

```
wstring x0;
```

length Each wstring `x` reports the *length* of its wide-character sequence with the
reserve call `x.length()`. It also reports its *reserve size* with the call `x.reserve()`. For a newly constructed `wstring` object, the reserve size suggests how much storage to initially allocate for the wide-character sequence. You can, for example, specify an initial reserve size of 100 wide characters by writing:

capacity
```
wstring x0(100, reserve);
```

For an object with a non-empty wide-character sequence, the reserve size suggests how much storage is currently available to hold the wide-character sequence. Thus, `x0.length() <= x0.reserve()` at all times. As a rule, you can ignore the reserve size. The implementation will guess it for you. (But see the discussion on page 279.)

To construct a `wstring` object and define its initial wide-character sequence, you have a number of choices. In each case below, the wide string literal in the comment shows the resulting wide-character sequence. The implied null wide character at the end of this wide string literal is *not* part of the wide-character sequence. You can write:

```
wstring x1(5, default_size);        // L"\0\0\0\0\0"
wstring x2('a');                            // L"a"
wstring x3('a', 5);                   // L"aaaaa"
wstring x4("abcde");                  // L"abcde"
wstring x5("abcdefg", 5);            // L"abcde"
```

substrings You can also define the initial wide-character sequence when you construct a `wstring` object by selecting a *substring* from another `wstring` object. Given the definition of `x5` above, you can write:

```
wstring x6(x5);                       // L"abcde"
wstring x7(x5, 1);                     // L"bcde"
wstring x8(x5, 1, 3);                   // L"bcd"
```

A substring thus has two default arguments. In order, these are:

- the initial position `pos` in the wide-character sequence, counting from zero (default is zero)

- the maximum number of wide characters `n` to include from the remainder of the wide-character sequence (default is `NPOS`, a huge value)

notation   Class **wstring** supports numerous combinations of argument types for practically every function that constructs or manipulates such objects. For brevity, I define here a terse and uniform style for writing various argument combinations. The resultant argument is:

- a single wide-character, with the argument **c**
- a repetition of wide characters, with the arguments **c, rep**
- a null-terminated array of wide characters, with the argument **s**
- an array of wide characters with a specified length, with the arguments **s, n**
- a substring, with the arguments **x**, or **x, pos**, or **x, pos, n**, as described above

With this notation, I can more quickly summarize all the ways you can perform various operations involving **wstring** objects. Here, for example, is a summary of most of the constructors I showed above:

```
wstring x2(c);
wstring x3(c, rep);
wstring x4(s);
wstring x5(s, n);
wstring x6(x);
wstring x7(x, pos);
wstring x8(x, pos, n);
```

A number of member functions alter the wide-character sequence controlled by a **wstring** object **x0**.

To assign a new wide-character sequence, in place of any existing one:

assign
```
x0.assign(c)              x0 = c
x0.assign(c, rep)
x0.assign(s)              x0 = s
x0.assign(s, n)
x0.assign(x)              x0 = x
x0.assign(x, pos)
x0.assign(x, pos, n)
```

To append to an existing wide-character sequence:

append
```
x0.append(c)              x0 += c
x0.append(c, rep)
x0.append(s)              x0 += s
x0.append(s, n)
x0.append(x)              x0 += x
x0.append(x, pos)
x0.append(x, pos, n)
```

To insert before position **px** in an existing wide-character sequence:

insert
```
x0.insert(px, c)
x0.insert(px, c, rep)
x0.insert(px, s)
x0.insert(px, s, n)
x0.insert(px, x)
x0.insert(px, x, pos)
x0.insert(px, x, pos, n)
```

To replace at most **m** wide characters beginning with position **px** in an existing wide-character sequence:

replace	`x0.replace(px, m, c)`
	`x0.replace(px, m, c, rep)`
	`x0.replace(px, m, s)`
	`x0.replace(px, m, s, n)`
	`x0.replace(px, m, x)`
	`x0.replace(px, m, x, pos)`
	`x0.replace(px, m, x, pos, n)`

You can remove a substring from a wide-character sequence in various ways:

remove	`x0.remove()` `// remove all wide characters`
	`x0.remove(px)` `// remove all from px to end`
	`x0.remove(px, n)` `// remove at most n beginning at px`

You can establish a new length **len** for a wide-character sequence. If the new length is greater than the existing length, the wide-character sequence is padded as stated in the comment below:

resize	`x0.resize(len)` `// pad to len with null wide characters`
	`x0.resize(len, c)` `// pad to len by repeating c`

As a final alteration, you can store a new value **c** in the element at position **px** two different ways:

put_at	`x0.put_at(px, c)`
	`x0[px] = c`
operator[]	Be warned, however, that the subscript notation is more delicate. It returns a reference that can be invalidated by all sorts of subsequent operations on **x0**. Use it only in a very localized context, as above.

Another set of functions lets you obtain part or all of the wide-character sequence controlled by a **wstring** object. The compaions to the functions immediately above are:

get_at	`x0.get_at(px)`
	`x0[px]`
operator[]	both of which return the wide-character value stored at position **px**.

You can get a pointer to the beginning of the entire wide-character sequence, complete with terminating null wide character, by calling:

c_wcs	`x0.c_wcs()`

The same caveats apply as for the subscript operator, above. Use the pointer to do any direct accessing of the wide-character sequence quickly, before you perform any subsequent operations on **x0**. The pointer may well become invalid.

You can also copy into a wide-character array beginning at **s** at most **n** wide characters from the wide-character sequence, by writing:

copy	`x0.copy(s, n)` `// copy at most n, from the beginning`
	`x0.copy(s, n, px)` `// copy at most n, beginning at px`

Yes, the arguments are backwards from the usual way for designating a substring.

Some functions each construct a **wstring** object to return as the value of the function, leaving the object **x0** unaltered. You can, for example, obtain a substring as a separate object:

```
substr        x0.substr()                                    // copy all
              x0.substr(pos)            // copy remainder beginning at pos
              x0.substr(pos, n)         // copy at most n beginning at pos
```

You can also construct a **wstring** object that appends the wide-character sequences defined by two operands:

```
operator+     x + c
              c + x
              x + s
              s + x
              x + x0
```

Comparing two **wstring** objects involves a wide-character-by-wide-character comparison of corresponding values in the two wide-character sequences, for the length of the shorter sequence. If two corresponding values are unequal, the wide-character sequence with the larger value compares larger. Otherwise, if the two wide-character sequences are of equal length, they compare equal. Otherwise, the longer wide-character sequence compares larger. To compare two complete wide-character sequences for equality (**==**) or inequality (**!=**), you can write any of:

```
operator==    x == c                           x != c
operator!=    c == x                           c != x
              x == s                           x != s
              s == x                           s != x
              x == x0                          x != x0
```

Or, you can call the member function **compare** to compare part or all of the wide-character sequences. The comment that follows shows the equivalent comparison in operator notation:

```
compare       x0.compare(x)                                  // x0 == x
              x0.compare(x, px)               // substr(x0, px) == x
              x0.compare(x, px, n)
                                 // substr(x0, px) == substr(x, 0, n)
```

Yes, the last example does *not* follow the usual pattern for specifying substrings.

A number of member functions look for substrings within a wide-character sequence. To find the first (lowest position) occurrence of the argument wide-character sequence within a wide-character sequence:

```
find          x0.find(c)
              x0.find(s)
              x0.find(s, 0, n)
              x0.find(x)
```

All such calls return the beginning position of a successful match, or **NPOS** to report failure. Yes, the third example does *not* follow the usual pattern for specifying substrings. That's because the second argument, when present, is always the position **px** within the wide-character sequence where the search begins. So to find the first occurrence of the argument wide-character sequence *beginning on or after* **px**:

```
              x0.find(c, px)
              x0.find(s, px)
              x0.find(s, px, n)
              x0.find(x)
```

Similarly, to find the last (highest position) occurrence of the argument wide-character sequence within a wide-character sequence:

rfind
```
x0.rfind(c)
x0.rfind(s)
x0.rfind(s, NPOS, n)
x0.rfind(x)
```

Note the use of **NPOS** to specify a very large position. To find the last occurrence of the argument wide-character sequence *beginning on or before* **px**:

```
x0.rfind(c, px)
x0.rfind(s, px)
x0.rfind(s, px, n)
x0.rfind(x)
```

Four sets of member functions treat the argument wide-character sequence as a *set* of wide characters. Each wide character in the set is compared against part or all of the wide-character sequence controlled by the **wstring** object. For example, to find the *first* element in the wide-character sequence that matches *any* wide character in the set (**find_first_of**), or that matches *no* wide character in the set (**find_first_not_of**):

find_
first_of

find_
first_not_of

```
x0.find_first_of(c)        x0.find_first_not_of(c)
x0.find_first_of(s)        x0.find_first_not_of(s)
x0.find_first_of(s, 0, n)  x0.find_first_not_of(s, 0, n)
x0.find_first_of(x)        x0.find_first_not_of(x)
x0.find_first_of(c, px)    x0.find_first_not_of(c, px)
x0.find_first_of(s, px)    x0.find_first_not_of(s, px)
x0.find_first_of(s, px, n) x0.find_first_not_of(s, px, n)
x0.find_first_of(x)        x0.find_first_not_of(x)
```

And to find the *last* element in the wide-character sequence that matches *any* wide character in the set (**find_last_of**), or that matches *no* wide character in the set (**find_last_not_of**):

find_last_of

find_last_
not_of

```
x0.find_last_of(c)         x0.find_last_not_of(c)
x0.find_last_of(s)         x0.find_last_not_of(s)
x0.find_last_of(s, 0, n)   x0.find_last_not_of(s, 0, n)
x0.find_last_of(x)         x0.find_last_not_of(x)
x0.find_last_of(c, px)     x0.find_last_not_of(c, px)
x0.find_last_of(s, px)     x0.find_last_not_of(s, px)
x0.find_last_of(s, px, n)  x0.find_last_not_of(s, px, n)
x0.find_last_of(x)         x0.find_last_not_of(x)
```

Implementing `<wstring>`

This implementation of **<wstring>** closely parallels that for **<string>**, as you might expect. To maximize that parallelism, I make extensive use of the functions declared in **<wchar.h>**. Note that these are *not* yet available in many implementations of the Standard C library. (See Appendix A: Interfaces.)

wstring
Figure 16.1 shows the file **wstring**, which implements the header **<wstring>**. I defined the static member object **_Nullwcs** as a handy source of a null wide character. (Not all implementations support wide literals.)

The class **wstring** defines also four secret protected member functions:

```
// wstring standard header
#ifndef _WSTRING_
#define _WSTRING_
#include <exception>
            // class wstring
class wstring {
public:
static const wchar_t _Nullwcs[];
    wstring()
        {_Tidy(); }
    wstring(size_t _N, capacity _C)
        {_Tidy(), _Res = _N;
        if (_C == default_size)
            assign((wchar_t)0, _N); }
    wstring(const wstring& _X, size_t _P = 0, size_t _N = NPOS)
        {_Tidy(), assign(_X, _P, _N); }
    wstring(const wchar_t *_S, size_t _N = NPOS)
        {_Tidy(), assign(_S, _N); }
    wstring(wchar_t _C, size_t _N = 1)
        {_Tidy(), assign(_C, _N); }
    ~wstring()
        {_Tidy(1); }
    wstring& operator=(const wstring& _X)
        {return (assign(_X)); }
    wstring& operator=(const wchar_t *_S)
        {return (assign(_S)); }
    wstring& operator=(wchar_t _C)
        {return (assign(_C)); }
    wstring& operator+=(const wstring& _X)
        {return (append(_X)); }
    wstring& operator+=(const wchar_t *_S)
        {return (append(_S)); }
    wstring& operator+=(wchar_t _C)
        {return (append(_C)); }
    wstring& append(const wstring&, size_t = 0, size_t = NPOS);
    wstring& append(const wchar_t *, size_t = NPOS);
    wstring& append(wchar_t, size_t = 1);
    wstring& assign(const wstring&, size_t = 0, size_t = NPOS);
    wstring& assign(const wchar_t *, size_t = NPOS);
    wstring& assign(wchar_t, size_t = 1);
    wstring& insert(size_t, const wstring&, size_t = 0,
        size_t = NPOS);
    wstring& insert(size_t, const wchar_t *, size_t = NPOS);
    wstring& insert(size_t, wchar_t, size_t = 1);
    wstring& remove(size_t = 0, size_t = NPOS);
    wstring& replace(size_t, size_t, const wstring&,
        size_t = 0, size_t = NPOS);
    wstring& replace(size_t, size_t, const wchar_t *,
        size_t = NPOS);
    wstring& replace(size_t, size_t, wchar_t, size_t = 1);
    wchar_t get_at(size_t) const;
    void put_at(size_t, wchar_t);
    wchar_t operator[](size_t _N) const
        {return (_Ptr[_N]); }
    wchar_t& operator[](size_t _N)
```

```
            {return (_Ptr[_N]); }
    const wchar_t *c_wcs() const
            {return (_Ptr != 0 ? _Ptr : _Nullwcs); }
    size_t length() const
            {return (_Len); }
    void resize(size_t _N, wchar_t _C = 0)
            {_N <= _Len ? remove(_N) : append(_C, _N - _Len); }
    size_t reserve() const
            {return (_Res); }
    void reserve(size_t _N)
            {if (_Ptr == 0)
                _Res = _N; }
    size_t copy(wchar_t *, size_t, size_t = 0);
    size_t find(const wstring& _X, size_t _P = 0) const
            {return (find(_X.c_wcs(), _P, _X.length())); }
    size_t find(const wchar_t *_S, size_t _P = 0,
        size_t _N = NPOS) const;
    size_t find(wchar_t _C, size_t _P = 0) const
            {return (find((const wchar_t *)&_C, _P, 1)); }
    size_t rfind(const wstring& _X, size_t _P = NPOS) const
            {return (rfind(_X.c_wcs(), _P, _X.length())); }
    size_t rfind(const wchar_t *, size_t = NPOS, size_t = NPOS)
        const;
    size_t rfind(wchar_t _C, size_t _P = NPOS) const
            {return (rfind((const wchar_t *)&_C, _P, 1)); }
    size_t find_first_of(const wstring& _X, size_t _P = 0) const
            {return (find_first_of(_X.c_wcs(), _P, _X.length())); }
    size_t find_first_of(const wchar_t *, size_t = 0,
        size_t = NPOS) const;
    size_t find_first_of(wchar_t _C, size_t _P = 0) const
            {return (find((const wchar_t *)&_C, _P, 1)); }
    size_t find_last_of(const wstring& _X, size_t _P = NPOS)
        const
            {return (find_last_of(_X.c_wcs(), _P, _X.length())); }
    size_t find_last_of(const wchar_t *, size_t = NPOS,
        size_t = NPOS) const;
    size_t find_last_of(wchar_t _C, size_t _P = NPOS) const
            {return (rfind((const wchar_t *)&_C, _P, 1)); }
    size_t find_first_not_of(const wstring& _X,
        size_t _P = 0) const
            {return (find_first_not_of(_X.c_wcs(), _P,
                _X.length())); }
    size_t find_first_not_of(const wchar_t *, size_t = 0,
        size_t = NPOS) const;
    size_t find_first_not_of(wchar_t _C, size_t _P = 0) const
            {return (find_first_not_of((const wchar_t *)&_C,
                _P, 1)); }
    size_t find_last_not_of(const wstring& _X,
        size_t _P = NPOS) const
            {return (find_last_not_of(_X.c_wcs(), _P,
                _X.length())); }
    size_t find_last_not_of(const wchar_t *, size_t = NPOS,
        size_t = NPOS) const;
    size_t find_last_not_of(wchar_t _C, size_t _P = NPOS) const
            {return (find_last_not_of((const wchar_t *)&_C,
```

```
                         _P, 1)); }
        wstring substr(size_t _P = 0, size_t _N = NPOS) const
            {return (wstring(*this, _P, _N)); }
        int compare(const wstring&, size_t = 0, size_t = NPOS)
            const;
        int compare(const wchar_t *, size_t = 0, size_t = NPOS)
            const;
        int compare(wchar_t, size_t = 0, size_t = 1) const;
private:
        _Bool _Grow(size_t, _Bool = 0);
        void _Tidy(_Bool = 0);
        void _Xlen() const
            {lengtherror("wstring too long").raise(); }
        void _Xran() const
            {outofrange("invalid wstring position").raise(); }
        wchar_t *_Ptr;
        size_t _Len, _Res;
        };
inline wstring operator+(const wstring& _L, const wstring& _R)
    {return (wstring(_L) += _R); }
inline wstring operator+(const wchar_t *_L, const wstring& _R)
    {return (wstring(_L) += _R); }
inline wstring operator+(wchar_t _L, const wstring& _R)
    {return (wstring(_L) += _R); }
inline wstring operator+(const wstring& _L, const wchar_t *_R)
    {return (wstring(_L) += _R); }
inline wstring operator+(const wstring& _L, wchar_t _R)
    {return (wstring(_L) += _R); }
inline _Bool operator==(const wstring& _L, const wstring& _R)
    {return (_L.compare(_R) == 0); }
inline _Bool operator==(const wchar_t * _L, const wstring& _R)
    {return (_R.compare(_L) == 0); }
inline _Bool operator==(wchar_t _L, const wstring& _R)
    {return (_R.compare(_L) == 0); }
inline _Bool operator==(const wstring& _L, const wchar_t *_R)
    {return (_L.compare(_R) == 0); }
inline _Bool operator==(const wstring& _L, wchar_t _R)
    {return (_L.compare(_R) == 0); }
inline _Bool operator!=(const wstring& _L, const wstring& _R)
    {return (!(_L == _R)); }
inline _Bool operator!=(const wchar_t *_L, const wstring& _R)
    {return (!(_L == _R)); }
inline _Bool operator!=(wchar_t _L, const wstring& _R)
    {return (!(_L == _R)); }
inline _Bool operator!=(const wstring& _L, const wchar_t *_R)
    {return (!(_L == _R)); }
inline _Bool operator!=(const wstring& _L, wchar_t _R)
    {return (!(_L == _R)); }
#endif                                                              □
```

_Grow ■ **_Grow**, which alters the storage reserved for the wide-character sequence

_Tidy ■ **_Tidy**, which initializes (**_Tidy()**) the member objects at construction time or discards any wide-character sequence (**_Tidy(1)**) and reinitializes the member objects

```
// wstring -- wstring basic members
#include <stdlib.h>
#include <wstring>

const size_t MIN_SIZE = 31;                                // 2^N - 1

const wchar_t wstring::_Nullwcs[] = {0};;

_Bool wstring::_Grow(size_t n, _Bool trim)
    {                                           // grow a wstring as needed
    size_t osize = _Ptr == 0 ? 0 : _Res;
    if (n == 0)
        {                                       // set up a null wstring
        if (trim && MIN_SIZE < osize)
            _Tidy(1);
        else if (_Ptr != 0)
            _Ptr[_Len = 0] = '\0';
        return (0);
        }
    else if (n == osize || n < osize && !trim)
        return (1);
    else
        {                                       // grow or alter the wstring
        size_t size = _Ptr == 0 && n < _Res ? _Res : n;
        if ((size |= MIN_SIZE) == NPOS)
            --size;
        wchar_t *s;
        if ((s = (wchar_t *)realloc(_Ptr,
            (size + 1) * sizeof (wchar_t))) == 0
            && (s = (wchar_t *)realloc(_Ptr,
                ((size = n) + 1) * sizeof (wchar_t))) == 0)
            _Nomemory();
        _Ptr = s;
        _Res = size;
        return (1);
        }
    }

void wstring::_Tidy(_Bool constructed)
    {                               // destroy any allocated wstring storage
    if (constructed && _Ptr != 0)
        free(_Ptr);
    _Ptr = 0, _Len = 0, _Res = 0;
    }
```

_Xlen ■ **_Xlen**, which reports a length error

_Xran ■ **_Xran**, which reports a range error

For a discussion of the exceptions associated with length and range errors, see Chapter 3: **<exception>**.

wstring.c   Figure 16.2 shows the file **wstring.c**. It defines the member functions **_Grow** and **_Tidy**, both of which are likely to be called for any object of class **wstring**.

Figure 16.3:
wstrasc.c

```
// wstrasc -- wstring::assign(wchar_t, size_t)
#include <wchar.h>
#include <wstring>

wstring& wstring::assign(wchar_t ch, size_t n)
    {                               // assign a repeated wchar_t to a wstring
    if (n == NPOS)
        _Xlen();
    if (_Grow(n, 1))
        {                                       // copy non-empty wstring
        wmemset(_Ptr, ch, n);
        _Ptr[_Len = n] = '\0';
        }
    return (*this);
    }                                                                      □
```

Figure 16.4:
wstrass.c

```
// wstrass -- wstring::assign(const wchar_t *, size_t)
#include <wchar.h>
#include <wstring>

wstring& wstring::assign(const wchar_t *s, size_t n)
    {                               // assign an NTWCS to a wstring
    if (n == NPOS)
        n = wcslen(s);
    if (_Grow(n, 1))
        {                                       // copy non-empty wstring
        wmemcpy(_Ptr, s, n);
        _Ptr[_Len = n] = '\0';
        }
    return (*this);
    }                                                                      □
```

Figure 16.5:
wstrasx.c

```
// wstrasx -- wstring::assign(const wstring&, size_t, size_t)
#include <wchar.h>
#include <wstring>

wstring& wstring::assign(const wstring& str, size_t pos,
    size_t ns)
    {                               // assign a substring to a wstring
    if (str.length() < pos)
        _Xran();
    size_t n = str.length() - pos;
    if (ns < n)
        n = ns;
    if (this == &str)
        remove(pos + n), remove(0, pos);
    else if (_Grow(n, 1))
        {                                       // copy non-empty wstring
        wmemcpy(_Ptr, &str.c_wcs()[pos], n);
        _Ptr[_Len = n] = '\0';
        }
    return (*this);
    }                                                                      □
```

Figure 16.6:
wstrapc.c

```
// wstrapc -- wstring::append(wchar_t, size_t)
#include <wchar.h>
#include <wstring>

wstring& wstring::append(wchar_t ch, size_t nr)
    {                           // append a repeated wchar_t to a wstring
    if (NPOS - _Len <= nr)
        _Xlen();
    size_t n;
    if (0 < nr && _Grow(n = _Len + nr))
        {                           // append to make non-empty wstring
        wmemset(_Ptr + _Len, ch, nr);
        _Ptr[_Len = n] = '\0';
        }
    return (*this);
    }                                                                        □
```

Figure 16.7:
wstraps.c

```
// wstraps -- wstring::append(const wchar_t *, size_t)
#include <wchar.h>
#include <wstring>

wstring& wstring::append(const wchar_t *s, size_t ns)
    {                           // append an NTWCS to a wstring
    if (ns == NPOS)
        ns = wcslen(s);
    if (NPOS - _Len <= ns)
        _Xlen();
    size_t n;
    if (0 < ns && _Grow(n = _Len + ns))
        {                           // append to make non-empty wstring
        wmemcpy(_Ptr + _Len, s, ns);
        _Ptr[_Len = n] = '\0';
        }
    return (*this);
    }                                                                        □
```

MIN_SIZE   The macro **MIN_SIZE** is both a minimum size for wide-character-sequence storage and a minimum increment for adding more. The function **_Grow** uses this parameter to round up requests for more storage, in the hopes of minimizing reallocations. It also uses the parameter **trim** as an indication that shrinking storage may be a good idea. The function is otherwise reluctant to do so.

realloc   Note that **_Grow** allocates, or reallocates, storage by calling **realloc**, declared in **<stdlib.h>**. That function can sometimes adjust the size of allocated storage more efficiently than the equivalent combination of *new* and *delete* expressions. For more on **_Nomemory**, see page 48.

Many member functions for class **wstring** come in groups of three. For members of such a group I chose source file names that have a common prefix, followed by:

Figure 16.8:
wstrapx.c

```
// wstrapx -- wstring::append(const wstring&, size_t, size_t)
#include <wchar.h>
#include <wstring>

wstring& wstring::append(const wstring& str, size_t pos,
    size_t ns)
    {                                    // append a substring to a wstring
    if (str.length() < pos)
        _Xran();
    size_t n = str.length() - pos;
    if (n < ns)
        ns = n;
    if (NPOS - _Len <= ns)
        _Xlen();
    if (0 < ns && _Grow(n = _Len + ns))
        {                                // append to make non-empty wstring
        wmemcpy(_Ptr + _Len, &str.c_wcs()[pos], ns);
        _Ptr[_Len = n] = '\0';
        }
    return (*this);
    }                                                                    □
```

Figure 16.9:
wstrinc.c

```
// wstrinc -- wstring::insert(size_t, wchar_t, size_t)
#include <wchar.h>
#include <wstring>

wstring& wstring::insert(size_t p0, wchar_t ch, size_t nr)
    {                                    // insert a repeated wchar_t into a wstring
    if (_Len < p0)
        _Xran();
    if (NPOS - _Len <= nr)
        _Xlen();
    size_t n;
    if (0 < nr && _Grow(n = _Len + nr))
        {                                // insert to make non-empty wstring
        wmemmove(_Ptr + p0 + nr, _Ptr + p0, _Len - p0);
        wmemset(_Ptr + p0, ch, nr);
        _Ptr[_Len = n] = '\0';
        }
    return (*this);
    }                                                                    □
```

- **c**, for an argument that is a single wide character or a repetition of wide characters
- **s**, for an argument that is a null-terminated wide string or an array of wide characters of specified length
- **x**, for an argument that is a substring or the entire wide-character sequence controlled by a **string** object

Often, the three flavors are just different enough to profit from distinct function definitions.

Figure 16.10:
wstrins.c

```
// wstrins -- wstring::insert(size_t, const wchar_t *, size_t)
#include <wchar.h>
#include <wstring>

wstring& wstring::insert(size_t p0, const wchar_t *s, size_t ns)
        {                               // insert an NTWCS into a wstring
        if (_Len < p0)
            _Xran();
        if (ns == NPOS)
            ns = wcslen(s);
        if (NPOS - _Len <= ns)
            _Xlen();
        size_t n;
        if (0 < ns && _Grow(n = _Len + ns))
            {                           // insert to make non-empty wstring
            wmemmove(_Ptr + p0 + ns, _Ptr + p0, _Len - p0);
            wmemcpy(_Ptr + p0, s, ns);
            _Ptr[_Len = n] = '\0';
            }
        return (*this);
        }                                                                    □
```

Figure 16.11:
wstrinx.c

```
// wstrinx -- wstring::insert(size_t, const wstring&, size_t,
//          size_t)
#include <wchar.h>
#include <wstring>

wstring& wstring::insert(size_t p0, const wstring& str,
        size_t pos, size_t ns)
        {                               // insert a substring into a wstring
        if (_Len < p0 || str.length() < pos)
            _Xran();
        size_t n = str.length() - pos;
        if (n < ns)
            ns = n;
        if (NPOS - _Len <= ns)
            _Xlen();
        if (0 < ns && _Grow(n = _Len + ns))
            {                           // insert to make non-empty wstring
            wmemmove(_Ptr + p0 + ns, _Ptr + p0, _Len - p0);
            wmemcpy(_Ptr + p0, &str.c_wcs()[pos], ns);
            _Ptr[_Len = n] = '\0';
            }
        return (*this);
        }                                                                    □
```

wstrasc.c   As the first example, here are the three source files that define the
wstrass.c variations of the member function **assign**. Figure 16.3 shows the file
wstrasx.c **wstrasc.c**. Figure 16.4 shows the file **wstrass.c**. And Figure 16.5 shows
the file **wstrasx.c**. You can see the common approach. First validate the
arguments, then call **_Grow** to adjust storage size for the character sequence,
then determine the new character sequence. The last act is to store the new

Figure 16.12:
wstrrem.c

```
// wstrrem -- wstring::remove(size_t, size_t)
#include <wchar.h>
#include <wstring>

wstring& wstring::remove(size_t p0, size_t nr)
    {                                           // remove a substring
    if (_Len < p0)
        _Xran();
    if (_Len - p0 < nr)
        nr = _Len - p0;
    if (0 < nr)
        {                                       // remove the substring
        wmemmove(_Ptr + p0, _Ptr + p0 + nr, _Len - p0 - nr);
        size_t n = _Len - nr;
        if (_Grow(n))
            _Ptr[_Len = n] = '\0';
        }
    return (*this);
    }                                                                        □
```

sequence length in the member object **_Len**. As is often the case, the substring version requires special handling because the substring may be controlled by the same object.

<wchar.h>   You can probably guess the behavior of the various wide-character functions declared in **<wchar.h>**, even if you are not yet familiar with this newer header. Functions whose names begin with **wcs** are direct analogs of those declared in **<string.h>** whose names begin with **str**. Similarly, functions whose names begin with **wmem** are direct analogs of those whose names begin with **mem**.

wstrapc.c   Another set of three source files define the variations of the member
wstraps.c function **append**. Figure 16.6 shows the file **wstrapc.c**. Figure 16.7 shows
wstrapx.c the file **wstraps.c**. And Figure 16.8 shows the file **wstrapx.c**. All follow much the same pattern as the previous trio. In this case, however, appending part or all of a substring to itself requires little additional caution.

wstrinc.c   Three more source files define the variations of the member function
wstrins.c **insert**. Figure 16.9 shows the file **wstrinc.c**. Figure 16.10 shows the file
wstrinx.c **wstrins.c**. And Figure 16.11 shows the file **wstrinx.c**. Here the special precaution is to sometimes call **wmemmove** instead of **wmemcpy**, both of which are declared in **<wchar.h>**. The former works properly even when copying a wide-character sequence to elements that overlap the original ones.

wstrrem.c   Figure 16.12 shows the file **wstrrem.c**, which implements the member function **remove**. It too calls **wmemmove** to close up any hole made in the character sequence.

wstrrec.c   Three source files define the variations of the member function **replace**.
wstrres.c Figure 16.13 shows the file **wstrrec.c**. Figure 16.14 shows the file
wstrrex.c **wstrres.c**. And Figure 16.15 shows the file **wstrrex.c**. The logic is a bit more complex than for the earlier trios, mostly because of the need to define

Figure 16.13:
wstrrec.c

```
// wstrrec -- wstring::replace(size_t, size_t, wchar_t, size_t)
#include <wchar.h>
#include <wstring>

wstring& wstring::replace(size_t p0, size_t n0, wchar_t ch,
    size_t nr)
    {                   // replace with a repeated wchar_t in a wstring
    if (_Len < p0)
        _Xran();
    if (_Len - p0 < n0)
        n0 = _Len - p0;
    if (NPOS - nr <= _Len - n0)
        _Xlen();
    size_t nm = _Len - n0 - p0;
    if (nr < n0)
        wmemmove(_Ptr + p0 + nr, _Ptr + p0 + n0, nm);
    size_t n;
    if ((0 < nr || 0 < n0) && _Grow(n = _Len + nr - n0))
        {                       // replace to make non-empty wstring
        if (n0 < nr)
            wmemmove(_Ptr + p0 + nr, _Ptr + p0 + n0, nm);
        wmemset(_Ptr + p0, ch, nr);
        _Ptr[_Len = n] = '\0';
        }
    return (*this);
    }
```

Figure 16.14:
wstrres.c

```
// wstrres -- wstring::replace(size_t, size_t, const wchar_t *,
//          size_t)
#include <wchar.h>
#include <wstring>

wstring& wstring::replace(size_t p0, size_t n0,
    const wchar_t *s, size_t ns)
    {                       // replace with an NTWCS into a wstring
    if (_Len < p0)
        _Xran();
    if (ns == NPOS)
        ns = wcslen(s);
    if (NPOS - ns <= _Len - n0)
        _Xlen();
    size_t nm = _Len - n0 - p0;
    if (ns < n0)
        wmemmove(_Ptr + p0 + ns, _Ptr + p0 + n0, nm);
    size_t n;
    if ((0 < ns || 0 < n0) && _Grow(n = _Len + ns - n0))
        {                       // replace to make non-empty wstring
        if (n0 < ns)
            wmemmove(_Ptr + p0 + ns, _Ptr + p0 + n0, nm);
        wmemcpy(_Ptr + p0, s, ns);
        _Ptr[_Len = n] = '\0';
        }
    return (*this);
    }
```

Figure 16.15:
wstrrex.c

```
// wstrrex -- wstring::replace(size_t size_t, const wstring&,
//          size_t, size_t)
#include <wchar.h>
#include <wstring>

wstring& wstring::replace(size_t p0, size_t n0,
    const wstring& str, size_t pos, size_t ns)
    {                               // replace a substring with a wstring
    if (_Len < p0 || str.length() < pos)
        _Xran();
    size_t n = str.length() - pos;
    if (n < ns)
        ns = n;
    if (NPOS - ns <= _Len - n0)
        _Xlen();
    size_t nm = _Len - n0 - p0;
    if (ns < n0)
        wmemmove(_Ptr + p0 + ns, _Ptr + p0 + n0, nm);
    if ((0 < ns || 0 < n0) && _Grow(n = _Len + ns - n0))
        {                           // replace to make non-empty wstring
        if (n0 < ns)
            wmemmove(_Ptr + p0 + ns, _Ptr + p0 + n0, nm);
        wmemcpy(_Ptr + p0, &str.c_wcs()[pos], ns);
        _Ptr[_Len = n] = '\0';
        }
    return (*this);
    }                                                               □
```

Figure 16.16:
wstrget.c

```
// wstrget -- wstring::get_at(size_t)
#include <wstring>

wchar_t wstring::get_at(size_t p0) const
    {                                           // get element of a wstring
    if (_Len <= p0)
        _Xran();
    return (_Ptr[p0]);
    }                                                               □
```

Figure 16.17:
wstrput.c

```
// wstrput -- wstring::put_at(size_t)
#include <wstring>

void wstring::put_at(size_t p0, wchar_t ch)
    {                                           // put element to a wstring
    if (_Len < p0)
        _Xran();
    else if (_Len == p0)
        append(ch);
    else
        _Ptr[p0] = ch;
    }                                                               □
```

```
// wstrcopy -- wstring::copy(const wchar_t *, size_t, size_t)
#include <wchar.h>
#include <wstring>

size_t wstring::copy(wchar_t *s, size_t n, size_t p0)
    {                                  // copy a wstring to an NTWCS
    if (_Len < p0)
        _Xran();
    if (_Len - p0 < n)
        n = _Len - p0;
    wmemcpy(s, _Ptr + p0, n);
    return (n);
    }
```

```
// wstrfis -- wstring::find(const wchar_t *, size_t, size_t)
#include <wchar.h>
#include <wstring>

size_t wstring::find(const wchar_t *s, size_t p0, size_t n)
    const
    {                              // find leftmost substring in a wstring
    if (n == 0 || n == NPOS && (n = wcslen(s)) == 0)
        return (0);
    size_t nmax;
    if (p0 < _Len && n <= (nmax = _Len - p0))
        {                          // find non-null substring in wstring
        const wchar_t *t, *u;
        for (nmax -= n - 1, u = _Ptr + p0;
            (t = wmemchr(u, *s, nmax)) != 0;
            nmax -= t - u + 1, u = t + 1)
            if (wmemcmp(t, s, n) == 0)
                return (t - _Ptr);
        }
    return (NPOS);
    }
```

both old and new substrings. It is otherwise much like what has gone before.

wstrget.c   Figure 16.16 shows the file **wstrget.c**, which defines the member
wstrput.c function **get_at**. And Figure 16.17 shows the file **wstrput.c**, which defines the companion function **put_at**. Both are simple, but as I noted earlier, the latter function has already been changed in the draft C++ Standard. It no longer appends the character when **_Len == p0**.

wstrcopy.c   Figure 16.18 shows the file **wstrcopy.c**, which defines the member function **copy**. It too is simple.

For the "find" member functions (names beginning with **find**), I found it sufficient to define the "wide string or array" versions (source files with names ending in **s**) only. All others are inline functions that call these versions.

Figure 16.20:
wstrrfis.c

```
// wstrrfis -- wstring::rfind(const wchar_t *, size_t, size_t)
#include <wchar.h>
#include <wstring>

size_t wstring::rfind(const wchar_t *s, size_t p0, size_t n)
    const
    {                               // find rightmost substring in a wstring
    if (n == 0 || n == NPOS && (n = wcslen(s)) == 0)
        return (0);
    if (n <= _Len)
        for (const wchar_t *t = _Ptr
            + (p0 < _Len - n ? p0 : _Len - n); ; --t)
            if (*t == *s && wmemcmp(t, s, n) == 0)
                return (t - _Ptr);
            else if (t == _Ptr)
                break;
    return (NPOS);
    }                                                                    □
```

Figure 16.21:
wstrffs.c

```
// wstrffs -- wstring::find_first_of(const wchar_t *, size_t,
//          size_t)
#include <wchar.h>
#include <wstring>

size_t wstring::find_first_of(const wchar_t *s, size_t p0,
    size_t n) const
    {                               // find leftmost set member in a wstring
    if (n == 0 || n == NPOS && (n = wcslen(s)) == 0)
        return (0);
    if (p0 < _Len)
        {                                   // find in non-null wstring
        const wchar_t *const u = _Ptr + _Len;
        for (const wchar_t *t = _Ptr + p0; t < u; ++t)
            if (wmemchr(s, *t, n) != 0)
                return (t - _Ptr);
        }
    return (NPOS);
    }                                                                    □
```

wstrfis.c   Figure 16.19 shows the file **wstrfis.c**, which defines the wide string or
wstrrfis.c array version of the member function **find**. As an optimization, it first scans
for the initial character of the wide character sequence to match. The (mildly
messy) logic could otherwise be made simpler. Figure 16.20 shows the file
wstrrfis.c, which defines the wide string or array version of the member
function **rfind**. It has no handy library function to perform the equivalent
reverse scan, so its logic is perforce simpler (and possibly slower).

wstrffs.c   Figure 16.21 shows the file **wstrffs.c**, which defines the wide string or
wstrfls.c array version of the member function **find_first_of**. And Figure 16.22
shows the file **wstrfls.c**, which defines the wide string or array version
of the member function **find_last_of**. Compare this pair with the pair
that follows.

Figure 16.22:
wstrfls.c

```
// wstrfls -- wstring::find_last_of(const char *, size_t, size_t)
#include <wchar.h>
#include <wstring>

size_t wstring::find_last_of(const wchar_t *s, size_t p0,
    size_t n) const
    {                           // find rightmost set member in a wstring
    if (n == 0 || n == NPOS && (n = wcslen(s)) == 0)
        return (0);
    if (0 < _Len)
        for (const wchar_t *t = _Ptr
            + (p0 < _Len ? p0 : _Len - 1); ; --t)
            if (wmemchr(s, *t, n) != 0)
                return (t - _Ptr);
            else if (t == _Ptr)
                break;
    return (NPOS);
    }
```

Figure 16.23:
wstrffns.c

```
// wstrffns -- wstring::find_first_not_of(const char *, size_t,
//          size_t)
#include <wchar.h>
#include <wstring>

size_t wstring::find_first_not_of(const wchar_t *s, size_t p0,
    size_t n) const
    {                           // find leftmost set member not in a wstring
    if (n == 0 || n == NPOS && (n = wcslen(s)) == 0)
        return (0);
    if (p0 < _Len)
        {                                       // find in non-null wstring
        const wchar_t *const u = _Ptr + _Len;
        for (const wchar_t *t = _Ptr + p0; t < u; ++t)
            if (wmemchr(s, *t, n) == 0)
                return (t - _Ptr);
        }
    return (NPOS);
    }
```

wstrffns.c Figure 16.23 shows the file **wstrffns.c**, which defines the wide string
wstrflns.c or array version of the member function **find_first_not_of**. And Figure
16.24 shows the file **wstrflns.c**, which defines the wide string or array
version of the member function **find_last_not_of**. All four functions are
very similar.

wstrcoc.c The last set of three source files define the variations of the member
wstrcos.c function **compare**. Figure 16.25 shows the file **wstrcoc.c**. Figure 16.26
wstrcox.c shows the file **wstrcos.c**. And Figure 16.27 shows the file **wstrcox.c**. The
messiest part of the logic occurs when the shorter of two wide-character
sequences is a prefix of the longer one, or when the wide-character sequences are equal.

Figure 16.24:
wstrflns.c

```
// wstrflns -- wstring::find_last_not_of(const wchar_t *,
//         size_t, size_t)
#include <wchar.h>
#include <wstring>

size_t wstring::find_last_not_of(const wchar_t *s, size_t p0,
    size_t n) const
    {                        // find rightmost set member not in a wstring
    if (n == 0 || n == NPOS && (n = wcslen(s)) == 0)
        return (0);
    if (0 < _Len)
        for (const wchar_t *t = _Ptr
            + (p0 < _Len ? p0 : _Len - 1); ; --t)
            if (wmemchr(s, *t, n) == 0)
                return (t - _Ptr);
            else if (t == _Ptr)
                break;
    return (NPOS);
    }                                                                    □
```

Figure 16.25:
wstrcoc.c

```
// wstrcoc -- wstring::compare(wchar_t, size_t, size_t)
#include <wstring>

int wstring::compare(wchar_t ch, size_t p0, size_t ns) const
    {                        // compare a repeated wchar_t to a wstring
    if (_Len < p0)
        _Xran();
    size_t n = _Len - p0;
    for (const wchar_t *s = _Ptr + p0,
        *t = s + (n < ns ? n : ns); s < t; ++s)
        if (*s != ch)
            return (*s < ch ? -1 : +1);
    return (n < ns ? -1 : n == ns ? 0 : +1);
    }                                                                    □
```

Figure 16.26:
wstrcos.c

```
// wstrcos -- wstring::compare(const wchar_t *, size_t, size_t)
#include <wchar.h>
#include <wstring>

int wstring::compare(const wchar_t *s, size_t p0, size_t ns)
    const
    {                                  // compare an NTWCS to a wstring
    if (_Len < p0)
        _Xran();
    size_t n = _Len - p0;
    if (ns == NPOS)
        ns = wcslen(s);
    size_t ans = wmemcmp(_Ptr + p0, s, n < ns ? n : ns);
    return (ans != 0 ? ans : n < ns ? -1 : n == ns ? 0 : +1);
    }                                                                    □
```

Figure 16.27:
wstrcox.c

```
// wstrcox -- wstring::compare(const wstring&, size_t, size_t)
#include <wchar.h>
#include <wstring>

int wstring::compare(const wstring& str, size_t p0, size_t ns)
    const
    {                            // compare a substring to a wstring
    if (_Len < p0)
        _Xran();
    size_t n = _Len - p0;
    if (str.length() < ns)
        ns = str.length();
    size_t ans = wmemcmp(_Ptr + p0, str.c_wcs(),
        n < ns ? n : ns);
    return (ans != 0 ? ans : n < ns ? -1 : n == ns ? 0 : +1);
    }
```

Testing `<wstring>`

twstring.c   Figure 16.28 shows the file **twstring.c**. It tests the basic properties of the class **wstring** defined in **<wstring>**. It does so by testing the various string operations in related groups, at least for their minimum functionality. This source file is long because I avoided the use of wide string literals. Otherwise, it is much the same as **tstring.c**, in the previous chapter.

> If all goes well, the program prints:
>
> **SUCCESS testing <wstring>**
>
> and takes a normal exit.

Exercises

Exercise 16.1 Type **wchar_t** can have a signed integer representation. What effect can this have on comparison of two **wstring** objects? What effect can it have on how you compate two null-terminated wide-character strings?

Exercise 16.2 What other element type, besides *char* or **wchar_t**, makes a sensible basis for a string class?

Exercise 16.3 Describe all the operations performed by functions declared in **<wchar.h>**, and how to do the same thing using only functions declared in **wstring**.

Exercise 16.4 Define the template class **basic_string** that behaves the same as class **string**, for the element type *char*, and class **wstring**, for the element type **wchar_t**. Do you need any template parameters besides the element type?

Exercise 16.5 [Harder] Implement an **mbstring** class that controls a multibyte character sequence. What functions do you define for converting to and from wide-character codes? How do you count multibyte characters?

Exercise 16.6 [Very hard] Define and implement a **text** class that you can access as either multibyte or wide-character sequences.

```
// test <wstring>
#include <assert.h>
#include <wchar.h>
#include <wstring>
#include <iostream>
#include <strstream>

static const wchar_t L_4[] = {0, 0, 0, 0, 0};
static const wchar_t Ls4[] = {_L('s'), _L('4'), 0};
static const wchar_t Ls5xxx[] = {_L('s'), _L('5'), _L('x'),
    _L('x'), _L('x'), 0};
static const wchar_t Ls5[] = {_L('s'), _L('5'), 0};
static const wchar_t Laaa[] = {_L('a'), _L('a'), _L('a'), 0};
static const wchar_t Lc[] = {_L('c'), 0};
static const wchar_t Lhello[] = {_L('h'), _L('e'), _L('l'),
    _L('l'), _L('o'), 0};
static const wchar_t Lx[] = {_L('x'), 0};
static const wchar_t LAB[] = {_L('A'), _L('B'), 0};
static const wchar_t LC[] = {_L('C'), 0};
static const wchar_t Labc[] = {_L('a'), _L('b'), _L('c'), 0};
static const wchar_t Ls4abc[] = {_L('s'), _L('4'), _L('a'),
    _L('b'), _L('c'), 0};
static const wchar_t Ls4abcd[] = {_L('s'), _L('4'), _L('a'),
    _L('b'), _L('c'), _L('d'), 0};
static const wchar_t Ls4abcds4[] = {_L('s'), _L('4'), _L('a'),
    _L('b'), _L('c'), _L('d'), _L('s'), _L('4'), 0};
static const wchar_t LA[] = {_L('A'), 0};
static const wchar_t LBC[] = {_L('B'), _L('C'), 0};
static const wchar_t LABC[] = {_L('A'), _L('B'), _L('C'), 0};
static const wchar_t LABCD[] = {_L('A'), _L('B'), _L('C'),
    _L('D'), 0};
static const wchar_t LABCDs4[] = {_L('A'), _L('B'), _L('C'),
    _L('D'), _L('s'), _L('4'), 0};
static const wchar_t Ls4s5[] = {_L('s'), _L('4'), _L('s'),
    _L('5'), 0};
static const wchar_t Ls45[] = {_L('s'), _L('4'), _L('5'), 0};
static const wchar_t L4s5[] = {_L('4'), _L('s'), _L('5'), 0};
static const wchar_t LDd[] = {_L('D'), _L('d'), 0};
static const wchar_t LAaBbCcDd[] = {_L('A'), _L('a'), _L('B'),
    _L('b'), _L('c'), _L('D'), _L('d'), 0};
static const wchar_t LAaBbCcDdEE[] = {_L('A'), _L('a'),
    _L('B'), _L('b'), _L('C'), _L('c'), _L('D'), _L('d'),
    _L('E'), _L('E'), 0};
static const wchar_t Ls4AaBbCcDdEEs4[] = {_L('s'), _L('4'),
    _L('A'), _L('a'), _L('B'), _L('b'), _L('C'), _L('c'),
    _L('D'), _L('d'), _L('E'), _L('E'), _L('s'), _L('4'), 0};
static const wchar_t LAaBbCcDdEEs4[] = {_L('A'), _L('a'),
    _L('B'), _L('b'), _L('C'), _L('c'), _L('D'), _L('d'),
    _L('E'), _L('E'), _L('s'), _L('4'), 0};
static const wchar_t LAaBbCcDd[] = {_L('A'), _L('a'), _L('B'),
    _L('b'), _L('C'), _L('c'), _L('D'), _L('d'), 0};
static const wchar_t L123ab789[] = {_L('1'), _L('2'), _L('3'),
    _L('a'), _L('b'), _L('7'), _L('8'), _L('9'), 0};
static const wchar_t L45678[] = {_L('4'), _L('5'), _L('6'),
    _L('7'), _L('8'), 0};
```

```
static const wchar_t L123456789[] = {_L('1'), _L('2'), _L('3'),
    _L('4'), _L('5'), _L('6'), _L('7'), _L('8'), _L('9'), 0};
static const wchar_t L01xx56789[] = {_L('0'), _L('1'), _L('x'),
    _L('x'), _L('5'), _L('6'), _L('7'), _L('8'), _L('9'), 0};
static const wchar_t L01s4456789[] = {_L('0'), _L('1'), _L('s'),
    _L('4'), _L('4'), _L('5'), _L('6'), _L('7'), _L('8'),
    _L('9'), 0};
static const wchar_t L012[] = {_L('0'), _L('1'), _L('2'), 0};
static const wchar_t L012XX_[] = {_L('0'), _L('1'), _L('2'),
    _L('X'), _L('X'), 0, 0};
static const wchar_t L12X[] = {_L('1'), _L('2'), _L('X'), 0};
static const wchar_t Ls4s4[] = {_L('s'), _L('4'), _L('s'),
    _L('4'), 0};
static const wchar_t Ls4XX[] = {_L('s'), _L('4'), _L('X'),
    _L('X'), 0};
static const wchar_t Labs[] = {_L('a'), _L('b'), _L('s'), 0};
static const wchar_t Ls4a[] = {_L('s'), _L('4'), _L('a'), 0};
static const wchar_t Ls44[] = {_L('s'), _L('4'), _L('4'), 0};
static const wchar_t Lxx[] = {_L('x'), _L('x'), 0};

int main()
    {                       // test basic workings of wstring definitions
    wstring s1, s2(30, reserve), s3(4, default_size);
    wstring s4(Ls4), s5(Ls5xxx, 2), s6(_L('a'), 3);
    wstring s8(_L('c'));
    s1.reserve(20);
    assert(s1.reserve() == 20 && s2.reserve() == 30);
    assert(wcscmp(s1.c_wcs(), L_4) == 0);
    assert(wcscmp(s2.c_wcs(), L_4) == 0);
    assert(wmemcmp(s3.c_wcs(), L_4, 5) == 0);
    assert(wcscmp(s4.c_wcs(), Ls4) == 0);
    assert(wcscmp(s5.c_wcs(), Ls5) == 0);
    assert(wcscmp(s6.c_wcs(), Laaa) == 0);
    assert(wcscmp(s8.c_wcs(), Lc) == 0);
        // test assignments
    s1 = Lhello, assert(wcscmp(s1.c_wcs(), Lhello) == 0);
    s1 = _L('x'), assert(wcscmp(s1.c_wcs(), Lx) == 0);
    s1 = s4, assert(wcscmp(s1.c_wcs(), Ls4) == 0);
    s1.assign(LAB), assert(wcscmp(s1.c_wcs(), LAB) == 0);
    s1.assign(_L('C')), assert(wcscmp(s1.c_wcs(), LC) == 0);
    s1.assign(s4), assert(wcscmp(s1.c_wcs(), Ls4) == 0);
        // test appends
    s1 += Labc, assert(wcscmp(s1.c_wcs(), Ls4abc) == 0);
    s1 += _L('d'), assert(wcscmp(s1.c_wcs(), Ls4abcd) == 0);
    s1 += s4, assert(wcscmp(s1.c_wcs(), Ls4abcds4) == 0);
    s1 = LA, s1.append(LBC);
    assert(wcscmp(s1.c_wcs(), LABC) == 0);
    s1.append(_L('D')), assert(wcscmp(s1.c_wcs(), LABCD) == 0);
    s1.append(s4), assert(wcscmp(s1.c_wcs(), LABCDs4) == 0);
    assert(wcscmp((s4 + s5).c_wcs(), Ls4s5) == 0);
    assert(wcscmp((s4 + Ls5).c_wcs(), Ls4s5) == 0);
    assert(wcscmp((Ls4 + s5).c_wcs(), Ls4s5) == 0);
    assert(wcscmp((s4 + _L('5')).c_wcs(), Ls45) == 0);
    assert(wcscmp((_L('4') + s5).c_wcs(), L4s5) == 0);
        // test inserts
```

```
s1 = Labc, s1.insert(3, LDd).insert(1, LBC, 1).insert(0, LA);
assert(wcscmp(s1.c_wcs(), LAaBbcDd) == 0);
s1.insert(7, _L('E'), 2).insert(4, _L('C'));
assert(wcscmp(s1.c_wcs(), LAaBbCcDdEE) == 0);
s1.insert(10, s4).insert(0, s4, 1).insert(0, s4, 0, 1);
assert(wcscmp(s1.c_wcs(), Ls4AaBbCcDdEEs4) == 0);
      // test removes
s1.remove(0, 2);
assert(wcscmp(s1.c_wcs(), LAaBbCcDdEEs4) == 0);
s1.remove(8), assert(wcscmp(s1.c_wcs(), LAaBbCcDd) == 0);
s1.remove(), assert(wcscmp(s1.c_wcs(), L_4) == 0);
      // test replace
s1.replace(0, 0, L123ab789), s1.replace(3, 2, L45678, 3);
assert(wcscmp(s1.c_wcs(), L123456789) == 0);
s1.replace(1, 3, _L('x'), 2).replace(0, 0, _L('0'));
assert(wcscmp(s1.c_wcs(), L01xx56789) == 0);
s1.replace(3, 1, s4, 1).replace(2, 1, s4);
assert(wcscmp(s1.c_wcs(), L01s4456789) == 0);
      // test accesses
s1.put_at(2, _L('2'));
assert(s1.get_at(1) == _L('1') && s1[2] == _L('2'));
assert((s1[3] = _L('3')) == _L('3'));
assert(s1.length() == 10);
s1.resize(3), assert(wcscmp(s1.c_wcs(), L012) == 0);
s1.resize(5, _L('X'));
assert(wcscmp(s1.c_wcs(), L012XX_) == 0);
s1.resize(6), assert(wmemcmp(s1.c_wcs(), L012XX_, 7) == 0);
wchar_t buf[10];
assert(s1.copy(buf, sizeof (buf) / sizeof (wchar_t)) == 6
      && wcscmp(buf, L012XX_) == 0);
assert(s1.copy(buf, 3, 1) == 3
      && wmemcmp(buf, L12X, 3) == 0);
      // test finds
s1 = Ls4s4;
assert(s1.find(s4) == 0 && s1.find(s4, 1) == 2
      && s1.find(s4, 3) == NPOS);
assert(s1.find(Ls4) == 0 && s1.find(Ls4, 3) == NPOS
      && s1.find(Ls4XX, 1, 2) == 2);
assert(s1.find(_L('s')) == 0 && s1.find(_L('s'), 1) == 2
      && s1.find(_L('x')) == NPOS);
assert(s1.rfind(s4) == 2 && s1.rfind(s4, 1) == 0
      && s1.rfind(s5, 3) == NPOS);
assert(s1.rfind(Ls4) == 2 && s1.rfind(Ls4, 3) == 2
      && s1.rfind(Ls4XX, 1, 3) == NPOS);
assert(s1.rfind(_L('s')) == 2 && s1.rfind(_L('s'), 2) == 2
      && s1.rfind(_L('x')) == NPOS);
assert(s1.find_first_of(s4) == 0
      && s1.find_first_of(s4, 1) == 1
      && s1.find_first_of(s4, 4) == NPOS);
assert(s1.find_first_of(Ls4) == 0
      && s1.find_first_of(Ls4, 3) == 3
      && s1.find_first_of(Labs, 1, 2) == NPOS);
assert(s1.find_first_of(_L('s')) == 0
      && s1.find_first_of(_L('s'), 1) == 2
      && s1.find_first_of(_L('x')) == NPOS);
```

```
    assert(s1.find_last_of(s4) == 3
        && s1.find_last_of(s4, 1) == 1
        && s1.find_last_of(s6) == NPOS);
    assert(s1.find_last_of(Ls4) == 3
        && s1.find_last_of(Ls4, 2) == 2
        && s1.find_last_of(Labs, 1, 2) == NPOS);
    assert(s1.find_last_of(_L('s')) == 2
        && s1.find_last_of(_L('s'), 1) == 0
        && s1.find_last_of(_L('x')) == NPOS);
    assert(s1.find_first_not_of(s5) == 1
        && s1.find_first_not_of(s5, 2) == 3
        && s1.find_first_not_of(s4) == NPOS);
    assert(s1.find_first_not_of(Ls5) == 1
        && s1.find_first_not_of(Ls5, 2) == 3
        && s1.find_first_not_of(Ls4a, 1, 2) == NPOS);
    assert(s1.find_first_not_of(_L('s')) == 1
        && s1.find_first_not_of(_L('s'), 2) == 3
        && s1.find_first_not_of(_L('s'), 4) == NPOS);
    assert(s1.find_last_not_of(s5) == 3
        && s1.find_last_not_of(s5, 2) == 1
        && s1.find_last_not_of(s4) == NPOS);
    assert(s1.find_last_not_of(Ls5) == 3
        && s1.find_last_not_of(Ls5, 2) == 1
        && s1.find_last_not_of(Ls4a, 1, 2) == NPOS);
    assert(s1.find_last_not_of(_L('s')) == 3
        && s1.find_last_not_of(_L('s'), 2) == 1
        && s1.find_last_not_of(_L('s'), 0) == NPOS);
        // test compares
    assert(s1.compare(s1) == 0 && s1.compare(s4, 2) == 0
        && s1.compare(s4, 2, 2) == 0);
    assert(s1.compare(Ls4s4) == 0 && s1.compare(Ls4, 2) == 0
        && s1.compare(Ls4XX, 2, 2) == 0);
    assert(s8.compare(_L('c')) == 0
        && s1.compare(_L('4'), 3) == 0
        && s6.compare(_L('a'), 0, 3) == 0);
    assert(s1.compare(s4) != 0 && s1.compare(s1, 1) != 0
        && s1.compare(s4, 0, 2) != 0);
    assert(s1.compare(Ls4s5) != 0 && s1.compare(Ls44, 3) != 0
        && s1.compare(Ls4XX, 0, 2) != 0);
    assert(s1.compare(_L('c')) != 0
        && s1.compare(_L('4'), 2) != 0
        && s6.compare(_L('a'), 0, 2) != 0);
    assert(s1 == s1 && s1 == Ls4s4 && s8 == _L('c')
        && Ls4 == s4 && _L('c') == s8);
    assert(s1 != s4 && s1 != Lxx && s1 != _L('s') && Ls4 != s1
        && _L('a') != s6);
    cout << "SUCCESS testing <wstring>" << endl;
    return (0);
    }
```
□

Chapter 17: `<bits>`

Background

A common practice among programmers has long been to use *flag* and *mask words*. Both of these are objects typically of some integer type. But they do not store a range of integer values. Rather:

flag word ■ Each bit field of a flag word represents an independent Boolean value.

mask word ■ Groups of one or more bits in a mask are set to select, by a bitwise AND operation, corresponding mask fields in integer values of the same size.

I group these two uses together because they often overlap. Consider the bitmask type `ios::fmtflags`. It has both bit fields, such as **skipws**, and mask fields, such as **floatfield**. (See Chapter 6: `<ios>`.)

The idiom in C has long been to define macros that specify each bit and mask field, as in:

```
#define SKIPWS       0x80
#define FLOATFIELD   0x70
.....
```

You can then define flag and mask words of some integer type and perform bitwise operations between such objects and these macros.

The limitations of this approach are obvious:

■ The translator can perform no type checking, to ensure that only the relevant macros mix with flag or mask words.

■ You have to contrive non-overlapping bit and mask fields by hand. Adding or changing a field is both tiresome and error prone.

■ When you exhaust the bits in the largest available integer type, you must indulge in significant rewrites to add more bit or mask fields.

bitmask types Enumerations help some with the first limitation. The draft C++ Standard improves matters further by tightening the type checking on enumerations. (See page 121.) Indeed, the bitmask types are used throughout the Standard C++ library to replace old-fashioned flag words. But bitmask types still suffer from the remaining limitations listed above.

`<bits>` The Committee adopted the header `<bits>` as a way to overcome all three limitations. It defines the template class **bits<N>**, and a handful of related functions. The parameter **N**, of type **size_t**, specifies the number of elements in an object of this class. You can perform bitwise operations on this class by much the same rules as for the basic integer types, and with the same notation, regardless of the number of bits in a particular instantiation. You can also designate an element by its position (counting from zero), rather than writing explicit shifting and masking code.

A good implementation of this template class is presumably economical in its use of storage. In particular, the idea is that:

- for small enough values of **N**, a single integer stores all the bits and the generated code is as efficient as traditional C code

- for larger values of **N**, multiple integers store all the bits and the generated code loops over these objects as needed

You still need to contrive names for the bits in a **bits<N>** object, but a conventional enumeration can now define positions for the distinct bit fields in the object. And, unlike older implementations of flag words, you can more easily loop over subranges of bits, just by varying a position value.

template   I've already shown one header that defines templates, for the iostreams
limitations manipulators that take an argument. (See Chapter 10: **<iomanip>**.) I've also discussed the current limitations of template technology, on page 120 and on page 252. The template class **bits<N>** is far more ambitious than any of these template classes. It is also an invention of the Committee. Some implementations, particularly those that endeavor to be portable, are still hampered by available technology. And some would-be users are still hampered by lack of implementations, and sheer lack of time to build experience. It is thus too soon to tell whether programmers will widely abandon conventional flag and mask words in favor of this newer and more disciplined technology.

What the Draft C++ Standard Says

The function declarations that follow the definition of the template class **bits<N>** are a bit equivocal. For **N** to be a true parameter, the declarations should properly be written as template functions. But it is not currently permissible to write a template function with no type parameters. (See page 252.) In this particular case, an integer parameter does indeed provide the information needed to enable overload resolution — all the template functions have at least one argument of class **bits<N>**. That's a hard point to get across to a translator, however, and the form shown here is *not* a valid way to do the job.

friend   One way to do so is to define the template functions as inline *friend*
functions functions within the template class **bits<N>**. The parameter **N** is then available to express all the necessary types. While this is a common implementation technique, it was not chosen as the way to specify this class. I won't discuss the reasons for the choice here (partly because I don't understand the issues well enough to articulate them clearly).

17.5.3 Header **<bits>**

The header **<bits>** defines a template class and several related functions for representing and manipulating fixed-size sequences of bits.

17.5.3.1 Template class **bits<N>**

```
template<size_t N> class bits {
public:
    bits();
    bits(unsigned long val);
    bits(const string& str, size_t pos = 0, size_t n = NPOS);
    bits<N>& operator&=(const bits<N>& rhs);
    bits<N>& operator|=(const bits<N>& rhs);
    bits<N>& operator^=(const bits<N>& rhs);
    bits<N>& operator<<=(size_t pos);
    bits<N>& operator>>=(size_t pos);
    bits<N>& set();
    bits<N>& set(size_t pos, int val = 1);
    bits<N>& reset();
    bits<N>& reset(size_t pos);
    bits<N> operator~() const;
    bits<N>& toggle();
    bits<N>& toggle(size_t pos);
    unsigned short to_ushort() const;
    unsigned long to_ulong() const;
    string to_string() const;
    size_t count() const;
    size_t length() const;
    int operator==(const bits<N>& rhs) const;
    int operator!=(const bits<N>& rhs) const;
    int test(size_t pos) const;
    int any() const;
    int none() const;
    bits<N> operator<<(size_t pos) const;
    bits<N> operator>>(size_t pos) const;
private:
//  char array[N];                                  exposition only
};
```

The template class **bits<N>** describes an object that can store a sequence consisting of a fixed number of bits, **N**.

Each bit represents either the value zero (reset) or one (set). To *toggle* a bit is to change the value zero to one, or the value one to zero. Each bit has a non-negative position **pos**. When converting between an object of class **bits<N>** and a value of some integral type, bit position **pos** corresponds to the *bit value* $1 << pos$. The integral value corresponding to two or more bits is the sum of their bit values.

For the sake of exposition, the maintained data is presented here as:

• **char array[N]**, the sequence of bits, stored one bit per element.[113]

The functions described in this subclause can report three kinds of errors, each associated with a distinct exception:

• an *invalid-argument* error is associated with exceptions of type **invalid-argument**;

• an *out-of-range* error is associated with exceptions of type **outofrange**;

• an *overflow* error is associated with exceptions of type **overflow**.

To report one of these errors, the function evaluates the expression **ex.raise()**, where **ex** is an object of the associated exception type.

17.5.3.1.1 bits<*N*>::bits()

```
bits();
```

Constructs an object of class **bits<*N*>**, initializing all bits to zero.

17.5.3.1.2 bits<*N*>::bits(unsigned long)

```
bits(unsigned long val);
```

Constructs an object of class **bits<*N*>**, initializing the first *M* bit positions to the corresponding bit values in **val**. *M* is the smaller of *N* and the value **CHAR_BIT * sizeof (unsigned long)**. The macro **CHAR_BIT** is defined in **<limits.h>**.

If *M* < *N*, remaining bit positions are initialized to zero.

17.5.3.1.3 bits<*N*>::bits(const string&, size_t, size_t)

```
bits(const string& str, size_t pos = 0, size_t n = NPOS);
```

Reports an out-of-range error if **pos > str.len**. Otherwise, the function determines the effective length **rlen** of the initializing string as the smaller of **n** and **str.len - pos**. The function then reports an invalid-argument error if any of the **rlen** characters in **str** beginning at position **pos** is other than **0** or **1**.

Otherwise, the function constructs an object of class **bits<*N*>**, initializing the first *M* bit positions to values determined from the corresponding characters in the string **str**. *M* is the smaller of *N* and **rlen**. An element of the constructed string has value zero if the corresponding character in **str**, beginning at position **pos**, is **0**. Otherwise, the element has the value one. Character position **pos + *M* - 1** corresponds to bit position zero. Subsequent decreasing character positions correspond to increasing bit positions.

If *M* < *N*, remaining bit positions are initialized to zero.

17.5.3.1.4 bits<*N*>::operator&=(const bits<*N*>&)

```
bits<N>& operator&=(const bits<N>& rhs);
```

Clears each bit in ***this** for which the corresponding bit in **rhs** is clear, and leaves all other bits unchanged. The function returns ***this**.

17.5.3.1.5 bits<*N*>::operator|=(const bits<*N*>&)

```
bits<N>& operator|=(const bits<N>& rhs);
```

Sets each bit in ***this** for which the corresponding bit in **rhs** is set, and leaves all other bits unchanged. The function returns ***this**.

17.5.3.1.6 bits<*N*>::operator^=(const bits<*N*>&)

```
bits<N>& operator^=(const bits<N>& rhs);
```

Toggles each bit in ***this** for which the corresponding bit in **rhs** is set, and leaves all other bits unchanged. The function returns ***this**.

17.5.3.1.7 bits<*N*>::operator<<=(size_t)

```
bits<N>& operator<<=(size_t pos);
```

Replaces each bit at position *I* in ***this** with a value determined as follows:
- If *I* < **pos**, the new value is zero;
- If *I* >= **pos**, the new value is the previous value of the bit at position *I* - **pos**.

The function returns ***this**.

17.5.3.1.8 bits<_N_>::operator>>=(size_t)

operator>>=

```
bits<N>& operator>>=(size_t pos);
```

Replaces each bit at position _I_ in ***this** with a value determined as follows:

- If _pos_ >= _N_ - _I_, the new value is zero;
- If _pos_ < _N_ - _I_, the new value is the previous value of the bit at position _I_ + _pos_.

The function returns ***this**.

17.5.3.1.9 bits<_N_>::set()

set

```
bits<N>& set();
```

Sets all bits in ***this**. The function returns ***this**.

17.5.3.1.10 bits<_N_>::set(size_t, int)

set

```
bits<N>& set(size_t pos, int val = 1);
```

Reports an out-of-range error if _pos_ does not correspond to a valid bit position. Otherwise, the function stores a new value in the bit at position _pos_ in ***this**. If _val_ is nonzero, the stored value is one, otherwise it is zero. The function returns ***this**.

17.5.3.1.11 bits<_N_>::reset()

reset

```
bits<N>& reset();
```

Resets all bits in ***this**. The function returns ***this**.

17.5.3.1.12 bits<_N_>::reset(size_t)

reset

```
bits<N>& reset(size_t pos);
```

Reports an out-of-range error if _pos_ does not correspond to a valid bit position. Otherwise, the function resets the bit at position _pos_ in ***this**. The function returns ***this**.

17.5.3.1.13 bits<_N_>::operator~()

operator~

```
bits<N> operator~() const;
```

Constructs an object _x_ of class **bits<_N_>** and initializes it with ***this**. The function then returns _x_.**toggle()**.

17.5.3.1.14 bits<_N_>::toggle()

toggle

```
bits<N>& toggle();
```

Toggles all bits in ***this**. The function returns ***this**.

17.5.3.1.15 bits<_N_>::toggle(size_t)

toggle

```
bits<N>& toggle(size_t pos);
```

Reports an out-of-range error if _pos_ does not correspond to a valid bit position. Otherwise, the function toggles the bit at position _pos_ in ***this**. The function returns ***this**.

17.5.3.1.16 bits<_N_>::to_ushort()

to_ushort

```
unsigned short to_ushort() const;
```

If the integral value _x_ corresponding to the bits in ***this** cannot be represented as type **unsigned short**, reports an overflow error. Otherwise, the function returns _x_.

17.5.3.1.17 bits<_N_>::to_ulong()

to_ulong

```
unsigned long to_ulong() const;
```

If the integral value _x_ corresponding to the bits in ***this** cannot be represented as type **unsigned long**, reports an overflow error. Otherwise, the function returns _x_.

17.5.3.1.18 bits<*N*>::to_string()

to_string

```
string to_string() const;
```

Constructs an object of type **string** and initializes it to a string of length *N* characters. Each character is determined by the value of its corresponding bit position in ***this**. Character position *N* - **1** corresponds to bit position zero. Subsequent decreasing character positions correspond to increasing bit positions. Bit value zero becomes the character **0**, bit value one becomes the character **1**.

The function returns the created object.

17.5.3.1.19 bits<*N*>::count()

count

```
size_t count() const;
```

Returns a count of the number of bits set in ***this**.

17.5.3.1.20 bits<*N*>::length()

length

```
size_t length() const;
```

Returns *N*.

17.5.3.1.21 bits<*N*>::operator==(const bits<*N*>&)

operator==

```
int operator==(const bits<N>& rhs) const;
```

Returns a nonzero value if the value of each bit in ***this** equals the value of the corresponding bit in *rhs*.

17.5.3.1.22 bits<*N*>::operator!=(const bits<*N*>&)

operator!=

```
int operator!=(const bits<N>& rhs) const;
```

Returns a nonzero value if **!(*this == rhs)**.

17.5.3.1.23 bits<*N*>::test(size_t)

test

```
int test(size_t pos) const;
```

Reports an out-of-range error if *pos* does not correspond to a valid bit position. Otherwise, the function returns a nonzero value if the bit at position *pos* in ***this** has the value one.

17.5.3.1.24 bits<*N*>::any()

any

```
int any() const;
```

Returns a nonzero value if any bit in ***this** is one.

17.5.3.1.25 bits<*N*>::none()

none

```
int none() const;
```

Returns a nonzero value if no bit in ***this** is one.

17.5.3.1.26 bits<*N*>::operator<<(size_t)

operator<<

```
bits<N> operator<<(size_t pos) const;
```

Returns **bits<*N*>(*this) <<= pos**.

17.5.3.1.27 bits<*N*>::operator>>(size_t)

operator>>

```
bits<N> operator>>(size_t pos) const;
```

Returns **bits<*N*>(*this) >>= pos**.

17.5.3.2 operator&(const bits<*N*>&, const bits<*N*>&)

operator&

```
bits<N> operator&(const bits<N>& lhs, const bits<N>& rhs);
```

Returns **bits<*N*>(lhs) &= pos**.

17.5.3.3 operator|(const bits<*N*>&, const bits<*N*>&)

operator|

```
bits<N> operator|(const bits<N>& lhs, const bits<N>& rhs);
```

Returns **bits<*N*>(lhs) |= pos**.

operator^ | **17.5.3.4 operator^(const bits<_N_>&, const bits<_N_>&)**

`bits<N> operator^(const bits<N>& lhs, const bits<N>& rhs);`

Returns **bits<_N_>(_lhs_) ^= _pos_**.

operator>> | **17.5.3.5 operator>>(istream&, bits<_N_>&)**

`istream& operator>>(istream& is, bits<N>& x);`

A formatted input function, extracts up to **_N_** (single-byte) characters from **_is_**. The function stores these characters in a temporary object **_str_** of type **string**, then evaluates the expression **_x_ = bits<_N_>(_str_)**. Characters are extracted and stored until any of the following occurs:

- **_N_** characters have been extracted and stored;
- end-of-file occurs on the input sequence;
- the next input character is neither **0** or **1** (in which case the input character is not extracted).

If no characters are stored in **_str_**, the function calls **_is_.setstate(ios::failbit)**.

The function returns **_is_**.

operator<< | **17.5.3.6 operator<<(ostream&, const bits<_N_>&)**

`ostream& operator<<(ostream& os, const bits<N>& x);`

Returns **_os_ << _x_.to_string()**.

Footnotes:

Footnotes | 113) An implementation is free to store the bit sequence more efficiently.

Future Directions

Standard Template Library A very ambitious recent addition to the Standard C++ Library is an extensive Standard Template Library, or STL (**S&L94**). It provides a uniform and powerful set of templates comparable in size to all the code shown in this book. It offers considerable promise for future implementations of the draft C++ Standard. At the moment, however, it strains the current template technology. Moreover, the defintion of STL makes extensive use of default template parameters and member templates, two extensions only recently added to the draft C++ Standard.

STL may eventually replace the header **<bits>**, and most of the headers that follow. Still, I've chosen to cover fully the header **<bits>** because:

- It is still part of the Informal Review Draft, which forms the basis for this implementation of the Standard C++ Library.

- It describes *functionality* that should be retained, in one form or another, in future versions of the draft C++ Standard.

- It has useful tutorial benefit, for those who want to see how a template class of this nature can be constructed and used.

- It has useful practical benefit, for those who want to use such a template class whether or not it remains a part of the draft C++ Standard.

I note for each of the headers that follow if it is likely to be in the same boat. But I also continue to describe each one, for much the same reasons.

Using `<bits>`

You include the header **`<bits>`** to make use of the template class **`bits<N>`**. Here, **N** is an integer constant expression that specifies the number of bits in an instantiation of the template class. Objects of such a template class let you represent and manipulate a fixed-length sequence of bits. Earlier in this chapter, I dubbed such objects flag and mask words. The advantage here is that you can manipulate all objects of template class **`bits<N>`** the same way irrespective of the number of words required for their representations.

construction   To construct a **`bits<N>`** object **x0**, say of size 20 bits, with all bits initially zero, you can simply write:

```
bits<20> x0;
```

length   Each object **x** reports the *length* of its bit sequence with the call **x.length()**. That way, you don't have to reconstruct the value **N**, or store it separately, from when you first instantiate the class until you later need it again.

One style for determining the size of a particular instantiation is in conjunction with the enumeration constants that designate its elements, as in:

```
enum color (red, green, blue, ....., N);
typedef bits<N> colorset;
```

You append **N** to the list of enumeration constants you define to access different elements (bits) of **colorset** objects. That way, the translator determines the number of bits for you.

You can also construct a **`bits<N>`** object and initialize its elements from an unsigned integer value, as in:

```
bits<32> x1(0x55555555);              // set every other bit
```

In this case, the least-significant bit in the integer argument determines element zero. More generally, the initializer stores the value one in element **j** if, for the argument **val**, the expression **val & (1 << j)** is nonzero.

Finally, you can construct a **`bits<N>`** object and initialize its elements from corresponding elements of a character sequence controlled by a **string** object. (See Chapter 15: **`<string>`**.) The character value **'0'** initializes the element to zero, and the character value **'1'** initializes the element to one. No other character values are permitted. As usual with **string** arguments, you can specify one or two additional arguments to select a substring. In the examples that follow, the comment after each constructor indicates the constructor with equivalent effect:

```
string alt("10101");
bits<10> x2(alt);                     // bits<10> x2(0x15)
bits<10> x3(alt, 1);                  // bits<10> x3(0x0a)
bits<10> x4(alt, 1, 3);               // bits<10> x4(0x02)
```

An unsigned integer or **string** object that specifies more than **N** bits causes no problems. The excess bits are simply ignored.

bitwise   Given two objects **x0** and **x1** of class **bits<N>** (for the same value of **N**,
operations of course), you can perform the usual bitwise operations:

```
x0 = x1
x0 &= x1              x0 & x1
x0 |= x1              x0 | x1
x0 ^= x1              x0 ^ x1
x0 <<= m              x0 << m
x0 >>= m              x0 >> m
x0 == x1              x0 != x1
```

Here, **m** is an expression with some integer type. The semantics of all these
operations involving **x0** and **x1** are a natural extension of those for unsigned integer values.

You can deal with all bits at once, by writing:

```
x0.set()                          // set all bits
x0.reset()                        // clear all bits
x0.toggle()                       // toggle (invert) all bits
~x0                               // toggle all bits
x0.count()                        // count all set bits
x0.any()                          // test if any bit set
x0.none()                         // test if no bit set
```

Or, given a valid bit position **n**, you can affect just that bit, by writing:

```
x0.set(n)                         // set bit n
x0.set(n, b)                 // set bit n to (b != 0)
x0.reset(n)                       // clear bit n
x0.toggle(n)                      // toggle bit n
x0.test(n)                        // test bit n
```

conversions   The constructors, shown above, define mappings from unsigned integers or **string** objects to **bits<N>** objects. You can perform the inverse
mappings as well:

```
x0.to_ushort()    // return unsigned short equivalent
x0.to_ulong()     // return unsigned long equivalent
x0.to_string()             // return string equivalent
```

The first two member functions can report an overflow error (by throwing
an exception) if the corresponding value is too large to represent as the
return type. Absent any overflow, such a return value should serve as a
constructor argument that generates a **bits<N>** object equal to **x0**.

Finally, you can insert and extract objects of class **bits<N>**. For example:

extractor   **cin >> x0**

effectively extracts a **string** object from the standard input stream and
assigns it to some temporary. (See Chapter 15: **<string>**.) Unlike the usual
string extractor, however, the function:

- does not use the width field stored in **cin**, nor does it set the field to zero

- extracts at most **N** characters, after skipping any white space

- otherwise extracts up to, but not including, the first character that is not
  0 or **1**

The function then converts the controlled character sequence, by the same
rules as for constructing a **bits<N>** object from a **string** argument, and
assigns it to **x0**.

Last of all, you can insert the character sequence into, say, the standard output stream, by writing:

inserter   `cout << x0`

As you might expect, this is equivalent to inserting `x0.to_string()`.

Implementing `<bits>`

bits   Figure 17.1 shows the file **bits**, which implements the standard header `<bits>`. All template functions appear within the header as inline definitions, as I discussed much earlier. (See page 253.) Nevertheless, you will find that not all translators will accept this header unmodified.

cfront   In particular, those based on the cfront preprocessor may refuse to translate inline functions that contain *for* statements. You have to reorganize the code for cfront. I present the header in this form because I believe it is clear and fairly simple. Hence, it should serve as a good starting point even if it is not completely acceptable to all currently available translators.

_Bitsxstr   I introduced a secret function **_Bitsxstr**, with external linkage. It extracts a **string** object by the special rules I gave above for a **bits<N>** object. Class **bitstring**, in the next chapter, also uses this function.

friend   I also moved the function declarations inside the template class defini-
functions tion as *friend* functions, for the reasons I described earlier in this chapter. (See page 422.) Thus, the header consists almost entirely of the definition of template class **bits<N>**.

_T   Within the template class definition, I introduced the type definition **_T**. An object of class **bits<N>** stores an array of one or more unsigned integer member objects. **_T** is the type of the array elements. I have chosen *unsigned long* for this type, but you might prefer *unsigned short* or *unsigned char*. Some implementations may manipulate the smaller element types more efficiently. Or you may declare large arrays of **bits<N>** elements and want to keep object sizes smaller.

Private to the class, I define two useful constants. They masquerade as elements in an enumeration — a common trick — but they are used independently as numeric values:

_Nb ▪ **_Nb**, the number of bits in an array element

_Nw ▪ **_Nw**, *one less than* the number of elements in the array

I won't recite all the reasons for choosing these particular derived parameter values. All I can say is, they were the result of several rewrites to make the code at once compact, robust, and readable.

_BITS_BYTE   The definition of **_Nb** involves the macro **_BITS_BYTE**. It is defined in `<yxvals.h>` with the obvious meaning — it counts the number of bits in a single byte. Yes, this is exactly the same value as the macro **CHAR_BITS**, defined in `<limits.h>`. The latter macro cannot, however, be defined in a program that includes only the header `<bits>`. So I use a secret alias instead.

Figure 17.1:
bits
Part 1 of 4

```
// bits standard header
#ifndef _BITS_
#define _BITS_
#include <string>
        // template class bits
string _Bitsxstr(istream&, size_t);
template<size_t _N> class bits {
    typedef unsigned long _T;
public:
    bits()
        {_Tidy(); }
    bits(unsigned long _X)
        {_Tidy();
        for (size_t _P = 0; _X != 0 && _P < _N; _X >>= 1, ++_P)
            if (_X & 1)
                set(_P); }
    bits(const string& _S, size_t _P = 0, size_t _L = NPOS)
        {if (_S.length() < _P)
            _Xran();
        if (_S.length() - _P < _L)
            _L = _S.length() - _P;
        if (_N < _L)
            _L = _N;
        _Tidy(), _P += _L;
        for (size_t _I = 0; _I < _L; ++_I)
            if (_S[--_P] == '1')
                set(_I);
            else if (_S[_P] != '0')
                _Xinv(); }
    bits<_N>& operator&=(const bits<_N>& _R)
        {for (int _I = _Nw; 0 <= _I; --_I)
            _A[_I] &= _R._W(_I);
        return (*this); }
    bits<_N>& operator|=(const bits<_N>& _R)
        {for (int _I = _Nw; 0 <= _I; --_I)
            _A[_I] |= _R._W(_I);
        return (*this); }
    bits<_N>& operator^=(const bits<_N>& _R)
        {for (int _I = _Nw; 0 <= _I; --_I)
            _A[_I] ^= _R._W(_I);
        return (*this); }
    bits<_N>& operator<<=(size_t _P)
        {if (_P < 0)
            return (*this >>= -_P);
        const int _D = _P / _Nb;
        if (_D != 0)
            for (int _I = _Nw; 0 <= _I; --_I)
                _A[_I] = _D <= _I ? _A[_I - _D] : 0;
        if ((_P %= _Nb) != 0)
            {for (int _I = _Nw; 0 < _I; --_I)
                _A[_I] = (_A[_I] << _P)
                    | (_A[_I - 1] >> (_Nb - _P));
            _A[0] <<= _P, _Trim(); }
        return (*this); }
    bits<_N>& operator>>=(size_t _P)
```

```
            {if (_P < 0)
                return (*this <<= -_P);
            const int _D = _P / _Nb;
            if (_D != 0)
                for (int _I = 0; _I <= _Nw; ++_I)
                    _A[_I] = _D <= _Nw - _I ? _A[_I + _D] : 0;
            if ((_P %= _Nb) != 0)
                {for (int _I = 0; _I < _Nw; ++_I)
                    _A[_I] = (_A[_I] >> _P)
                        | (_A[_I + 1] << (_Nb - _P));
                _A[_Nw] >>= _P; }
            return (*this); }
    bits<_N>& set()
        {_Tidy(~(_T)0);
        return (*this); }
    bits<_N>& set(size_t _P, _Bool _X = 1)
        {if (_N <= _P)
            _Xran();
        if (_X)
            _A[_P / _Nb] |= (_T)1 << _P % _Nb;
        else
            _A[_P / _Nb] &= ~((_T)1 << _P % _Nb);
        return (*this); }
    bits<_N>& reset()
        {_Tidy();
        return (*this); }
    bits<_N>& reset(size_t _P)
        {return (set(_P, 0)); }
    bits<_N> operator~() const
        {return (bits<_N>(*this).toggle()); }
    bits<_N>& toggle()
        {for (int _I = _Nw; 0 <= _I; --_I)
            _A[_I] = ~_A[_I];
        _Trim();
        return (*this); }
    bits<_N>& toggle(size_t _P)
        {if (_N <= _P)
            _Xran();
        _A[_P / _Nb] ^= (_T)1 << _P % _Nb;
        return (*this); }
    unsigned short to_ushort() const
        {unsigned long _V = to_ulong();
        if (~(unsigned short)0 < _V)
            _Xoflo();
        return (_V); }
    unsigned long to_ulong() const
        {enum {_Assert = 1 /
            (sizeof (unsigned long) % sizeof (_T) == 0)};
        int _I = _Nw;
        for (; sizeof (unsigned long) / sizeof (_T) <= _I; --_I)
            if (_A[_I] != 0)
                _Xoflo();
        for (unsigned long _V = _A[_I]; 0 <= --_I; )
            _V = _V << _Nb | _A[_I];
        return (_V); }
```

```
    string to_string() const
        {string _S(_N, reserve);
        for (size_t _P = _N; 0 < _P; )
            _S += test(--_P) ? '1' : '0';
        return (_S); }
size_t count() const
    {size_t _V = 0;
    for (int _I = _Nw; 0 <= _I; --_I)
        for (_T _X = _A[_I]; _X != 0; _X >>= 4)
            _V += "\0\1\1\2\1\2\2\3"
                    "\1\2\2\3\2\3\3\4"[_X & 0xF];
    return (_V); }
size_t length() const
    {return (_N); }
_Bool operator==(const bits<_N>& _R) const
    {for (int _I = _Nw; 0 <= _I; --_I)
        if (_A[_I] != _R._W(_I))
            return (0);
    return (1); }
_Bool operator!=(const bits<_N>& _R) const
    {return (!(*this == _R)); }
_Bool test(size_t _P) const
    {if (_N <= _P)
        _Xran();
    return ((_A[_P / _Nb] & ((_T)1 << _P % _Nb)) != 0); }
_Bool any() const
    {for (int _I = _Nw; 0 <= _I; --_I)
        if (_A[_I] != 0)
            return (1);
    return (0); }
_Bool none() const
    {return (!any()); }
bits<_N> operator<<(size_t _R) const
    {return (bits<_N>(*this) <<= _R); }
bits<_N> operator>>(size_t _R) const
    {return (bits<_N>(*this) >>= _R); }
friend bits<_N> operator&(const bits<_N>& _L,
    const bits<_N>& _R)
    {return (bits<_N>(_L) &= _R); }
friend bits<_N> operator|(const bits<_N>& _L,
    const bits<_N>& _R)
    {return (bits<_N>(_L) |= _R); }
friend bits<_N> operator^(const bits<_N>& _L,
    const bits<_N>& _R)
    {return (bits<_N>(_L) ^= _R); }
friend istream& operator>>(istream& _I, bits<_N>& _R)
    {_R = _Bitsxstr(_I, _N);
    return (_I); }
friend ostream& operator<<(ostream& _O, const bits<_N>& _R)
    {return (_O << _R.to_string()); }
_T _W(size_t _I) const
    {return (_A[_I]); }
private:
    enum {_Nb = _BITS_BYTE * sizeof (_T),
        _Nw = _N == 0 ? 0 : (_N - 1) / _Nb};
```

```
      void _Tidy(_T _X = 0)
          {for (int _I = _Nw; 0 <= _I; --_I)
              _A[_I] = _X;
          if (_X != 0)
              _Trim(); }
      void _Trim()
          {if (_N % _Nb != 0)
              _A[_Nw] &= ((_T)1 << _N % _Nb) - 1; }
      void _Xinv() const
          {invalidargument("invalid bits<N> char").raise(); }
      void _Xoflo() const
          {overflow("bits<N> conversion overflow").raise(); }
      void _Xran() const
          {outofrange("invalid bits<N> position").raise(); }
      _T _A[_Nw + 1];
      };
#endif                                                                □
```

The template class **bits<N>** also defines five secret protected member functions:

_Tidy ▪ **_Tidy**, which initializes the array elements all to the same value (usually zero)

_Trim ▪ **_Trim**, which sets to zero any unused bits in the last element of the array, both for good hygiene and to simplify several bitwise operations

_Xinv ▪ **_Xinv**, which reports an invalid-argument error

_Xoflo ▪ **_Xoflo**, which reports an overflow error

_Xran ▪ **_Xran**, which reports a range error

For a discussion of the exceptions associated with invalid-argument, overflow, and range errors, see Chapter 3: **<exception>**. As you can see, all of these functions are used throughout the member function definitions.

template limitations None of the member function definitions is particularly complex. Nevertheless, several of the larger ones are poor candidates for making inline, as they are declared here. As I have discussed earlier (page 253), some translators refuse to make inline any definition that includes a looping statement. (Some simply refuse to translate the code at all, even though they are supposed to.) Others may generate inline code, but slavishly loop even over a single word.

Obviously, this code works best in conjunction with a smart template optimizer. Such creatures are currently in short supply, but that should not always be the case. The draft C++ Standard is banking ever more heavily on template technology, and not just within the Standard C++ library. If such pressures continue to drive the commercial compiler industry, then the kind of code I show here will eventually come into its own.

Meanwhile, I can report that this code does translate successfully under at least some current implementations. To make more than nontrivial use of it, however, you should check carefully to see the kind of code it generates. You may well want to modify it.

Figure 17.2:
bitsxstr.c

```
// bitsxstr -- _Bitsxstr(istream&, size_t)
#include <bitstring>

string _Bitsxstr(istream& is, size_t n)
        {                               // extract into a string of text bits
        _Bool changed = 0;
        string str(n, reserve);
        if (n == NPOS)
                --n;
        _TRY_IO_BEGIN
        if (is.ipfx())
                {                               // extract arbitrary characters
                int ch;
                while (0 < n && (ch = is.rdbuf()->sbumpc()) != EOF)
                        if (ch != '0' && ch != '1')
                                {                       // put back non-bit and quit
                                is.rdbuf()->sputbackc(ch);
                                break;
                                }
                        else
                                str.append((char)ch), changed = 1, --n;
                }
        if (!changed)
                is.setstate(ios::failbit);
        is.isfx();
        _CATCH_IO_(is);
        return (str);
        }                                                                     □
```

bitsxstr.c The header **<bits>** needs only one additional source file. Figure 17.2 shows the file **bitsxstr.c**, which defines the function **_Bitsxstr**. It is quite similar to the corresponding extractor for class **string**. (See Chapter 15: **<string>**.) I described the differences earlier in this chapter, on page 429. The function extracts a character sequence of maximum length **n**, consisting only of the characters **0** and **1**.

For a description of the exception-handling macros, see page 128.

Testing <bits>

tbits.c Figure 17.3 shows the file **tbits.c**. It tests the basic properties of the template class **bits<N>** defined in **<bits>**. It does so by instantiating the class **bits<5>** and testing the various operations, at least for their minimum functionality. It then instantiates the class **<153>**, as an example of a larger parameter value, and performs a few more cursory tests.

If all goes well, the program prints:

SUCCESS testing <bits>

and takes a normal exit.

```
// test <bits>
#include <assert.h>
#include <string.h>
#include <bits>
#include <iostream>
#include <strstream>

int main()
    {                       // test basic workings of bits definitions
    bits<5> x50, x51(0xf), x52(string("xx10101ab"), 2, 15);
    bits<5> x53(x52);
    assert(x50.to_ushort() == 0x00);
    assert(x51.to_ulong() == 0x0f);
    assert(x52.to_ulong() == 0x15);
    assert(x53.to_ulong() == 0x15);
        // test arithmetic
    x50 |= x51, assert(x50.to_ulong() == 0x0f);
    x50 ^= x52, assert(x50.to_ulong() == 0x1a);
    x50 &= x51, assert(x50.to_ulong() == 0x0a);
    x50 <<= 2, assert(x50.to_ulong() == 0x08);
    x50 >>= 3, assert(x50.to_ulong() == 0x01);
    x50.set(2), assert(x50.to_ulong() == 0x05);
    x50.set(0, 0), assert(x50.to_ulong() == 0x04);
    x50.set(), assert(x50.to_ulong() == 0x1f);
    x50.reset(3), assert(x50.to_ulong() == 0x17);
    x50.reset(), assert(x50.to_ulong() == 0x00);
    x50.toggle(2), assert(x50.to_ulong() == 0x04);
    x50.toggle(), assert(x50.to_ulong() == 0x1b);
    assert(x50.to_string() == string("11011"));
    assert(x50.count() == 4 && x52.count() == 3);
    assert(x50.length() == 5 && x51.length() == 5);
    assert(x50 == x50 && x50 != x51);
    assert(x50.test(1) && !x50.test(2));
    assert(x50.any() && !x50.none());
    x50.reset(), assert(!x50.any() && x50.none());
        // test friend arithmetic functions
    x50 = x51;
    assert((x50 << 2).to_ulong() == 0x1c
        && (x50 >> 2).to_ulong() == 0x03);
    assert((x50 & x52) == bits<5>(0x05)
        && (x50 & 0x05) == bits<5>(0x05)
        && (0x05 & x50) == bits<5>(0x05));
    assert((x50 | x52) == bits<5>(0x1f)
        && (x50 | 0x15) == (0x15 | x50));
    assert((x50 ^ x52) == bits<5>(0x1a)
        && (x50 ^ 0x15) == bits<5>(string("11010"))
        && (0x15 ^ x50) == (x50 ^ 0x15));
        // test I/O
    istrstream ins("1 0101 11000");
    ostrstream outs;
    ins >> x50, assert(x50.to_ulong() == 0x01);
    outs << x50 << ' ';
    ins >> x50, assert(x50.to_ulong() == 0x05);
    outs << x50 << ' ';
    ins >> x50, assert(x50.to_ulong() == 0x18);
```

<table>
<tr><td>

Continuing
tbits.c
Part 2 of 2
</td><td>

```
outs << x50 << ends;
assert(strcmp(outs.str(), "00001 00101 11000") == 0);
        // test larger bits
bits<153> x153a, x153b;
(x153a.set(100) >>= 99) <<= 1;
assert(x153a.to_ulong() == 0x04);
x153b.set(121);
assert(x153b.any() && !x153b.test(105)
       && x153b.test(121) && x153b.count() == 1);
assert((x153a | x153b) ^ x153b == x153a);
cout << "SUCCESS testing <bits>" << endl;
return (0);
}                                                  □
```
</td></tr>
</table>

Exercises

Exercise 17.1 Describe how you might use template class **bits<N>** to perform extended-precision arithmetic.

Exercise 17.2 What is the meaning of the instantiation **bits<0>**? Is it permitted? Is it useful? Does the code in file **bits** survive such an instantiation?

Exercise 17.3 Does the code in file **bits** survive the instantiation **bits<NPOS>**?

Exercise 17.4 Implement the class **bits32** that has the same functionality as **bits<32>**.

Exercise 17.5 Change the definition of **_Nw** in file **bits** to be one greater, and hence count the number of words in the array of unsigned integers. Alter the remaining code to work correctly with this revised definition.

Exercise 17.6 [Harder] Rewrite the definition of template class **bits<N>** for your implementation so that it generates the most optimal code. Can you get the looping code to disappear for small enough values of **N**?

Exercise 17.7 [Very hard] Write a portable definition of template class **bits<N>** that assuredly contains no loops over array elements when **N <= 32**.

Chapter 18: `<bitstring>`

Background

The header `<bitstring>` defines the class `bitstring`, and a few supporting functions. Like an object of class `string`, described in an earlier chapter, a `bitstring` object controls a sequence that can vary in length as the program executes. (See Chapter 15: `<string>`.) Where the former controls a character sequence, however, the latter controls a bit sequence.

You could achieve the same effect by using only two values in a character sequence and recycling class `string`. Presumably, however, class `bitstring` offers greater storage economy. A reasonable implementation should pack those bits into integer objects of a more convenient size.

Class `bitstring` also borrows heavily from another predecessor in the Standard C++ library. The template class `bits<N>`, described in the previous chapter, deals with fixed-length sequences of bits. Both classes have reason to overload the bitwise operators defined on the integer types. And both classes have reason to define simple logical operations on individual bits.

What you will find here, then, is a heady mixture of operations. You can insert, delete, and replace subsequences within a bit sequence. You can also AND, OR, and EXCLUSIVE OR bit sequences. Class `bitstring` is thus more suitable for manipulating, say, sequences of pixels in an image than either class `string` or the template class `bits<N>`.

What the Draft C++ Standard Says

bit order For all their similarity, class `bitstring` and the template class `bits<N>` have a fundamental difference. When converting to and from integer values, the two classes have exactly opposite positional bit weighting schemes. Recall that element `j` of an object of class `bits<N>` corresponds to the value `1 << j`. (Bit zero is the *least* significant bit.) But for an object of class `bitstring` that controls a bit sequence of length `len`, the corresponding value is `1 << (len - j - 1)`. (Bit zero is the *most* significant bit.)

Good reasons exist for this difference in conventions, but it can still be a nuisance if you convert between integers and objects of these two classes.

17.5.4 Header `<bitstring>`

The header `<bitstring>` defines a class and several function signatures for representing and manipulating varying-length sequences of bits.

17.5.4.1 Class `bitstring`

```
class bitstring {
public:
    bitstring();
    bitstring(unsigned long val, size_t n);
    bitstring(const bitstring& str, size_t pos = 0,
        size_t n = NPOS);
    bitstring(const string& str, size_t pos = 0,
        size_t n = NPOS);
    bitstring& operator+=(const bitstring& rhs);
    bitstring& operator&=(const bitstring& rhs);
    bitstring& operator|=(const bitstring& rhs);
    bitstring& operator^=(const bitstring& rhs);
    bitstring& operator<<=(size_t pos);
    bitstring& operator>>=(size_t pos);
    bitstring& append(const bitstring& str, pos = 0, n = NPOS);
    bitstring& assign(const bitstring& str, pos = 0, n = NPOS);
    bitstring& insert(size_t pos1, const bitstring& str,
        size_t pos2 = 0, size_t n = NPOS);
    bitstring& remove(size_t pos = 0, size_t n = NPOS);
    bitstring& replace(size_t pos1, size_t n1,
        const bitstring& str; size_t pos2 = 0,
        size_t n2 = NPOS);
    bitstring& set();
    bitstring& set(size_t pos, int val = 1);
    bitstring& reset();
    bitstring& reset(size_t pos);
    bitstring& toggle();
    bitstring& toggle(size_t pos);
    string to_string() const;
    size_t count() const;
    size_t length() const;
    size_t resize(size_t n, int val = 0);
    size_t trim();
    size_t find(int val, size_t pos = 0, size_t n = NPOS) const;
    size_t rfind(int val, size_t pos = 0, size_t n = NPOS)
        const;
    bitstring substr(size_t pos, size_t n = NPOS) const;
    int operator==(const bitstring& rhs) const;
    int operator!=(const bitstring& rhs) const;
    int test(size_t pos) const;
    int any() const;
    int none() const;
    bitstring operator<<(size_t pos) const;
    bitstring operator>>(size_t pos) const;
    bitstring operator~() const;
private:
//    char* ptr;                                  exposition only
//    size_t len;                                 exposition only
};
```

The class **bitstring** describes an object that can store a sequence consisting of a varying number of bits. Such a sequence is also called a *bit string* (or simply a *string* if the type of the elements is clear from context). Storage for the string is allocated and freed as necessary by the member functions of class **bitstring**.

Each bit represents either the value zero (reset) or one (set). To *toggle* a bit is to change the value zero to one, or the value one to zero. Each bit has a non-negative position **pos**. When converting between an object of class **bitstring** of length **len** and a value of some integral type, bit position **pos** corresponds to the *bit value* **1 << (len - pos - 1)**.[114] The integral value corresponding to two or more bits is the sum of their bit values.

For the sake of exposition, the maintained data is presented here as:

- **char* ptr**, points to the sequence of bits, stored one bit per element;[115]
- **size_t len**, the length of the bit sequence.

The functions described in this subclause can report three kinds of errors, each associated with a distinct exception:

- an *invalid-argument* error is associated with exceptions of type **invalidargument**;
- a *length* error is associated with exceptions of type **lengtherror**;
- an *out-of-range* error is associated with exceptions of type **outofrange**.

To report one of these errors, the function evaluates the expression **ex.raise()**, where **ex** is an object of the associated exception type.

17.5.4.1.1 bitstring::bitstring()

constructor

```
bitstring();
```

Constructs an object of class **bitstring**, initializing:

- **ptr** to an unspecified value;
- **len** to zero.

17.5.4.1.2 bitstring::bitstring(unsigned long, size_t)

constructor

```
bitstring(unsigned long val, size_t n);
```

Reports a length error if **n** equals **NPOS**. Otherwise, the function constructs an object of class **bitstring** and determines its initial string value from **val**. If **val** is zero, the corresponding string is the empty string. Otherwise, the corresponding string is the shortest sequence of bits with the same bit value as **val**. If the corresponding string is shorter than **n**, the string is extended with elements whose values are all zero. Thus, the function initializes:

- **ptr** to point at the first element of the string;
- **len** to the length of the string.

17.5.4.1.3 bitstring::bitstring(const bitstring&, size_t, size_t)

constructor

```
bitstring(const bitstring& str, size_t pos = 0,
    size_t n = NPOS);
```

Reports an out-of-range error if **pos > str.len**. Otherwise, the function constructs an object of class **bitstring** and determines the effective length **rlen** of the initial string value as the smaller of **n** and **str.len - pos**. Thus, the uunction initializes:

- **ptr** to point at the first element of an allocated copy of **rlen** elements of the string controlled by **str** beginning at position **pos**;
- **len** to **rlen**.

17.5.4.1.4 `bitstring::bitstring(const string&, size_t,`
     `size_t)`

constructor

    `bitstring(const string& str, size_t pos = 0, size_t n = NPOS);`

Reports an out-of-range error if **pos** > **str.len**. Otherwise, the function determines the effective length **rlen** of the initializing string as the smaller of **n** and **str.len** - **pos**. The function then reports an invalid-argument error if any of the **rlen** characters in **str** beginning at position **pos** is other than **0** or **1**.

Otherwise, the function constructs an object of class **bitstring** and determines its initial string value from **str**. The length of the constructed string is **rlen**. An element of the constructed string has value zero if the corresponding character in **str**, beginning at position **pos**, is **0**. Otherwise, the element has the value one.

Thus, the function initializes:

• **ptr** to point at the first element of the string;
• **len** to **rlen**.

17.5.4.1.5 `bitstring::operator+=(const bitstring&)`

operator+=

    `bitstring& operator+=(const bitstring& rhs);`

Reports a length error if **len** >= **NPOS** - **rhs.len**.

Otherwise, the function replaces the string controlled by ***this** with a string of length **len** + **rhs.len** whose first **len** elements are a copy of the original string controlled by ***this** and whose remaining elements are a copy of the elements of the string controlled by **rhs**.

The function returns ***this**.

17.5.4.1.6 `bitstring::operator&=(const bitstring&)`

operator&=

    `bitstring& operator&=(const bitstring& rhs);`

Determines a length **rlen** which is the larger of **len** and **rhs.len**, then behaves as if the shorter of the two strings controlled by ***this** and **rhs** were temporarily extended to length **rlen** by adding elements all with value zero. The function then replaces the string controlled by ***this** with a string of length **rlen** whose elements have the value one only if both of the corresponding elements of ***this** and **rhs** are one.

The function returns ***this**.

17.5.4.1.7 `bitstring::operator|=(const bitstring&)`

operator|=

    `bitstring& operator|=(const bitstring& rhs);`

Determines a length **rlen** which is the larger of **len** and **rhs.len**, then behaves as if the shorter of the two strings controlled by ***this** and **rhs** were temporarily extended to length **rlen** by adding elements all with value zero. The function then replaces the string controlled by ***this** with a string of length **rlen** whose elements have the value one only if either of the corresponding elements of ***this** and **rhs** are one.

The function returns ***this**.

17.5.4.1.8 `bitstring::operator^=(const bitstring&)`

operator^=

    `bitstring& operator^=(const bitstring& rhs);`

Determines a length **rlen** which is the larger of **len** and **rhs.len**, then behaves as if the shorter of the two strings controlled by ***this** and **rhs** were temporarily extended to length **rlen** by adding elements all with value zero. The function then replaces the string controlled by ***this** with a string of length **rlen** whose elements have the value one only if the corresponding elements of ***this** and **rhs** have different values.

The function returns ***this**.

17.5.4.1.9 bitstring::operator<<=(size_t)

operator<<=

```
bitstring& operator<<=(size_t pos);
```

Replaces each element at position *I* in the string controlled by ***this** with a value determined as follows:

- If *pos* >= *len* - *I*, the new value is zero;
- If *pos* < *len* - *I*, the new value is the previous value of the element at position *I* + *pos*.

The function returns ***this**.

17.5.4.1.10 bitstring::operator>>=(size_t)

operator>>=

```
bitstring& operator>>=(size_t pos);
```

Replaces each element at position *I* in the string controlled by ***this** with a value determined as follows:

- If *I* < *pos*, the new value is zero;
- If *I* >= *pos*, the new value is the previous value of the element at position *I* - *pos*.

17.5.4.1.11 bitstring::append(const bitstring&, size_t, size_t)

append

```
bitstring& append(const bitstring& str, size_t pos = 0,
    size_t n = NPOS);
```

Reports an out-of-range error if *pos* > *str.len*. Otherwise, the function determines the effective length *rlen* of the string to append as the smaller of *n* and *str.len* - *pos*. The function then reports a length error if *len* >= NPOS - *rlen*.

Otherwise, the function replaces the string controlled by ***this** with a string of length *len* + *rlen* whose first *len* elements are a copy of the original string controlled by ***this** and whose remaining elements are a copy of the initial elements of the string controlled by *str* beginning at position *pos*.

The function returns ***this**.

17.5.4.1.12 bitstring::assign(const bitstring&, size_t, size_t)

assign

```
bitstring& assign(const bitstring& str, size_t pos = 0,
    size_t n = NPOS);
```

Reports an out-of-range error if *pos* > *str.len*. Otherwise, the function determines the effective length *rlen* of the string to assign as the smaller of *n* and *str.len* - *pos*.

The function then replaces the string controlled by ***this** with a string of length *rlen* whose elements are a copy of the string controlled by *str* beginning at position *pos*.

The function returns ***this**.

17.5.4.1.13 bitstring::insert(size_t, const bitstring&, size_t, size_t)

insert

```
bitstring& insert(size_t pos1, const bitstring& str,
    size_t pos2 = 0, size_t n = NPOS);
```

Reports an out-of-range error if *pos1* > *len* or *pos2* > *str.len*. Otherwise, the function determines the effective length *rlen* of the string to insert as the smaller of *n* and *str.len* - *pos2*. The function then reports a length error if *len* >= NPOS - *rlen*.

Otherwise, the function replaces the string controlled by **this** with a string of length **len + rlen** whose first **pos1** elements are a copy of the initial elements of the original string controlled by **this**, whose next **rlen** elements are a copy of the elements of the string controlled by **str** beginning at position **pos2**, and whose remaining elements are a copy of the remaining elements of the original string controlled by **this**.

The function returns **this**.

17.5.4.1.14 `bitstring::remove(size_t, size_t)`

remove

```
bitstring& remove(size_t pos = 0, size_t n = NPOS);
```

Reports an out-of-range error if **pos > len**. Otherwise, the function determines the effective length **xlen** of the string to be removed as the smaller of **n** and **len - pos**.

The function then replaces the string controlled by **this** with a string of length **len - xlen** whose first **pos** elements are a copy of the initial elements of the original string controlled by **this**, and whose remaining elements are a copy of the elements of the original string controlled by **this** beginning at position **pos + xlen**.

The function returns **this**.

17.5.4.1.15 `bitstring::replace(size_t, size_t, const bitstring&, size_t, size_t)`

replace

```
bitstring& replace(size_t pos1, size_t n1,
    const bitstring& str, size_t pos2 = 0, size_t n2 = NPOS);
```

Reports an out-of-range error if **pos1 > len** or **pos2 > str.len**. Otherwise, the function determines the effective length **xlen** of the string to be removed as the smaller of **n1** and **len - pos1**. It also determines the effective length **rlen** of the string to be inserted as the smaller of **n2** and **str.len - pos2**. The function then reports a length error if **len - xlen >= NPOS - rlen**.

Otherwise, the function replaces the string controlled by **this** with a string of length **len - xlen + rlen** whose first **pos1** elements are a copy of the initial elements of the original string controlled by **this**, whose next **rlen** elements are a copy of the initial elements of the string controlled by **str** beginning at position **pos2**, and whose remaining elements are a copy of the elements of the original string controlled by **this** beginning at position **pos1 + xlen**.

The function returns **this**.

17.5.4.1.16 `bitstring::set()`

set

```
bitstring& set();
```

Sets all elements of the string controlled by **this**. The function returns **this**.

17.5.4.1.17 `bitstring::set(size_t, int)`

set

```
bitstring& set(size_t pos, int val = 1);
```

Reports an out-of-range error if **pos > len**. Otherwise, if **pos == len**, the function replaces the string controlled by **this** with a string of length **len + 1** whose first **len** elements are a copy of the original string and whose remaining element is set according to **val**. Otherwise, the function sets the element at position **pos** in the string controlled by **this**. If **val** is nonzero, the stored value is one, otherwise it is zero. The function returns **this**.

17.5.4.1.18 `bitstring::reset()`

reset

```
bitstring& reset();
```

Resets all elements of the string controlled by **this**. The function returns **this**.

17.5.4.1.19 bitstring::reset(size_t)

reset

```
bitstring& reset(size_t pos);
```

Reports an out-of-range error if **pos > len**. Otherwise, if **pos == len**, the function replaces the string controlled by ***this** with a string of length **len + 1** whose first **len** elements are a copy of the original string and whose remaining element is zero. Otherwise, the function resets the element at position **pos** in the string controlled by ***this**.

17.5.4.1.20 bitstring::toggle()

toggle

```
bitstring& toggle();
```

Toggles all elements of the string controlled by ***this**. The function returns ***this**.

17.5.4.1.21 bitstring::toggle(size_t)

toggle

```
bitstring& toggle(size_t pos);
```

Reports an out-of-range error if **pos >= len**. Otherwise, the function toggles the element at position **pos** in ***this**.

17.5.4.1.22 bitstring::to_string()

to_string

```
string to_string() const;
```

Creates an object of type **string** and initializes it to a string of length **len** characters. Each character is determined by the value of its corresponding element in the string controlled by ***this**. Bit value zero becomes the character **0**, bit value one becomes the character **1**.

The function returns the created object.

17.5.4.1.23 bitstring::count()

count

```
size_t count() const;
```

Returns a count of the number of elements set in the string controlled by ***this**.

17.5.4.1.24 bitstring::length()

length

```
size_t length() const;
```

Returns **len**.

17.5.4.1.25 bitstring::resize(size_t, int)

resize

```
size_t resize(size_t n, int val = 0);
```

Reports a length error if **n** equals **NPOS**. Otherwise, the function alters the length of the string controlled by ***this** as follows:

- If **n <= len**, the function replaces the string controlled by ***this** with a string of length **n** whose elements are a copy of the initial elements of the original string controlled by ***this**.
- If **n > len**, the function replaces the string controlled by ***this** with a string of length **n** whose first **len** elements are a copy of the original string controlled by ***this**, and whose remaining elements all have the value one if **val** is nonzero, or zero otherwise.

The function returns the previous value of **len**.

17.5.4.1.26 bitstring::trim()

trim

```
size_t trim();
```

Determines the highest position **pos** of an element with value one in the string controlled by ***this**, if possible. If no such position exists, the function replaces the string with an empty string (**len** is zero). Otherwise, the function replaces the string with a string of length **pos + 1** whose elements are a copy of the initial elements of the original string controlled by ***this**.

The function returns the new value of **len**.

17.5.4.1.27 bitstring::find(int, size_t, size_t)

find

```
size_t find(int val, size_t pos = 0, size_t n = NPOS) const;
```

Returns **NPOS** if *pos* >= *len*. Otherwise, the function determines the effective length *rlen* of the string to be scanned as the smaller of *n* and *len* - *pos*. The function then determines the lowest position *xpos*, if possible, such that both of the following conditions obtain:

- *pos* <= *xpos*;
- The element at position *xpos* in the string controlled by ***this** is one if *val* is nonzero, or zero otherwise.

If the function can determine such a value for *xpos*, it returns *xpos*. Otherwise, it returns **NPOS**.

17.5.4.1.28 bitstring::rfind(int, size_t, size_t)

rfind

```
size_t rfind(int val, size_t pos = 0, size_t n = NPOS) const;
```

Returns **NPOS** if *pos* >= *len*. Otherwise, the function determines the effective length *rlen* of the string to be scanned as the smaller of *n* and *len* - *pos*. The function then determines the highest position *xpos*, if possible, such that both of the following conditions obtain:

- *pos* <= *xpos*;
- The element at position *xpos* in the string controlled by ***this** is one if *val* is nonzero, or zero otherwise.

If the function can determine such a value for *xpos*, it returns *xpos*. Otherwise, it returns **NPOS**.

17.5.4.1.29 bitstring::substr(size_t, size_t)

substr

```
bitstring substr(size_t pos, size_t n = NPOS) const;
```

Returns **bitstring(*this, pos, n)**.

17.5.4.1.30 bitstring::operator==(const bitstring&)

operator==

```
int operator==(const bitstring& rhs) const;
```

Returns zero if *len* != *rhs.len* or if the value of any element of the string controlled by ***this** differs from the value of the corresponding element of the string controlled by *rhs*.

17.5.4.1.31 bitstring::operator!=(const bitstring&)

operator!=

```
int operator!=(const bitstring& rhs) const;
```

Returns a nonzero value if **!(*this == rhs)**.

17.5.4.1.32 bitstring::test(size_t)

test

```
int test(size_t pos) const;
```

Reports an out-of-range error if *pos* >= *len*. Otherwise, the function returns a nonzero value if the element at position *pos* in the string controlled by ***this** is one.

17.5.4.1.33 bitstring::any()

any

```
int any() const;
```

Returns a nonzero value if any bit is set in the string controlled by ***this**.

17.5.4.1.34 bitstring::none()

none

```
int none() const;
```

Returns a nonzero value if no bit is set in the string controlled by ***this**.

17.5.4.1.35 bitstring::operator<<(size_t)

operator<<

```
bitstring operator<<(size_t pos) const;
```

Constructs an object **x** of class **bitstring** and initializes it with ***this**. The function then returns **x <<= pos**.

17.5.4.1.36 bitstring::operator>>(size_t)

operator>>

```
bitstring operator>>(size_t pos) const;
```

Constructs an object **x** of class **bitstring** and initializes it with ***this**. The function then returns **x >>= pos**.

17.5.4.1.37 bitstring::operator~()

operator~

```
bitstring operator~() const;
```

Constructs an object **x** of class **bitstring** and initializes it with ***this**. The function then returns **x.toggle()**.

17.5.4.2 operator+(const bitstring&, const bitstring&)

operator+

```
bitstring operator+(const bitstring& lhs,
    const bitstring& rhs);
```

Constructs an object **x** of class **bitstring** and initializes it with **lhs**. The function then returns **x += rhs**.

17.5.4.3 operator&(const bitstring&, const bitstring&)

operator&

```
bitstring operator&(const bitstring& lhs,
    const bitstring& rhs);
```

Constructs an object **x** of class **bitstring** and initializes it with **lhs**. The function then returns **x &= rhs**.

17.5.4.4 operator|(const bitstring&, const bitstring&)

operator|

```
bitstring operator|(const bitstring& lhs,
    const bitstring& rhs);
```

Constructs an object **x** of class **bitstring** and initializes it with **lhs**. The function then returns **x |= rhs**.

17.5.4.5 operator^(const bitstring&, const bitstring&)

operator^

```
bitstring operator^(const bitstring& lhs,
    const bitstring& rhs);
```

Constructs an object **x** of class **bitstring** and initializes it with **lhs**. The function then returns **x ^= rhs**.

17.5.4.6 operator>>(istream&, bitstring&)

operator>>

```
istream& operator>>(istream& is, bitstring& x);
```

A formatted input function, extracts up to **NPOS - 1** (single-byte) characters from **is**. The function behaves as if it stores these characters in a temporary object **str** of type **string**, then evaluates the expression **x = bitstring(str)**. Characters are extracted and stored until any of the following occurs:

- **NPOS - 1** characters have been extracted and stored;
- end-of-file occurs on the input sequence;
- the next character to read is neither **0** or **1** (in which case the input character is not extracted).

If no characters are stored in **str**, the function calls **is.setstate(ios::failbit)**.

The function returns **is**.

17.5.4.7 operator<<(ostream&, const bitstring&)

operator<<

```
ostream& operator<<(ostream& os, const bitstring& x);
```

Returns **os << x.to_string()**.

Footnotes:

114) Note that bit position zero is the *most-significant* bit for an object of class **bitstring**, while it is the *least-significant* bit for an object of class **bits<N>**.

115) An implementation is, of course, free to store the bit sequence more efficiently.

Future Directions

bit_string   The name of the class has been changed to **bit_string**.

Standard   As I first mentioned in the previous chapter, the Standard Template
Template Library (STL) may replace the header **<bitstring>**. Class **bitstring** is not
Library a template class, but neither does it enjoy the central importance of class
string, which is unlikely to be displaced by such a change. A combination
of more general templates from STL may prove to be an adequate substitute
for an explicit class **bitstring**. Nevertheless, I provide a full discussion of
the header **<bitstring>**, for the reasons I outlined on page 427.

If class **bitstring** survives, its behavior will probably be reconciled in
a number of small ways with class **string** (and class **wstring**).

Using <bitstring>

You include the header **<bitstring>** to make use of the class **bit-string**. Objects of this class let you manipulate in-memory bit sequences
that vary dynamically in length. The **bitstring** object allocates and frees
storage as needed to accommodate changes in length of the controlled
sequence.

construction   To construct a **bitstring** object **x0** with an initially empty bit sequence,
you can simply write:

```
bitstring x0;
```

length   Each object **x** reports the *length* of its bit sequence with the call **x.
length()**. (Class **bitstring** does not, however, support a reserve size as
does class **string**.)

To construct a **bitstring** and define its initial bit sequence, you have
several choices. In each case below, the comment shows the resulting bit
sequence, beginning with bit position zero. You can, for example, construct
a **bitstring** from an *unsigned int* initial value by writing such things as:

```
bitstring x1(0x12)                                    // 10010
bitstring x2(0x12, 1)                                 // 10010
bitstring x3(0x12, 8)                                 // 10010000
```

As I noted earlier in this chapter, on page 439, the significance of bits is
reversed from that for the template class **bits<N>**. If you omit the second
argument, the sequence exactly captures all significance. If the second
argument calls for more bits, the constructor effectively scales the initial
value by a power of 2. Bit zero is set for any nonzero initial value.

You can also construct a **bitstring** from a **string** object, by writing such things as:

```
string str("01001");
bitstring x4(str)                               // 01001
bitstring x5(str, 1)                            // 1001
bitstring x6(str, 1, 3)                         // 100
```

I described the rules for selecting a substring from a **string** object much earlier, on page 358.

substrings Finally, you can define the initial bit sequence when you construct a **bitstring** object by selecting a substring from another **bitstring** object. The arguments behave the same as those for selecting a substring from a **string** argument, above. Given the definition of **x4** above, you can write:

```
bitstring x7(x4);                               // 01001
bitstring x8(x4, 1);                            // 1001
bitstring x9(x4, 1, 3);                         // 100
```

notation For brevity, I define here a terse and uniform style for writing various argument combinations. The resultant argument is:

- an entire **bitstring** object, with the argument **x**
- a substring beginning at position **pos**, with the arguments **x, pos**
- a substring of **n** bits beginning at position **pos**, with the arguments **x, pos, n**

With this notation, I can more quickly summarize all the ways you can perform various operations involving **bitstring** objects. Here, for example, is a summary of the last three constructors I showed above:

```
bitstring x7(x);
bitstring x8(x, pos);
bitstring x9(x, pos, n);
```

string The presentation that follows shows the parallels first with class **string**,
operations then with template class **bits<N>**. A number of member functions alter the bit sequence controlled by a **bitstring** object **x0**.

To assign a new bit sequence, in place of any existing one:

assign
```
x0.assign(x)              x0 = x
x0.assign(x, pos)
x0.assign(x, pos, n)
```

To append to an existing bit sequence:

append
```
x0.append(x)              x0 += x
x0.append(x, pos)
x0.append(x, pos, n)
```

To insert before position **px** in an existing bit sequence:

insert
```
x0.insert(px, x)
x0.insert(px, x, pos)
x0.insert(px, x, pos, n)
```

To replace at most **m** bits beginning with position **px** in an existing bit sequence:

replace
```
x0.replace(px, m, x)
x0.replace(px, m, x, pos)
x0.replace(px, m, x, pos, n)
```

You can remove a substring from a bit sequence in various ways:

remove
```
x0.remove()                        // remove all bits
x0.remove(px)                      // remove all from px to end
x0.remove(px, n)          // remove at most n beginning at px
```

You can establish a new length **len** for a bit sequence. If the new length is greater than the existing length, the bit sequence is padded as stated in the comment below:

resize
```
x0.resize(len)                     // pad to len with zero bits
x0.resize(len, b)          // pad to len by repeating (b != 0)
```

As a final alteration, you can remove any trailing zero bits:

trim
```
x0.trim()                          // remove trailing zero bits
```

If the sequence has no bits set, it is removed completely. Otherwise, the last bit in the remaining sequence is set.

Some functions each construct a **string** object to return as the value of the function, leaving the object **x0** unaltered. You can, for example, obtain a substring as a separate object:

substr
```
x0.substr()                                  // copy all
x0.substr(pos)            // copy remainder beginning at pos
x0.substr(pos, n)         // copy at most n beginning at pos
```

You can also construct a **bitstring** object that appends the character sequences defined by two operands:

operator+
```
x + x0
```

Comparing two **bitstring** objects involves a bit-by-bit comparison of corresponding values in the two bit sequences. If the two bit sequences are not of equal length, they do not compare equal. To compare two bit sequences for equality (**==**) or inequality (**!=**), you can write:

operator==
```
x == x0
x != x0
```

A number of member functions look for a given bit setting within a bit sequence. To find the first (lowest position) occurrence that matches **b !=** **0** within a bit sequence:

find
```
x0.find(b)                             // find first in x0
x0.find(b, px)                // find first on or after px
x0.find(b, px, n)         // find first in x0.substr(px, n)
```

All such calls return the position of a successful match, or **NPOS** to report failure.

Similarly, to find the last (highest position) occurrence that matches **b !=** **0** within a bit sequence:

rfind
```
x0.rfind(b)                            // find last in x0
x0.rfind(b, px)               // find last on or after px
x0.rfind(b, px, n)        // find last in x0.substr(px, n)
```

Note that the arguments for the member functions **find** and **rfind** differ significantly between class **string** and class **bitstring**. Study both carefully lest you misuse either.

bitwise   Now for the operations that parallel those for the template class
operations **bits<N>**. Given two objects **x0** and **x1** of class **bitstring**, you can perform
the usual bitwise operations:

```
x0 &= x1            x0 & x1
x0 |= x1            x0 | x1
x0 ^= x1            x0 ^ x1
x0 <<= m            x0 << m
x0 >>= m            x0 >> m
```

Here, **m** is an expression with some integer type. The semantics of all these
operations involving **x0** and **x1** are a natural extension of those for unsigned integer values with an added proviso. If the two operands are of
differing length, the shorter is effectively padded to the same length by
appending zero bits. The resulting bit sequence has this greater length,
regardless of which operand was initially shorter.

You can deal with all bits at once, by writing:

```
x0.set()                          // set all bits
x0.reset()                        // clear all bits
x0.toggle()              // toggle (invert) all bits
~x0                            // toggle all bits
x0.count()                   // count all set bits
x0.any()                     // test if any bit set
x0.none()                     // test if no bit set
```

Or, given a valid bit position **n**, you can affect just that bit, by writing:

```
x0.set(n)                          // set bit n
x0.set(n, b)             // set bit n to (b != 0)
x0.reset(n)                       // clear bit n
x0.toggle(n)                     // toggle bit n
x0.test(n)                        // test bit n
```

conversions   The constructors, shown above, define mappings from unsigned integers or **string** objects to **bitstring** objects. To go the other way, write:

```
x0.to_string()              // return string equivalent
```

The return value can serve as a single constructor argument that generates
a **bitstring** object equal to **x0**. To map a bit sequence to a numerical value,
use the **to_ushort** or **to_ulong** member functions in class **string**. (See
Chapter 15: **<string>**.)

Finally, you can insert and extract objects of class **bitstring**, as in:

extractor   **cin >> x0**

effectively extracts a **bitstring** object from the standard input stream and
assigns it to some temporary. The function follows the same special rules
for extracting the string as does the extractor for the template class **bits<N>**,
as described on page 429. The function then converts the controlled character sequence, by the same rules as for constructing a **bitstring** object
from a **string** argument, and assigns it to **x0**.

Last of all, you can insert the character sequence into, say, the standard
output stream, by writing:

inserter   **cout << x0**

As you might expect, this is equivalent to inserting **x0.to_string()**.

Figure 18.1:
bitstrin
Part 1 of 3

```
// bitstring standard header
#ifndef _BITSTRING_
#define _BITSTRING_
#include <string>
        // class bitstring
string _Bitsxstr(istream&, size_t);
class bitstring {
public:
    typedef unsigned long _T;
    enum {_Nb = _BITS_BYTE * sizeof (_T)};
    enum _Source {_Zeros = 0, _Ones = -1};
    bitstring()
        {_Tidy(); }
    bitstring(unsigned long, size_t);
    bitstring(const bitstring& _X, size_t _P = 0,
        size_t _N = NPOS)
        {_Tidy(), assign(_X, _P, _N); }
    bitstring(const string&, size_t = 0, size_t = NPOS);
    bitstring(_Source _S)
        : _Ptr(0), _Src(_S), _Len(0), _Res(0) {}
    ~bitstring()
        {_Tidy(1); }
    bitstring& operator=(const bitstring& _R)
        {return (assign(_R)); }
    bitstring& operator+=(const bitstring& _R)
        {return (append(_R)); }
    bitstring& operator&=(const bitstring&);
    bitstring& operator|=(const bitstring&);
    bitstring& operator^=(const bitstring&);
    bitstring& operator<<=(size_t);
    bitstring& operator>>=(size_t);
    bitstring& append(const bitstring&, size_t = 0,
        size_t = NPOS);
    bitstring& assign(const bitstring&, size_t = 0,
        size_t = NPOS);
    bitstring& insert(size_t, const bitstring&, size_t = 0,
        size_t = NPOS);
    bitstring& remove(size_t = 0, size_t = NPOS);
    bitstring& replace(size_t, size_t, const bitstring&,
        size_t = 0, size_t = NPOS);
    bitstring& set();
    bitstring& set(size_t, _Bool = 1);
    bitstring& reset();
    bitstring& reset(size_t _P)
        {return (set(_P, 0)); }
    bitstring& toggle();
    bitstring& toggle(size_t);
    string to_string() const;
    size_t count() const;
    size_t length() const
        {return (_Len); }
    size_t resize(size_t, _Bool = 0);
    size_t trim()
        {resize(rfind(1) + 1);
        return (_Len); }
```

```
      size_t find(_Bool, size_t = 0, size_t = NPOS) const;
      size_t rfind(_Bool, size_t = 0, size_t = NPOS) const;
      bitstring substr(size_t _P, size_t _N = NPOS) const
          {return (bitstring(*this, _P, _N)); }
      _Bool operator==(const bitstring&) const;
      _Bool operator!=(const bitstring& _R) const
          {return (!(*this == _R)); }
      _Bool test(size_t) const;
      _Bool any() const;
      _Bool none() const
          {return (!any()); }
      bitstring operator<<(size_t _R) const
          {return (bitstring(*this) <<= _R); }
      bitstring operator>>(size_t _R) const
          {return (bitstring(*this) >>= _R); }
      bitstring operator~() const
          {return (bitstring(*this).toggle()); }
      _T _W(int _I) const
          {return (_Ptr[_I]); }
      _T _X(int _I, int _P) const
          {int _L = _Len == 0 ? -1 : (_Len - 1) / _Nb;
          return (_L < _I ?  _Src : _P == 0 ? _Ptr[_I]
              : _L == _I ? _Ptr[_I] << _P
              : _Ptr[_I] << _P | _Ptr[_I + 1] >> _Nb - _P); }
private:
      void _Copylr(const bitstring&, size_t, size_t, size_t);
      void _Copyrl(const bitstring&, size_t, size_t, size_t);
      _Bool _Grow(size_t, _Bool = 0);
      void _Setl(size_t _L)
          {_Len = _L, _L %= _Nb;
          if (_L != 0)
              _Ptr[(_Len - 1) / _Nb] &= ~(~(_T)0 >> _L); }
      void _Tidy(_Bool = 0);
      void _Xinv() const
          {invalidargument("invalid bitstring char").raise(); }
      void _Xlen() const
          {lengtherror("bitstring too long").raise(); }
      void _Xran() const
          {outofrange("invalid bitstring position").raise(); }
      _T *_Ptr, *_Src;
      size_t _Len, _Res;
      };
          // operators
inline bitstring operator+(const bitstring& _L,
      const bitstring& _R)
      {return (bitstring(_L) += _R); }
inline bitstring operator&(const bitstring& _L,
      const bitstring& _R)
      {return (bitstring(_L) &= _R); }
inline bitstring operator|(const bitstring& _L,
      const bitstring& _R)
      {return (bitstring(_L) |= _R); }
inline bitstring operator^(const bitstring& _L,
      const bitstring& _R)
      {return (bitstring(_L) ^= _R); }
```

```
inline istream& operator>>(istream& _I, bitstring& _R)
    {_R = _Bitsxstr(_I, NPOS - 1);
    return (_I); }
inline ostream& operator<<(ostream& _O, const bitstring& _R)
    {return (_O << _R.to_string()); }
#endif                                                        □
```

**Figure 18.2:
bitstrin.c**

```
// bitstring -- bitstring basic members
#include <stdlib.h>
#include <bitstring>

static inline size_t bytes(size_t bits)
    {                                   // find enough bytes to hold bits
    return (sizeof (bitstring::_T) * (bits / bitstring::_Nb
        + (bits % bitstring::_Nb != 0 ? 1 : 0)));
    }

_Bool bitstring::_Grow(size_t n, _Bool trim)
    {                                   // grow a bitstring as needed
    size_t osize = _Ptr == 0 ? 0 : _Res;
    if (n == 0)
        {                               // set up a null string
        const size_t MIN_SIZE = _Nb;
        if (trim && MIN_SIZE < osize)
            _Tidy(1);
        _Len = 0;
        return (0);
        }
    else if (n == osize || n < osize && !trim)
        return (1);
    else
        {                               // grow or alter the bitstring
        size_t size = _Ptr == 0 && n < _Res ? _Res : n;
        _T *s;
        if ((s = (_T *)realloc(_Ptr, bytes(size))) == 0
            && (s = (_T *)realloc(_Ptr, bytes(size = n))) == 0)
            _Nomemory();
        _Ptr = s;
        if ((_Res = bytes(size) * _BITS_BYTE) == 0)
            _Res = NPOS - 1;
        return (1);
        }
    }

void bitstring::_Tidy(_Bool constructed)
    {                       // destroy any allocated bitstring storage
    if (constructed && _Ptr != 0)
        free(_Ptr);
    _Ptr = 0, _Src = 0, _Len = 0, _Res = 0;
    }                                                        □
```

Implementing <bitstring>

bitstrin   Figure 18.1 shows the file **bitstrin**, which implements the header <bitstring>. Its principal business is to define the class **bitstring**.

_T   Class **bitstring** includes two type definitions and several enumeration constants. The first type definition is **_T**. An object of class **bitstring** stores an array of one or more unsigned integer member objects. **_T** is the type of the array elements. I have chosen *unsigned long* for this type, but you might prefer *unsigned short* or *unsigned char*. Some implementations may manipulate the smaller element types more efficiently. Or you may declare large arrays of **bitstring** and want to keep object sizes smaller.

_Source
_Zeros
_Ones   An added constructor has as its single parameter type the enumeration **_Source**. It constructs a special form of **bitstring** object jiggered to supply an arbitrary-length bit sequence. An argument value of **_Zeros** specifies that all bits in the sequence be zeros. An argument value of **_Ones** specifies that all bits in the sequence be ones.

_Nb
_BITS_BYTE   The last constant is **_Nb**, the number of bits in an array element Its definition involves the macro **_BITS_BYTE**, defined in <yxvals.h> as the number of bits in a single byte. (See page 430.)

Figure 18.3:
bitsculo.c

```
// bitsculong -- bitstring::bitstring(unsigned long, size_t)
#include <bitstring>

const size_t ULOBITS = _BITS_BYTE * sizeof (unsigned long);
const unsigned long UB0 = 1UL << ULOBITS - 1;

bitstring::bitstring(unsigned long ulo, size_t n)
    {                        // construct a bitstring from unsigned long
    if (n == NPOS)
        _Xlen();
    _Tidy();
    size_t ns;
    if (ulo == 0)
        ns = 0;
    else
        for (ns = ULOBITS; ulo < UB0; --ns)
            ulo <<= 1;
    if (n < ns)
        n = ns;
    if (_Grow(n))
        {                              // set first ns bits from ulo
        for (int i = (n - 1) / _Nb; 0 <= i; --i)
            _Ptr[i] = 0;
        _Len = n;
        for (size_t pos = 0; ulo != 0; ulo <<= 1, ++pos)
            if (ulo & UB0)
                set(pos);
        }
    }
```

```
// bitscstr -- bitstring::bitstring(const string&, size_t,
//    size_t)
#include <bitstring>

bitstring::bitstring(const string& str, size_t pos, size_t ns)
    {                               // construct bitstring from string
    if (str.length() < pos)
        _Xran();
    _Tidy();
    size_t n = str.length() - pos;
    if (ns < n)
        n = ns;
    if (_Grow(n))
        {                               // initialize bits from string
        for (int i = (n - 1) / _Nb; 0 <= i; --i)
            _Ptr[i] = 0;
        _Len = n;
        for (size_t p = 0; p < n; ++p, ++pos)
            {                               // set selected bits
            if (str[pos] == '1')
                set(p);
            else if (str[pos] != '0')
                _Xinv();
            }
        }
    }
```                                                          □

```
// bitsand -- bitstring::operator&=(const bitstring&)
#include <bitstring>

bitstring& bitstring::operator&=(const bitstring& str)
    {                               // AND a bitstring into a bitstring
    size_t m, n;
    if (str.length() < _Len)
        m = str.length(), n = _Len;
    else
        m = _Len, n = str.length();
    if (_Grow(n))
        {                               // AND into non-empty string
        int mw = m == 0 ? -1 : (m - 1) / _Nb;
        int nw = (n - 1) / _Nb;
        for (int i = 0; i <= mw; ++i)
            _Ptr[i] &= str._W(i);
        while (++mw <= nw)
            _Ptr[mw] = 0;
        _Len = n;
        }
    return (*this);
    }
```                                                          □

```
// bitsor -- bitstring::operator|=(const bitstring&)
#include <bitstring>

bitstring& bitstring::operator|=(const bitstring& str)
    {                                    // OR a bitstring into a bitstring
    size_t m, n;
    if (str.length() < _Len)
        m = str.length(), n = _Len;
    else
        m = _Len, n = str.length();
    if (_Grow(n))
        {                                        // OR into non-empty string
        int mw = m == 0 ? -1 : (m - 1) / _Nb;
        int nw = (n - 1) / _Nb;
        for (int i = 0; i <= mw; ++i)
            _Ptr[i] |= str._W(i);
        if (_Len < n)
            while (++mw <= nw)
                _Ptr[mw] = str._W(mw);
        _Len = n;
        }
    return (*this);
    }                                                                    □
```

```
// bitsxor -- bitstring::operator^=(const bitstring&)
#include <bitstring>

bitstring& bitstring::operator^=(const bitstring& str)
    {                                   // XOR a bitstring into a bitstring
    size_t m, n;
    if (str.length() < _Len)
        m = str.length(), n = _Len;
    else
        m = _Len, n = str.length();
    if (_Grow(n))
        {                                       // XOR into non-empty string
        int mw = m == 0 ? -1 : (m - 1) / _Nb;
        int nw = (n - 1) / _Nb;
        for (int i = 0; i <= mw; ++i)
            _Ptr[i] ^= str._W(i);
        if (_Len < n)
            while (++mw <= nw)
                _Ptr[mw] = str._W(mw);
        _Len = n;
        }
    return (*this);
    }                                                                    □
```

Figure 18.8:
bitslsh.c

```
// bitslsh -- bitstring::operator<<=(size_t)
#include <bitstring>

bitstring& bitstring::operator<<=(size_t pos)
    {                                   // shift left a bitstring
    if (pos < 0)
        *this >>= -pos;
    else if (0 < _Len && 0 < pos)
        _Copylr(*this, 0, pos, _Len);
```

Figure 18.9:
bitsrsh.c

```
// bitsrsh -- bitstring::operator>>=(size_t)
#include <bitstring>

const bitstring zeros(bitstring::_Zeros);

bitstring& bitstring::operator>>=(size_t pos)
    {                                   // shift right a bitstring
    if (pos < 0)
        *this <<= -pos;
    else if (0 < _Len && 0 < pos)
        {                               // shift non-empty string
        _Copyrl(*this, pos, 0, _Len);
        _Copylr(zeros, 0, pos, pos);
        }
```

_Bitsxstr   In the previous chapter, I introduced a secret function **_Bitsxstr**, with external linkage. For a description of the function, see page 430. It extracts a **string** object by the special rules for a **bits<N>** or **bitstring** object. The function is declared both in **<bits>** and **<bitstring>**.

The class **bitstring** defines eight secret protected member functions:

_Copylr ■ **_Copylr**, which copies a bit sequence from left to right

_Copyrl ■ **_Copyrl**, which copies a bit sequence from right to left

_Grow ■ **_Grow**, which alters the storage reserved for the bit sequence

_Setl ■ **_Setl**, which stores a new length for the controlled bit sequence and clears any unused least-significant bits in the last element of the array

_Tidy ■ **_Tidy**, which initializes (**_Tidy()**) the member objects at construction time or discards any bit sequence (**_Tidy(1)**) and reinitializes the member objects

_Xinv ■ **_Xinv**, which reports an invalid-argument error

_Xlen ■ **_Xlen**, which reports a length error

_Xran ■ **_Xran**, which reports a range error

For a discussion of the exceptions associated with invalid-argument, length, and range errors, see Chapter 3: **<exception>**.

bitstrin.c   Figure 18.2 shows the file **bitstrin.c**. It defines the member functions **_Grow** and **_Tidy**, both of which are likely to be called for any object of class **bitstring**. It also defines the local function **bytes**, which determines the number of bytes of storage to allocate for a bit sequence.

Figure 18.10:
bitscplr.c

```
// bitscplr -- bitstring::_Copylr(const bitstring&, size_t,
//    size_t, size_t)
#include <bitstring>

void bitstring::_Copylr(const bitstring& str, size_t p0,
    size_t pos, size_t n)
    {                               // copy a bitstring from left to right
    if (0 < n)
        {                                    // make non-empty string
        const int nb = n % _Nb;
        const int nl = p0 == 0 ? -1 : (p0 - 1) / _Nb;
        const int np = pos / _Nb;
        const int nw = (n - 1) / _Nb;
        const int off = np - nl - 1;
        _T mask, save;
        if (nb != 0)
            mask = ~(_T)0 >> nb, save = _Ptr[nw];
        pos %= _Nb;
        if ((p0 %= _Nb) == 0)
            for (int i = nl; ++i <= nw; )
                _Ptr[i] = str._X(i + off, pos);
        else
            {                         // copy shifted by p0 % _Nb bits
            _Ptr[nl] = _Ptr[nl] & ~(~(_T)0 >> p0)
                | str._X(np, pos) >> p0;
            for (int i = nl; ++i <= nw; )
                _Ptr[i] = str._X(i + off, pos) << _Nb - p0
                    | str._X(i + off + 1, pos) >> p0;
            }
        if (nb != 0)
            _Ptr[nw] = _Ptr[nw] & ~mask | save & mask;
        }
    }
```

□

The member function _Grow calls **bytes** to determine the size of requests for more storage. It also uses the parameter **trim** as an indication that shrinking storage may be a good idea. The function is otherwise reluctant to do so.

realloc   Note that _Grow allocates, or reallocates, storage by calling **realloc**, declared in **<stdlib.h>**. That function can sometimes adjust the size of allocated storage more efficiently than the equivalent combination of **new** and **delete** expressions. For a description of the function _Nomemory, see page 48.

bitsculo.c   Figure 18.3 shows the file **bitsculo.c**, which defines the constructor **bitstring(unsigned long ulo, size_t n)**. It converts **ulo** to an equivalent bit sequence whose length is at least **n**. Note that bits are packed into array elements from left (most significant) to right. Moreover, bit zero in the sequence is the *most* significant bit numerically. This convention is backwards from that for the template class **bits<N>**, described in the previous chapter.

Figure 18.11:
bitscprl.c

```
// bitscprl -- bitstring::_Copyrl(const bitstring&, size_t,
//     size_t, size_t)
#include <bitstring>

void bitstring::_Copyrl(const bitstring& str, size_t p0,
    size_t pos, size_t n)
    {                              // copy a bitstring from right to left
    if (0 < n)
        {                                      // make non-empty string
        const int nb = n % _Nb;
        const int nl = p0 == 0 ? -1 : (p0 - 1) / _Nb;
        const int np = pos / _Nb;
        const int nw = (n - 1) / _Nb;
        const int off = np - nl - 1;
        _T mask, save;
        if (nb != 0)
            mask = ~(_T)0 >> nb, save = _Ptr[nw];
        pos %= _Nb;
        if ((p0 %= _Nb) == 0)
            for (int i = nw; nl < i; --i)
                _Ptr[i] = str._X(i + off, pos);
        else
            {                           // copy shifted by p0 % _Nb bits
            for (int i = nw; nl < i; --i)
                _Ptr[i] = str._X(i + off, pos) << _Nb - p0
                    | str._X(i + off + 1, pos) >> p0;
            _Ptr[nl] = _Ptr[nl] & ~(~(_T)0 >> p0)
                | str._X(np, pos) >> p0;
            }
        if (nb != 0)
            _Ptr[nw] = _Ptr[nw] & ~mask | save & mask;
        }
    }
```

bitscstr.c   Figure 18.4 shows the file bitscstr.c, which defines the constructor
bitstring(const string& str, size_t pos, size_t ns). It converts
the substring str.substr(pos, ns) to an equivalent bit sequence of the
same length.

bitsand.c   Three source files define similar member functions for the assigning
bitsor.c bitwise operators between two bitstring objects. Figure 18.5 shows the
bitsxor.c file bitsand.c, which defines operator&=. Figure 18.6 shows the file
bitsor.c, which defines operator|=. And Figure 18.7 shows the file
bitsxor.c, which defines operator^=. The major difference between
these three member functions is how they handle the implicit padding of
a shorter operand with zero bits.

bitslsh.c   Another pair of source files defines similar member functions for the
bitsrsh.c assigning shift operators. Figure 18.8 shows the file bitslsh.c, which
defines operator<<=. And Figure 18.9 shows the file bitsrsh.c, which
defines operator>>=. They depend on the internal member functions
_Copylr and _Copyrl, mentioned earlier. Note the use of the constant
object zeros as a source of an arbitrary-length sequence of zero bits.

```
// bitsapp -- bitstring::append(const bitstring&, size_t, size_t)
#include <bitstring>

bitstring& bitstring::append(const bitstring& str, size_t pos,
    size_t ns)
    {                                    // append a bitstring to a bitstring
    if (str.length() < pos)
        _Xran();
    size_t n = str.length() - pos;
    if (n < ns)
        ns = n;
    if (NPOS - _Len <= ns)
        _Xlen();
    if (0 < ns)
        {                                    // make new non-empty string
        n = _Len + ns;
        _Grow(n);
        _Copylr(str, _Len, pos, n);
        _Setl(n);
        }
    return (*this);
    }                                                                    □
```

```
// bitsass -- bitstring::assign(const bitstring&, size_t, size_t)
#include <bitstring>

bitstring& bitstring::assign(const bitstring& str, size_t pos,
    size_t ns)
    {                                    // assign a bitstring to a bitstring
    if (str.length() < pos)
        _Xran();
    size_t n = str.length() - pos;
    if (ns < n)
        n = ns;
    if (this == &str)
        remove(pos + n), remove(0, pos);
    else if (_Grow(n, 1))
        {                                    // make non-empty string
        _Copylr(str, 0, pos, n);
        _Setl(n);
        }
    return (*this);
    }                                                                    □
```

Here is where the implementation pays the price for economical use of storage. Copying a substring within a bit sequence is not easy, given arbitrary bit offsets and an arbitrary length. How these interact with array element boundaries is tricky, and optimizing to move whole array elements wherever possible is even trickier. I simplified matters somewhat by defining two kinds of moves, copying bits from left to right or from right to left. The calling functions must decide which flavor is safer, if source and destination can possibly overlap.

Figure 18.14:
bitsins.c

```
// bitsins -- bitstring::insert(size_t, const bitstring&,
//    size_t, size_t)
#include <bitstring>

bitstring& bitstring::insert(size_t p0, const bitstring& str,
    size_t pos, size_t ns)
    {                                // insert a bitstring into a bitstring
    if (_Len < p0 || str.length() < pos)
        _Xran();
    size_t n = str.length() - pos;
    if (n < ns)
        ns = n;
    if (NPOS - _Len <= ns)
        _Xlen();
    if (0 < ns && _Grow(n = _Len + ns))
        {                            // insert to make non-empty string
        _Copyrl(*this, p0 + ns, p0, n);
        _Copylr(str, p0, pos, p0 + ns);
        _Setl(n);
        }
    return (*this);
    }                                                                    □
```

Figure 18.15:
bitsrem.c

```
// bitsrem -- bitstring::remove(size_t, size_t)
#include <bitstring>

bitstring& bitstring::remove(size_t p0, size_t nr)
    {                                // remove part of a bitstring
    if (_Len < p0)
        _Xran();
    if (_Len - p0 < nr)
        nr = _Len - p0;
    if (0 < nr)
        {                                    // remove the substring
        const int n = _Len - nr;
        _Copylr(*this, p0, p0 + nr, n);
        if (_Grow(n))
            _Setl(n);
        }
    return (*this);
    }                                                                    □
```

bitscplr.c   Figure 18.10 shows the file **bitscplr.c**, which defines the member
bitscprl.c   function **_Copylr**. And Figure 18.11 shows the file **bitscprl.c**, which
defines the member function **_Copyrl**. Each moves either whole elements
(**p0 % _Nb == 0**), or partial elements which the function must shift and
pack into existing elements. And each must tidy up the least-significant
element affected by the move. Be warned that this code is delicate.

Figure 18.16:
bitsrep.c

```
// bitsrep -- bitstring::replace(size_t size_t,
//     const bitstring&, size_t, size_t)
#include <bitstring>

bitstring& bitstring::replace(size_t p0, size_t n0,
    const bitstring& str, size_t pos, size_t ns)
    {                    // replace part of a bitstring with a bitstring
    if (_Len < p0 || str.length() < pos)
        _Xran();
    size_t n = str.length() - pos;
    if (n < ns)
        ns = n;
    if (NPOS - ns <= _Len - n0)
        _Xlen();
    n = _Len + ns - n0;
    if (ns < n0)
        _Copylr(*this, p0 + ns, p0 + n0, n);
    if ((0 < ns || 0 < n0) && _Grow(n))
        {                         // replace to make non-empty string
        if (n0 < ns)
            _Copyrl(*this, p0 + ns, p0 + n0, n);
        _Copylr(str, p0, pos, p0 + ns);
        _Setl(n);
        }
    return (*this);
    }
```

bitsapp.c   Six source files define similar member functions that edit the bit se-
bitsass.c   quence controlled by a **bitstring** object. Figure 18.12 shows the file
bitsins.c   **bitsapp.c**, which defines the member function **append**. Figure 18.13
bitsrem.c   shows the file **bitsass.c**, which defines the member function **assign**.
bitsrep.c   Figure 18.14 shows the file **bitsins.c**, which defines the member function
bitsresi.c   **insert**. Figure 18.15 shows the file **bitsrem.c**, which defines the member
function **remove**. Figure 18.16 shows the file **bitsrep.c**, which defines the
member function **replace**. And Figure 18.17 shows the file **bitsresi.c**,
which defines the member function **resize**. All perform their edits in terms
of calls to the secret member functions **_Copylr** and **_Copyrl**.

bitsset.c   Five more source files define small member functions that implement
bitset1.c   bit-manipulation operations. Figure 18.18 shows the file **bitsset.c**. It
bitsrese.c   defines the member function **set()**, which sets all bits in the sequence.
bitstog.c   Figure 18.19 shows the file **bitsset1.c**. It defines the member function
bitstog1.c   **set(size_t p0, _Bool val)**, which sets the bit at position **p0** to the value
val != 0. Figure 18.20 shows the file **bitsrese.c**. It defines the member
function **reset()**, which clears all bits. Figure 18.21 shows the file **bits-
tog.c**. It defines the member function **toggle()**, which toggles all bits.
And Figure 18.22 shows the file **bitstog1.c**. It defines the member function **toggle(size_t p0)**, which toggles the bit at position **p0**. All are
straightforward.

Figure 18.17:
bitsresi.c

```
// bitsresize -- bitstring::resize(size_t, _Bool)
#include <bitstring>

const bitstring ones(bitstring::_Ones);
const bitstring zeros(bitstring::_Zeros);

size_t bitstring::resize(size_t n, _Bool val)
    {                                       // change size of a bitstring
    const size_t len = _Len;
    if (n == NPOS)
        _Xlen();
    if (_Grow(n, 1))
        {                                   // clean up non-empty string
        if (_Len < n)
            _Copylr(val != 0 ? ones : zeros, _Len, 0, n);
        _Setl(n);
        }
    return (len);
    }
```

Figure 18.18:
bitsset.c

```
// bitsset -- bitstring::set()
#include <bitstring>

bitstring& bitstring::set()
    {                                       // set all bits in a bitstring
    if (0 < _Len)
        {                                   // set a non-empty string
        for (int i = (_Len - 1) / _Nb; 0 <= i; --i)
            _Ptr[i] = ~(_T)0;
        _Setl(_Len);
        }
    return (*this);
    }
```

Figure 18.19:
bitsset1.c

```
// bitsset1 -- bitstring::set(size_t, int)
#include <bitstring>

bitstring& bitstring::set(size_t p0, _Bool val)
    {                                       // set one bit in a bitstring
    if (_Len < p0)
        _Xran();
    if (_Len == p0)
        {                                   // extend bitstring
        _Grow(_Len + 1);
        _Setl(_Len + 1);
        }
    if (val != 0)
        _Ptr[p0 / _Nb] |= (_T)1 << (_Nb - 1 - p0 % _Nb);
    else
        _Ptr[p0 / _Nb] &= ~((_T)1 << (_Nb - 1 - p0 % _Nb));
    return (*this);
    }
```

Figure 18.20:
bitsrese.c

```
// bitsreset -- bitstring::reset()
#include <bitstring>

bitstring& bitstring::reset()
    {                                       // reset all bits in a bitstring
    if (0 < _Len)
        for (int i = (_Len - 1) / _Nb; 0 <= i; --i)
            _Ptr[i] = 0;
    return (*this);
    }
```

Figure 18.21:
bitstog.c

```
// bitstog -- bitstring::toggle()
#include <bitstring>

bitstring& bitstring::toggle()
    {                                       // toggle all bits in a bitstring
    if (0 < _Len)
        {                                   // toggle a non-empty string
        for (int i = (_Len - 1) / _Nb; 0 <= i; --i)
            _Ptr[i] ^= ~(_T)0;
        _Setl(_Len);
        }
    return (*this);
    }
```

Figure 18.22:
bitstog1.c

```
// bitstog1 -- bitstring::toggle(size_t, int)
#include <bitstring>

bitstring& bitstring::toggle(size_t p0)
    {                                       // toggle one bit in a bitstring
    if (_Len < p0)
        _Xran();
    _Ptr[p0 / _Nb] ^= (_T)1 << (_Nb - 1 - p0 % _Nb);
    return (*this);
    }
```

Figure 18.23:
bitscoun.c

```
// bitscount -- bitstring::count()
#include <bitstring>

size_t bitstring::count() const
    {                                       // count set bits in a bitstring
    size_t val = 0;
    if (0 < _Len)
        {                                   // count non-empty string
        for (int i = (_Len - 1) / _Nb; 0 <= i; --i)
            for (_T x = _Ptr[i]; x != 0; x >>= 4)
                val += "\0\1\1\2\1\2\2\3"
                    "\1\2\2\3\2\3\3\4"[x & 0xF];
        }
    return (val);
    }
```

Figure 18.24:
bitstost.c

```
// bitstost -- bitstring::to_string(size_t)
#include <bitstring>

string bitstring::to_string() const
    {                                      // make a string from a bitstring
    string str(_Len, reserve);
    for (size_t pos = 0; pos < _Len; ++pos)
        str += test(pos) ? '1' : '0';
    return (str);
    }                                                                    □
```

Figure 18.25:
bitsfind.c

```
// bitsfind -- bitstring::find(int, size_t, size_t)
#include <bitstring>

size_t bitstring::find(_Bool val, size_t p0, size_t n) const
    {                                      // find leftmost bit in a bitstring
    static const _T MSB = (_T)1 << (_Nb - 1);
    size_t pf = _Len <= p0 ? 0 : _Len - p0 < n ? _Len : p0 + n;
    if (p0 < pf)
        {                                      // find in non-empty string
        const int nw = pf / _Nb;
        int i = p0 / _Nb;
        size_t pos = i * _Nb;
        if (val)
            for (; i <= nw; ++i, pos += _Nb)
                {                                  // find leftmost one bit
                _T x = _Ptr[i];
                for (size_t j = pos; x != 0; x <<= 1, ++j)
                    if (x & MSB && p0 <= j && j < pf)
                        return (j);
                }
        else
            for (; i <= nw; ++i, pos += _Nb)
                {                                  // find leftmost zero bit
                _T x = _Ptr[i];
                for (size_t j = pos; ~x != 0;
                    x = x << 1 | 1, ++j)
                    if (!(x & MSB) && p0 <= j && j < pf)
                        return (j);
                }
        }
    return (NPOS);
    }                                                                    □
```

bitscoun.c   Two source files define small member functions that inspect each bit in
bitstost.c   a sequence. Figure 18.23 shows the file **bitscoun.c**. It defines the member
function **count()**, which counts the number of set bits. The cute code
processes bits four at a time. And Figure 18.24 shows the file **bitstost.c**,
which defines the member function **to_string**. Converting to a **string**
object is easy, given the member functions in both classes.

bitsfind.c   Two member functions search for a given bit value in a sequence. Figure
bitsrfin.c   18.25 shows the file **bitsfind.c**, which defines the member function **find**.

```
// bitsrfind -- bitstring::rfind(int, size_t, size_t)
#include <bitstring>

size_t bitstring::rfind(_Bool val, size_t p0, size_t n) const
    {                                // find rightmost bit in a bitstring
    static const _T MSB = (_T)1 << (_Nb - 1);
    size_t pf = _Len <= p0 ? 0 : _Len - p0 < n ? _Len : p0 + n;
    if (p0 < pf)
        {                                        // find in non-empty string
        const int nw = p0 / _Nb;
        int i = pf / _Nb;
        size_t pos = i * _Nb + _Nb - 1;
        if (val)
            for (; nw <= i; --i, pos -= _Nb)
                {                                // find rightmost one bit
                _T x = _Ptr[i];
                for (size_t j = pos; x != 0; x >>= 1, --j)
                    if (x & 1 && p0 <= j && j < pf)
                        return (j);
                }
        else
            for (; nw <= i; --i, pos -= _Nb)
                {                                // find rightmost zero bit
                _T x = _Ptr[i];
                for (size_t j = pos; ~x != 0;
                    x = x >> 1 | MSB, --j)
                    if (!(x & 1) && p0 <= j && j < pf)
                        return (j);
                }
        }
    return (NPOS);
    }
```                                                                                  □

```
// bitseq -- bitstring::operator==(const bitstring&)
#include <bitstring>

_Bool bitstring::operator==(const bitstring& str) const
    {                                // compare a bitstring to a bitstring
    if (_Len != str.length())
        return (0);
    else if (_Len == 0)
        return (1);
    else
        {                        // compare same-length non-empty strings
        for (int i = (_Len - 1) / _Nb; 0 <= i; --i)
            if (_Ptr[i] != _W(i))
                return (0);
        return (1);
        }
    }
```                                                                                  □

```
// bitstest -- bitstring::test(size_t, int)
#include <bitstring>

_Bool bitstring::test(size_t p0) const
    {                                  // test one bit in a bitstring
    if (_Len <= p0)
        _Xran();
    return ((_Ptr[p0 / _Nb] & (_T)1 << (_Nb - 1 - p0 % _Nb))
        != 0);
    }                                                              □
```

```
// bitsany -- bitstring::any()
#include <bitstring>

_Bool bitstring::any() const
    {                                  // test for any bits set in a bitstring
    if (_Len == 0)
        return (0);
    else
        {                                          // test non-empty string
        for (int i = (_Len - 1) / _Nb; 0 <= i; --i)
            if (_Ptr[i] != 0)
                return (1);
        return (0);
        }
    }                                                              □
```

And Figure 18.26 shows the file **bitsrfin.c**, which defines the member function **rfind**. Both are much more elaborate than they have to be, in the interest of improving performance over the obvious, simple code. Both functions separate the logic for searching for a set bit or a clear bit.

bitseq.c   The last three source files implement member functions that compare or
bitstest.c   test bit seqeunces in various ways. Figure 18.27 shows the file **bitseq.c**. It
bitsany.c   overloads **operator==** for comparing two **bitstring** objects. Figure 18.28
shows the file **bitstest.c**. It defines the member function **test(size_t p0)**, which tests the bit at position **p0**. Finally, Figure 18.29 shows the file **bitsany.c**. It defines the mmeber function **any**, which tests whether any bit in the sequence is set. As usual, these functions process a whole array element at a time whenever possible.

Testing <bitstring>

tbitstri.c   Figure 18.30 shows the file **tbitstri.c**. It tests the basic properties of class **bitstring** defined in **<bitstring>**. It does so by testing the various bit string operations in related groups, at least for their minimum functionality. If all goes well, the program prints:

    SUCCESS testing <bitstring>

and takes a normal exit.

Exercises

Exercise 18.1 Does it make sense to define **bitstring** member functions similar to the **string** member functions **find_first_of** and **find_last_not_of**? If so, describe how they might work.

Exercise 18.2 Define a class that represents an array of eleven-bit data samples, using a **bitstring** object to manage storage for the array efficiently. What member functions should your class have to be reasonably complete?

Exercise 18.3 Write a function that exchanges two bit sequences. (Hint: consider the EXCLUSIVE OR operation.)

Exercise 18.4 Write a function that reverses the bits in a sequence controlled by a **bitstring** object.

Exercise 18.5 Add a member function to class **bitstring** to find the leftmost occurrence of an argument bit sequence within the controlled bit sequence. What is a good name for the function? What parameters should it have?

Exercise 18.6 [**Harder**] Combine the classes **string** and **bitstring** so that you retain all the functionality of both classes. Aside from storage efficiency, the class should also behave the same as class **bitstring** if all the elements of the sequence are restricted to the values zero and one.

Exercise 18.7 [**Very hard**] Define and implement a **bitstring** class that has no limit on the length of a bit sequence.

```cpp
// test <bitstring>
#include <assert.h>
#include <bitstring>
#include <iostream>

int main()
    {                       // test basic workings of bitstring definitions
    string str("11110101");
    bitstring x0, x1(0x1230, 1), x2(x1), x3(x1, 1, 8);
    bitstring x4(str), x5(str, 4, 3);
    assert(x0.length() == 0 && x0.to_string() == "");
    assert(x1.length() == 13
        && x1.to_string() == "1001000110000");
    assert(x2.count() == 4
        && x2.to_string() == "1001000110000");
    assert(x3.to_string() == "00100011");
    assert(x4.to_string() == "11110101");
    assert(x5.to_string() == "010");
        // test assigns and appends
    x0 = x1, assert(x0.to_string() == "1001000110000");
    x0.assign(x3), assert(x0.to_string() == "00100011");
    x0.assign(x3, 1), assert(x0.to_string() == "0100011");
    x0.assign(x3, 2, 3), assert(x0.to_string() == "100");
    x0 += x5, assert(x0.to_string() == "100010");
    x0.append(x5), assert(x0.to_string() == "100010010");
    x0.append(x5, 1), assert(x0.to_string() == "10001001010");
    x0.append(x5, 2, 3);
    assert(x0.to_string() == "100010010100");
    x0.assign(x0, 3, 4), assert(x0.to_string() == "0100");
    assert((x1 + x1 + x1).to_string() == "1001000110000"
        "1001000110000" "1001000110000");
        // test logic
    x0 = x3;
    x0 |= x5, assert(x0.to_string() == "01100011");
    assert((x3 | x5).to_string() == "01100011");
    assert((x3 | str).to_string() == "11110111");
    x0 &= x4, assert(x0.to_string() == "01100001");
    assert((x3 & x4).to_string() == "00100001");
    x0 ^= x2, assert(x0.to_string() == "1111000010000");
    assert((x4 ^ x5).to_string() == "10110101");
    x0 <<= 2, assert(x0.to_string() == "1100001000000");
    assert((x4 << 3).to_string() == "10101000");
    x0 >>= 4, assert(x0.to_string() == "0000110000100");
    assert((x4 >> 2).to_string() == "00111101");
    assert((~x3).to_string() == "11011100");
    assert(((x1 + x1 + x1) ^ x1) == (x1 + x1 + x1) << 13);
        // test inserts, removes, replaces
    x0 = x5;
    x0.insert(1, x5), assert(x0.to_string() == "001010");
    x0.insert(1, x5, 1), assert(x0.to_string() == "01001010");
    x0.insert(1, x5, 1, 1);
    assert(x0.to_string() == "011001010");
    x0.remove(7), assert(x0.to_string() == "0110010");
    x0.remove(2, 3), assert(x0.to_string() == "0110");
    x0.replace(2, 1, x5), assert(x0.to_string() == "010100");
```

```
    x0.replace(2, 1, x5, 1);
    assert(x0.to_string() == "0110100");
    x0.replace(2, 3, x5, 1, 1);
    assert(x0.to_string() == "01100");
    x0.remove(), assert(x0.to_string() == "");
        // test bit twiddling
    x0 = x5;
    x0.set(2), assert(x0.to_string() == "011");
    x0.set(1, 0), assert(x0.to_string() == "001");
    x0.set(), assert(x0.to_string() == "111");
    x0.reset(0), assert(x0.to_string() == "011");
    x0.reset(), assert(x0.to_string() == "000");
    x0.toggle(2), assert(x0.to_string() == "001");
    x0.toggle(), assert(x0.to_string() == "110");
    assert(x0.trim() == 2 && x0.to_string() == "11");
    assert(x0.resize(4) == 2 && x0.to_string() == "1100");
    assert(x0.resize(3) == 4 && x0.to_string() == "110");
    assert(x0.resize(4, 1) == 3 && x0.to_string() == "1101");
        // test finds
    x0 = x3;
    assert(x0.to_string() == "00100011");
    assert(x0.find(0) == 0 && x0.find(1) == 2);
    assert(x0.find(0, 2) == 3 && x0.find(1, 3) == 6);
    assert(x0.find(0, 2, 1) == NPOS && x0.find(1, 1, 2) == 2);
        // test tests
    x0 = x5;
    assert(x0.any() && !x0.none());
    assert(!x0.test(0) && x0.test(1));
    assert(x0 == x5 && x0 != x3);
    x0.reset(), assert(!x0.any() && x0.none());
    x0.resize(145), x0.toggle(101);
    assert(!x0.test(100) && x0.test(101));
    cout << "SUCCESS testing <bitstring>" << endl;
    return (0);
    }                                                    □
```

Chapter 19: **<dynarray>**

Background

So far, I have discussed three different classes that manipulate varying-length sequences:

string ▪ **string**, which controls sequences of single-byte characters (see Chapter 15: **<string>**)

wstring ▪ **wstring**, which controls sequences of wide characters (see Chapter 16: **<wstring>**)

bitstring ▪ **bitstring**, which controls sequences of bits (see Chapter 15: **<bitstring>**)

You can argue that each of these kinds of sequences deserves special handling because it is likely to be widely used in C++ programs. Moreover, each of these presents special opportunities for improving performance or space efficiency. But after a while, making yet another string-like class gets old. You'd like to start recycling the common design features, and the common code.

value The header **<dynarray>** addresses this desire. It defines the template
semantics class **dynarray<T>**, which controls a sequence of elements of type **T**. Here, **T** can be any type with *value semantics*. Put simply, that means you can freely copy about objects of such a type. There is nothing magic about *where* the object resides. Put more formally, the type **T** must have:

▪ a default constructor

▪ a copy constructor

▪ an assignment operator

▪ a destructor

all with the expected behavior. All the scalar types (such as *char*, *float*, and pointers) meet these requirements. So do many Standard C++ library classes such as **ios** and **double_complex**. (See Chapter 6: **<ios>** and Chapter 21: **<complex>**.) Some do not, however, such as class **streambuf**. (See Chapter 7: **<streambuf>**.)

If you want to control varying-length sequences of objects that don't meet these requirements, do not despair. That's the topic of the next chapter. (See Chapter 20: **<ptrdynarray>**.)

What the Draft C++ Standard Says

I warned about several equivocal template function definitions in the description of the header **<bits>**. (See page 422.) That problem does *not* occur in the descriptions shown here. The template functions defined in the header **<dynarray>** have a type parameter, not an integer parameter. Thus, the template parameter participates in an obvious way in overload resolution. (See page 252.)

17.5.5 Header **<dynarray>**

<dynarray>

The header **<dynarray>** defines a template class and several related functions for representing and manipulating varying-size sequences of some object type *T*.

17.5.5.1 Template class **dynarray**

**Class
dynarray**

```
template<class T> class dynarray {
public:
    dynarray();
    dynarray(size_t size, capacity cap);
    dynarray(const dynarray& arr);
    dynarray(const T& obj, size_t rep = 1);
    dynarray(const T* parr, size_t n);
    dynarray& operator+=(const dynarray& rhs);
    dynarray& operator+=(const T& obj);
    dynarray& append(const T& obj, size_t rep = 1);
    dynarray& append(const T* parr, size_t n = 1);
    dynarray& assign(const T& obj, size_t rep = 1);
    dynarray& assign(const T* parr, size_t n = 1);
    dynarray& insert(size_t pos, const dynarray& arr);
    dynarray& insert(size_t pos, const T& obj, size_t rep = 1);
    dynarray& insert(size_t pos, const T* parr, size_t n = 1);
    dynarray& remove(size_t pos = 0, size_t n = NPOS);
    dynarray& sub_array(dynarray& arr, size_t pos,
          size_t n = NPOS);
    void swap(dynarray& arr);
    const T& get_at(size_t pos) const;
    void put_at(size_t pos, const T& obj);
    T& operator[](size_t pos);
    const T& operator[](size_t pos) const;
    T* base();
    const T* base() const;
    size_t length() const;
    void resize(size_t n);
    void resize(size_t n, const T& obj);
    size_t reserve() const;
    void reserve(size_t res_arg);
private:
//  T* ptr;                                   exposition only
//  size_t len, res;                          exposition only
};
```

The template class **dynarray** describes an object that can store a sequence consisting of a varying number of objects of type *T*. The first element of the sequence is at position zero. Such a sequence is also called a *dynamic array*. An object of type *T* shall have:

- a default constructor *T()*;
- a copy constructor *T(const T&)*;
- an assignment operator *T& operator=(const T&)*;
- a destructor *~T()*.

For the function signatures described in this subclause:

- it is unspecified whether an operation described in this subclause as "initializing an object of type *T* with a copy" calls its copy constructor, calls its default constructor followed by its assignment operator, or does nothing to an object that is already properly initialized;
- it is unspecified how many times objects of type *T* are copied, or constructed and destroyed.[116]

For the sake of exposition, the maintained data is presented here as:

- *T *ptr*, points to the sequence of objects;
- *size_t len*, counts the number of objects currently in the sequence;
- *size_t res*, for an unallocated sequence, holds the recommended allocation size of the sequence, while for an allocated sequence, becomes the currently allocated size.

In all cases, *len <= res*.

The functions described in this subclause can report three kinds of errors, each associated with a distinct exception:

- an *invalid-argument* error is associated with exceptions of type **invalidargument**;
- a *length* error is associated with exceptions of type **lengtherror**.
- an *out-of-range* error is associated with exceptions of type **outofrange**;

To report one of these errors, the function evaluates the expression *ex.raise()*, where *ex* is an object of the associated exception type.

17.5.5.1.1 dynarray::dynarray()

constructor

```
dynarray();
```

Constructs an object of class **dynarray**, initializing:

- *ptr* to an unspecified value;
- *len* to zero;
- *res* to an unspecified value.

17.5.5.1.2 dynarray::dynarray(size_t, capacity)

constructor

```
dynarray(size_t size, capacity cap);
```

Reports a length error if *size* equals **NPOS** and *cap* is **default_size**. Otherwise, the function constructs an object of class **dynarray**. If *cap* is *default_size*, the function initializes:

- *ptr* to point at the first element of an allocated array of *size* elements of type *T*, each initialized with the default constructor for type *T*;
- *len* to *size*;
- *res* to a value at least as large as *len*.

Otherwise, *cap* shall be *reserve* and the function initializes:

- *ptr* to an unspecified value;
- *len* to zero;
- *res* to *size*.

17.5.5.1.3 dynarray::dynarray(const dynarray&)

constructor

```
dynarray(const dynarray& arr);
```

Constructs an object of class **dynarray** and determines its initial dynamic array value by copying the elements from the dynamic array designated by **arr**. Thus, the function initializes:

- **ptr** to point at the first element of an allocated array of **arr.len** elements of type **T**, each initialized with a copy of the corresponding element from the dynamic array designated by **arr**;
- **len** to **arr.len**;
- **res** to a value at least as large as **len**.

17.5.5.1.4 dynarray::dynarray(const T&, size_t)

constructor

```
dynarray(const T& obj, size_t rep = 1);
```

Reports a length error if **rep** equals **NPOS**. Otherwise, the function constructs an object of class **dynarray** and determines its initial dynamic array value by copying **obj** into all **rep** values. Thus, the function initializes:

- **ptr** to point at the first element of an allocated array of **rep** elements of type **T**, each initialized by copying **obj**;
- **len** to **rep**;
- **res** to a value at least as large as **len**.

17.5.5.1.5 dynarray::dynarray(const T*, size_t)

constructor

```
dynarray(const T* parr, size_t n);
```

Reports a length error if **n** equals **NPOS**. Otherwise, the function reports an invalid-argument error if **parr** is a null pointer. Otherwise, **parr** shall designate the first element of an array of at least **n** elements of type **T**.

The function then constructs an object of class **dynarray** and determines its initial dynamic array value by copying the elements from the array designated by **parr**. Thus, the function initializes:

- **ptr** to point at the first element of an allocated array of **n** elements of type **T**, each initialized with a copy of the corresponding element from the array designated by **parr**;
- **len** to **n**;
- **res** to a value at least as large as **len**.

17.5.5.1.6 dynarray::operator+=(const dynarray&)

operator+=

```
dynarray& operator+=(const dynarray& rhs);
```

Reports a length error if **len >= NPOS - rhs.len**. Otherwise, the function replaces the dynamic array designated by ***this** with a dynamic array of length **len + rhs.len** whose first **len** elements are a copy of the original dynamic array designated by ***this** and whose remaining elements are a copy of the elements of the dynamic array designated by **rhs**.

The function returns ***this**.

17.5.5.1.7 dynarray::operator+=(const T&)

operator+=

```
dynarray& operator+=(const T& obj);
```

Returns **append(obj)**.

17.5.5.1.8 dynarray::append(const T&, size_t)

append

```
dynarray& append(const T& obj, size_t rep = 1);
```

Reports a length error if **len >= NPOS - rep**. Otherwise, the function replaces the dynamic array designated by ***this** with a dynamic array of length **len +**

rep whose first *len* elements are a copy of the original dynamic array designated by `*this` and whose remaining elements are each a copy of *obj*.

The function returns `*this`.

17.5.5.1.9 dynarray::append(const T*, size_t)

append
```
dynarray& append(const T* parr, size_t n = 1);
```

Reports a length error if *len* >= NPOS - *n*. Otherwise, the function reports an invalid-argument error if *n* > 0 and *parr* is a null pointer. Otherwise, *parr* shall designate the first element of an array of at least *n* elements of type *T*.

The function then replaces the dynamic array designated by `*this` with a dynamic array of length *len* + *n* whose first *len* elements are a copy of the original dynamic array designated by `*this` and whose remaining elements are a copy of the initial elements of the array designated by *parr*.

The function returns `*this`.

17.5.5.1.10 dynarray::assign(const T&, size_t)

assign
```
dynarray& assign(const T& obj, size_t rep = 1);
```

Reports a length error if *rep* == NPOS. Otherwise, the function replaces the dynamic array designated by `*this` with a dynamic array of length *rep* each of whose elements is a copy of *obj*.

The function returns `*this`.

17.5.5.1.11 dynarray::assign(const T*, size_t)

assign
```
dynarray& assign(const T* parr, size_t n = 1);
```

Reports a length error if *n* == NPOS. Otherwise, the function reports an invalid-argument error if *n* > 0 and *parr* is a null pointer. Otherwise, *parr* shall designate the first element of an array of at least *n* elements of type *T*.

The function then replaces the dynamic array designated by `*this` with a dynamic array of length *n* whose elements are a copy of the initial elements of the array designated by *parr*.

The function returns `*this`.

17.5.5.1.12 dynarray::insert(size_t, const dynarray&)

insert
```
dynarray& insert(size_t pos, const dynarray& arr);
```

Reports an out-of-range error if *pos* > *len*. Otherwise, the function reports a length error if *len* >= NPOS - *arr.len*.

Otherwise, the function replaces the dynamic array designated by `*this` with a dynamic array of length *len* + *arr.len* whose first *pos* elements are a copy of the initial elements of the original dynamic array designated by `*this`, whose next *arr.len* elements are a copy of the initial elements of the dynamic array designated by *arr*, and whose remaining elements are a copy of the remaining elements of the original dynamic array designated by `*this`.

The function returns `*this`.

17.5.5.1.13 dynarray::insert(size_t, const T&, size_t)

insert
```
dynarray& insert(size_t pos, const T& obj, size_t rep = 1);
```

Reports an out-of-range error if *pos* > *len*. Otherwise, the function reports a length error if *len* >= NPOS - *rep*.

Otherwise, the function replaces the dynamic array designated by `*this` with a dynamic array of length *len* + *rep* whose first *pos* elements are a copy of the initial elements of the original dynamic array designated by `*this`, whose next *rep* elements are each a copy of *obj*, and whose remaining elements are a copy of the remaining elements of the original dynamic array designated by `*this`.

The function returns *`this`.

17.5.5.1.14 dynarray::insert(size_t, const T*, size_t)

insert
    `dynarray& insert(size_t pos, const T* parr, size_t n = 1);`

Reports an out-of-range error if **`pos`** > **`len`**. Otherwise, the function reports a length error if **`len`** >= **NPOS** - **`n`**. Otherwise, the function reports an invalid-argument error if **`n`** > **0** and **`parr`** is a null pointer. Otherwise, **`parr`** shall designate the first element of an array of at least **`n`** elements of type **`T`**.

The function then replaces the dynamic array designated by *`this`* with a dynamic array of length **`len`** + **`n`** whose first **`pos`** elements are a copy of the initial elements of the original dynamic array designated by *`this`*, whose next **`n`** elements are a copy of the initial elements of the array designated by **`parr`**, and whose remaining elements are a copy of the remaining elements of the original dynamic array designated by *`this`*.

The function returns *`this`*.

17.5.5.1.15 dynarray::remove(size_t, size_t)

remove
    `dynarray& remove(size_t pos = 0, size_t n = NPOS);`

Reports an out-of-range error if **`pos`** > **`len`**. Otherwise, the function determines the effective length **`xlen`** of the sequence to be removed as the smaller of **`n`** and **`len`** - **`pos`**.

The function then replaces the dynamic array designated by *`this`* with a dynamic array of length **`len`** - **`xlen`** whose first **`pos`** elements are a copy of the initial elements of the original dynamic array designated by *`this`*, and whose remaining elements are a copy of the elements of the original dynamic array designated by *`this`* beginning at position **`pos`** + **`xlen`**. The original **`xlen`** elements beginning at position **`pos`** are destroyed.

The function returns *`this`*.

17.5.5.1.16 dynarray::sub_array(dynarray&, size_t, size_t)

sub_array
    `dynarray& sub_array(dynarray& arr, size_t pos,`
        `size_t n = NPOS);`

Reports an out-of-range error if **`pos`** > **`len`**. Otherwise, the function determines the effective length **`rlen`** of the dynamic array designated by *`this`* as the smaller of **`n`** and **`arr.len`** - **`pos`**.

The function then replaces the dynamic array designated by **`arr`** with a dynamic array of length **`rlen`** whose elements are a copy of the elements of the dynamic array designated by *`this`* beginning at position **`pos`**.

The function returns **`arr`**.

17.5.5.1.17 dynarray::swap(dynarray&)

swap
    `void swap(dynarray& arr);`

Replaces the dynamic array designated by *`this`* with the dynamic array designated by **`arr`**, and replaces the dynamic array designated by **`arr`** with the dynamic array originally designated by *`this`*.[117]

17.5.5.1.18 dynarray::get_at(size_t)

get_at
    `const T& get_at(size_t pos) const;`

Reports an out-of-range error if **`pos`** >= **`len`**. Otherwise, the function returns **`ptr[pos]`**.

17.5.5.1.19 dynarray::put_at(size_t, const T&)

put_at
    `void put_at(size_t pos, const T& obj);`

Reports an out-of-range error if **`pos`** >= **`len`**. Otherwise, the function assigns **`obj`** to the element at position **`pos`** in the dynamic array designated by *`this`*.

17.5.5.1.20 dynarray::operator[](size_t)

operator[]
```
T& operator[](size_t pos);
const T& operator[](size_t pos) const;
```
If **pos** < **len**, returns the element at position **pos** in the dynamic array designated by ***this**. Otherwise, the behavior is undefined.

The reference returned by the non-**const** version is invalid after any subsequent call any non-**const** member function for the object.

17.5.5.1.21 dynarray::base()

base
```
T* base();
const T* base() const;
```
Returns **ptr** if **len** is nonzero, otherwise a null pointer. The program shall not alter any of the values stored in the dynamic array. Nor shall the program treat the returned value as a valid pointer value after any subsequent call to a non-**const** member function of the class **dynarray** that designates the same object as **this**.

17.5.5.1.22 dynarray::length()

length
```
size_t length() const;
```
Returns **len**.

17.5.5.1.23 dynarray::resize(size_t)

resize
```
void resize(size_t n);
```
Reports a length error if **n** equals **NPOS**. Otherwise, if **n** != **len** the function alters the length of the dynamic array designated by ***this** as follows:

- If **n** < **len**, the function replaces the dynamic array designated by ***this** with a dynamic array of length **n** whose elements are a copy of the initial elements of the original dynamic array designated by ***this**. Any remaining elements are destroyed.
- If **n** > **len**, the function replaces the dynamic array designated by ***this** with a dynamic array of length **n** whose first **len** elements are a copy of the original dynamic array designated by ***this**, and whose remaining elements are all initialized with the default constructor for class **T**.

17.5.5.1.24 dynarray::resize(size_t, const T&)

resize
```
void resize(size_t n, const T& obj);
```
Reports a length error if **n** equals **NPOS**. Otherwise, if **n** != **len** the function alters the length of the dynamic array designated by ***this** as follows:

- If **n** < **len**, the function replaces the dynamic array designated by ***this** with a dynamic array of length **n** whose elements are a copy of the initial elements of the original dynamic array designated by ***this**. Any remaining elements are destroyed.
- If **n** > **len**, the function replaces the dynamic array designated by ***this** with a dynamic array of length **n** whose first **len** elements are a copy of the original dynamic array designated by ***this**, and whose remaining elements are all initialized by copying **obj**.

17.5.5.1.25 dynarray::reserve()

reserve
```
size_t reserve() const;
```
Returns **res**.

17.5.5.1.26 dynarray::reserve(size_t)

reserve
```
void reserve(size_t res_arg);
```
If no dynamic array is allocated, assigns **res_arg** to **res**. Otherwise, whether or how the function alters **res** is unspecified.

operator+	**17.5.5.2 operator+(const dynarray&, const dynarray&)**
	`template<class T> dynarray<T>`
	`    operator+(const dynarray<T>&lhs, const dynarray<T>& rhs);`
	Returns **dynarray<T>(lhs) += rhs**.

operator+	**17.5.5.3 operator+(const dynarray&, const T&)**
	`template<class T> dynarray<T>`
	`    operator+(const dynarray<T>& lhs, const T& obj);`
	Returns **dynarray<T>(lhs) += rhs**.

operator+	**17.5.5.4 operator+(const T&, const dynarray&)**
	`template<class T> dynarray<T>`
	`    operator+(const T& obj, const dynarray<T>& rhs);`
	Returns **dynarray<T>(lhs) += rhs**.

Footnotes:

Footnotes

116) Objects that cannot tolerate this uncertainty, or that fail to meet the stated requirements, can sometimes be organized into dynamic arrays through the intermediary of an object of class **ptrdynarray**.

117) Presumably, this operation occurs with no actual copying of array elements.

Future Directions

dyn_array   The name of the class has been changed to **dyn_array**.

base   The member function **dynarray<T>::base** has been changed to **dynarray<T>::data**.

Standard   As I mentioned earlier, the Standard Template Library (STL) will almost
Template   certainly replace the header **<dynarray>**. (See page 427.) A combination of
Library   more general templates from STL is an adequate substitute for an explicit template class **dynarray<T>**. Nevertheless, I provide here a full discussion of the header **<dynarray>**, for the reasons I outlined earlier.

Using **<dynarray>**

You include the header **<dynarray>** to make use of the template class **dynarray<T>**. Here, **T** is a type with value semantics, as described on page 473. Objects of such a template class let you represent and manipulate in-memory sequences that vary dynamically in length. The **dynarray<T>** object allocates and frees storage as needed to accommodate changes in length of the controlled sequence.

construction   To construct a **dynarray<T>** object **x0** with an initially empty sequence, you can simply write:

```
dynarray<T> x0;
```

length   Each object **x** reports the *length* of its sequence with the call **x.length()**.
reserve   It also reports its *reserve size* with the call **x.reserve()**. For a newly constructed **dynarray<T>** object, the reserve size suggests how much storage to initially allocate for the sequence. You can, for example, specify an initial reserve size of 100 elements by writing:

capacity   `dynarray<T> x0(100, reserve);`

For an object with a non-empty sequence, the reserve size suggests how much storage is currently available to hold the sequence of type **T**. Thus, `x0.length() <= x0.reserve()` at all times. As a rule, you can ignore the reserve size. The implementation will guess it for you. (But see the discussion on page 279.)

To construct a **dynarray<T>** and define its initial sequence, you have a number of choices. To give concrete examples, I show the explicit instantiation **dynarray<Char>**, given

```
class Char {
public:
    Char(char c = 'X')
        : ch(c) {};
private:
    char ch;
    };
Char b('B'), xxxx[4];
```

In each case below, the comment shows the character values stored in the elements of the resulting sequence. You can write:

```
dynarray<Char> x1(5, default_size);                 // XXXXX
dynarray<Char> x2(b);                                    // B
dynarray<Char> x3(b, 5);                             // BBBBB
dynarray<Char> x4(xxxx, 2);                             // XX
dynarray<Char> x5(x3);                               // BBBBB
```

notation   Class **dynarray<T>** supports several combinations of argument types for many functions that construct or manipulate such objects. For brevity, I define here a terse and uniform style for writing various argument combinations. The resultant argument is:

- a single element (of type **T**), with the argument **t**
- a repetition of elements, with the arguments **t, rep**
- a pointer to a single element, with the argument **s**
- an array of elements with a specified length, with the arguments **s, n**
- an object of class **dynarray<T>**, with the argument **x**

With this notation, I can more quickly summarize all the ways you can perform various operations involving **dynarray<T>** objects. Here, for example, is a summary of most of the constructors I showed above:

```
dynarray<T> x2(t);
dynarray<T> x3(t, rep);
dynarray<T> x4(s, n);
dynarray<T> x5(x);
```

A number of member functions alter the sequence controlled by a **dynarray<T>** object **x0**.

To assign a new sequence, in place of any existing one:

assign
```
x0.assign(t)
x0.assign(t, rep)
x0.assign(s)
x0.assign(s, n)
x0.assign(x)              x0 = x
```

To append to an existing sequence:

append
```
x0.append(t)                    x0 += t
x0.append(t, rep)
x0.append(s)
x0.append(s, n)
x0.append(x)                    x0 += x
```

To insert before position **px** in an existing sequence:

insert
```
x0.insert(px, t)
x0.insert(px, t, rep)
x0.insert(px, s)
x0.insert(px, s, n)
x0.insert(px, x)
```

You can remove a subsequence from a sequence in various ways:

remove
```
x0.remove()                        // remove all elements
x0.remove(px)                   // remove all from px to end
x0.remove(px, n)        // remove at most n beginning at px
```

You can establish a new length **len** for a sequence. If the new length is greater than the existing length, the sequence is padded as stated in the comment below:

swap   You can swap the controlled sequences with that controlled by another **dynarray<T>** object **x**:

```
x0.swap(x)
```

This call is presumably *much* faster than the conventional idiom:

```
dynarray<T> xt(x0);
x0 = x, x = xt;
```

You can establish a new length **len** for a sequence. If the new length is greater than the existing length, the sequence is padded as stated in the comment below:

resize
```
x0.resize(len)     // pad to len with default constructor
x0.resize(len, t)                // pad to len by repeating t
```

As a final alteration, you can store a new object **t** in the element at position **px** two different ways:

put_at
```
x0.put_at(px, t)
x0[px] = t
```

operator[] Be warned, however, that the subscript notation is more delicate. It returns a reference that can be invalidated by all sorts of subsequent operations on **x0**. Use it only in a very localized context, as above.

Another set of functions lets you obtain part or all of the sequence controlled by a **dynarray<T>** object. The compaions to the functions immediately above are:

get_at
```
x0.get_at(px)
x0[px]
```
operator[] both of which return the object stored at position **px**.

You can get a pointer to the beginning of the entire sequence by calling:

base
```
x0.base()
```

The same caveats apply as for the subscript operator, above. Use the pointer to do any direct accessing of the sequence quickly, before you perform any subsequent operations on **x0**. The pointer may well become invalid.

sub_array   You can copy a subsequence into another **dynarray<T>** object **x**:

```
x0.sub_array(x, px)              // copy from px to end
x0.sub_array(x, px, n)      // copy at most n beginning at px
```

Note that these calls return a reference to **x**.

Finally, some functions each construct a **dynarray<T>** object to return as the value of the function, leaving the object **x0** unaltered. You can, for example, construct a **dynarray<T>** object that appends the sequences defined by two operands:

operator+
```
x + t
t + x
x + x0
```

Implementing **<dynarray>**

dynarray   Figure 19.1 shows the file **dynarray**, which implements the standard header **<dynarray>**. It defines the template class **dynarray<T>** and a few related template functions. All template functions appear within the header as inline definitions, as I discussed much earlier. (See page 253.) Nevertheless, you will find that not all translators will accept this header unmodified. (See page 430.)

The template class **dynarray<T>** also defines five secret protected member functions:

_Grow ▪ **_Grow**, which alters the storage reserved for the sequence

_Tidy ▪ **_Tidy**, which initializes (**_Tidy()**) the member objects at construction time or discards any sequence (**_Tidy(1)**) and reinitializes the member objects

_Xinv ▪ **_Xinv**, which reports an invalid-argument error

_Xlen ▪ **_Xlen**, which reports a length error

_Xran ▪ **_Xran**, which reports a range error

For a discussion of the exceptions associated with invalid-argument, length, and range errors, see Chapter 3: **<exception>**. As you can see, all of these functions are used throughout the member function definitions.

I have added a default argument to several member functions. These are functions that accept a pointer to a sequence and a length (**const T***, **size_t**). Each has a companion function that accepts a reference to an element and a repetition count (**const T&, size_t = 1**). To enable the companion function to call the former version, I add to the former a pointer increment parameter (**size_t _D = 1**). Thus, the function steps by one to walk a sequence, and by zero to repeat a single element.

None of the functions is otherwise complex. For hints on what individual member functions do, see their analogs in class **string**.

```
// dynarray standard header
#ifndef _DYNARRAY_
#define _DYNARRAY_
#include <defines>
            // template class dynarray
template<class _T> class dynarray {
public:
    dynarray()
        {_Tidy(); }
    dynarray(size_t _N, capacity _C)
        {_Tidy(), _Res = _N;
        if (_C == default_size)
            _Grow(_N); }
    dynarray(const dynarray<_T>& _X)
        {_Tidy(), _Grow(_X.length());
        for (size_t _I = 0; _I < _Len; ++_I)
            _Ptr[_I] = _X[_I]; }
    dynarray(const _T& _X, size_t _N = 1)
        {_Tidy(), _Grow(_N, &_X); }
    dynarray(const _T *_S, size_t _N)
        {if (_S == 0)
            _Xinv();
        _Tidy(), assign(_S, _N); }
    ~dynarray()
        {_Tidy(1); }
    dynarray<_T>& operator=(const dynarray<_T>& _R)
        {return (this == &_R ? *this
            : assign(_R.base(), _R.length())); }
    dynarray<_T>& operator+=(const dynarray<_T>& _R)
        {return (append(_R.base(), _R.length())); }
    dynarray<_T>& operator+=(const _T& _R)
        {return (append(_R)); }
    dynarray<_T>& append(const _T& _X, size_t _N = 1)
        {return (append(&_X, _N, 0)); }
    dynarray<_T>& append(const _T *_S, size_t _N = 1,
        size_t _D = 1)
        {if (NPOS - _Len <= _N)
            _Xlen();
        size_t _I = _Len;
        for (_Grow(_N += _I); _I < _N; ++_I, _S += _D)
            _Ptr[_I] = *_S;
        return (*this); }
    dynarray<_T>& assign(const _T& _X, size_t _N = 1)
        {return (assign(&_X, _N, 0)); }
    dynarray<_T>& assign(const _T *_S, size_t _N = 1,
        size_t _D = 1)
        {_Grow(_N, 0, 1);
        for (size_t _I = 0; _I < _N; ++_I, _S += _D)
            _Ptr[_I] = *_S;
        return (*this); }
    dynarray<_T>& insert(size_t _P, const dynarray<_T>& _X)
        {return (insert(_P, _X.base(), _X.length())); }
    dynarray<_T>& insert(size_t _P, const _T& _X, size_t _N = 1)
        {return (insert(_P, &_X, _N, 0)); }
    dynarray<_T>& insert(size_t _P, const _T *_S, size_t _N = 1,
```

```
        size_t _D = 1)
        {if (_Len < _P)
            _Xran();
        if (NPOS - _Len <= _N)
            _Xlen();
        if (0 < _N)
            {size_t _I = _Len - _P;
            for (_Grow(_N + _Len); 0 < _I; )
                --_I, _Ptr[_P + _N + _I] = _Ptr[_P + _I];
            for (_I = 0; _I < _N; ++_I, _S += _D)
                _Ptr[_P + _I] = *_S; }
        return (*this); }
    dynarray<_T>& remove(size_t _P = 0, size_t _N = NPOS)
        {if (_Len < _P)
            _Xran();
        if (_Len - _P < _N)
            _N = _Len - _P;
        if (0 < _N)
            {size_t _M = _Len - _P - _N;
            for (size_t _I = 0; _I < _M; ++_I)
                _Ptr[_P + _I] = _Ptr[_P + _I + _N];
            _Grow(_Len - _N); }
        return (*this); }
    dynarray<_T>& sub_array(dynarray<_T>& _X, size_t _P,
        size_t _N = NPOS)
        {if (_Len < _P)
            _Xran();
        if (_Len - _P < _N)
            _N = _Len - _P;
        return (this == &_X ? (remove(_P + _N), remove(0, _P))
            : _X.assign(&_Ptr[_P], _N)); }
    void swap(dynarray<_T>& _X)
        {_T *_Tp = _Ptr; _Ptr = _X._Ptr, _X._Ptr = _Tp;
        size_t _Tl = _Len; _Len = _X._Len, _X._Len = _Tl;
        size_t _Tr = _Res; _Res = _X._Res, _X._Res = _Tr; }
    const _T& get_at(size_t _I) const
        {if (_Len <= _I)
            _Xran();
        return (_Ptr[_I]); }
    void put_at(size_t _I, const _T& _X)
        {if (_Len <= _I)
            _Xran();
        _Ptr[_I] = _X; }
    _T& operator[](size_t _I)
        {return (_Ptr[_I]); }
    const _T& operator[](size_t _I) const
        {return (_Ptr[_I]); }
    _T *base()
        {return (_Len != 0 ? _Ptr : 0); }
    const _T *base() const
        {return (_Len != 0 ? _Ptr : 0); }
    size_t length() const
        {return (_Len); }
    void resize(size_t _N)
        {_Grow(_N, 0, 1); }
```

```
        void resize(size_t _N, const _T& _X)
            {_Grow(_N, &_X, 1); }
    size_t reserve() const
        {return (_Res); }
    void reserve(size_t _R)
        {if (_Ptr == 0)
            _Res = _R; }
private:
    void _Grow(size_t _N, const _T *_S = 0, _Bool _Trim = 0)
        {size_t _Os = _Ptr == 0 ? 0 : _Res;
        if (_N == 0)
            {if (_Trim)
                _Tidy(1); }
        else if (_N == _Os || _N < _Os && !_Trim)
            ;
        else if (_N == NPOS)
            _Xlen();
        else
            {size_t _I, _M = _Ptr == 0 && _N < _Res ? _Res : _N;
            _T *_Np = new _T[_M];
            if (_Np == 0)
                _Nomemory();
            _Res = _M, _M = _N < _Len ? _N : _Len;
            for (_I = 0; _I < _M; ++_I)
                _Np[_I] = _Ptr[_I];
            if (_S != 0)
                for (; _I < _Res; ++_I)
                    _Np[_I] = *_S;
            _Tidy(1), _Ptr = _Np; }
        _Len = _N; }
    void _Tidy(_Bool _Constructed = 0)
        {if (_Constructed && _Ptr != 0)
            delete[] _Ptr;
        _Len = 0, _Ptr = 0, _Res = 0; }
    void _Xinv() const
        {invalidargument("invalid dynarray argument").raise(); }
    void _Xlen() const
        {lengtherror("dynarray too long").raise(); }
    void _Xran() const
        {outofrange("invalid dynarray position").raise(); }
    _T *_Ptr;
    size_t _Len, _Res;
    };
        // template operators
template<class _T> dynarray<_T>
    operator+(const dynarray<_T>& _L, const dynarray<_T>& _R)
    {return (dynarray<_T>(_L) += _R); }
template<class _T> dynarray<_T>
    operator+(const dynarray<_T>& _L, const _T& _R)
    {return (dynarray<_T>(_L) += _R); }
template<class _T> dynarray<_T>
    operator+(const _T& _L, const dynarray<_T>& _R)
    {return (dynarray<_T>(_L) += _R); }
#endif                                                              □
```

I discussed the pros and cons of this style of implementation in conjunction with the template class **bits<N>**. (See page 434.) Once again, I can report that this code does translate successfully under at least some current implementations. To make more than nontrivial use of it, however, you should check carefully to see the kind of code it generates. You may well want to modify it.

Testing `<dynarray>`

tdynarra.c   Figure 19.2 shows the file **tdynarra.c**. It defines the simple class **Char** that stores a single character. The default constructor for this class stores **'X'**. It also overloads **operator==** and **operator+** for various parameter combinations that all include at least one parameter of type **const dynarray<Char>&**. Some implementations need the three explicit declarations of **operator+** instantiated for **dynarray<Char>**. Others may not.

With this scaffolding, the function defines several objects of type **dynarray<Char>** and exercises at least the obvious features of the template class. If all goes well, the program prints:

    SUCCESS testing <dynarray>

and takes a normal exit.

Exercises

Exercise 19.1 Does the definition of the template class **dynarray<T>** guarantee that the sequence is always represented in contiguous storage?

Exercise 19.2 How would you instantiate the template class **dynarray<T>** to control a sequence of bits?

Exercise 19.3 What is the meaning of the instantiation **dynarray<const int>**? Is it permitted? Is it useful? Does the code in file **dynarray** survive such an instantiation?

Exercise 19.4 Compare the performance of objects of class **string** with that for objects of class **dynarray<char>**.

Exercise 19.5 Implement the class **double_array** that has the same functionality as **dynarray<double>**.

Exercise 19.6 Compare the performance of objects of class **double_array**, from the previous exercise, with that for objects of class **dynarray<double>**.

Exercise 19.7 [Harder] Rewrite the definition of template class **dynarray<T>** to provide predictable calling patterns for the copy constructor, assignment operator, and destructor supplied by **T**.

Exercise 19.8 [Very hard] Rewrite the definition of template class **dynarray<T>** for your implementation so that it generates the most optimal code for an arbitrary type **T** with value semantics.

```
// test <dynarray>
#include <assert.h>
#include <dynarray>
#include <iostream>

class Char {
public:
    Char(char c = 'X')
        : ch(c) {};
    char val() const
        {return (ch); }
    _Bool operator==(const Char& c) const
        {return (ch == c.val()); }
private:
    char ch;
    };

_Bool operator==(const dynarray<Char>& x, const char *s)
    {                              // test contents of a dynarray<Char>
    for (int i = 0; i < x.length(); ++i)
        if (x[i].val() != s[i])
            return (0);
    return (s[x.length()] == '\0');
    }

dynarray<Char> operator+(const dynarray<Char>&,
    const dynarray<Char>&);
dynarray<Char> operator+(const dynarray<Char>&, const Char&);
dynarray<Char> operator+(const Char&, const dynarray<Char>&);

int main()
    {                    // test basic workings of dynarray definitions
    Char c0, ca('a'), cb('b'), c3[3];
    dynarray<Char> s1, s2(30, reserve), s3(4, default_size);
    dynarray<Char> s4(s3), s5(ca), s6(cb, 10);
    const dynarray<Char> s7(c3, 3);
    assert(s1.length() == 0);
    s1.reserve(10);
    assert(s1.length() == 0 && s1.reserve() == 10);
    assert(s2.length() == 0 && s2.reserve() == 30);
    assert(s3.length() == 4 && s3 == "XXXX");
    assert(s4.length() == 4 && s4 == "XXXX");
    assert(s5.length() == 1 && s5[0] == ca);
    assert(s6.length() == 10 && s6 == "bbbbbbbbbb");
    assert(s7.length() == 3 && s7 == "XXX");
    s1.resize(2), assert(s1 == "XX");
    s1.resize(4, ca), assert(s1 == "XXaa");
    s1.resize(3), assert(s1 == "XXa");
        // test assigns
    s1 = s5, assert(s1 == "a");
    s1 = s1, assert(s1 == "a");
    s1.assign(cb), assert(s1 == "b");
    s1.assign(cb, 5), assert(s1 == "bbbbb");
    s1.assign(&cb), assert(s1 == "b");
    s1.assign(c3, 3), assert(s1 == "XXX");
```

```
    // test appends
s1 = s5, s1 += s5, assert(s1 == "aa");
s1 += cb, assert(s1 == "aab");
s1.append(cb), assert(s1 == "aabb");
s1.append(cb, 5), assert(s1 == "aabbbbbbb");
s1.append(&ca), assert(s1 == "aabbbbbbba");
s1.append(c3, 3), assert(s1 == "aabbbbbbbaXXX");
s1 = s4 + s5, assert(s1 == "XXXXa");
s1 = ca + s5, assert(s1 == "aa");
s1 = s4 + cb, assert(s1 == "XXXXb");
    // test inserts, removes, etc.
s1 = s4, s1.insert(1, s5), assert(s1 == "XaXXX");
s1.insert(2, cb), assert(s1 == "XabXXX");
s1.insert(0, ca, 3), assert(s1 == "aaaXabXXX");
s1.insert(9, &ca), assert(s1 == "aaaXabXXXa");
s1.insert(1, c3, 3), assert(s1 == "aXXXaaXabXXXa");
s1.remove(7), assert(s1 == "aXXXaaX");
s1.remove(2, 1), assert(s1 == "aXXaaX");
s1.remove(), assert(s1 == "");
s6.sub_array(s1, 2);
assert(s6 == "bbbbbbbbbb" && s1 == "bbbbbbbb");
s1.sub_array(s1, 3, 2), assert(s1 == "bb");
s1.swap(s3), assert(s1 == "XXXX" && s3 == "bb");
    // test access functions
s1 = s7, assert(s1[0] == c0);
s1[0] = ca, assert(s1[0] == ca);
s1.put_at(1, cb), assert(s1.get_at(1) == cb);
assert(s1.base()[1] == cb && s7.base()[2] == c0);
cout << "SUCCESS testing <dynarray>" << endl;
return (0);
}
```

Chapter 20: `<ptrdynarray>`

Background

The template class **dynarray<T>**, described in the previous chapter, has an important requirement. The parameter type **T** must have value semantics, so that objects of that type can be freely copied. This requirement is met by all scalar objects, but not necessarily for a class you define. If you want to organize objects of an arbitrary type **T** into varying-length sequences, all is not lost. You can construct a sequence of *pointers* to such objects, as **dynarray<T *>**. Then, only the pointers get copied about.

The header **<ptrdynarray>** supplies a bit of help in managing pointer sequences. It defines the template class **ptrdynarray<T>**, which has the public base class **dynarray<void *>**. The derived class then hides all member functions in the base class with versions tailored specifically for pointers to **T**. The template class **ptrdynarray<T>** thus controls a sequence of pointers to an object type **T**, maintained as a sequence of pointers to *void*.

What the Draft C++ Standard Says

The description of template class **ptrdynarray<T>** is tedious, pure and simple. It is admittedly a thin layer atop **dynarray<void *>**.

17.5.6 Header `<ptrdynarray>`

<ptr-dynarray>

The header **<ptrdynarray>** defines a template and several related functions for representing and manipulating varying-size sequences of pointers to some object type **T**.

17.5.6.1 Template class `ptrdynarray`

Class ptrdynarray

```
template<class T> class ptrdynarray : public dynarray<void*> {
public:
    ptrdynarray();
    ptrdynarray(size_t size, capacity cap);
    ptrdynarray(const ptrdynarray& arr);
    ptrdynarray(T* obj, size_t rep = 1);
    ptrdynarray(T** parr, size_t n = 1);
    ptrdynarray& operator+=(const ptrdynarray& rhs);
    ptrdynarray& operator+=(T* obj);
    ptrdynarray& append(T* obj, size_t rep = 1);
```

```
        ptrdynarray& append(T** parr, size_t n = 1);
        ptrdynarray& assign(T* obj, size_t rep = 1);
        ptrdynarray& assign(T** parr, size_t n = 1);
        ptrdynarray& insert(size_t pos, const ptrdynarray& arr);
        ptrdynarray& insert(size_t pos, T* obj, size_t rep = 1);
        ptrdynarray& insert(size_t pos, T** parr, size_t n = 1);
        ptrdynarray& remove(size_t pos = 0, size_t n = NPOS);
        ptrdynarray& sub_array(ptrdynarray& arr, size_t pos,
            size_t n = NPOS);
        void swap(ptrdynarray& arr);
        T* get_at(size_t pos) const;
        void put_at(size_t pos, T* obj);
        T*& operator[](size_t pos);
        T* const& operator[](size_t pos) const;
        T** base();
        const T** base() const;
        size_t length() const;
        void resize(size_t n);
        void resize(size_t n, T* obj);
        size_t reserve() const;
        void reserve(size_t res_arg);
    };
```

The template class **ptrdynarray** describes an object that can store a sequence consisting of a varying number of objects of type pointer to **T**. Such a sequence is also called a *dynamic pointer array*. Objects of type **T** are never created, destroyed, copied, assigned, or otherwise accessed by the function signatures described in this subclause.

17.5.6.1.1 ptrdynarray::ptrdynarray()

constructor

```
ptrdynarray();
```

Constructs an object of class **ptrdynarray**, initializing the base class with **dynarray<void*>()**.

17.5.6.1.2 ptrdynarray::ptrdynarray(size_t, capacity)

constructor

```
ptrdynarray(size_t size, capacity cap);
```

Constructs an object of class **ptrdynarray**, initializing the base class with **dynarray<void*>(size, cap)**.

17.5.6.1.3 ptrdynarray::ptrdynarray(const ptrdynarray&)

constructor

```
ptrdynarray(const ptrdynarray& arr);
```

Constructs an object of class **ptrdynarray**, initializing the base class with **dynarray<void*>(arr)**.

17.5.6.1.4 ptrdynarray::ptrdynarray(T*)

constructor

```
ptrdynarray(T* obj, size_t rep = 1);
```

Constructs an object of class **ptrdynarray**, initializing the base class with **dynarray<void*>((void*)obj, rep)**.

17.5.6.1.5 ptrdynarray::ptrdynarray(const T**, size_t)

constructor

```
ptrdynarray(const T** parr, size_t n);
```

Constructs an object of class **ptrdynarray**, initializing the base class with **dynarray<void*>((void**)parr, n)**.

17.5.6.1.6 ptrdynarray::operator+=(const ptrdynarray&)

operator+=

```
ptrdynarray& operator+=(const ptrdynarray& rhs);
```

Returns **(ptrdynarray&)dynarray<void*>::operator+=((const dynarray<void*>&)***rhs**).

17.5.6.1.7 ptrdynarray::operator+=(*T**)

operator+=   `ptrdynarray& operator+=(T* obj);`

Returns **(ptrdynarray&)dynarray<void*>::operator+=((void*)***obj**).

17.5.6.1.8 ptrdynarray::append(*T**, size_t)

append   `ptrdynarray& append(T* obj, size_t rep = 1);`

Returns **(ptrdynarray&)dynarray<void*>::append((void*)** *obj*, *rep*).

17.5.6.1.9 ptrdynarray::append(*T***, size_t)

append   `ptrdynarray& append(T** parr, size_t n = 1);`

Returns **(ptrdynarray&)dynarray<void*>::append((void**)***parr*, *n*).

17.5.6.1.10 ptrdynarray::assign(*T**, size_t)

assign   `ptrdynarray& assign(T* obj, size_t rep = 1);`

Returns **(ptrdynarray&)dynarray<void*>::assign((void*)** *obj*, *rep*).

17.5.6.1.11 ptrdynarray::assign(*T***, size_t)

assign   `ptrdynarray& assign(T** parr, size_t n = 1);`

Returns **(ptrdynarray&)dynarray<void*>::assign((void**)***parr*, *n*).

17.5.6.1.12 ptrdynarray::insert(size_t, const ptrdynarray&, size_t)

insert   `ptrdynarray& insert(size_t pos, const ptrdynarray& arr);`

Returns **(ptrdynarray&)dynarray<void*>::insert(***pos*, **(const dynarray<void*>&)** *arr*).

17.5.6.1.13 ptrdynarray::insert(size_t, *T**, size_t)

insert   `ptrdynarray& insert(size_t pos, T*obj, size_t rep = 1);`

Returns **(ptrdynarray&)dynarray<void*>::insert(***pos*, **(void*)** *obj*, *rep*).

17.5.6.1.14 ptrdynarray::insert(size_t, *T***, size_t)

insert   `ptrdynarray& insert(size_t pos, T**parr, size_t n = 1);`

Returns **(ptrdynarray&)dynarray<void*>::insert(***pos*, **(void**)***parr*, *n*).

17.5.6.1.15 ptrdynarray::remove(size_t, size_t)

remove   `ptrdynarray& remove(size_t pos = 0, size_t n = NPOS);`

Returns **(ptrdynarray&)dynarray<void*>::remove(***pos*, *n*).

17.5.6.1.16 ptrdynarray::sub_array(ptrdynarray&, size_t, size_t)

sub_array   `ptrdynarray& sub_array(ptrdynarray& arr, size_t pos, size_t n = NPOS);`

Returns **(ptrdynarray&)dynarray<void*>::sub_array(***arr*, *pos*, *n*).

17.5.6.1.17 ptrdynarray::swap(ptrdynarray&)

swap   `void swap(ptrdynarray& arr);`

Calls `dynarray<void*>::swap(arr)`.

17.5.6.1.18 ptrdynarray::get_at(size_t)

get_at
```
T* get_at(size_t pos) const;
```
Returns `(T*)dynarray<void*>::get_at(pos)`.

17.5.6.1.19 ptrdynarray::put_at(size_t, const T&)

put_at
```
void put_at(size_t pos, T* obj);
```
Calls `dynarray<void*>::put_at(pos, (void*)obj)`.

17.5.6.1.20 ptrdynarray::operator[](size_t)

operator[]
```
T*& operator[](size_t pos);
T* const& operator[](size_t pos) const;
```
Returns `(T* &)dynarray<void*>::operator[](pos)`.

17.5.6.1.21 ptrdynarray::base()

base
```
T** base();
const T** base() const;
```
Returns `(T*)dynarray<void*>::base()`.

17.5.6.1.22 ptrdynarray::length()

length
```
size_t length() const;
```
Returns `dynarray<void*>::length()`.

17.5.6.1.23 ptrdynarray::resize(size_t)

resize
```
void resize(size_t n);
```
Calls `dynarray<void*>::resize(n)`.

17.5.6.1.24 ptrdynarray::resize(size_t, T*)

resize
```
void resize(size_t n, T* obj);
```
Calls `dynarray<void*>::resize(n, (void*)obj)`.

17.5.6.1.25 ptrdynarray::reserve()

reserve
```
size_t reserve() const;
```
Returns `dynarray<void*>::reserve()`.

17.5.6.1.26 ptrdynarray::reserve(size_t)

reserve
```
void reserve(size_t res_arg);
```
Returns `dynarray<void*>::reserve(res_arg)`.

17.5.6.2 operator+(const ptrdynarray&, onst ptrdynarray&)

operator+
```
template<class T> ptrdynarray<T>
    operator+(const ptrdynarray<T>& lhs,
        const ptrdynarray<T>& rhs);
```
Returns `ptrdynarray<T>(lhs) += rhs)`.

17.5.6.3 operator+(const ptrdynarray&, T*)

operator+
```
template<class T> ptrdynarray<T>
    operator+(const ptrdynarray<T>& lhs, T* obj);
```
Returns `ptrdynarray<T>(lhs) += rhs)`.

17.5.6.4 operator+(T*, const ptrdynarray&)

operator+
```
template<class T> ptrdynarray<T>
    operator+(T* obj, const ptrdynarray<T>& rhs);
```
Returns `ptrdynarray<T>(lhs) += rhs)`.

Future Directions

The name of the class has been changed to **ptr_dyn_array**.

base The member function **ptrdynarray<T>::base** has been changed to **ptrdynarray<T>::data**.

Standard The header **<ptrdynarray>** is the last of the candidates in this book for
Template replacement by the Standard Template Library (STL). (See page 427.) A
Library combination of more general templates from STL is an adequate substitute
for an explicit template class **ptrdynarray<T>**. Once again, however, I
provide here a full discussion of the header **<ptrdynarray>**, for the reasons
I outlined earlier.

Using `<ptrdynarray>`

You include the header **<ptrdynarray>** to make use of the template class
ptrdynarray<T>. Here, **T** is an arbitrary object type. Objects of such a
template class let you represent and manipulate in-memory sequences, of
pointers to **T**, that vary dynamically in length. The **ptrdynarray<T>** object
allocates and frees storage as needed to accommodate changes in length of
the controlled sequence. For a description of how to use a **ptrdynarray<T>**
object, see the previous chapter. The only difference is that every reference
to **T**, in the description of class **dynarray<T>**, is replaced by a pointer to **T**.

Implementing `<ptrdynarray>`

ptrdynar Figure 20.1 shows the file **ptrdynar**, which implements the standard
header **<ptrdynarray>**. It defines the template class **ptrdynarray<T>** and
a few related template functions. All template functions appear within the
header as inline definitions, as I discussed much earlier. (See page 253.) In
this particular case, such an approach is eminently sensible.

Testing `<ptrdynarray>`

tptrdyna.c Figure 20.2 shows the file **tptrdyna.c**, a simple variant of the file
tdynarra.c in the previous chapter. (See page 488.) It defines the simple
class **Char** that stores a single character. The default constructor for this class
stores **'X'**. It also overloads **operator==** and **operator+** for various parameter combinations that all include at least one parameter of type **const
dynarray<Char>&**. With this scaffolding, the function defines several objects of type **ptrdynarray<Char>** and exercises at least the obvious features
of the template class.

If all goes well, the program prints:

```
SUCCESS testing <ptrdynarray>
```

and takes a normal exit.

```
// ptrdynarray standard header
#ifndef _PTRDYNARRAY_
#define _PTRDYNARRAY_
#include <dynarray>
            // template class ptrdynarray
template<class _T> class ptrdynarray
    : public dynarray<void *> {
public:
    ptrdynarray()
        : dynarray<void *>() {}
    ptrdynarray(size_t _N, capacity _C)
        : dynarray<void *>(_N, _C) {}
    ptrdynarray(const ptrdynarray<_T>& _X)
        : dynarray<void *>(_X) {}
    ptrdynarray(_T *_X, size_t _N = 1)
        : dynarray<void *>((void *)_X, _N) {}
    ptrdynarray(_T **_S, size_t _N = 1)
        : dynarray<void *>((void **)_S, _N) {}
    ptrdynarray<_T>& operator=(const ptrdynarray<_T>& _R)
        {return ((ptrdynarray<_T>&)dynarray<void *>::
            operator=((const dynarray<void *>&)_R)); }
    ptrdynarray<_T>& operator+=(const ptrdynarray<_T>& _R)
        {return ((ptrdynarray<_T>&)dynarray<void *>::
            operator+=((const dynarray<void *>&)_R)); }
    ptrdynarray<_T>& operator+=(_T *_R)
        {return ((ptrdynarray<_T>&)dynarray<void *>::
            operator+=((void *)_R)); }
    ptrdynarray<_T>& append(_T *_X, size_t _N = 1)
        {return ((ptrdynarray<_T>&)dynarray<void *>::
            append((void *)_X, _N)); }
    ptrdynarray<_T>& append(_T **_S, size_t _N = 1)
        {return ((ptrdynarray<_T>&)dynarray<void *>::
            append((void **)_S, _N)); }
    ptrdynarray<_T>& assign(_T *_X, size_t _N = 1)
        {return ((ptrdynarray<_T>&)dynarray<void *>::
            assign((void *)_X, _N)); }
    ptrdynarray<_T>& assign(_T **_S, size_t _N = 1)
        {return ((ptrdynarray<_T>&)dynarray<void *>::
            assign((void **)_S, _N)); }
    ptrdynarray<_T>& insert(size_t _P,
        const ptrdynarray<_T>& _X)
        {return ((ptrdynarray<_T>&)dynarray<void *>::
            insert(_P, (const dynarray<void *>&)_X)); }
    ptrdynarray<_T>& insert(size_t _P, _T *_X, size_t _N = 1)
        {return ((ptrdynarray<_T>&)dynarray<void *>::
            insert(_P, (void *)_X, _N)); }
    ptrdynarray<_T>& insert(size_t _P, _T **_S, size_t _N = 1)
        {return ((ptrdynarray<_T>&)dynarray<void *>::
            insert(_P, (void **)_S, _N)); }
    ptrdynarray<_T>& remove(size_t _P = 0, size_t _N = NPOS)
        {return ((ptrdynarray<_T>&)dynarray<void *>::
            remove(_P, _N)); }
    ptrdynarray<_T>& sub_array(ptrdynarray<_T>& _X, size_t _P,
        size_t _N = NPOS)
        {return ((ptrdynarray<_T>&)dynarray<void *>::
```

```
                 sub_array(_X, _P, _N)); }
     void swap(ptrdynarray<_T>& _X)
          {dynarray<void *>::swap(_X); }
     _T* get_at(size_t _P) const
          {return ((_T *)dynarray<void *>::get_at(_P)); }
     void put_at(size_t _P, _T *_X)
          {dynarray<void *>::put_at(_P, (void *)_X); }
     _T *& operator[](size_t _P)
          {return ((_T *&)dynarray<void *>::operator[](_P)); }
     _T *const& operator[](size_t _P) const
          {return ((_T *&)dynarray<void *>::operator[](_P)); }
     _T **base()
          {return ((_T **)dynarray<void *>::base()); }
     const _T **base() const
          {return ((_T **)dynarray<void *>::base()); }
     size_t length() const
          {return (dynarray<void *>::length()); }
     void resize(size_t _N)
          {dynarray<void *>::resize(_N); }
     void resize(size_t _N, _T * _X)
          {dynarray<void *>::resize(_N, (void *)_X); }
     size_t reserve() const
          {return (dynarray<void *>::reserve()); }
     void reserve(size_t _N)
          {dynarray<void *>::reserve(_N); }
     };
          // template operators
template<class _T> ptrdynarray<_T>
     operator+(const ptrdynarray<_T>& _L,
          const ptrdynarray<_T>& _R)
     {return (ptrdynarray<_T>(_L) += _R); }
template<class _T> ptrdynarray<_T>
     operator+(const ptrdynarray<_T>& _L, _T *_R)
     {return (ptrdynarray<_T>(_L) += _R); }
template<class _T> ptrdynarray<_T>
     operator+(_T *_L, const ptrdynarray<_T>& _R)
     {return (ptrdynarray<_T>(_L) += _R); }
#endif                                                      □
```

Exercises

Exercise 20.1 Is there ever any difference in effect between, say, **dynarray<int *>** and **ptrdynarray<int>**? If so, what is the difference? How might it affect program execution?

Exercise 20.2 Say you intend to instantiate **ptrdynarray<T>** for many different types. Is this approach better or worse, in any way, than instantiating **dynarray<T>** for the corresponding pointer types instead?

Exercise 20.3 Is it permissible to instantiate **ptrdynarray<fvoid_t>**? (For the definition of **fvoid_t**, see Chapter 2: **<defines>**.) If not, how would you achieve the desired effect?

Exercise 20.4 Why might you want to maintain a varying-length sequence of **streambuf** objects?

Exercise 20.5 [Harder] Rewrite the definition of template class **ptrdynarray<T>** so that it accepts the same parameter types (such as **T&** and **T ***) as **dynarray<T>** and converts them as needed to corresponding pointer types (such as **T *** and **T ****).

Exercise 20.6 [Very hard] Rewrite the definition of template class **dynarray<T>** for your implementation so that it adapts as needed to a class **T** that doesn't have value semantics.

Figure 20.2:
tptrdyna.c
Part 1 of 2

```
// test <ptrdynarray>
#include <assert.h>
#include <iostream>
#include <ptrdynarray>

class Char {
public:
    Char(char c = 'X')
        : ch(c) {};
    char val() const
        {return (ch); }
    _Bool operator==(const Char& c) const
        {return (ch == c.val()); }
private:
    char ch;
    };

_Bool operator==(const ptrdynarray<Char>& x, const char *s)
    {                       // test contents of a ptrdynarray<Char>
    for (int i = 0; i < x.length(); ++i)
        if (x[i]->val() != s[i])
            return (0);
    return (s[x.length()] == '\0');
    }

ptrdynarray<Char> operator+(const ptrdynarray<Char>&,
    const ptrdynarray<Char>&);
ptrdynarray<Char> operator+(const ptrdynarray<Char>&, Char *);
ptrdynarray<Char> operator+(Char *, const ptrdynarray<Char>&);

int main()
    {               // test basic workings of ptrdynarray definitions
    static Char c0, ca('a'), cb('b'), c3[3];
    static Char *pc3[] = {&ca, &cb, &c0};
    ptrdynarray<Char> s1, s2(30, reserve), s3(4, default_size);
    ptrdynarray<Char> s4(s3), s5(&ca), s6(&cb, 10);
    const ptrdynarray<Char> s7(pc3, 3);
    assert(s1.length() == 0);
    s1.reserve(10);
    assert(s1.length() == 0 && s1.reserve() == 10);
    assert(s2.length() == 0 && s2.reserve() == 30);
```

```
assert(s3.length() == 4);
assert(s4.length() == 4);
assert(s5.length() == 1 && s5[0] == &ca);
assert(s6.length() == 10 && s6 == "bbbbbbbbbb");
assert(s7.length() == 3 && s7 == "abX");
s1.resize(2), s1[0] = &c0, s1[1] = &c0, assert(s1 == "XX");
s1.resize(4, &ca), assert(s1 == "XXaa");
s1.resize(3), assert(s1 == "XXa");
    // test assigns
s1 = s5, assert(s1 == "a");
s1 = s1, assert(s1 == "a");
s1.assign(&cb), assert(s1 == "b");
s1.assign(&cb, 5), assert(s1 == "bbbbb");
s1.assign(pc3), assert(s1 == "a");
s1.assign(pc3, 3), assert(s1 == "abX");
    // test appends
s1 = s5, s1 += s5, assert(s1 == "aa");
s1 += &cb, assert(s1 == "aab");
s1.append(&cb), assert(s1 == "aabb");
s1.append(&cb, 5), assert(s1 == "aabbbbbbb");
s1.append(pc3), assert(s1 == "aabbbbbbba");
s1.append(pc3, 3), assert(s1 == "aabbbbbbbaabX");
s1 = s6 + s7, assert(s1 == "bbbbbbbbbbabX");
s1 = &ca + s7, assert(s1 == "aabX");
s1 = s7 + &cb, assert(s1 == "abXb");
    // test inserts, removes, etc.
s1 = s7, s1.insert(1, s7), assert(s1 == "aabXbX");
s1.insert(2, &cb), assert(s1 == "aabbXbX");
s1.insert(0, &ca, 3), assert(s1 == "aaaaabbXbX");
s1.insert(10, pc3), assert(s1 == "aaaaabbXbXa");
s1.insert(1, pc3, 3), assert(s1 == "aabXaaaabbXbXa");
s1.remove(7), assert(s1 == "aabXaaa");
s1.remove(2, 1), assert(s1 == "aaXaaa");
s1.remove(), assert(s1 == "");
s6.sub_array(s1, 2);
assert(s6 == "bbbbbbbbbb" && s1 == "bbbbbbbb");
s1.sub_array(s1, 3, 2), assert(s1 == "bb");
s1.swap(s6), assert(s1 == "bbbbbbbbbb" && s6 == "bb");
    // test access functions
s1 = s7, assert(s1[0] == &ca);
s1[0] = &cb, assert(s1[0] == &cb);
s1.put_at(1, &ca), assert(s1.get_at(1) == &ca);
assert(s1.base()[1] == &ca && s7.base()[2] == &c0);
cout << "SUCCESS testing <ptrdynarray>" << endl;
return (0);
}                                                                □
```

Chapter 21: `<complex>`

Background

Encapsulating complex arithmetic is one of the earliest applications for C++. One of the first libraries supplied with a C++ translator supported iostream-style input and output, complex arithmetic, and little else. Since those early days, it has become traditional to provide at least minimal support for making complex look more like a builtin type in C++.

complex.h Widespread current practice is to supply a header, such as **complex.h**, that defines at least a complex class based on type *double*. Addition, subtraction, and negation make easy inline functions. Multiplication and division are more involved, but still easy enough to supply. Other math functions are considerably harder. Support for them varies considerably.

Indeed, it is hard to find a better excuse for hiding implementation details of a class, or for overloading arithmetic operators, than providing complex arithmetic. A number of operators have well established meanings for complex values, dating back to the earliest days of FORTRAN. After integer and floating-point values, complex values probably have the richest culture in computer programming. Many scientists and engineers still bemoan the loss of complex data types in later languages such as Pascal and C. In a very real (and positive) sense, C++ allows C programs to look more like FORTRAN.

The header **<complex>** is rather more ambitious than the typical header **<complex.h>** of existing practice. It defines three classes, one for each of the three floating-point types of Standard C:

- **float_complex**, based on *float*
- **double_complex**, based on *double*
- **long_double_complex**, based on *long double*

Cartesian form The member objects are hidden inside each of these classes, as usual. In principle, the actual representation is equally hidden. But the functions that access stored values deliver only the *Cartesian* components of a complex value. Cartesian form represents a complex value as the pair (x, y) representing the sum $x + i{*}y$. Here, i is the notorious square root of -1, the unit vector along the imaginary axis in the complex plane. Thus, the *real* component is x and the *imaginary* component is y.

polar   Another way to represent complex values is with *polar* components.
form   Polar form represents a complex value as the pair (ρ, θ) representing the
product $\rho*exp(i*\theta)$. Thus, the *magnitude* is ρ and the *argument* (or *phase angle*)
is θ. Put simply, Cartesian form is far more convenient for addition and
subtraction, while polar form is sometimes more convenient for multiplication and division. On balance, however, Cartesian form is generally more
convenient.

Beyond this brief introduction, I won't even try to explain all the mysteries of complex mathematics. Nor will I make a case for why you might
want to use it. If you're familiar with complex math, you know it is often
useful in its own right. It also models well many processes of interest to
scientists and engineers, such as time-varying voltages and motion in two
dimensions. But if you don't already know how you might use complex
arithmetic, here is not the place for me to try to teach it.

What the Draft C++ Standard Says

The descriptions that follow are highly repetitious. You will find essentially the same functionality described for the classes **float_complex**,
double_complex, and **long_double_complex**. They differ only in the functions that convert between different precisions. Look closely at the constructors provided for each class, which sometimes raise precision. Look
also at the conversion functions with names such as **_float_complex**,
which lower precision. The descriptions are otherwise identical.

17.5.7 Header <complex>

<complex>   The header **<complex>** defines a macro, three types, and numerous functions
for representing and manipulating complex numbers.
The macro is:

__STD_COMPLEX   **__STD_COMPLEX**

whose definition is unspecified.

17.5.7.1 Complex numbers with float precision

17.5.7.1.1 Class float_complex

Class
float_complex
```
class float_complex {
public:
    float_complex(float re_arg = 0, im_arg = 0);
    float_complex& operator+=(float_complex rhs);
    float_complex& operator-=(float_complex rhs);
    float_complex& operator*=(float_complex rhs);
    float_complex& operator/=(float_complex rhs);
private:
//  float re, im;                                 exposition only
};
```
The class **float_complex** describes an object that can store the Cartesian
components, of type **float**, of a complex number.
For the sake of exposition, the maintained data is presented here as:

- **float** *re*, the real component;
- **float** *im*, the imaginary component.

17.5.7.1.1.1 float_complex::float_complex(float, float)

constructor

```
float_complex(float re_arg = 0, im_arg = 0);
```

Constructs an object of class **float_complex**, initializing *re* to *re_arg* and *im* to *im_arg*.

17.5.7.1.1.2 operator+=(float_complex)

operator+=

```
float_complex& operator+=(float_complex rhs);
```

Adds the complex value *rhs* to the complex value ***this** and stores the sum in ***this**. The function returns ***this**.

17.5.7.1.1.3 operator-=(float_complex)

operator-=

```
float_complex& operator-=(float_complex rhs);
```

Subtracts the complex value *rhs* from the complex value ***this** and stores the difference in ***this**. The function returns ***this**.

17.5.7.1.1.4 operator*=(float_complex)

operator*=

```
float_complex& operator*=(float_complex rhs);
```

Multiplies the complex value *rhs* by the complex value ***this** and stores the product in ***this**. The function returns ***this**.

17.5.7.1.1.5 operator/=(float_complex)

operator/=

```
float_complex& operator/=(float_complex rhs);
```

Divides the complex value *rhs* into the complex value ***this** and stores the quotient in ***this**. The function returns ***this**.

17.5.7.1.2 _float_complex(const double_complex&)

_float_complex

```
float_complex _float_complex(const double_complex& rhs);
```

Returns **float_complex((float)real(*rhs*), (float)imag(*rhs*))**.

17.5.7.1.3 _float_complex(const long_double_complex&)

_float_complex

```
float_complex _float_complex(const long_double_complex& rhs);
```

Returns **float_complex((float)real(*rhs*), (float)imag(*rhs*))**.

17.5.7.1.4 operator+(float_complex, float_complex)

operator+

```
float_complex operator+(float_complex lhs, float_complex rhs);
```

Returns **float_complex(*lhs*) += *rhs***.

17.5.7.1.5 operator+(float_complex, float)

operator+

```
float_complex operator+(float_complex lhs, float rhs);
```

Returns **float_complex(*lhs*) += float_complex(*rhs*)**.

17.5.7.1.6 operator+(float, float_complex)

operator+

```
float_complex operator+(float lhs, float_complex rhs);
```

Returns **float_complex(*lhs*) += *rhs***.

17.5.7.1.7 operator-(float_complex, float_complex)

operator-

```
float_complex operator-(float_complex lhs, float_complex rhs);
```

Returns **float_complex(*lhs*) -= *rhs***.

17.5.7.1.8 operator-(float_complex, float)

operator-

```
float_complex operator-(float_complex lhs, float rhs);
```

Returns **float_complex(*lhs*) -= float_complex(*rhs*)**.

17.5.7.1.9 operator-(float, float_complex)

operator- | `float_complex operator-(float lhs, float_complex rhs);`

Returns `float_complex(lhs) -= rhs`.

17.5.7.1.10 operator*(float_complex, float_complex)

operator* | `float_complex operator*(float_complex lhs, float_complex rhs);`

Returns `float_complex(lhs) *= rhs`.

17.5.7.1.11 operator*(float_complex, float)

operator* | `float_complex operator*(float_complex lhs, float rhs);`

Returns `float_complex(lhs) *= float_complex(rhs)`.

17.5.7.1.12 operator*(float, float_complex)

operator* | `float_complex operator*(float lhs, float_complex rhs);`

Returns `float_complex(lhs) *= rhs`.

17.5.7.1.13 operator/(float_complex, float_complex)

operator/ | `float_complex operator/(float_complex lhs, float_complex rhs);`

Returns `float_complex(lhs) /= rhs`.

17.5.7.1.14 operator/(float_complex, float)

operator/ | `float_complex operator/(float_complex lhs, float rhs);`

Returns `float_complex(lhs) /= float_complex(rhs)`.

17.5.7.1.15 operator/(float, float_complex)

operator/ | `float_complex operator/(float lhs, float_complex rhs);`

Returns `float_complex(lhs) /= rhs`.

17.5.7.1.16 operator+(float_complex)

operator+ | `float_complex operator+(float_complex lhs);`

Returns `float_complex(lhs)`.

17.5.7.1.17 operator-(float_complex)

operator- | `float_complex operator-(float_complex lhs);`

Returns `float_complex(-real(lhs), -imag(lhs))`.

17.5.7.1.18 operator==(float_complex, float_complex)

operator== | `int operator==(float_complex lhs, float_complex rhs);`

Returns `real(lhs) == real(rhs) && imag(lhs) == imag( rhs)`.

17.5.7.1.19 operator==(float_complex, float)

operator== | `int operator==(float_complex lhs, float rhs);`

Returns `real(lhs) == rhs && imag(lhs) == 0`.

17.5.7.1.20 operator==(float, float_complex)

operator== | `int operator==(float lhs, float_complex rhs);`

Returns `lhs == real(rhs) && imag(rhs) == 0`.

17.5.7.1.21 operator!=(float_complex, float_complex)

operator!= | `int operator!=(float_complex lhs, float_complex rhs);`

Returns `real(lhs) != real(rhs) || imag(lhs) != imag( rhs)`.

17.5.7.1.22 operator!=(float_complex, float)

operator!= | `int operator!=(float_complex lhs, float rhs);`

Returns `real(lhs) != rhs || imag(lhs) != 0`.

17.5.7.1.23 operator!=(float, float_complex)

operator!=
```
int operator!=(float lhs, float_complex rhs);
```
Returns *lhs* != real(*rhs*) || imag(*rhs*) != 0.

17.5.7.1.24 operator>>(istream&, float_complex&)

operator>>
```
istream& operator>>(istream& is, float_complex& x);
```
Evaluates the expression:
```
is >> ch && ch == '('
&& is >> re >> ch && ch == ','
&& is >> im >> ch && ch == ')';
```
where *ch* is an object of type **char** and *re* and *im* are objects of type **float**. If the result is nonzero, the function assigns **float_complex(re, im)** to *x*. The function returns *is*.

17.5.7.1.25 operator<<(ostream&, float_complex)

operator<<
```
ostream& operator<<(ostream& os, float_complex x);
```
Returns *os* << '(' << real(*x*) << ',' << imag(*x*) << ')'.

17.5.7.1.26 abs(float_complex)

abs
```
float abs(float_complex x);
```
Returns the magnitude of *x*.

17.5.7.1.27 arg(float_complex)

arg
```
float arg(float_complex x);
```
Returns the phase angle of *x*.

17.5.7.1.28 conj(float_complex)

conj
```
float_complex conj(float_complex x);
```
Returns the conjugate of *x*.

17.5.7.1.29 cos(float_complex)

cos
```
float_complex cos(float_complex x);
```
Returns the cosine of *x*.

17.5.7.1.30 cosh(float_complex)

cosh
```
float_complex cosh(float_complex x);
```
Returns the hyperbolic cosine of *x*.

17.5.7.1.31 exp(float_complex)

exp
```
float_complex exp(float_complex x);
```
Returns the exponential of *x*.

17.5.7.1.32 imag(float_complex)

imag
```
float imag(float_complex x);
```
Returns the imaginary part of *x*.

17.5.7.1.33 log(float_complex)

log
```
float_complex log(float_complex x);
```
Returns the logarithm of *x*.

17.5.7.1.34 norm(float_complex)

norm
```
float norm(float_complex x);
```
Returns the squared magnitude of *x*.

17.5.7.1.35 polar(float, float)

polar
```
float_complex polar(float rho, float theta);
```

Returns the **float_complex** value corresponding to a complex number whose magnitude is **rho** and whose phase angle is **theta**.

17.5.7.1.36 pow(float_complex, float_complex)

```
float_complex pow(float_complex x, float_complex y);
```
Returns **x** raised to the power **y**.

17.5.7.1.37 pow(float_complex, float)

```
float_complex pow(float_complex x, float y);
```
Returns **x** raised to the power **y**.

17.5.7.1.38 pow(float_complex, int)

```
float_complex pow(float_complex x, int y);
```
Returns **x** raised to the power **y**.

17.5.7.1.39 pow(float, float_complex)

```
float_complex pow(float x, float_complex y);
```
Returns **x** raised to the power **y**.

17.5.7.1.40 real(float_complex)

```
float real(float_complex x);
```
Returns the real part of **x**.

17.5.7.1.41 sin(float_complex)

```
float_complex sin(float_complex x);
```
Returns the sine of **x**.

17.5.7.1.42 sinh(float_complex)

```
float_complex sinh(float_complex x);
```
Returns the hyperbolic sine of **x**.

17.5.7.1.43 sqrt(float_complex)

```
float_complex sqrt(float_complex x);
```
Returns the square root of **x**.

17.5.7.2 Complex numbers with double precision

17.5.7.2.1 Class double_complex

```
class double_complex {
public:
    double_complex(re_arg = 0, im_arg = 0);
    double_complex(const float_complex& rhs);
    double_complex& operator+=(double_complex rhs);
    double_complex& operator-=(double_complex rhs);
    double_complex& operator*=(double_complex rhs);
    double_complex& operator/=(double_complex rhs);
private:
//  double re, im;                              exposition only
};
```

The class **double_complex** describes an object that can store the Cartesian components, of type **double**, of a complex number.

For the sake of exposition, the maintained data is presented here as:

- **double re**, the real component;
- **double im**, the imaginary component.

constructor

17.5.7.2.1.1 `double_complex::double_complex(double, double)`

```
double_complex(double re_arg = 0, im_arg = 0);
```

Constructs an object of class **double_complex**, initializing *re* to *re_arg* and *im* to *im_arg*.

constructor

17.5.7.2.1.2 `double_complex::double_complex(float_complex&)`

```
double_complex(float_complex& rhs);
```

Constructs an object of class **double_complex**, initializing *re* to **(double)real(*rhs*)** and *im* to **(double)imag(*rhs*)**.

operator+=

17.5.7.2.1.3 `operator+=(double_complex)`

```
double_complex& operator+=(double_complex rhs);
```

Adds the complex value *rhs* to the complex value ***this** and stores the sum in ***this**. The function returns ***this**.

operator-=

17.5.7.2.1.4 `operator-=(double_complex)`

```
double_complex& operator-=(double_complex rhs);
```

Subtracts the complex value *rhs* from the complex value ***this** and stores the difference in ***this**. The function returns ***this**.

operator*=

17.5.7.2.1.5 `operator*=(double_complex)`

```
double_complex& operator*=(double_complex rhs);
```

Multiplies the complex value *rhs* by the complex value ***this** and stores the product in ***this**. The function returns ***this**.

operator/=

17.5.7.2.1.6 `operator/=(double_complex)`

```
double_complex& operator/=(double_complex rhs);
```

Divides the complex value *rhs* into the complex value ***this** and stores the quotient in ***this**. The function returns ***this**.

**_double_
complex**

17.5.7.2.2 `_double_complex(const long_double_complex&)`

```
double_complex _double_complex(
    const long_double_complex& rhs);
```

Returns
double_complex((double)real(*rhs*), (double)imag(*rhs*)).

operator+

17.5.7.2.3 `operator+(double_complex, double_complex)`

```
double_complex operator+(double_complex lhs,
    double_complex rhs);
```

Returns **double_complex(*lhs*) += *rhs***.

operator+

17.5.7.2.4 `operator+(double_complex, double)`

```
double_complex operator+(double_complex lhs, double rhs);
```

Returns **double_complex(*lhs*) += double_complex(*rhs*)**.

operator+

17.5.7.2.5 `operator+(double, double_complex)`

```
double_complex operator+(double lhs, double_complex rhs);
```

Returns **double_complex(*lhs*) += *rhs***.

operator-

17.5.7.2.6 `operator-(double_complex, double_complex)`

```
double_complex operator-(double_complex lhs,
    double_complex rhs);
```

Returns **double_complex(*lhs*) -= *rhs***.

operator-

17.5.7.2.7 `operator-(double_complex, double)`

```
double_complex operator-(double_complex lhs, double rhs);
```

Returns `double_complex(`*`lhs`*`) -= double_complex(`*`rhs`*`)`.

17.5.7.2.8 operator-(double, double_complex)

operator-
```
double_complex operator-(double lhs, double_complex rhs);
```
Returns `double_complex(`*`lhs`*`) -= `*`rhs`*.

17.5.7.2.9 operator*(double_complex, double_complex)

operator*
```
double_complex operator*(double_complex lhs,
    double_complex rhs);
```
Returns `double_complex(`*`lhs`*`) *= `*`rhs`*.

17.5.7.2.10 operator*(double_complex, double)

operator*
```
double_complex operator*(double_complex lhs, double rhs);
```
Returns `double_complex(`*`lhs`*`) *= double_complex(`*`rhs`*`)`.

17.5.7.2.11 operator*(double, double_complex)

operator*
```
double_complex operator*(double lhs, double_complex rhs);
```
Returns `double_complex(`*`lhs`*`) *= `*`rhs`*.

17.5.7.2.12 operator/(double_complex, double_complex)

operator/
```
double_complex operator/(double_complex lhs, double_complex
rhs);
```
Returns `double_complex(`*`lhs`*`) /= `*`rhs`*.

17.5.7.2.13 operator/(double_complex, double)

operator/
```
double_complex operator/(double_complex lhs, double rhs);
```
Returns `double_complex(`*`lhs`*`) /= double_complex(`*`rhs`*`)`.

17.5.7.2.14 operator/(double, double_complex)

operator/
```
double_complex operator/(double lhs, double_complex rhs);
```
Returns `double_complex(`*`lhs`*`) /= `*`rhs`*.

17.5.7.2.15 operator+(double_complex)

operator+
```
double_complex operator+(double_complex lhs);
```
Returns `double_complex(`*`lhs`*`)`.

17.5.7.2.16 operator-(double_complex)

operator-
```
double_complex operator-(double_complex lhs);
```
Returns `double_complex(-real(`*`lhs`*`), -imag(`*`lhs`*`))`.

17.5.7.2.17 operator==(double_complex, double_complex)

operator==
```
int operator==(double_complex lhs, double_complex rhs);
```
Returns `real(`*`lhs`*`) == real(`*`rhs`*`) && imag(`*`lhs`*`) == imag( `*`rhs`*`)`.

17.5.7.2.18 operator==(double_complex, double)

operator==
```
int operator==(double_complex lhs, double rhs);
```
Returns `real(`*`lhs`*`) == `*`rhs`* `&& imag(`*`lhs`*`) == 0`.

17.5.7.2.19 operator==(double, double_complex)

operator==
```
int operator==(double lhs, double_complex rhs);
```
Returns *`lhs`* `== real(`*`rhs`*`) && imag(`*`rhs`*`) == 0`.

17.5.7.2.20 operator!=(double_complex, double_complex)

operator!=
```
int operator!=(double_complex lhs, double_complex rhs);
```
Returns `real(`*`lhs`*`) != real(`*`rhs`*`) || imag(`*`lhs`*`) != imag( `*`rhs`*`)`.

17.5.7.2.21 operator!=(double_complex, double)

`operator!=`

```
int operator!=(double_complex lhs, double rhs);
```

Returns **real(***lhs***)** != ***rhs*** || **imag(***lhs***)** != 0.

17.5.7.2.22 operator!=(double, double_complex)

`operator!=`

```
int operator!=(double lhs, double_complex rhs);
```

Returns ***lhs*** != **real(***rhs***)** || **imag(***rhs***)** != 0.

17.5.7.2.23 operator>>(istream&, double_complex&)

`operator>>`

```
istream& operator>>(istream& is, double_complex& x);
```

Evaluates the expression:

```
is >> ch && ch == '('
&& is >> re >> ch && ch == ','
&& is >> im >> ch && ch == ')';
```

where ***ch*** is an object of type **char** and ***re*** and ***im*** are objects of type **double**. If the result is nonzero, the function assigns **double_complex(***re, im***)** to ***x***. The function returns ***is***.

17.5.7.2.24 operator<<(ostream&, double_complex)

`operator<<`

```
ostream& operator<<(ostream& os, double_complex x);
```

Returns ***os*** << '(' << **real(***x***)** << ',' << **imag(***x***)** << ')'.

17.5.7.2.25 abs(double_complex)

`abs`

```
double abs(double_complex x);
```

Returns the magnitude of ***x***.

17.5.7.2.26 arg(double_complex)

`arg`

```
double arg(double_complex x);
```

Returns the phase angle of ***x***.

17.5.7.2.27 conj(double_complex)

`conj`

```
double_complex conj(double_complex x);
```

Returns the conjugate of ***x***.

17.5.7.2.28 cos(double_complex)

`cos`

```
double_complex cos(double_complex x);
```

Returns the cosine of ***x***.

17.5.7.2.29 cosh(double_complex)

`cosh`

```
double_complex cosh(double_complex x);
```

Returns the hyperbolic cosine of ***x***.

17.5.7.2.30 exp(double_complex)

`exp`

```
double_complex exp(double_complex x);
```

Returns the exponential of ***x***.

17.5.7.2.31 imag(double_complex)

`imag`

```
double imag(double_complex x);
```

Returns the imaginary part of ***x***.

17.5.7.2.32 log(double_complex)

`log`

```
double_complex log(double_complex x);
```

Returns the logarithm of ***x***.

17.5.7.2.33 norm(double_complex)

`norm`

```
double norm(double_complex x);
```

Returns the squared magnitude of *x*.

17.5.7.2.34 polar(double, double)

polar
```
double_complex polar(double rho, double theta);
```
Returns the **double_complex** value corresponding to a complex number whose magnitude is *rho* and whose phase angle is *theta*.

17.5.7.2.35 pow(double_complex, double_complex)

pow
```
double_complex pow(double_complex x, double_complex y);
```
Returns *x* raised to the power *y*.

17.5.7.2.36 pow(double_complex, double)

pow
```
double_complex pow(double_complex x, double y);
```
Returns *x* raised to the power *y*.

17.5.7.2.37 pow(double_complex, int)

pow
```
double_complex pow(double_complex x, int y);
```
Returns *x* raised to the power *y*.

17.5.7.2.38 pow(double, double_complex)

pow
```
double_complex pow(double x, double_complex y);
```
Returns *x* raised to the power *y*.

17.5.7.2.39 real(double_complex)

real
```
double real(double_complex x);
```
Returns the real part of *x*.

17.5.7.2.40 sin(double_complex)

sin
```
double_complex sin(double_complex x);
```
Returns the sine of *x*.

17.5.7.2.41 sinh(double_complex)

sinh
```
double_complex sinh(double_complex x);
```
Returns the hyperbolic sine of *x*.

17.5.7.2.42 sqrt(double_complex)

sqrt
```
double_complex sqrt(double_complex x);
```
Returns the square root of *x*.

17.5.7.3 Complex numbers with long double precision

17.5.7.3.1 Class long_double_complex

Class
long_double_
complex
```
class long_double_complex {
public:
    long_double_complex(re_arg = 0, im_arg = 0);
    long_double_complex(const float_complex& rhs);
    long_double_complex(const double_complex& rhs);
    long_double_complex&
        operator+=(long_double_complex rhs);
    long_double_complex&
        operator-=(long_double_complex rhs);
    long_double_complex& operator*=(long_double_complex rhs);
    long_double_complex& operator/=(long_double_complex rhs);
private:
//  long double re, im;                            exposition only
};
```

The class **`long_double_complex`** describes an object that can store the Cartesian components, of type **`long double`**, of a complex number.

For the sake of exposition, the maintained data is presented here as:

- **`long double`** *`re`*, the real component;
- **`long double`** *`im`*, the imaginary component.

17.5.7.3.1.1 `long_double_complex::long_double_complex(long double, long double)`

constructor

`long_double_complex(long double re_arg = 0, im_arg = 0);`

Constructs an object of class **`long_double_complex`**, initializing *`re`* to *`re_arg`* and *`im`* to *`im_arg`*.

17.5.7.3.1.2 `long_double_complex::long_double_complex(float_complex&)`

constructor

`long_double_complex(float_complex& rhs);`

Constructs an object of class **`long_double_complex`**, initializing *`re`* to `(long double)real(rhs)` and *`im`* to `(long double)imag(rhs)`.

17.5.7.3.1.3 `long_double_complex::long_double_complex(double_complex&)`

constructor

`long_double_complex(double_complex& rhs);`

Constructs an object of class **`long_double_complex`**, initializing *`re`* to `(long double)real(rhs)` and *`im`* to `(long double)imag(rhs)`.

17.5.7.3.1.4 `operator+=(long_double_complex)`

operator+=

`long_double_complex& operator+=(long_double_complex rhs);`

Adds the complex value *`rhs`* to the complex value **`*this`** and stores the sum in **`*this`**. The function returns **`*this`**.

17.5.7.3.1.5 `operator-=(long_double_complex)`

operator-=

`long_double_complex& operator-=(long_double_complex rhs);`

Subtracts the complex value *`rhs`* from the complex value **`*this`** and stores the difference in **`*this`**. The function returns **`*this`**.

17.5.7.3.1.6 `operator*=(long_double_complex)`

operator*=

`long_double_complex& operator*=(long_double_complex rhs);`

Multiplies the complex value *`rhs`* by the complex value **`*this`** and stores the product in **`*this`**. The function returns **`*this`**.

17.5.7.3.1.7 `operator/=(long_double_complex)`

operator/=

`long_double_complex& operator/=(long_double_complex rhs);`

Divides the complex value *`rhs`* into the complex value **`*this`** and stores the quotient in **`*this`**. The function returns **`*this`**.

17.5.7.3.2 `operator+(long_double_complex, long_double_complex)`

operator+

`long_double_complex operator+(long_double_complex lhs, long_double_complex rhs);`

Returns **`long_double_complex(lhs) += rhs`**.

17.5.7.3.3 `operator+(long_double_complex, long double)`

operator+

`long_double_complex operator+(long_double_complex lhs, long double rhs);`

Returns
`long_double_complex(lhs) += long_double_complex(rhs)`.

operator+

17.5.7.3.4 operator+(long double, long_double_complex)

```
long_double_complex operator+(long double lhs,
    long_double_complex rhs);
```

Returns `long_double_complex(lhs) += rhs`.

17.5.7.3.5 operator-(long_double_complex, long_double_complex)

operator-

```
long_double_complex operator-(long_double_complex lhs,
    long_double_complex rhs);
```

Returns `long_double_complex(lhs) -= rhs`.

17.5.7.3.6 operator-(long_double_complex, long double)

operator-

```
long_double_complex operator-(long_double_complex lhs,
    long double rhs);
```

Returns
`long_double_complex(lhs) -= long_double_complex(rhs)`.

17.5.7.3.7 operator-(long double, long_double_complex)

operator-

```
long_double_complex operator-(long double lhs,
    long_double_complex rhs);
```

Returns `long_double_complex(lhs) -= rhs`.

17.5.7.3.8 operator*(long_double_complex, long_double_complex)

operator*

```
long_double_complex operator*(long_double_complex lhs,
    long_double_complex rhs);
```

Returns `long_double_complex(lhs) *= rhs`.

17.5.7.3.9 operator*(long_double_complex, long double)

operator*

```
long_double_complex operator*(long_double_complex lhs,
    long double rhs);
```

Returns
`long_double_complex(lhs) *= long_double_complex(rhs)`.

17.5.7.3.10 operator*(long double, long_double_complex)

operator*

```
long_double_complex operator*(long double lhs,
    long_double_complex rhs);
```

Returns `long_double_complex(lhs) *= rhs`.

17.5.7.3.11 operator/(long_double_complex, long_double_complex)

operator/

```
long_double_complex operator/(long_double_complex lhs,
    long_double_complex rhs);
```

Returns `long_double_complex(lhs) /= rhs`.

17.5.7.3.12 operator/(long_double_complex, long double)

operator/

```
long_double_complex operator/(long_double_complex lhs,
    long double rhs);
```

Returns
`long_double_complex(lhs) /= long_double_complex( rhs)`.

17.5.7.3.13 operator/(long double, long_double_complex)

operator/

```
long_double_complex operator/(long double lhs,
    long_double_complex rhs);
```

Returns `long_double_complex(lhs) /= rhs`.

operator+

17.5.7.3.14 operator+(long_double_complex)

```
long_double_complex operator+(long_double_complex lhs);
```

Returns `long_double_complex(lhs)`.

operator-

17.5.7.3.15 operator-(long_double_complex)

```
long_double_complex operator-(long_double_complex lhs);
```

Returns `long_double_complex(-real(lhs), -imag(lhs))`.

operator==

17.5.7.3.16 operator==(long_double_complex, long_double_complex)

```
int operator==(long_double_complex lhs,
    long_double_complex rhs);
```

Returns `real(lhs) == real(rhs) && imag(lhs) == imag( rhs)`.

operator==

17.5.7.3.17 operator==(long_double_complex, long double)

```
int operator==(long_double_complex lhs, long double rhs);
```

Returns `real(lhs) == rhs && imag(lhs) == 0`.

operator==

17.5.7.3.18 operator==(long double, long_double_complex)

```
int operator==(long double lhs, long_double_complex rhs);
```

Returns `lhs == real(rhs) && imag(rhs) == 0`.

operator!=

17.5.7.3.19 operator!=(long_double_complex, long_double_complex)

```
int operator!=(long_double_complex lhs,
    long_double_complex rhs);
```

Returns `real(lhs) != real(rhs) || imag(lhs) != imag(rhs)`.

operator!=

17.5.7.3.20 operator!=(long_double_complex, long double)

```
int operator!=(long_double_complex lhs, long double rhs);
```

Returns `real(lhs) != rhs || imag(lhs) != 0`.

operator!=

17.5.7.3.21 operator!=(long double, long_double_complex)

```
int operator!=(long double lhs, long_double_complex rhs);
```

Returns `lhs != real(rhs) || imag(rhs) != 0`.

operator>>

17.5.7.3.22 operator>>(istream&, long_double_complex&)

```
istream& operator>>(istream& is, long_double_complex& x);
```

Evaluates the expression:

```
is >> ch && ch == '('
&& is >> re >> ch && ch == ','
&& is >> im >> ch && ch == ')';
```

where `ch` is an object of type `char` and `re` and `im` are objects of type `long double`. If the result is nonzero, the function assigns `long_double_complex(re, im)` to `x`.

The function returns `is`.

operator<<

17.5.7.3.23 operator<<(ostream&, long_double_complex)

```
ostream& operator<<(ostream& os, long_double_complex x);
```

Returns `os << '(' << real(x) << ',' << imag(x) << ')'`.

abs

17.5.7.3.24 abs(long_double_complex)

```
long double abs(long_double_complex x);
```

Returns the magnitude of `x`.

17.5.7.3.25 arg(long_double_complex)

arg

```
long double arg(long_double_complex x);
```
Returns the phase angle of **x**.

17.5.7.3.26 conj(long_double_complex)

conj

```
long_double_complex conj(long_double_complex x);
```
Returns the conjugate of **x**.

17.5.7.3.27 cos(long_double_complex)

cos

```
long_double_complex cos(long_double_complex x);
```
Returns the cosine of **x**.

17.5.7.3.28 cosh(long_double_complex)

cosh

```
long_double_complex cosh(long_double_complex x);
```
Returns the hyperbolic cosine of **x**.

17.5.7.3.29 exp(long_double_complex)

exp

```
long_double_complex exp(long_double_complex x);
```
Returns the exponential of **x**.

17.5.7.3.30 imag(long_double_complex)

imag

```
long double imag(long_double_complex x);
```
Returns the imaginary part of **x**.

17.5.7.3.31 log(long_double_complex)

log

```
long_double_complex log(long_double_complex x);
```
Returns the logarithm of **x**.

17.5.7.3.32 norm(long_double_complex)

norm

```
long double norm(long_double_complex x);
```
Returns the squared magnitude of **x**.

17.5.7.3.33 polar(long double, long double)

polar

```
long_double_complex polar(long double rho, long double theta);
```
Returns the **long_double_complex** value corresponding to a complex number whose magnitude is **rho** and whose phase angle is **theta**.

17.5.7.3.34 pow(long_double_complex, long_double_complex)

pow

```
long_double_complex pow(long_double_complex x,
    long_double_complex y);
```
Returns **x** raised to the power **y**.

17.5.7.3.35 pow(long_double_complex, long double)

pow

```
long_double_complex pow(long_double_complex x, long double y);
```
Returns **x** raised to the power **y**.

17.5.7.3.36 pow(long_double_complex, int)

pow

```
long_double_complex pow(long_double_complex x, int y);
```
Returns **x** raised to the power **y**.

17.5.7.3.37 pow(long double, long_double_complex)

pow

```
long_double_complex pow(long double x, long_double_complex y);
```
Returns **x** raised to the power **y**.

17.5.7.3.38 real(long_double_complex)

real

```
long double real(long_double_complex x);
```

Returns the real part of *x*.

17.5.7.3.39 sin(long_double_complex)

sin |
```
long_double_complex sin(long_double_complex x);
```
Returns the sine of *x*.

17.5.7.3.40 sinh(long_double_complex)

sinh |
```
long_double_complex sinh(long_double_complex x);
```
Returns the hyperbolic sine of *x*.

17.5.7.3.41 sqrt(long_double_complex)

sqrt |
```
long_double_complex sqrt(long_double_complex x);
```
Returns the square root of *x*.

Future Directions

Strong sentiment exists for using templates to capture the parallelism between the three complex arithmetic classes defined in **<complex>**. Unfortunately, template technology does not yet provide an easy way to handle the asymmetric conversion rules that many programmers find desirable for these classes.

Using **<complex>**

You include the header **<complex>** to make use of any of the three classes **float_complex**, **double_complex**, or **long_double_complex**. Objects of any of these classes let you represent complex values to a given floating-point precision. Numerous functions, overloaded for all three classes, perform many of the mathematical operations defined for complex values.

__STD_COMPLEX The header defines the macro **__STD_COMPLEX** as a reassurance. Presumably, you can write code such as:

```
#if !defined(__STD_COMPLEX)
 #error WRONG COMPLEX LIBRARY
#endif
```

The program should fail to translate if the implementation supplies a nonconforming version of the header **<complex>**. Unless you are *very* serious about writing highly portable code, you can probably omit such tests.

construction You can construct an object of a floating-point class in several ways:

```
float_complex f0;                    // becomes (0.0F, 0.0F)
float_complex f1(3.0F);              // becomes (3.0F, 0.0F)
float_complex f2(3.0, -2)            // becomes (3.0F, -2.0F)
double_complex d0;                   // becomes (0.0, 0.0)
double_complex d1(3.0F);             // becomes (3.0, 0.0)
double_complex d2(3.0, -2);          // becomes (3.0, -2.0)
double_complex d3(f1);               // becomes (3.0, 0.0)
long_double_complex ld0;             // becomes (0.0L, 0.0L)
long_double_complex ld1(3.0F);       // becomes (3.0L, 0.0L)
long_double_complex ld2(3.0, -2);    // becomes (3.0L, -2.0L)
long_double_complex ld3(f1);         // becomes (3.0L, 0.0L)
long_double_complex ld3(d2);         // becomes (3.0L, -2.0L)
```

In other words, you can specify in a complex class constructor: no components, just the real component, or both real and imaginary components of a complex value. Any components you omit become zero. You can also construct a complex class object from a complex class object of the same or lower precision. (I don't show the same-precision case, since that is the usual default copy constructor.) These single-argument constructors also supply a number of useful implicit conversions, in a variety of contexts. Thus, for example, you can often write a *double* value (real component) or a **float_complex** value where a **double_complex** value is required.

float complex   You can also convert to a complex class of lower precision by explicitly calling a conversion function. Using the objects declared in the examples above, you can write any of:

double complex
```
f0 = _float_complex(d1);
f0 = _float_complex(ld1);
d0 = _double_complex(ld1);
```

Naturally, such conversions can result in floating-point overflow, underflow, or loss of precision, in either or both components of the converted value. Use them cautiously.

notation   All other functions are common to all three complex classes. For brevity in describing them, I introduce the following common notation:

- **TC** is the complex class, such as **float_complex**.

- **T** is the corresponding floating-point type, such as *float*.

- **x0** and **x1** are objects of class **TC**.

- **f** is a value of type **T**.

I explain any other notation as needed.

arithmetic operators   The following arithmetic operators are overloaded for each of the complex classes. The operators have their usual arithmetic meaning, as extended into the complex plane:

```
x0 += x1        x0 + x1         x0 + f          f + x0
x0 -= x1        x0 - x1         x0 - f          f - x0
x0 *= x1        x0 * x1         x0 * f          f * x0
x0 /= x1        x0 / x1         x0 / f          f / x0
+x0             x0 == x1        x0 == f         f == x0
-x0             x0 != x1        x0 != f         f != x0
```

A number of functions are also overloaded for each of the complex classes. One group returns a value of type **T**:

abs   ■   **abs(x0)**, returns the magnitude of **x0** (the ρ polar component)

arg   ■   **arg(x0)**, returns the argument of **x0** (the θ polar component)

imag   ■   **imag(x0)**, returns the imaginary component of **x0** (the y Cartesian component)

norm   ■   **norm(x0)**, returns the squared magnitude of **x0** ($x^2 + y^2$)

real   ■   **real(x0)**, returns the imaginary component of **x0** (the x Cartesian component)

Note that a class **TC** supplies *no* member functions for accessing the stored components of the complex value. Use the above functions instead.

Another group of functions returns a value of type **TC**:

conjg ■ **conjg(x0)**, returns the conjugate of **x0** (the value *x–i*y*) in Cartesian components)

cos ■ **cos(x0)**, returns the cosine of **x0**

cosh ■ **cosh(x0)**, returns the hyperbolic cosine of **x0**

exp ■ **exp(x0)**, returns the exponential of **x0**

log ■ **log(x0)**, returns the natural logarithm of **x0**

polar ■ **polar(rho, theta)**, returns the complex value corresponding to the magnitude **rho** and argument **theta**, both of type **F**

pow ■ **pow(x0, x1)**, returns **x0** raised to the power **x1**

pow ■ **pow(f, x1)**, returns **f** raised to the power **x1**

pow ■ **pow(x0, f)**, returns **x0** raised to the power **f**

pow ■ **pow(x0, i)**, returns **x0** raised to the power **i**, where **i** has type *int*

sin ■ **sin(x0)**, returns the sine of **x0**

sinh ■ **sinh(x0)**, returns the hyperbolic sine of **x0**

sqrt ■ **sqrt(x0)**, returns the square root of **x0**

Finally, you can insert and extract objects of class **c**. For example:

extractor   `cin >> x0`

extracts a pair of Cartesian component values from the standard input stream, constructs from them an object of class **TC**, and assigns it to **x0**. The components are enclosed in parentheses and separated by a comma, as in **(2, -4.5)**.

And last of all, you can insert an object of class **TC** into, say, the standard output stream, by writing:

inserter   `cout << x0`

As you might expect, the components have a format acceptable to the extractor, above, such as **(2,-4.5)**. Format flags have their usual effect on each of the floating-point components. (See the general discussion beginning on page 124.) Be warned, however, that a nonzero width field affects only the first of the two components. It is set to zero, as usual, after the first floating-point component is inserted.

Implementing `<complex>`

complex   Figure 21.1 shows the file **complex**, which implements the standard header **<complex>**. It is very large, one of the largest files in this book. Nevertheless, it is also one of the simpler headers. Most of its bulk results from saying almost exactly the same thing for each of the three complex classes **float_complex**, **double_complex**, and **long_double_complex**. You should encounter just one or two surprises.

_Real   One surprise is the addition to each class of the secret member functions
_Imag   **_Real** and **_Imag**. These, of course, let you access the stored values of the two Cartesian components. I chose to add these member functions rather than make *friend* functions of **real** and **imag**.

```
// complex standard header
#ifndef _COMPLEX_
#define _COMPLEX_
#include <istream>
#include <ostream>
#define __STD_COMPLEX
                // class float_complex
class float_complex {
public:
    float_complex(float _R = 0, float _I = 0)
        : _Re(_R), _Im(_I) {}
    float_complex operator+=(float_complex _R)
        {_Re += _R._Real(), _Im += _R._Imag();
        return (*this); }
    float_complex operator-=(float_complex _R)
        {_Re -= _R._Real(), _Im -= _R._Imag();
        return (*this); }
    float_complex operator*=(float_complex);
    float_complex operator/=(float_complex);
    float _Real() const
        {return (_Re); }
    float _Imag() const
        {return (_Im); }
private:
    float _Re, _Im;
    };
                // class double_complex
class double_complex {
public:
    double_complex(double _R = 0, double _I = 0)
        : _Re(_R), _Im(_I) {}
    double_complex operator+=(double_complex _R)
        {_Re += _R._Real(), _Im += _R._Imag();
        return (*this); }
    double_complex operator-=(double_complex _R)
        {_Re -= _R._Real(), _Im -= _R._Imag();
        return (*this); }
    double_complex operator*=(double_complex);
    double_complex operator/=(double_complex);
    double _Real() const
        {return (_Re); }
    double _Imag() const
        {return (_Im); }
private:
    double _Re, _Im;
    };
                // class long_double_complex
class long_double_complex {
public:
    long_double_complex(long double _R = 0, long double _I = 0)
        : _Re(_R), _Im(_I) {}
    long_double_complex operator+=(long_double_complex _R)
        {_Re += _R._Real(), _Im += _R._Imag();
        return (*this); }
    long_double_complex operator-=(long_double_complex _R)
```

```
                    {_Re -= _R._Real(), _Im -= _R._Imag();
                    return (*this); }
            long_double_complex operator*=(long_double_complex);
            long_double_complex operator/=(long_double_complex);
            long double _Real() const
                    {return (_Re); }
            long double _Imag() const
                    {return (_Im); }
    private:
            long double _Re, _Im;
            };
                    // type definitions
    typedef float_complex _FC;
    typedef double_complex _DC;
    typedef long_double_complex _LDC;
                    // float_complex functions
    inline float imag(_FC _X)
            {return (_X._Imag()); }
    inline float real(_FC _X)
            {return (_X._Real()); }
    inline _FC _float_complex(const _DC& _X)
            {return (_FC((float)_X._Real(), (float)_X._Imag())); }
    inline _FC _float_complex(const _LDC& _X)
            {return (_FC((float)_X._Real(), (float)_X._Imag())); }
    inline _FC operator+(_FC _L, _FC _R)
            {return (_L += _R); }
    inline _FC operator+(_FC _L, float _R)
            {return (_L += _R); }
    inline _FC operator+(float _L, _FC _R)
            {return (_FC(_L) += _R); }
    inline _FC operator-(_FC _L, _FC _R)
            {return (_L -= _R); }
    inline _FC operator-(_FC _L, float _R)
            {return (_L -= _R); }
    inline _FC operator-(float _L, _FC _R)
            {return (_FC(_L) -= _R); }
    inline _FC operator*(_FC _L, _FC _R)
            {return (_L *= _R); }
    inline _FC operator*(_FC _L, float _R)
            {return (_L *= _R); }
    inline _FC operator*(float _L, _FC _R)
            {return (_FC(_L) *= _R); }
    inline _FC operator/(_FC _L, _FC _R)
            {return (_L /= _R); }
    inline _FC operator/(_FC _L, float _R)
            {return (_L /= _R); }
    inline _FC operator/(float _L, _FC _R)
            {return (_FC(_L) /= _R); }
    inline _FC operator+(_FC _L)
            {return (_L); }
    inline _FC operator-(_FC _L)
            {return (_FC(-real(_L), -imag(_L))); }
    inline _Bool operator==(_FC _L, _FC _R)
            {return (real(_L) == real(_R) && imag(_L) == imag(_R)); }
    inline _Bool operator==(_FC _L, float _R)
```

```
        {return (real(_L) == _R && imag(_L) == 0); }
inline _Bool operator==(float _L, _FC _R)
        {return (_L == real(_R) && 0 == imag(_R)); }
inline _Bool operator!=(_FC _L, _FC _R)
        {return (!(_L == _R)); }
inline _Bool operator!=(_FC _L, float _R)
        {return (!(_L == _R)); }
inline _Bool operator!=(float _L, _FC _R)
        {return (!(_L == _R)); }
istream& operator>>(istream&, _FC&);
ostream& operator<<(ostream&, _FC);
float abs(_FC);
float arg(_FC);
inline _FC conj(_FC _X)
        {return (_FC(real(_X), -imag(_X))); }
_FC cos(_FC);
_FC cosh(_FC);
_FC exp(_FC);
_FC log(_FC);
inline float norm(_FC _X)
        {return (real(_X) * real(_X) + imag(_X) * imag(_X)); }
_FC polar(float, float);
_FC pow(_FC, _FC);
_FC pow(_FC, float);
_FC pow(_FC, int);
_FC pow(float, _FC);
_FC sin(_FC);
_FC sinh(_FC);
_FC sqrt(_FC);
                // double_complex functions
inline double imag(_DC _X)
        {return (_X._Imag()); }
inline double real(_DC _X)
        {return (_X._Real()); }
inline _DC _double_complex(const _LDC& _X)
        {return (_DC((double)_X._Real(), (double)_X._Imag())); }
inline _DC operator+(_DC _L, _DC _R)
        {return (_L += _R); }
inline _DC operator+(_DC _L, double _R)
        {return (_L += _R); }
inline _DC operator+(double _L, _DC _R)
        {return (_DC(_L) += _R); }
inline _DC operator-(_DC _L, _DC _R)
        {return (_L -= _R); }
inline _DC operator-(_DC _L, double _R)
        {return (_L -= _R); }
inline _DC operator-(double _L, _DC _R)
        {return (_DC(_L) -= _R); }
inline _DC operator*(_DC _L, _DC _R)
        {return (_L *= _R); }
inline _DC operator*(_DC _L, double _R)
        {return (_L *= _R); }
inline _DC operator*(double _L, _DC _R)
        {return (_DC(_L) *= _R); }
inline _DC operator/(_DC _L, _DC _R)
```

```
        {return (_L /= _R); }
inline _DC operator/(_DC _L, double _R)
        {return (_L /= _R); }
inline _DC operator/(double _L, _DC _R)
        {return (_DC(_L) /= _R); }
inline _DC operator+(_DC _L)
        {return (_L); }
inline _DC operator-(_DC _L)
        {return (_DC(-real(_L), -imag(_L))); }
inline _Bool operator==(_DC _L, _DC _R)
        {return (real(_L) == real(_R) && imag(_L) == imag(_R)); }
inline _Bool operator==(_DC _L, double _R)
        {return (real(_L) == _R && imag(_L) == 0); }
inline _Bool operator==(double _L, _DC _R)
        {return (_L == real(_R) && 0 == imag(_R)); }
inline _Bool operator!=(_DC _L, _DC _R)
        {return (!(_L == _R)); }
inline _Bool operator!=(_DC _L, double _R)
        {return (!(_L == _R)); }
inline _Bool operator!=(double _L, _DC _R)
        {return (!(_L == _R)); }
istream& operator>>(istream&, _DC&);
ostream& operator<<(ostream&, _DC);
double abs(_DC);
double arg(_DC);
inline _DC conj(_DC _X)
        {return (_DC(real(_X), -imag(_X))); }
_DC cos(_DC);
_DC cosh(_DC);
_DC exp(_DC);
_DC log(_DC);
inline double norm(_DC _X)
        {return (real(_X) * real(_X) + imag(_X) * imag(_X)); }
_DC polar(double, double);
_DC pow(_DC, _DC);
_DC pow(_DC, double);
_DC pow(_DC, int);
_DC pow(double, _DC);
_DC sin(_DC);
_DC sinh(_DC);
_DC sqrt(_DC);
            // long_double_complex functions
inline long double imag(_LDC _X)
        {return (_X._Imag()); }
inline long double real(_LDC _X)
        {return (_X._Real()); }
inline _LDC operator+(_LDC _L, _LDC _R)
        {return (_L += _R); }
inline _LDC operator+(_LDC _L, long double _R)
        {return (_L += _R); }
inline _LDC operator+(long double _L, _LDC _R)
        {return (_LDC(_L) += _R); }
inline _LDC operator-(_LDC _L, _LDC _R)
        {return (_L -= _R); }
inline _LDC operator-(_LDC _L, long double _R)
```

```
        {return (_L -= _R); }
inline _LDC operator-(long double _L, _LDC _R)
        {return (_LDC(_L) -= _R); }
inline _LDC operator*(_LDC _L, _LDC _R)
        {return (_L *= _R); }
inline _LDC operator*(_LDC _L, long double _R)
        {return (_L *= _R); }
inline _LDC operator*(long double _L, _LDC _R)
        {return (_LDC(_L) *= _R); }
inline _LDC operator/(_LDC _L, _LDC _R)
        {return (_L /= _R); }
inline _LDC operator/(_LDC _L, long double _R)
        {return (_L /= _R); }
inline _LDC operator/(long double _L, _LDC _R)
        {return (_LDC(_L) /= _R); }
inline _LDC operator+(_LDC _L)
        {return (_L); }
inline _LDC operator-(_LDC _L)
        {return (_LDC(-real(_L), -imag(_L))); }
inline _Bool operator==(_LDC _L, _LDC _R)
        {return (real(_L) == real(_R) && imag(_L) == imag(_R)); }
inline _Bool operator==(_LDC _L, long double _R)
        {return (real(_L) == _R && imag(_L) == 0); }
inline _Bool operator==(long double _L, _LDC _R)
        {return (_L == real(_R) && 0 == imag(_R)); }
inline _Bool operator!=(_LDC _L, _LDC _R)
        {return (!(_L == _R)); }
inline _Bool operator!=(_LDC _L, long double _R)
        {return (!(_L == _R)); }
inline _Bool operator!=(long double _L, _LDC _R)
        {return (!(_L == _R)); }
istream& operator>>(istream&, _LDC&);
ostream& operator<<(ostream&, _LDC);
long double abs(_LDC);
long double arg(_LDC);
inline _LDC conj(_LDC _X)
        {return (_LDC(real(_X), -imag(_X))); }
_LDC cos(_LDC);
_LDC cosh(_LDC);
_LDC exp(_LDC);
_LDC log(_LDC);
inline long double norm(_LDC _X)
        {return (real(_X) * real(_X) + imag(_X) * imag(_X)); }
_LDC polar(long double, long double);
_LDC pow(_LDC, _LDC);
_LDC pow(_LDC, long double);
_LDC pow(_LDC, int);
_LDC pow(long double, _LDC);
_LDC sin(_LDC);
_LDC sinh(_LDC);
_LDC sqrt(_LDC);
#endif
```

The other surprise is the introduction of three abbreviations:

_FC   ■   _FC, for **float_complex**
_DC   ■   _DC, for **double_complex**
_LDC ■   _LDC, for **long_double_complex**

I wrote most of the header in terms of these type definitions to minimize the folding of long lines. Otherwise, the file would be noticeably longer.

The header supplies inline definitions of all the trivial functions. All other function definitions inhabit a host of additional source files. In principle, these source files come in sets of three, one version for each complex class. In practice, I found such triplets repeated a lot of code, but were just different enough to make for a maintenance headache. So I settled on a slightly unorthodox organization for all this code.

xcomplex   The most orthodox part of the approach is to add an internal header, to capture declarations and definitions needed across all functions. Figure 21.2 shows the file **xcomplex**, which implements the internal header **<xcomplex>**. Unlike the often used internal header **<yxvals.h>**, it is *not* intended to be included in any user-supplied translation units, either directly or indirectly. Only the source files that define functions declared in **<complex>** need include **<xcomplex>**.

An important role for **<xcomplex>** is to define two types and a macro:

TC   ■   **TC** is the complex class, such as **float_complex**.
T   ■   **T** is the corresponding floating-point type, such as *float*.
XFLOAT ■ **_XFLOAT_** is the macro guard that, once defined, prevents a redefinition of **TC** and **T**.

xfloat   The obvious effect of including **<xcomplex>** is to define **TC** as class **double_complex** and **T** as type *double*. Less obvious is the effect of first defining these types another way. For example, Figure 21.3 shows the file **xfloat**, which implements yet another secret internal header **<xfloat>**. Consider the effect of including this header. It first defines the macro guard **_XFLOAT_**, then includes the header **<xcomplex>**. It is then free to define **TC** as class **float_complex** and **T** as type *float*.

Now for the rest of the trick. Consider, for example, the file **dcabs.c**, described later in this chapter, which defines the function **abs**. It includes the header **<xcomplex>**. Translating this source file yields a definition for **abs(double_complex)**, as you will soon see. Nothing unusual here. But the corresponding file **fcabs.c** can simply read:

fcabs.c
```
// fcabs -- abs(float_complex)
#include <xfloat>
#include "dcabs.c"
```

Translating this source file yields a definition for **abs(float_complex)**. While it is unusual to include a source file in this way, it is perfectly permissible. The effect is a kind of poor man's template instantiation. I chose this method, instead of the more modern template notation, simply because the latter is still not universally supported. Since **fcabs.c** and its ilk are trivial and repetitious, I don't show them in this book.

```
// xcomplex internal header -- PJP C LIBRARY VERSION
#ifndef _XCOMPLEX_
#define _XCOMPLEX_
#include "xmath.h"
#include <complex>
 #ifndef _XFLOAT_
 #define _XFLOAT_
typedef double T;                        // default base type is double
typedef double_complex TC;
 #endif
            // float functions
inline float _Cosh(float _X, float _Y)
    {return (_FCosh(_X, _Y)); }
inline short _Exp(float *_P, float _Y, short _E)
    {return (_FExp(_P, _Y, _E)); }
float _Fabs(float_complex, int *);
inline float _Infv(float)
    {return (_FInf._F); }
inline _Bool _Isinf(float _X)
    {return (_FDtest(&_X) == INF); }
inline _Bool _Isnan(float _X)
    {return (_FDtest(&_X) == NAN); }
inline float _Nanv(float)
    {return (_FNan._F); }
inline float _Sinh(float _X, float _Y)
    {return (_FSinh(_X, _Y)); }
inline float atan2(float _Y, float _X)
    {return (atan2f(_Y, _X)); }
inline float cos(float _X)
    {return (cosf(_X)); }
inline float exp(float _X)
    {return (expf(_X)); }
inline float ldexp(float _R, int _E)
    {return (ldexpf(_R, _E)); }
inline float log(float _X)
    {return (logf(_X)); }
inline float pow(float _X, float _Y)
    {return (powf(_X, _Y)); }
inline float sin(float _X)
    {return (sinf(_X)); }
inline float sqrt(float _X)
    {return (sqrtf(_X)); }
            // double functions
double _Fabs(double_complex, int *);
inline double _Infv(double)
    {return (_Inf._D); }
inline _Bool _Isinf(double _X)
    {return (_Dtest(&_X) == INF); }
inline _Bool _Isnan(double _X)
    {return (_Dtest(&_X) == NAN); }
inline double _Nanv(double)
    {return (_Nan._D); }
            // long double functions
inline long double _Cosh(long double _X, long double _Y)
    {return (_LCosh(_X, _Y)); }
```

Continuing
xcomplex
Part 2 of 2

```
inline short _Exp(long double *_P, long double _Y, short _E)
     {return (_LExp(_P, _Y, _E)); }
long double _Fabs(long_double_complex, int *);
inline long double _Infv(long double)
     {return (_LInf._L); }
inline _Bool _Isinf(long double _X)
     {return (_LDtest(&_X) == INF); }
inline _Bool _Isnan(long double _X)
     {return (_LDtest(&_X) == NAN); }
inline long double _Nanv(long double)
     {return (_LNan._L); }
inline long double _Sinh(long double _X, long double _Y)
     {return (_LSinh(_X, _Y)); }
inline long double atan2(long double _Y, long double _X)
     {return (atan2l(_Y, _X)); }
inline long double cos(long double _X)
     {return (cosl(_X)); }
inline long double exp(long double _X)
     {return (expl(_X)); }
inline long double ldexp(long double _R, int _E)
     {return (ldexpl(_R, _E)); }
inline long double log(long double _X)
     {return (logl(_X)); }
inline long double pow(long double _X, long double _Y)
     {return (powl(_X, _Y)); }
inline long double sin(long double _X)
     {return (sinl(_X)); }
inline long double sqrt(long double _X)
     {return (sqrtl(_X)); }
#endif
```

**Figure 21.3:
xfloat**

```
// xfloat internal header
#ifndef _XFLOAT_
#define _XFLOAT_
#include <xcomplex>
typedef float T;                          // base type is float
typedef float_complex TC;
#endif
```

**Figure 21.4:
xldouble**

```
// xldouble internal header
#ifndef _XFLOAT_
#define _XFLOAT_
#include <xcomplex>
typedef long double T;                 // base type is long double
typedef long_double_complex TC;
#endif
```

xldouble   Naturally, the same trick works for the third member of each triplet as well. Figure 21.4 shows the file **xldouble**, which implements the internal header **<xldouble>**. It defines the types needed to generate the **long_double_complex** version of each function definition (also not shown).

The other business of the header **<xcomplex>** is to define a number of internal functions used by many of the functions declared in **<complex>**. These internal functions perform calculations that need delicate attention to avoid spurious floating-point overflow, or to return exotic codes, or to test for those exotic codes.

<xmath.h> The version of the file **xcomplex** I show here is designed to work with an enhanced version of my implementation of the Standard C library (**Pla92**). It includes yet another secret header from that older library, called **<xmath.h>**. That header defines the magic functions used by the inline function definitions in **xcomplex**. To support the remaining source code in this chapter, you have three choices:

■ Use the enhanced Standard C library, which defines **<xmath.h>** as required.

■ Write your own version of the file **xmath.h**, as described more fully in Appendix A: Interfaces.

■ Write your own version of the file **xcomplex**, implementing the functions as described below.

Whichever approach you take, you should know what functions the header **<xcomplex>** must declare, either directly or indirectly. All are overloaded for all three complex classes and/or the corresponding floating-point type. All also implicitly assume floating-point arithmetic compatible with (or strongly resembling) the IEEE-754 Standard for floating-point arithmetic (**IEE85**). For a discussion of the merits of that assumption, see **Pla92**.

In the descriptions that follow, I call the complex class **TC** and the corresponding floating-point type **T**. Note that the function **_Fabs**, in all three precisions, is defined later in this chapter. It is the *only* function declared in **<xcomplex>** that is supplied as a separate source file here:

_Cosh ■ **T _Cosh(T x, T y)** returns **y** times the hyperbolic cosine of **x**.

_Exp ■ **T _Exp(T *px, T y, short e)** returns **y** times the exponential of ***px** times 2 raised to the **e** power.

_Fabs ■ **T _Fabs(TC x0, int *pe)** stores a scale factor in ***pe** and returns the value **z** such that the magnitude of **x0** is **z** times 2 raised to the ***pe** power. For any finite **z**, ***pe** is nonzero and even.

_Infv ■ **T _Infv(T)** returns the code for infinity, or Inf. The argument value is unused.

_Isinf ■ **_Bool _Isinf(T x)** returns a nonzero value if **x** is any code for infinity, either +Inf or –Inf.

_Isnan ■ **_Bool _Isnan(T x)** returns a nonzero value if **x** is any code for not-a-number, or NaN.

_Nanv ■ **T _Nanv(T)** returns some code for not-a-number, or NaN. The argument value is unused.

_Sinh ■ **T _Sinh(T x, T y)** returns **y** times the hyperbolic sine of **x**.

Figure 21.5:
dcdiv.c

```
// dcdiv -- TC::operator/=(TC)
#include <xcomplex>

TC TC::operator/=(TC rop)
    {                                           // divide TC by TC
    T re = real(rop);
    T im = imag(rop);
    if (_Isnan(re) || _Isnan(im))
        _Re = _Nanv(_Re), _Im = _Re;
    else
        {                       // rop has ordered components, divide
        if (re < 0)
            re = -re;
        if (im < 0)
            im = -im;
        if (im < re)
            {                           // |imag| is smaller for rop
            T r = imag(rop) / real(rop);
            T d = real(rop) + r * imag(rop);
            if (_Isnan(d) || d == 0)
                _Re = _Nanv(_Re), _Im = _Re;
            else
                {                           // denom is nonzero
                T t = (_Re + _Im * r) / d;
                _Im = (_Im - _Re * r) / d;
                _Re = t;
                }
            }
        else if (im == 0)
            _Re = _Nanv(_Re), _Im = _Re;
        else
            {                               // |real| is smaller for rop
            T r = real(rop) / imag(rop);
            T d = imag(rop) + r * real(rop);
            if (_Isnan(d) || d == 0)
                _Re = _Nanv(_Re), _Im = _Re;
            else
                {                           // denom is finite
                T t = (_Re * r + _Im) / d;
                _Im = (_Im * r - _Re) / d;
                _Re = t;
                }
            }
        }
    return (*this);
    }
```

The header **\<xcomplex\>** also declares a number of functions declared in **\<math.h\>**. The version shown here does so by including **\<xmath.h\>**, as described earlier, which in turn includes **\<math.h\>**. The functions are **atan2**, **cos**, **exp**, **ldexp**, **log**, **pow**, **sin**, and **sqrt**. These too must be overloaded for all three floating-point types.

Figure 21.6:
dcmul.c

```
// dcmul -- TC::operator*=(TC)
#include <xcomplex>

TC TC::operator*=(TC rop)
    {                                                    // multiply TC by TC
    T t = _Re * real(rop) - _Im * imag(rop);
    _Im = _Re * imag(rop) + _Im * real(rop);
    _Re = t;
    return (*this);
    }                                                                    □
```

The version of **xcomplex** shown here assumes that **<math.h>** (or **<xmath.h>**) declares the *float* and *long double* versions with the names reserved in the C Standard (**ISO90**). For example, the *float* version of **exp** is **expf** and the *long double* version is **expl**. These functions are *not* required of all implementations of Standard C, and hence may not be present. As a (barely adequate) substitute, you can call the *double* versions in all cases. Those should always be present. (Again, see Appendix A: Interfaces.)

dcdiv.c   With that long preamble, I can now describe the remaining source files.
dcmul.c Figure 21.5 shows the file **dcdiv.c**. It defines the member function **operator/=** for the class **TC**. And Figure 21.6 shows the file **dcmul.c**. It defines the member function **operator*=** for the class **TC**. The former is far more cautious, and hence more complex. It avoids dividing by zero, or a NaN, returning a NaN instead. It also performs the actual division in one of two different ways, to avoid intermediate overflow.

Neither of these two functions is as safe as it could be. To be completely portable, a function should avoid evaluating an expression that can contain a Nan or Inf operand. Otherwise, the program is at the mercy of the implementation. It can terminate execution or do other undesirable things. More and more often, however, computers take these special codes in stride. They also generate them properly as needed.

Choosing between complete safety and good performance always involves a bit of guessing on the part of the library designer. In this case, I chose to follow common practice with complex arithmetic. I assumed that most people would prefer small inline code and fast execution. If the hardware is well behaved, that gamble pays off. Otherwise, you can expect surprises from time to time when you exercise the complex classes.

dcabsx.c   Figure 21.7 shows the file **dcabsx.c**. It defines the function **_Fabs**, which I described briefly above. Computing the magnitude of a complex value warrants careful handling, for several reasons:

- Several other functions compute the magnitude along the way.
- The magnitude can be slightly too large to represent, yet still contribute to a representable result.
- It is easy to lose precision, or to generate a spurious intermediate overflow, in computing the magnitude.

Figure 21.7:
dcabsx.c

```
// dcabsx -- _Fabs(TC, int *)
#include <xcomplex>

T _Fabs(TC x, int *pexp)
    {                                       // find magnitude of TC
    *pexp = 0;
    T a = real(x);
    T b = imag(x);
    if (_Isnan(a))
        return (a);
    else if (_Isnan(b))
        return (b);
    else
        {                       //  both ordered, compute modulus
        if (a < 0)
            a = -a;
        if (b < 0)
            b = -b;
        if (a < b)
            {                               // swap to make b smaller
            T t = a;
            a = b, b = t;
            }
        if (a == 0 || _Isinf(a))
            return (a);
        if (1 <= a)
            *pexp = 2, a *= 0.25, b *= 0.25;
        else
            *pexp = -2, a *= 4, b *= 4;
        T t = a - b;
        if (t == a)
            return (a);
        else if (b < t)
            {                                   // 2 < a/b <= 1/eps
            const T q = a / b;
            return (a + b / (q + sqrt(q * q + 1)));
            }
        else
            {                                   // 1 <= a/b <= 2
            static const T r2 = 1.4142135623730950488L;
            static const T xh = 2.4142L;
            static const T xl = 0.00001356237309504880016887L;
            const T q = t / b;
            const T r = (q + 2) * q;
            const T s = r / (r2 + sqrt(r + 2)) + xl + q + xh;
            return (a + b / s);
            }
        }
    }
```

Thus, _Fabs returns a scaled value to postpone overflow concerns as long as possible. And it does a bit of extra work to sidestep overflow or loss of magnitude.

Figure 21.8:
dcabs.c

```
// dcabs -- abs(TC)
#include <xcomplex>

T abs(TC x)
    {                                           // find magnitude of TC
    int xexp;
    T rho = _Fabs(x, &xexp);
    return (xexp == 0 ? rho : ldexp(rho, xexp));
    }                                                                    □
```

Figure 21.9:
dcarg.c

```
// dcarg -- arg(TC)
#include <xcomplex>

T arg(TC x)
    {                                           // find argument of TC
    return (atan2(imag(x), real(x)));
    }                                                                    □
```

Figure 21.10:
dcpolar.c

```
// dcpolar -- polar(T, T)
#include <xcomplex>

TC polar(T rho, T theta)
    {                                           // convert polar to TC
    return (TC(rho * cos(theta), rho * sin(theta)));
    }                                                                    □
```

The algorithm is a bit tricky, and hard to describe. (See **Kah87.**) Put simply, it works progressively harder the closer the two Cartesian components get in magnitude. In the extreme case, it indulges in a kind of extended precision to paste the final answer together.

dcabs.c   Figure 21.8 shows the file **dcabs.c**. It defines the function **abs**, the visible interface to **_Fabs**. Any scaling occurs in the function **ldexp**, which presumably can deal with floating-point overflow or underflow gracefully.

dcarg.c   Figure 21.9 shows the file **dcarg.c**. It defines the function **arg**, which computes the argument, or phase angle. Fortunately, the function **atan2** does exactly this job, given the Cartesian components. **arg** is not defined inline in the header only because **atan2** must not be made visible there.

dcpolar.c   Figure 21.10 shows the file **dcpolar.c**. It defines the function **polar** in the obvious way. Again, it is almost a candidate for defining inline, except for name visibility issues.

dccos.c   Four functions are very similar. Figure 21.11 shows the file **dccos.c**,
dccosh.c   which defines the function **cos**. Figure 21.12 shows the file **dccosh.c**,
dcsin.c   which defines the function **cosh**. Figure 21.13 shows the file **dcsin.c**,
dcsinh.c   which defines the function **sin**. And Figure 21.14 shows the file **dcsinh.c**, which defines the function **sinh**. All form the components of the complex result by calling **_Cosh** and **_Sinh** with various arguments. These functions presumably avoid any intermediate overflow.

Figure 21.11:
dccos.c

```
// dccos -- cos(TC)
#include <xcomplex>

TC cos(TC x)
    {                                         // find double_complex cos
    return (TC(_Cosh(imag(x), cos(real(x))),
        -_Sinh(imag(x), sin(real(x))))));
    }                                                                    □
```

Figure 21.12:
dccosh.c

```
// dccosh -- cosh(TC)
#include <xcomplex>

TC cosh(TC x)
    {                                                    // find TC cosh
    return (TC(_Cosh(real(x), cos(imag(x))),
        _Sinh(real(x), sin(imag(x))))));
    }                                                                    □
```

dcexp.c   Figure 21.15 shows the file dcexp.c, which defines the function exp. It faces a problem similar to that faced by the previous group of functions. It also handles the problem in a similar way, by calling _Exp to form the final product carefully. In principle, the function need compute the exponential only once. Doing so, however, sidesteps the safety provided by the function _Exp.

dclog.c   Figure 21.16 shows the file dclog.c, which defines the function log. It essentially computes the logarithm by first converting to polar form:

$$ln(\rho*exp(i*\theta)) = ln(\rho) + i*\theta$$

The result ends up neatly in Cartesian form. The code takes some care to handle and generate Inf and NaN codes. Beyond that, the only trickery lies in the careful way the function assembles the real component. The sum of c1 and c2 is $ln(2)$, with c1 contrived to have at most fifteen nonzero fraction bits. This is again a simple form of extended precision.

dcsqrt.c   Figure 21.17 shows the file dcsqrt.c, which defines the function sqrt. Several methods exist for computing the complex square root. The one I chose here is about as twisty as the logic in _Fabs, and for much the same reasons. It endeavors to minimize computations, and preserve precision, by hand crafting the simple solution for an argument value in each of the four different quadrants.

dcpowcc.c
dcpowcf.c
dcpowfc.c   The function pow(x0, x1) is overloaded for each complex class with four combinations of parameter types. Three of these functions work particularly closely together. Figure 21.18 shows the file dcpowcc.c, which defines the function pow(TC, TC). Figure 21.19 shows the file dcpowcf.c, which defines the function pow(TC, T). And Figure 21.20 shows the file dcpowfc.c, which defines the function pow(T, TC). These filter out zero components one at a time, in the hopes of achieving useful strength reduction.

Figure 21.13:
dcsin.c

```
// dcsin -- sin(TC)
#include <xcomplex>

TC sin(TC x)
    {                                              // find TC sin
    return (TC(_Cosh(imag(x), sin(real(x))),
        _Sinh(imag(x), cos(real(x))))));
    }                                                              □
```

Figure 21.14:
dcsinh.c

```
// dcsinh -- sinh(TC)
#include <xcomplex>

TC sinh(TC x)
    {                                              // find TC sinh
    return (TC(_Sinh(real(x), cos(imag(x))),
        _Cosh(real(x), sin(imag(x))))));
    }                                                              □
```

Figure 21.15:
dcexp.c

```
// dcexp -- exp(TC)
#include <xcomplex>

TC exp(TC x)
    {                                              // find TC exp
    T re(real(x)), im(real(x));
    _Exp(&re, cos(imag(x)), 0);
    _Exp(&im, sin(imag(x)), 0);
    return (TC(re, im));
    }                                                              □
```

Figure 21.16:
dclog.c

```
// dclog -- log(TC)
#include <xcomplex>

TC log(TC x)
    {                                              // find logarithm of TC
    int xexp;
    T rho = _Fabs(x, &xexp);
    if (_Isnan(rho))
        return (TC(rho, rho));
    else
        {                                          // not a NaN, compute log
        static const T c1 = 22713.0 / 32768.0;
        static const T c2 = 1.428606820309417232e-6L;
        T xn = xexp;
        return (TC(rho == 0 ? -_Infv(rho) : _Isinf(rho) ? rho
            : log(rho) + xn * c2 + xn * c1,
            atan2(imag(x), real(x))));
        }
    }                                                              □
```

Figure 21.17:
dcsqrt.c

```
// dcsqrt -- sqrt(TC)
#include <xcomplex>

TC sqrt(TC x)
    {                                           // find square root of TC
    int xexp;
    T rho = _Fabs(x, &xexp);
    if (xexp == 0)
        return (TC(rho, rho));
    else
        {                       //  magnitude finite, compute square root
        T remag = ldexp(real(x) < 0 ? - real(x) : real(x),
            -xexp);
        rho = ldexp(sqrt(2 * (remag + rho)), xexp / 2 - 1);
        if (0 <= real(x))
            return (TC(rho, imag(x) / (2 * rho)));
        else if (imag(x) < 0)
            return (TC(-imag(x) / (2 * rho), -rho));
        else
            return (TC(imag(x) / (2 * rho), rho));
        }
    }                                                              □
```

Figure 21.18:
dcpowcc.c

```
// dcpowcc -- pow(TC, TC)
#include <xcomplex>

TC pow(TC x, TC y)
    {                                       // find TC raised to TC power
    return (imag(y) == 0 ? pow(x, real(y))
        : imag(x) == 0 ? TC(pow(real(x), y))
        : exp(y * log(x)));
    }                                                              □
```

Figure 21.19:
dcpowcf.c

```
// dcpowcf -- pow(TC, double)
#include <xcomplex>

TC pow(TC x, T y)
    {                                       // find TC x raised to T power
    return (imag(x) == 0 ? TC(pow(real(x), y))
        : exp(y * log(x)));
    }                                                              □
```

Figure 21.20:
dcpowfc.c

```
// dcpowfc -- pow(T, TC)
#include <xcomplex>

TC pow(T x, TC y)
    {                                       // find T x raised to TC power
    return (imag(y) == 0 ? TC(pow(x, real(y)))
        : exp(y * log(x)));
    }                                                              □
```

Figure 21.21:
dcpowci.c

```
// dcpowci -- pow(TC, int)
#include <xcomplex>

TC pow(TC x, int y)
    {                               // find TC x raised to int power
    if (imag(x) == 0)
        return (TC(pow(real(x), (T)y)));
    unsigned int n = y;
    if (y < 0)
        n = -n;
    for (TC z(1); ; x *= x)
        {                               // scale by x^2^n
        if (n & 1)
            z *= x;
        if ((n >>= 1) == 0)
            return (y < 0 ? TC(1) / z : z);
        }
    }
```

Figure 21.22:
dcext.c

```
// dcext -- operator>>(istream&, TC&)
#include <xcomplex>

istream& operator>>(istream& is, TC& x)
    {                               // extract TC
    char ch;
    T re, im;
    if (is >> ch && ch == '('
        && is >> re >> ch && ch == ','
        && is >> im >> ch && ch == ')')
        x = TC(re, im);
    return (is);
    }
```

Figure 21.23:
dcins.c

```
// dcins -- operator<<(ostream&, TC)
#include <xcomplex>

ostream& operator<<(ostream& os, TC x)
    {                               // insert TC
    return (os << '(' << real(x) << ',' << imag(x) << ')');
    }
```

If both imaginary components are zero, the real component is computed by calling the function $pow(T, T)$. Otherwise, the fallback is to compute $exp(x1 * log(x0))$. While this method is mathematically correct, it can sometimes lose precision. Still, it is adequate for many needs.

dcpowci.c   Function $pow(x0, x1)$ has a fourth form. Figure 21.21 shows the file dcpowci.c, which defines the function $pow(TC, int)$. It too checks for a zero imaginary component, and it too calls $pow(T, T)$ where possible. But to raise an arbitrary complex value to an integer power, the function uses a classic square-and-multiply approach, which can be quite efficient.

dcext.c   The last two generic files implement the extractor and inserter for a
dcins.c   complex class. Figure 21.22 shows the file **dcext.c**, which defines the
extractor. And Figure 21.23 shows the file **dcins.c**, which implements the
inserter. Both follow directly from their specification in the draft C++
Standard.

Testing `<complex>`

tcomplex.c   Figure 21.24 shows the file **tcomplex.c**. It tests the basic properties of
the three classes defined in **`<complex>`**. It does so by repeating much the
same sequence of tests for class **float_complex** (in function **tf()**), class
double_complex (in function **td()**), and **long_double_complex** (in function **tld()**).

Three versions of the function **approx** test the accuracy of computed
values. In all three precisions, **approx** permits an error in at most the two
least-significant bits of the result. That's not to say, however, that the tested
functions meet this criterion for all meaningful argument values. The tests
are merely anecdotal, and are far from complete by any reasonable metric
for test coverage. If all goes well, the program prints:

SUCCESS testing `<complex>`

and takes a normal exit.

Exercises

Exercise 21.1 Determine what your implementation does when a program:

- divides by zero
- performs arithmetic on an Inf or NaN code
- generates a floating-point overflow
- generates a floating-point underflow

Exercise 21.2 Alter the classes and functions defined in header **`<complex>`** to avoid all
arithmetic operations on Inf or NaN values. What does this do to perform-
ance?

Exercise 21.3 Are there ever circumstances, in floating-point arithmetic, where $(0 + B*i)$
does not have the same effect as $B*i$? If so, describe one or more cases. If
not, explain why not.

Exercise 21.4 [Harder] Define the class **double_imaginary**, which represents only the
imaginary component of a **double_complex** object. Extend the capabilities
defined for **double_complex** to include this new class, as well as all sensible
combinations of **double_imaginary** and **double_complex** operands.

Exercise 21.5 [Very hard] Rewrite the classes defined in header **`<complex>`** to represent
all complex values within the three classes in polar form, then alter the
functions to work with this new representation.

```
// test <complex>
#include <assert.h>
#include <float.h>
#include <math.h>
#include <string.h>
#include <complex>
#include <iostream>
#include <strstream>

#ifndef __STD_COMPLEX
 #error macro __STD_COMPLEX is not defined
#endif


        // static data
static float feps;
static double eps;
static long double ldeps;

static int approx(float d1, float d2)
    {                           // test for approximate float equality
    return ((d2 ? fabsf((d2 - d1) / d2) : fabsf(d1)) < feps);
    }

static int approx(double d1, double d2)
    {                           // test for approximate double equality
    return ((d2 ? fabs((d2 - d1) / d2) : fabs(d1)) < eps);
    }

static int approx(long double d1, long double d2)
    {                   // test for approximate long double equality
    return ((d2 ? fabsl((d2 - d1) / d2) : fabsl(d1)) < ldeps);
    }

void tf()
    {                                   // test float_complex properties
    float_complex fc0, fc1(1), fc2(2, 2);
    feps = FLT_EPSILON * 4.0;
    assert(real(fc0) == 0 && imag(fc0) == 0);
    assert(real(fc1) == 1 && imag(fc1) == 0);
    assert(real(fc2) == 2 && imag(fc2) == 2);
    fc0 += fc2, assert(real(fc0) == 2 && imag(fc0) == 2);
    fc0 -= fc1, assert(real(fc0) == 1 && imag(fc0) == 2);
    fc0 *= fc2, assert(real(fc0) == -2 && imag(fc0) == 6);
    fc0 /= fc2, assert(real(fc0) == 1 && imag(fc0) == 2);
        // test arithmetic
    fc0 = _float_complex(double_complex(2, 3));
    assert(real(fc0) == 2 && imag(fc0) == 3);
    fc0 = _float_complex(long_double_complex(-4, -5));
    assert(real(fc0) == -4 && imag(fc0) == -5);
    fc0 = 2 + fc2 + 3, assert(real(fc0) == 7 && imag(fc0) == 2);
    fc0 = 2 - fc2 - 3;
    assert(real(fc0) == -3 && imag(fc0) == -2);
    fc0 = 2 * fc2 * 3;
    assert(real(fc0) == 12 && imag(fc0) == 12);
    fc0 = 8 / fc2 / 2;
```

```
        assert(real(fc0) == 1 && imag(fc0) == -1);
        fc0 = +fc1 + -fc2;
        assert(real(fc0) == -1 && imag(fc0) == -2);
        assert(fc2 == fc2 && fc1 == 1 && 1 == fc1);
        assert(fc1 != fc2 && fc1 != 0 && 3 != fc1);
            // test I/O
        istrstream istr("(3, -1) (002,  2e1)");
        ostrstream ostr;
        istr >> fc0, assert(real(fc0) == 3 && imag(fc0) == -1);
        ostr << fc0, istr >> fc0;
        assert(real(fc0) == 2 && imag(fc0) == 20);
        ostr << fc0 << ends;
        assert(strcmp(ostr.str(), "(3,-1)(2,20)") == 0);
            // test math functions
        static const float e = {2.7182818284590452353602875};
        static const float ln2 = {0.6931471805599453094172321};
        static const float piby4 = {0.7853981633974483096156608};
        static const float rthalf = {0.7071067811865475244008444};
        float c1 = rthalf * (e + 1 / e) / 2;
        float s1 = rthalf * (e - 1 / e) / 2;
        assert(approx(abs(float_complex(5, -12)), 13));
        assert(arg(fc1) == 0 && approx(arg(fc2), piby4));
        assert(conj(fc2) == float_complex(2, -2));
        fc0 = cos(float_complex(piby4, -1));
        assert(approx(real(fc0), c1) && approx(imag(fc0), s1));
        fc0 = cosh(float_complex(-1, piby4));
        assert(approx(real(fc0), c1) && approx(imag(fc0), -s1));
        fc0 = exp(fc1);
        assert(approx(real(fc0), e) && imag(fc0) == 0);
        fc0 = exp(float_complex(1, -piby4));
        assert(approx(real(fc0), e * rthalf)
            && approx(imag(fc0), -e * rthalf));
        fc0 = log(float_complex(1, -1));
        assert(approx(real(fc0), ln2 / 2)
            && approx(imag(fc0), -piby4));
        assert(norm(float_complex(3, -4)) == 25 && norm(fc2) == 8);
        fc0 = polar(1, -piby4);
        assert(approx(real(fc0), rthalf)
            && approx(imag(fc0), -rthalf));
        fc0 = pow(fc2, fc2);
        fc0 = pow(fc2, 5);
        assert(real(fc0) == -128 && imag(fc0) == -128);
        fc0 = pow(fc2, (float)2);
        assert(approx(real(fc0), 0) && approx(imag(fc0), 8));
        fc0 = pow((float)2, fc2);
        fc0 = sin(float_complex(piby4, -1));
        assert(approx(real(fc0), c1) && approx(imag(fc0), -s1));
        fc0 = sinh(float_complex(-1, piby4));
        assert(approx(real(fc0), -s1) && approx(imag(fc0), c1));
        fc0 = sqrt(float_complex(0, -1));
        assert(approx(real(fc0), rthalf)
            && approx(imag(fc0), -rthalf));
        }

void td()
```

```
{                                    // test double_complex properties
double_complex fc0, fc1(1), fc2(2, 2);
eps = DBL_EPSILON * 4.0;
assert(real(fc0) == 0 && imag(fc0) == 0);
assert(real(fc1) == 1 && imag(fc1) == 0);
assert(real(fc2) == 2 && imag(fc2) == 2);
fc0 += fc2, assert(real(fc0) == 2 && imag(fc0) == 2);
fc0 -= fc1, assert(real(fc0) == 1 && imag(fc0) == 2);
fc0 *= fc2, assert(real(fc0) == -2 && imag(fc0) == 6);
fc0 /= fc2, assert(real(fc0) == 1 && imag(fc0) == 2);
        // test arithmetic
fc0 = _double_complex(long_double_complex(-4, -5));
assert(real(fc0) == -4 && imag(fc0) == -5);
fc0 = 2 + fc2 + 3, assert(real(fc0) == 7 && imag(fc0) == 2);
fc0 = 2 - fc2 - 3;
assert(real(fc0) == -3 && imag(fc0) == -2);
fc0 = 2 * fc2 * 3;
assert(real(fc0) == 12 && imag(fc0) == 12);
fc0 = 8 / fc2 / 2;
assert(real(fc0) == 1 && imag(fc0) == -1);
fc0 = +fc1 + -fc2;
assert(real(fc0) == -1 && imag(fc0) == -2);
assert(fc2 == fc2 && fc1 == 1 && 1 == fc1);
assert(fc1 != fc2 && fc1 != 0 && 3 != fc1);
        // test I/O
istrstream istr("(3, -1) (002,   2e1)");
ostrstream ostr;
istr >> fc0, assert(real(fc0) == 3 && imag(fc0) == -1);
ostr << fc0;
istr >> fc0, assert(real(fc0) == 2 && imag(fc0) == 20);
ostr << fc0 << ends;
assert(strcmp(ostr.str(), "(3,-1)(2,20)") == 0);
        // test math functions
static const double e = {2.7182818284590452353602875};
static const double ln2 = {0.6931471805599453094172321};
static const double piby4 = {0.7853981633974483096156608};
static const double rthalf = {0.7071067811865475244008444};
double c1 = rthalf * (e + 1 / e) / 2;
double s1 = rthalf * (e - 1 / e) / 2;
assert(approx(abs(double_complex(5, -12)), 13));
assert(arg(fc1) == 0 && approx(arg(fc2), piby4));
assert(conj(fc2) == double_complex(2, -2));
fc0 = cos(double_complex(piby4, -1));
assert(approx(real(fc0), c1) && approx(imag(fc0), s1));
fc0 = cosh(double_complex(-1, piby4));
assert(approx(real(fc0), c1) && approx(imag(fc0), -s1));
fc0 = exp(fc1);
assert(approx(real(fc0), e) && imag(fc0) == 0);
fc0 = exp(double_complex(1, -piby4));
assert(approx(real(fc0), e * rthalf)
    && approx(imag(fc0), -e * rthalf));
fc0 = log(double_complex(1, -1));
assert(approx(real(fc0), ln2 / 2)
    && approx(imag(fc0), -piby4));
assert(norm(double_complex(3, -4)) == 25 && norm(fc2) == 8);
```

```
    fc0 = polar(1, -piby4);
    assert(approx(real(fc0), rthalf)
        && approx(imag(fc0), -rthalf));
    fc0 = pow(fc2, fc2);
    fc0 = pow(fc2, 5);
    assert(real(fc0) == -128 && imag(fc0) == -128);
    fc0 = pow(fc2, (double)2);
    assert(approx(real(fc0), 0) && approx(imag(fc0), 8));
    fc0 = pow((double)2, fc2);
    fc0 = sin(double_complex(piby4, -1));
    assert(approx(real(fc0), c1) && approx(imag(fc0), -s1));
    fc0 = sinh(double_complex(-1, piby4));
    assert(approx(real(fc0), -s1) && approx(imag(fc0), c1));
    fc0 = sqrt(double_complex(0, -1));
    assert(approx(real(fc0), rthalf)
        && approx(imag(fc0), -rthalf));
    }

void tld()
    {                               // test long_double_complex properties
    long_double_complex fc0, fc1(1), fc2(2, 2);
    ldeps = LDBL_EPSILON * 4.0;
    assert(real(fc0) == 0 && imag(fc0) == 0);
    assert(real(fc1) == 1 && imag(fc1) == 0);
    assert(real(fc2) == 2 && imag(fc2) == 2);
    fc0 += fc2, assert(real(fc0) == 2 && imag(fc0) == 2);
    fc0 -= fc1, assert(real(fc0) == 1 && imag(fc0) == 2);
    fc0 *= fc2, assert(real(fc0) == -2 && imag(fc0) == 6);
    fc0 /= fc2, assert(real(fc0) == 1 && imag(fc0) == 2);
        // test arithmetic
    fc0 = 2 + fc2 + 3, assert(real(fc0) == 7 && imag(fc0) == 2);
    fc0 = 2 - fc2 - 3;
    assert(real(fc0) == -3 && imag(fc0) == -2);
    fc0 = 2 * fc2 * 3;
    assert(real(fc0) == 12 && imag(fc0) == 12);
    fc0 = 8 / fc2 / 2;
    assert(real(fc0) == 1 && imag(fc0) == -1);
    fc0 = +fc1 + -fc2;
    assert(real(fc0) == -1 && imag(fc0) == -2);
    assert(fc2 == fc2 && fc1 == 1 && 1 == fc1);
    assert(fc1 != fc2 && fc1 != 0 && 3 != fc1);
        // test I/O
    istrstream istr("(3, -1) (002,  2e1)");
    ostrstream ostr;
    istr >> fc0, assert(real(fc0) == 3 && imag(fc0) == -1);
    ostr << fc0;
    istr >> fc0, assert(real(fc0) == 2 && imag(fc0) == 20);
    ostr << fc0 << ends;
    assert(strcmp(ostr.str(), "(3,-1)(2,20)") == 0);
        // test math functions
    static const long double e =
        {2.7182818284590452353602875L};
    static const long double ln2 =
        {0.6931471805599453094172321L};
    static const long double piby4 =
```

```
            {0.78539816339744483096156608L};
      static const long double rthalf =
            {0.70710678118654752440084444L};
      long double c1 = rthalf * (e + 1 / e) / 2;
      long double s1 = rthalf * (e - 1 / e) / 2;
      assert(approx(abs(long_double_complex(5, -12)), 13));
      assert(arg(fc1) == 0 && approx(arg(fc2), piby4));
      assert(conj(fc2) == long_double_complex(2, -2));
      fc0 = cos(long_double_complex(piby4, -1));
      assert(approx(real(fc0), c1) && approx(imag(fc0), s1));
      fc0 = cosh(long_double_complex(-1, piby4));
      assert(approx(real(fc0), c1) && approx(imag(fc0), -s1));
      fc0 = exp(fc1);
      assert(approx(real(fc0), e) && imag(fc0) == 0);
      fc0 = exp(long_double_complex(1, -piby4));
      assert(approx(real(fc0), e * rthalf)
            && approx(imag(fc0), -e * rthalf));
      fc0 = log(long_double_complex(1, -1));
      assert(approx(real(fc0), ln2 / 2)
            && approx(imag(fc0), -piby4));
      assert(norm(long_double_complex(3, -4)) == 25
            && norm(fc2) == 8);
      fc0 = polar(1, -piby4);
      assert(approx(real(fc0), rthalf)
            && approx(imag(fc0), -rthalf));
      fc0 = pow(fc2, fc2);
      fc0 = pow(fc2, 5);
      assert(real(fc0) == -128 && imag(fc0) == -128);
      fc0 = pow(fc2, (long double)2);
      assert(approx(real(fc0), 0) && approx(imag(fc0), 8));
      fc0 = pow((long double)2, fc2);
      fc0 = sin(long_double_complex(piby4, -1));
      assert(approx(real(fc0), c1) && approx(imag(fc0), -s1));
      fc0 = sinh(long_double_complex(-1, piby4));
      assert(approx(real(fc0), -s1) && approx(imag(fc0), c1));
      fc0 = sqrt(long_double_complex(0, -1));
      assert(approx(real(fc0), rthalf)
            && approx(imag(fc0), -rthalf));
      }

int main()
      {                       // test basic workings of complex definitions
      tf();
      td();
      tld();
      cout << "SUCCESS testing <complex>" << endl;
      return (0);
      }                                                                  □
```

Appendix A: Interfaces

This appendix summarizes what you have to provide to construct an object-module library from the source code presented in this book. It assumes as a starting point the existence of a Standard C library that you can link with C++ code. Basically, that's a library that conforms to the ISO C Standard (**ISO90**). While any such library will do, I can't help but recommend the one I present in my earlier book, *The Standard C Library* (**Pla92**, hereafter the PJP C library). Like the code in this book, it is published code that emphasizes readability and portability.

I'd like to be able to say that a Standard C library is all you need. Unfortunately, life is seldom so simple:

- The Standard C++ library has to know how to cooperate with the Standard C library in such matters as defining the same type in multiple headers. Non-standard method must invariably be employed.

- Extractors in the Standard C++ library need to make floating-point conversions not adequately supported by the Standard C library. Extra functions must be supplied.

- Buffering of file reads and writes requires both close coordination between the two libraries and the greatest possible optimization for each. Knowledge of internal structures must be shared to achieve both goals.

- C++ exists in multiple dialects, thanks to the addition of major language features over several years of standardization. Macros and type definitions must be defined to gloss over these differences.

- The C Standard itself is changing with the acceptance of Amendment 1 (**ISO94**). For full compliance, extra functionality must be supplied.

For all these reasons, a typical implementation of the Standard C library needs supplementing. And a typical implementation of C++ needs to provide a few hints about what it can and cannot do.

`<yxvals.h>`   I've concentrated all the hints — in the form of implementation-dependent macros and type definitions — in a single "internal" header called **`<yxvals.h>`**. (Yes, the name is weird. It is modeled after the analogous file **`<yvals.h>`** in the PJP C library.) Figure A.1 shows one way to write the file **`yxvals.h`**, to implement this header. This particular version represents a full implementation of the language described by the draft C++ Standard. It also assumes that the underlying Standard C library is from **Pla92**.

Figure A.1:
yxvals.h

```
// yxvals.h sample values header for C++
#ifndef _YXVALS_
#define _YXVALS_
          // translator/library features
#define _CATCH_IO_EXCEPTIONS          /* try blocks in iostreams */
#define _HAS_ARRAY_NEW                /* operator new[] implemented */
#define _HAS_PJP_CLIB                 /* running atop PJP C Library */
#define _HAS_SIGNED_CHAR              /* char/signed char distinct */
#define _HAS_TYPEINFO                 /* typeid implemented */
          // bitmask macros -- enum overloading implemented
#define _BITMASK(E, T)    \
E& operator&=(E& _X, E _Y) \
    {_X = (E)(_X & _Y); return (_X); } \
E& operator|=(E& _X, E _Y) \
    {_X = (E)(_X | _Y); return (_X); } \
E& operator^=(E& _X, E _Y) \
    {_X = (E)(_X ^ _Y); return (_X); } \
E& operator&(E _X, E _Y) \
    {return ((E)(_X & _Y)); } \
E& operator|(E _X, E _Y) \
    {return ((E)(_X | _Y)); } \
E& operator^(E _X, E _Y) \
    {return ((E)(_X ^ _Y)); } \
E& operator~(E _X) \
    {return ((E)~_X); } \
typedef E T
          // exception macros -- exceptions implemented
#define _TRY_BEGIN  try {
#define _CATCH_ALL  } catch (...) {
#define _CATCH_END  }
#define _RAISE(x)   throw (x)
#define _RERAISE    throw
          // numeric representation macros
#define _BITS_BYTE      8
#define _MAX_EXP_DIG    8
#define _MAX_INT_DIG    32
#define _MAX_SIG_DIG    36
          // type definitions
typedef bool _Bool;
struct _Filet;
struct _Fpost;
/* #define _PTRDIFFT       /* only if ptrdiff_t already defined */
typedef int _Ptrdifft;
/* #define _SIZET          /* only if size_t already defined */
typedef unsigned int _Sizet;
typedef int _Typedesc;
#define _WCHART            /* only if wchar_t already defined */
typedef unsigned short _Wchart;
/* #define _WINTT          /* only if wint_t already defined */
typedef unsigned short _Wintt;
#endif /* _YXVALS_ */                                            □
```

Here is a summary of all the types and macros defined in **<yxvals.h>**. It suggests changes to make if these assumptions do not all hold:

_BITS_BYTE ■ **_BITS_BYTE** — defined as a macro that expands to an integer constant expression. Its value is the number of bits in a byte (at least 8).

_Bool ■ **_Bool** — a synonym for the newly added type *bool*. For an implementation that does not support the keyword **bool**, define this type as *int*.

_CATCH_ALL ■ **_CATCH_ALL** — the macro that introduces an all-purpose *catch* clause, after **_TRY_BEGIN** and before **_CATCH_END**. For an implementation that does not support exceptions, you can define this macro as **} if (0) {**.

_CATCH_END ■ **_CATCH_END** — the macro that terminates an all-purpose *catch* clause, after **_TRY_BEGIN** and **_CATCH_END**. For an implementation that does not support exceptions, you can define this macro as **}}**.

_CATCH_IO_ ■ **_CATCH_IO_EXCEPTIONS** — defined as a macro if you want each inserter
EXCEPTIONS and extractor to be wrapped in a *try* block, as the draft C++ Standard requires. Omit the macro definition if you don't want all this code.

_Filet ■ **_Filet** — a synonym for the type **FILE**, declared in **<stdio.h>**. The PJP C library actually defines **FILE** as **struct _Filet**. For another Standard C library, you may have to add a type definition.

_Fpost ■ **_Fpost** — a synonym for the type **fpos_t**, defined in **<stdio.h>**. The PJP C library actually defines **fpos_t** as **struct _Fpost**. For another Standard C library, you may have to add a type definition.

HAS ■ **_HAS_ARRAY_NEW** — defined as a macro if the implementation accepts
ARRAY_NEW the function names **operator delete[]** and **operator new[]**. (See the code for **delaop.c** on page 92 and for **newaop.c** on page 92.) Omit the macro definition if such function names are not accepted.

HAS ■ **_HAS_PJP_CLIB** — defined as a macro if you want the **filebuf** virtual
PJP_CLIB member functions to directly manipulate **FILE** objects as defined in the PJP C library. (See the code for **filebuf.c** beginning on page 330.) Omit the macro definition for more portable, but slower, code.

HAS ■ **_HAS_SIGNED_CHAR** — defined as a macro if the implementation distin-
SIGNED_CHAR guishes the types *char* and *signed char*, as it should. Omit the macro definition if the types are not distinct.

HAS ■ **_HAS_TYPEINFO** — defined as a macro if the implementation accepts the
TYPEINFO keyword **typeid**. (See the code for **ttypeinf.c** on page 102.) Omit the macro definition if the keyword is not accepted.

_MAX_EXP_DIG ■ **_MAX_EXP_DIG** — defined as a macro that expands to an integer constant expression. Its value should be at least the maximum number of decimal digits required to represent the exponent part of an arbitrary floating-point value in scientific format.

_MAX_INT_DIG ■ **_MAX_INT_DIG** — defined as a macro that expands to an integer constant expression. Its value should be at least the maximum number of decimal digits required to represent an arbitrary *unsigned long* value.

_MAX_SIG_DIG ■ **_MAX_SIG_DIG** — defined as a macro that expands to an integer constant expression. Its value should be at least the maximum number of decimal digits required to represent all the significance in a floating-point value.

_PTRDIFFT ■ **_PTRDIFFT** — defined as a macro if a definition is visible for the type **ptrdiff_t**. The PJP C library uses this macro to guard against multiple definitions of the type. For another Standard C library, the machinery may differ.

_Ptrdifft ■ **_Ptrdifft** — a synonym for the type **ptrdiff_t**.

_RAISE(x) ■ **_RAISE(x)** — the macro that generates a *raise* expression for the object **x**. For an implementation that does not support exceptions, you can define this macro as **xmsg::_Throw(&(x))**.

_RERAISE ■ **_RERAISE** — the macro that generates a *raise* expression to rethrow an exception. For an implementation that does not support exceptions, you can define this macro as **xmsg::_Throw(0)**.

_SIZET ■ **_SIZET** — defined as a macro if a definition is visible for the type **size_t**. The PJP C library uses this macro to guard against multiple definitions of the type. For another Standard C library, the machinery may differ.

_Sizet ■ **_Sizet** — a synonym for the type **size_t**.

_TRY_BEGIN ■ **_TRY_BEGIN** — the macro that introduces a *try* block, followed by **_CATCH_ALL** and **_CATCH_END**. For an implementation that does not yet support exceptions, you can define this macro as **{{**.

_Typedesc ■ **_Typedesc** — a synonym for the type of the **typeinfo** member object that captures ordering information. (See Chapter 5: **<typeinfo>**.) For an implementation that does not accept the keyword **typeid**, I define this type as a synonym for *int*.

_WCHART ■ **_WCHART** — defined as a macro if a definition is visible for the type **wchar_t**. The PJP C library uses this macro to guard against multiple definitions of the type. For another Standard C library, the machinery may differ. If the implementation defines **wchar_t** as a keyword, as it should, guard against *any* attempt to (re)define **wchar_t**.

_Wchart ■ **_Wchart** — a synonym for the type **wchar_t**.

_WINTT ■ **_WINTT** — defined as a macro if a definition is visible for the type **wint_t**. The PJP C library uses this macro to guard against multiple definitions of the type. For another Standard C library, the machinery may differ.

_Wintt ■ **_Wintt** — a synonym for the type **wint_t**.

stdio.h If you define the macro **_HAS_PJP_CLIB** in **<yxvals.h>**, then the code in the source file **filebuf.c** makes certain assumptions about the member objects in a **_Filet** (or **FILE**) object. In particular, the code assumes the existence of four pointers to *char*, with the following semantics:

_Buf ■ **_Buf** points to the beginning of either the input or output sequence.

_Next ■ **_Next** points to the next element to extract in the input sequence or the next element to insert in the output sequence.

_Rend ■ **_Rend** points just beyond the last element of the input sequence.

_Wend ■ **_Wend** points just beyond the last element of the output sequence.

None of these member objects ever stores a null pointer. Nor does a **_Filet** object ever define both a non-empty input sequence and a non-empty output sequence at the same time.

extended   The interface I have described so far is compatible with the PJP C library
PJP C library as described in **Pla92**. What follows requires rather more than that library.
To provide complete support for the Standard C++ library, I have found it
necessary to *extend* my published version of the Standard C library in
several dimensions. You will find earlier versions of many of these new
features in *The Standard C Library*, but never the whole story.

So if you want comply fully with the specification of the Standard C++
library in the Informal Review Draft, you have two choices:

- obtain a copy of the extended PJP C library

- supply the functionality described in the remainder of this appendix
  some other way

(The former is included in the Professional Media for the Draft Standard
C++ Library marketed by Plum Hall Inc. See the Preface and/or the order
card inserted in this book.) End of advertisement.

<stdlib.h>   The extractors for floating-point values assume the existence of three
additional functions. The extended PJP C library declares the following in
<stdlib.h>, but you can also declare them in **<yxvals.h>**:

_Stod
```
double _Stod(const char *s, char **ep, long eoff);
float _Stof(const char *s, char **ep, long eoff);
long double _Stold(const char *s, char **ep, long eoff);
```

Each function behaves much like **stod(s, ep)**, declared in **<stdlib.h>**.
But each multiplies the converted value by ten raised to the power **eoff**. A
good implementation performs all conversions to essentially full precision
over the representable range of values. It also safely handles any true
overflow or underflow. I provide portable, but less than safe, substitutes
for these three functions in Chapter 8: **<istream>**.

<xmath.h>   Full support of the classes in **<complex>** requires quite a few additional
floating-point math functions. The extended PJP C library declares or
defines the following in the internal header **<xmath.h>**, but you can also
declare them in **<yxvals.h>**. You can also alter the definitions in the header
<xcomplex> to provide comparable facilities in a different way. (See the
source file **xcomplex** beginning on page 524.)

The implementation of **<complex>** I provide here requires the following:

INF
NAN
_Dtest
```
short INF;
short NAN;
short _Dtest(double *p)
short _FDtest(float *p)
short _LDtest(long double *p)
```

Each function returns **INF** if ***p** is one of the special codes for (plus or
minus) Infinity. It returns **NAN** if ***p** is one of the special codes for Not a
Number.

_Cosh
```
double _Cosh(double x, double y)
float _FCosh(float x, float y)
long double _LCosh(long double x, long double y)
```

Each function behaves the same as **y * cosh(x)**, but avoids intermediate overflow.

_Sinh
```
double _Sinh(double x, double y)
float _FSinh(float x, float y)
long double _LSinh(long double x, long double y)
```

Each function behaves the same as `y * sinh(x)`, but avoids intermediate overflow.

_Exp
```
short _Exp(double *p, double y, short boff)
short _FExp(float *p, float y, short boff)
short _LExp(long double *p, long double y, short boff)
```

Each function behaves as if it stores in `*p` the value `ldexp(y * exp(*p),
boff)` (to suitable precision), but avoids intermediate overflow. It returns
INF or **NAN** as above, or zero for a zero floating-point result, or a negative
number for a finite floating-point result.

_Inf
```
double _Inf._D
float _FInf._F
long double _LInf._L
```

Each object stores a representation of positive Infinity.

_Nan
```
double _Nan._D
float _FNan._F
long double _LNan._L
```

Each object stores a representation of Not a Number.

atan2
cos
exp
ldexp
log
pow
sin
sqrt
```
float atan2f(float, float)
float cosf(float);
float expf(float);
float ldexpf(float, int);
float logf(float);
float powf(float, float);
float sinf(float);
float sqrtf(float);
long double atan2l(long double, long double)
long double cosl(long double);
long double expl(long double);
long double ldexpl(long double, int);
long double logl(long double);
long double powl(long double, long double);
long double sinl(long double);
long double sqrtl(long double);
```

Each function behaves the same as the standard *double* version without
the **f** or **l** suffix, declared in **<math.h>**. These functions can also be declared
in **<math.h>**.

Amendment 1   This implementation of **<wstring>** calls several functions declared in
<wchar.h>. Moreover, a full implementation of the Standard C++ library
requires a Standard C library that complies with Amendment 1 to the C
Standard, as I mentioned earlier. To comply, a Standard C library must have:

- the new headers **<iso646.h>**, **<wchar.h>**, and **<wctype.h>**

- objects of type **FILE** augmented to support wide-character streams as
  well as conventional single-byte streams

An existing implementation of the Standard C library typically gets about
half again larger when all this functionality is added, which represents no
small amount of effort. The extended PJP C library complies fully with
Amendment 1 to the C Standard.

Appendix B: Names

This appendix lists the names of entities that are visible when a program includes a header. They are the names that your program sees, for good or for ill. Following each name is the header that declares or defines it at least once (or **keyword** for a newly minted keyword), possibly followed by the source file that defines the name in this implementation (which may be the header itself) and by the page number where the listing for that source file begins. File names that begin with **fdc** or **ldc** are trivial, and hence not shown in this book. (See page 523.) A name defined in a C header has no source file or page number.

With rare exception, a name that begins with an underscore is *not* mandated by the draft C++ Standard. I list these "secret" names last.

NAME		HEADER	FILE	PAGE
BUFSIZ	BUFSIZ	`<stdio.h>`		
	CHAR_BIT	`<limits.h>`		
	CHAR_MAX	`<limits.h>`		
	CHAR_MIN	`<limits.h>`		
	CLOCKS_PER_SEC	`<time.h>`		
	DBL_DIG	`<float.h>`		
	DBL_EPSILON	`<float.h>`		
	DBL_MANT_DIG	`<float.h>`		
	DBL_MAX	`<float.h>`		
	DBL_MAX_10_EXP	`<float.h>`		
	DBL_MAX_EXP	`<float.h>`		
	DBL_MIN	`<float.h>`		
	DBL_MIN_10_EXP	`<float.h>`		
	DBL_MIN_EXP	`<float.h>`		
	EDOM	`<errno.h>`		
	EFPOS	`<errno.h>`		
	EOF	`<stdio.h>`		
	EOF	`<streambuf>`	streambu	163
	ERANGE	`<errno.h>`		
	EXIT_FAILURE	`<stdlib.h>`		
	EXIT_SUCCESS	`<stdlib.h>`		
FILE	FILE	`<stdio.h>`		
	FILENAME_MAX	`<stdio.h>`		
	FLT_DIG	`<float.h>`		
	FLT_EPSILON	`<float.h>`		
	FLT_MANT_DIG	`<float.h>`		
	FLT_MAX	`<float.h>`		
	FLT_MAX_10_EXP	`<float.h>`		
	FLT_MAX_EXP	`<float.h>`		
	FLT_MIN	`<float.h>`		
	FLT_MIN_10_EXP	`<float.h>`		
	FLT_MIN_EXP	`<float.h>`		

NAME		HEADER	FILE	PAGE
	FLT_RADIX	`<float.h>`		
	FLT_ROUNDS	`<float.h>`		
	FOPEN_MAX	`<stdio.h>`		
HUGE_VAL	HUGE_VAL	`<math.h>`		
	INT_MAX	`<limits.h>`		
	INT_MIN	`<limits.h>`		
	LC_ALL	`<locale.h>`		
	LC_COLLATE	`<locale.h>`		
	LC_CTYPE	`<locale.h>`		
	LC_MONETARY	`<locale.h>`		
	LC_NUMERIC	`<locale.h>`		
	LC_TIME	`<locale.h>`		
	LDBL_DIG	`<float.h>`		
	LDBL_EPSILON	`<float.h>`		
	LDBL_MANT_DIG	`<float.h>`		
	LDBL_MAX	`<float.h>`		
	LDBL_MAX_10_EXP	`<float.h>`		
	LDBL_MAX_EXP	`<float.h>`		
	LDBL_MIN	`<float.h>`		
	LDBL_MIN_10_EXP	`<float.h>`		
	LDBL_MIN_EXP	`<float.h>`		
	LONG_MAX	`<limits.h>`		
	LONG_MIN	`<limits.h>`		
	L_tmpnam	`<stdio.h>`		
	MB_CUR_MAX	`<stdlib.h>`		
	MB_LEN_MAX	`<limits.h>`		
NPOS	NPOS	`<defines>`	defines	46
	NULL	`<locale.h>`		
	NULL	`<stddef.h>`		
	NULL	`<stdio.h>`		
	NULL	`<stdlib.h>`		
	NULL	`<string.h>`		
	NULL	`<time.h>`		
	NULL	`<wchar.h>`		
	RAND_MAX	`<stdlib.h>`		
	SCHAR_MAX	`<limits.h>`		
	SCHAR_MIN	`<limits.h>`		
	SEEK_CUR	`<stdio.h>`		
	SEEK_END	`<stdio.h>`		
	SEEK_SET	`<stdio.h>`		
	SHRT_MAX	`<limits.h>`		
	SHRT_MIN	`<limits.h>`		
	SIGABRT	`<signal.h>`		
	SIGFPE	`<signal.h>`		
	SIGILL	`<signal.h>`		
	SIGINT	`<signal.h>`		
	SIGSEGV	`<signal.h>`		
	SIGTERM	`<signal.h>`		
	SIG_DFL	`<signal.h>`		
	SIG_ERR	`<signal.h>`		
	SIG_IGN	`<signal.h>`		
	TMP_MAX	`<stdio.h>`		
	UCHAR_MAX	`<limits.h>`		
	UINT_MAX	`<limits.h>`		
	ULONG_MAX	`<limits.h>`		
	USHRT_MAX	`<limits.h>`		
	WCHAR_MAX	`<wchar.h>`		
	WCHAR_MIN	`<wchar.h>`		
	WEOF	`<wchar.h>`		
	WEOF	`<wctype.h>`		
	_IOFBF	`<stdio.h>`		
	_IOLBF	`<stdio.h>`		
	_IONBF	`<stdio.h>`		
	_double_complex	`<complex>`	complex	518
	_float_complex	`<complex>`	complex	518
abort	abort	`<stdlib.h>`		
	abs	`<complex>`	dcabs.c	530

Appendix C: Terms

This appendix lists terms that have special meaning within this book. Check here if you suspect that a term means more (or less) than you might ordinarily think.

A **access** — to obtain the value stored in an object or to store a new value in the object

address constant expression — an expression that you can use to initialize a static object of some pointer type

allocated storage — objects whose storage is obtained during program execution

alphabetic character — a lowercase or uppercase letter

alphanumeric character — an alphabetic character or a digit

Amendment 1 — the first amendment to the ISO C Standard

ANSI — American National Standards Institute, the organization authorized to formulate computer-related standards in the U.S.

argument — an expression that provides the initial value for one of the parameters in a function call

arithmetic type — an integer or floating-point type

array type — an object type consisting of a prespecified repetition of an object element

assembly language — a programming language tailored to a specific computer architecture

assertion — a predicate that must be true for a program to be correct

assign — to store a value in an object

assignment operator — an operator that stores a value in an object, such as **operator=**,

B **base** — the value used to weigh the digits in a positional number representation, such as base 8 (octal) or base 10 (decimal)

base class — a class from which another class is derived by inheriting the properties of the base class

beginning-of-file — the file position just before the first byte in a file

benign redefinition — a macro definition that defines an existing macro to have the same sequence of tokens spelled the same way and with white space between the same pairs of tokens

binary — as opposed to text, containing arbitrary patterns of bits

binary stream — a stream that can contain arbitrary binary data

block — a group of statements in a C++ function enclosed in braces

Boolean — an expression with two meaningful values, zero and nonzero

buffer — an array object used as a convenient work area or for temporary storage, often between a program and a file

C   **C header** — one of the headers in the Standard C++ library inherited from the Standard C library, having a name ending in **.h**

C++ header — one of the headers unique to the Standard C++ library, having a name *not* ending in **.h**

C Standard — a description of the C programming language adopted by ANSI and ISO to minimize variations in C implementations and programs

calling environment — the information in a stack frame that must be preserved on behalf of the calling function

Cartesian representation — a representation of complex numbers whose two components are the real and imaginary parts, usually as distinct from polar representation

catch **clause** — a sequence of tokens that specifies how to handle an exception thrown within an associated *try* block

cfront — a translator from C++ to C, developed at AT&T Bell Labs and used in several commercial C++ translators

category — part of a locale that deals with a specific group of services, such as character classification or time and date formatting

character — an object type in C++ that occupies one byte of storage and that can represent all the codes in the basic C++ character set

character constant — a token in a C++ program, such as **'a'**, whose integer value is the code for a character in the execution character set

class — an object type consisting of a sequence of function, object, and type members of different types

close — to terminate a connection between a stream and a file

code — colloquial term for programming language text or the executable binary produced from that text

compiler — a translator that produces an executable file

complex number — a number with two components, which in Cartesian form measures distances along the "real axis" (conventional numbers) and the "imaginary axis" (multiplied by the square root of –1)

computer architecture — a class of computers that can all execute a common executable-file format

constant type — the type of an object that you cannot store into (it is read-only) once it is initialized because it has the **const** type qualifier

constructor — a member function that constructs an object, typically by constructing its subobjects and storing initial values in its scalar member objects

conversion specification — a sequence of characters within a print or scan format that begins with a per cent and specifies the next conversion or transmission to perform

conversion specifier — the last character in a conversion specification, which determines the type of conversion or transmission to perform

conversion, type — altering the representation of a value of one type (as necessary) to make it a valid representation of a value of another type

copy constructor — a constructor that can be called with a single argument that is a const reference to another object of the same class, whose stored value provides the initial value of the object being constructed

D **decimal** — the positional representation for numbers with base ten

decimal point — the character that separates the integer part from the fraction part in a decimal number

declaration — a sequence of tokens in a C++ program that gives meaning to a name, allocates storage for an object, defines the initial content of an object or the behavior of a function, and/or specifies a type

default — the choice made when a choice is required and none is specified

definition — a declaration that, among other things, allocates storage for an object, associates a value with a *const* object, specifies the behavior of a function, or gives a name to a type; also the *define* directive for a macro

delete **expression** — an expression involving **operator delete**, which destroys the object, then calls the operator function to free storage for the object

derived class — a class that inherits properties from one or more base classes

destructor — a member function that destroys an object, typically by freeing any storage or other resources associated with the constructed object

destroy — to call the destructor for an object

diagnostic — a message emitted by a C++ translator reporting an invalid program

digit — one of ten characters used to represent numbers, such as **3**

domain error — calling a function with a numeric argument value (or values) for which the function is not defined

dot — the character **.**, often used as a decimal point

draft C++ Standard — the working version of a description of the C++ programming language being developed by ANSI and ISO to minimize variations in C++ implementations and programs

dynamic-cast **expression** — use of the **dynamic_cast** operator to obtain a valid reference to an object with a derived type, or a null pointer

dynamic storage — objects whose storage is allocated on entry to a block (or function) and freed when the activation of that block terminates, such as function parameters, **auto** declarations, and **register** declarations

E **element** — one of the repeated components of an array object

encapsulation — localizing a design decision so that a change of design results in changes within a small and easily identified region of source text

end-of-file — the file position just after the last byte in a file

exception — an object specified by a *throw* expression within a *try* block and caught by a *catch* clause that specifies the object type, used to report an abnormal condition

exception handler — the part of a *catch* clause that responds to a thrown exception

exception specification — a qualifier appended to a function declaration that specifies the types of exceptions that can propagate out of the function when it executes

executable file — a file that the operating system can execute without further translation or interpretation

exponent — the component of a floating-point value that specifies to what power the base is raised before it is multiplied by the fraction

expression — a sequence of tokens in a C++ program that specifies how to compute a value and generate side effects

extract — to obtain the value of the next character in a sequence controlled by a stream, and to point past that character position in the stream

extractor — a function that extracts one or more characters from a stream, converts them to the value of some object type, and stores the value in the object

F **field** — a contiguous group of characters that matches a pattern specified by a scan format conversion specification, and hence by an extractor

file — a contiguous sequence of bytes that has a name, maintained by the environment

file descriptor — a non-negative integer that designates a file while it is opened by a C program

file-level — that portion of a C++ source file outside any declaration

file-position indicator — an encoded value associated with an open file that specifies the next byte within the file to be read or written

file-positioning error — a request to alter the file-position indicator that cannot be honored

file-positioning functions — those functions that read or alter the file-position indicator

file name — the name used t designate a file by several functions in the Standard C++ library

FILE object — an object used in the Standard C library to control transfers of character data between a file and the program

floating-point type — any of the types *float, double,* or *long double*

format — a null-terminated string that determines the actions of a print or scan function

formatted input — reading text and converting it to encoded values under control of a format, as with a scan function

formatted output — converting encoded values and writing them as text under control of a format, as with a print function

free — to release storage allocated for an object during earlier program execution

friend — a class or function declaration within a class that makes the name space of the class available within the declared class or function

function — a contiguous group of executable statements that accepts argument values corresponding to its parameters when called from within an expression and (possibly) returns a value for use in that expression

function signature — the name of a function, along with the type information for its parameters, used in overload resolution to determine which function to call in an expression

G **GNU C++ compiler** — a portable C++ compiler developed by an organization based in Massachusetts that makes its software widely available

graphic — the visible representation of a printing character

H **handle** — an alternate term for a file descriptor

handler — a function registered with some agency to assume control when the agency detects some corresponding condition

header file — a text file that is made part of a translation unit by being named in an **#include** directive in a C++ source file

heap — that portion of memory that an executable program uses to store allocated objects

hexadecimal — the positional representation for numbers with base 16

hole — a contiguous group of bits or bytes within an object or argument list that does not participate in determining its value

I **identifier** — a name

IEEE — Institute of Electrical and Electronic Engineers, one of the ANSI-authorized bodies that develops computer-related standards

implementation — a working version of a specification, such as a programming language

include file — a text file made part of a translation unit by being named in an **#include** directive in a C++ source file or another include file

infinity — (Inf) a floating-point code that represents a value too large for finite representation

Informal Review Draft — the description of the C++ programming language being developed by ANSI and ISO as it was first presented to ISO Committee JTC1/SC22 for informal public review

inheritance — obtaining the member definitions and type equivalence from a base class

insert — to store a value in the next character in a sequence controlled by a stream, and to point past that character position in the stream

inserter — a function that converts a value of some object type to a sequence of one or more characters and inserts those characters into a stream

instantiate — to write a template class or template function and supply any parameter values to specify a particular instance of the template, as in **bits<5>**

integer — a whole number, possibly negative or zero

integer constant expression — an expression that the translator can reduce to a known integer value at translation time

integer type — an object type that can represent some contiguous range of integers including zero

interface — a collection of functions and conventions that makes a service, such as input/output, available to a C++ program

interpreter — a translator that maintains control during program execution

invalid — not conforming to the draft C++ Standard

invalid argument error — calling a function with an invalid argument value

I/O — input and output

ISO — International Organization for Standardization, the organization charged with developing international computer-related standards

K **knock out** — to prevent the linker from incorporating a library object module by providing a definition for a name with external linkage

L **length error** — specifying a sequence length that is too large

letter — one of the 52 characters, **a-z** and **A-Z**, in the English alphabet, plus possibly additional characters in other than the **"C"** locale

librarian — a program that maintains libraries of object modules

library — a collection of object modules that a linker can selectively incorporate into an executable program to provide definitions for names with external linkage

linker — a program that combines object modules to form an executable file

locale — a collection of information that modifies the behavior of the Standard C library to suit the conventions of a given culture or profession

locale-specific — subject to variation among locales

lowercase letter — one of the 26 characters, **a-z**, in the English alphabet, plus possibly additional characters in other than the **"C"** locale

lvalue — an expression that designates an object

M machine — colloquial term for a distinct computer architecture

macro — a name defined by the **#define** directive that specifies replacement text for subsequent invocations of the macro in the translation unit

macro definition — the replacement text associated with a macro name

macro guard — a macro name used to ensure that a text sequence is incorporated in a translation unit at most once

macro, masking — a macro definition that masks a declaration of the same name earlier in the translation unit

member — an object declaration that specifies one of the components of a class, struct, or union declaration

mode — a qualifier that specifies two or more alternate behaviors, such as text versus binary mode for an open file

modifiable lvalue — an expression that designates an object that you can store a new value into (having neither a constant nor an array type)

monetary — concerning currency, such as a monetary value

MS-DOS — a popular operating system by Microsoft Corporation for PC-compatible computers

multibyte character — a character from a large character set that is encoded as sequences of one or more conventional (one-byte) characters

multiple inheritance — inheriting the properties from more than one base class

multithread — supporting more than one program execution in a given time interval, possibly allowing interactions between the separate program executions

N name — a token from a large set used to designate a distinct entity — such as a function, macro, or member — in a translation unit

name space — a set of names distinguishable by context within a C program

namespace — a region of source code qualified by a namespace name

native — the locale named by the empty string **" "**

new **expression** — an expression involving **operator new**, which calls the operator function to allocate storage for an object, then constructs the object

new **handler** — a function registered with **set_new_handler** that **operator new** calls when it cannot satisfy a storage allocation request

not-a-number — (NaN) a floating-point code that designates no numeric value, such as an undefined result

null character — the character with code value zero

null pointer — the value of a pointer object that compares equal to zero, and hence designates no function or object

null-pointer constant — an integer constant expression with value zero, that can serve in some context as a null pointer

O **object** — a group of contiguous bytes in memory that can store a value of a given type

object module — the translated form of a translation unit, suitable for linking as part of an executable program

object type — a type that describes an object, as opposed to a function type

octal — the positional representation for numbers with base eight

offset — the relative address of a member or element within a containing object, often expressed in bytes

open — to form an association between a file and a stream

operand — a subexpression in a C++ expression acted on by an operator

operating system — a program that runs other programs, usually masking many variations among computers that share a common architecture

operator — a token in a C++ expression that yields a value of a given type, and possibly produces side effects, given one to three subexpressions as operands

operator function — a function called implicitly by the evaluation of an operator in an expression

overflow error — computation of a value too large to be represented as the required numeric type

overload — to provide more than one definition for a name in a given scope

overload resolution — to determine which of two or more overloaded functions to call within an expression

override — to provide a definition in a derived class that masks a definition in its base class

P **parameter** — an object declared in a function that stores the value of its corresponding argument on a function call

parse — to determine the syntactic structure of a sequence of tokens

period — alternate name for the dot character

pointer type — an object type that represents addresses of a function or object type

polar representation — a representation of complex numbers whose two components are the distance from the origin (magnitude) and angle made with the positive real axis (phase), usually as distinct from Cartesian representation

portability — cheaper to move to another environment than to rewrite for that environment

POSIX — the IEEE 1003 Standard operating-system interface based on the system services provided by UNIX to application programs

precision — the number of distinct values that can be represented, often expressed in bits or decimal digits (which indicates the *logarithm* of the number of distinct values)

predicate — an expression that yields a binary result, usually nonzero for true and zero for false

preprocessor — that portion of a C++ translator that processes text-oriented directives and macro invocations

primitive — an interface function that performs an essential service, often one that cannot be performed another way

print function — one of the functions that convert encoded values to text under control of a format string

printable — giving a meaningful result, such as displaying a graphic or controlling the print position, when written to a display device

program — a collection of functions and objects that a computer can execute to carry out the semantic intent of a corresponding set of C++ source files

program startup — the period in the execution of a program just before `main` is called

program termination — the period in the execution of a program just after `main` returns or `exit` is called

push back — to return a character to an input stream so that it is the next character read

punctuation — printable characters other than letters and digits, used to separate and delimit character sequences

R **raise** — to throw an exception by calling the member function `xmsg::raise` for an exception object

raise **handler** — a function registered with `xmsg::set_raise_handler` that `xmsg::raise` calls before it throws an exception

range error — calling a function with a numeric argument value (or values) for which the result is too large or too small to represent as a finite value

read-only — containing a stored value that cannot be altered

recursion — calling a function while an invocation of that function is active

register — to store a pointer to a *handler* function so that it can be called under specified circumstances at a later time

representation — the number of bits used to represent an object type, along with the meanings ascribed to various bit patterns

reserved name — a name available for use only for a restricted purpose

round — to obtain a representation with reduced precision by some rule, such as round to nearest

runtime type identification — (RTTI) using the operator **typeid** to determine the actual derived type of an object

rvalue — an expression that designates a value of some type (without necessarily designating an object)

S **scan function** — one of the functions that convert text to encoded values under control of a format string

scan set — a conversion specifier for a scan function that specifies a set of matching characters

secret name — a name from the space of names reserved to the implementor, such as **_Abc**

seek — to alter the file-position indicator for a stream to designate a given character position within a file

semantics — the meaning ascribed to valid sequences of tokens in a language

sequence point — a place in a program where the values stored in objects are in a known state

side effect — a change in the value stored in an object or in the state of a file when an expression executes

signed integer — an integer type that can represent negative as well as positive values

significance loss — a reduction in meaningful precision of a floating-point addition or subtraction caused by cancellation of high-order bits

source file — a text file that a C++ translator can translate to an object module

space — a character that occupies one print position but displays no graphic

specialize — to write a template class or template function definition by hand that replaces a particular instantiation of the template

stack — a list with a last in/first out protocol

stack frame — the data allocated on the call stack when a function is called

Standard C — that dialect of the C programming language defined by the ANSI/ISO C Standard

Standard C++ — that dialect of the C++ programming language defined by the draft ANSI/ISO C++ Standard

Standard C library — the set of functions, objects, and headers defined by the C Standard, usable by any hosted C or C++ program

Standard C++ library — the set of functions, objects, and headers defined by the C++ Standard, usable by any hosted C++ program

standard header — one of many headers defined by the draft C++ Standard

state table — an array that defines the actions of a finite-state machine

statement — an executable component of a function that specifies an action, such as evaluating an expression or altering flow of control

static storage — objects whose lifetime extends from program startup to program termination, initialized prior to program startup

store — to replace the value stored in an object with a new value

stream — an object that maintains the state of a sequence of reads, writes, and file-positioning requests for an open file

string — a sequence of characters stored in an array whose last (highest subscripted) stored value is a null character

string literal — a token in a C++ source file delimited by double quotes, such as **"abc"**, that designates a read-only *array of char* initialized to the specified character sequence with a null character added at the end

structure type — an object type consisting of a sequence of function, object, and type members of different types

Sun UNIX — a version of the UNIX operating system provided for the Sun workstation

synonym — an alternate way of designating a type that is otherwise equivalent to the original type

syntax — the grammatical constraints imposed on valid sequences of tokens in a language

system call — alternate term for a system service

system service — a request to an operating system to perform a service, such as writing to a device or obtaining the current time

T template — a class or function declaration written in terms of one or more type or value parameters for later instantiation with specific parameter values

terminate **handler** — a function registered with **set_terminate** that exception handling calls when it cannot determine which *catch* clause to execute

text — a sequence of characters nominally suitable for writing to a display device (to be read by people)

text stream — a stream that contains text

thousands separator — the character used to separate groups of digits to the left of the decimal point (not necessarily groups of three)

thread of control — the execution of a program by a single agent

throw **expression** — an expression of the form **throw ex** that throws the object **ex** as an exception

token — a sequence of characters treated as a single element in a higher-level grammar

translation table — an array that specifies a mapping from one encoding to another

translation unit — a C++ source file plus all the files included by **#include** directives, excluding any source lines skipped by conditional directives

translator — a program that converts a translation unit to executable form

truncate — to round toward zero

try **block** — a block followed by one or more *catch* clauses prepared to handle exceptions thrown within the block

type — the attribute of a value that determines its representation and what operations can be performed on it, or the attribute of a function that determines what arguments it expects and what it returns

type definition — a declaration that gives a name to a type

U underflow — computation of a value too small to be represented as the required floating-point type

unexpected **handler** — a function registered with **set_unexpected** that exception handling calls when it transfers control out of a function with an exception specification that does not include the thrown exception

union type — an object type consisting of an alternation of object members, only one of which can be represented at a time

UNIX — a machine-independent operating system developed in the early 1970s at AT&T Bell Laboratories, the first host for the C language

unsigned integer — an integer type that can represent values between zero and some positive upper limit

uppercase letter — one of the 26 characters, **A-Z**, in the English alphabet, plus possibly additional characters in other than the **"C"** locale

V variable — older term for an object

variable argument list — a list of arguments to a function that accepts additional arguments beyond its last declared parameter

virtual member — a member function whose overriding definition is called even when accessed as an object of its base class

void type — a type that has no representation and no values

volatile type — a qualified type for objects that may be accessed by more than one thread of control

W WG21 — the ISO-authorized committee responsible for C++ standardization

white space — a sequence of one or more space characters, possibly mixed with other spacing characters such as horizontal tab

wide character — a code value of type **wchar_t** used to represent a very large character set

width — part of a conversion specification in a format that partially controls the number of characters to be transmitted

writable — can have its value altered, opposite of read-only

X X3J16 — the ANSI-authorized committee responsible for C++ Standard

Appendix D: References

The literature on C++ is vast, but not always useful. What follows is an assortment of books and documents that are either directly related to the material in this book or useful in their own right as tutorial material. This list is *not* intended as an exhaustive list of books on the subject.

ANS89 *ANSI Standard X3.159-1989* (New York NY: American National Standards Institute, 1989). The original C Standard, developed by the ANSI-authorized committee X3J11. The Rationale that accompanies the C Standard explains many of the decisions that went into it, if you can get your hands on it.

C&W80 William J. Cody, Jr. and William Waite, *Software Manual for the Elementary Functions* (Englewood Cliffs NJ: Prentice Hall, 1980). The definitive work on writing and testing math functions.

E&S90 Margaret A. Ellis and Bjarne Stroustrup, *The Annotated C++ Reference Manual* (Reading MA: Addison Wesley, 1990). Known popularly as the *ARM*. This is the *base document* for the language portion of the draft C++ Standard. You will find that the draft C++ Standard has already evolved well beyond the *ARM*, at least in places.

IEE85 *ANSI/IEEE Standard 754-1985* (Piscataway, N.J.: Institute of Electrical and Electronics Engineers, Inc., 1985). The floating-point standard widely used in modern microprocessors.

ISO90 *ISO/IEC Standard 9899:1990* (Geneva: International Standards Organization, 1990). The official C Standard around the world. Aside from formatting details and section numbering, the ISO C Standard is identical to the ANSI C Standard.

ISO94 *ISO/IEC Amendment 1 to Standard 9899:1990* (Geneva: International Standards Organization, 1994). The first (and only) amendment to the C Standard. It provides substantial support for manipulating large character sets.

K&S89 Andrew Koenig and Bjarne Stroustrup, "C++: As Close to C as Possible — But No Closer," *The C++ Report*, July 1989. An article from the early days of the C++ standardization effort. It spells out ground rules for allowing Standard C++ to differ from from Standard C in sensible ways.

Kah87 W. Kahan, "Branch Cuts for Complex Elementary Functions or Much Ado About Nothing's Sign Bit," *Proceedings of the joint IMA/SIAM Conference on The State of the Art in Numerical Analysis*, University of Birmingham, April

1986, edited by A. Iserles and M.J.D. Powell (Oxford: Clarendon Press, 1987). Describes some of the peculiarities of computing complex functions, particularly using of IEEE 754 floating-point arithmetic.

Koe94 Andrew Koenig, editor, *Working Paper for Draft Proposed International Standard for Information Systems — Programming Language* C++ (committee working paper: WG21/N0414, X3J16/94-0027, 25 January 1994). The draft C++ Standard distributed within SC22, herein referred to as the Informal Review Draft. It is subject to change by Committee vote three times per year until approved.

Mey92 Scott Meyers, *Effective C++* (Reading MA: Addison Wesley, 1992. Provides "50 specific ways to improve your programs and designs," many of which are gems.

Pla92 P.J. Plauger, *The Standard C Library* (Englewood Cliffs NJ: Prentice Hall, 1992) Contains a complete implementation of the Standard C library, as well a text from the library portion of the C Standard and guidance in using the Standard C library. It is the predecessor and companion volume to this book.

P&B92 P.J. Plauger and Jim Brodie, *ANSI and ISO Standard C: Programmer's Reference* (Redmond WA: Microsoft Press, 1992). Provides a complete but succinct reference to the entire C Standard. It covers both the language and the library.

Plu89 Thomas Plum, *C Programming Guidelines* (Cardiff NJ: Plum Hall, Inc., 1989). An excellent style guide for writing C programs. It also contains a good discussion of first-order correctness testing, on pp. 194-199.

P&S91 Thomas Plum and Dan Saks, *C++ Programming Guidelines* (Cardiff NJ: Plum Hall, Inc., 1991). Another excellent style guide, this time for writing C++ programs.

S&L94 A.A. Stepanov and M. Lee, "The Standard Template Library," *Technical Report HPL-94-34* (Hewlett-Packard Laboratories, April 1994). The basis for the STL addition to the draft Standard C++ Library.

Str91 Bjarne Stroustrup, *The C++ Programming Language, Second Edition* (Reading MA: Addison Wesley, 1991). An excellent overview by the developer of the C++ language.

Str94 Bjarne Stroustrup, *The Design and Evolution of C++* (Reading MA: Addison Wesley, 1994). More recent reflections on changes made to C++, including those made as part of the standardization process.

Tea93 Steve Teale, *C++ IOStreams Handbook* (Reading MA: Addison-Wesley, 1993). Describes many of the inner workings of the iostreams portion of a typical C++ library. The version covered predates the one chosen as the basis for standardization, however.

Vil93 Mike Vilot, *C++ Programming PowerPack* (Carmel IN: Sams Publishing, 1993). An excellent example of the use of templates in building a powerful library atop the Standard C++ library.

Index

This index makes no attempt to provide all references to names defined in the code. For a complete list of such names, and associated source files, see Appendix B: Names. For a list of specialized terms used in this book, see Appendix C: Terms.

586

X

Y